MW00611211

WESTERN WORLD GEOGRAPHY

Copyright © 2019 by Houghton Mifflin Harcourt Publishing Company

All rights reserved. No part of this work may be reproduced or transmitted in any form or by any means, electronic or mechanical, including photocopying or recording, or by any information storage or retrieval system, without the prior written permission of the copyright owner unless such copying is expressly permitted by federal copyright law. Requests for permission to make copies of any part of the work should be submitted through our Permissions website at https://customercare.hmhco.com/contactus/Permissions.html or mailed to Houghton Mifflin Harcourt Publishing Company, Attn: Intellectual Property Licensing, 9400 Southpark Center Loop, Orlando, Florida 32819-8647.

Portions © 2010 A&E Television Networks, LLC. All rights reserved.

HISTORY® and the HISTORY® H Logo are trademarks of A&E Television Networks, LLC. All rights reserved.

Unless otherwise indicated, all maps © Maps.com LLC.

If you have received these materials as examination copies free of charge, Houghton Mifflin Harcourt Publishing Company retains title to the materials and they may not be resold. Resale of examination copies is strictly prohibited.

Possession of this publication in print format does not entitle users to convert this publication, or any portion of it, into electronic format.

Printed in the U.S.A.

ISBN 978-0-544-66938-3

4 5 6 7 8 9 10 0868 26 25 24 23 22 21 20 19

4500787059   D E F G

Educational Advisory Panel

The following educators have provided review during development of HMH programs.

Jose Colon
Berkeley High School
Berkeley, California

Bethany Copeland
Peach County High School
Fort Valley, Georgia

Darrel Dexter
Egyptian Community Unit School
Tamms, Illinois

Charles Dietz
Burnett Middle School
San Jose, California

John Hogan
Brevard High School
Brevard, North Carolina

Jeffrey Kaufman
Aspirations Diploma Plus High School
Brooklyn, New York

Beth E. Kuhlman
Queens Metropolitan High School
Forest Hills, New York

Beatrice Nudelman
Aptakisic Junior High School
Buffalo Grove, Illinois

Kyle Race
Greene High School
Greene, New York

Gretchen Ritter Varela
Northville High School
Northville, Michigan

Sharon Shirley
Branford High School
Branford, Connecticut

Yvette Snopkowski
Davis Junior High School
Sterling Heights, Michigan

La-Shanda West
Cutler Bay Senior High School
Cutler Bay, Florida

Contents

Videos related to each module can be accessed through your digital Student Edition.

Module 1

Module 2

Module 3

Module 4

Module 5

Module 6

The United States 188

Module 7

Canada 222

Module 8

Early Civilizations of Latin America 246

Module 9

Module 10

Module 11

🌐

Module 12

🌐

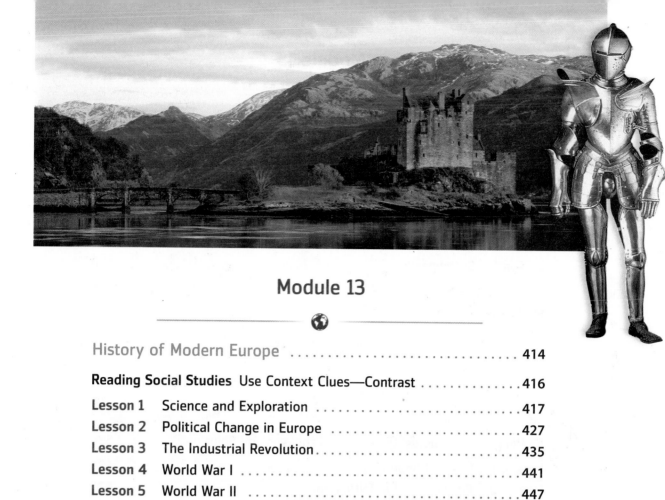

Module 13

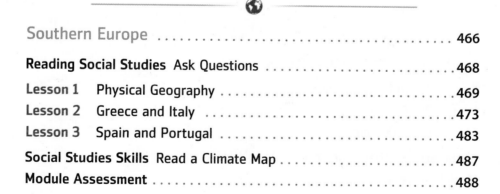

Module 14

Module 15

Module 16

Module 17

References

Available Online

Reading Like a Historian

Biographical Dictionary

Economics Handbook

Geography and Map Skills Handbook

Skillbuilder Handbook

Multimedia Connections

These online lessons feature award-winning content and include short video segments, maps and visual materials, primary source documents, and more.

The American Revolution　　　**Ancient Greece**

The Maya　　　**Dear Home: Letters from WWI**

Mexico

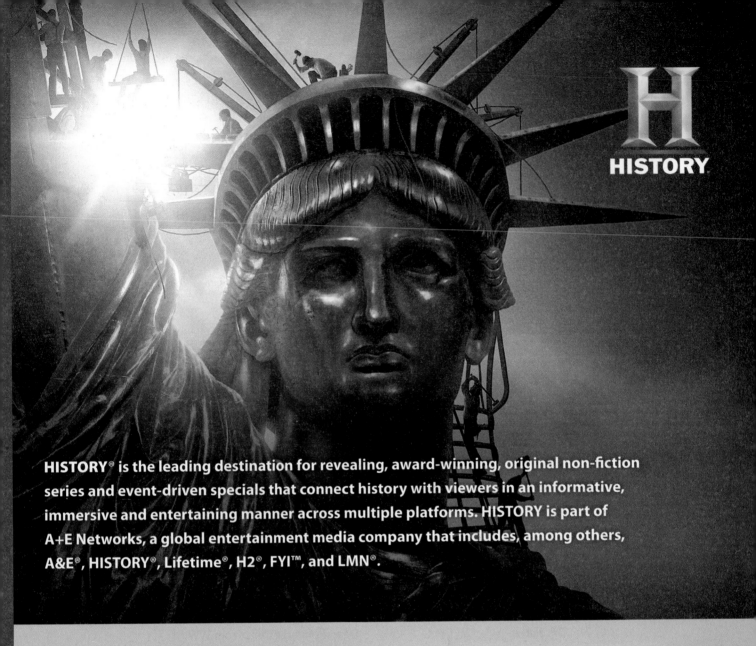

HISTORY® is the leading destination for revealing, award-winning, original non-fiction series and event-driven specials that connect history with viewers in an informative, immersive and entertaining manner across multiple platforms. HISTORY is part of A+E Networks, a global entertainment media company that includes, among others, A&E®, HISTORY®, Lifetime®, H2®, FYI™, and LMN®.

HISTORY programming greatly appeals to educators and young people who are drawn into the visual stories our documentaries tell. Our Education Department has a long-standing record in providing teachers and students with curriculum resources that bring the past to life in the classroom. Our content covers a diverse variety of subjects, including American and world history, government, economics, the natural and applied sciences, arts, literature and the humanities, health and guidance, and even pop culture.

The HISTORY website, located at **www.history.com**, is the definitive historical online source that delivers entertaining and informative content featuring broadband video, interactive timelines, maps, games, podcasts and more.

"We strive to engage, inspire and encourage the love of learning..."

Since its founding in 1995, HISTORY has demonstrated a commitment to providing the highest quality resources for educators. We develop multimedia resources for K–12 schools, two- and four-year colleges, government agencies, and other organizations by drawing on the award-winning documentary programming of A&E Television Networks. We strive to engage, inspire and encourage the love of learning by connecting with students in an informative and compelling manner. To help achieve this goal, we have formed a partnership with Houghton Mifflin Harcourt.

©2010 A&E Television Networks, LLC. All Rights Reserved. 01762.

The Idea Book for Educators

Classroom resources that bring the past to life

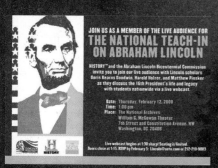
Live webcasts

HISTORY Take a Veteran to School Day

In addition to premium video-based resources, **HISTORY** has extensive offerings for teachers, parents, and students to use in the classroom and in their in-home educational activities, including:

● *The Idea Book for Educators* is a biannual teacher's magazine, featuring guides and info on the latest happenings in history education to help keep teachers on the cutting edge.

● **HISTORY** Classroom (www.history.com/classroom) is an interactive website that serves as a portal for history educators nationwide. Streaming videos on topics ranging from the Roman aqueducts to the civil rights movement connect with classroom curricula.

● **HISTORY** email newsletters feature updates and supplements to our award-winning programming relevant to the classroom with links to teaching guides and video clips on a variety of topics, special offers, and more.

● **Live webcasts** are featured each year as schools tune in via streaming video.

● **HISTORY** Take a Veteran to School Day connects veterans with young people in our schools and communities nationwide.

In addition to **Houghton Mifflin Harcourt**, our partners include the *Library of Congress*, the *Smithsonian Institution, National History Day, The Gilder Lehrman Institute of American History,* the Organization of American Historians, and many more. HISTORY video is also featured in museums throughout America and in over 70 other historic sites worldwide.

Reading Social Studies

Did you ever think you would begin reading your social studies book by reading about reading? Actually, it makes better sense than you might think. You would probably make sure you learned soccer skills and strategies before playing in a game. Similarly, you need to learn reading skills and strategies before reading your social studies book. In other words, you need to make sure you know whatever you need to know in order to read this book successfully.

Tip #1

Use the Reading Social Studies Page

Take advantage of the page on reading at the beginning of every module. This page introduces the reading skill you will learn and the reading strategy you will use. Then you will have an opportunity to practice that skill and strategy.

Reading Focus

The Reading Focus describes the reading skill you will learn and explains why it is important to master and use that skill.

Reading Strategy

Good readers use a number of strategies to make sure they understand what they are reading. These strategies are the basic tools you need to read and understand social studies.

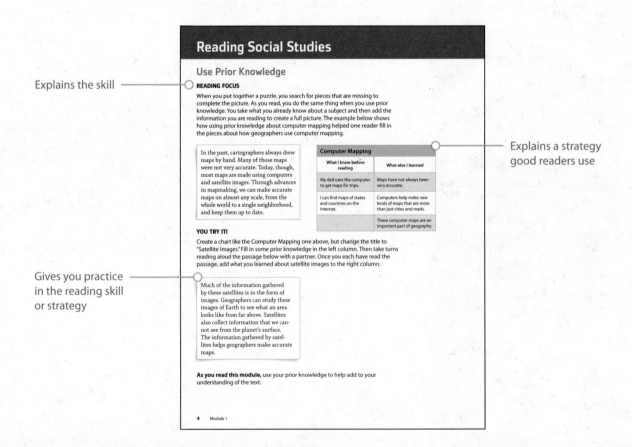

Explains the skill

Explains a strategy good readers use

Gives you practice in the reading skill or strategy

Tip #2

Read like a Skilled Reader

You will never get better at reading your social studies book—or any book for that matter—unless you spend some time thinking about how to be a better reader.

Skilled readers do the following:

- They preview what they are supposed to read before they actually begin reading. They look for vocabulary words, titles of lessons, information in the margin, or maps or charts they should study.

- They divide their notebook paper into two columns. They title one column "Notes from the Lesson" and the other column "Questions or Comments I Have."

- They take notes in both columns as they read.

- They read like **active readers.** The Active Reading list below shows you what that means.

- They use clues in the text to help them figure out where the text is going. The best clues are called signal words.

Chronological Order Signal Words:

first, second, third, before, after, later, next, following that, earlier, finally

Cause and Effect Signal Words:
because of, due to, as a result of, the reason for, therefore, consequently

Comparison/Contrast Signal Words:

likewise, also, as well as, similarly, on the other hand

Active Reading

Successful readers are **active readers.** These readers know that it is up to them to figure out what the text means. Here are some steps you can take to become an active, and successful, reader.

Predict what will happen next based on what has already happened. When your predictions don't match what happens in the text, reread the confusing parts.

Question what is happening as you read. Constantly ask yourself why things have happened, what things mean, and what caused certain events.

Summarize what you are reading frequently. Do not try to summarize the entire module! Read a bit and then summarize it. Then read on.

Connect what is happening in the part you're reading to what you have already read.

Clarify your understanding. Stop occasionally to ask yourself whether you are confused by anything. You may need to reread to clarify, or you may need to read further and collect more information before you can understand.

Visualize what is happening in the text. Try to see the events or places in your mind by drawing maps, making charts, or jotting down notes about what you are reading.

Tip #3

Pay Attention to Vocabulary

It is no fun to read something when you don't know what the words mean, but you can't learn new words if you use or read only the words you already know. In this book, we know we probably have used some words you don't know. But we have followed a pattern as we have used more difficult words.

Key Terms and Places

At the beginning of each lesson you will find a list of key terms and places that you will need to know. Be on the lookout for those words as you read through the lesson.

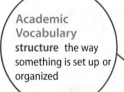

Academic
Vocabulary
structure the way
something is set up or
organized

Academic Vocabulary

When we use a word that is important in all classes, not just social studies, we define it in the margin under the heading Academic Vocabulary. You will run into these academic words in other textbooks, so you should learn what they mean while reading this book.

Academic and Social Studies Words

As you read this social studies textbook, you will be more successful if you know or learn the meanings of the words on this page. Academic words are important in all classes, not just social studies. Social studies words are special to the study of world history and other social studies topics.

Academic Words

abstract   expressing a quality or idea without reference to an actual thing

affect   to change or influence

agreement   a decision reached by two or more people or groups

aspects   parts

cause   the reason something happens

circumstances   conditions that influence an event or activity

concrete   specific, real

consequences   the effects of a particular event or events

contemporary   modern

criteria   rules for defining

develop/development   1. to grow or improve; 2. creation

distinct   clearly different and separate

distribute   to divide among a group of people

effect   the result of an action or decision

efficient/efficiency   productive and not wasteful

element   part

establish   to set up or create

execute   to perform, carry out

factor   cause

features   characteristics

function   use or purpose

impact   effect, result

implement   to put in place

implications   effects of a decision

incentive   something that leads people to follow a certain course of action

influence   change or have an effect on

innovation   a new idea or way of doing something

method   a way of doing something

monumental   impressively large, sturdy, and enduring

motive   a reason for doing something

neutral   unbiased, not favoring either side in a conflict

policy   rule, course of action

primary   main, most important

procedure   a series of steps taken to accomplish a task

process   a series of steps by which a task is accomplished

purpose   the reason something is done

reaction   a response to something

role   1. a part or function; 2. assigned behavior

structure   the way something is set up or organized

traditional   customary, time-honored

values   ideas that people hold dear and try to live by

vary/various   1. to be different; 2. of many types

Social Studies Words

AD   refers to dates after the birth of Jesus of Nazareth

BC   refers to dates before the birth of Jesus

BCE   refers to "Before Common Era," dates before the birth of Jesus

CE   refers to "Common Era," dates after the birth of Jesus

century   a period of 100 years

civilization   the culture of a particular time or place

climate   the weather conditions in a certain area over a long period of time

culture   the knowledge, beliefs, customs, and values of a group of people

custom   a repeated practice, tradition

decade   a period of 10 years

democracy   governmental rule by the people, usually on a majority rule principle

economy   the system in which people make and exchange goods and services

era   a period of time

geography   the study of Earth's physical and cultural features

monarchy   governmental rule by one person, a king or queen

physical features   features on the earth's surface, such as mountains and rivers

politics   government

region   an area with one or more features that make it different from surrounding areas

resources   materials found on the earth that people need and value

society   a group of people who share common traditions

trade   the exchange of goods and service

Using This Book

Studying geography will be easy for you using this textbook. Take a few minutes to become familiar with the easy-to-use structure and special features of your book. See how it will make geography come alive for you!

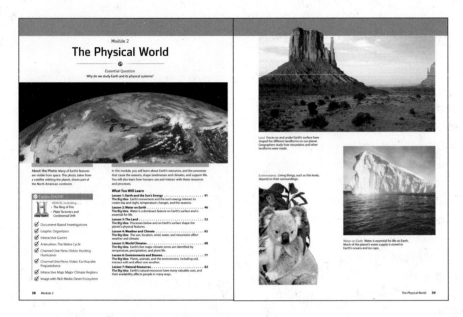

Module

Each module begins with an Essential Question and a preview of what you will learn and ends with a Module Assessment.

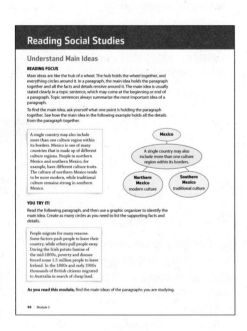

Reading Social Studies

These reading lessons teach you skills and provide opportunities for practice to help you read the textbook more successfully. There are questions in the Module Assessment to make sure you understand the reading skill.

Social Studies Skills

The Social Studies Skills lessons give you an opportunity to learn and use a skill you will most likely use again while in school. You will also be given a chance to make sure you understand each skill by answering related questions in the Module Assessment.

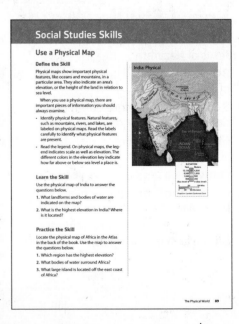

Lesson

The lesson opener includes an overarching Big Idea statement, Main Ideas, and Key Terms and Places.

If YOU lived there . . .

introductions begin each lesson with a situation for you to respond to, placing you in a location related to the content you will be studying in the lesson.

Headings and subheadings

organize the information into manageable chunks of text that will help you learn and understand the lesson's main ideas.

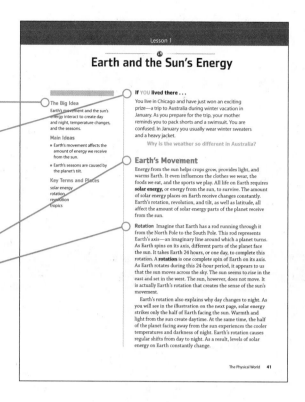

Earth and the Sun's Energy

The Big Idea
Earth's movement and the sun's energy interact to create day and night, temperature changes, and the seasons.

Main Ideas
- Earth's movement affects the amount of energy we receive from the sun.
- Earth's seasons are caused by the planet's tilt.

Key Terms and Places
solar energy
rotation
revolution
tropics

If YOU lived there . . .
You live in Chicago and have just won an exciting prize—a trip to Australia during winter vacation in January. As you prepare for the trip, your mother reminds you to pack shorts and a swimsuit. You are confused. In January you usually wear winter sweaters and a heavy jacket.

Why is the weather so different in Australia?

Earth's Movement

Energy from the sun helps crops grow, provides light, and warms Earth. It even influences the clothes we wear, the foods we eat, and the sports we play. All life on Earth requires **solar energy**, or energy from the sun, to survive. The amount of solar energy places on Earth receive changes constantly. Earth's rotation, revolution, and tilt, as well as latitude, all affect the amount of solar energy parts of the planet receive from the sun.

Rotation Imagine that Earth has a rod running through it from the North Pole to the South Pole. This rod represents Earth's axis—an imaginary line around which a planet turns. As Earth spins on its axis, different parts of the planet face the sun. It takes Earth 24 hours, or one day, to complete this rotation. A **rotation** is one complete spin of Earth on its axis. As Earth rotates during this 24-hour period, it appears to us that the sun moves across the sky. The sun seems to rise in the east and set in the west. The sun, however, does not move. It is actually Earth's rotation that creates the sense of the sun's movement.

Earth's rotation also explains why day changes to night. As you will see in the illustration on the next page, solar energy strikes only the half of Earth facing the sun. Warmth and light from the sun create daytime. At the same time, the half of the planet facing away from the sun experiences the cooler temperatures and darkness of night. Earth's rotation causes regular shifts from day to night. As a result, levels of solar energy on Earth constantly change.

The Physical World **41**

Water's Benefits: for Fun
This surfer rides a wave at the beach. Many people enjoy swimming, boating, fishing, and other recreational activities on water.

Recognizing all of these benefits, some communities work together to manage freshwater supplies. For example, in Florida, long-term population growth strains the freshwater supply. That, combined with drought conditions, inspired the creation of the Central Florida Water Initiative (CFWI). This organization works to protect and conserve water resources in a 5,300 square mile area. The CFWI works with businesses, utilities, environmental groups, agricultural groups, and others to meet people's water needs. Many regions around the world have similar organizations.

Reading Check
Summarize How does water affect people's lives?

Summary and Preview In this lesson you learned that water is essential for life on Earth. Next, you will learn about the shapes on Earth's surface

Lesson 2 Assessment

Review Ideas, Terms, and Places
1. a. Describe Name and describe the different types of water that make up Earth's water supply.
   b. Analyze Why is only a small percentage of Earth's freshwater available to us?
   c. Elaborate In your opinion, which is more important—surface water or groundwater? Why?
2. a. Recall What drives the water cycle?
   b. Make Inferences From what bodies of water do you think most evaporation occurs? Why?
3. a. Define What is a drought?
   b. Analyze How does water support life on Earth?
   c. Evaluate What water problem do you think is most critical in your community? Why?

Critical Thinking
4. Sequence Draw the graphic organizer. Then use your notes and the graphic organizer to identify the stages in Earth's water cycle.

| Heat from the sun evaporates water on Earth. |
| The water cycle repeats. |

The Physical World **51**

Reading Check

questions are at the end of each main heading so you can test whether or not you understand what you have just studied.

Summary and Preview

statements connect what you have just studied in the lesson to what you will study in the next lesson.

Lesson Assessment

boxes provide an opportunity for you to make sure you understand the main ideas of the lesson.

HMH Social Studies
Dashboard

Designed for today's digital natives, **HMH® Social Studies** offers you an informative and exciting online experience.

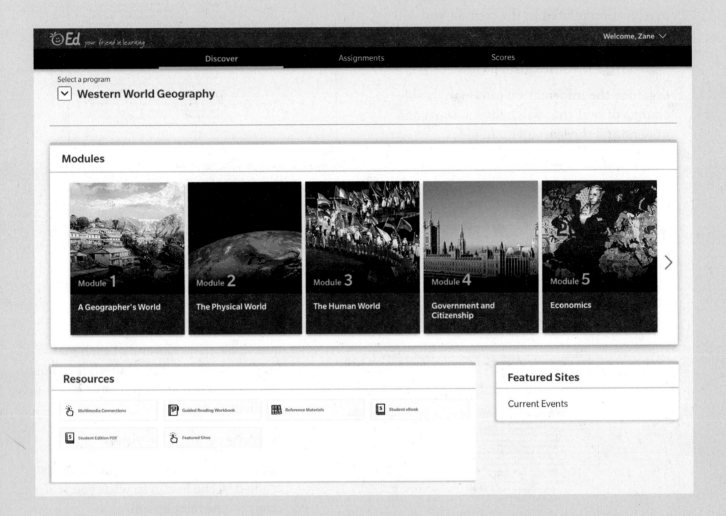

Your personalized Student Dashboard is organized into three main sections:

1. **Discover**—Quickly access content and search program resources
2. **Assignments**—Review your assignments and check your progress on them
3. **Scores**—Monitor your progress in the course

and places enriched with media, we're connecting you to geography through experiences that are energizing, inspiring, and memorable. The following pages highlight some digital tools and instructional support that will help you approach geography through active inquiry, so you can connect to the wider world while becoming active and informed citizens for the future.

The Student eBook is the primary learning portal.

More than just the digital version of a textbook, the Student eBook serves as the primary learning portal for you. The text is supported by a wealth of multimedia and learning resources to bring geography to life and give you the tools you need to succeed.

Bringing Content to Life

HISTORY® videos and Multimedia Connections bring content to life through primary source footage, dramatic storytelling, and expert testimonials.

In-Depth Understanding

Close Read Screencasts model an analytical conversation about primary sources.

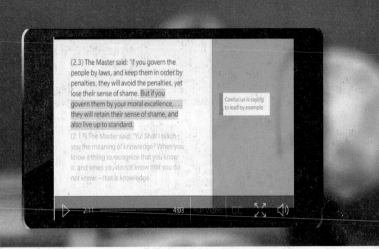

Content in a Fun Way

Interactive Features, Maps, and **Games** provide quick, entertaining activities and assessments that present important content in a fun way.

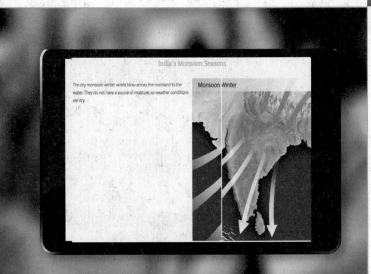

Focusing on Sources

Document-Based Investigations in lessons build to end-of-module DBI performance tasks so you can examine and assess primary and secondary sources as geographers and historians do.

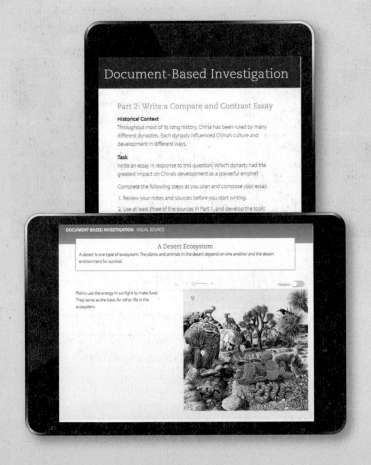

The **Guided Reading Workbook** and **Spanish/English Guided Reading Workbook** offer you lesson summaries with vocabulary, reading, and note-taking support.

Current Events features trustworthy articles on today's news that connect what you learn in class to the world around you.

Full-Text Audio Support

You can listen while you read.

Skills Support

Point-of-use support is just a click away, providing instruction on critical reading and social studies skills.

Personalized Annotations

Notes encourages you to take notes while you read and allows you to customize them to your study preferences. You can easily access them to review later as you prepare for exams.

Interactive Lesson Graphic Organizers

Graphic organizers help you process, summarize, and keep track of your learning for end-of-module performance tasks.

No Wi-Fi®? No problem!

HMH Social Studies Western World Geography will allow you to connect to content and resources by downloading it when online and accessing it when offline.

Module 1

A Geographer's World

Essential Question

How does the use of geographic tools help us view the world in new ways?

About the Photo: This village is in the country of Nepal. It rests high in the Himalayas, the highest mountains in the world.

In this module, you will learn that geography is the study of the world. You will find out how geographic studies are organized and what tools are used.

Explore ONLINE!

- ✓ Document-Based Investigations
- ✓ Graphic Organizers
- ✓ Interactive Games
- ✓ Animation: How Satellites Gather Map Data
- ✓ Channel One News Video: Making Art with GPS
- ✓ Animation: Map Projections
- ✓ Animation: How to Read a Map

What You Will Learn

Physical Geography Geography is the study of the world's land features, such as this windswept rock formation in Arizona.

Human Geography Geography is also the study of people. It asks where people live, what they eat, what they wear, and even what kinds of animals they keep.

Studying the World Exploring the world takes people to exciting and interesting places.

Reading Social Studies

Use Prior Knowledge

READING FOCUS

When you put together a puzzle, you search for pieces that are missing to complete the picture. As you read, you do the same thing when you use prior knowledge. You take what you already know about a subject and then add the information you are reading to create a full picture. The example below shows how using prior knowledge about computer mapping helped one reader fill in the pieces about how geographers use computer mapping.

In the past, cartographers always drew maps by hand. Many of those maps were not very accurate. Today, though, most maps are made using computers and satellite images. Through advances in mapmaking, we can make accurate maps on almost any scale, from the whole world to a single neighborhood, and keep them up to date.

Computer Mapping	
What I know before reading	**What else I learned**
My dad uses the computer to get maps for trips.	Maps have not always been very accurate.
I can find maps of states and countries on the Internet.	Computers help make new kinds of maps that are more than just cities and roads.
	These computer maps are an important part of geography.

YOU TRY IT!

Create a chart like the Computer Mapping one above, but change the title to "Satellite Images." Fill in some prior knowledge in the left column. Then take turns reading aloud the passage below with a partner. Once you each have read the passage, add what you learned about satellite images to the right column.

Much of the information gathered by these satellites is in the form of images. Geographers can study these images of Earth to see what an area looks like from far above. Satellites also collect information that we cannot see from the planet's surface. The information gathered by satellites helps geographers make accurate maps.

As you read this module, use your prior knowledge to help add to your understanding of the text.

Studying Geography

The Big Idea

The study of geography helps us view the world in new ways.

Main Ideas

- Geography is the study of the world, its people, and the landscapes they create.
- Geographers look at the world in many different ways.

Key Terms and Places

geography
landscape
social science
regions

If YOU lived there . . .

You have just moved to Miami, Florida, from your old home in Pennsylvania. Everything seems very different—from the weather and the trees to the way people dress and talk. Even the streets and buildings look different. One day you get an email from a friend at your old school. "What's it like living there?" your friend asks.

How will you describe your new home?

What Is Geography?

Think about the place where you live. What does the land look like? Are there tall mountains nearby, or is the land so flat that you can see for miles? Is the ground covered with bright green grass and trees, or is the area part of a sandy desert?

Now think about the weather in your area. What is it like? Does it get really hot in the summer? Do you see snow every winter? How much does it rain? Do tornadoes ever strike?

Finally, think about the people who live in your town or city. Do they live mostly in apartments or houses? Do most people own cars or do they get around town on buses or trains? What kinds of jobs do adults in your town have? Were most of the people you know born in your town or did they move there?

The things that you have been thinking about are part of your area's geography. **Geography** is the study of the world, its people, and the landscapes they create. To a geographer, a place's **landscape** is all the human and physical features that make it unique. When they study the world's landscapes, geographers ask questions much like the ones you just asked yourself.

Geography as a Science Many of the questions that geographers ask deal with how the world works. They want to know what causes mountains to form and what creates tornadoes. To answer questions like these, geographers have to think and act like scientists.

As scientists, geographers do field work to gather data, or information, about places. Gathering data can sometimes lead geographers to fascinating places. They might have to crawl deep into caves or climb tall mountains to make observations and take measurements. At other times, geographers study sets of images collected by satellites orbiting high above Earth. These scientists make observations about the places they study. Then they record those observations.

However geographers make observations and gather data, they have to study it carefully. Like other scientists, geographers must examine their findings in great detail before they can learn what all the information means. These scientists interpret and summarize the data gathered. Then they make their conclusions.

Geography as a Social Science Not everything that geographers study can be measured in numbers, however. Some geographers study people and their lives. For example, they may ask why countries change their governments or why people in a place speak a certain language. This kind of information cannot be measured.

Because it deals with people and how they live, geography is sometimes called a **social science.** A social science is a field that studies people and the relationships among them.

The geographers who study people do not dig in caves or climb mountains. Instead, they visit places and talk to the people who live there. That is the field work they do to gather information about people's lives and communities. These geographers may design and conduct surveys to gather information. They also might record oral histories from what people tell them about their communities.

Reading Check
Compare In what ways is geography both a science and a social science?

What Is Geography?

Geography is the study of the world, its people, and the landscapes they create. To study a place's geography, we look at its physical and human features.

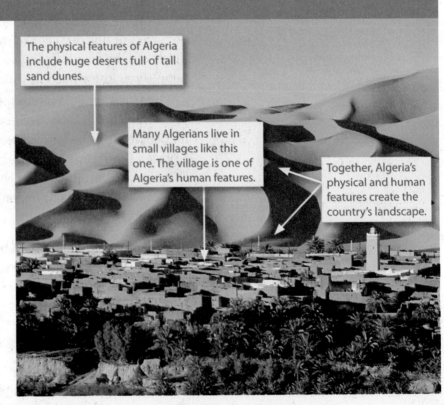

The physical features of Algeria include huge deserts full of tall sand dunes.

Many Algerians live in small villages like this one. The village is one of Algeria's human features.

Together, Algeria's physical and human features create the country's landscape.

Analyze Visuals
What is the landscape of this part of Algeria like?

Looking at the World

Whether they study volcanoes and storms or people and cities, geographers have to look carefully at the world around them. To fully understand how the world works, geographers often look at places at three different levels.

Local Level Some geographers study issues at a local level. They ask the same types of questions we asked at the beginning of this module: How do people in a town or community live? What is the local government like? How do the people who live there get around? What do they eat?

By asking these questions, geographers can figure out why people live and work the way they do. They can also help people improve their lives. For example, they can help town leaders figure out the best place to build new schools, shopping centers, or sports complexes. They can also help the people who live in the city or town plan for future changes.

Regional Level Sometimes, though, geographers want to study a bigger chunk of the world. To do this, they divide the world into **regions.** A region is a part of the world that has one or more common features that distinguish it from surrounding areas.

Some regions are defined by physical characteristics such as mountain ranges, climates, or plants native to the area. As a result, these types of regions are often easy to identify. The Rocky Mountains of the western United States, for example, make up a physical region. Another example of this kind of region is the Sahara, a huge desert in northern Africa.

Other regions may not be so easy to define, however. These regions are based on the human characteristics of a place, such as language, religion, or history. A place in which most people share these kinds of characteristics can also be seen as a region. For example, most people in Scandinavia, a region in northern Europe, speak similar languages and practice the same religion.

Regions come in all shapes and sizes. Some are small, like the neighborhood called Chinatown in San Francisco. Other regions are huge, like the Americas. This huge region includes two continents—North America and South America. The size of the area does not matter, as long as the area shares some characteristics. These shared characteristics define the region.

Geographers divide the world into regions for many reasons. The world is a huge place and home to billions of people. Studying so large an area can be extremely difficult. Dividing the world into regions makes it easier to study. A small area is much easier to examine than a large area.

Other geographers study regions to see how people interact with one another. For example, they may study a city such as London, England, to learn how the city's people govern themselves. Then they can compare what they learn about one region to what they learn about another region. In this way, they can learn more about life and landscapes in both places.

Global Level Sometimes, geographers do not want to study the world just at a regional level. Instead, they want to learn how people interact globally, or around the world. To do so, geographers ask how events and ideas from one region of the world affect people in other regions. In other words, they study the world on a global level.

Geographers who study the world on a global level try to find relationships among people who live far apart. They may, for example, examine the products that a country exports to see how those products are used in other countries.

Looking at the World

Geographers look at the world at many levels. At each level, they ask different questions and discover different types of information. By putting information gathered at different levels together, geographers can better understand a place and its role in the world.

Local Level
This busy neighborhood in London, England, is a local area. A geographer here might study local foods, housing, or clothing.

Regional Level
As a major city, London is also a region. At this level, a geographer might study the city's population or transportation systems.

Global Level
London is one of the world's main financial centers. Here, a geographer might study how London's economy affects the world.

Analyze Visuals
Based on these photos, what are some questions a geographer might ask about London?

In recent decades, worldwide trade and communication have increased. As a result, we need to understand how our actions affect people around the world. Through their studies, geographers provide us with information that helps us figure out how to live in a rapidly changing world.

Summary and Preview Geography is the study of the world, its people, and its landscapes. In the next lesson, you will explore the branches into which the field is divided.

Lesson 1 Assessment

Review Ideas, Terms, and Places

1. a. Define What is geography?
   b. Explain Why is geography considered a science?
2. a. Identify What is a region? Give two examples.
   b. Elaborate What global issues do geographers study?

Critical Thinking

3. Summarize Draw two ovals like the ones shown here. Use your notes to fill the ovals with information about geography and geographers.

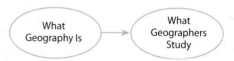

The Branches of Geography

The Big Idea

Geography is divided into two main branches—physical geography and human geography.

Main Ideas

- Physical geography is the study of landforms, water bodies, and other physical features.

- Human geography focuses on people, their cultures, and the landscapes they create.

- Other branches of geography examine specific aspects of the physical or human world.

Key Terms and Places

physical geography
human geography
cartography
meteorology

If YOU lived there . . .

You are talking to two friends about the vacations their families will take this summer. One friend says that his family is going to the Grand Canyon. He is very excited about seeing the spectacular landscapes in and around the canyon. Your other friend's family is going to visit Nashville, Tennessee. She is looking forward to trying new foods at the city's restaurants and touring its museums.

Which vacation sounds more interesting? Why?

Physical Geography

Think about a jigsaw puzzle. Seen as a whole, the puzzle shows a pretty or interesting picture. To see that picture, though, you have to put all the puzzle pieces together. Before you assemble them, the pieces do not give you a clear idea of what the puzzle will look like when it is assembled. After all, each piece contains only a tiny portion of the overall image.

In many ways, geography is like a huge puzzle. It is made up of many branches, or divisions. Each of these branches focuses on a single part of the world. Viewed separately, none of these branches shows us the whole world. Together, however, the many branches of geography improve our understanding of our planet and its people.

Geography's two main branches are physical geography and human geography. Geographers identify and locate major physical and human geographic features of various places and regions in the world. The first branch, **physical geography,** is the study of the world's physical geographic features—its landforms, bodies of water, climates, soils, and plants.

The Physical World What does it mean to say that physical geography is the study of physical geographic features? Physical geographers want to know all about the different features found on our planet. They want to know where mountain ranges are, how rivers flow across the landscape, and why different amounts of rain fall from place to place.

Eratosthenes (c. 276–c. 194 BC)

Did you know that geography is over two thousand years old? Actually, the study of the world is even older than that, but the first person ever to use the word *geography* lived then. His name was Eratosthenes (er-uh-TAHS-thuh-neez), and he was a Greek scientist and librarian. With no modern instruments of any kind, Eratosthenes figured out how large Earth is. He also drew a map that showed all of the lands that the Greeks knew about. Because of his many contributions to the field, Eratosthenes has been called the Father of Geography.

Generalize
Why is Eratosthenes called the Father of Geography?

More importantly, however, physical geographers want to know what causes the different shapes on Earth. They want to know why mountain ranges rise up where they do and what causes rivers to flow in certain directions. They also want to know why various parts of the world have very different weather and climate patterns.

To answer these questions, physical geographers take detailed measurements. They study the heights of mountains and the temperatures of places. To track any changes that occur over time, physical geographers keep careful records of all the information they collect.

Uses of Physical Geography Earth is made up of hundreds of types of physical geographic features. Without a complete understanding of what these features are and the effect they have on the world's people and landscapes, we cannot fully understand our world. This is the major reason that geographers study the physical world—to learn how it works.

There are also other, more specific reasons for studying physical geography, though. Studying the changes that take place on our planet can help us prepare to live with those changes. For example, knowing what causes volcanoes to erupt can help us predict eruptions. Knowing what causes terrible storms can help us prepare for them. In this way, the work of physical geographers helps us adjust to the dangers and changes of our world.

Human Geography

The physical world is only one part of the puzzle of geography. People are also part of the world. **Human geography** is the study of the world's human geographic features—people, communities, and landscapes. It is the second major branch of geography.

The Human World Put simply, human geographers study the world's people, past and present. They look at where people live and why. They ask why some parts of the world have more people than others, and why some places have almost no people at all.

Reading Check
Identify Points of View
What are some features in your area that a physical geographer might study?

Human geographers also study what people do. What jobs do people have? What crops do they grow? What makes them move from place to place? These are the types of questions that geographers ask about people around the world.

Because people's lives are so different in different places, no one can study every aspect of human geography. As a result, human geographers often specialize in a smaller area of study. Some may choose to study only the people and landscapes in a certain region. For example, a geographer may study only the lives of people who live in West Africa.

Other geographers choose not to limit their studies to one place. Instead, they may choose to examine only one aspect of people's lives. For example, a geographer could study only economics, politics, or city life. However, that geographer may compare economic patterns in various parts of the world to see how they differ.

Uses of Human Geography Although every culture is different, people around the world have some common needs. All people need food and water. All people need shelter. All people need to deal with other people in order to survive.

Human geographers study how people in various places address their needs. They look at the foods people eat and the types of governments they form. The knowledge they gather can help us better understand people in other cultures. Sometimes, this type of understanding can help people improve their landscapes and situations.

On a smaller scale, human geographers can help people design their cities and towns. By understanding where people go and what they need, geographers can help city planners place roads, shopping malls, and schools. Geographers also study the effect people have on the world. As a result, they often work with private groups and government agencies that want to protect the environment.

Partnering with Archaeology and History Human geography can also help other types of social scientists, such as archaeologists. Archaeologists engage in digs and study artifacts and features in a particular location. They gather evidence about groups of people and how those groups lived at particular times in history. The human geography of a place is part of archaeologists' gathered evidence.

Human geography also contributes to the work of historians. Historians use archaeological, geographical, and other types of evidence to investigate patterns in history. They identify turning points. A turning point can be an event, era, or development in history that brought about social, cultural, ecological, political, or economic change. The geography of places can affect historic turning points.

Reading Check
Summarize
What do human geographers study?

Other Fields of Geography

Physical geography and human geography are the two largest branches of the subject, but they are not the only ones. Many other fields of geography exist, each one devoted to studying one aspect of the world.

Geography is the study of Earth's physical and human geographic features.

Physical Geography
The study of Earth's physical geographic features, including rivers, mountains, oceans, weather, and other features, such as Victoria Falls in southern Africa

Human Geography
The study of Earth's people, including their ways of life, homes, cities, beliefs, and customs, like those of these children in Malawi, a country in Central Africa

Most of these fields are smaller, more specialized areas of either physical or human geography. For example, economic geography—the study of how people make and spend money—is a branch of human geography. Another specialized branch of human geography is urban geography, the study of cities and how people live in them. Physical geography also includes many fields, such as the study of climates. Other fields of physical geography are the studies of soils and plants.

Cartography One key field of geography is **cartography,** the science of making maps. Without maps, geographers would not be able to study where things are in the world. In addition to locations, maps can display other information about people, places, and environments. Cartographers decide which information to include on a given map and how it is displayed.

In the past, cartographers always drew maps by hand. Many of those maps were not very accurate. Today, though, most maps are made using computers and satellite images. Through advances in mapmaking, we can make accurate maps on almost any scale, from the whole world to a single

Computer Mapping

In the past, maps were drawn by hand. Making a map was a slow process. Even the simplest map took a long time to make. Today, however, cartographers have access to tools people in the past—even people who lived just 50 years ago—never imagined. The most important of these tools are computers.

Computers allow us to make maps quickly and easily. In addition, they let us make new types of maps that people could not make in the past.

The map shown here, for example, was drawn on a computer. It shows the number of computer users in the United States who were connected to the Internet on a particular day. Each of the lines that rises off of the map represents a city in which people were using the Internet. The color of the line indicates the number of computer users in that city. As you can see, this data resulted in a very complex map.

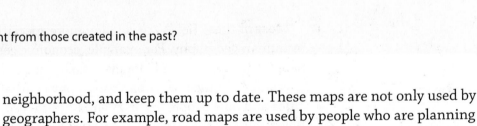

Making such a map required cartographers to sort through huge amounts of complex data. Such sorting would not have been possible without computers.

Contrast
How are today's maps different from those created in the past?

neighborhood, and keep them up to date. These maps are not only used by geographers. For example, road maps are used by people who are planning long trips.

Hydrology Another important branch of geography is hydrology, the study of water on Earth. Geographers in this field study the world's river systems and rainfall patterns. They study what causes droughts and floods and how people in cities can get safe drinking water. They also work to measure and protect the world's supply of water.

Meteorology Have you ever seen the weather report on television? If so, you have seen the results of another branch of geography. This branch is called **meteorology,** the study of weather and what causes it. Meteorologists use computers to follow and predict weather.

Meteorologists study weather patterns in a particular area. Then they use the information to predict what the weather will be like in the coming days. Their work helps people plan what to wear and what to do on any given day. At the same time, their work can save lives by predicting the arrival of terrible storms. These predictions are among the most visible ways in which the work of geographers affects our lives every day.

Summary and Preview In this lesson you learned about two main branches of geography—physical and human. Next, you will learn about two systems geographers use to organize their studies.

Lesson 2 Assessment

Review Ideas, Terms, and Places

1. **a. Define** What is physical geography?
   b. Explain Why do we study physical geography?
2. **a. Identify** What are some things that people study as part of human geography?
   b. Summarize What are some ways in which the study of human geography can influence our lives?
   c. Evaluate Which do you think would be more interesting to study: physical geography or human geography? Why?
3. **a. Identify** What are two specialized fields of geography?
   b. Analyze How do cartographers contribute to the work of other geographers?

Critical Thinking

4. **Compare and Contrast** Draw a diagram like the one shown here. In the left circle, list three features of physical geography from your notes. In the right circle, list three features of human geography. Where the circles overlap, list one feature they share.

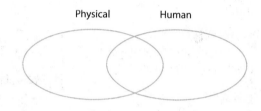

Physical   Human

Themes of Geography

The Big Idea

Geographers have created two different but related systems for organizing geographic studies.

Main Ideas

- The five themes of geography help us organize our studies of the world.
- The six essential elements of geography highlight some of the subject's most important ideas.

Key Terms and Places

absolute location
relative location
environment

If YOU lived there . . .

Your older sister has offered to drive you to a friend's house across town, but she doesn't know how to get there. You know your friend's street address and what the apartment building looks like. You know it's near the public library. You also would recognize some landmarks in the neighborhood, such as the gas station and the supermarket.

What might help your sister find the house?

The Five Themes of Geography

Geographers use themes, or ideas, in their work. These geography themes can be applied to nearly everything that geographers study. The five major themes of geography are Location, Place, Human-Environment Interaction, Movement, and Regions.

Location Every point on Earth has a location, a description of where it is. This location can be expressed in many ways. Sometimes a site's location is expressed in specific, or absolute, terms, such as an address. For example, the White House is located at 1600 Pennsylvania Avenue in the city of Washington, DC. A specific description like this one is called an **absolute location.** Other times, the site's location is expressed in general terms. For example, Canada is north of the United States. This general description of where a place lies is called its **relative location.**

Place Another theme, Place, is closely related to Location. However, Place does not refer simply to where an area is. It refers to the area's landscape, the features that define the area and make it different from other places. Such features could include land, climate, and people. Together, they give a place its own character.

Human-Environment Interaction In addition to looking at the features of places, geographers examine how those features interact. In particular, they want to understand how people interact with their environment—how people and their physical environment affect each other. An area's **environment** includes its land, water, climate, plants, and animals.

The Five Themes of Geography

Geographers use five major themes to organize and guide their studies: Location, Place, Human-Environment Interaction, Movement, and Regions.

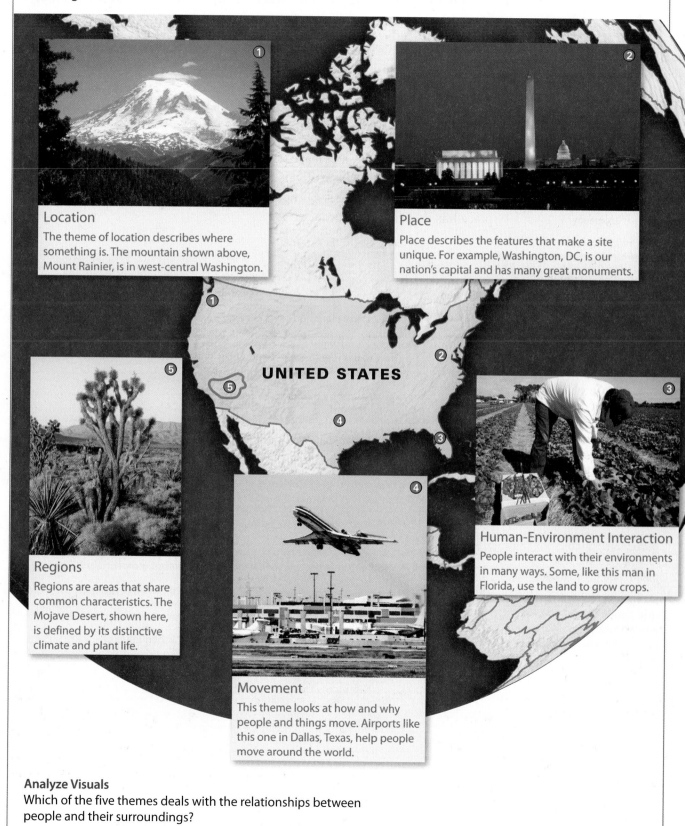

Location
The theme of location describes where something is. The mountain shown above, Mount Rainier, is in west-central Washington.

Place
Place describes the features that make a site unique. For example, Washington, DC, is our nation's capital and has many great monuments.

UNITED STATES

Regions
Regions are areas that share common characteristics. The Mojave Desert, shown here, is defined by its distinctive climate and plant life.

Human-Environment Interaction
People interact with their environments in many ways. Some, like this man in Florida, use the land to grow crops.

Movement
This theme looks at how and why people and things move. Airports like this one in Dallas, Texas, help people move around the world.

Analyze Visuals
Which of the five themes deals with the relationships between people and their surroundings?

People interact with their environment every day in all sorts of ways. They clear forests to plant crops, level fields to build cities, and dam rivers to prevent floods. At the same time, physical environments affect how people live. People in cold areas, for example, build houses with thick walls and wear heavy clothing to keep warm. People who live near oceans look for ways to protect themselves from storms.

Movement People are constantly moving. They move within cities, between cities, and between countries. Geographers want to know why and how people move. For example, they ask if people are moving to find work or to live in a more pleasant area. Geographers also study the roads and routes that make movement so common.

Regions You have already learned how geographers divide the world into many regions to help the study of geography. Creating regions also makes it easier to compare places. Comparisons help geographers learn why each place has developed the way it has.

Reading Check
Find Main Ideas
What are the five themes of geography?

Geography's Themes, Essential Elements, and Standards

Themes of Geography	Essential Elements	Geography Standards
Location The theme of Location describes where something is.	The World in Spatial Terms	1. How to use maps and other geographic representations, tools, and technologies to acquire, process, and report information from a spatial perspective 2. How to use mental maps to organize information about people, places, and environments in a spatial context 3. How to analyze the spatial organization of people, places, and environments on Earth's surface
Place Place describes the features that make a site unique. **Regions** Regions are areas that share common characteristics.	Places and Regions	4. The physical and human characteristics of places 5. How people create regions to interpret Earth's complexity 6. How culture and experience influence people's perceptions of places and regions
Movement This theme looks at how and why people and things move. **Human-Environment Interaction** People interact with their environment in many ways.	Physical Systems	7. The physical processes that shape the patterns of Earth's surface 8. The characteristics and spatial distribution of ecosystems on Earth's surface
	Human Systems	9. The characteristics, distribution, and migration of human populations on Earth's surface 10. The characteristics, distribution, and complexity of Earth's cultural mosaics 11. The patterns and networks of economic interdependence on Earth's surface 12. The processes, patterns, and functions of human settlement 13. How the forces of cooperation and conflict among people influence the division and control of Earth's surface
	Environment and Society	14. How human actions modify the physical environment 15. How physical systems affect human systems 16. Changes that occur in the meaning, use, distribution, and importance of resources
	The Uses of Geography	17. How to apply geography to interpret the past 18. How to apply geography to interpret the present and plan for the future

The Six Essential Elements

Academic Vocabulary
element part

The five themes of geography are not the only system geographers use to study the world. They also use a system of essential **elements** and national standards. Together, these themes, essential elements, and standards identify the most important ideas in the study of geography. Refer to the chart on the previous page.

The geography standards are 18 basic ideas that are central to the study of geography. The essential elements are based on the geography standards and act as a bridge between the themes and standards. Each element links several standards together. The six essential elements are The World in Spatial Terms, Places and Regions, Physical Systems, Human Systems, Environment and Society, and The Uses of Geography.

Read through that list again. Do you see any similarities between geography's six essential elements and its five themes? You probably do. The two systems are very similar because the six essential elements build on the five themes.

For example, the element Places and Regions combines two of the five themes of geography—Place and Regions. Also, the element called Environment and Society deals with many of the same issues as the theme Human-Environment Interaction.

There are also some basic differences between the essential elements and the themes. For example, the last element, The Uses of Geography, deals with issues not covered in the five themes. This element examines how people can use geography to plan the landscapes in which they live.

Throughout this book, you will notice references to both the themes and the essential elements. As you read, use these themes and elements to help you organize your own study of geography.

Reading Check
Summarize
What are the six essential elements of geography?

Summary and Preview You have just learned about the themes, elements, and standards of geography. In the next lesson, you will learn about the tools geographers use.

Lesson 3 Assessment

Review Ideas, Terms, and Places

1. a. Contrast How are the themes of Location and Place different?

b. Elaborate How does using the five themes help geographers understand the places they study?

2. a. Identify Which of the five themes of geography is associated with airports, highways, and the migration of people from one place to another?

b. Explain How are the geography standards and the six essential elements related?

c. Compare How are the six essential elements similar to the five themes of geography?

d. Recall To which essential element does the theme of Location relate?

Critical Thinking

3. Categorize Draw a chart like the one below. Use your notes to list the five themes of geography, explain each of the themes, and list one feature of your city or town that relates to each.

Theme					
Explanation					
Feature					

The Geographer's Tools

The Big Idea
Geographers use many tools to study the world.

Main Ideas
- Maps and globes are the most commonly used tools of geographers.
- Many geographers study information gathered by satellites.
- Geographers use many other tools, including graphs, charts, databases, and models, in their work.

Key Terms and Places
map
globe
Global Positioning System (GPS)
Geographic Information System (GIS)

If YOU lived there . . .

Your family's apartment has a leaking pipe under the kitchen sink. The landlord has sent a plumber to your apartment to fix the leak. The plumber arrives carrying a tool chest. You know that plumbers need specific tools to do their jobs correctly.

Can you think of a tool the plumber might use for this job?

Maps and Globes

Like all people with jobs to do, geographers need tools to study the world. The tools that geographers use most often in their work are maps and globes. A **map** is a flat drawing that shows all or part of Earth's surface. A **globe** is a spherical, or ball-shaped, model of the entire planet.

Both maps and globes show what the world looks like. They can show where mountains, deserts, and oceans are. They can also identify and describe the world's countries and major cities.

There are, however, major differences between maps and globes. Because a globe is spherical like Earth, it can show the world as it really is. A map, though, is flat. It is not possible to show a spherical area perfectly on a flat surface. To understand what this means, think about an orange. If you took the peel off of an orange, could you make it lie completely flat? No, you could not, unless you stretched or tore the peel first.

The same principle is true with maps. To draw Earth on a flat surface, people have to distort, or alter, some details. For example, places on a map might look to be farther apart than they really are, or their shapes or sizes might be changed slightly.

Still, maps have many advantages over globes. Flat maps are easier to work with than globes. Also, it is easier to show small areas like cities on maps than on globes. In addition, maps usually show more information than globes. Because globes are more expensive to make, they do not usually show anything more than where places are and what features they have.

Reading Check
Summarize
What are the tools geographers most often use?

Maps, on the other hand, can show all sorts of information. Besides showing land use and cities, maps can include a great deal of information about a place. A map might show what languages people speak or where their ancestors came from. Maps like the one below can even show how many students in an area play soccer.

The Geographer's Tools

Geographers use many tools to study the world. Each tool provides part of the information a geographer needs to learn what a place is like.

High School Soccer Participation

Participation in High School Soccer
- More than 9%
- 5–9%
- 3–5%
- Fewer than 3%
- Data not available

Maps usually give geographers more information about a place than globes do. This map, for example, shows rates of soccer participation in the United States.

A geographer can use a globe to see where a place, such as the United States, is located.

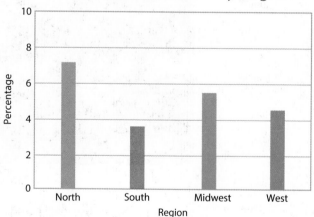

Percentage of Students on High School Soccer Teams by Region

Charts and graphs are also tools geographers can use to study information. They are often used when geographers want to compare numbers, such as the number of students who play soccer in each region of the country.

Analyze Visuals
What information could you learn from each of these tools?

Satellites

Maps and globes are not the only tools that geographers use in their work. As you have already read, many geographers study information gathered by satellites.

Much of the information gathered by these satellites is in the form of images. Geographers can study these images of Earth to see what an area looks like from far above. Satellites also collect information that we cannot see from the planet's surface. The information gathered by satellites helps geographers make accurate maps.

Satellites also collect and transmit information for a technology called **Global Positioning System (GPS).** The system uses 24 satellites to transmit information to Earth. This GPS information gives the exact location of a given object on our planet. The information is displayed on a small receiver. Vehicle drivers are some of the people who use GPS to find out how to get from where they are to other locations. There are many other uses of GPS. These include locating people in need of rescue on boats or in the wilderness. Scientists also use GPS to track and study wildlife.

Reading Check
Summarize
What satellite technology transmits data to people with receivers?

Satellite image of Italy

Other Geographic Tools

Geographers also use many other tools. To depict aspects of various countries and world regions, geographers create graphs, charts, databases, and models. They also use these tools to gather data and compare various world regions.

There is a geography tool that is made up of a group of databases. It is called **Geographic Information System (GIS).** GIS combines and provides information from many different sources. People use GIS by posing questions to the system. For example, a city planner might be looking for the best site near a city to build an airport. To find out, a geographer asks GIS, "What geographic characteristics are important for a good airport site?" GIS pulls together many layers of information, including different types of maps, to answer the question.

In less complex cases, the best tools a geographer can use are a notebook and digital voice recorder to take notes while talking to people. Armed with the proper tools, geographers learn about the world's people and places.

Summary and Preview You have learned that geographers use maps, globes, and other tools to study the world. In the next lesson, you will learn map skills, new geographic terms, and geographic themes and elements.

Reading Check
Summarize
Of what does Geographic Information System (GIS) consist?

Lesson 4 Assessment

Review Ideas, Terms, and Places

1. **a. Compare and Contrast** How are maps and globes similar? How are they different?
   b. Identify What are the advantages maps have over globes?
2. **a. Describe** How do geographers use satellite images?
   b. Recall What are some uses of GPS?
3. **a. Describe** What is GIS?
   b. Recall What is the purpose of GIS for geographers?

Critical Thinking

4. **Summarize** Make a chart like the one below that lists some of the geographer's tools.

The Geographer's Tools	

Geography Handbook

The Big Idea

Geographers study the world by understanding maps and geographic features of Earth.

Main Ideas

- When creating maps, cartographers use a pattern of latitude and longitude lines that circle Earth.

- Cartographers have created map projections to show the round surface of Earth on a flat piece of paper.

- Cartographers provide features to help users read maps.

- There are different kinds of maps for different uses.

- There are many kinds of landforms and other features on Earth.

Key Terms and Places

grid
latitude
parallels
equator
degrees
minutes
longitude
meridians
prime meridian
hemispheres
continents
map projections

Latitude and Longitude

As you learned in Lesson 4, a globe is a spherical model of Earth. It is useful for showing the entire Earth or studying large areas of Earth's surface.

To study the world, geographers use a pattern of imaginary lines that circle the globe in east–west and north–south directions. It is called a **grid.** The intersection of these imaginary lines helps us find places on Earth.

The east–west lines in the grid are lines of **latitude.** These lines are called **parallels** because they are always the same distance apart. Lines of latitude measure distance north and south of the **equator.** The equator is an imaginary line that circles the globe halfway between the North and South Poles. It divides the globe into north and south halves. Parallels measure distance from the equator in **degrees.** The symbol for degrees is °. Degrees are further divided into **minutes.** The symbol for minutes is ´. There are 60 minutes in a degree. Parallels north of the equator are labeled with an *N.* Those south of the equator are labeled with an *S.*

The north–south imaginary lines are lines of **longitude.** Lines of longitude are called **meridians.** These imaginary lines pass through the poles. They measure distance east and west of the **prime meridian.** The prime meridian is an imaginary line that divides the globe into east and west halves. It runs through Greenwich, England, and represents 0° longitude.

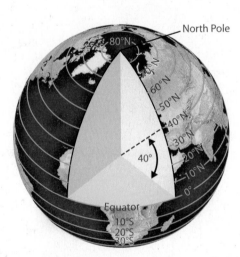

Lines of Latitude

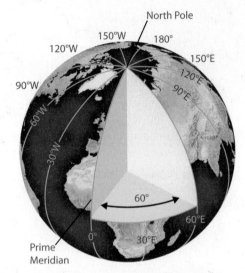

Lines of Longitude

Lines of latitude range from 0°, for locations on the equator, to 90°N or 90°S, for locations at the poles. Lines of longitude range from 0° on the prime meridian to 180° on a meridian in the mid–Pacific Ocean. Meridians west of the prime meridian to 180° are labeled with a *W*. Those east of the prime meridian to 180° are labeled with an *E*. Using latitude and longitude, geographers can identify the exact location of any place on Earth.

The equator divides the globe into two halves, called **hemispheres.** The half north of the equator is the Northern Hemisphere. The southern half is the Southern Hemisphere. The prime meridian and the 180° meridian divide the world into the Eastern and Western Hemispheres.

Earth's land surface is divided into seven large landmasses that are called **continents.** Landmasses smaller than continents and completely surrounded by water are called islands.

Geographers organize Earth's water surface into major regions, too. The largest is the world ocean. Geographers divide the world ocean into the Pacific Ocean, the Atlantic Ocean, the Indian Ocean, the Arctic Ocean, and the Southern Ocean.

Reading Check
Summarize
How do geographers use a grid of imaginary lines to study the world?

Northern Hemisphere

Southern Hemisphere

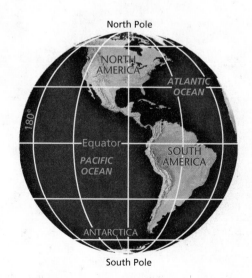

Western Hemisphere

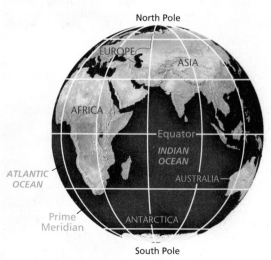

Eastern Hemisphere

Map Projections

A map is a flat diagram of all or part of Earth's surface. Mapmakers have created different ways of showing our round planet on flat maps. These different ways are called **map projections.** Because Earth is round, there is no way to show it accurately on a flat map. All flat maps are distorted in some way. Mapmakers must choose the type of map projection that is best for their purposes. Many map projections are one of three kinds: cylindrical, conic, or flat-plane.

Cylindrical Projections These projections are based on a cylinder wrapped around the globe. See the "Paper cylinder" illustration below. The cylinder touches the globe only at the equator. The meridians are pulled apart and are parallel to each other instead of meeting at the poles. This causes landmasses near the poles to appear larger than they really are.

A Mercator projection is one type of cylindrical projection. The Mercator projection is useful for navigators because it shows true direction and shape. However, it distorts the size of land areas near the poles.

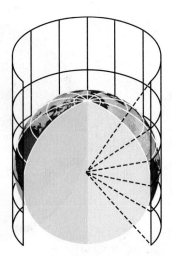

Paper cylinder

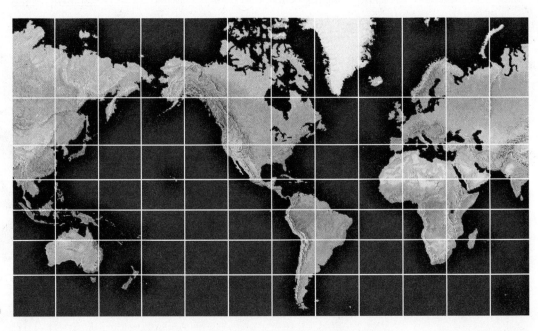

Mercator projection

Conic Projections These projections are based on a cone placed over the globe. See the "Paper cone" illustration below. A conic projection is most accurate along the lines of latitude where it touches the globe. It retains almost true shape and size. Conic projections are most useful for showing areas that have long east–west dimensions, such as the United States.

Flat-plane Projections These projections are based on a plane touching the globe at one point, such as at the North Pole or South Pole. See the "Flat plane" illustration below. A flat-plane projection can show true direction to airplane pilots and ship navigators. It also shows true area. However, it distorts the true shapes of landmasses.

Reading Check
Identify Problems
Why is it impossible to accurately show large parts of the world on flat maps?

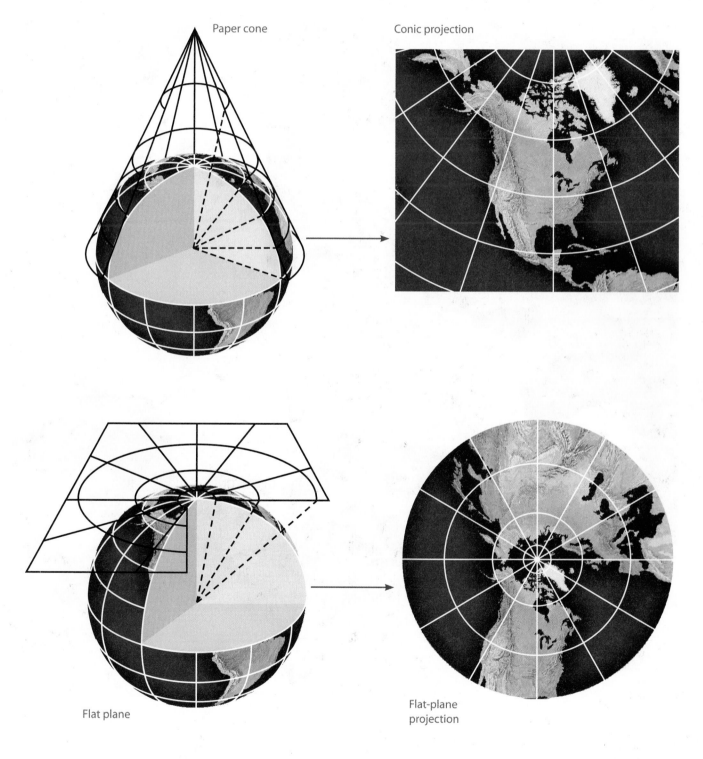

Paper cone

Conic projection

Flat plane

Flat-plane projection

Map Features

Maps are like messages sent out in code. To help us translate the code, mapmakers provide certain features. These features help us understand the message they are presenting about a particular part of the world. Of these features, almost all maps have a title, a compass rose, a scale, and a legend. The map below has these four features plus a fifth—a locator map.

1 Title A map's title shows what the subject of the map is. The map title is usually the first thing you should look at when studying a map, because it tells you what the map is trying to show.

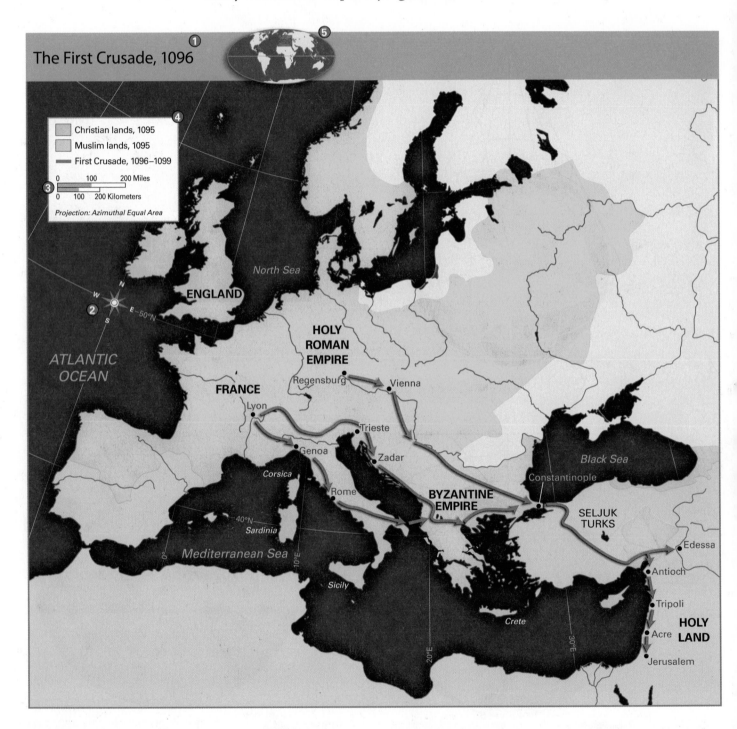

The First Crusade, 1096

Christian lands, 1095
Muslim lands, 1095
First Crusade, 1096–1099

0   100   200 Miles
0   100   200 Kilometers

Projection: Azimuthal Equal Area

North Sea

ENGLAND

ATLANTIC OCEAN

HOLY ROMAN EMPIRE

FRANCE

Lyon

Regensburg   Vienna

Genoa   Trieste
Zadar

Corsica

Rome

BYZANTINE EMPIRE

Black Sea

Constantinople

SELJUK TURKS

Sardinia

Mediterranean Sea

Sicily

Crete

Edessa

Antioch

Tripoli

Acre   HOLY LAND

Jerusalem

2 Compass Rose A directional indicator shows which way north, south, east, and west lie on the map. Some mapmakers use a "north arrow," which points toward the North Pole. Remember, "north" is not always at the top of a map. The way a map is drawn and the location of directions on that map depend on the perspective of the mapmaker. Most maps indicate direction with a compass rose. A compass rose has arrows that point to all four principal directions, also called cardinal points. The principal directions are north (N), east (E), south (S), and west (W). Some compass roses also show the intermediate directions. These are northeast (NE), southeast (SE), southwest (SW), and northwest (NW).

3 Scale Mapmakers use scales to represent the distances between points on a map. Scales may appear on maps in several different forms. Some maps provide a bar scale. Scales give distances in miles and kilometers.

To find the distance between two points on the map, place a piece of paper so that the edge connects the two points. Mark the location of each point on the paper with a line or dot. Then compare the distance between the two dots with the map's bar scale. The number on the top of the scale gives the distance in miles. The number on the bottom gives the distance in kilometers. Because the distances are given in large intervals, you may have to approximate the actual distance on the scale.

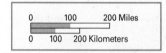

4 Legend The legend, or key, explains what the symbols on the map represent. Point symbols are used to specify the location of things, such as cities, that do not take up much space on the map. Some legends show colors that represent certain features like empires or other regions. Other maps might have legends with symbols or colors that represent features such as roads. Legends can also show economic resources, land use, population density, and climate. Some legends include the map scale as well.

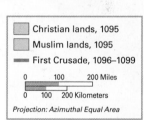

Reading Check
Summarize What four features do most maps have?

5 Locator Map A locator map shows where in the world the area on the map is located. In this example, the area shown on the main map is shown in red on the locator map. The locator map also shows surrounding areas so the reader can see how the information on the map relates to neighboring lands.

Different Kinds of Maps

As you study the world's regions and countries, you will use a variety of maps. Political maps and physical maps are two of the most common types of maps you will study. In addition, you will use thematic maps. These maps might show climate, population, resources, ancient empires, or other topics. By working with these maps, you will see what the physical geography of places is like, where people live, and how the world has changed over time.

Political Maps Political maps show the major political features of a region. These features include country borders, capital cities, and other places. Political maps use different colors to represent countries, and capital cities are often shown with a special star symbol.

North Africa: Political

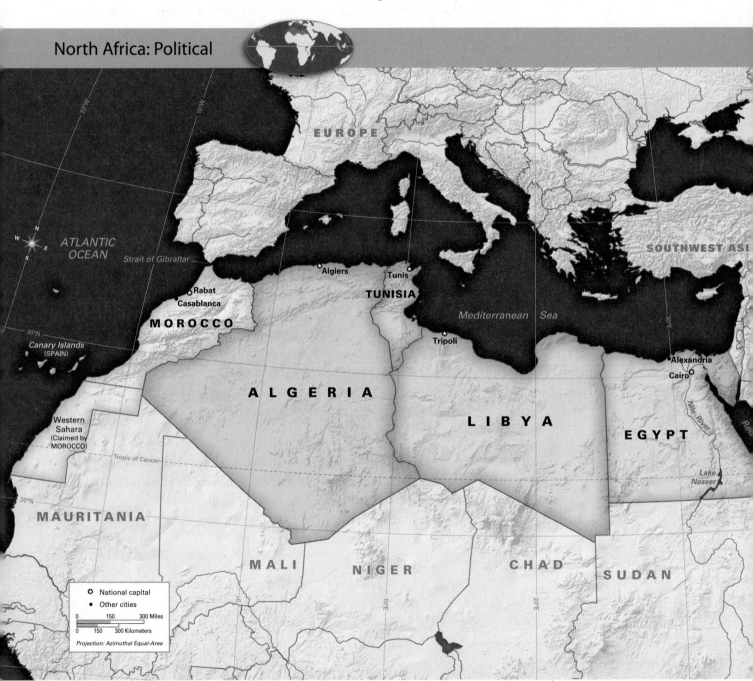

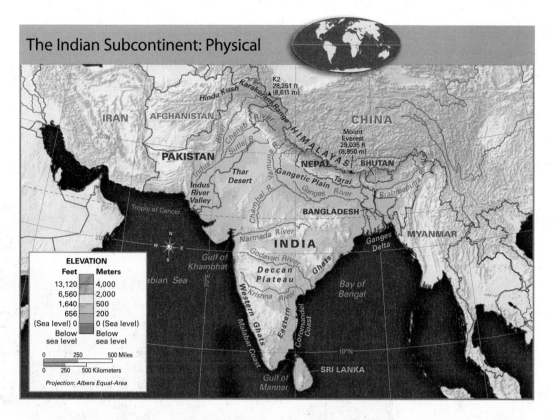

The Indian Subcontinent: Physical

ELEVATION

Feet	Meters
13,120	4,000
6,560	2,000
1,640	500
656	200
(Sea level) 0	0 (Sea level)
Below sea level	Below sea level

Projection: Albers Equal-Area

Physical Maps Physical maps show the major physical features of a region. See the map above. These features may include mountain ranges, rivers, oceans, islands, deserts, and plains. Often, these maps use different colors to represent different elevations of land. The reader can easily see which areas are high elevations, such as mountains, and which areas are lower.

Thematic Maps Thematic maps focus on one special topic, such as climate, resources, or population. See the map below. These maps present information on the topic that is particularly important in the region. Depending on the type of thematic map, the information may be shown with different colors, arrows, dots, or other symbols.

Reading Check
Summarize
What are two of the most common kinds of maps used in geography?

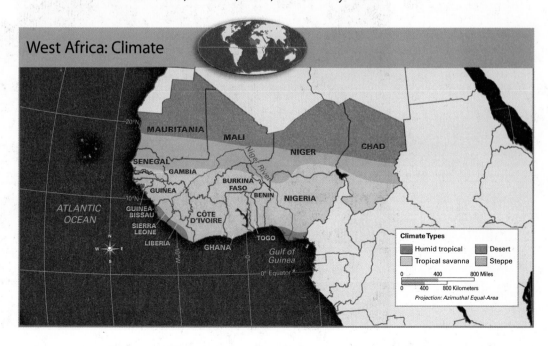

West Africa: Climate

Climate Types
- Humid tropical
- Tropical savanna
- Desert
- Steppe

Projection: Azimuthal Equal-Area

Earth's Surface Features

A landform is a naturally formed feature on Earth's surface. There are many kinds of landforms and water features on Earth. Many of these features are shown in this illustration.

Feature Descriptions

1	ocean	large body of water
2	cape	point of land that extends into water
3	coastal plain	area of flat land along a sea or ocean
4	coast	area of land near the ocean
5	glacier	large area of slow-moving ice
6	lake	inland body of water
7	plain	nearly flat area
8	inlet	area of water extending into the land from a larger body of water
9	floodplain	flat land next to a river formed by silt deposited by floods
10	timberline	line on a mountain above which it is too cold for trees to grow
11	river	natural flow of water that runs through the land
12	source of river	place where a river begins
13	foothill	hilly area at the base of a mountain
14	riverbank	land along a river
15	mouth of river	place where a river empties into another body of water
16	hill	rounded, elevated area of land smaller than a mountain
17	mountain	area of rugged land that generally rises higher than 2,000 feet
18	island	area of land surrounded entirely by water
19	basin	bowl-shaped area of land surrounded by higher land
20	mountain range	row of mountains
21	plateau	large, flat, elevated area of land
22	bluff	high, steep face of rock or earth
23	isthmus	narrow piece of land connecting two larger land areas
24	valley	area of low land between hills or mountains
25	marsh	lowland with moist soil and tall grasses
26	lagoon	body of shallow water
27	strait	narrow body of water connecting two larger bodies of water
28	canyon	deep, narrow valley with steep walls
29	peninsula	area of land that sticks out into a lake or ocean
30	volcano	opening in Earth's crust where lava, ash, and gases erupt
31	waterfall	steep drop from a high place to a lower place in a stream or river
32	delta	area where a river deposits soil into the ocean
33	cliff	high, steep face of rock or earth
34	reef	ocean ridge made up of coral, rock, or sand
35	gulf	large part of the ocean that extends into land
36	peak	top of a mountain
37	swamp	area of low, wet land with trees
38	bay	part of a large body of water that is smaller than a gulf
39	dune	hill of sand shaped by wind
40	tributary	stream or river that flows into a larger stream or river
41	mountain pass	gap between mountains
42	sea	body of salt water smaller than an ocean
43	desert	extremely dry area with little water and few plants
44	oasis	area in the desert with a water source
45	mesa	flat-topped mountain with steep sides
46	savanna	area of grassland and scattered trees

Summary As you study geography, one of the main tools you will use is the map—the primary tool of geographers. In this lesson, you learned about some of the basic features of maps. You discovered how maps are made, how to read them, and how they can show the round surface of Earth on a flat piece of paper. You learned about latitude and longitude and map projections. You read about map features, such as titles, compass roses, scales, legends, and locator maps, and different kinds of maps designed for different uses. You've discovered names and descriptions of some of Earth's features. Now use your new knowledge to explore the world from a geographer's perspective.

Lesson 5 Assessment

Review Ideas, Terms, and Places

1. **a. Define** What is the equator?

   b. Identify How is the prime meridian used?

2. **a. Define** What is a map projection?

   b. Explain Why are cylindrical and flat-plane projections useful for airplane pilots and ship navigators?

3. **a. Describe** Describe a compass rose and the information it contains.

   b. Identify and Explain What is a bar scale? How is it used?

4. **a. Analyze** Which kind of map would you use if you wanted to know which part of the mapped area was highest? Why?

   b. Identify What characteristic makes a map a thematic map?

5. **a. Define** What is a delta?

   b. Define What is a glacier?

Critical Thinking

6. **Compare and Contrast** Create a chart like the one shown that compares and contrasts kinds of map projections.

Map Projections			
	Cylindrical	Conic	Flat-plane
Based on			
Accurately shows			
Distorts			

Social Studies Skills

Analyze Satellite Images

Define the Skill

In addition to maps and globes, satellite images are among the geographer's most valuable tools. Geographers use two basic types of these images. The first type is called true color. These images are like photographs taken from high above Earth's surface. The colors in these images are similar to what you would see from the ground. Vegetation, for example, appears green.

The other type of satellite image is called an infrared image. Infrared images are taken using a special type of light. These images are based on heat patterns, and so the colors on them are not what we might expect. Bodies of water appear black, for example, since they give off little heat.

True-color satellite image of Italy

Learn the Skill

Use the satellite images on this page to answer the following questions.

1. On which image is vegetation red?
2. Which image do you think probably looks more like Italy from the ground?

Practice the Skill

Search the Internet to find a satellite image of your state or region. Determine whether the image is true color or infrared. Then write three statements that describe what you see on the image.

Infrared satellite image of Italy

Module 1 Assessment

Review Vocabulary, Terms, and Places

Match the words in the columns with the correct definitions listed below.

1. geography
2. physical geography
3. human geography
4. element
5. meteorology
6. region
7. cartography
8. map
9. landscape
10. globe

a. a part of the world that has one or more common features that make it different from surrounding areas

b. a flat drawing of part of Earth's surface

c. a part

d. a spherical model of the planet

e. the study of the world's physical features

f. the study of weather and what causes it

g. the study of the world, its people, and the landscapes they create

h. the science of making maps

i. the physical and human features that define an area and make it different from other places

j. the study of people and communities

Comprehension and Critical Thinking

Lesson 1

11. a. Explain In what ways do geographers become scientists when working to answer questions?

    b. Recall What are three levels at which a geographer might study the world?

    c. Identify Which of these levels covers the largest area?

Lesson 2

12. a. Locate Choose a country to locate on the political map of the world in this book's atlas. Use latitude and longitude to determine the absolute location of the country.

    b. Explain Why did geographers create the five themes and the six essential elements?

    c. Predict How might the five themes and six essential elements help you in your study of geography?

Lesson 3

13. a. Identify What are the two main branches of geography? What does each include?

    b. Summarize How can physical geography help people adjust to the dangers of the world?

    c. Elaborate Why do geographers study both physical and human geographic features of places?

Lesson 4

14. a. Elaborate How might satellite images and computers help geographers improve their knowledge of the world?

    b. Define What is GPS?

    c. Explain How might a geographer use a notebook and a digital voice recorder to gather data?

Lesson 5

15. a. Define What is a hemisphere of a globe?

    b. Explain What features are shown in a political map?

    c. Identify What is a peninsula?

Reading Skills

16. **Use Prior Knowledge** Use the Reading Social Studies activity in this module to help you create a chart. With a partner, create a three-column chart titled A Geographer's World. In the first column, list what you each knew about geography before you read the module. In the second column, list what you each learned about geography. In the third column, list questions that you each still have about geography.

Social Studies Skills

Analyze Satellite Images *Use the images from the Social Studies Skills activity in this module to answer the questions below.*

17. On which image do forests appear more clearly: the true color or the infrared image?

18. What color do you think represents mountains on the infrared satellite image?

19. Why might geographers use satellite images like these while making maps of Italy?

Map Activity

20. **Sketch Map** Look for and read environmental print to help you sketch a map of your school. Environmental print can be found all around you in the form of signs, labels, symbols, words, and numbers that provide information. Your map should include environmental print found in and around classrooms and buildings. Use the basic sketch map shown here as an example.

Focus on Writing

21. **Write a Job Description** Review your notes on the different jobs geographers do. Then write a job description of a geographer that could be included in a career planning guide. You should begin your description by explaining why the job is important. Then identify the job's tasks and responsibilities. Finally, tell what kind of person might do well as a geographer.

Module 2

The Physical World

Essential Question

Why do we study Earth and its physical systems?

About the Photo: Many of Earth's features are visible from space. This photo, taken from a satellite orbiting the planet, shows part of the North American continent.

In this module, you will learn about Earth's resources, and the processes that cause the seasons, shape landmasses and climates, and support life. You will also learn how humans use and interact with these resources and processes.

What You Will Learn

▶ *Explore ONLINE!*

HISTORY

VIDEOS, including . . .
- The Ring of Fire
- Plate Tectonics and Continental Drift

☑ Document-Based Investigations

☑ Graphic Organizers

☑ Interactive Games

☑ Animation: The Water Cycle

☑ Channel One News Video: Hunting Hurricanes

☑ Channel One News Video: Earthquake Preparedness

☑ Interactive Map: Major Climate Regions

☑ Image with Rich Media: Desert Ecosystem

Land Forces on and under Earth's surface have shaped the different landforms on our planet. Geographers study how mountains and other landforms were made.

Environments Living things, such as this koala, depend on their surroundings.

Water on Earth Water is essential for life on Earth. Much of the planet's water supply is stored in Earth's oceans and ice caps.

Reading Social Studies

Use Word Parts

READING FOCUS

Many English words are made up of several word parts: roots, prefixes, and suffixes. A root is the base of the word and carries the main meaning. A prefix is a letter or syllable added to the beginning of a root. A suffix is a letter or syllable added to the end to create new words. When you come across a new word, you can sometimes figure out the meaning by looking at its parts. Study the charts of common word parts and their meanings.

Common Prefixes		
Prefix	Meaning	Sample Words
geo-	earth	geology
inter-	between, among	interpersonal, intercom
in-	not	ineffective
re-	again	restate, rebuild

Common Suffixes		
Suffix	Meaning	Sample Words
-ible	capable of	visible, responsible
-less	without	penniless, hopeless
-ize	make	equalize
-ment	result, action	commitment
-al	relating to	directional
-tion	the act or condition of	rotation, selection

Common Roots		
Word Root	Meaning	Sample Words
-graph-	write, writing	autograph, biography
-vid-, -vis-	see	videotape, visible

YOU TRY IT!

Use your knowledge of word parts to understand challenging words such as the ones listed below. Work with a partner to read the words. First separate any prefixes or suffixes and identify the word's root. Use the charts to define the root, the prefix, or the suffix. Then work with your partner to write a definition for each word.

geography   regardless   reshaping   movement   invisible   seasonal

visualize   separation   interact

As you read this module, look for words that include these word parts.

Earth and the Sun's Energy

The Big Idea

Earth's movement and the sun's energy interact to create day and night, temperature changes, and the seasons.

Main Ideas

- Earth's movement affects the amount of energy we receive from the sun.
- Earth's seasons are caused by the planet's tilt.

Key Terms and Places

solar energy
rotation
revolution
tropics

If YOU lived there . . .

You live in Chicago and have just won an exciting prize—a trip to Australia during winter vacation in January. As you prepare for the trip, your mother reminds you to pack shorts and a swimsuit. You are confused. In January you usually wear winter sweaters and a heavy jacket.

Why is the weather so different in Australia?

Earth's Movement

Energy from the sun helps crops grow, provides light, and warms Earth. It even influences the clothes we wear, the foods we eat, and the sports we play. All life on Earth requires **solar energy,** or energy from the sun, to survive. The amount of solar energy places on Earth receive changes constantly. Earth's rotation, revolution, and tilt, as well as latitude, all affect the amount of solar energy parts of the planet receive from the sun.

Rotation Imagine that Earth has a rod running through it from the North Pole to the South Pole. This rod represents Earth's axis—an imaginary line around which a planet turns. As Earth spins on its axis, different parts of the planet face the sun. It takes Earth 24 hours, or one day, to complete this rotation. A **rotation** is one complete spin of Earth on its axis. As Earth rotates during this 24-hour period, it appears to us that the sun moves across the sky. The sun seems to rise in the east and set in the west. The sun, however, does not move. It is actually Earth's rotation that creates the sense of the sun's movement.

Earth's rotation also explains why day changes to night. As you will see in the illustration on the next page, solar energy strikes only the half of Earth facing the sun. Warmth and light from the sun create daytime. At the same time, the half of the planet facing away from the sun experiences the cooler temperatures and darkness of night. Earth's rotation causes regular shifts from day to night. As a result, levels of solar energy on Earth constantly change.

Solar Energy

Earth's tilt and rotation cause changes in the amount of energy we receive from the sun. As Earth rotates on its axis, energy from the sun creates periods of day and night. Earth's tilt causes some locations, especially those close to the equator, to receive more direct solar energy than others.

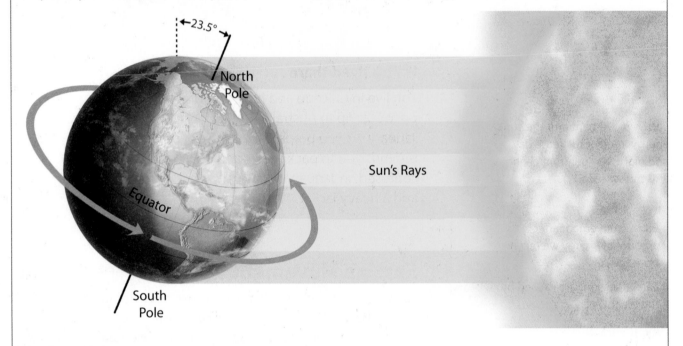

←23.5°

North Pole

Sun's Rays

Equator

South Pole

Analyze Visuals
Is the region north or south of the equator receiving more solar energy? How can you tell?

Revolution As Earth spins on its axis, it also follows a path, or orbit, around the sun. Earth's orbit around the sun is not a perfect circle. Sometimes the orbit takes Earth closer to the sun, and at other times the orbit takes it farther away. It takes 365¼ days for Earth to complete one **revolution,** or trip around the sun. We base our calendar year on the time it takes Earth to complete its orbit around the sun. To allow for the fraction of a day, we add an extra day—February 29—to our calendar every four years.

Academic Vocabulary
factor cause

Tilt and Latitude Another **factor** affecting the amount of solar energy we receive is the planet's tilt. As the illustration shows, Earth's axis is not straight up and down. It is actually tilted at an angle of 23.5 degrees from vertical. At any given time of year, some locations on Earth are tilting away from the sun, and others are tilting toward it. Places tilting toward the sun receive more solar energy and experience warmer temperatures. Those tilting away from the sun receive less solar energy and experience cooler temperatures.

A location's latitude, the distance north or south of Earth's equator, also affects the amount of solar energy it receives. Low-latitude areas, those near the equator like Hawaii, receive direct rays from the sun all year. These direct rays are more intense and produce warmer temperatures. Regions with high latitudes, like Antarctica, are farther from the equator. As a result, they receive indirect rays from the sun and have colder temperatures.

Reading Check
Find Main Ideas
What factors affect the solar energy Earth receives?

The Seasons

Does snow in July or high temperatures in January seem odd to you? It might if you live in the Northern Hemisphere, where cold temperatures are common in January, not July. The planet's changing seasons explain why we often connect certain weather with specific times of the year, like snow in January. Seasons are periods during the year that are known for certain types of weather. Many places on Earth experience four seasons—winter, spring, summer, and fall—based on temperature and length of day. In some parts of the world, seasons are based on the amount of rainfall.

Winter and Summer Earth's tilt creates the change in seasons. While one of Earth's poles is tilted away from the sun, the other is tilted toward it. During winter part of Earth tilts away from the sun, causing less direct solar energy, cool temperatures, and less daylight. Summer occurs when part of Earth tilts toward the sun, causing more direct solar energy, warmer temperatures, and longer periods of daylight.

The Seasons: Northern Hemisphere

As Earth orbits the sun, the tilt of its axis toward and away from the sun causes the seasons to change. Seasons in the Northern Hemisphere change at about the same time every year.

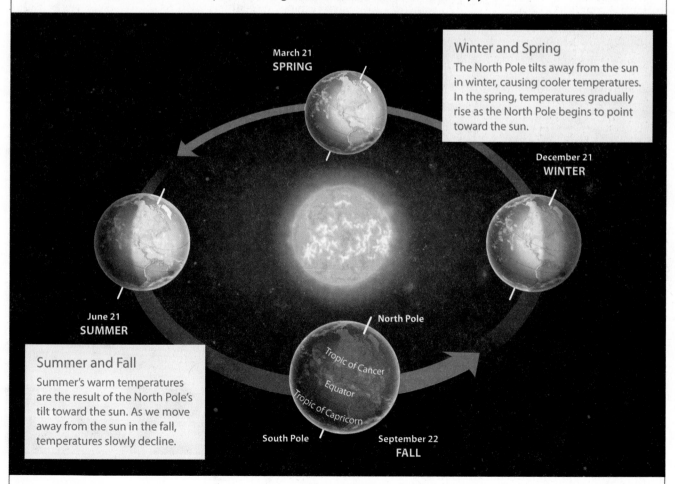

March 21
SPRING

Winter and Spring
The North Pole tilts away from the sun in winter, causing cooler temperatures. In the spring, temperatures gradually rise as the North Pole begins to point toward the sun.

December 21
WINTER

June 21
SUMMER

Summer and Fall
Summer's warm temperatures are the result of the North Pole's tilt toward the sun. As we move away from the sun in the fall, temperatures slowly decline.

North Pole

Tropic of Cancer

Equator

Tropic of Capricorn

South Pole

September 22
FALL

Analyze Visuals
As the Northern Hemisphere experiences winter, what season is it in the Southern Hemisphere?

Because of Earth's tilt, the Northern and Southern Hemispheres experience opposite seasons. As the North Pole tilts toward the sun in summer, the South Pole tilts away from it. As a result, the Southern Hemisphere experiences winter. Likewise, when it is spring in the Northern Hemisphere, it is fall in the Southern Hemisphere.

Spring and Fall As Earth orbits the sun, there are periods when the poles tilt neither toward nor away from the sun. These periods mark spring and fall. During the spring, as part of Earth begins to tilt toward the sun, solar energy increases. Temperatures slowly start to rise, and days grow longer. In the fall the opposite occurs as winter approaches. Solar energy begins to decrease, causing cooler temperatures and shorter days.

Focus on Culture

The Midnight Sun

Can you imagine going to sleep late at night with the sun shining in the sky? People who live near the Arctic and Antarctic Circles experience this every summer, when they can receive up to 24 hours of sunlight a day. The time-lapse photo below shows a typical sunset during this period—except the sun never really sets! This phenomenon is known as the midnight sun. For locations like Tromso, Norway, this means up to two months of constant daylight each summer. People living near Earth's poles often use the long daylight hours to work on outdoor projects in preparation for winter, when they can receive 24 hours of darkness a day.

Predict
How might people's daily lives be affected by the midnight sun?

Reading Check
Identify Cause and Effect What causes the seasons to change?

Rainfall and Seasons Some regions on Earth have seasons marked by rainfall rather than temperature. This is true in the **tropics,** regions close to the equator. At certain times of year, winds bring either dry or moist air to the tropics, creating wet and dry seasons. In India, for example, seasonal winds called monsoons bring heavy rains from June to October and dry air from November to January.

Summary and Preview Solar energy is crucial for all life on the planet. Earth's position and movements affect the amount of energy we receive from the sun and determine our seasons. The Northern and Southern Hemispheres have opposite seasons. Some regions experience four seasons while others experience only two. In the next lesson you will learn about Earth's water supply and its importance to us.

Lesson 1 Assessment

Review Ideas, Terms, and Places

1. a. **Identify** What is solar energy, and how does it affect Earth?

   b. **Analyze** How do rotation and tilt each affect the amount of solar energy that different parts of Earth receive?

   c. **Predict** What might happen if Earth received less solar energy than it currently does?

2. a. **Describe** Name and describe Earth's seasons.

   b. **Contrast** How are seasons different in the Northern and Southern Hemispheres?

   c. **Elaborate** How might the seasons affect human activities?

Critical Thinking

3. Identify Cause and Effect Use your notes and the chart to identify the causes of seasons.

Water on Earth

The Big Idea

Water is a dominant feature on Earth's surface and is essential for life.

Main Ideas

- Salt water and freshwater make up Earth's water supply.
- In the water cycle, water circulates from Earth's surface to the atmosphere and back again.
- Water plays an important role in people's lives.

Key Terms and Places

freshwater
glaciers
surface water
precipitation
groundwater
water vapor
water cycle

If YOU lived there...

You live in the desert Southwest, where heavy water use and a lack of rainfall have led to water shortages. Your city plans to begin a water conservation program that asks people to limit how much water they use. Many of your neighbors have complained that the program is unnecessary. Others support the plan to save water.

How do you feel about the city's water plan?

Earth's Water Supply

Think of the different uses for water. We use water to cook and clean, we drink it, and we grow crops with it. Water is used for recreation, to generate electricity, and even to travel from place to place. Water is perhaps the most important and abundant resource on Earth. In fact, water covers some two-thirds of the planet. Understanding Earth's water supply and how it affects our lives is an important part of geography.

Salt Water Although water covers much of the planet, we cannot use most of it. About 97 percent of Earth's water is salt water. Because salt water contains high levels of salt and other minerals, it is unsafe to drink.

In general, salt water is found in Earth's oceans. Oceans are vast bodies of water covering some 71 percent of the planet's

Salt Water
Earth's oceans contain some 97 percent of the planet's water supply. Unfortunately, this water is too salty to drink.

Glaciers

Tremendous bodies of ice consist of frozen freshwater. This cruise ship looks like a toy next to San Rafael Glacier at Laguna San Rafael National Park on the Pacific coast of southern Chile.

Freshwater

Freshwater from lakes, rivers, and streams makes up only a fraction of Earth's water supply.

surface. Earth's oceans are made up of smaller bodies of water such as seas, gulfs, bays, and straits. Altogether, Earth's oceans cover some 139 million square miles (360 million square km) of the planet's surface.

Some of Earth's lakes contain salt water. The Great Salt Lake in Utah, for example, is a saltwater lake. As salt and other minerals have collected in the lake, which has no outlet, the water has become salty.

Freshwater Since the water in Earth's oceans is too salty to use, we must rely on other sources for freshwater. **Freshwater**, or water without salt, makes up only about 3 percent of our total water supply. Much of that freshwater is locked in Earth's **glaciers**, large areas of slow-moving ice, and in the ice of the Antarctic and Arctic regions. Most of the freshwater we use every day is found in lakes, in rivers, and under Earth's surface.

One form of freshwater is surface water. **Surface water** is water that is found in Earth's streams, rivers, and lakes. It may seem that there is a great deal of water in our lakes and rivers, but only a tiny amount of Earth's water supply—less than 1 percent—comes from surface water.

Streams and rivers are a common source of surface water. Streams form when precipitation collects in a narrow channel and flows toward the ocean. **Precipitation** is water that falls to Earth's surface as rain, snow, sleet, or hail. In turn, streams join together to form rivers. Any smaller stream or river that flows into a larger stream or river is called a tributary. For example, the Missouri River is the largest tributary of the Mississippi River.

Lakes are another important source of surface water. Some lakes were formed as rivers filled low-lying areas with water. Other lakes, like the Great Lakes along the U.S.-Canada border, were formed when glaciers carved deep holes in Earth's surface and deposited water as they melted.

Most of Earth's available freshwater is stored underground. As precipitation falls to Earth, much of it is absorbed into the ground, filling spaces in the soil and rock.

Water found below Earth's surface is called **groundwater**. In some places on Earth, groundwater naturally bubbles from the ground as a spring. More often, however, people obtain groundwater by digging wells, or deep holes dug into the ground to reach the water.

Reading Check
Contrast Ideas How is salt water different from freshwater?

The Water Cycle

When you think of water, you probably visualize a liquid—a flowing stream, a glass of ice-cold water, or a wave hitting the beach. But did you know that water is the only substance on Earth that occurs naturally as a solid, a liquid, and a gas? We see water as a solid in snow and ice and as a liquid in oceans and rivers. Water also occurs in the air as an invisible gas called **water vapor**.

Water is always moving. As water heats up and cools down, it moves from the planet's surface to the atmosphere, or the mass of air that surrounds Earth. One of the most important processes in nature is the water cycle. The **water cycle** is the movement of water from Earth's surface to the atmosphere and back.

The sun's energy drives the water cycle. As the sun heats water on Earth's surface, some of that water evaporates, or turns from liquid to gas, or water vapor. Water vapor then rises into the air. As the vapor rises, it cools. The cooling causes the water vapor to condense, or change from a vapor into tiny liquid droplets. These droplets join together to form clouds. If the droplets become heavy enough, precipitation occurs—that is, the water falls back to Earth as rain, snow, sleet, or hail.

When that precipitation falls back to Earth's surface, some of the water is absorbed into the soil as groundwater. Excess water, called runoff, flows over land and collects in streams, rivers, and oceans. Because the water cycle is constantly repeating, it allows us to maintain a fairly constant supply of water on Earth.

Reading Check
Find Main Ideas
What is the water cycle?

Energy from the sun drives the water cycle. Surface water evaporates into Earth's atmosphere, where it condenses, then falls back to Earth as precipitation. This cycle repeats continuously, providing us with a fairly constant water supply.

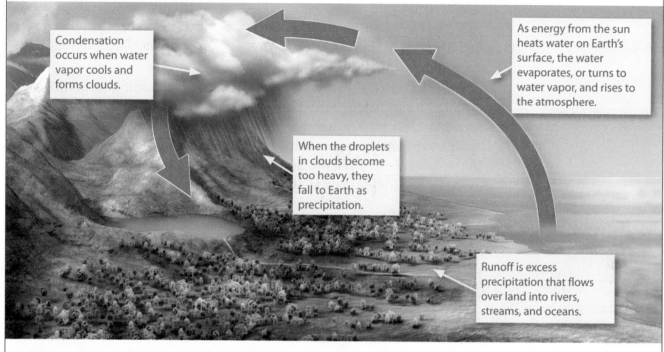

Condensation occurs when water vapor cools and forms clouds.

As energy from the sun heats water on Earth's surface, the water evaporates, or turns to water vapor, and rises to the atmosphere.

When the droplets in clouds become too heavy, they fall to Earth as precipitation.

Runoff is excess precipitation that flows over land into rivers, streams, and oceans.

Analyze Visuals
How does evaporation differ from precipitation?

Water and People

How many times a day do you think about water? Many of us rarely give it a second thought, yet water is crucial for survival. Water problems such as the lack of water, polluted water, and flooding are concerns for people all around the world. Water also provides us with countless benefits, such as energy and recreation.

Water Problems One of the greatest water problems people face is a lack of available freshwater. Many places face water shortages as a result of droughts, or long periods of lower-than-normal precipitation. Another cause of water shortages is overuse. In places like the southwestern United States, where the population has grown rapidly, the heavy demand for water has led to shortages.

Water shortages lead to many problems. Crops and livestock die without enough water, leading to food shortages. In many places in Africa, women and girls spend hours every day walking to distant water sources instead of doing other work or going to school.

Water shortages can even lead to or worsen conflict. Because water is necessary for survival, people will fight to control it in an attempt to control other groups.

Even where water is plentiful, it may not be clean enough to use. If chemicals and household wastes make their way into streams and rivers, they can contaminate the water supply. Polluted water can carry diseases. These diseases may harm humans, plants, and animals.

Flooding is another water problem that affects people around the world. Heavy rains often lead to flooding, which can damage property and threaten lives. One example of dangerous flooding occurred in Bangladesh in 2004. Severe floods there destroyed roads and schools, affecting about 25 million people.

Water dramatically impacts the physical environment in other ways as well. In Florida, where limestone is plentiful, sinkholes can arise with little warning. Over time, water dissolves and weakens limestone, leaving the surface with little support. The ground layer collapses. The resulting hole in the ground can swallow cars and houses. The Devil's Millhopper is one example of a well-known sinkhole.

Water's Benefits Water does more than just quench our thirst. It provides us with many benefits, such as food, power, and even recreation.

Water's most important benefit is that it provides us with food to eat. Everything we eat depends on water. For example, fruits and vegetables need water to grow. Animals also need water to live and grow. As a result, we use water to farm and raise animals so that we will have food to eat.

Water is also an important source of energy. Using dams, we harness the power of moving water to produce electricity. Electricity provides power to air-condition or heat our homes, to run our washers and dryers, and to keep our food cold.

Water also provides us with recreation. Rivers, lakes, and oceans make it possible for us to swim, to fish, to surf, or to sail a boat. Although recreation is not critical for our survival, it does make our lives richer and more enjoyable.

Water's Benefits: for Life

Without water, plants won't grow. This modern irrigation system, used for large agricultural projects, ensures that plants get the water they need and humans get the food they need.

Water's Benefits: for Fun
This surfer rides a wave at the beach. Many people enjoy swimming, boating, fishing, and other recreational activities on water.

Recognizing all of these benefits, some communities work together to manage freshwater supplies. For example, in Florida, long-term population growth strains the freshwater supply. That, combined with drought conditions, inspired the creation of the Central Florida Water Initiative (CFWI). This organization works to protect and conserve water resources in a 5,300-square-mile (13,727-sq-km) area. The CFWI works with businesses, utilities, environmental groups, agricultural groups, and others to meet people's water needs. Many regions around the world have similar organizations.

Reading Check
Summarize How does water affect people's lives?

Summary and Preview In this lesson you learned that water is essential for life on Earth. Next, you will learn about the shapes on Earth's surface.

Lesson 2 Assessment

Review Ideas, Terms, and Places

1. **a. Describe** Name and describe the different types of water that make up Earth's water supply.

   b. Analyze Why is only a small percentage of Earth's freshwater available to us?

   c. Elaborate In your opinion, which is more important—surface water or groundwater? Why?

2. **a. Recall** What drives the water cycle?

   b. Make Inferences From what bodies of water do you think most evaporation occurs? Why?

3. **a. Define** What is a drought?

   b. Analyze How does water support life on Earth?

   c. Evaluate What water problem do you think is most critical in your community? Why?

Critical Thinking

4. **Sequence** Draw the graphic organizer. Then use your notes and the graphic organizer to identify the stages in Earth's water cycle.

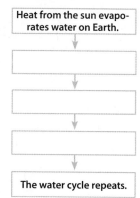

Heat from the sun evaporates water on Earth.

↓

↓

↓

The water cycle repeats.

The Land

The Big Idea

Processes below and on Earth's surface shape the planet's physical features.

Main Ideas

- Earth's surface is covered by many different landforms.
- Forces below Earth's surface build up our landforms.
- Forces on the planet's surface shape Earth's landforms.
- Landforms influence people's lives and culture.

Key Terms and Places

landforms
continents
plate tectonics
lava
earthquakes
weathering
erosion
alluvial deposition

Reading Check
Summarize
What are some common landforms?

If YOU lived there...

You live in the state of Washington. All your life, you have looked out at the beautiful, cone-shaped peaks of nearby mountains. One of them is Mount Saint Helens, an active volcano. You know that in 1980 it erupted violently, blowing a hole in the mountain and throwing ash and rock into the sky. Since then, scientists have watched the mountain carefully.

How do you feel about living near a volcano?

Landforms

Do you know the difference between a valley and a volcano? Can you tell a peninsula from a plateau? If you answered yes, then you are familiar with some of Earth's many landforms. **Landforms** are shapes on the planet's surface, such as hills or mountains. Landforms make up the landscapes that surround us, whether it's the rugged mountains of central Colorado or the flat plains of Oklahoma.

Earth's surface is covered with landforms of many different shapes and sizes. Some important landforms include:

- mountains, land that rises higher than 2,000 feet (610 m)
- valleys, areas of low land located between mountains or hills
- plains, stretches of mostly flat land
- islands, areas of land completely surrounded by water
- peninsulas, land surrounded by water on three sides

Because landforms play an important role in geography, many scientists study how landforms are made and how they affect human activity.

Landforms

Natural forces shaped this canyon, one of many different types of landforms on Earth's surface.

The theory of plate tectonics states that the plates that make up Earth's crust are moving, usually only a few inches per year. As Earth's plates collide, separate, and slide past each other, they create forces that shape many of Earth's landforms.

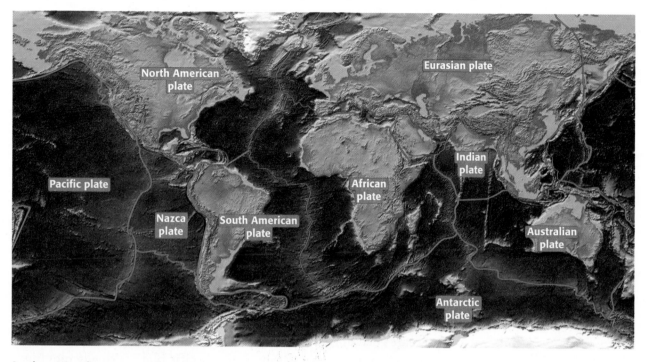

Analyze Visuals
Looking at the map, what evidence indicates that plates have collided or separated?

Forces below Earth's Surface

Geographers often study how landforms are made. One explanation for how landforms have been shaped involves forces below Earth's surface.

Academic
Vocabulary
structure the way
something is set up or
organized

Earth's Plates To understand how these forces work, we must examine Earth's <u>structure</u>. The planet is made up of three layers. A solid inner core is surrounded by a liquid layer, or mantle. The solid outer layer of Earth is called the crust. The planet's **continents**, or large landmasses, are part of Earth's crust.

Geographers use the theory of plate tectonics to explain how forces below Earth's surface have shaped our landforms. The theory of **plate tectonics** suggests that Earth's surface is divided into a dozen or so slow-moving plates, or pieces of Earth's crust. As you can see in the image above, some plates, like the Pacific plate, are quite large. Others, like the Nazca plate, are much smaller. These plates cover Earth's entire surface. Some plates are under the ocean. These are known as ocean plates. Other plates, known as continental plates, are under Earth's continents.

Why do these plates move? Energy deep inside the planet puts pressure on Earth's crust. As this pressure builds up, it forces the plates to shift. Earth's tectonic plates all move. However, they move in different directions and at different speeds.

The Movement of Continents Earth's tectonic plates move slowly—up to several inches per year. The continents, which are part of Earth's plates, shift as the plates move. If we could look back some 200 million years, we would see that the continents have traveled great distances. This idea is known as continental drift.

The theory of continental drift, first developed by Alfred Wegener, states that the continents were once united in a single supercontinent. Wegener's inspiration came from the similarity he observed between the western coast of Africa and the eastern coast of South America. According to this theory, Earth's plates shifted over millions of years. As a result, the continents slowly separated and moved to their present positions.

Earth's continents are still moving. Some plates move toward each other and collide. Other plates separate and move apart. Still others slide past one another. Over time, colliding, separating, and sliding plates have shaped Earth's landforms.

Plates Collide As plates collide, the energy created from their collision produces distinct landforms. The collision of different types of plates creates different shapes on Earth's surface. Ocean trenches and mountain ranges are two examples of landforms produced by the collision of tectonic plates.

When two ocean plates collide, one plate pushes under the other. This process creates ocean trenches. Ocean trenches are deep valleys in the ocean floor. Near Japan, for example, the Pacific plate is slowly moving under other plates. This collision has created several deep ocean trenches, including the world's deepest trench, the Mariana Trench.

Mountains Form When Plates Collide

The movement of Earth's tectonic plates has produced many of Earth's landforms. For example, the Himalayas in South Asia resulted from the collision of two massive continental plates.

Plate A

Plate B

Analyze Visuals
What type of landform is created by the collision of two continental plates?

Lava Flows When Plates Separate

The separation of Earth's tectonic plates produces landforms, just as the collision of plates does. The separation of plates can allow magma to rise up and create volcanic islands like Surtsey Island, near Iceland.

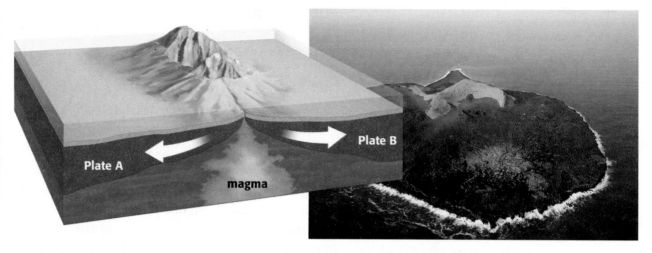

Analyze Visuals
What other landform involves flowing lava?

Ocean plates and continental plates can also collide. When this occurs, the ocean plate drops beneath the continental plate. This action forces the land above to crumple and form a mountain range. The Andes in South America, for example, were formed when the South American and Nazca plates collided.

The collision of two continental plates also results in mountain-building. When continental plates collide, the land pushes up, sometimes to great heights. The world's highest mountain range, the Himalayas, formed when the Indian plate crashed into the Eurasian plate. In fact, the Himalayas are still growing as the two plates continue to crash into each other.

Plates Separate A second type of plate movement causes plates to separate. As plates move apart, gaps between the plates allow magma, a liquid rock from the planet's interior, to rise to Earth's crust. **Lava**, or magma that reaches Earth's surface, emerges from the gap that has formed. As the lava cools, it builds a mid-ocean ridge, or underwater mountain. For example, the separation of the North American and Eurasian plates formed the largest underwater mountain, the Mid-Atlantic Ridge. If these mid-ocean ridges grow high enough, they can rise above the surface of the ocean, forming volcanic islands. Iceland, on the boundary of the Eurasian and North American plates, is an example of such an island.

Plates Slide Tectonic plates also slide past each other. As plates pass by one another, they sometimes grind together. This grinding produces **earthquakes**—sudden, violent movements of Earth's crust. Earthquakes often take place along faults, or breaks in Earth's crust where movement occurs. In California, for example, the Pacific plate is sliding by the edge of the North American plate. This has created the San Andreas Fault zone, an area where earthquakes are quite common.

Reading Check
Find Main Ideas
What forces below Earth's surface shape landforms?

The San Andreas Fault zone is one of many areas that lie along the boundaries of the Pacific plate. The frequent movement of this plate produces many earthquakes and volcanic eruptions along its edges. In fact, the region around the Pacific plate, called the Ring of Fire, is home to most of the world's earthquakes and volcanoes.

Processes on Earth's Surface

For millions of years, the movement of Earth's tectonic plates has been building up landforms on Earth's surface. At the same time, other physical environmental processes are working to change those very same landforms.

Imagine a small pile of dirt and rock on a table. If you poured water on the pile, it would move the dirt and rock from one place to another. Likewise, if you were to blow at the pile, the rock and dirt would also move. The same process happens in nature. Weather, water, and other forces change Earth's landforms by wearing them away or reshaping them.

Weathering One force that wears away landforms is weathering. **Weathering** is the process by which rock is broken down into smaller pieces. Several factors cause rock to break down. In desert areas, daytime heating and nighttime cooling can cause rocks to crack. Water may get into cracks in rocks and freeze. The ice then expands with a force great enough to break the rock. Even the roots of trees can pry rocks apart.

Regardless of which weathering process is at work, rocks eventually break down. These small pieces of rock are known as sediment. Once weathering has taken place, wind, ice, and water often move sediment from one place to another.

Erosion Another force that changes landforms is the process of erosion. **Erosion** is the movement of sediment from one location to another. Erosion can wear away or build up landforms. Wind, ice, and water all cause erosion.

Wind Erosion

Landforms in Utah's Canyonlands National Park have been worn away, mostly by thousands of years of powerful winds.

Powerful winds often cause erosion. Winds lift sediment into the air and carry it across great distances. On beaches and in deserts, wind can deposit large amounts of sand to form dunes. Blowing sand can also wear down rock. The sand acts like sandpaper to polish and wear away at rocks. As you can see in the photo, wind can have a dramatic effect on landforms.

Earth's glaciers also have the power to cause massive erosion. Glaciers, or large, slow-moving sheets of ice, build

Water Erosion
For millions of years, the Colorado River has worn away the rock at Horseshoe Bend in Arizona.

up when winter snows do not melt the following summer. Glaciers can be huge. Glaciers in Greenland and Antarctica, for example, are great sheets of ice up to two miles (3 km) thick. Some glaciers flow slowly downhill like rivers of ice. As they do so, they erode the land by carving large U-shaped valleys and sharp mountain peaks. As the ice flows downhill, it crushes rock into sediment and can move huge rocks long distances.

Water is the most common cause of erosion. Waves in oceans and lakes can wear away the shore, creating jagged coastlines, like those on the coast of Oregon. Rivers also cause erosion. Over many years, the flowing water can cut through rock, forming canyons, or narrow areas with steep walls. Arizona's Horseshoe Bend and Grand Canyon are examples of canyons created in this way.

Flowing water shapes other landforms as well. When water deposits sediment in new locations, it creates new landforms. For example, in a process called **alluvial deposition**, rivers create floodplains when they flood their banks and deposit sediment along the banks. Sediment that is carried by a river all the way out to sea creates a delta. The sediment settles to the bottom, where the river meets the sea. The Nile and Mississippi rivers have created two of the world's largest river deltas.

Reading Check
Compare
How are weathering and erosion similar?

Landforms Influence Life

Why do you live where you do? Perhaps your family moved to the desert to avoid harsh winter weather. Or possibly one of your ancestors settled near a river delta because its fertile soil was ideal for growing crops. Maybe your family wanted to live near the ocean to start a fishing business. As these examples show, landforms exert a strong influence on people's lives. Earth's landforms affect our settlements and our culture. At the same time, we affect the landforms around us.

Earth's landforms can influence where people settle. People sometimes settle near certain landforms and avoid others. For example, many settlements are built near fertile river valleys or deltas. The earliest urban civilization, for example, was built in the valley between the Tigris and Euphrates rivers. Other times, landforms discourage people from settling in a certain place. Tall, rugged mountains, like the Himalayas, and harsh desert climates, like the Sahara, do not usually attract large settlements.

Landforms affect our culture in ways that we may not have noticed. Landforms often influence what jobs are available in a region. For

Living with Landforms

The people of Rio de Janeiro, Brazil, have learned to adapt to the mountains and bays that dominate their landscape.

Analyze Visuals
How have people in Rio de Janeiro adapted to their landscape?

example, rich mineral deposits in the mountains of Colorado led to the development of a mining industry there. Landforms even affect language. On the island of New Guinea in Southeast Asia, rugged mountains have kept the people so isolated that more than 700 languages are spoken on the island today.

People sometimes change landforms to suit their needs. People may choose to modify landforms in order to improve their lives. For example, engineers built the Panama Canal to make travel from the Atlantic Ocean to the Pacific Ocean easier. In Southeast Asia, people who farm on steep hillsides cut terraces into the slope to create more level space to grow their crops. People have even built huge dams along rivers to divert water for use in nearby towns or farms.

Summary and Preview Landforms are created by actions deep within the planet's surface, and they are changed by forces on Earth's surface, like weathering and erosion. In the next lesson you will learn how other forces, like weather and climate, affect Earth's people.

Reading Check
Analyze Effects
What are some examples of humans adjusting to and changing landforms?

Lesson 3 Assessment

Review Ideas, Terms, and Places

1. a. Describe What are some common landforms?
   b. Analyze Why do geographers study landforms?
2. a. Identify What is the theory of plate tectonics?
   b. Compare and Contrast How are the effects of colliding plates and separating plates similar and different?
   c. Predict How might Earth's surface change as tectonic plates continue to move?
3. a. Recall What is the process of weathering?
   b. Elaborate How does water affect sediment?
4. a. Recall How do landforms affect life on Earth?
   b. Predict How might people adapt to life in an area with steep mountains?

Critical Thinking

5. Identify and Describe Use your notes and a two-column chart to identify and describe different physical environmental processes and their effects on Earth's surface.

Physical Environmental Process	Effect on Earth's Surface

Case Study

The Ring of Fire

Background

"The Ring of Fire" names not a fantasy novel, but a region that circles the Pacific Ocean. Known for its fiery volcanoes and powerful earthquakes, it stretches from the tip of South America to Alaska and from Japan to the islands east of Australia. Along this belt, the Pacific plate moves against several other tectonic plates. Thousands of earthquakes occur there every year, and dozens of volcanoes erupt.

The Eruption of Mount Saint Helens

One of the best-known volcanoes in the Ring of Fire is Mount Saint Helens in Washington State. Mount Saint Helens had been dormant, or quiet, since 1857. Then in March 1980, it released puffs of steam and ash. Officials warned people to leave the area. Scientists brought in equipment to measure the growing bulge in the mountainside.

The Ring of Fire

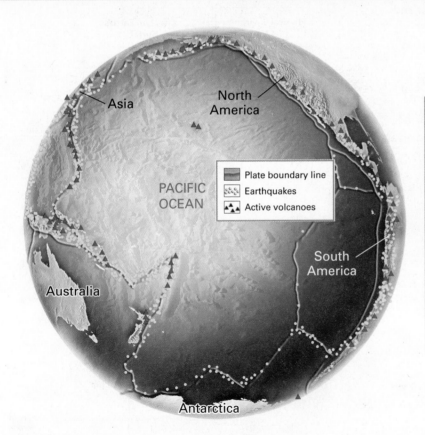

Major Eruptions in the Ring of Fire	
Volcano	**Year**
Tambora, Indonesia	1815
Krakatau, Indonesia	1883
Mount Saint Helens, United States	1980
Nevado del Ruiz, Colombia	1985
Mount Pinatubo, Philippines	1991
Source: *Volcanoes of the World,* Smithsonian Institution.	

On May 18, after a sudden earthquake, Mount Saint Helens let loose a massive explosion of rock and lava. Heat from the blast melted snow on the mountain, which mixed with ash to create deadly mudflows. As the mud quickly poured downhill, it flattened forests, swept away cars, and destroyed buildings. Clouds of ash covered the land, killing crops, clogging waterways, and blanketing towns as far as 200 miles (330 km) away. When the volcano finally quieted down, 57 people had died. Damage totaled nearly $1 billion. If it were not for the early evacuation of the area, the destruction could have been much worse.

What It Means

By studying Mount Saint Helens, scientists learned a great deal about stratovolcanoes. These are tall, steep, cone-shaped volcanoes that have violent eruptions. Stratovolcanoes often form in areas where tectonic plates collide.

Because stratovolcanoes often produce deadly eruptions, scientists try to predict when they might erupt. The lessons learned from Mount Saint Helens helped scientists warn people about another stratovolcano, Mount Pinatubo in the Philippines. That eruption in 1991 was the second-largest of the 1900s. It was far from the deadliest, however. Careful observation and timely warnings saved thousands of lives.

The Ring of Fire will always remain a threat. However, the better we understand its volcanoes, the better prepared we'll be when they erupt.

Mount Saint Helens, 1980 The 1980 eruption of Mount Saint Helens blew ash and hot gases miles into the air. Today, scientists study the volcano to learn more about predicting eruptions.

Geography for Life Activity

1. **Summarize** Why do scientists monitor volcanic activity?

2. **Investigate the Effects of Volcanoes** Some volcanic eruptions affect environmental conditions around the world. Research the eruption of either Mount Saint Helens or the Philippines' Mount Pinatubo to find out how its eruption affected the global environment.

Weather and Climate

The Big Idea

The sun, location, wind, water, and mountains affect weather and climate.

Main Ideas

- While weather is short term, climate is a region's average weather over a long period.

- The amount of sun at a given location is affected by Earth's tilt, movement, and shape.

- Wind and water move heat around Earth, affecting how warm or wet a place is.

- Mountains influence temperature and precipitation.

Key Terms and Places

weather
climate
prevailing winds
ocean currents
front

If YOU lived there . . .

You live in Buffalo, New York, at the eastern end of Lake Erie. One evening in January, you are watching the local TV news. The weather forecaster says, "A huge storm is brewing in the Midwest and moving east. As usual, winds from this storm will drop several feet of snow on Buffalo as they blow off Lake Erie."

Why will winds off the lake drop snow on Buffalo?

Understanding Weather and Climate

What is it like outside right now where you live? Is it hot, sunny, wet, cold? Is this what it is usually like outside for this time of year? The first two questions are about **weather,** the short-term changes in the air for a given place and time. The last question is about **climate,** a region's average weather conditions over a long period.

Weather is the temperature and precipitation from hour to hour or day to day. "Today is sunny, but tomorrow it might rain" is a statement about weather. Climate is the expected weather for a place based on data and experience. "Summer here is usually hot and muggy" is a statement about climate. The factors that shape weather and climate include the sun, location on Earth, wind, water, and mountains.

Stormy Weather Sometimes weather can be extreme. This photo shows a severe thunderstorm. These storms produce heavy rainfall and strong winds.

Reading Check
Find Main Ideas How are weather and climate different from each other?

Global Wind Systems

Prevailing winds blow in circular belts across Earth. These belts occur at about every 30° of latitude.

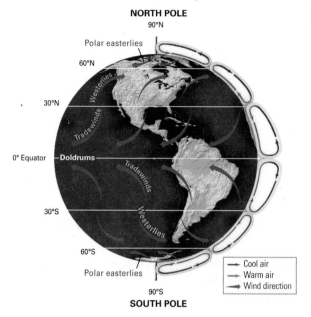

NORTH POLE
90°N

Polar easterlies

60°N

Westerlies

30°N

Tradewinds

0° Equator — Doldrums

Tradewinds

30°S

Westerlies

60°S

Polar easterlies

90°S
SOUTH POLE

→ Cool air
→ Warm air
→ Wind direction

Analyze Visuals
Which direction do the prevailing winds blow across the United States?

Reading Check
Summarize How does Earth's tilt on its axis affect climate?

Sun and Location

Energy from the sun heats the planet. Different locations receive different amounts of sunlight, though. Thus, some locations are warmer than others. The differences are due to Earth's tilt, movement, and shape.

You have learned that Earth is tilted on its axis. The part of Earth tilted toward the sun receives more solar energy than the part tilted away from the sun. As Earth revolves around the sun, the part of Earth that is tilted toward the sun changes during the year. This process creates the seasons. In general, temperatures in summer are warmer than in winter.

Earth's shape also affects the amount of sunlight different locations receive. Because Earth is a sphere, its surface is rounded. Therefore, solar rays are more direct and concentrated near the equator. Nearer the poles, the sun's rays are less direct and more spread out.

As a result, areas near the equator, called the lower latitudes, are mainly hot year-round. Areas near the poles, called the higher latitudes, are cold year-round. Areas about halfway between the equator and poles have more seasonal change. In general, the farther from the equator, or the higher the latitude, the colder the climate.

Wind and Water

Heat from the sun moves across Earth's surface. The reason is that air and water warmed by the sun are constantly on the move. You might have seen a gust of wind or a stream of water carrying dust or dirt. In a similar way, wind and water carry heat from place to place. As a result, they make different areas of Earth warmer or cooler.

Global Winds Wind, or the sideways movement of air, blows in great streams around the planet. **Prevailing winds** are winds that blow in the same direction over large areas of Earth. The illustration under Global Wind Systems shows the patterns of Earth's prevailing winds.

To understand Earth's wind patterns, you need to think about the weight of air. Although you cannot feel it, air has weight. This weight changes with the temperature. Cold air is heavier than warm air. For this reason, when air cools, it gets heavier and sinks. When air warms, it gets lighter and rises. As warm air rises, cooler air moves in to take its place, creating wind.

On a global scale, this rising, sinking, and flowing of air creates Earth's prevailing wind patterns. At the equator, hot air rises and flows toward the poles. At the poles, cold air sinks and flows toward the equator. Meanwhile, Earth is rotating. Earth's rotation causes prevailing winds to curve east or west rather than flowing directly north or south.

Depending on their source, prevailing winds make a region warmer or colder. In addition, the source of the winds can make a region drier or wetter. Winds that form from warm air or pass over lots of water often carry moisture. In contrast, winds that form from cold air or pass over lots of land often are dry.

Ocean Currents Like wind, **ocean currents**—large streams of surface seawater—move heat around Earth. Winds drive these currents. The map below shows how Earth's ocean currents carry warm or cool water to different areas. The water's temperature affects air temperature near it. Warm currents raise temperatures; cold currents lower them.

The Gulf Stream is a warm current that flows north along the U.S. East Coast. It then flows east across the Atlantic, to become the North Atlantic Drift. As the warm current flows along northwestern Europe, it heats the air. Westerlies blow the warmed air across Europe. This process makes Europe warmer than it otherwise would be.

Large Bodies of Water Large bodies of water, such as an ocean or sea, also affect climate. Water heats and cools more slowly than land does. For this reason, large bodies of water make the temperature of the land nearby

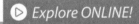

Major Ocean Currents

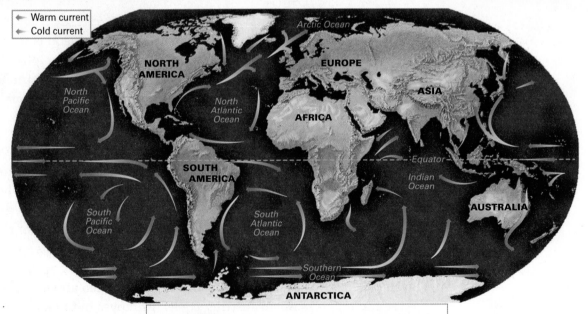

Interpret Maps

1. **Regions** Does a warm or cold ocean current flow along the lower west coast of North America?

2. **Movement** How do ocean currents move heat between warmer and colder areas of Earth?

Severe weather is often dangerous and destructive. In the photo to the left, rescuers search for people during a flood in Yardley, Pennsylvania. In the photo to the right, a tornado races across a wheat field in North Dakota.

Analyze Visuals
How might weather like that shown in these photos affect the people living nearby?

milder. Thus, coastal areas, such as the California coast, usually do not have as wide of temperature ranges as inland areas.

As an example, the state of Michigan is largely surrounded by the Great Lakes. The lakes make temperatures in the state milder than other places as far north.

Wind, Water, and Storms If you watch weather reports, you will hear about storms moving across the United States. Tracking storms is important to us because the United States has so many of them. As you will see, some areas of the world have more storms than others do.

Most storms occur when two air masses collide. An air mass is a large body of air. The place where two air masses of different temperatures or moisture content meet is a **front.** Cold air masses from the north and warm air masses from the south frequently collide over the United States, producing dramatic storms.

Fronts can produce rain or snow as well as severe weather such as thunderstorms and icy blizzards. Thunderstorms produce rain, lightning, and thunder. In the United States, they are most common in spring and summer. Blizzards produce strong winds and large amounts of snow and are most common during winter.

Thunderstorms and blizzards can also produce tornadoes, another type of severe storm. A tornado is a small, rapidly twisting funnel of air that touches the ground. Tornadoes usually affect a limited area and last only a

Rain Shadow Effect Most of the moisture in the ocean air falls on the mountainside facing the wind. Little moisture remains to fall on the other side, creating a rain shadow.

few minutes. However, they can be highly destructive, uprooting trees and tossing large vehicles through the air. Tornadoes can be extremely deadly as well. In 1925 a tornado that crossed Missouri, Illinois, and Indiana left 695 people dead. It is the deadliest U.S. tornado on record.

The largest and most destructive storms, however, are hurricanes. These large, rotating storms form over tropical waters in the Atlantic Ocean, usually from late summer to fall. Did you know that hurricanes and typhoons are the same? Typhoons are just hurricanes that form in the Pacific Ocean.

Hurricanes produce drenching rain and strong winds that can reach speeds of 155 miles per hour (250 kph) or more. This is more than twice as fast as most people drive on highways. In addition, hurricanes form tall walls of water called storm surges. When a storm surge smashes into land, it can wipe out an entire coastal area.

Reading Check
Analyze Causes Why do coastal areas have milder climates than inland areas?

Mountains

Mountains can influence an area's climate by affecting both temperature and precipitation. Many high mountains are located in warm areas yet have snow at the top all year. How can this be? The reason is that temperature decreases with elevation, the height on Earth's surface above sea level.

Mountains also create wet and dry areas. Look at the diagram titled Rain Shadow Effect. A mountain forces air blowing against it to rise. As it rises, the air cools and precipitation falls as rain or snow. Thus, the side of the mountain facing the wind is often green and lush. However, little moisture remains for the other side. This effect creates a rain shadow, a dry area on the mountainside facing away from the direction of the wind.

Summary and Preview As you can see, the sun, location on Earth, wind, water, and mountains affect weather and climate. In the next lesson you will learn what the world's different climate regions are like.

Lesson 4 Assessment

Review Ideas, Terms, and Places

1. a. Recall What shapes weather and climate?

   b. Contrast How do weather and climate differ?

2. a. Identify What parts of Earth receive the most heat from the sun?

   b. Explain Why do the poles receive less solar energy than the equator does?

3. a. Form Generalizations Examine the model of Global Wind Systems in this lesson. Pose and answer a question about the geographic patterns of winds shown on the model.

   b. Summarize How do ocean currents and large bodies of water affect climate?

4. a. Define What is a rain shadow?

   b. Explain Why might a mountaintop and a nearby valley have widely different temperatures?

Critical Thinking

5. Identify Cause and Effect Use your notes and a cause-and-effect chart like the one shown. Use your notes to explain how each factor affects climate.

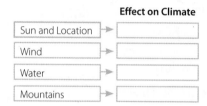

Effect on Climate

Sun and Location	→	
Wind	→	
Water	→	
Mountains	→	

World Climates

The Big Idea

Earth's five major climate zones are identified by temperature, precipitation, and plant life.

Main Ideas

- Geographers use temperature, precipitation, and plant life to identify climate zones.

- Tropical climates are wet and warm, while dry climates receive little or no rain.

- Temperate climates have the most seasonal change.

- Polar climates are cold and dry, while highland climates change with elevation.

Key Terms and Places

monsoons
savannas
steppes
permafrost

Reading Check
Make Inferences
Why do you think geographers consider native plant life when categorizing climates?

If YOU lived there . . .

You live in Colorado and are on your first serious hike in the Rocky Mountains. Since it is July, it is hot in the campground in the valley. But your guide insists that you bring a heavy fleece jacket. By noon, you have climbed to 11,000 feet (3,353 m). You are surprised to see patches of snow in shady spots. Suddenly, you are very happy that you brought your jacket!

Why does it get colder as you climb higher?

Major Climate Zones

In January, how will you dress for the weekend? In some places, you might get dressed to go skiing. In other places, you might head out in a swimsuit to go to the beach. What the seasons are like where you live depends on climate.

Earth is a patchwork of climates. Geographers identify these climates by looking at temperature, precipitation, and native plant life. Using these items, we can divide Earth into five general climate zones—tropical, temperate, polar, dry, and highland.

The first three climate zones relate to latitude. Tropical climates occur near the equator, in the low latitudes. Temperate climates occur about halfway between the equator and the poles, in the middle latitudes. Polar climates occur near the poles, in the high latitudes. The last two climate zones occur at many different latitudes. In addition, geographers divide some climate zones into more specific climate regions. The map and chart titled World's Climate Regions describe these specific regions. Read the chart and study the map to see if you can identify some climate patterns.

World Climate Regions

	Climate	Where is it?	What is it like?	Plants
Tropical	HUMID TROPICAL	On and near the equator	Warm with high amounts of rain year-round; in a few places, monsoons create extreme wet seasons	Tropical rain forest
	TROPICAL SAVANNA	Higher latitudes in the tropics	Warm all year; distinct rainy and dry seasons; at least 20 inches (50 cm) of rain during the summer	Tall grasses and scattered trees
Dry	DESERT	Mainly center on 30° latitude; also in middle of continents, on west coasts, or in rain shadows	Sunny and dry; less than 10 inches (25 cm) of rain a year; hot in the tropics; cooler with wide daytime temperature ranges in middle latitudes	A few hardy plants, such as cacti
	STEPPE	Mainly bordering deserts and interiors of large continents	About 10–20 inches (25–50 cm) of precipitation a year; hot summers and cooler winters with wide temperature ranges during the day	Shorter grasses; some trees and shrubs by water
Temperate	MEDITERRANEAN	West coasts in middle latitudes	Dry, sunny, warm summers; mild, wetter winters; rain averages 15–20 inches (30–50 cm) a year	Scrub woodland and grassland
	HUMID SUBTROPICAL	East coasts in middle latitudes	Humid with hot summers and mild winters; rain year-round; in paths of hurricanes and typhoons	Mixed forest
	MARINE WEST COAST	West coasts in the upper-middle latitudes	Cloudy, mild summers and cool, rainy winters; strong ocean influence	Evergreen forests
	HUMID CONTINENTAL	East coasts and interiors of upper-middle latitudes	Four distinct seasons; long, cold winters and short, warm summers; average precipitation varies	Mixed forest
Polar	SUBARCTIC	Higher latitudes of the interior and east coasts of continents	Extremes of temperature; long, cold winters and short, warm summers; little precipitation	Northern evergreen forests
	TUNDRA	Coasts in high latitudes	Cold all year; very long, cold winters and very short, cool summers; little precipitation; permafrost	Moss, lichens, low shrubs
	ICE CAP	Polar regions	Freezing cold; snow and ice; little precipitation	No vegetation
Highland	HIGHLAND	High mountain regions	Wide range of temperatures and precipitation amounts, depending on elevation and location	Ranges from forest to tundra

Interpret Maps

1. Location Which climates are found mainly in the Northern Hemisphere?

2. Region Where are many of the world's driest climates found on Earth?

Tropical and Dry Climates

Are you the type of person who likes to go to extremes? Then tropical and dry climates might be for you. These climates include the wettest, driest, and hottest places on Earth.

Tropical Climates Our tour of Earth's climates starts at the equator, in the heart of the tropics. This region extends from the Tropic of Cancer to the Tropic of Capricorn. Look back at the map to locate this region.

Humid Tropical Climate At the equator, the hot, damp air hangs like a thick, wet blanket. Sweat quickly coats your body. Welcome to the humid tropical climate. This climate is warm, muggy, and rainy year-round. Temperatures average about 80°F (26°C). Showers or storms occur almost daily, and rainfall ranges from 70 to more than 450 inches (180 to 1,140 cm) a year. In comparison, only a few parts of the United States average more than 70 inches (180 cm) of rain a year.

Some places with a humid tropical climate have **monsoons**, seasonal winds that bring either dry or moist air. During one part of the year, a moist ocean wind creates an extreme wet season. The winds then shift direction, and a dry land wind creates a dry season. Monsoons affect several parts of Asia. For example, the town of Mawsynram, India, receives on average more than 450 inches (1,140 cm) of rain a year—all in about six months! That is about 37 feet (11 m) of rain. As you can imagine, flooding during wet seasons is common and can be severe.

The humid tropical climate's warm temperatures and heavy rainfall support tropical rain forests. These lush forests contain more types of plants and animals than anywhere else on Earth. The world's largest rain forest is in the Amazon River basin in South America. There you can find more than 50,000 species, including giant lily pads, poisonous tree frogs, and toucans.

Tropical Climate Known for high temperatures and rainfall, tropical climates may support grasslands or full-blown forests.

The Tuareg of the Sahara

In the Sahara, the world's largest desert, temperatures can top 130°F (54°C). Yet the Tuareg (TWAH-reg) of North and West Africa call the Sahara home—and prefer it. The Tuareg have raised camels and other animals in the Sahara for more than 1,000 years. The animals graze on sparse desert plants. When the plants are gone, the Tuareg move on.

In camp, Tuareg families live in tents made from animal skins. Some wealthier Tuareg live in adobe homes. The men traditionally wear blue veils wrapped around their face and head. The veils help protect against windblown desert dust.

Summarize
How have the Tuareg adapted to life in a desert?

Tropical Savanna Climate Moving north and south away from the equator, we find the tropical savanna climate. This climate has a long, hot, dry season followed by short periods of rain. Rainfall is much lower than at the equator but still high. Temperatures are hot in the summer, often as high as 90°F (32°C). Winters are cooler but rarely get cold.

This climate does not receive enough rainfall to support dense forests. Instead, it supports **savannas**—areas of tall grasses and scattered trees and shrubs.

Dry Climates Leaving Earth's wettest places, we head to its driest. These climates are found in a number of locations on the planet.

Desert Climate Picture the sun baking down on a barren wasteland. This is the desert, Earth's hottest and driest climate. Deserts receive less than 10 inches (25 cm) of rain a year. Dry air and clear skies produce high daytime temperatures and rapid cooling at night. In some deserts, highs can top 130°F (54°C)! Under such conditions, only very hardy plants and animals can live. Many plants grow far apart so as not to compete for water. Others, such as cacti, store water in fleshy stems and leaves.

Steppe Climate Semidry grasslands or prairies—called **steppes** (STEPS)—often border deserts. Steppes receive slightly more rain than deserts do. Short grasses are the most common plants, but shrubs and trees grow along streams and rivers.

Reading Check
Contrast What are some ways in which tropical and dry climates differ?

Dry Climate Lots of heat and very little rain characterize dry climates. Any plants or animals living here need to be hardy to survive these extremes.

Temperate Climates

If you enjoy hot, sunny days as much as chilly, rainy ones, then temperate climates are for you. *Temperate* means "moderate" or "mild." These mild climates tend to have four seasons, with warm or hot summers and cool or cold winters.

Temperate climates occur in the middle latitudes, the regions halfway between the equator and the poles. Air masses from the tropics and the poles often meet in these regions, which creates a number of different temperate climates. You very likely live in one, because most Americans do.

Mediterranean Climate Named for the region of the Mediterranean Sea, this sunny, pleasant climate is found in many popular vacation areas. In a Mediterranean climate, summers are hot, dry, and sunny. Winters are mild and somewhat wet. Plant life includes shrubs and short trees with scattered larger trees. The Mediterranean climate occurs mainly in coastal areas. In the United States, much of California has this climate.

Humid Subtropical Climate The southeastern United States is an example of the humid subtropical climate. This climate occurs along east coasts near the tropics. In these areas, warm, moist air blows in from the ocean. Summers are hot and muggy. Winters are mild, with occasional frost and snow. Storms occur year-round. In addition, hurricanes can strike, bringing violent winds, heavy rain, and high seas.

A humid subtropical climate supports mixed forests. These forests include both deciduous trees, which lose their leaves each fall, and coniferous trees, which are green year-round. Coniferous trees are also known as evergreens.

Marine West Coast Climate Parts of North America's Pacific coast and of western Europe have a marine west coast climate. This climate occurs on west coasts where winds carry moisture in from the seas. The moist air keeps temperatures mild year-round. Winters are foggy, cloudy, and rainy, while summers can be warm and sunny. Dense evergreen forests thrive in this climate.

Academic
Vocabulary
distinct clearly
different and separate

Reading Check
Categorize Which
of the temperate
climates is too dry to
support forests?

Humid Continental Climate Closer to the poles, in the upper-middle latitudes, many inland and east coast areas have a humid continental climate. This climate has four **distinct** seasons. Summers are short and hot. Spring and fall are mild, and winters are long, cold, and, in general, snowy.

This climate's rainfall supports vast grasslands and forests. Grasses can grow very tall, such as in parts of the American Great Plains. Forests contain both deciduous and coniferous trees, with coniferous forests occurring in the colder areas.

Mediterranean Climate

The climate graph shows average temperatures and precipitation for Nice (NEECE), France, which has a Mediterranean climate.

Climate for Nice, France

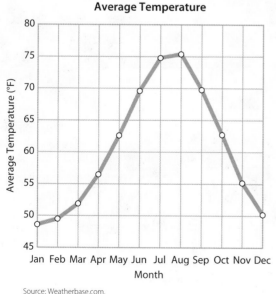

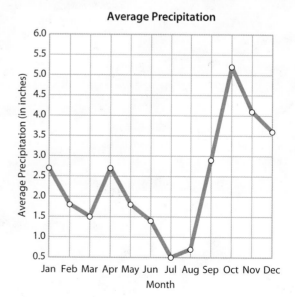

Source: Weatherbase.com.

Analyze Graphs
During which month is precipitation lowest?

Polar and Highland Climates

Get ready to feel the chill as we end our tour in the polar and highland climates. The three polar climates are found in the high latitudes near the poles. The varied highland climate is found on mountains.

Subarctic Climate The subarctic climate and the tundra climate described below occur mainly in the Northern Hemisphere south of the Arctic Ocean. In the subarctic climate, winters are long and bitterly cold. Summers are short and cool. Temperatures stay below freezing for about half the year. The climate's moderate rainfall supports vast evergreen forests, or taiga (TY-guh).

Tundra Climate The tundra climate occurs in coastal areas along the Arctic Ocean. As in the subarctic climate, winters are long and bitterly cold. Temperatures rise above freezing only during the short summer. Rainfall is light, and only plants such as mosses, lichens, and small shrubs grow.

In parts of the tundra, soil layers stay frozen all year. Permanently frozen layers of soil are called **permafrost**. Frozen earth absorbs water poorly, which creates ponds and marshes in summer. This moisture causes plants to burst forth in bloom.

Highland Climates

Mount Kilimanjaro is the tallest mountain in Africa. Although Kilimanjaro is only about 200 miles (320 km) south of the equator, snow blankets its highest peak.

Kilimanjaro rises to 19,341 ft (5,895 m). The snow-covered summit has an ice cap climate.

A tropical savanna climate is found around the base of Mount Kilimanjaro.

Climate and plant life ranges from rain forest, to steppe, to desert, to tundra.

Analyze Visuals
Which type of climate is found on the top of Mount Kilimanjaro?

Polar Climate Mountains often sustain polar climates, especially at their peaks. Different kinds of plants and animals may be found at different elevations.

Ice Cap Climate The harshest places on Earth may be the North and South poles. These regions have an ice cap climate. Temperatures are bone-numbingly cold, and lows of more than –120°F (–84°C) have been recorded. Snow and ice remain year-round, but precipitation is light. It is too cold for the water to evaporate into the atmosphere to become precipitation. In fact, the average precipitation is so low that these regions are technically deserts. Not surprisingly, no vegetation grows. However, mammals such as penguins and polar bears thrive. Seals can also live in the ice cap climate, and many birds travel through these cold regions.

Highland Climates Highland climates are cool to cold climates in mountain areas. They are unique because they contain several climate zones. This is because as you climb to higher elevations on a mountain, the climate changes. Temperatures drop, and plant life grows sparser. Going up a mountain can be like going from the tropics to the poles. On very tall mountains, ice coats the summit year-round.

Summary and Preview As you can see, Earth has many climates, which we identify based on temperature, precipitation, and native plant life. In the next lesson you will read about how nature and all living things are connected.

Lesson 5 Assessment

Review Ideas, Terms, and Places

1. **a. Recall** Which three major climate zones are most closely related to latitude?

   b. Summarize How do geographers categorize Earth's different climates?

2. **a. Define** What are monsoons?

   b. Make Inferences In which type of dry climate do you think the fewest people live, and why?

   c. Compare Look at the photographs in this lesson of a polar climate and a dry climate. What similarities do you notice in the physical characteristics of these regions?

3. **a. Identify** What are the four temperate climates?

   b. Geographic Questions Use the climate graph of Nice, France, to pose and answer a question about its climate patterns.

4. **a. Describe** What are some effects of permafrost?

   b. Explain How are highland climates unique?

Critical Thinking

5. **Categorize** Create a chart like the one below for each climate region. Then use your notes to describe each climate region's average temperatures, precipitation, and native plant life.

| Climate Region | → | Temperature | Precipitation | Plant Life |

Environments and Biomes

The Big Idea

Plants, animals, and the environment, including soil, interact with and affect one another.

Main Ideas

- The environment and life are interconnected and exist in a fragile balance.
- Soils play an important role in the environment.

Key Terms and Places

environment
ecosystem
biome
habitat
extinct
humus
desertification

If YOU lived there . . .

When your family moved to the city, you were sure you would miss the woods and pond near your old house. Then one of your new friends at school told you there's a large park only a few blocks away. You wondered how interesting a city park could be. But you were surprised at the many plants and animals that live there.

What environments might you see in the park?

The Environment and Life

If you saw a wild polar bear outside your school, you would likely be shocked. In most parts of the United States, polar bears live only in zoos. This is because plants and animals must live where they are suited to the **environment,** or surroundings. Polar bears are suited to very cold places with lots of ice, water, and fish. As you will see, living things and their environments are connected and affect each other in many ways.

Suitable Environment

With thick fur and a layer of fat, this polar bear, wading in shallow water in Svalbard, Norway, is well suited to its cold environment.

Limits on Life The environment limits life. As our tour of the world's climates showed, factors such as temperature, rainfall, and soil conditions limit where plants and animals can live. Palm trees cannot survive at the frigid North Pole. Ferns will quickly wilt and die in deserts, but they thrive in tropical rain forests.

At the same time, all plants and animals are adapted to specific environments. For example, kangaroo rats are adapted to dry desert environments. These small rodents can get all the water they need from food, so they seldom have to drink water.

Connections in Nature The interconnections between living things and the environment form ecosystems. An **ecosystem** is a group of plants and animals that depend on each other and the environment in which they live for survival. Ecosystems can be any size and can occur wherever air, water, and soil support life. A garden pond, a city park, a prairie, and a rain forest are all examples of ecosystems.

In addition to environments and ecosystems, geographers might use the term **biome.** A biome is much larger than an ecosystem. It may be made up of several ecosystems. An entire tropical rain forest can be a biome. Earth itself can be thought of as one big biome.

A Desert Ecosystem

A desert is one type of ecosystem. The plants and animals in the desert depend on one another and the desert environment for survival.

Sunlight is the source of energy for most living things.

Larger predators, such as mountain lions, compete for the prey that is available.

Predators, such as wolves and snakes, eat rabbits and other prey for energy.

Animals such as rabbits eat plants and gain some of their energy.

Plants use the energy in sunlight to make food. They serve as the basis for other life in the ecosystem.

Analyze Visuals
What might happen in the desert ecosystem above if the number of rabbits fell significantly?

The diagram on the previous page shows a desert ecosystem. Each part of this ecosystem fills a certain role. The sun provides energy to the plants, which use the energy to make their own food. The plants then serve as food, either directly or indirectly, for all other life in the desert. When the plants and animals die, their remains break down and provide nutrients for the soil and new plant growth. Thus, the cycle continues.

Changes to Environments The interconnected parts of an ecosystem exist in a fragile balance. For this reason, a small change to one part can affect the whole system. A lack of rain in the forest ecosystem could kill off many of the plants that feed the rabbits. If the rabbits die, there will be less food for the wolves and mountain lions. Then they too may die.

Extinction The dodo is not the only bird to go extinct. The passenger pigeon, shown in this Audubon illustration, went extinct in 1914. Commercial overhunting played a role in its end.

Academic Vocabulary
consequences the effects of a particular event or events

Many actions can affect ecosystems. For example, people need places to live and food to eat, so they clear land for homes and farms. Clearing land has **consequences**, however. It can cause the soil to erode. In addition, the plants and animals that live in the area might be left without food and shelter. Actions such as clearing land and polluting can destroy habitats. A **habitat** is the place where a plant or animal lives. The most diverse habitats on Earth are tropical rain forests. People are clearing Earth's rain forests for farmland, lumber, and other reasons, though. As a result, these diverse habitats are being lost.

Extreme changes in ecosystems can cause species to die out, or become **extinct.** For example, flightless birds called dodos once lived on Mauritius, an island in the Indian Ocean. When people first settled there, they hunted dodos and introduced predators, such as dogs. First seen in 1507, dodos were extinct by 1681.

Recognizing these problems, many countries are working to balance people's needs with the needs of the environment. The United States, for example, has passed many laws to limit pollution, manage forests, and protect valuable ecosystems. These laws rarely please everyone. A law that restricts logging in a forest, for example, may please hikers but frustrate logging companies. A law that bans hunting of threatened species may please wildlife photographers but disappoint hunters.

Reading Check
Make Inferences
How might one change affect an entire ecosystem?

Nevertheless, laws can produce positive results. For example, since the Endangered Species Act of 1973 became law, 47 species have been removed from the endangered species list because their populations have recovered.

Soil and the Environment

As you know, plants are the basis for all food that animals eat. Soils help determine what plants will grow and how well. Because soils support plant life, they play an important role in the environment.

Fertile soils are rich in minerals and **humus** (HYOO - muhs), decayed plant or animal matter. These soils can support abundant plant life. Like air and water, fertile soil is essential for life. Without it, we could not grow much of the food we eat.

Soils can lose fertility in several ways. Erosion from wind or water can sweep topsoil away. Planting the same crops over and over can also rob

Soil Factory

The next time you see a fallen tree in the forest, do not think of it as a dead log. Think of it as a soil factory. A fallen tree is buzzing with the activity of countless insects, bacteria, and other organisms. These organisms invade the fallen log and start to break the wood down.

As the tree decays and crumbles, it turns into humus. Humus is a rich blend of organic material. The humus mixes with the soil and broken rock material. These added nutrients then enrich the soil, making it possible for new trees and plants to grow. Fallen trees provide as much as one-third of the organic material in forest soil.

Summarize
What causes a fallen tree to change into soil?

Soil Layers

The three layers of soil are the topsoil, subsoil, and broken rock. The thickness of each layer depends on the conditions in a specific location. For example, soil can be as much as 100 feet thick in tropical regions.

Topsoil

Subsoil

Broken Rock

Solid Rock

Analyze Visuals
In which layer of soil are most plant roots and insects found?

Reading Check
Analyze Information What do fertile soils contain, and why are these soils important?

soil of its fertility. When soil becomes worn out, it cannot support as many plants. In fragile, dry environments, this can lead to the spread of desert-like conditions, or **desertification.** The spread of desertlike conditions is a serious problem in many parts of the world.

Summary and Preview Living things and the environment are connected, but changes can easily upset the balance in an ecosystem. Because they support plant life, soils are important parts of ecosystems. In the next lesson you will learn about Earth's many resources.

Lesson 6 Assessment

Review Ideas, Terms, and Places

1. **a. Define** What is an ecosystem, and what are two examples of ecosystems?

   b. Summarize How do nature and people change ecosystems?

   c. Elaborate Why can plants and animals not live everywhere?

   d. Contrast How is a biome different from an ecosystem?

2. **a. Recall** What is humus, and why is it important to soil?

   b. Identify Cause and Effect What actions can cause desertification, and what might be some possible effects?

   c. Elaborate Why is it important for geographers and scientists to study soils?

Critical Thinking

3. **Identify Cause and Effect** Review your notes. Then draw a two-row, two-column chart. Label one column Causes and the other Effects. Use the chart to identify some of the causes and effects of changes to ecosystems.

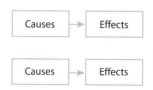

| Causes | → | Effects |

| Causes | → | Effects |

Natural Resources

The Big Idea

Earth's natural resources have many valuable uses, and their availability affects people in many ways.

Main Ideas

- Earth provides valuable resources for our use.
- Energy resources provide fuel, heat, and electricity.
- Mineral resources include metals, rocks, and salt.
- Resources shape people's lives and countries' wealth.

Key Terms and Places

natural resource
renewable resources
nonrenewable resources
deforestation
reforestation
fossil fuels
hydroelectric power

If YOU lived there . . .

You live in Southern California, where the climate is warm and dry. Every week, you water the grass around your house to keep it green. Now the city has declared a "drought emergency" because of a lack of rain. City officials have put limits on watering lawns and on other uses of water.

How can you help conserve scarce water?

Earth's Valuable Resources

Think about the materials in nature that you use. You have learned about the many ways we use sun, water, and land. They are just a start, though. Look at the human-made products around you. They all required the use of natural materials in some way. We use trees to make paper for books. We use petroleum, or oil, to make plastics for cell phones. We use metals to make machines, which we then use to make many items. Without these materials, our lives would change drastically.

Using Natural Resources Trees, oil, and metals are all examples of natural resources. A **natural resource** is any material in nature that people use and value. Earth's most important natural resources include air, water, soils, forests, and minerals.

Understanding how and why people use natural resources is an important part of geography. We use some natural resources just as they are, such as wind. Usually, though, we change natural resources to make something new. For example, we change metals to make products such as bicycles and watches. Thus, most natural resources are raw materials for other products.

Types of Natural Resources We group natural resources into two types: those we can replace and those we cannot. **Renewable resources** are resources Earth replaces naturally. For example, when we cut down a tree, another tree can grow in its place. Renewable resources include water, soil, trees, plants, and animals. These resources can last forever if used wisely.

Members of the Green Belt Movement plant trees in Kenya. Although trees are a renewable resource, some forests are being cut down faster than new trees can replace them. Reforestation helps protect Earth's valuable forestlands.

Analyze Visuals
How does reforestation help the environment?

Other natural resources will run out one day. These **nonrenewable resources** are resources that cannot be replaced. For example, coal formed over millions of years. Once we use the coal up, it is gone.

Managing Natural Resources People need to manage natural resources to protect them for the future. Consider how your life might change if we ran out of forests, for example. Although forests are renewable, we can cut down trees far faster than they can grow. The result is the clearing of trees, or **deforestation.**

By managing resources, we can repair and prevent resource loss. For example, some groups are engaged in **reforestation,** planting trees to replace lost forestland.

Reading Check
Contrast How do renewable and nonrenewable resources differ?

──────── BIOGRAPHY ────────

Wangari Maathai (1940–2011)

Can planting a tree improve people's lives? Wangari Maathai thinks so. Born in Kenya in East Africa, Maathai wanted to help people in her country, many of whom were poor. She asked herself what Kenyans could do to improve their lives. "Planting a tree was the best idea that I had," she says. In 1977 Maathai founded the Green Belt Movement to plant trees and protect forestland. The group has now planted more than 30 million trees across Kenya! These trees provide wood and prevent soil erosion. In 2004 Maathai was awarded the Nobel Peace Prize. She is the first African woman to receive this famous award.

Analyze Effects:
How has Maathai's Green Belt Movement helped Kenya?

The Physical World   **83**

Energy Resources

Every day you use plants and animals from the dinosaur age—in the form of energy resources. These resources power vehicles, produce heat, and generate electricity. They are some of our most important and valuable natural resources.

Nonrenewable Energy Resources Most of the energy we use comes from **fossil fuels,** nonrenewable resources that formed from the remains of ancient plants and animals. The most important fossil fuels are coal, petroleum, and natural gas.

Coal has long been a reliable energy source for heat. However, burning coal causes some problems. It pollutes the air and can harm the land. For these reasons, people have used coal less as other fuel options became available.

Today we use coal mainly to create electricity at power plants, not to heat single buildings. Because coal is plentiful, people are looking for cleaner ways to burn it.

Petroleum, or oil, is a dark liquid used to make fuels and other products. When first removed from the ground, petroleum is called crude oil. This oil is shipped or piped to refineries, factories that process the crude oil to make products. Fuels made from oil include gasoline, diesel fuel, and jet fuel. Oil is also used to make petrochemicals, which are processed to make products such as plastics and cosmetics.

As with coal, burning oil–based fuels comes with a tradeoff. Such fuels can pollute the air and land. In addition, oil spills can harm wildlife. International concern over the effect of oil spills inspired the creation of international regulations. These regulations address pollution from oil spills and help ensure a coordinated response. Because we are so dependent on oil for energy, it is an extremely valuable resource.

The cleanest-burning fossil fuel is natural gas. We use it mainly for heating and cooking. For example, your kitchen stove may use natural gas. Some vehicles run on natural gas as well. These vehicles cause less pollution than those that run on gasoline.

Many scientists believe that pollution from burning fossil fuels has caused Earth's temperature to increase. This increase, they argue, is bringing about climate change. The growing scientific agreement on this issue has inspired international action. The Kyoto Protocol to the United Nations Framework Convention on Climate Change was adopted in 1997. The Kyoto Protocol, as it is known, sets internationally binding targets to reduce emissions from burning fossil fuels. More than 190 countries have signed the agreement.

Renewable Energy Resources Unlike fossil fuels, renewable energy resources will not run out. They also are generally better for the environment. On the other hand, they are not available everywhere and can be costly.

The main alternative to fossil fuels is **hydroelectric power**—the production of electricity from water power. We obtain energy from moving water by damming rivers. The dams harness the power of moving water to generate electricity.

Hydroelectric power has both pros and cons. On the positive side, it produces power without polluting and lessens our use of fossil fuels. On the negative side, dams create lakes that replace existing resources, such as farmland, and disrupt wildlife habitats.

Another renewable energy source is wind. People have long used wind to power windmills. Today we use wind to power wind turbines, a type of modern windmill. At wind farms, hundreds of turbines create electricity in windy places.

A third source of renewable energy is heat from the sun and Earth. We can use solar power, or power from the sun, to heat water or homes. Using special solar panels, we turn solar energy into electricity. We can also use geothermal energy, or heat from within Earth. Geothermal power plants use steam and hot water located within Earth to create electricity.

Hydroelectric Power

Glen Canyon Dam, near Page, Arizona, provides roughly 4 billion kilowatt hours per year of hydroelectric power. It also created Lake Powell, which filled to capacity in 1980.

Nuclear Energy A final energy source is nuclear energy. We obtain this energy by splitting atoms, small particles of matter. This process uses the metal uranium, so some people consider nuclear energy a nonrenewable resource. Nuclear power does not pollute the air, but it does produce dangerous wastes. These wastes must be stored for thousands of years before they are safe. In addition, an accident at a nuclear power plant can have terrible effects.

All countries need energy. Yet, energy resources are not evenly spread across Earth. As a result, energy production differs by region. For example, the Middle East has rich oil deposits. For this reason, the Middle East leads the world in oil production.

Mineral Resources

Like energy resources, mineral resources can be quite valuable. Whether used locally or traded to distant regions to obtain other valuable goods, mineral resources help an area's economic growth. These resources include metals, salt, rocks, and gemstones.

Minerals fulfill countless needs. Look around you to see a few. Your school building likely includes steel, made from iron. The outer walls might be granite or limestone. The window glass is made from quartz, a mineral in sand. From staples to jewelry to coins, metals are everywhere.

Minerals are nonrenewable, so we need to conserve them. Recycling items such as aluminum cans and personal electronics will make the supply of these valuable resources last longer.

Reading Check
Make Inferences
Why might people look for alternatives to fossil fuels?

Reading Check
Categorize
What are the major types of mineral resources?

From the Ground to the Air

Humans gather and process minerals before using them. In nature, minerals are often mixed into rock or other solid material, called ore. People mine, or dig in the earth, to extract the ore. Then the ore is processed to get the mineral, which is used to create final products.

Bauxite, a rock, is mined and used to make aluminum.

Aluminum is used in many products, such as jet planes.

Identify
How many other aluminum products can you name?

This Ohio family shows some common products made from petroleum, or oil.

Analyze Visuals
What petroleum-based products can you identify in this photo?

Resources and People

Natural resources vary from place to place. The resources available in a region can shape life and wealth for the people there.

Resources and Daily Life The natural resources available to people affect their lifestyles and needs. In the United States, we have many different kinds of natural resources. We can choose among many different ways to dress, eat, live, travel, and entertain ourselves. People in places with fewer natural resources will likely have fewer choices and different needs than Americans.

For example, people who live in remote rain forests depend on forest resources for most of their needs. These people may craft containers by weaving plant fibers together. They may make canoes by hollowing out tree trunks. Instead of being concerned about money, they might be more concerned about food.

In areas where more than one group wants to use the same resources, conflicts can arise. For example, the Aka people of Central Africa sometimes struggle to find enough resources. Logging companies have been harvesting trees from the forests in which the Aka hunt and gather. The loss of trees has reduced animals' habitats, which makes it harder for the Aka to find food.

Resources and Wealth The availability of natural resources affects countries' economies as well. For example, the many natural resources available in the United States have helped it become one of the world's wealthiest countries. In contrast, countries with few natural resources often have weak economies.

Some countries have one or two valuable resources but few others. For example, Saudi Arabia is rich in oil but lacks water for growing food. As a result, Saudi Arabia must use its oil profits to import food. Indeed, a number of countries in Southwest Asia face similar challenges. In 1960, Iran, Iraq, Kuwait, Saudi Arabia and Venezuela founded the Organization of Petroleum Exporting Countries (OPEC). OPEC works to stabilize the oil markets and ensure a steady income to member states. OPEC has grown to 13 countries.

Summary You can see that Earth's natural resources have many uses. Important natural resources include air, water, soils, forests, fuels, and minerals.

Reading Check
Identify Cause and Effect
How can having few natural resources affect life and wealth in a region or country?

Lesson 7 Assessment

Review Ideas, Terms, and Places

1. **a. Define** What are renewable resources and nonrenewable resources?

   b. Explain Why is it important for people to manage Earth's natural resources?

   c. Identify What are some things you can do to help manage and conserve natural resources?

2. **a. Define** What are fossil fuels, and why are they significant?

   b. Summarize What are three examples of renewable energy resources?

3. **a. Recall** What are the main types of mineral resources?

   b. Analyze What are some products that we get from mineral resources?

4. **a. Summarize** How do resources affect people?

   b. Make Inferences How might a country with only one valuable resource develop its economy?

Critical Thinking

5. **Categorize** Draw a chart like this one. Use your notes to describe and evaluate each type of energy resource.

Fossil Fuels	Renewable Energy	Nuclear Energy
Pros	Pros	Pros
Cons	Cons	Cons

Social Studies Skills

Use a Physical Map

Define the Skill

Physical maps show important physical features, like oceans and mountains, in a particular area. They also indicate an area's elevation, or the height of the land in relation to sea level.

When you use a physical map, there are important pieces of information you should always examine.

- Identify physical features. Natural features, such as mountains, rivers, and lakes, are labeled on physical maps. Read the labels carefully to identify what physical features are present.

- Read the legend. On physical maps, the legend indicates scale as well as elevation. The different colors in the elevation key indicate how far above or below sea level a place is.

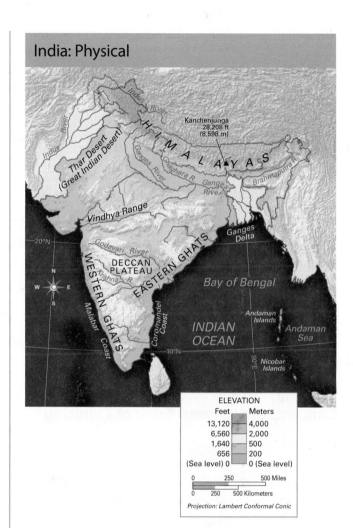

India: Physical

Learn the Skill

Use the physical map of India to answer the questions below.

1. What landforms and bodies of water are indicated on the map?

2. What is the highest elevation in India? Where is it located?

Practice the Skill

Locate the physical map of Africa in the Atlas in the back of the book. Use the map to answer the questions below.

1. Which region has the highest elevation?

2. What bodies of water surround Africa?

3. What large island is located off the east coast of Africa?

Module 2 Assessment

Review Vocabulary, Terms, and Places

For each statement below, write T if it is true and F if it is false. If the statement is false, write the correct term that would make the sentence a true statement.

1. **Weathering** is the movement of sediment from one location to another.
2. Most of our **groundwater** is stored in Earth's streams, rivers, and lakes.
3. It takes 365¼ days for Earth to complete one **rotation** around the sun.
4. Streams are formed when **precipitation** collects in narrow channels.
5. **Earthquakes** cause erosion as they flow downhill, carving valleys and mountain peaks.
6. The planet's tilt affects the amount of **erosion** Earth receives from the sun.
7. When plant or animal matter has decayed, it is called **humus**.
8. Conditions or changes in the air in a certain time and place are called **climate**.
9. **Reforestation** is the act of planting trees where forests once stood.
10. A species is **extinct** when it has completely died out.
11. **Steppes** are areas of tall grasses and scattered shrubs and trees.
12. Winds that change direction with the season and create wet and dry periods are known as **savannas**.

Comprehension and Critical Thinking

Lesson 1

13. **a. Identify** What factors influence the amount of energy that different places on Earth receive from the sun?

    b. Predict What might happen to the amount of solar energy we receive if Earth's axis were straight up and down?

Lesson 2

14. **a. Describe** What different sources of water are available on Earth?

    b. Draw Conclusions How does the water cycle keep Earth's water supply relatively constant?

    c. Elaborate What water problems affect people around the world? What solutions can you think of for one of those problems?

Lesson 3

15. **a. Define** What is a landform? What are some common types of landforms?

    b. Analyze effects What are some things that can happen when two tectonic plates interact?

    c. Elaborate What physical features dominate the landscape in your community? How do they affect life there?

Lesson 4

16. **a. Identify** What five factors affect climate?

    b. Analyze Is average annual precipitation an example of weather or climate?

Lesson 5

17. **a. Recall** What are the five major climate zones?

    b. Explain How does latitude relate to climate?

Lesson 6

18. **a. Define** What is an ecosystem, and why does it exist in a fragile balance?

    b. Explain Why are plants an important part of the environment?

Lesson 7

19. a. Define What are minerals?

b. Contrast How do nonrenewable resources and renewable resources differ?

c. Elaborate How might a scarcity of natural resources affect life in a region?

Reading Skills

Use Word Parts *Use what you learned about prefixes, suffixes, and word roots to answer the questions.*

20. The prefix *in-* sometimes means "not." What do the words *invisible* and *inactive* mean?

21. The suffix *–ment* means "action" or "process." What does the word *movement* mean?

Social Studies Skills

Use a Physical Map *Use the physical map of the United States in the World Atlas to answer these questions.*

22. What physical feature extends along the Gulf of Mexico?

23. What mountain range in the West lies above 6,560 feet (2,000 m)?

Map Activity

Physical Map *Use the map to answer the questions that follow.*

24. Which letter indicates a river?

25. Which letter on the map indicates the highest elevation?

26. The lowest elevation on the map is indicated by which letter?

27. An island is indicated by which letter?

28. Which letter indicates a large body of water?

29. Which letter indicates an area of land between 1,640 feet (500 m) and 6,560 feet (2,000 m) above sea level?

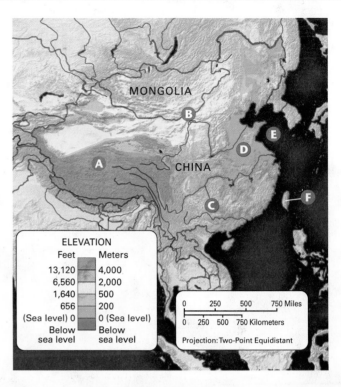

ELEVATION

Feet	Meters
13,120	4,000
6,560	2,000
1,640	500
656	200
(Sea level) 0	0 (Sea level)
Below sea level	Below sea level

0   250   500   750 Miles
0   250 500 750 Kilometers

Projection: Two-Point Equidistant

Focus on Reading and Viewing

30. Present and View a Weather Report Select a place and a season to write a weather report about. Watch weather reports online or on TV as part of your research. Note interesting vocabulary, and look up words you do not understand. Use what you learn in your research to describe the weather and predict upcoming weather. Include vocabulary from this module. Then present your report to the class. Speak using a professional, friendly tone and a variety of sentence types. Make frequent eye contact with your audience. Listen and take notes as your classmates present their reports. Be prepared to give feedback on the content and their presentation techniques.

Module 3
The Human World

Essential Question
Which geographic concepts are most useful for understanding the world's people?

About the Photo: Many of the world's people come together every four years to compete in the Olympics.

Explore ONLINE!

VIDEOS, including . . .
- Henry Ford's Motor Company
- Computers
- Hoover Dam

☑ Document-Based Investigations

☑ Graphic Organizers

☑ Interactive Games

☑ Channel One News Video: Young People Keep Mariachi Alive

☑ Interactive Map: Cultural Diffusion of Baseball

☑ Interactive Graph: World Population Growth, 1500–2000

☑ Image with Hotspots: How Fracking Works

In this module, you will learn about geographic concepts that help to explain the human world.

What You Will Learn

Human-Environment Interaction Farming is one way that humans interact with the environment. These rice farmers in Vietnam utilize the area's rich soil.

Culture Thousands of different cultures make up our world. Clothing, language, and music are just some parts of culture.

Population Geographers study human populations, like this one in India, to learn where and why people live in certain places.

Reading Social Studies

Understand Main Ideas

READING FOCUS

Main ideas are like the hub of a wheel. The hub holds the wheel together, and everything circles around it. In a paragraph, the main idea holds the paragraph together and all the facts and details revolve around it. The main idea is usually stated clearly in a topic sentence, which may come at the beginning or end of a paragraph. Topic sentences always summarize the most important idea of a paragraph.

To find the main idea, ask yourself what one point is holding the paragraph together. See how the main idea in the following example holds all the details from the paragraph together.

A single country may also include more than one culture region within its borders. Mexico is one of many countries that is made up of different culture regions. People in northern Mexico and southern Mexico, for example, have different culture traits. The culture of northern Mexico tends to be more modern, while traditional culture remains strong in southern Mexico.

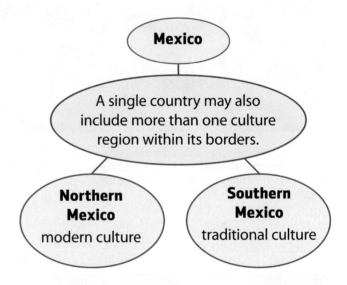

YOU TRY IT!

Read the following paragraph, and then use a graphic organizer to identify the main idea. Create as many circles as you need to list the supporting facts and details.

People migrate for many reasons. Some factors push people to leave their country, while others pull people away. During the Irish potato famine of the mid-1800s, poverty and disease forced some 1.5 million people to leave Ireland. In the 1800s and early 1900s thousands of British citizens migrated to Australia in search of cheap land.

As you read this module, find the main ideas of the paragraphs you are studying.

Elements of Culture

The Big Idea

Culture, a group's shared practices and beliefs, differs from group to group and changes over time while maintaining features common to all societies.

Main Ideas

- Culture is the set of beliefs, goals, and practices that a group of people share.

- The world includes many different culture groups.

- New ideas and events lead to changes in culture.

- The features common to all cultures are called cultural universals.

- All societies have social institutions that help their groups survive.

- Every culture expresses itself creatively in a variety of ways.

- All societies use technology to help shape and control the environment.

Key Terms and Places

culture
culture trait
culture region
ethnic group
multicultural society
cultural diffusion
cultural universals
social institutions
heritage
universal theme
technology

If YOU lived there . . .

You live in New York City, and your young cousin from out of state has come to visit. As you take her on a tour, you point out the different cultural neighborhoods, like Chinatown, Little Italy, Spanish Harlem, and Koreatown. People speak in other languages as they venture to the nearby shops and restaurants that offer a variety of cultural goods. Your cousin can see that shopping and eating special foods are common activities for many cultures. Still, she isn't quite sure what *culture* means or why these neighborhoods are so different from her own.

How can you explain what culture is?

What Is Culture?

If you traveled around the world, you would experience many different sights and sounds. You would probably hear unique music, eat a variety of foods, listen to different languages, see distinctive landscapes, and learn new customs. You would see and take part in the variety of cultures that exist in our world.

A Way of Life What exactly is culture? **Culture** is the set of beliefs, values, and practices that a group of people have in common. Culture includes many aspects of life, such as language and religion, that we may share with people around us. Everything in your day-to-day life is part of your culture— from the clothes you wear to the music you hear to the foods you eat.

On your world travels, you might notice that all societies share certain cultural features. All people have some kind of government, educate their children in some way, and create some type of art or music. However, not all societies practice their culture in the same way. For example, in Japan, the school year begins in the spring and students wear school uniforms. In the United States, however, the school year begins in the late summer and most schools do not require uniforms. Differences like these are what make each culture unique.

These students in Japan and Kenya have some culture traits in common, like eating lunch at school. Other culture traits are different.

Analyze Visuals
What culture traits do these students share?
Which are different?

Culture Traits Cultural features like starting the school year in the spring or wearing uniforms are types of culture traits. A **culture trait** is an activity or behavior in which people often take part. The language you speak and the sports you play are some of your culture traits. Sometimes a culture trait is shared by people around the world. For example, all around the globe, people participate in the game of soccer. In places as different as Germany, Nigeria, and Saudi Arabia, many people enjoy playing and watching soccer.

While some culture traits are shared around the world, others change from place to place. One example of this is how people around the world eat. In China, most people use chopsticks to eat their food. In Europe, however, people use forks and spoons. In Ethiopia, many people use bread or their fingers to scoop their food.

Development of Culture How do cultures develop? Culture traits are often learned or passed down from one generation to the next. Most culture traits develop within families as traditions, foods, or holiday customs are handed down over the years. Laws and moral codes are also passed down within societies. For example, many laws in the United States can be traced back to England in the 1600s and were brought by colonists to America. Among these are the right to a speedy trial, freedom of petition, and due process of law.

Cultures also develop as people learn new culture traits. Immigrants who move to a new country, for example, might learn to speak the language or eat the foods of their adopted country.

Reading Check
Find Main Ideas
What practices and customs make up culture?

Other factors, such as history and the environment, also affect how cultures develop. For example, historical events changed the language and religion of much of Central and South America. In the 1500s, when the Spanish conquered the region, they introduced their language and Roman Catholic faith. The environment in which we live can also shape culture. For example, the desert environment of Africa's Sahara influences the way people who live there earn a living. Rather than grow crops, they herd animals that have adapted to the harsh environment. As you can see, history and the environment affect how cultures develop.

Culture Groups

Earth is home to thousands of different cultures. People who share similar culture traits are members of the same culture group. Culture groups can be based on a variety of factors, such as age, language, or religion. American teenagers, for example, can be said to form a culture group based on location and age. They share similar tastes in music, clothing, and sports.

Culture Regions When we refer to culture groups, we are speaking of people who share a common culture. At other times, however, we need to refer to the area, or region, where the culture group is found. A **culture region** is an area in which people have many shared culture traits.

Arab Culture Region

Culture regions are based on shared culture traits. Southwest Asia and North Africa make up an Arab culture region based on ethnic heritage, a common language, and religion. Most people in this region are Arab, speak and write Arabic, and practice Islam.

Many people share Arab culture traits. An Omani boy, above, and Palestinian girls, at left, share the same language and religion.

Analyze Visuals
What culture traits do you see in the photos?

Sports are played in cultures around the world. These Lenape teens enjoy a game of lacrosse.

In a specific culture region, people share certain culture traits, such as religious beliefs, language, or lifestyle. One well-known culture region is the Arab world. As you can see in the Arab Culture Region feature, this culture region spreads across Southwest Asia and North Africa. In this region, most people write and speak Arabic and are Muslim. They also share other traits, such as foods, music, styles of clothing, and architecture.

Occasionally, a single culture region dominates an entire country. In Japan, for example, one primary culture dominates the country. Nearly everyone in Japan speaks the same language and follows the same practices. Many Japanese bow to their elders as a sign of respect and remove their shoes when they enter a home.

A single country may also include more than one culture region within its borders. Mexico is one of many countries that is made up of different culture regions. People in northern Mexico and southern Mexico, for example, have different culture traits. The culture of northern Mexico tends to be more modern, while traditional culture remains strong in southern Mexico.

A culture region may also stretch across country borders. As you have already learned, an Arab culture region dominates much of Southwest Asia and North Africa. Another example is the Kurdish culture region, home to the Kurds, a people that live throughout Turkey, Iran, and Iraq.

Cultural Diversity As you just learned, countries may contain several culture regions within their borders. Often, these culture regions are based on ethnic groups. An **ethnic group** is a group of people who share a common culture and ancestry. Members of ethnic groups often share certain culture traits such as language and special foods. Religion can also be a shared culture trait within an ethnic group.

People in different ethnic groups can be part of the same religious group. For example, many people around the world practice the religion of Judaism. However, a Jewish person from Hungary would not be in the same ethnic group as a Jewish person from Ethiopia. These two people may share religious beliefs, but they do not have the same ethnic background. In contrast, people can be in the same ethnic group and have different religious beliefs. For example, there are Christian and Muslim Arabs.

Some countries are home to a variety of ethnic groups. For example, more than 100 different ethnic groups live in the East African country of Tanzania. Countries with many ethnic groups are culturally diverse. A **multicultural society** is a society that includes a variety of cultures in the same area. While multiculturalism creates an interesting mix of ideas, behaviors, and practices, it can also lead to conflict.

In some countries, ethnic groups have been in conflict. In Canada, for example, some French Canadians want to separate from the rest of Canada to preserve their language and culture. In the 1990s, ethnic conflict in the African country of Rwanda led to extreme violence and bloodshed.

Reading Check
Make Inferences
Why might
multiculturalism
cause conflict?

Academic
Vocabulary
innovation a new
idea or way of doing
something

Although ethnic groups have clashed in some culturally diverse countries, they have cooperated in others. In the United States, for example, many different ethnic groups live side by side. One major reason for this diversity is that people have migrated to the United States from all over the world. Cities and towns often celebrate their ethnic heritage with festivals and parades, like the Saint Patrick's Day Parade in Boston or Philadelphia's Puerto Rican Festival.

Changes in Culture

You've read books or seen movies set in the time of the Civil War or in the Wild West of the late 1800s. Think about how our culture has changed since then. Clothing, food, music—all have changed drastically. When we study cultural change, we try to find out what factors influence the changes and how those changes spread from place to place.

How Cultures Change Cultures change constantly. Some changes happen rapidly, while others take many years. What causes cultures to change? <u>Innovation</u> and contact with other people are two key causes of cultural change.

New ideas often bring about cultural changes. For example, when Alexander Graham Bell invented the telephone, it changed how people communicate with each other. Other innovations, such as motion pictures, changed how people spend their free time. More recently, the creation of the Internet dramatically altered the way people find information, communicate, and shop.

Cultures also change as societies come into contact with each other. For example, when the Spanish arrived in the Americas, they introduced firearms and horses to the region, changing the lifestyle of some Native American groups. At the same time, the Spaniards learned about new foods like potatoes and chocolate. These foods then became an important part of Europeans' diet. The Chinese had a similar influence on Korea and Japan, where they introduced Buddhism and written language.

How Cultural Traits Spread You have probably noticed that a new slang word might spread from teenager to teenager and state to state. In the same way, clothing styles from New York or Paris might become popular all over the world. More serious cultural traits spread as well. Religious beliefs or ideas about government may spread from place to place. The spread of culture traits from one region to another is called **cultural diffusion.**

Cultural diffusion often occurs when individuals move from one place to another. For example, when European immigrants settled in the Americas, they brought their culture along with them. As a result, English, French, Spanish, and Portuguese are all spoken in the Americas. American culture also spread as pioneers moved west, taking with them their form of government, religious beliefs, and customs.

Another factor that leads to cultural diffusion is trade. An example of this developed along the Silk Road of ancient China. The trade route encouraged the exchange of goods and practices between Asia and the

Middle East. Also, the Phoenicians were an early trading civilization that moved Middle Eastern culture throughout the Mediterranean region. They are often called the "carriers of civilization" because of their strong influence on other cultures.

Conflict can also be a reason for cultural diffusion. Recently, millions of Syrians fled their country in a mass migration to escape civil war. Some refugees moved to neighboring countries in the Middle East. Other Syrian people traveled great distances to places such as Europe and North America. This migration contributed to the diversity of each region.

Cultural diffusion also takes place as new ideas spread from place to place. As you can see on the map, the game of baseball first began in New York, then spread throughout the United States. As more and more people learned the game, it spread even faster and farther. Baseball eventually spread to other world societies. Wearing blue jeans became part of our culture in a similar way. Blue jeans originated in the American West in the mid-1800s. They gradually became popular all over the country and the world.

Reading Check
Find Main Ideas
How do cultures change over time?

What Do All Cultures Have in Common?

You may be wondering how cultures can be so different when all people have the same basic needs. All people need food, clothing, and shelter to survive. Geographers and other social scientists believe that some needs

Focus on Culture

Cultural Diffusion of Baseball

Like many other ideas and customs, baseball has spread around the world through the process of cultural diffusion. Since its beginnings in New York in the 1800s, baseball has spread throughout the United States, into Central and South America, and to Asia.

American missionaries introduced baseball to Korea in 1905.

Organized baseball began in New York around 1845 and quickly spread around the world.

American students first brought baseball to Cuba in the 1800s.

NORTH AMERICA

PACIFIC OCEAN

UNITED STATES
New York
Origin of baseball

ATLANTIC OCEAN

SOUTH AMERICA

Spread of baseball
0   1,000   2,000 Miles
0 1,000 2,000 Kilometers
Projection: Miller Cylindrical

Analyze Visuals
Where did baseball begin, and to what parts of the world did it eventually spread?

Reading Check
Find Main Ideas
What can geographers
learn from cultural
universals?

are so basic that societies everywhere have developed certain features to meet them. These features, common to all cultures, are called **cultural universals.** In this section, you will learn about three important cultural universals: social institutions, creative expressions, and technology.

Basic Social Institutions

Societies, like people, have basic needs that must be met for a group to survive. **Social institutions** are organized patterns of belief and behavior that focus on meeting these needs. The most basic social institutions are family, education, religion, government, and economy. The core principles and ideals of a society are known as cultural values. They help to shape the group and all of its social institutions. Cultural values and social institutions exist in all societies. However, their specific characteristics and customs, or ways of doing things, vary from culture to culture.

Family Family is the most basic social institution. In all societies, its purpose is the same. The family ensures that children are cared for until old enough to fend for themselves. Families provide emotional and physical support. They also teach the accepted values, traditions, and customs of a culture.

The traditions of a culture hold great significance and get passed along from one generation to the next. One custom in Greece is that people celebrate a "name day" for the saint that bears their name instead of their own birthday. Another tradition is the Battle of Oranges in Northern Italy. Groups of people throw oranges to reenact a famous battle.

Cultural values are also important and often have a long history within a specific culture. For example, the foundation of African cultural values is based on the past and present. This is one reason why elders are so respected there. The elders are to always be acknowledged and served their meals first.

The size of a family can vary from one culture to another. Family members may live together under one roof or they might inhabit an entire village. For example, India's joint family system includes grandparents, parents, uncles, aunts, and all of their children living in one household.

Government To keep order and resolve conflicts, people need a government. A government is a system of leaders and laws that help people live safely together in their community or country. Laws help people live safely with each other because they define standards, protect property and people's rights, and help settle disagreements. Laws can apply to any of a society's social institutions. For example, a country may impose a minimum wage law, which affects the country's economy. Perhaps a government creates new laws for its nation's education system. This may impact what students learn in school.

Economy To support its people, a society must have an economy, or a system of using resources to meet needs. People must be able to make, buy, sell, and trade goods and services to get what they need and want. They must consider the questions of what to produce, for whom to produce, and how to produce. Prosperous nations have strong economic principles in place to guide their business decisions and actions.

In the United States and in Peru, schools teach knowledge, skills, and cultural norms to prepare students for adult roles.

Analyze Visuals
What similarities and differences do you detect between the two classroom environments?

Education Societies rely on education to pass on knowledge to young people. For example, schools across the world teach reading, writing, math, and technical skills that prepare students to take on adult roles. Schools also teach the norms and values that sustain, or support, a society. For instance, one goal of U.S. public schools is to develop informed citizens who contribute to the good of their communities.

Religion The world's religions are incredibly diverse. Still, in all societies, religion helps explain the meanings of life and death and the difference between good and bad behavior. Over time, religion is passed down and supported by traditional practices, literature, sacred texts and stories, and sacred places. All of this makes religion a powerful force. It is often the foundation of a culture's philosophical beliefs and attitudes. Moreover, in all world regions, it has inspired and sustained itself through great works of devotion, including art and **monumental** architecture.

Creative Expressions

All people are creative. Everyone has the ability to imagine, think, and create. Not surprisingly, all societies express themselves creatively, too. The main types of creative expression are:

- **Performing Arts**—art forms that combine sound and movement for an audience, such as music, theater, and dance
- **Visual Arts**—creative expressions that have both a visual and material form, such as painting, jewelry, sculpture, textiles, and architecture
- **Literary Arts**—art forms rooted in words and language, such as literature, folktales, and stories

Academic Vocabulary
monumental
impressively large, sturdy, and enduring

Reading Check
Summarize
What are the main social institutions?

Religion inspires creative expressions, including monumental architecture such as France's Notre Dame Cathedral and Shwedagon Pagoda, a Buddhist temple in Myanmar (Burma).

Analyze Visuals
How do examples of monumental architecture express the power of religion?

Creative Forces As you explore creative expressions from all world regions, note how they are influenced by the availability of natural materials and resources. Look, too, for how creative expressions reflect a specific **heritage,** or the wealth of cultural elements that has been passed down over generations.

Creative expressions also express individual choices. People use artistic forms to express individual as well as cultural ideas about what is pleasing, proper, and beautiful. They also use them to address contemporary issues such as politics, war, and social inequality. This is because the arts can inspire us. Creative forms communicate ideas and emotions that stir people to action.

Universal Themes Some creative expressions communicate universal themes. A **universal theme** is a message about life or human nature that is meaningful across time and in all places. Because they express basic human truths, universal themes transcend, or move beyond, the boundaries of a particular society. They speak to people everywhere.

Masterpieces of art have qualities that are meaningful and timeless. Examples include Egyptian hieroglyphics and the sculptures of ancient Greece. The woodblock prints made by the Japanese painter Katsushika Hokusai are also an example of this type of art. They express a love of nature's beauty, simplicity, and power.

Reading Check
Describe
What are the main types of cultural expressions?

Other art forms also gain worldwide appreciation. For example, literature such as *The Lord of the Rings* contains a universal theme of a hero's search for truth, goodness, and honor. Blues music is another example. Derived from African American work songs and spirituals in the American South, blues songs express feelings of sadness and struggle in the face of great challenges.

Science and Technology

All people use technology to shape and control their environments, and they use science to try and understand it. **Technology** refers to the use of knowledge, tools, and skills to solve problems. Science is a way of understanding the world through observation and the testing of ideas.

Factors Shaping Technology Use Historically, the type of technology a culture developed has been strongly tied to environmental factors. Not only were tools and technology made from local resources, they were also designed to solve specific problems posed by nature. For example, farmers might build dams to prevent rivers from flooding and destroying their crops.

Other factors such as belief systems, political decisions, and economic factors can influence technology use, too. Some religious groups, like the Amish people of the United States, selectively use technology. They readily use gas and horse-drawn buggies. However, they reject technology they think will undermine their traditions, including cars and computers.

Government decisions also affect technology use. North Korea, for example, restricts Internet use. To use the Internet, a North Korean must have special permission and may use it for government purposes only. Worldwide, however, the primary barrier between people and technology is economic. New technologies are simply too expensive for many of the world's people to access them.

Impact of Technology Throughout time, advances in science and technology have made life easier. Some discoveries even changed the world.

Consider, for example, the work of French scientist Louis Pasteur. His work revolutionized health and medicine. In 1870 Pasteur discovered that germs caused infections. To prevent the spread of disease, he urged people to wash their hands. He also developed vaccines to prevent deadly diseases and a process for removing bacteria from food. Today, most milk, cheese, and juice on our grocery shelves have been sterilized, or made germ-free, through pasteurization.

Inventors, too, change the world. For example, in 1879, Thomas Edison developed an affordable and practical light bulb. At the time, the invention caused a sensation. People no longer had to burn candles and oil lamps for light at night. Over time, electricity transformed daily life and work for many of the world's people.

Nature's awesome power is a universal theme in the painting of a great wave created by Japanese artist Katsushika Hokusai.

In fact, Thomas Edison had a friend in the auto industry who would greatly benefit from the new technology. In 1913 automaker Henry Ford launched the world's first moving assembly line. This new process allowed workers to decrease construction time on a single vehicle from 12 hours to roughly 90 minutes.

The introduction of computers into the workplace has demanded new skill sets from employees. Consider the work of an auto mechanic from 50 years ago and today. Every car manufactured today contains at least one computer system. Auto mechanics must understand these systems in order to effectively work on a vehicle.

All of these technologies greatly increased the rate of production. People were able to work faster and more efficiently, which resulted in a larger supply of available goods.

Today, scientists and inventors continue to identify and solve problems. They often work in groups to make discoveries or invent new devices or products that will benefit future generations. This involves careful thinking about the future and making predictions about the social, political, economic, cultural, and environmental impact of their work.

Summary and Preview In this lesson you learned about the role that culture plays in our lives, how our cultures change over time and move around the world, and the features that make cultures similar. Next, you will learn about human populations and how we keep track of Earth's changing population.

Reading Check
Form Generalizations
What are the basic purposes of technology and science?

Lesson 1 Assessment

Review Ideas, Terms, and Places

1. **a. Define** What is culture?
   b. Analyze What influences the development of culture?
   c. Elaborate How might the world be different if we all shared the same culture?

2. **a. Identify** What are the different types of culture regions?
   b. Analyze How does cultural diversity affect societies?

3. **a. Describe** Identify an example of a cultural trait that has spread. How did that culture trait spread?
   b. Identify Which factors influence cultural change?
   c. Evaluate Do you think that cultural diffusion has a positive or a negative effect? Explain your answer.

4. **a. Identify and Explain** What are five basic social institutions? What purposes do they serve?
   b. Analyze What efforts and activities are most important for a religious institution to last over time? Explain.

5. **a. Describe** What forces influence cultural expressions?

   b. Identify List and explain examples of art, music, and literature with universal themes.

6. **a. Explain** How can factors related to belief systems, government, and economics affect technology use?
   b. Make Inferences How might a resource such as river water affect how farmers use technology?
   c. Explain Give an example of a scientific discovery and an example of a technological innovation that have changed the world. Discuss the role of scientists and inventors in making the discovery and innovation.

Critical Thinking

7. **Find Main Ideas** Using your notes and a chart like the one here, explain the main idea of each aspect of culture in your own words.

Culture Traits	Culture Groups	Cultural Change

Population

The Big Idea

Population studies are an important part of geography.

Main Ideas

- The study of population patterns helps geographers learn about the world.
- Population statistics and trends are important measures of population change.

Key Terms and Places

population
population density
birthrate
migration

If YOU lived there . . .

You live in Mexico City, one of the largest and most crowded cities in the world. You realize just how crowded it is whenever you ride the subway at rush hour! You love the excitement of living in a big city. There is always something interesting to do. At the same time, the city has a lot of crime. Heavy traffic pollutes the air.

What do you like and dislike about living in a large city?

Population Patterns

How many people live in your community? Do you live in a small town, a huge city, or somewhere in between? Your community's **population,** or the total number of people in a given area, determines a great deal about the place in which you live. Population influences the variety of businesses, the types of transportation, and the number of schools in your community.

Because population has a huge impact on our lives, it is an important part of geography. Geographers who study human populations are particularly interested in patterns that emerge over time. They study such information as how many people live in an area, why people live where they do, and how populations change. Population patterns like these can tell us much about our world.

Population Density Some places on Earth are crowded with people. Others are almost empty. One statistic geographers use to examine populations is **population density,** a measure of the number of people living in an area. Population density is expressed as persons per square mile or square kilometer.

Population density provides us with important information about a place. The more people per square mile in a region, the more crowded, or dense, it is. Japan, for example, has a population density of about 897 people per square mile (around 347 per square km). That is a high population density. In many parts of Japan, people are crowded together in large cities and space is very limited. In contrast, Australia has a very low

World Population Density

Interpret Maps

1. **Place** Which continent is the most densely populated? Which is the least densely populated?

2. **Region** Why might the population density of far Northern America be so low?

population density. Only around 8 people per square mile (about 3 per square km) live there. Australia has many wide-open spaces with very few people.

How do you think population density affects life in a particular place? In places with high population densities, the land is often expensive, roads are crowded, and buildings tend to be taller. On the other hand, places with low population densities tend to have more open spaces, less traffic, and more available land.

Population density also affects the economic development of a region. These effects can be positive or negative depending on the circumstances. Areas with higher population densities and abundant resources have the potential to create more job opportunities, which can add value to the region. In contrast, a larger population density in regions with limited resources can present many challenges. It may be difficult to provide goods and services to every person when resources are in short supply.

Where People Live Can you tell where most of the world's people live by examining the world population density map above? The reds and purples on the map indicate areas of very high population density, while the light

Many parts of Japan have a high population density. Space is extremely limited in the city of Tokyo.

Australia has a very low population density. There is plenty of space for people living along the Noosa River.

yellow areas indicate sparse populations. When an area is thinly populated, it is often because the land does not provide a very good life. These areas may have rugged mountains or harsh deserts where people cannot grow crops. Some areas may be frozen all year long, making survival there very difficult. For these reasons, very few people live in parts of far North America, Greenland, northern Asia, and Australia.

Notice on the world population density map that some areas have large clusters of population. Such clusters can be found in East and South Asia, Europe, and eastern North America. Fertile soil, plentiful vegetation, reliable sources of water and minerals, and a good agricultural climate make these regions favorable for settlement. For example, the North China Plain in East Asia is one of the most densely populated regions in the world. The area's plentiful agricultural land, many rivers, and mild climate have made it an ideal place to settle. The natural resources in these regions offer job opportunities in farming, mining, and timber production. These industries can provide great economic benefits to the area.

As populations swell in desirable areas, there is a higher demand for resources. These demands can drastically affect the environment. Many developed nations consume resources faster than they can regenerate them. In some areas, population has been growing faster than food supplies. The amount of available farmland is shrinking as regions make room for more people. Coastal ecosystems are being pressured by urban development. The demand for fresh water also increases with population. Some countries may even face shortages in the future.

Reading Check
Form Generalizations
What types of information can population density provide?

Calculate Population Density

Population density measures the number of people living in an area. To calculate population density, divide a place's total population by its area in square miles (or square kilometers). For example, if your city has a population of 100,000 people and an area of 100 square miles, you would divide 100,000 by 100. This would give you a population density of 1,000 people per square mile (100,000 ÷ 100 = 1,000).

City	Population	Total Area (square miles)	Population Density (people per square mile)
Adelaide, Australia	1,255,516	705	1,781
Lima, Peru	9,897,033	1,032	9,590
Nairobi, Kenya	3,914,791	269	14,553

Source: *World Urbanization Prospects*, Population Division, UN Dept. of Economic and Social Affairs

Evaluate

If a city had a population of 615,000 and a total land area of 250 square miles, what would its population density be?

Population Change

The study of population is much more important than you might realize. The number of people living in an area affects all elements of life—the availability of housing and jobs, whether hospitals and schools open or close, even the amount of available food. Geographers track changes in populations by examining important statistics, studying the movement of people, and analyzing population trends.

Tracking Population Changes Geographers examine three key statistics to learn about population changes. These statistics are important for studying a country's population over time.

Three key statistics—birthrate, death rate, and the rate of natural increase—track changes in population. Births add to a population. Deaths subtract from it. The annual number of births per 1,000 people is called the **birthrate.** Similarly, the death rate is the annual number of deaths per 1,000 people. The birthrate minus the death rate equals the percentage of natural increase, or the rate at which a population is changing. For example, Denmark has a rate of natural increase of 0.01 percent. This means it has slightly more births than deaths and a very slight population increase.

Population growth rates differ from one place to another. In some countries, populations are growing very slowly or even shrinking. Many countries in Europe and North America have very low rates of natural increase. In Russia, for example, the birthrate is about 11 and the death rate is around 14. The result is a negative rate of natural increase and a shrinking population.

In most countries around the world, however, populations are growing. Mali, for example, has a rate of natural increase of about 3.1 percent. While that may sound small, it means that Mali's population is expected to double in the next 20 years! High population growth rates can pose

The failure of Ireland's most important food crop, the potato, caused widespread starvation. Disease and high food prices forced many Irish to flee to America in search of a better life.

Irish Migration to The United States, 1845–1855

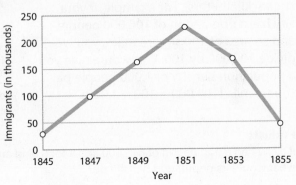

Source: *Historical Statistics of the United States.*

Analyze Graphs
In what year did Irish migration to the United States peak?

Push Factors

- Climate changes, exhausted resources, earthquakes, volcanoes, drought/famine
- Unemployment, slavery
- Religious, ethnic, or political persecution, war

Migration Factors

Environmental • Economic • Political

Pull Factors

- Abundant land, new resources, good climate
- Employment opportunities
- Political and/or religious freedom

some challenges, as governments try to provide enough jobs, education, and medical care for their rapidly growing populations.

Many governments track their regional population patterns and trends. Analyzing current data and making population projections can help leaders address present and future needs of citizens. This might involve enacting new laws that protect the natural resources of an area. A government could also develop policies that provide more economic opportunities for a region. For example, China's most recent Five-Year Plan promotes the use of cleaner energy sources to reduce pollution. The plan also outlines ways that China will strengthen support for farmers, increase agricultural income, and improve rural infrastructure.

Migration A common cause of population change is migration. **Migration** is the process of moving from one place to live in another. As one country loses citizens as a result of migration, its population can decline. At the same time, another country may gain population as people settle there.

People migrate for many reasons. Some factors push people to leave their country, while other factors pull, or attract, people to new countries. Warfare, a lack of jobs, or a lack of good farmland are common push factors. For example, during the Irish potato famine of the mid-1800s, poverty and disease forced some 1.5 million people to leave Ireland. Opportunities for a better life often pull people to new countries. For example, in the 1800s and early 1900s, thousands of British citizens migrated to Australia in search of cheap land.

Political conditions such as freedom or persecution can also cause movement. The political system of apartheid in South Africa imposed a regime of segregation and racial oppression from the mid-1900s until 1994. Thousands of black South Africans were forced to migrate to other parts of Africa. Environmental factors such as climate can also lead to migration. For example, people who live in harsh climates are often attracted to regions with milder climates.

World Population Trends In the last 200 years, Earth's population has exploded. For thousands of years, world population growth was low and relatively steady. About 2,000 years ago, the world had some 300 million people. By 1800 there were almost 1 billion people. Since 1800, better health care and improved food production have supported tremendous population growth. By 2012 the world's population passed 7 billion people.

World Population Growth

Advances in food production and health care have dramatically lowered death rates. As a result, the global population has seen incredible growth over the last 200 years.

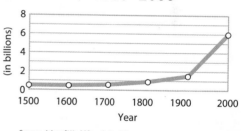

World Population Growth, 1500–2000

Source: *Atlas of World Population History*

Analyze Graphs
By how much did the world's population increase between 1800 and 2000?

Reading Check
Summarize
What population
statistics do
geographers study?
Why?

Population trends are an important part of the study of the world's people. Two important population trends are clear today. The first trend indicates that the population growth in some of the more industrialized nations has begun to slow. For example, Germany and France have low rates of natural increase. A second trend indicates that less industrialized countries, like Nigeria and Bangladesh, often have high growth rates. These trends affect a country's work force and government aid.

Summary and Preview In this lesson you learned where people live, how crowded places are, and how population changes. Geographers study population patterns and trends to plan for the future. In the next lesson, you will learn about factors that influence the settlement patterns of people.

Lesson 2 Assessment

Review Ideas, Terms, and Places

1. a. Identify What regions of the world have the highest levels of population density?

   b. Draw Conclusions What information can be learned by studying population density?

   c. Evaluate Would you prefer to live in a region with a dense or a sparse population? Why?

2. a. Describe What is natural increase? What can it tell us about a country?

   b. Analyze What effect does migration have on human populations?

   c. Predict What patterns do you think world population might have in the future?

Critical Thinking

3. Summarize Draw a chart with two columns. Label one column Population Patterns and the other column Population Change. Use your notes to write a sentence that summarizes each aspect of the study of population.

Population Patterns	Population Change

Settlement Patterns

The Big Idea

Many factors influence where people settle and how settlements develop.

Main Ideas

- Natural resources and trade routes are important factors in determining location for settlements.
- Areas can be defined as urban or rural.
- Spatial patterns describe ways that people build settlements.
- New technology has improved the interaction of regions with nearby and distant places.

Key Terms and Places

settlement
trade route
urban
suburb
metropolitan area
megalopolis
rural
spatial pattern
linear settlements
cluster settlements
grid settlements
commerce

If YOU lived there . . .

You live in Phoenix and your parents tell you that they must relocate for work. The family asks for your opinion on where to move. Do you prefer the city lights and skyscrapers of Chicago or the Smoky Mountains in North Carolina?

How do people decide where to live?

The Importance of Location

A **settlement** is any place where a community is established. Settlements vary in size, ranging anywhere from a heavily populated city to a remote island village. Where people choose to settle depends on many factors. These factors may be economic, political, or related to natural resources.

Natural Resources People have always settled near natural resources. Some of the earliest settlements were started near sources of freshwater or on tracts of land that were good for farming. As people began to use other resources, the places where they settled changed. During the late 1800s, the cities of Pittsburgh, Pennsylvania, and Birmingham, Alabama, grew considerably. This was due to their location near deposits of iron ore and coal. The steel manufacturing industry led to booms in both cities.

Trade Routes Because resources are not distributed evenly, trade routes have always been important to settlements. A **trade route** is a path used by traders for buying and selling goods. Villages, towns, and cities were often started along trade routes, and these places grew as the routes grew. For example,

Birmingham, Alabama, was founded in 1871 at the crossing of two railroad lines, near rich deposits of iron and coal.

Singapore's location along a major shipping route has helped make the tiny island nation rich.

Singapore, in Southeast Asia, grew along a major shipping route. The city of Timbuktu in western Africa was founded at the place where major caravan routes met. The Niger River, an important water trade route, was also located nearby. Timbuktu thrived not only as a trading center but also as a political center because of the different groups that met there to trade.

Reading Check
Find Main Ideas Why are natural resources and trade routes important to a settlement?

Urban and Rural

Geographers often classify patterns of settlement by size. One way they do this is by defining areas as urban or rural.

Urban areas are cities and the surrounding areas. They are heavily populated and very developed. This means that urban areas have many structures such as houses, roads, and commercial buildings. Most people work in jobs not related to agriculture.

Small urban areas might include a city center or a **suburb.** A suburb is an area immediately outside of a city, often a smaller residential community. Large urban areas might include an entire city and nearby suburbs. A city, its suburbs, and surrounding areas form a large urban area called a **metropolitan area.** When several metropolitan areas grow together, they form a **megalopolis.** A megalopolis in the northeastern United States is the tract of cities including Boston, New York, Philadelphia, Baltimore, and Washington, DC.

Rural areas are found outside of cities. They are less densely populated and have fewer structures. The economic activities of rural areas are usually tied to the land. Agriculture, forestry, mining, and recreation are examples of rural economic activities. Settlements in rural areas are often built around these activities.

Reading Check
Contrast What is the difference between rural and urban areas?

Times Square in Manhattan is an urban area.

The economic activities in rural areas are usually tied to the land.

Spatial Patterns

There are many factors that influence settlement design. Within urban and rural areas, settlements are built in certain ways. Geographers use spatial patterns to describe and classify how people build settlements. A **spatial pattern** is the placement of people and objects on Earth and the space between them.

Types of Settlements **Linear settlements** are grouped along the length of a resource, such as a river. They usually form a long and narrow pattern. In the eastern United States, many linear settlements were started along the Fall Line. This is a place where the land drops sharply to the Coastal Plain. This drop causes rivers to form waterfalls and rapids. In the past, people used the fast-moving water along the Fall Line to power factories and machines. Today, this water is used to generate electricity.

Cluster settlements are grouped around or at the center of a resource. Coal became an important resource in Europe in the early 1800s. Settlements were founded on the outskirts of coal deposits, or seams, to support mining operations. The Corn Belt is located in the midwestern United States and includes Iowa, Illinois, and Indiana, as well as parts of Nebraska, Kansas, Minnesota, and Missouri. Since the 1850s, this area has been a leading producer of corn. Settlements in the Corn Belt, like many agricultural areas, are designed to maximize the available land for farming.

Grid settlements are purposefully laid out with a network of transportation routes. Streets form a grid by running at right angles to each other. These settlements are commonly found in urban areas. Transportation networks are commonly made of roads, though some places also have networks of water routes or underground subway and train routes. Washington, DC, is one example of a grid settlement. It was designed using a grid plan that includes diagonal avenues often connected by traffic circles. This layout continued as the capital expanded.

Reading Check
Identify Problems
What is one problem that could occur in a cluster settlement?

Types of Settlement Patterns

Some basic types of settlement patterns include linear, cluster, and grid.

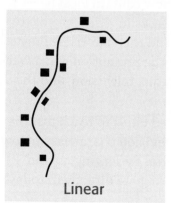

Linear

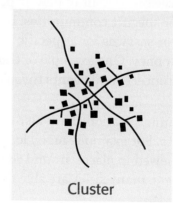

Cluster

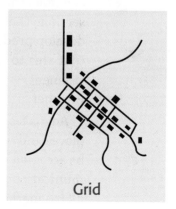

Grid

Analyze Visuals
How would you classify the settlement pattern of your community?

Planned transportation networks, such as this highway system in Los Angeles, California, are a feature of grid settlements.

Regions Interact

People live in or near urban areas because they are centers for commerce and trade. **Commerce** refers to the substantial exchange of goods between cities, states, or countries. Usually, urban areas are also centers of government services for a region. Moreover, cities are often known as hubs for education, communication, transportation, and innovation.

Advances in Technology Starting during the mid-1900s, new inventions including television and satellites greatly improved communications. Later, computers and the Internet also improved communications and changed the ways people collected, stored, shared, and used information.

Technological advances affected cities and the places near them. Cities were able to tailor services and communications to nearby regions. For example, some large metropolitan newspapers now contain local news sections that cover specific communities. Businesses in cities are able to develop products or services for a specific area and then advertise only to that area to save money. One example of this is the promotion and advertisement of local concerts and events through radio, television, and the Internet.

Advances in communications have also enabled cities to reach distant places and markets. For example, many local television channels can now be accessed and viewed in places around the world. By serving as communications centers, many cities are able to participate directly in today's global market.

Advances in transportation have also changed how people and ideas move around the world. Today, people can travel great distances in a

Traders work on the floor of the New York Stock Exchange on Wall Street in New York City. The New York Stock Exchange is one of the world's largest trading marketplaces. Wall Street and New York City have long been hubs of interaction for the financial industry.

Reading Check
Summarize How has new technology changed interaction between regions?

shorter amount of time. For example, the 7,500-mile (17,070-km) flight from Los Angeles to Sydney, Australia, takes less than 15 hours. Transportation hubs such as airports, train stations, and subway systems connect major cities across the globe. In a sense, new technology has allowed our enormous world to seem much smaller.

Summary and Preview In this lesson you learned about the many factors that influence where people settle and how settlements develop. In the next lesson, you will learn about how people interact with their environments.

Lesson 3 Assessment

Review Ideas, Terms, and Places

1. a. Define What is a settlement?
   b. Analyze Effects How do natural resources and human activities affect settlements?

2. a. Identify What terms do geographers use to classify settlement patterns by size?
   b. Form Opinions Would you prefer to live in a rural or urban area? Explain your choice.

3. a. Explain How do geographers use spatial patterns?
   b. Synthesize What pattern would you choose to design a settlement? Provide reasons for your selection.

4. a. Analyze How do cities affect nearby and distant places?
   b. Elaborate How does technology make the world seem smaller?

Critical Thinking

5. Summarize Use a three-column chart to write a sentence that summarizes each type of settlement. Include an example for each.

Linear Settlement	Cluster Settlement	Grid Settlement

Human-Environment Interaction

The Big Idea

Specific environments present distinct opportunities for people to meet their needs and unique challenges to which they must adapt.

Main Ideas

- Geographers examine how environmental conditions shape people's lives.

- Human activity changes specific places, regions, and the world as a whole.

Key Terms and Places

terraced farming
slash-and-burn agriculture
center-pivot irrigation
fracking

If YOU lived there . . .

You live on the beach in Southern California and enjoy daily walks by the water. Lately you have noticed the sand littered with trash and debris. Last week your friend rescued a small turtle that was entangled in a plastic bag. You can't help but wonder why these things are happening to such a beautiful place.

How do people affect the environment?

Responding to the Environment

How does geography shape human behavior? Geographers interested in this question investigate how environmental conditions—such as terrain, climate, vegetation, wildlife, variations in soil, and the availability of water resources—shape people's lives. They also study the human systems, or cultural practices, that people develop in response to environmental conditions. Some human systems, like farming, allow people to benefit from what their environment offers. Other systems develop to protect people from conditions beyond their control, such as natural hazards.

The colorful, traditional clothes worn by the Sami, Norway's original population, help them survive harsh winters.

Using slash-and-burn agriculture, farmers cut trees, brush, and grasses and burn debris to clear land for farming. The ash produced creates fertile soils for farming.

Terraced farming is an ancient technique for growing crops on hillsides or mountain slopes. Farmers cut steps into hillsides. This creates flat land for growing crops.

Center-pivot irrigation uses a sprinkler unit in the center of a large, circular field. The sprinkler's long arm circles over the field, sprinkling water on the crops.

Analyze Visuals
How does each type of farming help resolve a challenge presented by the environment?

Farming Farming is one of the best examples of human-environment interaction. Over time, people across the globe have developed farming practices to grow food under specific environmental conditions. Most notably, farming is affected by climate, vegetation, and soil conditions.

Moreover, with these practices, people refashion the land, leaving their mark on the environment as they make the most of natural resources. For example, the ancient Inca of Peru created farmland by using a method called **terraced farming.** They carved steps into steep hillsides to create flat land for growing crops. In thickly forested areas, such as the Amazon rain forest, farmers developed **slash-and-burn agriculture.** Using this technique, farmers cut down trees and plants with knives and machetes. Then they burn the fallen trees to clear land for farming. After a few years, when the soil's nutrients have been used up, farmers move to a new area. Today, in dry regions of the United States, farmers use a technique called **center-pivot irrigation,** which uses a sprinkler system in the center of a large, circular field. The long arms of the sprinkler circle over the field to water crops.

Natural Hazards Weather can be harsh and sometimes deadly. People can adapt to their environment by preparing for natural hazards such as fires, tornadoes, earthquakes, and hurricanes. They change what they do to stay safe based on the climate. These preparations may include building storm shelters or having drills to practice what to do in an emergency. Most schools have fire drills to practice leaving the building. Depending on the weather in a location, some schools have tornado drills or earthquake drills. Cities also have building codes for new buildings and structures. These codes are rules that tell what must be done to keep a building safe when people use it.

In the past, people did not have the tools to prepare for natural hazards. One example is the 1815 eruption of Mount Tambora in Indonesia. The eruption scattered tons of ash, dust, and gas into the atmosphere. In the aftermath, there were food shortages and disease outbreaks. This led to a mass migration of people searching for a better place to live.

During tornadoes, people often seek shelter in basements or interior rooms.

Reading Check
Summarize How can people prepare for natural hazards?

Although we are more prepared for natural disasters in today's world, the impacts can still be devastating. In 2011 an earthquake in the Tohoku region of Japan caused a tsunami and damaged a nuclear power station. Thousands of people fled the area due to earthquake aftershocks, power outages, a lack of food, and fear of radiation from the nuclear reactors.

Changing the Environment

How do people affect the environment? Geographers interested in this question are particularly concerned with how human activity changes specific places, regions, and the world as a whole. They look at how people use the environment to meet their needs and explore the damaging effects that some human activities have on the environment.

Using Resources People are constantly modifying, or changing, their environment. For example, they build roads and bridges to make it easier to move people and goods. They build dams to create steady water sources and to control floods, and they clear land for farming or for new housing developments. People also dig deep into Earth's surface to obtain natural resources to heat their homes, make clothing, and power their cars and businesses. Human activities that change the environment often improve people's lives. New buildings, roads, and bridges help people live, travel, and work, but they are not always beneficial to the environment.

Dams provide necessary water for communities but also disrupt water flow and surrounding ecosystems.

Water pollution harms our food supplies, drinking water, and environment.

Effects of Human Activity Human activities can have negative effects for people and the environment. For example, when a dam is built, it could disrupt an aquatic ecosystem, or the community of plants and animals that live along the river. Blocking the flow of water could change the amount of water downstream, block migration routes, and even change the water chemistry. These changes could, in turn, affect the survival of many river species.

Human activities can also change environmental conditions in larger regions. An urban heat island occurs in large cities that are densely covered with roads, concrete, and buildings. These human features make an area drier and trap heat, causing parts of the city to be hotter than surrounding, less developed areas.

Geographers are especially concerned with how human activities contribute to global environmental challenges, such as pollution, acid rain, land degradation, ozone depletion, and global warming. Such challenges pose a threat to all people and places. For example, the ozone layer helps protect living things from the sun's harmful rays. Scientists have found that human activities have depleted, or used up, areas of the ozone layer. Specifically, chemicals called chlorofluorocarbons (CFCs) cause ozone depletion. For many years, people released CFCs into the atmosphere when

Most air pollution comes from the production and use of energy.

they made or used products such as spray cans, refrigerators, and Styrofoam cups. CFCs were phased out beginning in 1987, but the ozone layer was already damaged. Scientists think this aggravated problems associated with global warming, such as severe storms and rising sea levels.

People have different perspectives on environmental issues. The argument over hydraulic fracturing offers an example. Also known as **fracking,** this process breaks up rock by injecting large amounts of water and chemicals into cracks. This procedure forces cracks in the rock to widen, which allows oil and gas to flow out. In the United States, those against fracking have concerns that the process will significantly damage the environment or contaminate drinking water. Supporters claim that it will reduce dependence on foreign oil and boost economies with the production of homeland fuel.

Some people believe that government intervention is the best way to prevent businesses and individuals from depleting natural resources. Governments around the world have enacted policies in an effort to protect land, freshwater, air, and ocean resources. For instance, Brazil's government designated more than half of the Brazilian Amazon as national parks or indigenous lands. By establishing these protected areas, rates of deforestation and illegal logging have been drastically reduced.

No matter the viewpoint, environmental issues impact every person on the planet. Deforestation has led to the loss of habitat for many species and increased global warming. The burning of fossil fuels causes high levels of pollution, acid rain, and health issues. Desertification damages soil and vegetation, which can lead to food shortages for a region.

Many countries and organizations are working together to improve environmental quality around the globe. For example, the Environmental Protection Agency (EPA) is working with groups in West Africa to improve drinking water standards. The EPA also helped India introduce technologies to manage air quality and decrease vehicle emissions.

Summary In this lesson you learned that geographers investigate how environmental conditions shape people's lives. You also learned about how people interact with their environments.

Reading Check
Identify Problems
What are some environmental problems caused by humans?

Lesson 4 Assessment

Review Ideas, Terms, and Places

1. a. **Define** What is slash-and-burn agriculture?

   b. **Draw Conclusions** What might happen if people did not develop human systems to deal with natural disasters?

2. a. **Explain** How do human activities in one place impact the global environment?

   b. **Form Opinions** Do you support or disagree with fracking? Provide reasons for your opinion.

Critical Thinking

3. **Evaluate** Draw a chart to explain how land is used in your community. Use the chart to help answer the following questions: What changes have been made to the environment to benefit people? How might human activities harm the environment? How can people use resources wisely?

Beneficial Changes	Negative Effects	Conservation Ideas

Social Studies Skills

Organize Information

Define the Skill

Remembering new information is easier if you organize it clearly. As you read and study, try to organize what you are learning. One way to do this is to create a graphic organizer. As you read:

1. Identify the main idea of the text you are reading and write it in a circle.

2. Look for subtopics under the main idea. Write the subtopics in the circles below the main idea.

3. Below each subtopic, draw a big box. Look for facts and supporting details for each sub-topic to list in the box.

4. Organizing information is not limited to text. You can organize information found in visuals, too. Take a look at the Irish Migration to the United States, 1845–1855 graph in Lesson 2. You could create a graphic organizer such as a chart showing the changing levels of migration, or you could write a summary that organizes the information.

Learn the Skill

Study the chart about new legal permanent residents in the United States. Then create a graphic organizer or write a summary to organize the information.

Top Five Countries of Birth of New Legal Permanent Residents to the United States (by percent)	
Mexico	13.2
India	7.7
China	7.5
Philippines	4.9
Cuba	4.6
Other	62.1

Source: *U.S. Department of Homeland Security*

Practice the Skill

Turn to Lesson 1 and read the passage titled *Culture Regions.* Draw a graphic organizer and then follow the steps to organize the information you have read. The passage will have two or more subtopics. Add additional circles for each additional subtopic you find.

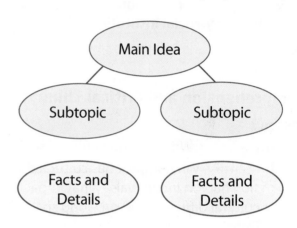

Module 3 Assessment

Review Vocabulary, Terms, and Places

Complete each sentence by filling in the blank with the correct term from the word pair.

1. Members of a/an _____ often share the same religion, traditions, and language. (**ethnic group/population**)

2. Music, art, and literature that transcend the boundaries of one society have _____. (**cultural universals/universal themes**)

3. _____, the process of moving from one place to live in another, is a cause of population change. (**Population density/Migration**)

4. Family, education, religion, government, and economy are all examples of basic _____. (**technology/social institutions**)

5. A _____ is a path used by traders for buying and selling goods. (**settlement/trade route**)

Comprehension and Critical Thinking

Lesson 1

6. a. Describe What is a multicultural society?

    b. Identify What impact has cultural diffusion had on individuals? What impact has cultural diffusion had on world societies? Define these impacts.

    c. Elaborate Describe some of the culture traits practiced by people in your community.

7. a. Evaluate Which social institution do you think is most important? Why?

    b. Explain What relationship exists between a society and its art, music, literature, and architecture?

    c. Predict Make a prediction about a future scientific discovery and a future technological innovation. What problem will each solve? What social, political, economic, cultural, or environmental impacts will each have?

Lesson 2

8. a. Describe What does population density tell us about a place?

    b. Draw Conclusions Why do certain areas attract large populations?

    c. Elaborate Why do you think it is important for geographers to study population trends?

Lesson 3

9. a. Evaluate Think about your own city or town. Why did people decide to establish a settlement in that location?

    b. Make Inferences Why does a grid settlement design easily support transportation routes?

    c. Analyze How can new technology negatively impact interaction between regions?

Lesson 4

10. a. Form Opinions Some areas of the world are at a greater risk for certain types of natural disasters such as hurricanes or earthquakes. Would the risk of a natural disaster impact your decision about where to live?

    b. Identify Problems Think about one environmental issue that affects your state. What can be done to improve the situation?

    c. Describe Give an example of new technology that is environmentally friendly. How does it work to benefit the environment?

Reading Skills

11. **Understand Main Ideas** *Use the Reading Skills taught in this module to answer a question about the reading selection below.*

> The ancient Greeks were the first to practice democracy. Since then many countries have adopted democratic governments. The United Kingdom, South Korea, and Ghana all practice democracy. Democracy is the most widely used type of government in the world today.

What is the main idea of the paragraph?

Social Studies Skills 🌐 21ST CENTURY

12. **Organize Information** *Use the Social Studies Skills taught in this module to create a graphic organizer for Lesson 3.*

Use the main ideas on the first page of the lesson for your large circles. Then write the subtopics under each main idea. Finally, identify supporting details for each subtopic.

Map Activity 🌐 21ST CENTURY

Population Density *Use the map to answer the questions that follow.*

13. What letter on the map indicates the least crowded area?

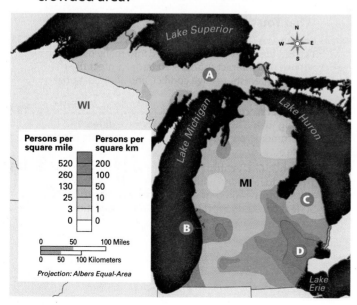

14. What letter on the map indicates the most densely crowded area?

15. Which letter indicates a region with 260–520 people per square mile (100–200 people per square km)?

Focus on Writing

16. **Write a Report** Population changes have a huge effect on the world around us. Countries around the globe must deal with shrinking populations, growing populations, and other population issues. Use Lesson 2 and other primary and secondary sources to explore the issues surrounding world population. Formulate appropriate questions to guide your research. You should use both print and digital sources. Collect information from non-print sources such as maps and graphs. Then imagine you have been asked to report on global population trends to the United Nations. Write a report in which you identify and describe world population trends and their impact on the world today. Be sure to apply key terms acquired from the lesson in your writing. Include at least one graphic that presents information related to the topic. Your report should be focused and organized with a clear introduction, supporting paragraphs, and conclusion. Check your report for spelling, grammar, capitalization, and punctuation.

Government and Citizenship

Essential Question
How do systems of government affect the roles of citizens across the globe?

About the Photo: The Palace of Westminster in London is where Parliament meets. Parliament is the United Kingdom's highest legislative authority.

Explore ONLINE!

VIDEOS, including . . .
- Could You Pass the U.S. Citizenship Test?
- Birth of Democracy

HISTORY.

☑ Document-Based Investigations

☑ Graphic Organizers

☑ Interactive Games

☑ Channel One News Video: Students Bring Climate Change Lawsuit

☑ Image with Hotspots: The DMZ Separates the Koreas

☑ Interactive Map: Freedom in Governments of the World

In this module, you will learn about how nations across the globe interact and form a world community. You will also learn about the different world governments and how people participate in those governments.

What You Will Learn

Citizenship Voting is an important responsibility for citizens of India and other free countries.

Global Community The United Nations Headquarters in New York City is where more than 190 member states meet to promote international cooperation.

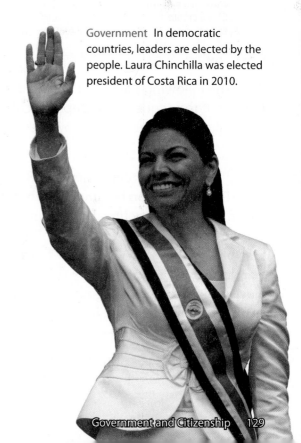

Government In democratic countries, leaders are elected by the people. Laura Chinchilla was elected president of Costa Rica in 2010.

Reading Social Studies

Sequence

READING FOCUS

Sequence is the order in which events follow one another. To show the order of events or steps in a process, writers use words like *before, after, next, first, then, later,* and *finally.* They also use words and phrases that indicate specific times, such as *the next day* and *on July 4, 1776.* Making a visual such as a sequence chain or a timeline can help you sequence events.

Read the passage below, noting the underlined clue words and dates. Notice how they reveal the order of the events shown in the timeline.

In <u>1949</u> Chinese leader Mao Zedong created an authoritarian Communist system, imprisoning or killing those who spoke out against his policies. He implemented Soviet-style five-year plans for industrial development. <u>Early</u> efforts, begun in 1953, had some success, but widespread food shortages led to the deaths of tens of millions by <u>1961</u>. In 1966, Mao began the Cultural Revolution, a violent effort to rid China of its pre-Communist customs and beliefs.

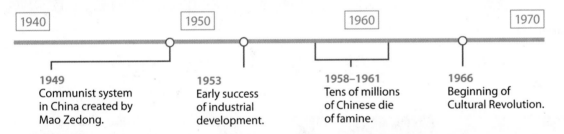

1940		1950		1960		1970

1949
Communist system in China created by Mao Zedong.

1953
Early success of industrial development.

1958–1961
Tens of millions of Chinese die of famine.

1966
Beginning of Cultural Revolution.

YOU TRY IT!

Read the following passage. Look for dates and clue words to help you figure out the sequence of steps described in it. Then make a sequence chain like the one above to show that order.

Brazil was a Portuguese colony for 300 years before gaining independence in 1822. The nation became a republic in 1889, but wealthy coffee planters held much of the political power until a series of military-led uprisings began in the 1920s. In 1930 Getúlio Vargas took power in a nonviolent revolution; by 1937 Vargas ruled as a dictator. After alternating attempts at democracy and at military rule, in 1985 the military finally turned over power to a civilian government. Three years later, Brazil enacted a constitution that is still in effect today.

As you read this module, look for clues that show the sequence of events.

A World of Nations

The Big Idea

The world is divided into many different nations that interact together to trade, protect their national interests, resolve conflict, and address global issues.

Main Ideas

- The world is divided into physical and human borders.

- The nations of the world interact through trade and foreign policy.

- The nations of the world form a world community that resolves conflicts and addresses global issues.

Key Terms and Places

borders
sovereign nation
foreign policy
diplomacy
national interest
United Nations
human rights
humanitarian aid

If YOU lived there . . .

You are living through a drought in Sacramento, California. Your teacher splits your class into groups to discuss ways to solve the drought problem. One student thinks using less water is the solution, and another believes people should try to find more water. Your group begins arguing over whose solution is the best. You want everyone to get along, but nobody seems to agree.

How could you help your classmates work together?

Boundaries and Borders

There are about 200 countries in the world today. Each country has political boundaries, or **borders.** Within a country there are also many smaller political units, such as cities, counties, and states, each with its own set of borders. There are two main types of borders used to set political boundaries—physical borders and human borders.

Physical Borders Borders sometimes follow natural boundaries. Mountains, deserts, and oceans make good natural boundaries because they are often difficult to cross and are permanent markers. For example, the Andes Mountains form the eastern border of Chile, while the Pacific Ocean forms Chile's western border. These two physical features give Chile a long, skinny shape.

Rivers and lakes are other natural boundaries used to set borders. For example, the Chattahoochee River forms part of the border between Alabama and Georgia. The Great Lakes form part of the border between the United States and Canada. However, rivers can be troublesome boundaries. Sometimes the flow of a river might shift course, changing the border.

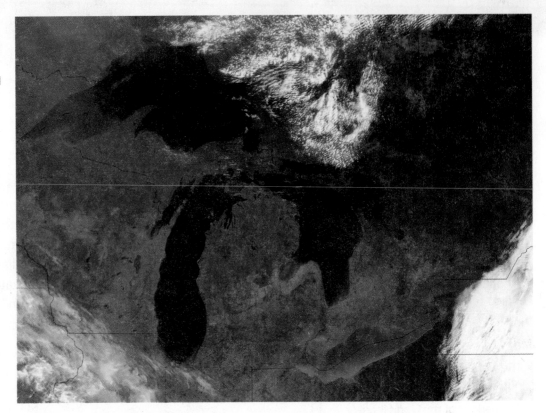

The Great Lakes are a natural boundary between the United States and Canada.

Human Borders Sometimes, borders are determined by humans, with no input from the physical landscape. There are two main types of boundaries used to set human borders: cultural and geometric.

Cultural boundaries are based on cultural traits, such as language or religion. For example, the border between mostly Muslim Pakistan and mostly Hindu India was established largely along religious lines. The border between Portugal and Spain is an example of a cultural boundary based on language.

Geometric boundaries are borders that are not based on natural or cultural patterns. Often, they are straight lines based on lines of latitude or longitude. For example, the border between North Korea and South Korea follows near the 38th parallel, or 38°N latitude. Another example is the part of the border between the United States and Canada that follows 93°N latitude. The borders of many states and counties in the United States are also geometric boundaries.

Reading Check
Identify
What natural boundaries are used to form borders?

Nations of the World

Having set borders is one characteristic of a **sovereign nation,** or a government that has complete authority over a geographic area. Sovereign nations rule independently from governments outside their borders. They can make their own laws and enforce them. They can collect taxes, build a military, and make treaties, or written agreements, with other nations. They can also defend themselves against foreign invasion.

Trade and Foreign Policy Though sovereign nations rule independently, they **interact** with other nations. One way nations interact with each other is through trade. Different nations have different resources, and they also lack different resources. Trade allows nations to exchange the goods that they have or can make for goods that they cannot make.

Another way that nations act together is through **foreign policy,** or a nation's plan for how to act toward other countries. Foreign policy is important because the actions one nation takes affect other nations. For example, when Germany invaded Poland in 1939, Great Britain and France declared war on Germany. This was the start of World War II, a conflict that grew to involve almost every part of the world. Because leaders of the world are concerned with keeping their nations safe, or national security, many leaders try to secure friendly relations with other countries as part of their foreign policy.

The foreign policy work nations do to keep friendly relations with each other is called **diplomacy.** Diplomacy is used to prevent war, solve problems, and open communication between countries. For example, the United States ended diplomatic ties with Cuba in 1961. In late 2014 President Obama announced that the United States and Cuba would have diplomatic relations for the first time in decades. President Obama traveled to Cuba in 2016. An American president had not done that in almost 90 years.

Another important foreign policy tool is foreign aid, or assistance that a country provides to another country. For example, the United States gave large amounts of foreign aid during and after World War II. It sent soldiers to help fight during the war. After the war, the people of Western Europe needed food, clothing, and housing, which the United States helped provide.

The DMZ Separates the Koreas

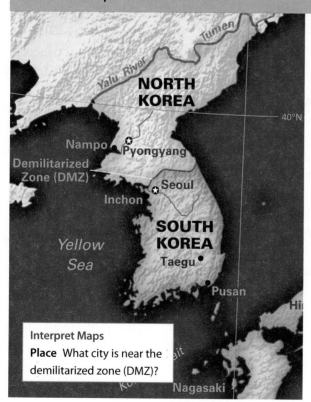

Interpret Maps
Place What city is near the demilitarized zone (DMZ)?

Following World War II, the 38th parallel was used to divide North and South Korea. Above, South Korean soldiers patrol the barbed wire fence along the demilitarized zone (DMZ), which separates the two Koreas today. The DMZ stretches east to west near the old boundary at the 38th parallel.

National Interest Each nation has its own goals to help it succeed. These goals make up a country's **national interest.** Different countries have different national interests. Part of the United States' national interest, for example, is to grow its economy and defend its national security. For New Zealand, protecting its natural resources against climate change is one of its national interests.

When nations have similar national interests, they sometimes become allies, or a group that gives support. For example, in 1949 the United States and 11 other nations formed the North Atlantic Treaty Organization (NATO) to stop a common adversary, or enemy. The Soviet Union was taking over other countries in Eastern Europe and spreading communism. NATO wanted to protect other nations from being invaded and to stop the spread of communism. Today, the Soviet Union no longer exists, but NATO has grown to include 28 nations who share common interests, such as promoting democratic values and peace.

Reading Check
Summarize
How do nations interact with each other?

A World Community

Together, the nations of the world form a world community. Countries are connected to each other through trade and diplomacy. What happens in one part of the world can affect the entire planet. Because of this, the world community works together to promote cooperation among countries in times of conflict and crisis.

Resolving Conflict From time to time, conflicts erupt among the countries of the world. Wars, trade disputes, and political disagreements can threaten the peace. Countries often join together to settle such conflicts. In 1945, for example, 51 nations created the **United Nations** (UN), an organization of the world's countries that promotes peace and security around the globe.

The United Nations now has more than 190 member states. The UN promotes security by calling on quarreling countries to work out a peaceful

---

Historical Source

The Charter of the United Nations

Created in 1945, the United Nations is an organization of the world's countries that works to solve global problems. The Charter of the United Nations outlines the goals of the UN, some of which are included here.

"We the Peoples of the United Nations Determined . . . to save succeeding generations from the scourge [terror] of war . . . to practice tolerance and live together in peace with one another as good neighbors, and to unite our strength to maintain international peace and security, and to ensure . . . that armed forces shall not be used, save [except] in the common interest, and to employ international machinery [systems] for the promotion of the economic and social advancement of all peoples, Have Resolved to Combine our Efforts to Accomplish these Aims."

—from the Charter of the United Nations

Analyze Sources
What are some of the goals of the United Nations?

Many people believe that health care is a basic human right. Here, a Doctors Without Borders medical team leader examines refugees from Libya.

settlement. It also places sanctions, or penalties, on those who have broken international laws. Sanctions restrict or ban trade, travel, or economic activity with law violators. For example, the United Nations has placed sanctions against the terrorist groups and militant organizations in the Middle East, such as al Qaeda and the Islamic State of Iraq and the Levant (ISIL), as a way to combat terrorism.

The United Nations also works to guarantee **human rights,** or rights that all people deserve. Human rights include political rights, such as the right to vote. Freedom of expression and equality before the law are other examples of human rights. Over the years, the UN has passed several declarations setting standards for such rights.

Nations also form organizations to help out in areas of conflict. These organizations provide **humanitarian aid,** or assistance to people in distress. For example, during the Syrian civil war, the International Committee of the Red Cross (ICRC) brought food, clean water, and essential aid to civilians. Another organization, the United States Agency for International Development (USAID), offers assistance to conflict and poverty-stricken countries all over the world. In Pakistan, USAID has built or rehabilitated 1,040 schools since 2009. Some groups lend aid to refugees, or people who have been forced to flee their homes. Doctors Without Borders, for example, provides medical aid to those fleeing areas of armed conflict, such as South Sudan, Libya, Syria, and Afghanistan.

Organizations are able to help conflict zones because the Geneva Conventions of 1949 protect them. The Geneva Conventions are international agreements that tell countries at war how to treat people. Under the Geneva Conventions, for example, people cannot be held hostage, enslaved, or tortured. The Geneva Conventions protect the human rights of civilians, medics, and aid workers who are not taking part in the fighting. They also protect those who can no longer fight, such as the wounded, the sick, and prisoners of war.

Promoting Cooperation The world community also promotes cooperation in times of crisis. A disaster may leave thousands of people in need. Earthquakes, floods, and droughts can cause crises around the world. Groups from many nations often come together to help out. For example, in 2004 a tsunami, or huge tidal wave, devastated parts of Southeast Asia. Many organizations, like the United Nations Children's Fund (UNICEF) and the International Red Cross, stepped in to provide humanitarian aid to the victims of the tsunami. In addition to providing medical aid in conflict zones, Doctors Without Borders also provides care in places hit by epidemics or natural disasters, such as the Central African Republic and Nepal.

Deadly diseases such as tuberculosis, malaria, and acquired immune deficiency syndrome (AIDS) can spread quickly and devastate entire communities. This is why nations work with health-care initiatives, or organizations that raise money to combat diseases. Examples of global health initiatives include the World Bank's Multi-Country AIDS Programme (MAP), Gavi, the Vaccine Alliance, and the Global Fund to Fight AIDS, Tuberculosis and Malaria (Global Fund). Through their efforts, millions of people in regions such as West and Central Africa have received vaccinations, medications, and disease-prevention education to fight the spread of deadly diseases.

Summary and Preview In this lesson you learned about borders and how nations work together to solve conflicts and crises. In the next lesson, you will learn about the different ways nations govern themselves.

Reading Check
Summarize How do nations promote cooperation?

Lesson 1 Assessment

Review Ideas, Terms, and Places

1. a. **Define** What are borders?
   b. **Identify** What are two types of human boundaries?
2. a. **Describe** What are the characteristics of a sovereign nation?
   b. **Demonstrate** How do nations benefit from interacting with each other?
3. a. **Analyze** How do global organizations help with conflict resolution and cooperation?
   b. **Explain** How do the Geneva Conventions protect individual rights and the common good?

Critical Thinking

4. **Evaluate** Draw a three-column chart to list the global organizations you read about in this lesson. Describe their efforts to combat poverty and promote world peace. If needed, use the Internet for additional research. Then use the chart to help answer this question: Why do you think these organizations are needed to protect human rights?

Organization	Combat Poverty	Promote World Peace

World Governments

The Big Idea

The world's countries have different governments, and some countries struggle with human rights abuses.

Main Ideas

- Limited governments of the world include democracies.

- Unlimited governments of the world include totalitarian governments.

- Most human rights abuses occur under unlimited governments of the world.

Key Terms and Places

limited government
constitution
democracy
direct democracy
representative democracies
common good
unlimited government
totalitarian governments

If YOU lived there . . .

You live in Dallas, Texas. Your class at school is planning a presentation about life in the United States for a group of visitors from Japan. Your teacher wants you to discuss government in the United States. As you prepare for your speech, you wonder what you should say.

How does government affect your life?

Limited Government

Can you imagine what life would be like if there were no rules? Without ways to establish order and ensure justice, life would be chaotic. This explains why societies have governments. Our governments make and enforce laws, regulate business and trade, and provide aid to people. Governments help shape the culture and economy of a country and the daily lives of the people who live there.

One system of government is **limited government.** A limited government has legal limits on its power. These limits are often stated in a **constitution,** or a written plan of government that outlines its purposes, powers, and limitations. A **democracy,** a form of government in which the people elect leaders and rule by majority, is an example of limited government. Many countries—including the United States, Canada, and Mexico—are democracies.

Origins of Democracy Ancient Athens and other Greek city-states were among the first democratic governments. The Athenian government was a **direct democracy,** which means the people made decisions through a process of majority rule. Whatever the majority of voters wanted became law. The citizens met regularly in a popular assembly to discuss issues and vote for leaders. Athenians liked to boast that in their government, everyone had equal say. In truth, Athenian democracy was an elite-based system. Only a small fraction of the male population was eligible to participate in political life. Neither women nor slaves, who formed the majority of the population, could participate.

Modern Democratic Governments Today, most countries have too many people to gather together to make political decisions. That is why most modern democratic governments are indirect democracies, or **representative democracies.** Instead of the citizens making all of the political decisions, they vote for representatives to make and enforce the laws.

Presidential and parliamentary democracies are the two most common democratic systems. In a presidential democracy, the people elect the head of state, called the president. The president heads the executive branch. The president shares power with the legislative branch, which is also elected by the people, and the judicial branch.

In a parliamentary democracy, the voters elect the legislature, or parliament. The parliament chooses the government leader, called the prime minister or chancellor. The head of state in some parliamentary democracies is a constitutional monarch. Constitutional monarchs are often figureheads, or leaders without real power. Instead, the elected parliament holds most of the power. Most of the world's democratic governments are parliamentary democracies.

Modern governments also distribute their powers in different ways. For example, the United Kingdom and Japan are unitary states, in which a central government has all the power and does not share it with its regions or states. The opposite of a unitary state is a confederation. In a confederation, a country's states or regions hold most of the power. Federal governments, on the other hand, divide their power between a central national government and its states. The United States is an example of a federal government.

Characteristics of Limited Governments Because power can be misused, limiting government's reach reduces the chances of abuse and creates freer and fairer societies. Limited governments are governed by rule of law, meaning that no person or government is above the law. This is why many limited governments have a constitution that outlines their laws.

Modern Democracies			
Country	Government Power	Type of Democracy	System of Government
United States	Federal	Presidential	Constitutional republic
United Kingdom	Unitary	Parliamentary	Constitutional monarchy
Canada	Federal	Parliamentary	Constitutional monarchy
Japan	Unitary	Parliamentary	Constitutional monarchy
India	Federal	Parliamentary	Constitutional republic

Analyze Information
Which countries are republics with federal governments?

Systems of Government

Dictatorship **Example: Cuba**	• Single dictator or a small group holds absolute authority and makes all decisions • Violence and force used to maintain rule
Totalitarian Regimes **Example: North Korea**	• Dictator holds ultimate authority • Government tightly controls all aspects of life—political, social, and economic • No formal or informal limits on government
Theocracy **Example: Iran**	• Government by officials regarded to have religious authority • Laws rooted in a particular religion or religious doctrine • Government power is unlimited
Direct Democracy **Example: ancient Greece (Athens)**	• Government by the people; citizens are the ultimate source of government authority • Citizens come together to discuss and pass laws and select leaders • Works best in small communities
Republic/Representative Democracy **Example: ancient Rome, United States**	• Government by the people; citizens are the ultimate source of government authority • Indirect form of democracy; citizens elect representatives to make government decisions and pass laws on their behalf • Representatives elected for set terms

Analyze Information
What is the difference between a direct democracy and a republic?

Nations governed by rule of law protect the rights of individuals. In many limited governments, for example, individuals have the right to a fair trial if they are accused of a crime. Limited governments also balance the welfare of the community, or the **common good,** with individual welfare. For example, individuals might be forced to sell their land to the government so that a new highway or school can be built. This challenges an individual's right to own property. However, a new highway or school benefits the whole community.

Today, nearly half of the almost 200 countries in the world are democratic or partly democratic with a limited system of government. Although the level of freedom in these nations varies, they share some basic characteristics:

- Democratic systems tend to have social welfare policies that seek to improve the quality of their citizens' lives.
- Most democratic governments protect their citizens' rights and freedoms. For this reason, citizens of these countries generally enjoy a high degree of economic and political freedom.
- Strong democratic countries can generally withstand national crises such as war, economic troubles, or civil unrest without major changes to their basic systems or structures.

Mexico

Government Characteristics
- Presidential, federal system of government
- Three branches of government
- Some legislative seats given to major parties
- President elected directly by the people to a six-year term
- Voting compulsory for people 18 and older

Brazil

Government Characteristics
- Presidential, federal system of government
- Three branches of government
- All legislative seats filled by direct election
- President elected directly by the people to a four-year term
- Voting compulsory for people 18 to 70

The seat of power for Mexico's president is the National Palace in Mexico City.

This map shows the locations of Mexico and Brazil.

Brazil's legislative body meets at the National Congress in Brasília.

Comparing Mexico and Brazil As you know, the United States is a democracy with a limited system of government. Mexico and Brazil are examples of other nations with limited systems. Their governments have much in common with our own.

Mexico's Government Mexico's federal government, like ours, has three branches: legislative, executive, and judicial. In a federal system, powers are divided between central and state governments. Mexico's central government is based in Mexico City, and its 31 states make up its state government.

Mexico's legislative branch has two houses. Three-fifths of the legislators in each house are elected, but the remaining seats are distributed to the major political parties in proportion to the parties' overall share of the popular vote.

The executive branch is led by a president elected directly by the people for a single six-year term. By law, voting is compulsory for people over age 18, although no formal penalty is enforced. Mexico does not have the office of vice-president.

Mexico has an independent judicial branch. Its highest court is the Supreme Court of Justice. Its judges are appointed by the president and must be approved by a single of the houses of the legislature.

Brazil's Government Brazil has a federal system with 26 states and a federal district. In many ways, Brazil's government is similar to that of Mexico and the United States, with three branches and a separation of powers. Brazil's legislature is bicameral and includes a senate and a chamber of deputies. All members are elected.

The executive branch is led by the president. The president and vice-president are elected by a direct vote of the people. Voting is compulsory for literate Brazilians between the ages of 18 and 70, and those who do not vote may be fined.

Brazil's Supreme Court is made up of two courts: the Superior Court of Justice, which deals with nonconstitutional issues, and the Supreme Federal Court, which handles cases involving constitutional interpretation.

Reading Check **Compare and Contrast** How are the governments of Mexico and Brazil similar and different?

Unlimited Governments

We categorize governments based on who holds governmental power, as well as by how much power they are allowed to execute. Recall that in a limited government, everyone—including leaders—must obey the law. By contrast, an **unlimited government** is a government in which there are no limits set on a ruler's power. They do not govern by a rule of law that balances individual rights with the common good. Many rulers of unlimited governments view individual rights as a threat to the common good. They define the common good as people doing their part to strengthen the leader, nation, and community.

Totalitarianism Authoritarian governments are unlimited governments, in which power is concentrated in the hands of a single person, such as a dictator, or a small group. Leaders can set laws without input from those they rule. This allows change and decision-making to work more quickly in unlimited governments than in limited governments. Leaders, however, can also break laws without punishment because they answer to no one.

At its most extreme, authoritarian rule becomes totalitarian. **Totalitarian governments** control all aspects of society—the government, the economy, and even people's personal beliefs and actions. The Soviet Union under Joseph Stalin, China under Mao Zedong, and North Korea under Kim Jong-un are examples of totalitarian regimes.

In these societies, citizens have no way to influence or change the government. The government sometimes maintains the appearance of democratic rule. For example, the totalitarian government of North Korea calls itself the Democratic People's Republic of Korea, holds elections, and has a written constitution. But these displays of democracy are nothing more than exhibitions to deceive the nation's people or outside observers.

Characteristics of Unlimited Governments All forms of unlimited government share certain features. In authoritarian and totalitarian systems, ordinary citizens have limited political and economic freedoms. Their rights are rarely recognized or protected, and they may not be able to effectively take part in government or openly express their views.

Totalitarian rulers often use force to put down opposition, such as human rights or pro-democracy movements demanding change. Moreover, because they are not subject to law, totalitarian rulers can change or ignore constitutions or laws intended to restrict their power. For example, before Saddam Hussein of Iraq was overthrown in a 2003 U.S.-led invasion, he used torture and violence against his political opponents, even though torture was officially banned under Iraqi law.

China's Government In 1949 Chinese leader Mao Zedong created an authoritarian Communist system, imprisoning or killing those who spoke out against his policies. He instituted Soviet-style five-year plans for industrial development. Early efforts, begun in 1953, had some success, but widespread food shortages led to the deaths of tens of millions by 1961. In 1966 Mao began the Cultural Revolution, a violent effort to rid China of its pre-Communist customs and beliefs.

Mao's death in 1976 saw a gradual retreat from many of his policies. Deng Xiaoping eventually became China's leader and slowly introduced many economic and a few political reforms. There were limits to what officials would allow, however. In 1989 the government violently crushed a peaceful pro-democracy student demonstration in China's capital, Beijing, in what became known as the Tiananmen Square Massacre.

China's leaders today are balancing authoritarian rule, economic growth, and slow political reform. China continues to limit its citizens' basic freedoms and rights, and the government exercises strict control over the media and the Internet.

Human Rights Abuses

Though many people and governments support human rights, human rights abuses occur in both limited and unlimited governments. These abuses include torture, slavery, and murder, and are most common in countries that are not free or are partially free. In many countries,

Reading Check
Summarize What are the characteristics of unlimited government?

Unlimited Government in China

A 1971 propaganda poster portrays people as happy with China's communist government.

毛主席万岁！万万岁！

A pro-democracy demonstrator confronts Chinese troops in Tiananmen Square, Beijing, in 1989.

Freedom in Governments of the World

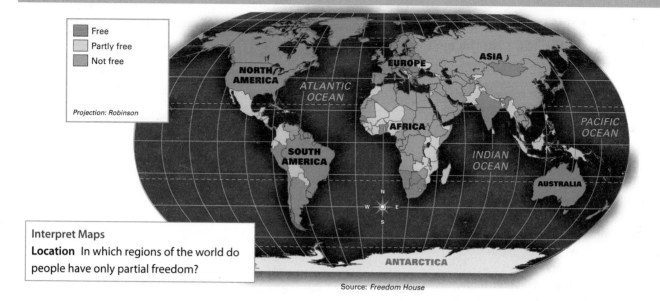

Free
Partly free
Not free

Projection: Robinson

Source: *Freedom House*

Interpret Maps

Location In which regions of the world do people have only partial freedom?

individuals and groups have been arrested or mistreated for political dissent. For example, countries including Iran, Pakistan, Cuba, El Salvador, and the former Soviet Union have persecuted people for their political views.

In unfree or partially free countries, children face the highest risk of becoming victims of human rights abuses. In some countries, such as northern Uganda, fighters have kidnapped thousands of children. These children have been made to fight as soldiers, while other have been enslaved. The United Nations has taken action to try to protect children. For example, the UN Convention on the Rights of the Child was adopted in 1989. The convention focused on trying to keep children free from hunger, neglect, and abuse.

Human rights abuses are also common in countries in the process of establishing democracy. For example, in 2013 the Sudanese government demolished several Christian churches in Sudan as part of an effort to force Christians out of the country. As a result, many Sudanese Christians have fled to South Sudan to avoid persecution.

Abuses in democratic countries are far fewer, but they do occur, often as a result of inaction. For example, the European Union was criticized for not adequately helping asylum seekers fleeing the civil war in Syria in 2013, which left some refugees homeless and without food or water.

As a country with a democratic government, the United States recognizes that respect for human rights promotes peace and deters aggression. To that end, the United States has made promoting human rights a major part of its foreign policy. According to the U.S. Department of State, the United States uses a three-part approach in its work on human rights. Those three parts are learning the truth and stating the facts, taking consistent

Reading Check
Draw Conclusions
Why would human
rights abuses
occur more often
in countries
with unlimited
governments?

positions about human rights abuses, and partnering with organizations and governments committed to human rights.

Summary and Preview The world's countries have different governments. In the next lesson, you will learn about citizenship in various countries.

Lesson 2 Assessment

Review Ideas, Terms, and Places

1. a. Define What is a direct democracy, and what are its origins?

b. Contrast What are the differences between presidential and parliamentary democracies?

2. a. Describe What is life like in a country with a totalitarian leader?

b. Contrast In what ways do limited governments differ from unlimited governments?

c. Analyze How does the definition of the common good differ in limited and unlimited governments?

3. a. Elaborate How does China's government limit human rights?

b. Contrast Look at the map Freedom in Governments of the World. How does government in North America differ from government in Asia?

Critical Thinking

4. Compare and Contrast Review your notes on the limited and unlimited governments of the United States, Mexico, Brazil, and China. Then use a chart like this one to compare and contrast how each government functions and is organized.

United States	Mexico	Brazil	China

🌐 Citizenship

The Big Idea

Along with the rights and freedoms of citizenship in representative democracies like the United States come important duties and responsibilities.

Main Ideas

- The duties and roles of citizenship help to make representative government work.

- Good citizens accept their responsibilities for maintaining a strong democracy.

- Citizens influence government through public opinion.

- The type of government in some societies influences the roles of the citizens in those societies.

Key Terms and Places

representative government
draft
jury duty
political parties
interest groups
public opinion
nonrepresentative governments

If YOU lived there . . .

Your older brother and his friends have just turned 18. That means they must register with the Selective Service System. But it also means that they are old enough to vote in national elections. You are interested in the upcoming elections and think it would be exciting to have a real voice in politics. But your brother and his friends don't even plan to register to vote.

How would you persuade your brother that voting is important?

Duties and Roles of Citizenship

The United States has a democratic, **representative government.** In such a system, people are the ultimate source of government authority. Elections are free and fair. Elected representatives closely follow the wishes of the people. Citizens typically enjoy rights and privileges such as freedom of speech and freedom of religion. For a representative government to work well, citizens must participate actively and perform certain duties. Let's look at some duties of U.S. citizens.

Obeying the Law Of course, all Americans must obey the law. Otherwise, our society would collapse. To obey laws, you must know what they are. For example, if you are stopped for speeding, it will not help to claim that you did not know the speed limit. It is your duty to find out what the speed limit is and to obey it.

Attending School You have to go to school, at least until age 16. A democracy cannot function without educated citizens. That is why we have free public schools. People need good reading and thinking skills so they can wisely choose their leaders and understand issues that affect them. Education also provides workforce skills so people can get jobs and help the economy grow.

Cadets from the U.S. Air Force Academy commit to several years of military service.

Paying Taxes If you work or buy things, then you probably have to pay taxes. We might not love paying taxes, but we enjoy the services that result from them, such as police and fire protection, road maintenance, public schools, and countless other services. Tax money also pays the huge costs of national security and defense.

All levels of government rely on a variety of taxes for funding. For example, the federal government relies on income taxes, a tax on personal earnings. These taxes go toward programs such as Social Security, which helps fund your retirement; Medicare, a health insurance program for certain qualifying Americans; and national defense. You are probably familiar with sales taxes, which state and local governments depend on for their revenue. Sales taxes help fund public safety, education, and programs to build and repair roads, buildings, and power plants.

Serving in the Armed Forces Volunteers have fought in every war in U.S. history. When the country's need has exceeded the number of volunteers, however, it sometimes has had to establish a **draft.** Draft laws require men of certain ages and qualifications to serve in the military.

The United States has not had a draft since 1973, during the Vietnam War. However, 18-year-old men must still register their names and addresses with the Selective Service System. If a crisis required that the country quickly expand its armed forces, a draft could be launched and registered citizens could be called up.

Appearing in Court Citizens must report to serve as members of a jury if they are called to do so. This service is called **jury duty.** Jury duty often involves sacrifice. Many citizens must take time off work to serve on a jury, and they are paid very small sums. This sacrifice is necessary because the Constitution guarantees citizens the right to a trial by jury of their peers—that is, their fellow citizens. Citizens must also testify in court if called as witnesses. For our system of justice to function, citizens must fulfill their duty to serve on juries and appear as witnesses.

Reading Check
Summarize
Describe five duties of American citizenship.

Rights and Responsibilities

Civic participation in representative government includes both duties, or the things we *must* do, and responsibilities. Responsibilities are the things we *should* do as citizens. These tasks are not required by law; yet, in the United States, most people accept them as their responsibility. Several of these responsibilities are listed below.

Voting United States government is based on the consent, or the approval, of the governed. Therefore, we must let our legislators know when we approve or disapprove of their actions. One way to do this is by voting for people whose views we support and who we believe to be good, honest candidates. As a citizen of your community, state, and nation, it is your responsibility to vote in local, state, and national elections so that your voice is heard.

There are several different types of elections in the United States. Elections allow citizens to choose leaders for every level of government. Because congressional elections take place every two years, citizens often elect some members of Congress when they vote for the president. State and local elections may also coincide with presidential and congressional elections.

Being Informed To cast your vote wisely, you must be well informed about candidates, current events, and key issues. There are many ways to stay informed. You can go to town meetings to learn about the key issues in your community. To learn about the candidates running for political offices, you can attend debates and forums. You can sit in on legislative sessions to watch public officials decide public policy.

U.S. Elections

Election Type	When Election Occurs	Purpose
Presidential	every 4 years	• vote for the U.S. president/vice-president
Congressional	every 2 years	• elect 1/3 of all U.S. Senate members • elect all 435 members of the U.S. House of Representatives
State	varies by state	• elect state governor • elect state legislators • elect state judges (in some states) • vote on state ballot initiatives
Local	varies by location	• elect various local offices • elect local judges (in some localities) • vote on local ballot initiatives

Analyze Information
Why is it important for citizens to vote in every type of election?

You can also use other tools at your home, school, or library to stay informed. Visiting government websites is a good way to learn about local, state, and national issues and laws. Reading newspapers, watching the news, listening to the radio, and watching televised debates can also keep you up to date on current events and important issues.

Taking Part in Government For a representative government to remain strong, people must participate at all levels. In addition to voting, people can work as public servants, serve in a political office, join a political party, or support other politically active organizations. You can also contact your state representatives and tell them what you think about topics of public concern.

Governments cannot provide services to their citizens without citizen participation. They need people to work as public servants to provide these services. Public servants deliver mail, inspect food and medicines for safety, operate national parks, fight fires, and perform a number of other services.

People are also needed to run for political office and serve wisely if elected. The quality of any democratic government depends on the quality of the people who serve it. Political leaders, for example, take on important roles. They may create laws or decide which programs will receive funding. Some decide the best course of action during local, state, or national emergencies.

Citizens can help shape government by joining **political parties.** Political parties nominate, or select, candidates to run for political office. They also try to convince voters to elect their candidates. Many citizens in the United States have joined one of two political parties—the Democratic Party or the Republican Party. Sometimes, citizens who believe their views are not represented by these parties will form a third party. For example, citizens formed the Green Party to focus on environmental issues.

Responsible Citizenship

Volunteers help citizens sign in to vote at a polling station.

By planting a tree, these volunteers are beautifying their community.

Citizens can also join **interest groups,** or organizations that try to influence government policies and decisions. Members of interest groups share a common goal. Members of the National Association for the Advancement of Colored People (NAACP), for example, work to promote racial equality.

On occasion, you may even need to stand in protest for what you believe. Yet protest, like civic participation in any form, must also be peaceful, respectful of the law, and tolerant of others' rights and liberties.

Helping Your Community Have you ever volunteered to help your community? There are so many ways to help—from giving your time at the public library to participating in a walk for hunger. Citizens should volunteer to improve their communities. The government cannot be aware of every small problem, much less fix them all. Yet solving small problems is something volunteers can do in many ways. Think of how small acts of kindness—such as cheering up a sick person or working in an animal shelter—can make community life better.

Respecting and Protecting Others' Rights In return for performing civic duties and responsibilities, people in the United States enjoy the privileges and rights of citizenship. The lasting success and the strength of the United States depend on the protection of its citizens' rights. You can play an important role in protecting these rights by knowing your own rights as an American citizen and knowing and respecting the rights of the people around you. For example, it is essential that community members respect others' property.

You should also know when people's rights are being violated. All Americans must help defend human rights. As a citizen, you have the responsibility to help make sure that our society works for everyone.

Reading Check
Form Generalizations
How can U.S. citizens contribute to society?

Citizens and the Media

You may not realize it, but you are surrounded by political messages every day. You might see people on the news protesting a government action. You might hear a radio host talk about raising taxes to fund education. Your friends or relatives might share websites or online news articles that support their favorite political candidate. As you have learned, forms of media such as newspapers, magazines, radio, television, film, and books help you stay informed. They also help influence the way you think about political leaders and issues.

Public Opinion The media plays an important role in free societies like the United States. News organizations report on important events and government actions. This allows citizens to stay informed and make their own decisions.

What citizens learn from the media shapes **public opinion,** or the way large groups of citizens think about issues and people. For example, when the media reports the dishonest actions of an elected official, the public may choose not to elect this person again. This puts pressure on political leaders to act honestly and keep their campaign promises.

Sometimes the media, political leaders, and citizens use political symbols to influence others' opinions. Political symbols include images, objects, or music that represent ideas or a political view. For example, a donkey is used as a symbol for the Democratic Party and an elephant is used to represent the Republican Party in the United States.

Have you ever seen a cartoon drawing of an elephant or donkey acting like a politician? Or a cartoon version of the president with exaggerated features? These are political cartoons used in the media to communicate a political view. The creators of these cartoons sometimes use humor as a way to persuade people to side with their political opinion.

Politicians often create political symbols to represent their ideas during campaigns. For example, President Barack Obama's campaign designed a letter O that looked like a rising sun. This was to make voters feel hopeful about the future if they voted for him. Citizens also use political symbols to influence public opinion. During the Vietnam War, for example, American citizens used the peace sign to show that they wanted peace. This was a way to gain public support for their protest against the war.

Citizens rely on the media to help them decide how to vote on important issues and how to pick the best candidates. Sometimes, however, the information you receive is inaccurate, misleading, or one-sided. Some sources might be biased, or favor some ideas over others. A newspaper, for example, might give the candidate it agrees with better coverage than another. A part of being a good citizen means you must think critically about what you see, hear, and read.

Reading Check
Analyze Effects How does public opinion help shape government policy and action?

Symbols in Political Cartoons

This cartoon titled "You Can't Have Everything" was created by Herbert Block around 1938. In 1937 President Franklin D. Roosevelt proposed a controversial plan to increase the number of justices on the Supreme Court.

Analyze Visuals
What symbols do you see in this cartoon? What do you think the artist is trying to say?

Citizenship in Other Societies

In other societies with representative governments, citizens' roles and rights are similar to, but not always the same as, those of U.S. citizens. For instance, German citizens are not called to serve on juries, because German courts do not use the jury system. The German constitution guarantees its citizens freedom of the press, but that freedom can be limited in order to protect youth or preserve a person's honor.

There are major differences, however, between the roles and rights of U.S. citizens and those of citizens from societies with **nonrepresentative governments.** In such systems, government power is unlimited and citizens have few, if any, rights. For example, citizens of Iran do not have the right of freedom of speech. Without this freedom, Iranians cannot voice their concerns to their leaders.

Citizens of nonrepresentative governments also have different responsibilities than citizens of representative governments. In autocratic governments, which are ruled by one person who makes all the decisions, citizens do not get to vote. This is the same for citizens of an oligarchy, or a government by a small group of individuals.

Citizens' perception of opportunities to participate in and influence the political process vary among various contemporary societies. For example, in countries where citizens do not trust the people who run their governments, voting turnout is much lower than in countries where citizens tend to trust their governments. Sometimes, distrust leads citizens to revolt against their leaders in an attempt to change governments. The people of Tunisia, for example, led a revolution that ousted their longtime president Zine al-Abidine Ben Ali and established a

Politicians and Political Symbols

Former Vice-President Joe Biden stands in front of the vice-presidential seal of the United States.

Analyze Visuals
What political symbols do you see in the vice-presidential seal? Why do you think those symbols were used?

Reading Check
Contrast How do
nonrepresentative
governments differ
from representative
democracies?

democracy in January 2011. Other times, a group of people or the military will overthrow the government and establish their own leader. These attempts are called coups d'état or military coups.

Summary In this lesson, you learned about the rights, duties, and responsibilities of citizenship. Effective citizenship is an important part of representative governments. Without citizens participating in their governments, their governments cannot represent their interests.

Lesson 3 Assessment

Review Ideas, Terms, and Places

1. **a. Define** What is a representative government?

   b. Predict What would happen in a representative government if only a small group of people performed their civic duties?

2. **a. Interpret** How are a citizen's duties, rights, and responsibilities connected?

   b. Summarize What are the rights and responsibilities of citizens to their community, state, and nation?

3. **a. Summarize** How can citizens influence the political process?

   b. Compare How are the methods citizens use to resolve issues in government and society alike?

   c. Draw Conclusions How do you think the media helps influence government policy and action?

4. **a. Identify** What is an example of a nonrepresentative government?

   b. Explain Why do the levels of civic engagement vary among different contemporary societies?

   c. Compare Do you think an election, revolution, or coup is the best way to change governments?

Critical Thinking

5. **Evaluate** **Draw** a two-column chart to list and describe citizens' duties and responsibilities in representative governments. Use the chart to help answer this question: In your opinion, which duty or responsibility expected of citizens is the most important? Explain your answer.

DUTIES	RESPONSIBILITIES

Social Studies Skills

Use a Problem-Solving Process

Define the Skill

Solving problems is a process for finding solutions to difficult situations. Being able to use a problem-solving process is an important skill that will help you identify problems and solve challenges as they appear.

Learn the Skill

Use the following steps to solve problems.

1. Identify the problem. Study the issue to learn about the problem.

2. Gather information. Research and ask questions to learn more about the problem.

3. List options. Identify possible options for solving the problem.

4. Evaluate your options. Consider their advantages and disadvantages.

5. Choose and implement a solution. After comparing your options, choose the one that seems best and apply it to solve your problem.

6. Evaluate the solution. Once the solution has been tried, evaluate how effectively it solved the problem. If the solution does not work, go back to your list of options and start again.

Practice the Skill

With a partner, use the steps of a problem-solving process to address the issue of graffiti in a local park. Express your ideas orally based on your experiences. Also share information that you learn from research. Then, create a graphic organizer like the sample on this page.

Problem

Voter turnout in elections for local government officials is decreasing in your hometown.

- In 2003, 51 percent of registered voters voted in local elections.
- By 2013, only 37 percent of registered voters voted in local elections.
- More people vote in local elections when they are held with state or national elections.

Possible Options

Option 1 Start a campaign to encourage voters to participate in local elections

Option 2 Hold local elections on the same day as state or national elections

Evaluation

Option 1 might persuade more people to vote, but could be expensive

Option 2 might increase voter turnout, but might not always be possible

Solution

An advertising campaign promoting voting in local elections increased voter turnout by 7 percent and cost an estimated $500,000.

Module 4 Assessment

Review Vocabulary, Terms, and Places

For each pair of terms below, write one or two sentences describing how the terms in the pair are related.

1. borders
   sovereign nation
2. foreign policy
   diplomacy
3. democracy
   limited government

4. totalitarian government
   unlimited government
5. draft
   jury duty
6. interest group
   political party

Comprehension and Critical Thinking

Lesson 1

7. a. Contrast What are differences between physical and human borders?
   b. Identify What are the various interests of different nations?
   c. Contrast What are the differences between allies and adversaries?

Lesson 2

8. a. Recall What group created and practiced direct democracy?
   b. Analyze What are some ways that governments can misuse power?
   c. Compare Create a table like the one below to compare the advantages and disadvantages of limited and unlimited governments.

Limited Government	Unlimited Government
Advantages:	Advantages:
Disadvantages:	Disadvantages:

Lesson 3

9. a. Explain Why is public service important in representative governments?
   b. Analyze How does volunteering help your community?
   c. Elaborate Why would citizens in countries with a nonrepresentative government participate less in civic life?

Reading Skills

10. Sequence *Use the Reading Skills taught in this module to sequence the events in the reading section below.*

    After three centuries of control by Spain, in 1810 Mexican revolutionaries rose up against Spanish authority. In 1821 Mexico declared independence. The country's current governmental structure and constitution were established in 1917, after a civil war that began in 1910.

Social Studies Skills

11. **Use a Problem-Solving Process** *Use the Social Studies Skills taught in the module to create a problem-solving graphic organizer. Use the problem-solving process to address the issue of human rights in China. Gather information about the problem, such as the Chinese government's reaction to pro-democracy protests and social media use. Then create a graphic organizer like the one from the Social Studies Skills. List and consider options for solving the problem. Discuss the advantages and disadvantages of each. Express your ideas based on your experiences and research. Be sure to address China's reactions to pro-democracy movements and social media use and evaluate its effect on human rights. Finally, choose what you think is the best solution to improve human rights in China.*

Map Activity

Freedom in Governments of the World *Use the map below to answer the questions.*

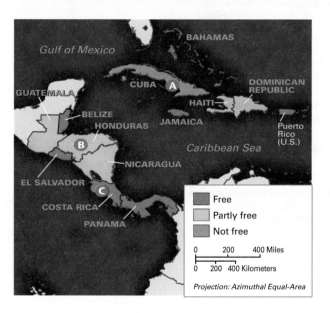

12. Which letter indicates a country whose government does not allow its citizens any rights or freedoms?

13. Which letter indicates a country whose government allows its citizens only partial rights and freedoms?

14. List the countries whose governments allow their citizens rights and freedoms. What system of government do you think is practiced in these countries?

Focus on Writing

15. **Write an Article** Research the direct democracy of ancient Athens and the representative democracy of the United States. Your purpose is to write an article that compares and contrasts the procedures for making decisions in each of these governments. Give your article a headline and write a brief introduction that expresses your main idea. Then write a paragraph comparing and contrasting the procedures each government uses to make decisions. Be sure to describe the roles of citizens in making laws and electing leaders. Then write a paragraph on ways you think you could improve each system's procedures. Write a conclusion that summarizes your main points. Your article should be focused and organized with a clear introduction, supporting paragraphs, and conclusion. Check your article for spelling, grammar, and punctuation.

Module 5

Economics

Essential Question
How does studying economics give us more insight into a country or region?

This map collage is made from the currency, or money, that is used around the world.

In this module, you will learn how economics plays an important role in the way people interact throughout the world.

What You Will Learn

▷ Explore ONLINE!

- ☑ Document-Based Investigations
- ☑ Graphic Organizers
- ☑ Interactive Games
- ☑ Channel One News Video: Generation Money: Teens and Financial Literacy
- ☑ Channel One News Video: Millennial Banking
- ☑ Channel One News Video: Teen Chef
- ☑ Image Carousel: Factors of Production
- ☑ Collapsible Table: Compare Economic Systems

Global Connections Technology allows people in remote places around the world to communicate.

Economics People buy and sell goods in marketplaces around the world.

Global Trade Around the world, major banking and financial centers such as Wall Street use common currencies for international trade.

Reading Social Studies

Draw Conclusions

READING FOCUS

You have probably heard the phrase, "Put two and two together." When people say that, they don't mean "2 + 2 = 4." They mean, "put the information together." When you put together information you already know with information you have read, you can draw a conclusion. Reach a conclusion by reading the passage carefully. Then think about what you already know about the topic. Put the two together to draw a conclusion.

Read the following text, then add what you know to reach a conclusion.

Today, federal, state, and local governments provide expensive or important services to large groups of people who might otherwise have to do without the service. These government goods and services that the public consumes are called public goods. The government pays for public goods with the taxes they collect.

For example, by establishing schools, government makes it possible for all children to receive a good education. Governments also provide police to protect lives and property, and fire departments to protect homes and businesses.

Information gathered from the passage:
These government goods and services that the public consumes are called public goods. The government pays for public goods with the taxes they collect.

+

What you already know:
Our school band director said we might get new instruments and uniforms next year if the parents approve it.

=

Put the two together to reach your conclusion:
Our parents will probably need to pay more school taxes in order to pay for the new instruments and uniforms.

YOU TRY IT!

Read the following paragraph. Next, think about something you like to do that might be part of our popular culture. Then, put the two together and draw a conclusion.

People around the world are linked through popular culture. Popular culture refers to culture traits that are well known and widely accepted by the general population. Food, sports, music, and movies are all examples of our popular culture. The United States has great influence on global popular culture. At the same time, the United States is influenced by global culture.

As you read this module, look for new facts. Then, add them to what you already know to draw your own conclusions.

Economic Basics

Big Idea

Economic systems help people buy the goods and services they need.

Main Ideas

- The main problem in economics is scarcity.
- Scarcity shapes how societies use factors of production.

Key Terms and Places

economy
scarcity
opportunity cost
profit
factors of production
income
contraction
expansion
economic interdependence

If YOU lived there...

You pour cereal into a bowl for breakfast and discover that you have no milk. How can you get more? Do you have to go to the farm and milk the cows? Of course not. With a quick trip to the store, you can buy a carton of milk.

How are you able to buy what you want or need?

Key Concepts

Every day, people all over the world purchase goods and services from other people. Goods are products that people consume or use, such as food or tools. Services are things that people do. For example, a school nurse provides a service by helping students who are sick or hurt. How people get goods and services is determined by global, national, and local economies. An **economy** is a system of producing, selling, and buying goods and services. The study of economies is called economics.

Scarcity and Choice Economists, who study economics, say that we all face the same basic problem. This problem is scarcity. **Scarcity** is when there are not enough resources to meet people's wants. People's wants are unlimited, but the resources available to satisfy their wants are limited.

When a resource becomes scarce, it is harder for producers to get. So, products made with that resource become more difficult for consumers to find. As a result, the prices for these items usually rise.

Scarcity forces us to make choices. We must decide what things we need and want. Choices always come with costs. For every choice you make, you give up something else. In economics, this choice is called a tradeoff. The value of the thing you give up in the tradeoff is called an **opportunity cost.** For example, suppose you get some money for your birthday. You want to use it to buy a new video game, but your friends invite you to play laser tag. You don't have enough money for both. If you choose the video game, the value of the laser tag games is the opportunity cost. It's the value of the next best choice you gave up in order to get what you wanted more.

▶ *Explore ONLINE!*

Interpret Graphs

Demand for Products

Supply of Products

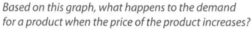

Based on this graph, what happens to the demand for a product when the price of the product increases?

If the price of the product changes from $50 to $70, what is likely to happen to the supply?

Supply and Demand Whenever you buy something, you make a choice about the product and the price. Your choice and those of other consumers help determine what sellers will produce and what they will charge for it. The price of a good or service is usually determined by the laws of supply and demand. *Supply* is the amount of a good or service that businesses are willing and able to produce. *Demand* is the desire to have a good or service and the number of people who are ready to buy it at a certain price.

The *law of supply* states that businesses will produce more of a good or service when they can charge a higher price. The *law of demand* states that consumers will want to buy more of a good or service when its price is low. As the price of a good or service rises, consumers will buy less of it.

Incentives Incentives, or benefits, also influence economic activity. **Profit** is a major incentive for both individuals and businesses. Profit is the money an individual or business has left after paying expenses. For example, suppose you help your school sell boxes of popcorn to raise money for your school band. The band's profit is the amount of money that your customers pay, minus the cost that your school actually paid for the popcorn. The profit motive, or the desire to make a profit, is essential in many economies. Without a profit incentive, many people would not start businesses. Then, the consumers in that economy would have no way to get goods and services.

Another type of consumer incentive is saving money. Businesses often offer coupons or advertisements to buy a good or service at a lower price. If enough people use the coupons, the business makes a profit. That's because the business will sell more of the lower-priced or discounted item than other businesses who offer the same thing at a higher price. A third type of incentive is receiving something extra. Has your family ever shopped at a "buy one, get one free" sale? When people buy a particular good or service during these kinds of sales, they also receive a free good or service.

Reading Check
Summarize
What is the connection between scarcity and tradeoffs?

Scarcity and Resource Use

Every day, the interaction between consumers and producers for goods and services happens at the local, state, national, and international levels. In the winter, your family might heat your home with oil that comes from Saudi Arabia or Texas, is refined in Louisiana, is shipped by train to Pittsburgh, and finally is delivered to your home's furnace. How do you think businesses in these diverse places decide what to make or sell?

Factors of Production Scarcity forces businesses to choose which goods and services to provide and how much to charge for them. Individuals, businesses, and societies must answer three basic questions: What will be produced? How will it be produced? For whom will it be produced? To understand how societies answer these questions, economists study **factors of production.** These four main factors are the basic economic resources needed to produce goods and services. They include natural resources, capital, labor, and entrepreneurs. These factors have one thing in common—their supply is limited.

The first factor of production is natural resources, such as oceans, mines, and forests, that provide the raw materials needed to produce goods. Another important natural resource for businesses is land. Every business needs a place to locate. Companies that provide services need to be located near their potential customers. Companies that make goods choose areas with transportation so they can ship their goods.

Factors of Production

Natural Resources

Capital

Labor

Entrepreneurs

The second factor is capital. Businesses need capital. Capital is the goods used to make other goods and services. Capital includes tools, trucks, machines, factories, and office equipment. These items are often called capital goods to distinguish them from financial capital. Financial capital is the money a business uses to buy the tools and equipment, or capital goods that they use in production.

The third factor of production is labor. Labor is the human time, effort, skills, and talent needed to produce goods and services. Workers sell their labor in exchange for payment, called **income.** Many workers earn a form of income called hourly wages. Other workers, such as those who manage companies or have a great deal of responsibility, are paid salaries. Salaries are fixed earnings rather than hourly wages. A salaried person is paid the same amount no matter how many hours he or she works.

Entrepreneurs are the fourth factor of production. An entrepreneur is a person who organizes, manages, and assumes the risk of a business. Entrepreneurs often come up with an idea for a new product or a new way of doing business. They use their own labor or capital and take the risks of failure. In return for the willingness to take risks, an entrepreneur hopes to make a substantial profit.

If a factor of production is in short supply, problems can arise. Suppose a farmer uses skills (labor) and tools (capital) to grow strawberries on a farm (natural resource), and he or she sells them at a market (role of entrepreneur). If a drought destroys farmland, the farmer might produce fewer, if any, crops. The farmer's business would be hurt. Strawberries would be scarce. Consumers would have to buy them at a higher price. This situation would cause what is called a **contraction,** or reduction of the strawberry farmer's business.

On the other hand, if a factor in production is increased, benefits can occur. How might this scenario affect the same farmer? Suppose rain is plentiful, and the farmer has a record crop of strawberries. Although the strawberry prices might be lower, the profits from the greater crop yields could allow the **expansion** of the farmer's business. The farmer could afford to hire more workers, buy more farm equipment, or buy more land to farm.

Availability of Resources

The availability of resources influences economic activity. Rwanda's agricultural economy relies heavily on a large number of workers.

By contrast, the availability of capital resources, such as combine harvesters, helps a small number of U.S. farmers tend large fields.

Resources and Economies The factors of production are not distributed equally. That's why countries decide what to produce based on the resources they have. This situation can create specialization. Specialization occurs when individuals or businesses produce a narrow range of products. For example, South Africa is rich in gold, diamonds, and mineral resources. Developing a mining industry has helped make South Africa one of the richest countries in Africa.

The availability of resources also shapes how a society produces goods and services. For example, Rwanda's economy is based on agriculture. Rwandans are rich in agricultural labor. In fact, nearly 80 percent of Rwandans work in agriculture. Farmers grow crops on small plots of land near their homes. In terms of capital, they have simple farming tools but few tractors and roads. By contrast, only about 2 percent of Americans work in agriculture. U.S. farmers rely heavily on capital. Using machinery and technology, they produce surplus crops on large farms.

Scarcity and Trade When a resource is relatively scarce in one place, people may trade with others to get that resource. This happens within a society as well as between nations. In this way, scarcity contributes to **economic interdependence.** Economic interdependence happens when producers in one nation depend on others to provide goods and services that they don't produce. It is a driving force behind international trade.

For instance, Japan manufactures cars, which require a great deal of steel. However, Japan lacks the iron ore needed to make steel. To obtain iron ore, Japan has formed international trading relationships with Australia and Brazil.

Reading Check
Analyze Effects
How does availability of the factors of production affect a society's economy?

Summary and Preview In this lesson you learned how economic systems help people buy the goods and services they need. In the next lesson, you will learn how geographers categorize various world economies and their peoples.

Lesson 1 Assessment

Review Ideas, Terms, and Places

1. **a. Compare** How do the laws of supply and demand work together?
   b. Summarize In economics, what is scarcity?
2. **a. Describe** What are the factors of production?
   b. Predict What problems might a homebuilder face if one of the factors of production, such as land or labor, was in short supply?

Critical Thinking

3. **Compare** You are supposed to babysit Friday night, but your friend wants you to sleep over and watch a new movie. List the opportunity cost of each tradeoff, then explain what you think is the best action and why.

4. **Identify Problems** Give an example of how the relative scarcity of resources might impact economic interdependence within a country.
5. **Synthesize** Draw a table like the one below. Then list some of the factors of production that were needed to produce a recent meal you had.

Natural Resources	Labor	Capital	Entrepreneurship

Economic Systems

Big Idea

Geographers understand world economies by studying factors of production, economic activities, and levels of development.

Main Ideas

- There are three basic types of economic systems.

- Contemporary societies have mixed economies.

- The United States benefits from a free enterprise system.

- Governments provide public goods.

- Geographers categorize countries based on levels of economic development and range of economic activities.

Key Terms and Places

traditional economy
command economy
market economy
mixed economies
free enterprise system
public goods
agricultural industries
manufacturing industries
wholesale industries
retail industries
service industries
gross domestic product (GDP)
developed countries
developing countries

Reading Check
Summarize
What are the three basic types of economic systems?

If YOU lived there . . .

You farm a small plot of land in southern India, and you have a decision to make. You can grow food for your family, or you can grow cassava, a cash crop that can be sold for profit if demand for the crop remains high.

What choice will you make?

Main Types of Economic Systems

An economic system is the way in which a society organizes the production and distribution of goods and services. Economic systems can be divided into three types: traditional, command, and market.

In a **traditional economy,** the work that people do is based on long-established customs. People in these groups hunt, fish, and tend animals and crops. Often, the focus of work is survival. The good of the group is more important than individual desires. The group's leaders decide what to produce and which group members will provide services. Typically, the men hunt and fish and the women tend to crops, animals, and children. In earlier times, all societies had traditional economies.

Today, traditional economies are rare and under pressure to change. Still, you can find this system in many places. For example, the Aymara people of the South American Andes and the Inuit people in northern Canada have traditional economies.

In a **command economy,** the government controls the economy. The government decides what goods and services to produce, how and how much to produce, and how goods and services are distributed. It also sets wages and prices. Some economists refer to command economies as centrally planned economies.

The most common economic system used today is a **market economy.** A market economy is based on private ownership, free trade, and competition. Individuals and businesses are free to buy and sell what they wish, with little interference from government. Prices are determined by the supply of and demand for goods.

Traditional

The Inuit of Canada use fishing techniques passed down over many generations.

Command

Food was scarce and expensive in this store in the former Soviet Union, a command economy.

Market

Advertisements, like these billboards in New York City, are a common sight in a market economy.

Modern Economies

Few, if any, pure economic systems exist today. Most countries have **mixed economies,** which combine elements of traditional, market, and command economic systems. The most common types of mixed economies are communist, capitalist, and socialist.

Communist Economies Modern economies tend to emphasize features of one system over others. For example, communist economies are closest to the command model. In a communist economy, the government owns all the factors of production. There is no private ownership of property or resources and little or no political freedom.

How do communist nations decide what, how, and for whom to produce? In countries such as North Korea and Cuba, the government collectivized, or took ownership of, the factors of production. Then government workers, called central planners, make long-term plans. They make all decisions about the production, price, and distribution of goods and services. They may even decide what types of work people are able to do.

Capitalist Economies By contrast, capitalist economies emphasize features of market systems. In capitalist economies, individuals and businesses own the factors of production. They play a major role in answering the basic economic questions, and no central government authority tells them what to do. Consumers buy goods and services that they like best. Their choices push producers to make better products at lower prices.

The economies of the United States, Canada, and Taiwan are capitalist. In these countries, government plays an important but limited role in the economy. For example, in the United States, government agencies enforce health and safety standards. These actions benefit U.S. workers and consumers but affect business planning in complicated ways. Regulations can increase the cost of running a business. On the other hand, the government spends money that it collects in taxes on services that support economic development, such as education, roads, and social welfare programs. Businesses save money by not having to pay for these services themselves.

Socialist Economies The third type of economy falls between communism and capitalism. In socialist economies, the government controls some of the basic factors of production. In most cases, that control is limited to industries and services that are key to a nation's well-being, such as electrical utilities, communications networks, and health care. Other industries are privately controlled.

Today, many nations with elements of a socialist economy, such as Sweden and India, have democratic governments. Still, central planners make decisions about government-owned industries. They also make decisions about other sectors, such as health care, to ensure that everyone has access to services.

Compare Economic Systems			
	Communism	**Socialism**	**Free Enterprise**
Who owns resources?	Government	Government owns basic resources; the rest are privately owned	Individuals and businesses
Who distributes resources?	Government decides how resources are used	Government regulates basic resources; market allocates privately owned resources	Market allocates resources
What role does government play?	Government makes all economic decisions	Government makes decisions in the basic industries	Government has a limited role, acting mostly to ensure market forces are free to work

Trends Since the Fall of Communism The record of collective, or communist, non-free market economies is poor. From the 1940s until the 1990s, between one-quarter and one-third of the world's people lived under communist regimes. The former Soviet Union and several of its Eastern European neighbors, China and much of Southeast Asia, Cuba, and North Korea all had centrally planned economies.

The failure of these economies is due largely to the shortcomings of communism. Often, central planners had too many decisions to make and too little understanding of local conditions. With wages set, workers had little **incentive** to work hard. Communism's greatest failing, however, was the suffering that it caused. Shortages of food and goods were common. Millions of people died building huge collective farms in China and the Soviet Union. Millions more were imprisoned for criticizing government policies.

Academic Vocabulary
incentive motivation, or reason to do something

Reading Check
Compare How are socialist economies similar to both communist and capitalist economies?

With the collapse of communism in the early 1990s, most communist countries adopted some form of market economy. Five communist countries are left—China, Cuba, Laos, North Korea, and Vietnam. All allow greater market competition, except for North Korea.

The Free Enterprise System

U.S. capitalism is sometimes called the **free enterprise system.** Under this system, Americans enjoy a number of freedoms. They are free to exchange goods and services and choose careers. They are also free to own and operate enterprises, or businesses, with little government intervention.

The ability to make a profit is one of the chief advantages of the free enterprise system. In this system, profit can reward hard work and innovation. The desire to make a profit also encourages competition, forcing producers to offer higher-quality products at lower prices. Another advantage is that people often have greater freedoms in societies with free enterprise systems. They can own property, make economic decisions, and participate in open elections.

Maintaining a functioning free enterprise system requires people to act in a morally responsible and ethical way. Businesses and individuals must obey laws, be truthful, and avoid behaviors harmful to others.

Reading Check
Summarize How does the ability to make a profit help the economy?

Unethical behavior can lead to business failure and a loss of trust in the system. For example, if company officials begin to lie about a business's financial condition, then investors can lose thousands, even billions of dollars. Finally, the company itself could go bankrupt.

Focus on Economics

Young Entrepreneurs

Let's take a look at one American entrepreneur who took advantage of the free enterprise system. In 2006, eight-year-old Madison Robinson from Galveston, Texas, had an idea to sell light-up flip-flops for kids. With financing from friends and family, she started her own company, Fish Flops. By 2013 Fish Flops had over $1 million in sales, enough profit to cover Robinson's college tuition.

At age eight, Madison Robinson started a business selling flip-flops that she designed.

Government and Public Goods

Today, federal, state, and local governments provide expensive or important services to large groups of people who might otherwise have to do without the service. These government goods and services that the public consumes are called **public goods.** The government pays for public goods with the taxes they collect.

For example, by establishing schools, government makes it possible for all children to receive a good education. Governments also provide police to protect lives and property and fire departments to protect homes and businesses.

This firefighter battles a raging fire to protect public safety.

Because of government, we can travel highways that stretch from border to border. We have a system of money that makes it easy for us to buy and sell things and to know the price of these things. Trash is collected, and health and safety laws are enforced to protect us. We can go to public libraries. By maintaining our infrastructure of bridges, airports, and roads as well as many more services, government helps economic activity.

Government Scarcity Scarcity affects government, too. It has unlimited wants but limited resources. Government collects taxes to pay for the public goods. Some economists believe that if taxes are too high, businesses won't make as much profit. Other economists believe that if taxes are too low, it reduces the public services that protect our quality of life. Therefore, government must determine the opportunity cost of investing in education, national defense, social services, and other programs and try to find a balance.

In addition, federal, state, and local governments use regulations, or a set of rules or laws, to control business behavior. Government regulations must be effective and fairly enforced. These regulations often include protections for public health and safety and the environment. For example, a town in a mountain ski area might determine the opportunity cost of regulations to preserve land versus the rights of property owners to develop it for tourism. Then, it must make tradeoffs.

Reading Check
Find Main Ideas
Why does the government provide public goods?

Economic Activities and Development

Every nation's economy includes a variety of economic activities. Economic activities are the ways in which people make a living. Some people farm, others manufacture goods, and still others provide services. Geographers categorize these economic activities into four levels of industry.

Levels of Industry The first level is called primary industry. People working at this level harvest products from the earth. **Agricultural industries** are primary activities that focus on growing crops and raising livestock. Fishing and mining are also primary activities. Raw materials such as grain, cattle, seafood, and coal are all products of primary activities.

At the next level, secondary industry, people use natural resources and raw materials to make products to sell. In **manufacturing industries,** people and businesses manufacture, or make, finished products from raw materials. For example, a furniture maker could use wood to make a table or a chair.

Economic Activity

Primary Industry

Primary industries use natural resources to make money. This farmer sells milk from dairy cows to earn a living.

Secondary Industry

Secondary economic activities use raw materials to produce or manufacture something new. In this case, the milk from dairy cows is used to make cheese.

Tertiary Industry

Tertiary economic activities provide goods and services to people and businesses. This grocer selling cheese in a market is involved in a tertiary activity.

Quaternary Industry

Quaternary industries process and distribute information. Skilled workers research and gather information. Here, inspectors examine and test the quality of cheese.

In the third level, or tertiary industry, people provide goods and services to customers. Workers at this level may sell goods and products from primary and secondary industries. Some work in **wholesale industries,** businesses that sell to businesses. They help move goods from manufacturer to market. Others work in **retail industries,** businesses that sell directly to final consumers. For example, a furniture wholesaler buys tables from a manufacturer. Then, the wholesaler sells the tables to a retail store, such as a department store, that sells directly to consumers.

Still other tertiary workers, like health-care workers and mechanics, work in **service industries,** businesses that provide services rather than goods. Teachers, store clerks, and doctors are all tertiary workers.

The fourth level of economic activity, quaternary industry, involves the research and distribution of information. People making a living at this level work with information rather than goods and often have specialized knowledge and skills. Architects, librarians, computer programmers, and scientists all work in quaternary industries.

Economic Indicators Economic systems and activities affect a country's economic development, or the level of economic growth and quality of life. Geographers group countries into two basic categories: developed countries and developing countries. To decide if a country is developed or developing, geographers use economic indicators, or measures of a country's wealth.

A Developed and a Developing Country	
Australia	**Afghanistan**
Per Capita GDP (U.S. $): $56,311	Per Capita GDP (U.S. $): $594
Life Expectancy at Birth: 82.2	Life Expectancy at Birth: 51.3
Literacy Rate: 99%	Literacy Rate: 38.2%
Physicians Per 10,000 People: 32.7	Physicians Per 10,000 People: 2.7
Sources: CIA, The World Factbook 2016; World Bank	

Contrast
How does the quality of life in Afghanistan differ from that in Australia?

Academic
Vocabulary
per capita the
average per person

One indicator, **gross domestic product (GDP),** is the value of all goods and services produced within a country in a single year. Another indicator is a country's <u>per capita</u> GDP, or the total GDP divided by the number of people in a country. As you can see in the chart, per capita GDP allows us to compare incomes among countries. Other indicators include literacy and life expectancy and the overall level of industrialization. We also look at the types of industries a country has and at its level of health care and education.

Developed and Developing Countries Many of the world's wealthiest and most powerful nations are **developed countries,** countries with strong economies and a high quality of life. Developed countries like Germany and the United States have a high per capita GDP and high levels of industrialization. Their health care and education systems are among the best in the world.

The world's poorer nations are known as **developing countries.** These countries have less productive economies and a lower quality of life. Almost two-thirds of the world's people live in developing countries. These countries have a lower per capita GDP than developed countries. Most of their citizens work in farming or other primary industries. Although these countries typically have large cities, much of their population still lives in rural areas. People in developing countries usually have less access to health care, education, and technology. Guatemala, Nigeria, and Afghanistan are all developing countries.

Often, a country's economic activities reflect its economic development. In the poorest developing countries, the vast majority of people work in primary industries, such as farming. As a country becomes more

Focus on Culture

Female Literacy

Literacy rates are improving around the world, particularly for women and girls. Still, women lag behind men. Of the 774 million illiterate adults (about 17% of the world's population), two-thirds are women. Religious and cultural beliefs and economic conditions contribute to the problem. Illiteracy severely impacts a country's economic growth, quality of life, and its population's overall health and well-being. At 24.2%, Afghanistan has one of the lowest female literacy rates in the world. In many areas, women and girls are not allowed to attend school or to hold a job.

Reading Check
Contrast How
does GDP differ
in developed and
developing countries?

developed, fewer people work in primary industries. In the mid-1800s about two-thirds of U.S. workers worked in primary activities. Today, 80 percent work in tertiary industries, including wholesale, retail, and service industries. Only 3 percent of Americans work in primary industries.

Summary and Preview In this lesson you learned some of the ways in which geographers categorize world economies and their peoples. In the next lesson, you will learn about how the money and banking systems work.

Lesson 2 Assessment

Review Vocabulary, Terms, and Places

1. a. Compare Who makes the economic decisions in a traditional economy? Compare this with market and command economies.

   b. Analyze Effects Why are most modern economies called mixed economies?

2. a. Identify What types of industries does a socialist government control?

   b. Evaluate What explains the record of collective, non-free market economies in the world today?

3. a. Identify What are the advantages of the free enterprise system?

   b. Analyze Effects How can unethical and immoral behavior hurt the free enterprise system?

4. a. Define What are public goods? Give examples, and describe why they are important.

   b. Evaluate What are some of the tradeoffs of government regulations? Include examples in your answer.

5. a. Define Describe and give examples of agricultural, wholesale, retail, manufacturing, and service industries.

   b. Explain What are developed and developing countries? Include examples of economic indicators in your answer.

Critical Thinking

6. Form Generalizations How might economic factors affect the use of technology in a developing country?

7. Compare Use your notes to complete a chart like the one below that compares economic systems. For each system, list how some societies organize the production and distribution of goods and services.

Free Enterprise	Socialist	Communist

Money and Banking

The Big Idea

People and businesses sell goods and services to earn income, which they can then use to build wealth.

Main Ideas

- Money is used as a medium of exchange, a store of value, and a unit of account.
- Banks are places to store money, earn money, and borrow money.
- People can use their earnings to build wealth.

Key Terms and Places

barter
money
medium of exchange
store of value
unit of account
interest rate
assets
savings
investment

If YOU lived there . . .

Sadly, your favorite elderly grandmother has passed away. As a parting gift, she left some money in her will for your college education. Since you are not 18 years old, your parents will manage the money. But, they want you to help them decide the best way to keep it safe and to make it grow.

How would you decide what to do with the money until you are ready for college?

Purposes of Money

Imagine what life would be like if money did not exist. How would people get the goods that they need? One way is to **barter,** or trade a good or service for a good or service provided by someone else. Trading like this is hard because two people who want to barter must at the same time want what the other has to offer. For example, suppose you want to trade two T-shirts for a pair of jeans. One friend may have the jeans but not want your shirts. Another might want your shirts but not have jeans to trade. As a result of these kinds of trading challenges, people created money to use as payment.

The History of Money What do the following things have in common: cattle, corn, salt, copper, gold, silver, seashells, stones, and whale teeth? At different times and in different places, they have all been used as money. **Money** is anything that people will accept as payment for goods and services.

Historians do not know exactly when and where metal coins were first used as money, but most agree that coins were invented in the sixth or seventh century BC. Over time, more and more civilizations began minting, or stamping, their own coins. Eventually, they began producing paper money as well. Today, every country in the world has a currency, or type of money. For example, the United States has the dollar, Mexico has the peso, and many European countries have the euro.

The Functions of Money Money performs three important functions. It serves as a medium of exchange, a store of value, and a unit of account. As you have read, bartering is an

Yen
Japan

Peso
Mexico

Euro
European Union

Yuan
China

Dollar
United States

Real
Brazil

Rupee
India

inefficient way for people to meet economic needs. By contrast, money is an efficient **medium of exchange,** or a means through which goods and services can be exchanged. It allows precise, flexible pricing of goods and services.

A **store of value** is something that holds its value over time. People do not have to spend their money all at one time. They can save it and spend it in the future. They know that it will be accepted wherever and whenever they need to use it to make purchases.

Money serves as a good **unit of account,** or yardstick of economic value in exchanges. It allows people to measure the relative costs of goods and services. For example, a $20 T-shirt is worth two $10 gift cards, four $5 burritos, or ten $2 bus rides. In the United States, the economic value of all goods and services can be measured by the dollar, the nation's basic monetary unit.

Reading Check
Draw Conclusions
Why did civilizations begin using coins as money?

Banks and the Economy

Banks offer services that allow them to act like "money stores." Just as stores are places where goods can be bought and sold, banks are places where money can be bought (borrowed) and sold (loaned). Services offered by banks allow customers to store money, earn money, and borrow money. Banks are businesses that earn money by charging interest or fees on these services.

Banks store money and other valuables for their customers in vaults.

Banking Services Although banks can offer many services, they have three main functions. Customers can store money in banks, they can earn money from banks, and they can borrow money from banks. Each of these services is important.

Banks are safe places where people can store money and valuables. Customers deposit money in the bank, and the bank stores the money in vaults. The money stored in banks is insured against theft and other loss. Customers' bank accounts are also insured in case the bank fails.

Customers can earn money when they store their savings in banks. Savings accounts and some checking accounts offer a payment called interest. Interest is a payment that a borrower pays to a lender as a fee for use of the money borrowed. When a person deposits money in a savings account, he or she is loaning money to the bank. In addition to savings accounts, many banks offer types of accounts that have special rules and higher interest rates.

Banks also offer loans to customers. They offer different loans for different reasons. Customers apply for loans, and their applications for each loan must be approved by the bank. In addition, when borrowing money from a bank, the customer must pay interest to the bank. One common loan is a mortgage. A mortgage loan allows a buyer to purchase property such as a house without having all of the money. The lending bank and the borrower agree on a time period for the loan and an interest rate. Then, customers pay the bank a certain amount every month until the loan is paid off.

How Interest Works When customers leave money in a bank, the bank pays the customer for use of that money in the form of interest. The amount of interest paid is determined by the **interest rate,** which is usually a percentage of the total amount of money in the customer's account. The bank doesn't simply store its customers' money, though. It uses the money to make loans to other customers. It charges these borrowing customers a higher interest rate than the rate that it pays on savings accounts. In this way, the bank hopes to make a profit.

Interest rates affect economic activity of businesses and individuals. When interest rates are high, more bank customers will save money so that they can earn more money in interest. When interest rates are low, customers tend to borrow more money to take advantage of the low cost of borrowing. Or, if they have no need to borrow money, they may look for savings products or investments that offer high interest rates so that they can earn more with their money.

Reading Check
Explain
What are the effects of high and low interest rates?

Money Management

As you have learned, wants are unlimited and the resources available to meet these wants are limited. For this reason, people and businesses are motivated to save and invest money, which increases their financial resources. Savings and investments are good ways to gain **assets.** An asset is something of economic value that a person or company owns. Some assets, such as houses, are physical and acquired by spending. Other assets, such as savings and investments, are **intangible** but still valuable.

Academic Vocabulary
intangible not perceivable by the senses; not physical

Fastest-Growing Occupations
(projected for 2014–2024)

 High school   Some college or training   College degree

Number of New Jobs in These Occupations		% Change	Average Salary*	Education Needed
Wind turbine service technicians	4,800	108	$51,050	✔ ✔ ✔
Web developers	39,500	26.6	$64,970	✔ ✔
Registered nurses	439,300	16.0	$67,490	✔ ✔ ✔
Home health aides	348,400	38.1	$21,920	✔
Nurse practitioners	44,700	35.2	$98,190	✔ ✔ ✔
Retail salespersons	314,200	6.8	$21,780	✔
Occupational therapy assistants	14,100	42.7	$57,870	✔ ✔

Source: United States Bureau of Labor Statistics, 2017

*Median average salary, 2015

The Relationship of Risk and Return

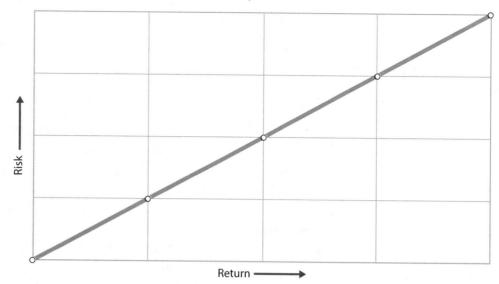

The higher the risk of the investment, the greater the possible return.

Income Every person who has a job that pays a wage earns income. They offer a service (their labor) to a company (their employer) and are paid money in return. Businesses also earn income by selling goods and services. Supply and demand help determine how much businesses and individuals can charge for their goods and services, but a worker can sometimes increase earnings by being especially productive. Why would a business pay a worker more for being productive? It is because the productive worker completes more work in less time than the other workers do.

People can do two things with the money they earn. They can spend it or save it. Much income is spent on basic costs such as housing, food, and utilities. Any money left after these essentials have been covered is called discretionary income. The earner can spend this money on other wants or save it.

Building Wealth **Savings** is income not spent on immediate wants. People have many options for saving money. Common options include savings accounts, certificates of deposit (CDs), and stocks. Savings accounts are good when the money may be needed soon, because these accounts allow customers to withdraw money anytime. However, they pay only a small interest rate. For this reason, savers who do not expect to need their money soon may choose a different way to save.

CDs are offered for a fixed term like six months or a year. Because customers agree to leave the money in the account for a specific time period, banks pay higher interest than they do for savings accounts. In general, the longer the time period of the CD, the higher the interest rate that a bank will pay.

Another option for earners is to invest their money. **Investment** is the use of money today in a way that earns future benefits. One way to invest is to buy stock, or partial ownership, in a company. Savers do this in the hope that the stock price will increase. They could then sell their stock and make a profit. Unlike deposits in savings accounts of banks and credit unions, money invested in stock is not insured. There is always the risk that stock prices could drop instead of rise. In such cases, the investor loses money because the investment is not insured. In addition, investors pay fees to buy stock.

Risk and Reward When deciding whether to save or invest, earners must first choose an investment goal. Are they saving up for a car? a vacation? retirement? The goal will help them determine the best method to save. Savers must also consider how much risk they are able to accept and how much reward (earnings) they are hoping to earn.

In general, investments that carry higher risk—that is, risk of losing some or all of the invested money—are most likely to earn high rewards. Safe investments such as savings accounts are less risky, but they also earn lower rewards. Because stock investments are risky in the short-term, they are not a good way to save money for short-term goals such as vacation or a new car. However, because they tend to earn high returns over many years, they are a good way to save for retirement. Savings accounts and CDs are better savings options for short-term goals.

Inflation is another risk that savers must consider. Because it affects the purchasing power of money, it can affect all types of accounts. Savings accounts may not pay enough interest to keep up with inflation. This means that, over time, the money in the account will buy less and less. For this reason, savers often seek products that can offer a higher rate of return, such as those available from stock investments. Because a higher rate of return comes with a higher risk, savers leave the money in the account for a long time in the hopes that any losses can eventually be regained.

Reading Check
Identify Which types of savings would work best when saving to buy a car?

Summary and Preview In this lesson you learned how our money and banking systems help people spend and save money. In the next lesson, you will learn how world economies interact and trade.

Lesson 3 Assessment

Review Vocabulary, Terms, and Places

1. **a. Summarize** What are the three main functions of money?
   b. Predict Effects What did the invention of coined money likely do for trade?
2. **a. Recall** What are the three main functions of banks?
   b. Explain Why do banks charge more interest to borrowers than they pay to lenders?
3. **a. Elaborate** What are the advantages of savings accounts? their disadvantages?
   b. Identify and Explain Which tool for savers has the potential for the most earnings? What is the downside of this tool?

Critical Thinking

4. **Compare and Contrast** Use your notes to complete a chart like the one below to compare and contrast different savings and investment options. For each option, list the positive and negative aspects.

Savings Account	CDs	Stocks

Living in a Global Economy

Big Idea

Fast, easy global connections have made cultural exchange, trade, and a cooperative world community possible.

Main Ideas

- Globalization links the world's countries together through culture and trade.

- Multinational corporations make global trade easier and allow countries to become more interdependent.

- The world community works together to solve global conflicts and crises.

Key Terms and Places

globalization
popular culture
trade barrier
free trade

If YOU lived there . . .

You live in Louisville, Kentucky, and you have never traveled out of the United States. However, when you got ready for school this morning, you put on a T-shirt made in Guatemala and jeans made in Malaysia. Your shoes came from China. You rode to school on a bus with parts manufactured in Mexico. At school, your class even took part in an online discussion with students who live in Canada.

What makes your global connections possible?

Globalization

In just seconds, an email message sent by a teenager in India beams all the way to a friend in London. A band in Seattle releases a song that becomes popular in China. People from New York to Singapore respond to a crisis in Brazil. These are all examples of **globalization,** the process in which countries are increasingly linked to each other through culture and trade.

What caused globalization? Over the past 100 years, improvements in transportation and communications—like airplanes, telecommunications, and the Internet—have brought the world closer together. As a result, global culture and trade have increased.

Popular Culture What might you have in common with a teenager in Brazil? You probably have more in common than you think. You may use similar technology, wear similar clothes, and watch many of the same movies. You share the same global **popular culture.**

More and more, people around the world are linked through popular culture. *Popular culture* refers to culture traits that are well known and widely accepted by the general population. Food, sports, music, and movies are all examples of our popular culture.

T-shirt from Vietnam

scarf from India

notebook from Canada

pencil from the United States

smartphone case from China

backpack from China

The United States has great influence on global popular culture. For example, American soft drinks are sold in almost every country in the world. Many popular American television shows are broadcast internationally. English has become the major global language. One-quarter of the world's people speak English. It has become the main language for international music, business, science, and education.

At the same time, the United States is influenced by global culture. Martial arts movies from Asia attract large audiences in the United States. Radio stations in the United States play music by African, Latin American, and European musicians. We even adopt many foreign words, like *sushi* and *plaza*, into English.

Reading Check
Find Main Ideas
How has globalization affected the world?

Global Trade

Globalization not only links the world's people, it also connects businesses and affects trade. Societies have traded with each other for centuries. Today, global trade takes place at a much faster pace than ever. Cargo ships have grown larger and faster, and specially designed airplanes now move goods at record speeds. Telecommunication, computers, and the Internet have globalized trade and made global buying and selling quick and easy. For example, a shoe retailer in Chicago can order the running shoes she needs on a website from a company in China. The order can be flown to Chicago the next day and sold to customers that afternoon.

Large container ships, such as these in the port of Seattle, are a cost-efficient way to transport goods across the globe.

The expansion of global trade has increased interdependence among the world's countries. Interdependence is a relationship between countries in which they rely on one another for resources, goods, or services. Many companies in one country often rely on goods and services produced in another country. For example, automakers in Europe might purchase auto parts made in the United States or Japan. Consumers also rely on goods produced elsewhere. For example, American shoppers buy bananas from Ecuador and tomatoes from Mexico. Global trade gives us access to goods from around the world.

Multinational Corporations Multinational companies operate in a number of different countries. Examples include Apple, Nike, and Toyota. These companies sell the products and services they offer to places throughout the world. They also have manufacturing plants, offices, and stores in many countries and continents.

To keep costs low, companies often build their manufacturing plants in locations where raw materials or labor is cheapest. They may produce different parts of their products on different continents. Then, the companies ship the various parts to another location to be assembled. The corporations find that if they locate part of their business in a country, local residents are more likely to buy its products and services.

Arguments For and Against Economic Globalization

For

- promotes peace through trade
- raises the standard of living and GDP
- creates jobs in developing countries
- promotes investment in developing nations' education, technology, and infrastructure
- creates a sense of world community

Against

- creates conflict because of an unfair system
- benefits developed nations more than developing nations
- takes jobs from high-paid laborers in developed countries
- may underpay workers in developing nations
- hurts local cultures

Reading Check
Analyze Effects
How might the location of multinational companies affect the gross domestic product (GDP) of a developed and developing country?

Many developing nations want multinational corporations to invest in them because they create jobs. Some developing nations offer multinational corporations a promise of low taxes to encourage them to do business there. After all, multinational corporations create jobs and expand the economy of a nation. With additional money coming in because of globalization, developing countries can improve their infrastructure. In this way, governments are better able to meet the needs of their citizens.

Global Economic Issues

Countries trade with each other to obtain resources, goods, and services. However, as you learned, scarcity is not equally divided across nations. While developed nations have found ways to strengthen their economies, developing nations still struggle to gain economic stability. They lack the necessary technologies, well-trained workers, and money for investments.

Economic Aid Organizations Developed nations provide aid to developing nations through the work of international organizations. One of these organizations is the World Bank. The World Bank provides loans for large projects in countries that need them, but might not otherwise be able to pay

Trade Barriers

Type of Trade Barrier	Definition	Example
Tariff	A tax that must be paid on imported items	A country taxes imports of Chinese steel at higher rates to protect steel production within its own country.
Quota	A limit on the amount of product imported or a limit on the amount of product imported at a lower tariff	A country imposes more quotas on goods and materials from developed countries than those from less-developed countries.
Embargo	A restriction or ban of trade with a country for political purposes	The United States restricts trade with Cuba because of concerns about the dictatorship of Raúl Castro.

Analyze Information
Which type of trade barrier do you think is used least often? Why?

for them. These loans often are used to pay for health care, education projects, or infrastructure, such as roads or power plants. Another organization is the International Monetary Fund (IMF). The IMF offers emergency loans to countries in financial trouble. These loans help countries keep a stable money and banking system so people can continue to buy and sell goods and services and their economy can begin to grow and prosper.

While these economic aid organizations can play an important role in development, they also have weaknesses. For example, the World Bank might fund a project that it considers worthy, like the building of a large dam. But, the project may not help the people of a country. Some have criticized the IMF for setting harsh financial conditions for countries receiving loans. For example, the IMF might require a country to cut its government spending drastically, which could affect jobs. Still, developed nations remain interested in helping developing nations. They see developing nations as sources of raw materials and as potential markets for goods. That is why developed nations would like the economies of developing nations to become strong and stable.

U.S. president Donald Trump and Chinese president Xi Jinping shake hands before a G20 (Group of 20) meeting in Hamburg, Germany. G20 meetings bring together the world's 20 leading industrialized and emerging economies for discussions on important issues, such as trade.

The Economics of Free Trade Global trading helps many countries around the world expand their economies. Yet sometimes governments pass laws to try to protect their country's jobs and industries. A **trade barrier** is any law that limits free trade between nations. One type of trade barrier is quotas. Quotas limit the amount of a lower-priced imported product. Another trade barrier is a tariff, or tax on imported goods to protect the price of domestic goods. An embargo is a law that cuts off most or all trade with a specific country. It is often used for political purposes. Since the early 1960s, for example, the United States has had an embargo on trade with communist Cuba. In 2016 President Obama visited Cuba and met with Cuba's president Raúl Castro in an effort to begin to ease relations between the two countries. In 2017 President Trump reversed Obama's policies and created new restrictions on traveling to or doing any business with Cuba.

Trade barriers exist for many reasons. However, some countries look for ways to make it easier for other nations to trade with them. For example, many countries now encourage free trade. **Free trade** removes trade barriers between nations. Since 1995 the World Trade Organization (WTO) has worked with other nations to help trade among nations flow as smoothly and freely as possible. In 2016, there were 164 member countries.

Summary Economic systems help people around the world buy the goods and services they need. These systems also provide a way for people and businesses to sell goods and services to earn income. Geographers learn more about a country by studying its factors of production, economic activities, and levels of development. Fast and easy global connections have made cultural exchange, trade, and a cooperative world community possible.

Reading Check
Compare and Contrast
List the differences among the following types of trade barriers: tariffs, quotas, and embargoes.

Lesson 4 Assessment

Review Ideas, Terms, and Places

1. a. **Describe** What is globalization?
   b. **Make Inferences** How has popular culture influenced countries around the world?

2. a. **Evaluate** Describe the impact of globalization and improved communications technology on cultures.
   b. **Analyze Motives** What benefits do multinational companies receive by locating business in a developing country? What benefits does the government of the developing country receive?

3. a. **Evaluate** In your opinion, has globalization hurt or helped the people of the world? Why?
   b. **Analyze Causes** Why might governments use trade barriers?

Critical Thinking

4. **Identify Cause and Effect** Use your notes and make a graphic organizer like the one below to identify the effects that globalization has on our world.

Globalization		
Effects	Effects	Effects

Social Studies Skills

Determine the Strength of an Argument

Define the Skill

Studying economics and geography often involves learning about different opinions. In order to understand these opinions, it is important to recognize strong arguments. An **argument** is a piece of writing that expresses a particular view. A strong argument presents a position, or claim about a topic, and supports that claim with reasons and evidence. Examples and points should be true and should relate to the argument. It is also important to consider any evidence against the argument.

Claim - a writer's position on a problem or issue

Reason - a statement that explains to readers why they should believe your claim

Evidence - proof that supports or backs up each reason, including facts, examples, statistics, and quotations

Although each piece of evidence supports a specific reason, all of the evidence should clearly relate to the writer's position or claim. The evidence must also come from credible, reliable sources.

Learn the Skill

Read the following paragraph. Notice how the claim is supported by a reason and evidence.

> The term literacy means a person's ability to read, write, do basic math, and use technology.
>
> Increasing literacy rates is the best way to overcome poverty and disadvantage.
>
> People who master these skills are more likely to achieve a higher level of education and get better jobs. Studies have shown that illiterate people earn 30%-42% less than similar literate people. A UNESCO study shows that the income of a person with poor literacy changes very little during his or her working career. However, incomes of people with higher literacy and math skills will increase two to three times more than what they earned at the beginning of their working career.

Claim

Reason

Evidence 1

Evidence 2

Practice the Skill

Use the library or Internet to find an editorial or a reader's letter to the editor in your local newspaper. Print it out or copy it. Then highlight the claim, at least one reason, and one supporting piece of evidence.

Module 5 Assessment

Review Vocabulary, Terms, and Places

For each group of terms below, write one or two sentences to describe how the terms in the group are related.

1. scarcity

   factors of production

2. agricultural industries

   manufacturing industries

   wholesale industries

   retail industries

3. income

   savings

4. developed country

   developing country

Comprehension and Critical Thinking

Lesson 1

5. **a.** Describe What is the relationship between scarcity and international trade?

   b. Explain How do the factors of production influence a nation's economy? Give two examples.

   c. Compare and Contrast Study the images and text on page 162. How do economic factors affect how U.S. and Rwandan farmers use technology?

Lesson 2

6. **a.** Elaborate Why do you think that market economies are more successful today than command economies are?

   b. Analyze Effects In general, how does a country's access to education and technology affect its GDP per capita and standard of living?

Lesson 3

7. **a.** Describe How does a barter system work?

   b. Make Inferences Why might a low interest rate lead people to borrow more money?

   c. Form Opinions Is a savings account or a stock investment a better way to accumulate intangible assets? Explain.

Lesson 4

8. **a.** Identify Cause and Effect What role does government regulation and taxation play in economic development and business planning?

   b. Make Inferences Identify a local business in your community that sells or provides goods or services that were made globally. List two or three examples of the globally produced goods or services, and why you think they are.

Module 5 Assessment, continued

Reading Skills

9. **Draw Conclusions** *Use the Reading Skills taught in this module to answer a question about the reading selection below.*

> The ability to make a profit is one of the chief advantages of the free enterprise system. In this system, profit can reward hard work and innovation.
>
> The desire to make a profit also encourages competition, forcing producers to offer higher-quality products at lower prices.

Think about a popular product. How does the free enterprise system help it to be successful?

Social Studies Skills

10. **Determine the Strength of an Argument** Use the Internet or library to find a magazine or newspaper article. Highlight its claim, at least one reason that backs up the claim, and at least one piece of supporting evidence.

Focus on Writing

11. **Sequence** Describe the sequence of steps for moving goods from maker to consumer Use sequence clue words in your answer.

12. **Write an Online Article** Choose two economic systems, one in a developing country and one in a developed country. Your purpose is to compare the main characteristics of these systems. Write a headline and a brief introduction that expresses your main idea. Then write a paragraph that compares their economic systems. Be sure to describe for each country who decides what to produce, how to produce it, and for whom to produce it. Write a conclusion that summarizes your main points.

The United States

Essential Question
Why does where you live in the United States matter?

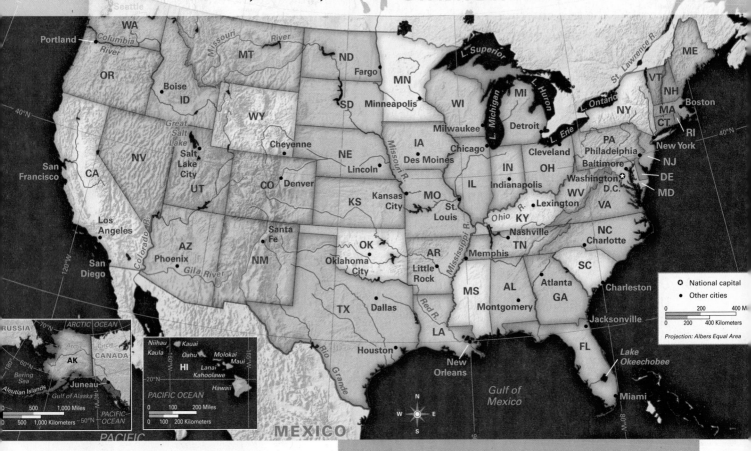

Explore ONLINE!

VIDEOS, including . . .
- Mount Saint Helens Erupts

HISTORY.

- ☑ Document-Based Investigations
- ☑ Graphic Organizers
- ☑ Interactive Games
- ☑ Channel One News Video: Climate Change: Extreme Weather
- ☑ Interactive Graph: Top Oil-Producing States, 2015
- ☑ Image with Hotspots: Wagon Train
- ☑ Interactive Chart: How a Bill Becomes a Law

In this module, you will learn about the United States and how this large and diverse country is often divided into regions that share common characteristics.

What You Will Learn

Geography The Grand Canyon in Arizona is one example of the many spectacular landscapes in the United States.

Culture People of many different ethnic groups and cultures make up the population of the United States.

History The Statue of Liberty in New York Harbor symbolizes our freedom and our history as a democratic nation.

Reading Social Studies

Categorize

READING FOCUS

When you sort things into groups of similar items, you are categorizing. When you read, categorizing helps you to identify the main groups of information. Then you can find and see the individual facts in each group. Notice how the information in the paragraph below has been sorted into three main groups, or categories, with details listed under each group.

Category 1:
Atlantic Coastal Plain
Details: low, flat, close to sea level

Category 2:
Piedmont
Details: farther west and higher than Atlantic Coastal Plain

Category 3:
Appalachian Mountains
Details: main eastern mountain range, higher than Piedmont

If you were traveling across the United States, you might start on the country's eastern coast. This low area, which is flat and close to sea level, is called the Atlantic Coastal Plain. As you go west, the land gradually rises higher to a region called the Piedmont. The Appalachian Mountains, which are the main mountain range in the East, rise above the Piedmont.

YOU TRY IT!

Read the following paragraph, and then use a graphic organizer like the one used above to categorize the groups and details in the paragraph. Create as many ovals as you need to list the main groups.

The eastern United States has three climate regions. In the Northeast, people live in a humid continental climate with snowy winters and warm, humid summers. Southerners, on the other hand, experience milder winters and the warm, humid summers of a humid subtropical climate. Most of Florida is warm all year.

As you read this module, think about how you could categorize the information you read.

Physical Geography

The Big Idea

The United States is a large country with diverse physical features, climates, and resources.

Main Ideas

- Major physical features of the United States include mountains, rivers, and plains.
- The climate of the United States is wetter in the East and South and drier in the West.
- The United States is rich in natural resources such as farmland, oil, forests, and minerals.

Key Terms and Places

Appalachian Mountains
Great Lakes
Mississippi River
tributary
Rocky Mountains
continental divide

If YOU lived there . . .

You live in St. Louis, Missouri, which is located on the Mississippi River. For the next few days, you will travel down the river on an old-fashioned steamboat. The Mississippi begins in Minnesota and flows south through ten states in the heart of the United States. On your trip, you bring a video camera to film life along this great river.

What will you show in your video about the Mississippi?

Physical Features

The United States is the third-largest country in the world, behind Russia and Canada. Our country is home to an incredible variety of physical features. All but 2 of the 50 states—Alaska and Hawaii—make up the main part of the country. Look at the physical map of the United States. It shows the main physical features of our country. Use the map as you read about America's physical geography in the East and South, the Interior Plains, and the West.

The East and South If you were traveling across the United States, you might start on the country's eastern coast. This low area, which is flat and close to sea level, is called the Atlantic Coastal Plain. As you go west, the land gradually rises higher, to a region called the Piedmont. The **Appalachian Mountains,** which are the main mountain range in the East, rise above the Piedmont. These mountains are very old. For many millions of years, rain, snow, and wind have eroded and smoothed their peaks. As a result, the highest mountain in the Appalachians is about 6,700 feet (2,040 m).

The Appalachians The smooth peaks of the Appalachian Mountains dominate the landscape of western North Carolina.

The Interior Plains As you travel west from the Appalachians, you come across the vast Interior Plains that stretch to the Great Plains just east of the Rocky Mountains. The Interior Plains are filled with hills, lakes, and rivers. The first major water feature that you see here is called the **Great Lakes.** These lakes make up the largest group of freshwater lakes in the world. The Great Lakes are also an important waterway for trade between the United States and Canada.

West of the Great Lakes lies North America's largest and most important river, the **Mississippi River.** Tributaries in the Interior Plains flow to the Mississippi. A **tributary** is a smaller stream or river that flows into a larger stream or river.

Along the way, these rivers deposit rich silt. The silt creates fertile farmlands that cover most of the Interior Plains. The Missouri and Ohio rivers are huge tributaries of the Mississippi. They help drain the entire Interior Plains.

Look at the physical map of the United States. Notice that the land begins to increase in elevation west of the Interior Plains. This higher region is called the Great Plains. Vast areas of grasslands cover these plains. There are fewer rivers and not very many trees.

The West In the region called the West, several of the country's most rugged mountain ranges make up the **Rocky Mountains.** These enormous mountains, also called the Rockies, stretch as far as you can see. Many of

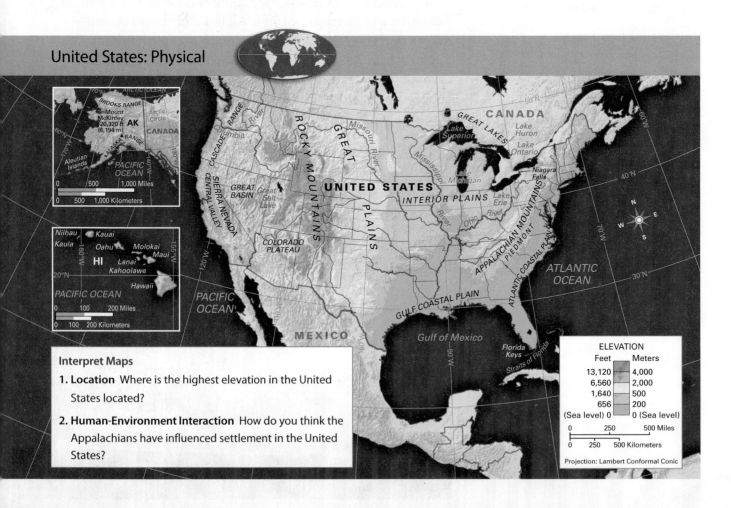

United States: Physical

Interpret Maps

1. **Location** Where is the highest elevation in the United States located?

2. **Human-Environment Interaction** How do you think the Appalachians have influenced settlement in the United States?

ELEVATION

Feet		Meters
13,120		4,000
6,560		2,000
1,640		500
656		200
(Sea level) 0		0 (Sea level)

Projection: Lambert Conformal Conic

From its source in Minnesota, the Mississippi River flows south across the central United States. It ends at the tip of Louisiana, which is shown here. This satellite image shows the area where the Mississippi River meets the Gulf of Mexico. This area is called a delta. A river's delta is formed from sediment that a river carries downstream to the ocean. Sediment is usually made up of rocks, soil, sand, and dead plants. Each year, the Mississippi dumps more than 400 million tons of sediment into the Gulf of Mexico.

The light blue and green areas in this image are shallow areas of sediment. The deeper water of the Gulf of Mexico is dark blue. Also, notice that much of the delta looks fragile. This is new land that the river has built up by depositing sediment.

Analyze Visuals
What natural hazards might people living in the Mississippi Delta experience?

The river branches out in several places here as it tries to find the shortest way to the gulf.

the mountains' jagged peaks rise above 14,000 feet (4,270 m). The Rockies are more jagged than the Appalachian Mountains because they are younger and haven't eroded as much.

In the Rocky Mountains is a line of high peaks called the Continental Divide. A **continental divide** is an area of high ground that divides the flow of rivers toward opposite ends of a continent. Rivers east of the divide in the Rockies mostly flow eastward and empty into the Mississippi River. Most of the rivers west of the divide flow westward and empty into the Pacific Ocean.

Farther west, mountain ranges include the Cascade Range and the Sierra Nevada. Most of the mountains in the Cascades are dormant volcanoes. One mountain, Mount Saint Helens, is an active volcano. A tremendous eruption in 1980 blew off the mountain's peak and destroyed 150 square miles (390 sq km) of forest.

Mountains also stretch north along the Pacific coast. At 20,310 feet (6,190 m), Alaska's Denali, which used to be known as Mount McKinley, is the highest mountain in North America. Alaska is home to 39 mountain ranges and 17 out of 20 of the tallest peaks in the United States. Some of its mountains are active volcanoes.

Far out in the Pacific Ocean are the islands that make up the state of Hawaii. Volcanoes formed these islands millions of years ago. Today, hot lava and ash continue to erupt from the islands' volcanoes.

Climate

Did you know that the United States has a greater variety of climates than any other country? Look at the map United States: Climate to see the different climates of the United States.

Reading Check
Summarize
What are the major physical features of the United States?

The East and South The eastern United States has three climate regions. In the Northeast, people live in a humid continental climate with snowy winters and warm, humid summers. Southerners, on the other hand, experience milder winters and the warm, humid summers of a humid subtropical climate. Most of Florida is warm all year.

The Interior Plains Temperatures throughout the year can vary greatly in the Interior Plains. Summers are hot and dry in the Great Plains. However, most of the region has a humid continental climate with long, cold winters.

The West Climates in the West are mostly dry. The Pacific Northwest Coast, however, has a wet, mild coastal climate. The region's coldest climates are in Alaska, which has both subarctic and tundra climates. In contrast, Hawaii is the only state with a warm, tropical climate.

Natural Resources

The United States is extremely rich in natural resources. Do you know that your life is affected in some way every day by these natural resources? For example, if you ate bread today, it was probably made with wheat grown in the fertile soils of the Interior Plains. If you rode in a car or on a bus recently, it may have used gasoline from Alaska, California, or Louisiana.

The United States is a major oil producer but uses more oil than it produces. In fact, we import more than one-fourth of the oil we need.

Valuable nonrenewable natural resources are mined in the Appalachians and Rockies. One resource, coal, supplies the energy for about a third of the electricity produced in the United States. The United States has about 25 percent of the world's coal reserves and is a major coal exporter.

Reading Check
Summarize
What types of climates are found in the United States?

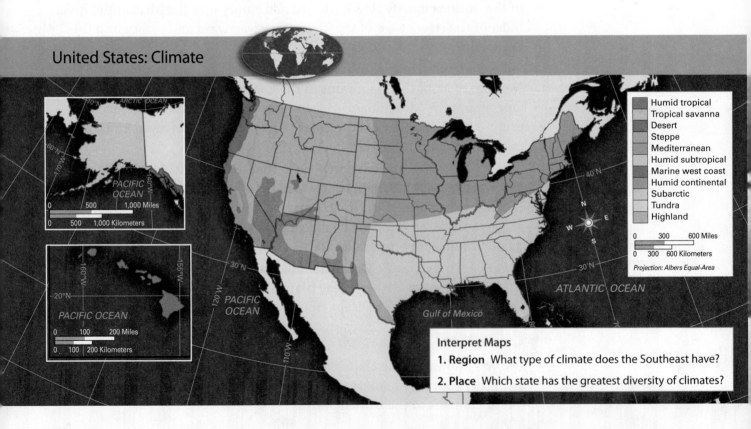

United States: Climate

Humid tropical
Tropical savanna
Desert
Steppe
Mediterranean
Humid subtropical
Marine west coast
Humid continental
Subarctic
Tundra
Highland

Projection: Albers Equal-Area

Interpret Maps
1. **Region** What type of climate does the Southeast have?
2. **Place** Which state has the greatest diversity of climates?

The Varied Climates of the United States

With a humid continental climate, New York City experiences cold winters with snowfall. In this climate, people can ice skate during the winter.

With a humid subtropical climate, most of Florida has warm, sunny days during most of the year. In this climate, people can enjoy the region's beaches.

Analyze Visuals
How do the human characteristics of New York City differ from a Florida beach? How does climate impact those characteristics?

Reading Check
Summarize
What are important natural resources in the United States?

Other important resources include forests and farmland, which cover much of the country. The trees in our forests provide timber that is used in constructing buildings. Wood from these trees is also used to make paper. Farmland produces a variety of crops including wheat, corn, soybeans, cotton, fruits, and vegetables.

Summary and Preview In this lesson you learned about the geography, climates, and natural resources of the United States. In the next lesson, you will learn about the history, government, and culture of the United States.

Lesson 1 Assessment

Review Ideas, Terms, and Places

1. a. **Describe** What is a tributary?

   b. **Contrast** How are the Appalachian Mountains different from the Rocky Mountains?

   c. **Elaborate** Look at the U.S. physical map in this lesson to locate the Great Lakes. Why are the Great Lakes an important waterway?

2. a. **Describe** Look at the U.S. climate map in this lesson. What is the climate like in the Northeast?

   b. **Draw Conclusions** What would winter be like in Alaska?

3. a. **Recall** What kinds of crops are grown in the United States?

   b. **Explain** Why is coal an important nonrenewable natural resource? Where is it mined?

   c. **Predict** What natural resources might not be as important to your daily life in the future?

Critical Thinking

4. **Categorize** Copy the graphic organizer below. Use it to organize the key ideas about physical features, climate, and natural resources by region of the country.

Region	East and South	Interior Plains	West
Physical features			
Climate			
Natural resources			

Natural Hazards in the United States

Background

Earth's physical systems create patterns around us, and these patterns influence our lives. For example, every region of the United States has distinctive natural hazards. Volcanoes threaten the Pacific Northwest. Earthquakes rattle California. Wildfires strike forests in the West. Hurricanes endanger the Atlantic and Gulf of Mexico coasts, and major rivers are prone to flooding. Tornadoes regularly rip across flat areas of central and southeast United States.

In fact, the United States lies in danger of getting hit by an average of six hurricanes a year. Formed by the warm waters of the Atlantic Ocean and Caribbean Sea and the collision of strong winds, hurricanes are the most powerful storms on Earth. Most hurricanes look like large doughnuts with a hole, or eye, in the middle of the storm. Around the eye, high winds and rain bands rotate counterclockwise. Once the hurricane moves over land or cold water, it weakens.

Natural Hazards in the United States

Tornado Alley

Earthquakes

Wildfires

Hurricanes

Flood areas

Volcanoes

Tornadoes

Tornado Risk
Moderate
High

After Hurricane Katrina hit New Orleans, people escaped the floodwaters by fleeing to rooftops and high-rise apartment buildings like this one.

Hurricane Katrina

On August 29, 2005, one of the most destructive hurricanes ever hit the United States. Hurricane Katrina devastated coastal regions of Louisiana, the city of New Orleans, and the entire coast of Mississippi.

With winds as high as 145 mph (235 km), Katrina destroyed hundreds of thousands of homes and businesses. In addition, Katrina pushed water from the Gulf of Mexico onto land to a height of about two stories. As a result, low-lying areas along the Gulf coast experienced massive flooding.

The storm also caused several levees that protected New Orleans from Lake Pontchartrain to break. The loss of these levees, which was a technological hazard, caused the lake's waters to flood most of the city. About 150,000 people who did not evacuate before the storm were left stranded in shelters, high-rise buildings, and on rooftops. Using boats and helicopters, emergency workers rescued thousands of people. Total damages from the storm were estimated to be nearly $151 billion. More than 1,800 people died and over a million were displaced.

What It Means

Natural hazards can influence where we live, how we build our homes, and how we prepare for storms. For example, in Tornado Alley, special warning sirens go off when storms develop that might form a dangerous tornado.

Using satellite images like this one of Hurricane Katrina, scientists saw how large the storm was and warned people along the Gulf coast to evacuate.

Geography for Life Activity

1. **Analyze Effects** What types of natural hazards affect people in the United States? How do they affect people?

2. **Contrast** Do some research to find out how tornadoes and hurricanes differ. Summarize the differences in a chart that includes information about how these storms start, where and when they tend to occur in the United States, and their wind strength.

🌐 History and Culture

It is 1803, and President Jefferson just arranged the purchase of a huge area of land west of the Mississippi River. It almost doubles the size of the United States. Living on the frontier in Ohio, you are a skillful hunter and trapper. One day, you see a poster calling for volunteers to explore the new Louisiana Territory. An expedition is heading west soon. You think it would be exciting but dangerous.

Will you join the expedition to the West? Why or why not?

The Big Idea

Democratic ideas and immigration have shaped the history, government, and culture of the United States.

Main Ideas

- The United States, the world's first modern democracy, expanded from the Atlantic coast to the Pacific coast over time.

- In the United States, different levels of government have different roles, but all levels require the participation of the citizens.

- The people and culture of the United States are very diverse.

Key Terms and Places

colony
Boston
New York
plantation
pioneers
U.S. Constitution
legislative branch
executive branch
judicial branch
bilingual

First Modern Democracy

Long before Italian explorer Christopher Columbus sailed to the Americas in 1492, native people lived on the land that is now the United States. These Native Americans developed many distinct cultures. Soon after Columbus and his crew explored the Americas, other Europeans began to set up colonies there.

The American Colonies Europeans began settling in North America and setting up colonies in the 1500s. A **colony** is a territory inhabited and controlled by people from a foreign land. By 1733, the British had 13 colonies along the Atlantic coast. New cities in the colonies such as **Boston** and **New York** became major seaports. As European colonies grew, many indigenous, or native, people were forced off the land or died of diseases brought by Europeans.

Some British colonists lived on plantations. A **plantation** is a large farm that grows mainly one crop. Many colonial plantations produced tobacco, rice, or cotton. From 1619 to 1808, about 453,000 enslaved Africans were forcibly brought to what is now the United States to work on plantations.

During the colonial period, Europeans from various ethnic and religious groups arrived in the colonies, looking for religious freedom and economic opportunity. For example, Anabaptists from Germany settled in places like Pennsylvania. Jews,

Fight for Independence

This painting shows General George Washington leading American troops across the Delaware River to attack British forces.

first from Spain and Portugal and later from Germany and Eastern Europe, moved to port cities like New York and Charleston, South Carolina.

By the 1770s many colonists in America were unhappy with the British monarchy. They wanted independence from Britain. In July 1776 the colonial representatives created and adopted the Declaration of Independence. The document stated that "all men are created equal" and have the right to "life, liberty, and the pursuit of happiness." Although not everyone in the colonies was considered equal, the Declaration was a great step toward equality and justice.

To win their independence, the American colonists fought the British in the Revolutionary War. First, colonists from Massachusetts fought in the early battles of the war in and around Boston. As the war spread west and south, soldiers from all the American colonies joined the fight against Britain.

In 1781 the American forces under General George Washington defeated the British army at the Battle of Yorktown in Virginia. With this defeat, Britain recognized the independence of the United States. As a consequence, Britain granted all its land east of the Mississippi River to the new nation. The colonists then worked to form a new government based on rule by representatives of the people instead of rule by a monarch. They formed the first modern democracy.

--- BIOGRAPHY ---

George Washington 1732–1799

As the first president of the United States, George Washington is known as the Father of His Country. Washington was admired for his heroism and leadership as the commanding general during the Revolutionary War. Delegates to the Constitutional Convention chose him to preside over their meetings. Washington was then elected president in 1789 and served two terms.

Make Inferences
Why do you think Washington was elected president?

Benjamin Franklin 1706–1790

Benjamin Franklin was a scientist, an inventor, a diplomat, a writer, and a printer. Franklin was born in Boston, Massachusetts, but he thought of Philadelphia, Pennsylvania, as his home. His most famous published work was *Poor Richard's Almanack,* a yearly journal that included many sayings that are still part of American culture today.

Franklin worked to improve society by starting Philadelphia's first fire and police departments and hospital. He started the first lending library in the colonies and a school that became the University of Pennsylvania.

Benjamin Franklin also made important contributions to American politics. He worked in France to gain support for the American Revolution. He helped edit the Declaration of Independence and was a signer of the Constitution. Benjamin Franklin's many achievements still affect the United States today.

Summarize
What types of contributions did Benjamin Franklin make to the United States?

Expansion and Industrial Growth After gaining independence, the United States gradually expanded west. Despite the challenges of crossing swift-moving rivers and traveling across rugged terrain and huge mountains, people moved west for land and plentiful resources.

These first settlers who traveled west were called **pioneers.** Many followed the 2,000-mile (3,219-km) Oregon Trail west from Missouri to the

Wagon Train

Many pioneers headed west in covered wagons like those in this photograph.

Analyze Visuals
What do you think the westward journey was like for the pioneers?

Oregon Territory. Groups of families traveled together in wagons pulled by oxen or mules. The trip was harsh. Food, supplies, and water were scarce.

While many pioneers headed west seeking land, others went in search of gold. The discovery of gold in California in 1848 had a major impact on the country. The lure of gold brought hundreds of thousands of people to California.

By 1850 the population of the United States exceeded 23 million and the country stretched all the way to the Pacific Ocean. In order to promote the settling of the rural West, the federal government enacted laws giving away land to anyone, including women, immigrants, and African Americans, willing to farm it. This public policy was called the Homestead Act. One-tenth of all land in the United States was settled under this act.

As the United States expanded, the nation's economy also grew. By the late 1800s the country was a major producer of goods like steel, oil, and textiles, or cloth products. The steel industry grew around cities that were located near coal and iron ore deposits. Most of those new industrial cities were in the Northeast and Midwest. The country's economy also benefited from the **development** of canals and railroads. These technologies helped industry and people move farther into the interior.

Academic Vocabulary
development the process of growing or improving

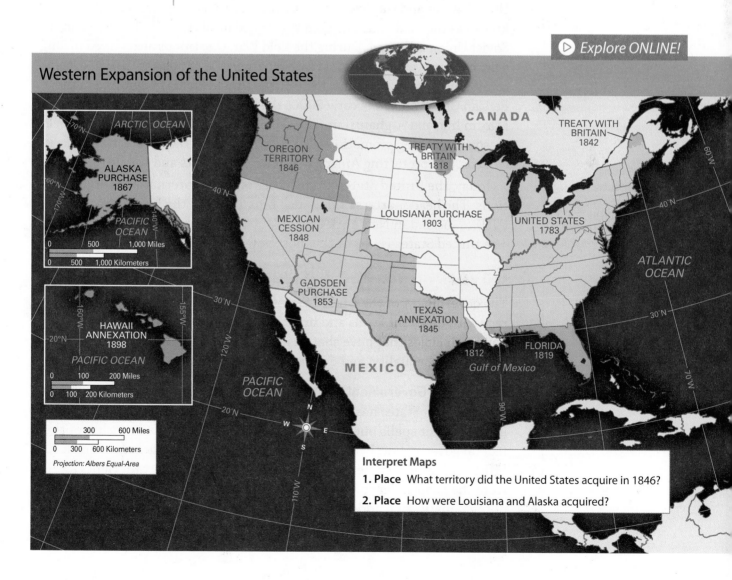

Western Expansion of the United States

Explore ONLINE!

Interpret Maps

1. Place What territory did the United States acquire in 1846?

2. Place How were Louisiana and Alaska acquired?

Attracted by a strong economy, millions of people immigrated, or came to, the United States for better jobs and land. Immigration from European countries was especially heavy in the late 1800s and early 1900s. Immigrants supplied labor to fuel the economy. Immigration also brought groups of people who had not previously interacted with each other. Sometimes, this created conflict as groups competed with each other for jobs and space.

The growth of industry had some negative effects. Mines and factories were often unsafe for workers. People were injured or killed on the job. Employers' desire to make money conflicted with workers' concerns. In the early 1900s, workers of different backgrounds began to work together in unions and with others, like politicians and journalists, to make factories and mines safer. Laws were passed, making workplaces safer. Unions and workplace reforms helped more workers achieve economic stability. Other groups and organizations also worked together to solve issues of over-crowding and poor living conditions in cities.

Wars and Peace The United States came into conflict with other countries and fought in several wars during the 1900s. Many Americans died in two major wars, World War I and World War II. After World War II, most of the once-strong European and Asian nations were struggling to rebuild. The United States and the Soviet Union became rival superpowers in what was known as the Cold War. The Cold War lasted until the early 1990s, when the Soviet Union collapsed. During the Cold War, U.S. troops also served in long wars in Korea in the 1950s and in Vietnam in the 1960s and 1970s to keep communism from spreading. In 1991 the United States fought Iraq in the Persian Gulf War. In the early 2000s the United States military fought long wars in Iraq and Afghanistan. The United States fought these wars for several reasons, including promoting and protecting democracy, protecting American citizens, and protecting American economic interests and stability.

Today, the United States is a member of many international organizations. The headquarters of one such organization, the United Nations (UN), is located in New York City. About 190 countries are UN members. The United States is one of the most powerful members.

Reading Check
Sequence
What were some major events in the history of the United States?

Government and Citizenship

The government of the United States is a complex, representative democracy with different levels and branches. It is a type of limited government. Some principles that have shaped its structure and function include freedom, justice, equality, and democracy.

The Federal Government Since 1787 the federal, or national, government of the United States has been based on the **U.S. Constitution.** This founding document spells out the powers and functions of the branches of the federal government. Everyone has to follow the Constitution, even elected officials. The government is limited and cannot take certain rights away from the people. Part of the Constitution is the Bill of Rights. The framers of the Constitution added the first ten amendments to help protect individual rights. For example, the Bill of Rights protects freedom of speech, press, and religion, as well as the right to a fair trial.

The federal government includes an elected president and Congress. Congress, the **legislative branch,** is responsible for making laws. There are two parts of Congress—the House of Representatives and the Senate. The **executive branch,** which includes the president, vice-president, and the president's cabinet, carries out and enforces laws. The federal government also includes a **judicial branch** of judges, who are appointed, not elected. The judicial branch interprets the laws in court cases. Sometimes, judges decide if laws violate the Constitution.

In general, the federal government handles issues affecting the whole country, like trade between countries and states and issues relating to national security. The federal government also provides services like national parks, Social Security, and military protection. Under the U.S. Constitution, many powers are left to the 50 state governments.

State and Local Governments State governments are based on each state's constitution. State constitutions set the rules for how each state's government works. State constitutions must not violate the U.S. Constitution or individual freedoms protected by the Constitution. Since state

Historical Source

The Constitution

On September 17, 1787, state delegates gathered in Philadelphia to create a constitution, a written statement of the powers and functions of the new government of the United States. The Preamble, or introduction, to the U.S. Constitution is shown below. It states the document's general purpose.

"We the People of the United States, in order to form a more perfect Union, establish justice, insure domestic tranquility, <u>provide for the common defense</u>, promote the general welfare, and secure the blessings of liberty to <u>ourselves and our posterity</u>, do ordain and establish this Constitution for the United States of America."

Americans wanted peace within the United States and a national military force.

They wanted to ensure freedoms for themselves and for future generations.

Analyze Sources
How do you think the ideas that appear in the Preamble affect your daily life?

constitutions are different from each other, each state's government is unique. However, all state governments have three branches, just like the federal government.

All states have an elected governor as the head of the executive branch, a legislative branch of elected members, and a judicial branch. In some states, judges are elected, while in others, they are appointed. State governments issue licenses, birth certificates, and death certificates; set, enforce, and interpret state laws; and run elections.

Counties and cities also have their own local governments, usually with executive, legislative, and judicial branches. Local elected leaders may include mayors, county commissioners, city councilors, judges, and school board members. Many local governments provide services to the community such as trash collection, road building, water, and public transportation. Local governments also run public schools. Federal, state, and local governments all provide services paid for with revenue from taxes.

Rights and Responsibilities of Citizens American citizens have many rights and responsibilities, including the right to vote. Voting for leaders is one way that the value of democracy is shown at all levels of government. Starting at age 18, U.S. citizens are allowed to vote. In order to vote, you have to register. In many states, you register for a particular political party. Political parties are organized groups of people who have similar views about government and issues. People in political parties work together to win elections and shape policies. Political parties also raise money to fund candidates' campaigns and promote the party's agenda, or platform.

During an election, there are usually primary elections where voters choose which candidates will represent each political party. In states with closed primaries, like Pennsylvania and Maryland, only voters registered in a particular party can vote in that party's primary. Other states, like Georgia and Montana, allow voters to choose which party's primary to vote in on Election Day. After each political party chooses a candidate in the primary election, these candidates run against each other in the general election. The winner of the general election takes office and helps to lead the community.

Link to Civics

How a Bill Becomes a Law

Laws can be written and changed by Congress. The steps for how to write laws are part of the Constitution.

❶ A member of the House or the Senate introduces a bill and refers it to a committee.

❷ The House or Senate Committee may approve, rewrite, or kill the bill.

❸ The House or the Senate debates and votes on its version of the bill.

❹ House and Senate conference committee members work out the differences between the two versions.

❺ Both houses of Congress pass the revised bill.

❻ The president signs or vetoes the bill.

❼ Two-thirds majority vote of Congress is needed to approve a vetoed bill. The bill becomes a law.

Analyze Information
Why do you think the framers created this complex system for adopting laws?

The Bill of Rights

The Bill of Rights is the first ten amendments to the Constitution.	
1st Amendment	Protects freedom of religion, speech, press, assembly, petition
2nd Amendment	Protects the right to keep and bear arms
3rd Amendment	Provides restrictions on quartering soldiers in citizens' homes
4th Amendment	Bans unreasonable searches or seizures
5th Amendment	Protects citizens against self-incrimination and being tried twice for the same crime; prohibits the government from depriving citizens of life, liberty, or property without due process of law
6th Amendment	Protects citizens' right to a swift and fair trial
7th Amendment	Guarantees right to trial by jury
8th Amendment	Protects citizens against cruel and unusual punishment
9th Amendment	States that citizens have rights beyond those specifically written in the Constitution
10th Amendment	States that powers not given to the government are reserved to the states, or to the people

Analyze Information
What problems with government do you think the framers wanted to avoid by writing these amendments?

In addition to voting, citizens are also encouraged to play an active role in government. For example, Americans can call or write their public officials to ask them to help solve problems in their communities. When many citizens have the same goal about a specific issue, they may form an interest group. Interest groups lobby, or advocate, at a federal, state, or local level to persuade elected officials. Citizens can also run for state, local, or federal elected office.

Other responsibilities include paying taxes and serving on a jury. By serving on a jury, citizens help the court system resolve conflicts between people and make sure justice is carried out. Jurors decide if people are guilty and sometimes decide what a fair outcome or punishment would be. Without people participating in their government, the democratic process suffers.

Reading Check Compare How are federal, state, and local governments similar?

People and Culture

Many Americans are descended from European immigrants. However, the United States is also home to people of many other cultures and ethnic groups. Immigration has led to cultural diffusion. As a result, the United States is a diverse nation, where many languages are spoken and different religions and customs are practiced. The blending of these different cultures has helped produce a unique American culture.

Ethnic Groups in the United States Some ethnic groups in the United States include Native Americans, African Americans, Hispanic Americans, and Asian Americans. As you will see on the maps about the distribution of ethnic groups in the United States, higher percentages of these ethnic groups are concentrated in different areas of the United States.

For thousands of years, Native Americans were the only people living in the Americas. Today, most Native Americans live in the western United States. Many Native Americans are concentrated in Arizona and New Mexico.

Even though African Americans live in every region of the country, some areas of the United States have a higher percentage of African Americans. For example, a higher percentage of African Americans live in southern states. Many large cities also have a high percentage of African Americans. On the other hand, descendants of people who came from Asian countries, or Asian Americans, are mostly concentrated in California.

Many Hispanic Americans originally migrated to the United States from Mexico, Cuba, and other Latin American countries. As you can see on the map of Hispanic Americans, a higher percentage of Hispanic Americans live in the southwestern states. These states border Mexico.

People and organizations from all of these ethnic groups have made important contributions in the areas of history, culture, government, and economy. For example, Chinese immigrants constructed a lot of the railroads in the 1800s. They helped to connect the vast country and allowed goods and people to flow from coast to coast. George Washington Carver, an African American man, improved the economy of the South by developing new uses for crops, including using peanuts to make peanut butter.

Language In many parts of the country, English is just one of many languages you might hear. Are you or is someone you know bilingual? People who speak two languages are **bilingual.**

Today, more than 60 million U.S. residents speak a language other than English at home. These languages include Spanish, French, Chinese, Vietnamese, Arabic, Tagalog, and many others. After English, Spanish is the most widely spoken language in the United States. About 37 million Americans speak Spanish at home. Many of these people live near the border between the United States and Mexico and in Florida and Puerto Rico.

Religion Americans also practice many religious faiths. Over time, people with different religious beliefs have come to the United States and brought their religious traditions with them. The majority are Christians, as were the first European colonists. However, some are Jewish or Muslim, and a smaller percentage are Hindu, Buddhist, or Sikh. To many, religious groups are important social organizations. Your community might have Christian churches, Jewish synagogues, Islamic mosques, Hindu temples, or Sikh gurdwaras, as well as other places of worship. Many religious groups also provide services like soup kitchens and homeless shelters to those in need.

A variety of traditional religious holidays are celebrated in the United States. Christians celebrate Jesus' birth at Christmas and Jesus' resurrection at Easter. Jews observe Yom Kippur—also known as Day of Atonement—and Rosh Hashanah, the Jewish New Year. Muslims fast during the month of Ramadan, a time when they believe the Qur'an, their holy scripture, was revealed to Muhammad. Hindus celebrate Diwali, a festival of lights that symbolizes the victory of good over evil. Sikhs commemorate the establishment of a formalized Sikh community called the Khalsa in the 1690s with a festival called Vaisakhi.

Distribution of Selected Ethnic Groups, 2010

These maps show population information from the U.S. Census. Every ten years, Americans answer census questions about their race or ethnic group.

Hispanic Americans

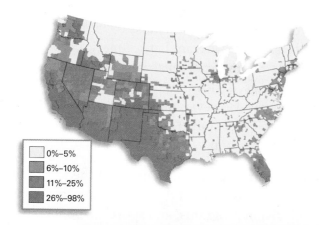

- 0%–5%
- 6%–10%
- 11%–25%
- 26%–98%

Native Americans

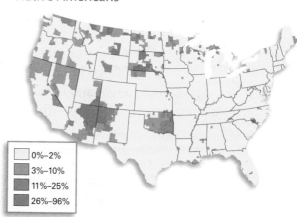

- 0%–2%
- 3%–10%
- 11%–25%
- 26%–96%

Diverse America

People of different ethnic groups enjoy a parade in Washington, DC. Like most large American cities, Washington has a very diverse population. About 50 percent of Washington's population is African American. Hispanic Americans make up about 10 percent of the city's population, and Asian Americans make up about 4 percent.

African Americans

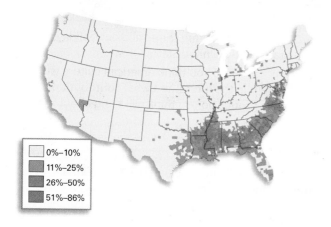

- 0%–10%
- 11%–25%
- 26%–50%
- 51%–86%

Asian Americans

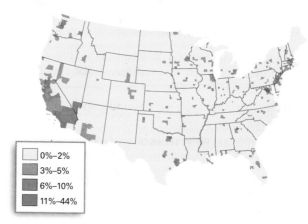

- 0%–2%
- 3%–5%
- 6%–10%
- 11%–44%

Source: U.S. Census Bureau

Interpret Maps

1. **Region** In what region of the United States does the highest percentage of African Americans live?

2. **Region** Why do you think many Hispanic Americans live in the southwestern United States?

Foods and Music Diversity shows itself through cultural practices. In addition to language and religion, cultural practices include the food we eat and the music we listen to.

America's food is as diverse as the American people. Think about some of the foods you have eaten this week. You may have eaten Mexican tacos, Italian pasta, or Japanese sushi. These dishes are now part of the American diet.

Different types of music from around the world have also influenced American culture. For example, salsa music from Latin America is popular in the United States today. Many American musicians now combine elements of salsa into their pop songs. African rhythms and instruments have also influenced American music. However, music that originated in the United States is also popular in other countries. American musical styles include blues, jazz, rock, and hip hop.

American Popular Culture As the most powerful country in the world, the United States has tremendous influence around the world. American popular culture, such as movies, television programs, and sports, is popular elsewhere. For example, American movies are seen by millions of people around the world. Other examples of American culture in other places include the popularity of baseball in Japan, American fast food restaurants in almost every major city in the world, and American television programs and channels broadcasting around the world. As you can see, Americans influence the rest of the world in many ways through their culture.

Reading Check
Form Generalizations
How has cultural diversity enriched life in the United States?

Summary and Preview The history of the United States has helped shape the diverse, democratic nation it is today. In the next lesson, you will learn about the different regions of the United States and the issues the country is facing today.

Lesson 2 Assessment

Review Ideas, Terms, and Places

1. **a. Identify and Explain** What are some cities that were important locations in U.S. history? What happened in those cities?

   b. Analyze What role did covered wagons play in U.S. history?

   c. Summarize What types of conflicts impacted the history of the United States?

2. **a. Identify** What ideals have shaped government in the United States?

   b. Describe What are the different levels of government, and what services do they provide?

   c. Evaluate Which right or responsibility of American citizens do you think is most important? Why?

3. **a. Recall** What language other than English is widely spoken in the United States?

   b. Summarize What are some religious holidays celebrated in the United States?

   c. Predict How do you think American culture will be different in the future, and what contributions of diverse groups do you think will bring about the changes?

Critical Thinking

4. **Summarize** Fill out the diagram and label the three branches of government. In the box for each branch, write a sentence summarizing that branch's responsibilities.

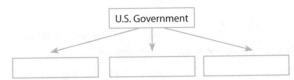

U.S. Government

The United States Today

The Big Idea

The United States has four main regions and faces opportunities and challenges.

Main Ideas

- The United States has four regions—the Northeast, the South, the Midwest, and the West.
- The United States has a strong economy and a powerful military but is facing the challenge of world terrorism.

Key Terms and Places

Washington, DC
Detroit
Chicago
Seattle
terrorism

If YOU lived there . . .

You and your family run a small resort hotel in Fort Lauderdale, on the east coast of Florida. You love the sunny weather and the beaches there. Now your family is thinking about moving the business to another region where the tourist industry is important. They have looked at ski lodges in Colorado, lake cottages in Michigan, and hotels on the coast of Maine.

How will you decide among these different regions?

Regions of the United States

Because the United States is such a large country, geographers often divide it into four main geographic and economic regions. These are the Northeast, the South, the Midwest, and the West. You can see the four regions on the map Regions of the United States. Find the region where you live. You probably know more about your own region than you do the other three. The population, resources, and economies of the four regions are similar in some ways and unique in others.

The Northeast The Northeast shares a border with Canada. The economy in this region is heavily dependent on banks, investment firms, and insurance companies. Education also contributes to the economy. The area's respected universities include Harvard and Yale.

Some natural resources of the Northeast states include rich farmland and huge pockets of coal. Having a valuable natural resource can lead to specialization in a region's economy. Since coal is used in the steelmaking process, the steel industry grew around the coal industry. The steel industry helped make Pittsburgh, in western Pennsylvania, the largest industrial city in the Appalachians. Today, Pittsburgh is no longer an industrial center, but it is still known as the "Steel City."

Today, fishing remains an important industry in the Northeast. Major seaports allow companies to ship their products to markets around the world. Cool, shallow waters off the Atlantic coast are good fishing areas. Cod and shellfish such as lobster are the most valuable seafood.

Population of Major U.S. Cities, 2015		
Rank	City	Population
1	New York	8,550,405
2	Los Angeles	3,971,883
3	Chicago	2,720,546
4	Houston	2,296,224
5	Philadelphia	1,567,442

Source: U.S. Census Bureau

Interpret Charts

Using the chart and the map Regions of the United States, what geographical feature are many populous cities located near?

The Northeast is the most densely populated region of the United States. Much of the Northeast is a megalopolis, a string of large cities that have grown together. This area stretches along the Atlantic coast from Boston to **Washington, DC.** The three other major cities in the megalopolis are New York, Philadelphia, and Baltimore.

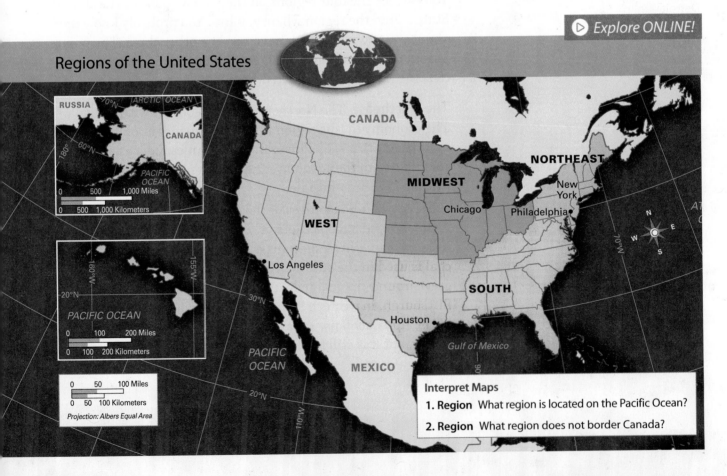

▶ Explore ONLINE!

Regions of the United States

Interpret Maps

1. **Region** What region is located on the Pacific Ocean?

2. **Region** What region does not border Canada?

New York, New York, is the largest city in the United States.

More than 51 million people live in this urban area. All of these cities, except for Washington, DC, were founded during the colonial era. They grew because they were important seaports. Today, these cities are industrial and financial centers. Cities with high population density tend to have more people employed as executives and scientists than rural areas. But with so many people, there are workers doing almost any job you can imagine—from chefs and window washers to court reporters and engineers.

The South The South is a region that includes long coastlines along the Atlantic Ocean and the Gulf of Mexico. Along the coastal plains, rich soils provide farmers with abundant crops of cotton, tobacco, and citrus fruit.

In recent years, the South has become more urban and industrial and is one of the country's fastest-growing regions. The warm climate attracts people and businesses to the South. The South's cities, such as Atlanta, have grown along with the economy. The Atlanta metropolitan area has grown from a population of only about 1 million in 1960 to more than 5 million today. As Atlanta has grown, the culture has become more diverse as people from all over the globe have settled there, bringing traditions with them from places like Somalia, Ethiopia, Korea, and Mexico.

Other places in the South have also experienced growth in population and industry. The Research Triangle in North Carolina is an area of high-tech companies and several large universities. The Texas Gulf Coast and the lower Mississippi River area have huge oil refineries and petrochemical plants. Their products, which include gasoline, are mostly shipped from the ports of Houston and New Orleans.

Millions of Americans vacation in the South, which makes the travel industry profitable in the region. Warm weather and beautiful beaches draw many vacationers to resorts in the South. You may not think of weather and beaches when you think about industry, but you should. Resort areas are an industry because they provide jobs and help local economies grow.

Many cities in the South trade goods and services with Mexico and countries in Central and South America. This trade is possible because several of the southern states are located near these countries. For example, Miami is an important trading port and travel connection with Caribbean countries, Mexico, and South America. Atlanta, Houston, and Dallas are also major transportation centers.

The Midwest The Midwest is one of the most productive farming regions in the world. The Mississippi River and many of its tributaries carry materials that help create the region's rich soils, which are good for farming. Midwestern farmers grow mostly corn, wheat, and soybeans. Farmers in the region also raise livestock such as dairy cows. Raising cattle for beef is also an important part of the economy in the Midwest, especially in states like Nebraska and Kansas.

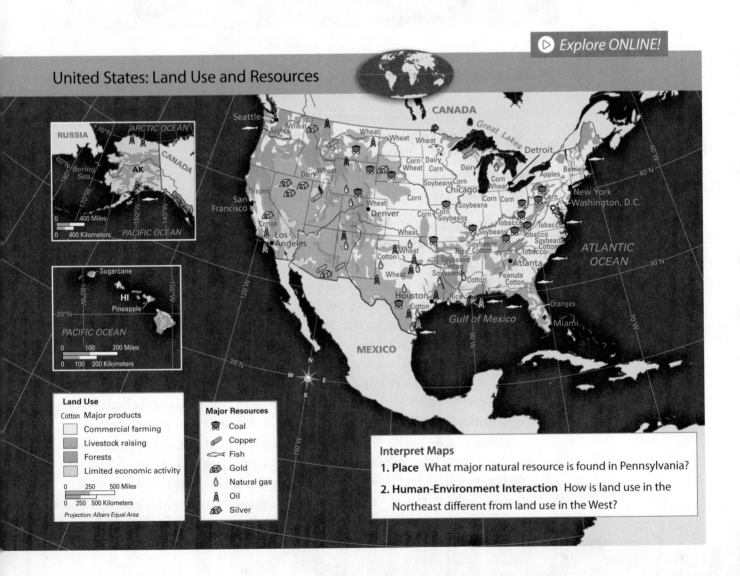

Explore ONLINE!

United States: Land Use and Resources

Land Use

Cotton Major products

☐ Commercial farming
☐ Livestock raising
☐ Forests
☐ Limited economic activity

0   250   500 Miles
0   250   500 Kilometers
Projection: Albers Equal Area

Major Resources

🜨 Coal
▱ Copper
🐟 Fish
⬗ Gold
◊ Natural gas
⚲ Oil
▱ Silver

Interpret Maps

1. **Place** What major natural resource is found in Pennsylvania?

2. **Human-Environment Interaction** How is land use in the Northeast different from land use in the West?

Farms with fertile soils, like this one in Wisconsin, cover much of the rural Midwest.

Large white containers, shown here at the Port of Houston, store oil from the Gulf Coast.

Analyze Visuals
How do the natural resources of these two areas impact the way the land is used?

The core of the Midwest's corn-growing region stretches from Ohio to Nebraska. Much of the corn is used to feed livestock, such as cattle and hogs.

To the north of the corn-growing region is an area of dairy farms. States with dairy farms are major producers of milk, cheese, and other dairy products. This area includes Wisconsin and most of Michigan and Minnesota. Much of the dairy farm region is pasture, but farmers also grow crops to feed dairy cows.

Many of the Midwest's farm and factory products are shipped to markets by water routes, such as those along the Ohio and Mississippi rivers. Another route is through the Great Lakes and the St. Lawrence Seaway to the Atlantic Ocean.

Most major cities in the Midwest are located on rivers or the Great Lakes. As a result, they are important transportation centers. Farm products, coal, and iron ore are easily shipped to these cities from nearby farms and mines. These natural resources support industries such as automobile manufacturing, so these cities are also often industrial areas. **Detroit,** Michigan, is one of many Midwest cities producing automobiles.

One of the busiest shipping ports on the Great Lakes is **Chicago,** Illinois. The city also has one of the world's busiest airports. Chicago's industries attracted many immigrants in the late 1800s. People moved here to work in the city's steel mills. Today, Chicago is the nation's third-largest city.

The West The West is the largest region in the United States. Many western states have large open spaces with few people. The West is not all open spaces, however. Many large cities are on the Pacific coast.

One state on the coast, California, is home to more than 10 percent of the U.S. population. California's mild climate and wealth of resources attract people to the state. Most Californians live in Los Angeles, San Diego, and the San Francisco Bay area. The center of the country's

One of the largest sections of coastal wilderness in the United States, shown here, stretches along the Pacific coast in Washington's Olympic National Park.

Academic Vocabulary
process a series of steps by which a task is accomplished

entertainment industry, Hollywood, is in Los Angeles. Farming and the technology industry are also important to California's economy.

The economy of other states in the West is dependent on ranching and growing wheat. Wheat is grown mostly in Montana, Idaho, and Washington.

Much of the farmland in the West must be irrigated, or watered. One method of irrigation uses long sprinkler systems mounted on huge wheels. The wheels rotate slowly. This sprinkler system waters the area within a circle. From the air, parts of the irrigated Great Plains resemble a series of green circles.

Other parts of the West are desert areas. Historically, people have not settled in these areas in large numbers.

The West also has rich deposits of coal, oil, gold, silver, copper, and other minerals. However, mining these minerals can cause problems. For example, coal miners in parts of the Great Plains use a **process** called strip mining, which strips away soil and rock to reach the coal. This kind of mining leads to soil erosion and other problems. Today, laws require miners to restore mined areas.

In Oregon and Washington, forestry and fishing are two of the most important economic activities. Seattle is Washington's largest city. The **Seattle** area is home to many important industries, including technology and aerospace companies. More than half of the people in Oregon live in and around Portland.

Alaska's economy is largely based on oil, forests, and fish. As in Washington and Oregon, people debate about developing these resources. Some people want to limit oil drilling in wild areas of Alaska. They are concerned about technological hazards such as oil spills. In the past, oil spills have damaged the environment, harmed animals, and impacted Native Alaskans. Other people want to expand drilling to produce more oil. They argue that expansion will provide more jobs and lower the cost of fuel.

Hawaii's natural beauty, mild climate, and fertile soils are its most important resources. The islands' major crops are seeds, macadamia nuts, and pineapples. Millions of tourists visit the islands each year.

Changes in the Nation

Because of its economic and military strength, the United States is often called the world's only superpower. In recent years, however, the United States has faced many challenges and changes.

Economy Technology, an abundance of natural resources, and plentiful jobs have helped make the United States' economy strong. The United States also benefits by cooperating with other countries. The three largest trading partners of the United States are Canada, China, and Mexico. In 1992 the United States, Mexico, and Canada signed the North American Free Trade Agreement, or NAFTA. This agreement made trade easier and cheaper between the three neighboring nations. However, some people worry that agreements like NAFTA harm workers in the United States. They believe that manufacturing jobs will be lost because workers in other countries will work for lower wages. They are concerned that companies will move their factories to these countries to save money on labor.

The U.S. economy has experienced significant ups and downs since the 1990s. In the 1990s the nation experienced the longest period of economic growth in its history. By the end of 2007, the United States faced a recession, or a sharp decrease in economic activity. In this recession, the housing market collapsed, major banks and businesses failed, and an estimated 8.4 million jobs were lost in the United States. Since markets around the world are increasingly connected due to globalization, the recession affected economies around the world.

The U.S. federal government responded to the economic crisis in several ways. The Federal Reserve, the central bank of the United States, lowered its interest rates. These rates determine the amount of interest that private banks pay to borrow money. When banks have to pay less, they lower their interest rates and charge their customers less. When people can borrow at lower rates, they spend more money. Increased spending can help improve the economy. Another way the federal government encouraged spending was by cutting taxes. With less money going to taxes, individuals would have more money to spend.

The United States also implemented policies and laws increasing government spending on projects such as building roads and schools in order to create more jobs and put more money into the economy. Another step the U.S. government took was to help banks that were failing. After these policies were implemented, the U.S. economy began to recover. While the recession was officially over in June 2009, some of its effects are still felt today, especially in areas where unemployment remains high.

The War on Terror In the 1990s the United States began to experience acts of terrorism. **Terrorism** is the threat or use of violence against civilians to intimidate or cause fear for political or social reasons. Some terrorists have been from foreign countries, whereas others have been U.S. citizens.

On September 11, 2001, the United States suffered the deadliest terrorist attack in the country's history when 19 terrorists hijacked four American jets. They crashed two into the World Trade Center in New York City and one into the Pentagon.

In response, President George W. Bush declared a "war on terrorism." He sent military forces to Afghanistan to kill or capture members of a terrorist group called al-Qaeda, which had planned the 9/11 attacks. Troops from other allied counties joined U.S. forces there. President Bush also viewed Iraqi dictator Saddam Hussein as a serious threat to Americans. In 2003 Bush sent U.S. troops into Iraq to remove Hussein from power.

President Obama took over the U.S. war on terror in 2009. U.S. forces killed Osama bin Laden, the mastermind of the 9/11 attacks in 2011. However, since then, other terrorist groups, such as the Islamic State in Iraq and the Levant (ISIL), and individuals influenced by ISIL have become a threat.

Today, world leaders continue to work with the United States to combat terrorism. In the United States, the Department of Homeland Security was established to prevent terrorist attacks on American soil. This federal department oversees many organizations including the U.S. Coast Guard, the Transportation Security Administration (TSA), and the Federal Emergency Management Agency (FEMA). Many other countries have also increased security within their borders, especially at airports.

Government In 2008 Barack Obama won the presidential election, becoming the nation's first African American president. President Obama succeeded in passing health care reform legislation and oversaw the

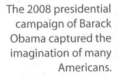

The 2008 presidential campaign of Barack Obama captured the imagination of many Americans.

Donald Trump and Hillary Clinton were the two major party candidates in the 2016 election.

withdrawal of U.S. troops from Iraq. Slow economic growth, unemployment, and high federal deficits were major issues during Obama's successful bid to win a second term in 2012.

During his second term, Obama worked on a variety of issues, including continuing to work to solve unemployment and combat terrorism. He also worked on improving relations with Cuba. Since 1961 the United States did not have diplomatic relations with Cuba, even though the two countries are only about 100 miles away from each other. The United States was opposed to Cuba's communist dictatorship, and Cold War hostilities between the countries led to tense situations. Beginning in 2014 President Obama set policies and made agreements with Cuba, allowing more travel to and trade with Cuba. He also reopened the U.S. Embassy in Cuba's capital, Havana.

During the 2016 election, Donald Trump, a business leader, was the Republican Party candidate. He defeated the Democratic Party candidate, Hillary Clinton, a former first lady, senator, and secretary of state. As in other recent elections, the economy and terrorism were two issues that concerned voters. Some voters were concerned about expanding trade with other countries and the decline of manufacturing jobs in the United States.

Issues of cultural conflict within the United States also were discussed during the election. These issues included the role racism plays in society and who should be allowed to immigrate to the United States. The candidates and their supporters also differed in how they thought religious values should be reflected in government and laws.

Summary In this lesson you learned about the geographic features, resources, and economic activities found in different regions of the United States. You also learned that the economy and terrorism are two important issues facing the country today.

Lesson 3 Assessment

Review Ideas, Terms, and Places

1. **a. Identify** What major cities are part of the largest megalopolis in the United States?

   b. Compare and Contrast How is the modification of the physical environment in the Midwest similar to and different from the modification of the physical environment in the South?

   c. Elaborate How are the regions of the United States different from one another?

   d. Explain How has the physical geography of the United States influenced the way people have settled there?

2. **a. Define** What is terrorism? What terrorist attack occurred in September 2001?

   b. Predict Effects What might happen to the national and local economies if the government cut spending on building roads and schools?

   c. Elaborate What have been the impacts of agreements that the United States has made with other countries in recent years?

Critical Thinking

3. **Find Main Ideas** In a table like the one below, list at least one main idea about the population, resources, and economy of each region.

	Northeast	South	Midwest	West
Population				
Resources				
Economy				

Social Studies Skills

Use a Political Map

Define the Skill

Many types of maps are useful in studying geography. Political maps are one of the most frequently used types of maps. These maps show human cultural features such as cities, states, and countries. Look at the map's legend to figure out how these features are represented on the map.

Most political maps show national boundaries and state boundaries. The countries on political maps are sometimes shaded different colors to help you tell where the borders of each country are located.

Learn the Skill

Use the political map here to answer the following questions.

1. What countries does this map show?

2. How does the map show the difference between state boundaries and national boundaries?

3. What is the capital of Canada?

Practice the Skill

Using an atlas or the Internet, find a political map of your state. Use that map to answer the following questions.

1. What is the state capital, and where is it located?

2. What other states or countries border your state?

3. What are two other cities in your state besides the capital and the city you live in?

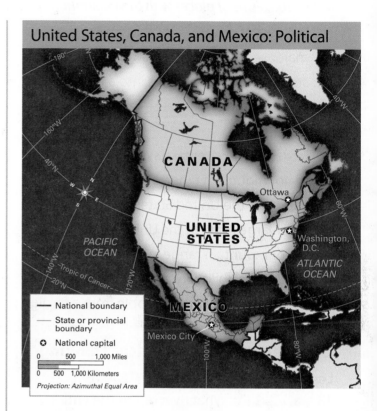

United States, Canada, and Mexico: Political

Module 6 Assessment

Review Vocabulary, Terms, and Places

Match the terms or places with their definitions or descriptions.

1. the part of government that makes the laws
2. major seaport in the British colonies
3. stream or river that flows into a larger stream or river
4. violent attacks that cause fear
5. first settlers
6. largest freshwater lake system in the world
7. major mountain range in the West
8. capital of the United States
9. third-largest city in the United States
10. major mountain range in the East
11. having the ability to speak two languages
12. territory controlled by people from a foreign land

a. Boston
b. Great Lakes
c. tributary
d. Rocky Mountains
e. colony
f. Appalachian Mountains
g. pioneers
h. bilingual
i. legislative branch
j. Washington, DC
k. Chicago
l. terrorism

Comprehension and Critical Thinking

Lesson 1

13. a. **Identify** What river drains the entire Interior Plains and is the longest river in North America?

    b. **Contrast** How are the Appalachians different from the Rocky Mountains?

    c. **Elaborate** Imagine you live in Tornado Alley. How would your life be affected by the interaction of physical processes and the environment?

Lesson 2

14. a. **Define** Who were the pioneers?

    b. **Compare and Contrast** Look at a copy of your state's constitution and a copy of the U.S. Constitution. How are the basic ideals in them alike? How are the specific rules about the structure and function of government different?

    c. **Draw Conclusions** How has the United States changed since its beginnings? What has remained the same?

    d. **Elaborate** How has American culture influenced cultures around the world?

Lesson 3

15. a. **Recall** What are the four regions of the United States?

    b. **Compare** Is corn grown mostly in the Midwest or the South?

    c. **Identify and Explain** What is one example of the United States cooperating with another culture? Explain how the United States cooperates with this culture.

    d. **Make Inferences** Look at the map United States: Land Use and Resources and the photos in Lesson 3. How might the location of natural resources affect technology use?

Reading Skills

Categorize *Use the Reading Skills taught in this module to answer the question about the reading selection below.*

> The federal government includes an elected president and Congress. Congress, the legislative branch, is responsible for writing laws. The executive branch, which includes the president, vice-president, and president's cabinet, carries out and enforces laws. The federal government also includes a judicial branch of judges, who are appointed, not elected. The judicial branch interprets the laws in court cases. Sometimes, judges decide if laws violate the Constitution.

16. What are two or three possible categories into which you could place information from the passage?

17. List one detail that could go in each possible category.

Social Studies Skills

Use a Political Map *Use the Social Studies Skills taught in this module to answer the questions about a political map of the United States.*

18. What four states border Mexico?

19. What river forms the boundary between Illinois and Missouri?

Map Activity

20. **The United States** On a sheet of paper, match the letters on the map with their correct labels.

Great Lakes	Rocky Mountains
Mississippi River	Pacific Ocean
Atlantic Ocean	Alaska

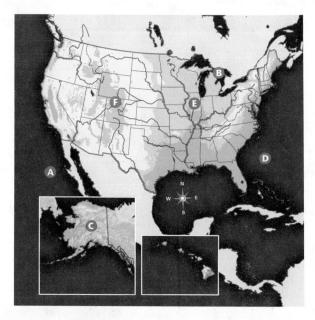

Focus on Writing

21. **Make a Brochure** The United States has a diverse population and a varied landscape. Your community is a part of this country. Decide whether you would like to research your state or local community. Make a brochure that explains your community's history, government, geography, and culture. First, research and gather valid and relevant primary and secondary sources and images you need to explain your community in your brochure. Then, create your brochure. Be sure to include at least one image for each topic you cover. Also include at least one historical artifact that helps to explain your community. Write captions for your images. Make sure your brochure is organized and clear. Check your brochure for spelling and grammar.

THE *American* REVOLUTION

The American Revolution led to the formation of the United States of America in 1776. Beginning in the 1760s, tensions grew between American colonists and their British rulers when Britain started passing a series of new laws and taxes for the colonies. With no representation in the British government, however, colonists had no say in these laws, which led to growing discontent. After fighting broke out in 1775, colonial leaders met to decide what to do. They approved the Declaration of Independence, announcing that the American colonies were free from British rule. In reality, however, freedom would not come until after years of fighting.

Explore some of the people and events of the American Revolution online. You can find a wealth of information, video clips, primary sources, activities, and more through your online textbook.

> "I know not what course others may take; but as for me, give me liberty or give me death!"
>
> —Patrick Henry

"Give Me Liberty or Give Me Death!"
Read an excerpt from Patrick Henry's famous speech, which urged the colonists to fight against the British.

Seeds of Revolution
Watch the video to learn about colonial discontent in the years before the Revolutionary War.

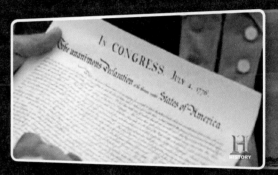

Independence!
Watch the video to learn about the origins of the Declaration of Independence.

Victory!
Watch the video to learn how the American colonists won the Revolutionary War.

Canada

GREENLAND
(DENMARK)

Essential Question

Do Canada's many regional differences strengthen or weaken the country?

In this module, you will learn about Canada, our neighbor to the north, including its history, diverse culture, and natural beauty and resources.

What You Will Learn

▷ Explore ONLINE!

HISTORY.

VIDEOS, including . . .
• Technology of the Ice Road
• The Vikings: Voyage to America

✓ Document-Based Investigations

✓ Graphic Organizers

✓ Interactive Games

✓ Channel One News Video: Geo Quiz: Arctic Summer

✓ Image with Hotspots: An Early Inuit Family

✓ Image Carousel: Canada's Diverse History

✓ Interactive Map: Regions of Canada

Geography Canada's physical geography ranges from the rocky Atlantic coast, shown here, to vast interior plains and mountains in the west.

Culture Ice hockey is Canada's national sport. Many Canadians grow up playing on frozen lakes.

History Since 1867, leaders of Canada's democratic government have met in the nation's parliament building in Ottawa.

Reading Social Studies

Understand Lists

READING FOCUS

A to-do list can keep you focused on what you need to get done. Keeping lists while you read can keep you focused on understanding the main points of a text. In the example below, a list helps the reader identify and focus on the types of cold climates found in central and northern Canada.

The farther north you go in Canada, the colder it gets. The coldest areas of Canada are located close to the Arctic Circle. Much of central and northern Canada has a subarctic climate. The far north has tundra and ice cap climates. About half of Canada lies in these extremely cold climates.

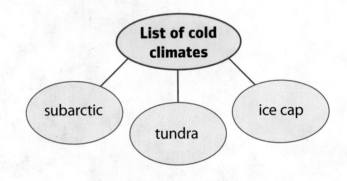

YOU TRY IT!

Read the sentences and then list the territories that make up the Canadian North region.

Northern Canada is extremely cold because of its location close to the Arctic Circle. The region called the Canadian North includes the Yukon Territory, the Northwest Territories, and Nunavut. These three territories cover more than a third of Canada but are home to only about 100,000 people.

As you read this module, look for lists that help you focus on the main points you are studying.

Physical Geography

The Big Idea

Canada is a huge country with a northerly location, cold climates, and rich resources.

Main Ideas

- A huge country, Canada has a wide variety of physical features, including rugged mountains, plains, and swamps.

- Because of its northerly location, Canada is dominated by cold climates.

- Canada is rich in natural resources like fish, minerals, fertile soil, and forests.

Key Terms and Places

Rocky Mountains
St. Lawrence River
Niagara Falls
Canadian Shield
Grand Banks
pulp
newsprint

If YOU lived there . . .

You live in Winnipeg, Manitoba, in central Canada. Your hiking club is trying to decide where to go on a trip this summer. Since you live on the plains, some people want to visit the rugged Rocky Mountains in the west. Others want to travel north to Hudson Bay to see polar bears and other wildlife. Others would rather hike in the east near the Great Lakes and Niagara Falls.

Which place will you choose for this year's trip?

Physical Features

Did you know that Canada is the second-largest country in the world? Russia is the only country in the world that is larger than Canada. The United States is the third-largest country in the world and shares many physical features with Canada.

Locate Canada on the map further on in this section, and see if you can find the physical features that the United States and Canada share. You may notice that mountains along the Pacific coast and the **Rocky Mountains** extend north into western Canada from the western United States. Broad plains stretch across the interiors of both countries. In the east, the two countries share a natural border formed by the **St. Lawrence River.** An important international waterway, the St. Lawrence links the Great Lakes to the Atlantic Ocean.

The United States and Canada also share a spectacular physical feature called **Niagara Falls.** The falls are located on the Niagara River between the province of Ontario and New York

Mist rises over Niagara Falls, where the Niagara River forms a natural boundary between the United States and Canada.

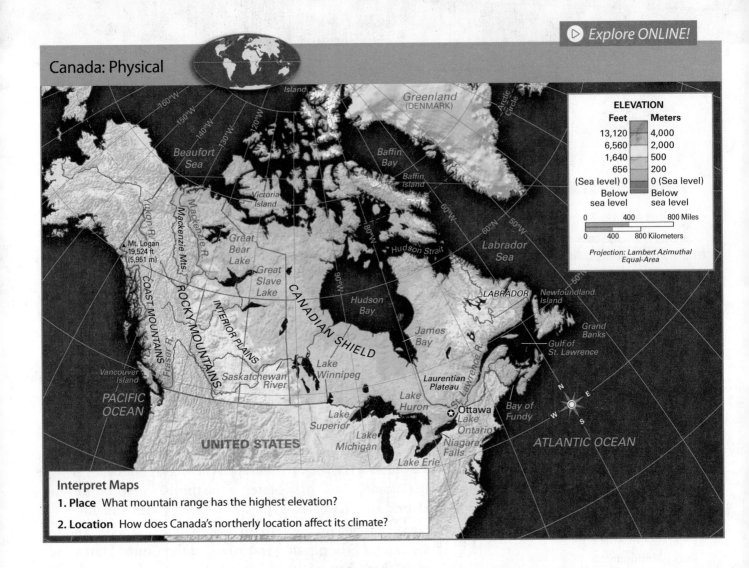

Canada: Physical

ELEVATION

Feet		Meters
13,120		4,000
6,560		2,000
1,640		500
656		200
(Sea level) 0		0 (Sea level)
Below sea level		Below sea level

0 400 800 Miles
0 400 800 Kilometers

Projection: Lambert Azimuthal Equal-Area

Interpret Maps

1. **Place** What mountain range has the highest elevation?

2. **Location** How does Canada's northerly location affect its climate?

State. Created by the waters of the Niagara River, the falls flow between two of the Great Lakes—Lake Erie and Lake Ontario. The falls here plunge an average of 162 feet (49 m) down a huge ledge. That is higher than many 15-story buildings!

Canada has a region of rocky uplands, lakes, and swamps called the **Canadian Shield.** See on the map how this feature curves around Hudson Bay. The Shield covers about half the country.

Farther north, Canada stretches all the way up to the Arctic Ocean. The land here is covered with ice year-round. Ellesmere Island is very rugged, with snow-covered mountains and jagged coastlines. Very few people live this far north, but wildlife such as the polar bear and the Arctic wolf have adapted to the harsh environment.

Climate

Canada's location greatly influences the country's climate. Canada is located far from the equator at much higher latitudes than the United States. This more northerly location gives Canada cool to freezing temperatures year-round.

Reading Check
Summarize
What are the major physical features of Canada?

Banff National Park
Some of Canada's most spectacular scenery is found here in the Rockies at Banff National Park.

Reading Check
Categorize
What are Canada's climates?

The farther north you go in Canada, the colder it gets. The coldest areas of Canada are located close to the Arctic Circle. Much of central and northern Canada has a subarctic climate. The far north has tundra and ice cap climates. About half of Canada lies in these extremely cold climates.

The central and eastern parts of southern Canada have a much different climate. It is humid and relatively mild. However, the mildest area of Canada is along the coast of British Columbia. This location on the Pacific coast brings rainy winters and mild temperatures. Inland areas of southern Canada are colder and drier.

More than 80 percent of Canadians live in urban areas. Many of these cities are located in provinces that border the United States, where the weather is relatively mild.

Resources

Canada is incredibly rich in natural resources such as fish, minerals, and forests. Canada's Atlantic and Pacific coastal waters are among the world's richest fishing areas. Off the Atlantic coast lies a large fishing ground near Newfoundland and Labrador called the **Grand Banks.** Here, cold waters from the Labrador Sea meet the warm waters of the Gulf Stream. These conditions are ideal for the growth of tiny organisms, or plankton, that fish like to eat. As a result, large schools of fish gather at the Grand Banks.

Canada   **227**

Agriculture in Ontario

In this satellite image, crop fields in different stages of growth appear scattered throughout the province of Ontario. These rectangular fields of vegetation appear red at their height of growth and white after the crops are harvested. Rich soils and a mild climate in this region, which lies north of Lake Erie, make it one of Canada's most fertile regions. Crops grown here include wheat, soybeans, corn, and a variety of vegetables. Some of these crops are exported to the United States through the Canadian port of Windsor to Detroit, Michigan, just across the Detroit River. Both cities appear in this image as shades of blue and brown.

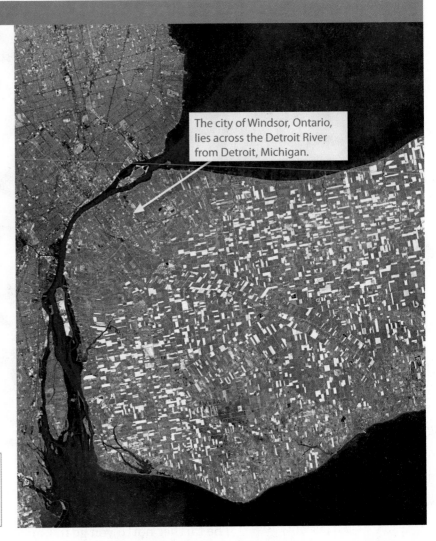

The city of Windsor, Ontario, lies across the Detroit River from Detroit, Michigan.

Analyze Information
What is the economy of southern Ontario based on?

Canada faces challenges protecting some of its water-related resources. For instance, recent overfishing of the Grand Banks region has left many fishers in Canada unemployed. Also, acid rain has harmed its lakes and rivers, including the Great Lakes region. Acid rain is a form of pollution in which rain becomes acidic because of the particles that are released when cars, factories, and power stations burn fuels. In response to this problem, Canada passed a law limiting this kind of pollution and instituted a program to watch for and measure it. The goal of the law is to protect this sensitive area from acid rain.

Minerals are also valuable resources in Canada. The Canadian Shield contains many mineral deposits. Canada is a main source of the world's nickel, zinc, and uranium. Lead, copper, gold, and silver are also important resources. Saskatchewan has large deposits of potash, a mineral used to make fertilizer. Alberta produces most of Canada's oil and natural gas.

Canada's climate supports vast areas of forests, which stretch across most of the country from Labrador to the Pacific coast. These trees provide lumber and pulp. **Pulp**—softened wood fibers—is used to make paper. The

Reading Check
Draw Conclusions
How do Canada's
major resources affect
its economy?

United States, the United Kingdom, and Japan get much of their newsprint from Canada. **Newsprint** is cheap paper used mainly for newspapers. Canada's many exports allow it to trade for items that it cannot produce as readily due to its climate, such as some kinds of fresh fruit and vegetables.

Summary and Preview In this lesson you learned that Canada shares many physical features with the United States. However, Canada's geography is also different. Due to its northerly location, Canada has a cold climate. Fish, minerals, fertile soil, and forests are all important natural resources. In the next lesson, you will learn about the history and culture of Canada.

Lesson 1 Assessment

Review Ideas, Terms, and Places

1. **a. Recall** What river links the Great Lakes to the Atlantic Ocean?

   b. Explain What physical features does Niagara Falls flow between?

   c. Geographic Questions Look at the map in this lesson. Pose and answer a question about Canada's physical geography.

2. **a. Describe** How is Canada's climate related to its northerly location?

   b. Draw Conclusions Locate Canada on the map in this lesson. Where would you expect to find Canada's coldest climate? Why?

3. **a. Define** What is the Grand Banks?

   b. Interpret How are Canada's forests a valuable resource?

Critical Thinking

4. **Generalize** Using your notes on Canada's resources, identify the location of each type of resource.

Resource	Location

History and Culture

The Big Idea

Canada's history and culture reflect Native Canadian and European settlement, immigration, and migration to cities.

Main Ideas

- Beginning in the 1600s, Europeans settled the region that would later become Canada.

- Immigration and migration to cities have shaped Canadian culture.

Key Terms and Places

Quebec
provinces
British Columbia
Toronto

If YOU lived there . . .

You own a general store in Calgary, Alberta, in the early 1880s. Your town is a center for agriculture and ranching on the prairies around you. Still, it sometimes feels very isolated. You miss your family in Ontario. Now the news comes that the Canadian Pacific Railway will soon reach Calgary. It will connect the town with all of central and eastern Canada.

How will the railroad change your life?

History

As the ice sheets of the ice ages melted, people moved into all areas of what is now Canada. As they did elsewhere in the Americas, these ancient settlers adapted to the physical environment.

Native Canadians Native peoples such as the Inuit (IH-nu-wuht) peoples and others were the first Canadians. Over the years, some of these native peoples divided into groups that became known as the First Nations. One group living on Canada's vast interior plains, the Cree, were skilled bison hunters. In the far north, the Inuits adapted to the region's extreme cold, where farming was impossible. By hunting seals, whales, walruses, and other animals, the Inuits could feed, clothe, and house themselves. Today more than 1 million Aboriginals and Inuits live in Canada.

European Settlement Other people migrated to Canada from Europe. The first Europeans in Canada were the Vikings, or Norse. They settled on Newfoundland Island in about AD 1000 but later abandoned their settlements. In the late 1400s other Europeans arrived and explored Canada. Soon more explorers and fishers from western Europe began crossing the Atlantic.

Trade quickly developed between the Europeans and Native Canadians. Europeans valued the furs that Native Canadians supplied. The Canadians wanted European metal goods like axes and guns. Through trading, they began to also exchange food, clothing, and methods of travel.

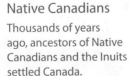

Native Canadians

Thousands of years ago, ancestors of Native Canadians and the Inuits settled Canada.

British settlement

The British built forts throughout Canada, like this one in Halifax, Nova Scotia.

Academic Vocabulary
establish to set up or create

New France France was the first European country to successfully settle parts of what would become Canada. The French <u>established</u> Quebec City in 1608. They called their new territories New France. At its height, New France included much of eastern Canada and the central United States.

New France was important for several reasons. It was part of the French Empire, which provided money and goods to French settlers. It also served as a base to spread French culture.

France had to compete with Britain, another European colonial power, for control of Canada. To defend their interests against the British, the French built trade and diplomatic relationships with Native Canadians. They exported furs, fish, and other products from New France to other parts of their empire. In addition, the French sent manufactured goods from France to New France. French missionaries also went to New France to convert people to Christianity.

All of these efforts protected French interests in New France for 150 years, until the British finally defeated the French. Although it did not last, New France shaped Canada's cultural makeup. The descendants of French settlers form one of Canada's major ethnic groups today.

New France

Known as the founder of New France, explorer Samuel de Champlain established Quebec in 1608.

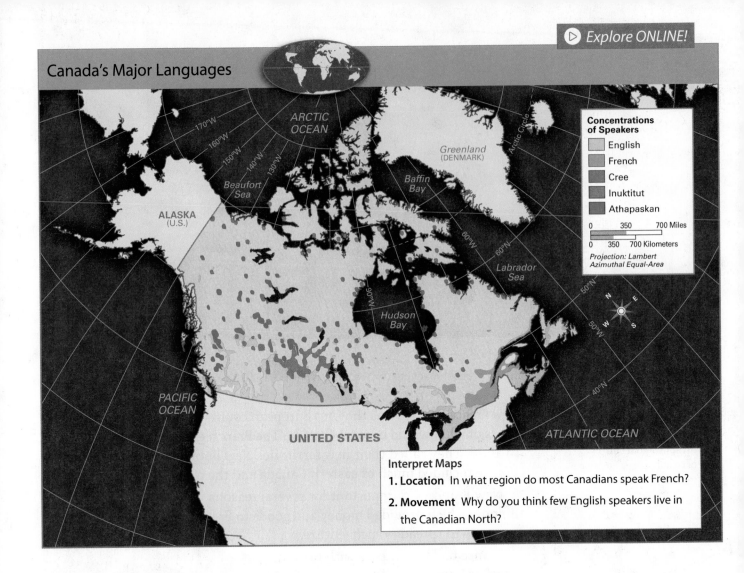

Explore ONLINE!

Concentrations of Speakers

- English
- French
- Cree
- Inuktitut
- Athapaskan

0   350   700 Miles
0   350   700 Kilometers

Projection: Lambert Azimuthal Equal-Area

Interpret Maps

1. **Location** In what region do most Canadians speak French?

2. **Movement** Why do you think few English speakers live in the Canadian North?

British Conquest In the mid-1700s the rivalry between France and England turned to war. The conflict was called the French and Indian War. This was the war that resulted in the British taking control of New France away from the French.

A small number of French went back to France. However, the great majority stayed. For most of them, few changes occurred in their daily activities. They farmed the same land, prayed in the same churches, and continued to speak French. England's passage of the Quebec Act in 1774 supported the French-speaking colonists by making it legal for Roman Catholics in Quebec to hold public office. Most of the French in Quebec were Roman Catholic, while English-speaking Canadian settlers tended to be Protestant. Few English-speaking settlers came to what is now called **Quebec.**

The British divided Quebec into two colonies. Lower Canada was mostly French-speaking, and Upper Canada was mostly English-speaking. The boundary between Upper and Lower Canada forms part of the border between the provinces of Quebec and Ontario today. **Provinces** are administrative divisions of a country. To the east, the colony of Nova Scotia (noh-vuh SKOH-shuh) was also divided. A new colony called New Brunswick was created where many of the British settlers lived.

Creation of Canada For several decades, these new colonies developed separately from each other. The colonists viewed themselves as different from other parts of the British Empire. Therefore, the British Parliament created the Dominion of Canada in 1867. A dominion is a territory or area of influence.

This founding document encouraged the colonists to look at themselves in a slightly different light. For Canadians, the creation of the Dominion was a step toward independence from Britain. Now the colonists needed to make some changes that might better help to unite their sprawling land. The motto of the new Dominion was "from sea to sea."

How would Canadians create a nation from sea to sea? With railroads. When the Dominion was established, Ontario and Quebec were already well served by railroads. **British Columbia,** on the Pacific coast, was not. To connect British Columbia with the provinces in the east, the Canadians built a transcontinental railroad. Completed in 1885, the Canadian Pacific Railway was Canada's first transcontinental railroad.

After the Canadian Pacific Railway linked the original Canadian provinces to British Columbia, Canada acquired vast lands in the north. Much of this land was bought from the Hudson's Bay Company, a large British fur-trading business. Most of the people living in the north were Native Canadians and people of mixed European and native ancestry. With the building of the railroad and the signing of treaties with Native Canadians, early Canadian settlers created a way for more people to settle Canada's new territories.

Reading Check
Summarize How was Canada linked from sea to sea?

Dominion of Canada
After 1867 Canadians created their own government and a mounted police force patrolled the border with the United States.

Canadian Pacific Railroad

Since 1885 the Canadian Pacific Railway has snaked through the Canadian Rockies on its way to the Pacific coast.

Canadian Ethnic Groups

Canada's ethnic diversity reflects its history, with settlers and immigrants coming to the country from all over the world. Many Canadians see the country's diversity as one of its strengths.

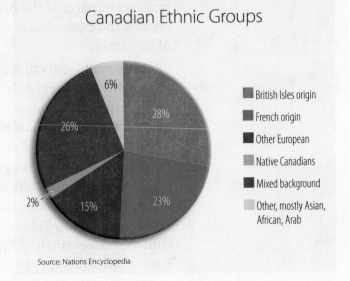

Canadian Ethnic Groups

- British Isles origin
- French origin
- Other European
- Native Canadians
- Mixed background
- Other, mostly Asian, African, Arab

28%
26%
6%
2%
15%
23%

Source: Nations Encyclopedia

Analyze Graphs
Which ethnic group makes up the largest percentage of Canada's population?

Culture

Canada's people reflect a history of British and French colonial rule. In addition, the country has experienced waves of immigration. The country is home to a great variety of people who belong to different ethnic groups and cultures. Although individual groups still keep their own cultural ways, many Canadians have tried to create a single national identity.

Immigration During the late 1800s and early 1900s, many immigrants came to Canada from Europe. Most were from Britain, Russia, and Germany. Some people also came from the United States. While most of these immigrants farmed, others worked in mines, forests, and factories. Other immigrants were lured to Canada in 1897 by the discovery of gold in the Yukon Territory. Many people from the United States migrated north in search of Canada's gold.

Immigrants also came to Canada from Asian countries, especially China, Japan, and India. British Columbia became the first Canadian province to have a large Asian minority. Many Chinese immigrants migrated to Canada to work on the railroads. Chinese immigrants built most of the Canadian Pacific Railway, one of the railroad lines linking eastern Canada to the Pacific coast.

All of these immigrants played an important part in an economic boom that Canada experienced in the early 1900s. During these prosperous times, Quebec, New Brunswick, and Ontario produced wheat, pulp, and paper. British Columbia and Ontario supplied the country with minerals and hydroelectricity. As a result, Canadians enjoyed one of the highest standards of living in the world by the 1940s.

Today, Canada values its immigrants. The government recognizes not only that immigrants historically helped build the country but continue to help build it today. In 2010 the country launched the Canadian Immigrant Integration Program (CIIP) to help immigrants prepare for success in their new country even before they leave their old one. The program connects them directly with resources they need, including employers and colleges, so that they are better prepared to take their place as part of the national fabric.

Many immigrant families strongly encourage their children to excel in school. While a good education often helps these second-generation Canadians to succeed, it can have less intended consequences. Immigrant children often learn and adopt the language and culture of their new country faster than their parents. In some families, parents depend on their children as translators in certain situations, but still expect their children to submit completely to their authority. This expectation, often seen in families from countries with strict cultural beliefs surrounding family roles, can lead to tension between the generations.

Movement to Cities After World War II, another wave of immigrants from Europe arrived in Canada. Many settled in Canada's large cities. For example, **Toronto** has become one of the most culturally diverse cities in the world. The Europeans were joined by other people from Africa, the Caribbean, Latin America, and particularly Asia. Asian businesspeople have brought a great deal of wealth to Canada's economy.

Toronto

With about 6 million people, Toronto is Canada's largest city.

Analyze Visuals
How is Toronto's history reflected in this city square?

Vancouver's Chinatown

If you walked around Vancouver, British Columbia, you would quickly realize when you entered the neighborhood of Chinatown. First you would notice that most signs are in Chinese and you would hear some people speaking Chinese. Then you would realize most restaurants serve Chinese food and shops sell colorful silk clothing, herbs, and art imported from China. If you were in the city for the Chinese New Year, you would probably see a parade of people in traditional Chinese dress. Vancouver's Chinatown is a unique place where Chinese culture is kept alive in Canada today.

Draw Conclusions
How is Vancouver's Chinatown a unique neighborhood?

Reading Check
Analyze How has immigration changed Canada?

Many Canadians have recently moved from farms to the country's cities. Some settlements in rural Canada have even disappeared because so many people left. Many Canadians have moved to cities in Ontario to find jobs. Others moved to Vancouver, British Columbia, for its good job opportunities, mild climate, and location near plentiful resources. Resources such as oil, gas, potash, and uranium have provided wealth to many cities in the Western Provinces. However, the political and economic center of power remains in the cities of Ottawa, Toronto, and Montreal.

Summary and Preview In this lesson you learned that Canada was greatly influenced by British and French settlement, the building of the railroad to the Pacific coast, immigration, and movement to cities. In the next lesson, you will learn about Canada's regions and economy today.

Lesson 2 Assessment

Review Ideas, Terms, and Places

1. **a. Recall** What is a province?
   b. Evaluate What are some cultural contributions of groups in Canada's past?
   c. Elaborate How do you think the Canadian Pacific Railway changed Canada?
2. **a. Identify** What immigrant group helped build the railroads?
   b. Draw Conclusions Why did people migrate to Canada?
   c. Elaborate Why do you think many Canadians moved from farms to the cities?

Critical Thinking

3. **Analyze** Draw a diagram like the one below. Using your notes, write a sentence in each box about how each topic influenced the next topic.

Railroad	Immigration	Cities

🌐
Canada Today

The Big Idea

Canada's democratic government oversees the country's regions and economy.

Main Ideas

- Canada has a democratic government with a prime minister and a parliament.
- Canada has four distinct geographic and cultural regions.
- Canada's economy is largely based on trade with the United States.

Key Terms and Places

regionalism
maritime
Montreal
Ottawa
Vancouver

If YOU lived there . . .

You and your family live in Toronto, Ontario. Your parents, who are architects, have been offered an important project in Montreal. If they accept it, you would live there for two years. Montreal is a major city in French-speaking Quebec. You would have to learn a new language. In Montreal, most street signs and advertisements are written in French.

How do you feel about moving to a city with a different language and culture?

Canada's Government

"Peace, order, and good government" is a statement from Canada's constitution that Canadians greatly value. The country's 1867 founding document provided the framework for Canada's current government. It has been amended and modified a number of times since then, but the constitution has maintained its basic structure. It still holds the force of the highest law in the land.

In part for historical reasons, Canada's government can be characterized as a constitutional monarchy. The monarch in the United Kingdom inherits the right to rule. Laws strictly limit the monarch's role in government. On the other hand, the royal influence can be seen in the often ceremonial duties of the governor general as the Queen's representative and head of state.

It's more accurate, however, to describe the country as a parliamentary democracy. Canadians are proud of their democratic government, which is led by a prime minister. Similar to a president, a prime minister is the head of a country's government.

Canada's prime minister oversees the country's parliament, Canada's governing body. Parliament consists of the House of Commons and the Senate. Canadians elect members of the House of Commons. Using the prime minister's recommendations, the governor general appoints senators. Legislation is proposed and debated in Parliament and must be approved by both the House and the Senate to become law.

Reading Check
Compare
How is Canada's government similar to that of the United States?

Canada's provincial governments are each led by a premier. These provincial governments take responsibility for education, health and social services, highways, the administration of justice, and local government within their province. They are much like our state governments.

Canada's central government is similar to our federal government. A federal government, or federation, unites several partially self-governing areas under one central (federal) umbrella. This idea was built into Canada's constitution right from the beginning. The Canadian federal system lets people keep their feelings of loyalty to their own province.

Canada's Regions

Canada's physical geography separates the country into different regions. For example, people living on the Pacific coast in British Columbia are isolated from Canadians living in the eastern provinces on the Atlantic coast. Just as geographic distance separates much of Canada, differences in culture also define regions.

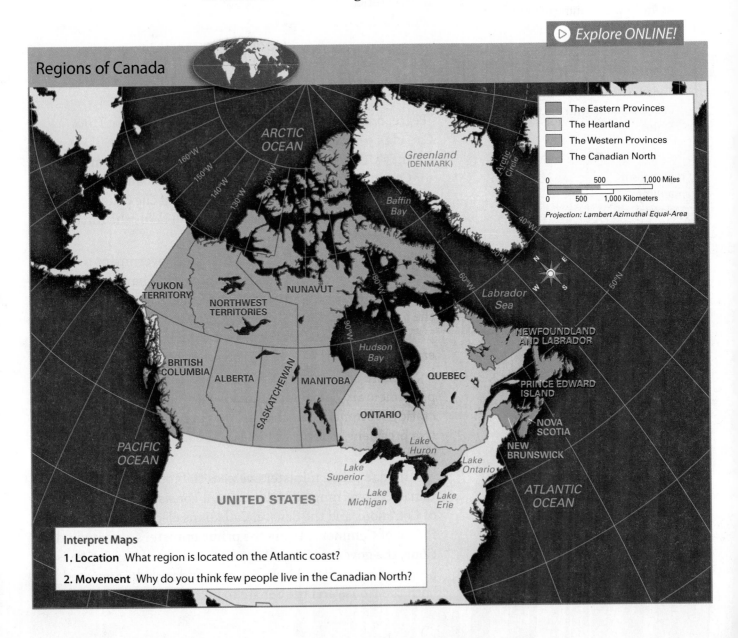

▷ Explore ONLINE!

Regions of Canada

- The Eastern Provinces
- The Heartland
- The Western Provinces
- The Canadian North

0   500   1,000 Miles
0   500   1,000 Kilometers
Projection: Lambert Azimuthal Equal-Area

Interpret Maps

1. **Location** What region is located on the Atlantic coast?

2. **Movement** Why do you think few people live in the Canadian North?

Regionalism The cultural differences between English-speaking and French-speaking Canadians have led to problems. English is the main language in most of Canada. In Quebec, however, French is the main language. When Canadians from different regions discuss important issues, they are often influenced by regionalism. **Regionalism** refers to the strong connection that people feel toward the region in which they live. In some places, this connection is stronger than people's connection to their country as a whole. To better understand regionalism in Canada, we will now explore each region of the country. As you read, use the Regions of Canada map to locate each region.

The Eastern Provinces The region called the Eastern Provinces lies on the Atlantic coast. The provinces of New Brunswick, Nova Scotia, and Prince Edward Island are often called the Maritime Provinces. **Maritime** means on or near the sea. The province of Newfoundland and Labrador is usually not considered one of the Maritime Provinces. It includes the island of Newfoundland and a large region of the mainland called Labrador.

A short growing season due to Canada's climate limits farming in the Eastern Provinces. However, farmers in Prince Edward Island grow potatoes. Most of the economy in Canada's Eastern Provinces is related to the forestry and fishing industries.

Many people in the Eastern Provinces are descendants of immigrants from the British Isles. In addition, French-speaking families have moved from Quebec to New Brunswick. Most of the region's people live in coastal cities. Many cities have industrial plants and serve as fishing and shipping ports. Along the Atlantic coast lies Halifax, Nova Scotia, the region's largest city.

The Heartland Inland from the Eastern Provinces are Quebec and Ontario, which together are sometimes referred to as the Heartland. More than half of all Canadians live in these two provinces. In fact, the chain of cities that extends from Windsor, Ontario, to the city of Quebec is the country's most urbanized region.

The provincial capital of Quebec is also called Quebec. The city's older section has narrow streets, stone walls, and French-style architecture. **Montreal** is Canada's second-largest city and one of the largest French-speaking cities in the world. About 3.8 million people live in the Montreal metropolitan area. It is the financial and industrial center of the province. Winters in Montreal are very cold. To deal with this harsh environment, Montreal's people use underground passages and overhead tunnels to move between buildings in the city's downtown.

In Canada many residents of Quebec, called Quebecois (kay-buh-KWAH), believe their province should be given a special status. Quebecois argue that this status would recognize the cultural differences between their province and the rest of Canada. Some even want Quebec to become an independent country. Indeed, referendums have been held twice in Quebec on that very issue, in 1980 and 1995. A third one was discussed, though not held, as recently as 2014. This separatist movement at times puts Quebec at odds with Canada's central government.

Many English-speaking Canadians think Quebec already has too many privileges. Most Canadians, however, still support a united Canada. Strong feelings of regionalism will continue to be an important issue.

With an even larger population than Quebec, the province of Ontario is Canada's leading manufacturing province. Hamilton, Ontario, is the center of Canada's steel industry. Canada exports much of its steel to the United States.

Ontario's capital, Toronto, is a major center for industry, finance, education, and culture. Toronto's residents come from many different parts of the world, including China, Europe, and India.

Canada's national capital, **Ottawa,** is also in Ontario. In Ottawa, many people speak both English and French. The city is known for its grand government buildings, parks, and several universities.

The Western Provinces West of Ontario are the prairie provinces of Manitoba, Saskatchewan, and Alberta. On the Pacific coast is the province of British Columbia. Together, these four provinces make up Canada's Western Provinces.

More people live in Quebec than in all of the prairie provinces combined. The southern grasslands of these provinces are part of a rich wheat belt. Farms here produce far more wheat than Canadians need. The extra wheat is exported. Oil and natural gas production is a very important economic activity in Alberta. The beauty of the Canadian Rockies attracts many visitors to national parks in western Alberta and eastern British Columbia.

British Columbia is Canada's westernmost province and home to almost 4 million people. This mountainous province has rich natural resources, including forests, salmon, and valuable minerals. Nearly half of British Columbia's population lives in and around the coastal city of **Vancouver.** The city's location on the Pacific coast helps it to trade with countries in Asia.

Daily Life in Nunavut
Even in June, snow covers the small town of Pond Inlet, Nunavut. The Inuits here travel by snowmobile and enjoy ice fishing.

The Canadian North Northern Canada is extremely cold because of its location close to the Arctic Circle. The region called the Canadian North includes the Yukon Territory, the Northwest Territories, and Nunavut (NOO-nuh-voot). These three territories cover more than a third of Canada but are home to only about 100,000 people.

Academic Vocabulary
distinct separate

Reading Check
Draw Conclusions
How does geography affect the location of economic activities in the Western Provinces?

Nunavut is a new territory created for the native Inuit people who live there. Nunavut means "Our Land" in the Inuit language. Even though Nunavut is part of Canada, the people there have their own **distinct** culture and government. About 30,000 people live in Nunavut.

The physical geography of the Canadian North includes forests and tundra. The frozen waters of the Arctic Ocean separate isolated towns and villages. During some parts of the winter, sunlight is limited to only a few hours.

Canada's Economy

As you learned in Lesson 1, Canada has many valuable natural resources. Canada's economy is based on the industries associated with these resources. In addition, Canada's economy also benefits from trade. Like the United States, Canada has a market-based, though mixed, economy. Some observers have noted that Canada's government involves itself more with its country's economy than the U.S. government involves itself with the U.S. economy.

Industries Thanks in part to the Canadian Shield, Canada is one of the world's leading mineral producers. Canadians mine valuable titanium, zinc, iron ore, gold, and coal. Canada's iron and steel industry uses iron ore to manufacture products like planes, automobiles, and household appliances. However, most Canadians work in the services industry. For example, tourism is Canada's fastest-growing services industry. Canada's economy also benefits from the millions of dollars visitors spend in the country each year.

Trade Canada's economy depends on trade. Many of Canada's natural resources that you have learned about are exported to countries around the world. Industries successful in trading grow and hire more workers. Trade also allows foreign companies to invest in Canada, which provides jobs to Canadians. Canada's leading trading partner is the United States.

As the world's largest trading relationship, Canada and the United States rely heavily on each other. About 50 percent of Canada's imported goods are from the United States. About 75 percent of Canada's exports, such as lumber, go to the United States.

However, the United States has placed tariffs, or added fees, on Canadian timber. American lumber companies accused Canada of selling their lumber at unfairly low prices. Canada argued that the tariffs were unfair according to the North American Free Trade Agreement (NAFTA).

The export of cattle to the United States has also been an area of dispute between the two countries. When a Canadian cow was discovered with

Trade with the United States	
Major Exports	**Major Imports**
• Petroleum products	• Automobiles and parts
• Automobiles and parts	• Chemicals
• Lumber	• Plastics

Lumber is just one of many items that make up the trade between Canada and the United States.

Advertising Canada to Tourists

Tourism is a huge part of Canada's economy. According to the country's national tourism marketing organization, tourism-related businesses supported more than 608,000 jobs in the Canadian economy. In 2010 the organization stopped promoting Canada as a vacation spot in the United States, focusing on China and other markets instead.

Canada did see more tourists from these developing markets, but visits from the U.S. declined. The head of Canada's national tourism marketing organization noted in 2015 that the country saw 3.8 million fewer international visitors since 2002, and 80 percent of those tourists lost were from the U.S. In response, Canada launched a three-year, $30 million advertising campaign, "Connecting America," to encourage more travelers from the United States to vacation in Canada.

Draw Conclusions
Why did tourism from the United States to Canada drop off between 2010 and 2015?

Canoeing is just one activity popular with tourists in Canada's Lake Algonquin National Park.

Reading Check
Summarize
What goods does Canada export?

mad cow disease in 2003, the United States placed an embargo, or ban, on the import of all cattle from Canada. Canadian ranchers now claim that all their cows are free of the disease. As of 2015, more than half of all Canadian meat exports go to the United States.

Canada does trade with a wide range of other countries for the commodities they offer. For example, in 2016 Canada began implementing a trade agreement with the European Union. Under this agreement, Canada increased its import quota for cheese. This agreement allows the EU to export more cheese to Canada.

Summary In this lesson you learned that Canada has distinct regions that are separated by both geography and culture. The United States and Canada share a common history, a border, and the English language.

Lesson 3 Assessment

Review Ideas, Terms, and Places

1. **a. Recall** What office heads Canada's government?
   b. Summarize How is Canada's parliament structured?
2. **a. Define** What is regionalism?
   b. Contrast How are Canada's Western Provinces different from the Canadian North?
   c. Evaluate Why do you think the Quebecois want to break away from Canada?
3. **a. Describe** How are Canada's natural resources important to the country's economy?
   b. Draw Conclusions Why do Canada and the United States rely on each other as trading partners?

Critical Thinking

4. **Compare and Contrast** Use your notes to complete this chart. List the similarities and differences between the Eastern Provinces and Western Provinces.

Similarities	Differences
1.	1.
2.	2.

Social Studies Skills

Use Mental Maps and Sketch Maps

Define the Skill

We create maps in our heads of all kinds of places—our schools, communities, country, and the world. These images, or mental maps, are shaped by what we see and experience.

We use mental maps of places when we draw sketch maps. A sketch map uses very simple shapes to show the relationship between places and regions and the relative size of places and regions. Notice the sketch map of the world shown here. It may not look like any other map in your book, but it does give you an idea of what the world looks like.

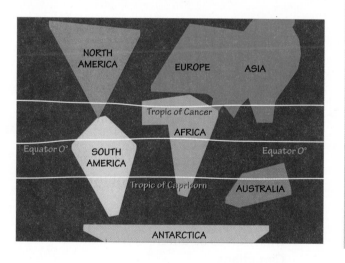

Learn the Skill

Does your mental map of the world look like the sketch map here? It is all right if they do not look exactly alike. Now think about the places in your own neighborhood. Use your mental map to draw a sketch map of your neighborhood. Then use your sketch map to answer the following questions and discuss your answers with a partner.

1. What are the most important features of your map? Describe these features to your partner.

2. What is the largest building in your neighborhood? Describe the building to your partner.

3. What labels did you use on your map?

Practice the Skill

Draw a sketch map of Canada. Make sure to include the cities, regions, and physical features you learned about in this module. Then exchange your map with another student. Ask your partner to make corrections to your map if he or she does not understand it.

Module 7 Assessment

Review Vocabulary, Terms, and Places

Choose the letter of the answer that best completes the statement or answers the question below.

1. A physical feature of rocky uplands, lakes, and swamps in Canada is called the
   - a. Niagara Falls.
   - b. Great Lakes.
   - c. Grand Banks.
   - d. Canadian Shield.

2. Which part of Canada did the French settle?
   - a. Ontario
   - b. New Brunswick
   - c. Quebec
   - d. British Columbia

3. What province was the first to have a large Asian population?
   - a. Manitoba
   - b. British Columbia
   - c. Quebec
   - d. Saskatchewan

4. A strong connection that people feel toward their region is called
   - a. maritime.
   - b. province.
   - c. heartland.
   - d. regionalism.

Comprehension and Critical Thinking

Lesson 1
5. a. **Define** What is pulp?
   b. **Make Inferences** What is the coldest area in Canada?
   c. **Evaluate** What makes the Grand Banks an ideal fishing ground?

Lesson 2
6. a. **Identify** Who were the first Canadians?
   b. **Draw Conclusions** Why did Canadians build a rail line across Canada?
   c. **Predict** Do you think Canada's cities will increase or decrease in population in the future? Explain your answers.

Lesson 3
7. a. **Recall** What kind of government does Canada have?
   b. **Compare and Contrast** How are the Eastern Provinces different from the Western Provinces?
   c. **Evaluate** Why do the Quebecois see themselves as different from other Canadians?

Module 7 Assessment, continued

Reading Skills

Understand Lists *Use the Reading Skills taught in this module to answer a question about the reading selection below.*

> Canada is one of the world's leading mineral producers. Canadians mine valuable titanium, zinc, iron ore, gold, and coal. Canada's iron and steel industry uses iron ore to manufacture products like planes, automobiles, and household appliances.

8. What minerals does Canada produce?

Social Studies Skills

9. **Use Mental Maps and Sketch Maps** Without looking at a map of Canada, think about what the Eastern Provinces look like. Then create a sketch map of the Eastern Provinces. Make sure to include a compass rose and important physical features.

Map Activity

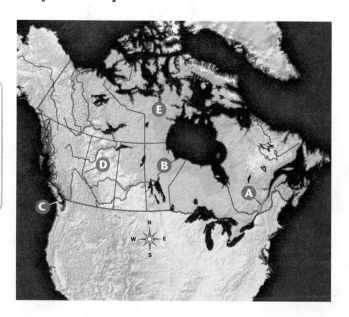

10. **Canada** On a separate sheet of paper, match the letters on the map with their correct labels.

Rocky Mountains   Manitoba

Nunavut   St. Lawrence River

Vancouver

11. **Create a Tourism Ad** Now that you have collected notes on Canada's geography, history, and culture, choose the information you think will most appeal to visitors. Write a one-minute radio script using descriptive and persuasive language to convince your audience to visit Canada. Consult the Internet and other sources for more information or examples of tourism ads. Describe Canada in a way that will capture your audience's imagination. Ask the class to listen carefully as you read your radio ad to them. Then ask the class to evaluate your ad on how persuasive it was or was not. When viewing other ads, make sure to listen and take note of any basic or academic vocabulary terms you may hear.

Early Civilizations of Latin America

Essential Question

Which early Latin American civilization was most successful?

About the Photo: The Maya built impressive pyramids in Central America. These ruins are in Tikal, Guatemala.

▶ *Explore ONLINE!*

HISTORY.

VIDEOS, including . . .
- Mexico's Ancient Civilizations
- Studying Glyphs
- The Search for Inca Gold

✓ Document-Based Investigations

✓ Graphic Organizers

✓ Interactive Games

✓ Interactive Map: Maya Civilization, c. 900

✓ Image with Hotspots: Tenochtitlán

✓ Image Carousel: Inca Arts

In this module, you will learn about the location, growth, and decline of early Latin American societies, including the Olmec, Maya, Aztec, and Inca civilizations.

What You Will Learn

The Maya Maya cities, ruled by local kings, traded items like jade and cacao with each other.

The Aztecs The Aztecs were known for warfare as well as for their art.

The Inca The Inca built well-crafted stone cities high in the Andes.

Reading Social Studies

Set a Purpose

READING FOCUS

When you go on a trip, you have a purpose or a destination in mind before you start. Maps can help you get to your destination. When you read, you should also have a purpose in mind before you start. This purpose keeps you focused and moving toward your goal of understanding. Textbooks often provide "maps" to help you set a purpose for your reading. A textbook's "map" includes a module's headings, pictures, and study tips. To determine a purpose for your reading, look over the headings, pictures, and study tips. Then ask yourself a question that can guide you. See how looking over the module's first page can help you set a purpose.

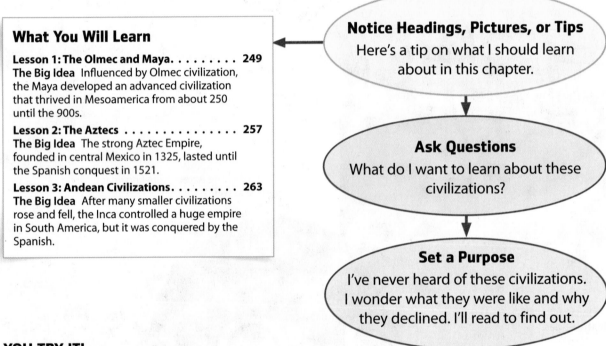

What You Will Learn

Notice Headings, Pictures, or Tips
Here's a tip on what I should learn about in this chapter.

Ask Questions
What do I want to learn about these civilizations?

Set a Purpose
I've never heard of these civilizations. I wonder what they were like and why they declined. I'll read to find out.

YOU TRY IT!

You can also use the method described above to set a purpose for reading the main text in your book. Look at the heading for the following caption. Then write down one or two questions about what you will read. Finally, develop a purpose for reading about Tenochtitlán. State this purpose in one or two sentences.

Tenochtitlán

The Aztecs turned a swampy, uninhabited island into one of the largest and grandest cities in the world. The first Europeans to visit Tenochtitlán were amazed. At the time, the Aztec capital was about five times bigger than London.

As you read this module, set a purpose for reading as you begin reading each segment.

The Olmec and Maya

The Big Idea

Influenced by Olmec civilization, the Maya developed an advanced civilization that thrived in Mesoamerica from about 250 until the 900s.

Main Ideas

- The Olmec were the first complex civilization in Mesoamerica and influenced other cultures.
- Geography helped shape the lives of the early Maya.
- During the Classic Age, the Maya built great cities linked by trade.
- Maya culture included a strict social structure, a religion with many gods, and achievements in science and the arts.
- The decline of Maya civilization began in the 900s.

Key Terms and Places

civilization
maize
Palenque
observatories

If YOU lived there . . .

You live in a rural Maya village in Mesoamerica. You and your family farm maize, beans, and other vegetables. One day you go with your father to bring crops to the king, and you see a big city with large pyramids, plazas, and observatories. You also see people playing a ball game. You learn that the winners get rewarded with jewels, but the losers are often killed.

Would you want to learn to play the ball game?

The Olmec

The region known as Mesoamerica stretches from the central part of Mexico south to include the northern part of Central America. It was in this region that a people called the Olmec (OHL-mek) developed the first complex civilization in Mesoamerica.

A **civilization** is an organized society within a specific area. Civilizations often include large cities in which different social classes of people live. Writing, formal education, art, and architecture are often features of civilizations. In civilizations, governments are made up of leaders or family groups. The governments make decisions that help the civilization develop. These characteristics improve people's quality of life.

Around 1200 BC, the Olmec settled in the lowlands along the Gulf of Mexico in what are today the southern Mexico states of Veracruz and Tabasco. This region's climate is hot and humid. Abundant rainfall and rich, fertile soil made this a perfect area for the Olmec to grow **maize,** or corn. Olmec also grew beans, squash, peppers, and avocados. In some places, the Olmec could harvest crops twice a year.

Olmec Life and Achievements Most Olmec lived in small villages, but some lived in larger towns. These towns were religious and government centers with temples and plazas. Impressive sculptures and buildings and planned-out settlements show that the Olmec were a complex civilization with a class structure. The ruling class ordered the large building projects that the Olmec completed.

The Olmec used basalt to create huge stone sculptures of heads. This rock was not from the area and had to be transported, probably by raft or by rolling the stone along logs, as shown here.

The Olmec built the first pyramids in the Americas. They also made sculptures of huge stone heads. Each head probably represented a different Olmec ruler. Other sculptures, such as jaguars, probably represented Olmec gods.

The Olmec created one of the first writing systems in the Americas. Unfortunately, historians and archaeologists don't know how to read their writing, so what they wrote remains a mystery. Other innovations developed by the Olmec include a calendar and a ball game using a rubber ball. Harvesting latex and making rubber were technological advances made by the Olmec. Similar elements of culture were later used by other Mesoamerican civilizations.

Olmec Trade and Influence The Olmec civilization also had a large trading network. Villages traded with each other and with other peoples farther away. Through trade, the Olmec got valuable goods, such as the stones they used for building and sculpture. This interaction with nearby people also spread Olmec culture.

Olmec civilization ended around 400 BC. By then, trade had spread Olmec influence across Mesoamerica. Later peoples were able to build on their achievements. Some also followed Olmec traditions. One group influenced by the Olmec was the Maya.

Reading Check
Summarize
What characteristics made the Olmec a civilization?

Geography and the Early Maya

Around 1000 BC the Maya began settling in the lowlands of what is now northern Guatemala. Thick tropical forests covered most of the land, but the people cleared areas to farm. They grew a variety of crops, including beans, squash, avocados, and maize. The forests provided valuable resources, too. Forest animals such as deer, rabbits, and monkeys were sources of food. In addition, trees and other forest plants made good building materials. For example, some Maya used wooden poles and vines, along with mud, to build their houses.

Reading Check
Find Main Ideas
How did the early
Maya make use of their
physical environment?

The early Maya lived in small, isolated villages. Eventually, though, these villages started trading with one another and with other groups in Mesoamerica. As trade increased, the villages grew. By about AD 200, the Maya had begun to build large cities in Mesoamerica.

The Classic Age

The Maya civilization reached its height between about AD 250 and 900. This time in Maya history is known as the Classic Age. During this time, Maya territory grew to include more than 40 large cities. Each had its own government and its own king. No single ruler united the many cities into one empire. Sometimes the different cities fought with each other for control of land and resources.

Maya cities were linked through trade. The Maya established trade routes throughout Mesoamerica. People exchanged goods for products that were not available locally. Look at the trade routes on the map to see the goods that were available in different areas of Maya civilization. For example, the warm lowlands were good for growing cotton and cacao (kuh-KOW), the

▷ Explore ONLINE!

Maya Civilization, c. 900

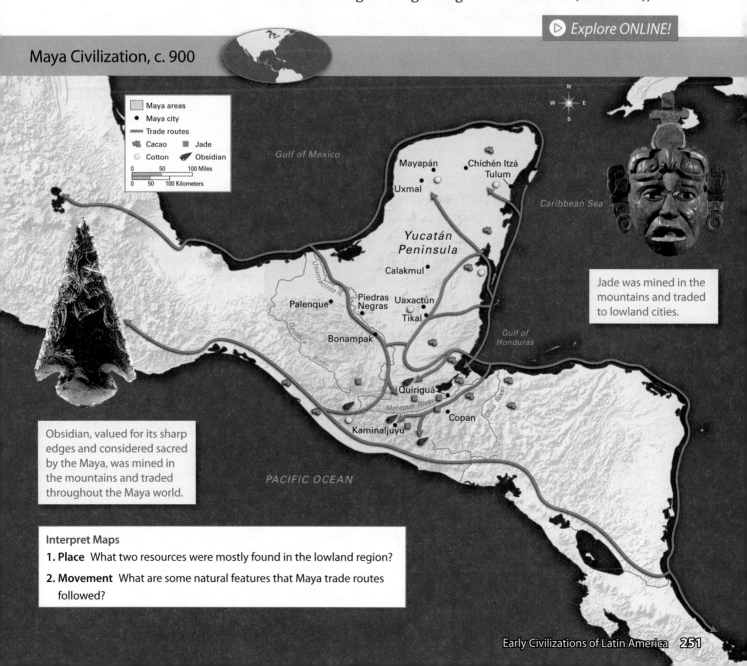

Maya areas
● **Maya city**
━ **Trade routes**
🌰 Cacao   ■ Jade
○ Cotton   ⚑ Obsidian

0   50   100 Miles
0   50   100 Kilometers

Gulf of Mexico

Mayapán
Chichén Itzá
Tulum
Uxmal
Caribbean Sea

Yucatán Peninsula

Calakmul

Usumacinta R.

Palenque
Piedras Negras
Uaxactún
Tikal

Grijalva River

Bonampak

Gulf of Honduras

Quiriguá
Motagua River
Copán
Ulúa River
Kaminaljuyú

PACIFIC OCEAN

Jade was mined in the mountains and traded to lowland cities.

Obsidian, valued for its sharp edges and considered sacred by the Maya, was mined in the mountains and traded throughout the Maya world.

Interpret Maps

1. **Place** What two resources were mostly found in the lowland region?

2. **Movement** What are some natural features that Maya trade routes followed?

Palenque

The ancient Maya city of Palenque was a major power on the border between the Maya highlands and lowlands. Its great temples and plazas were typical of the Classic Age of Maya civilization.

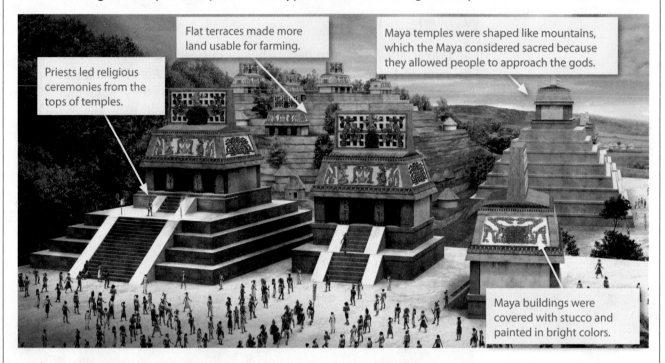

Priests led religious ceremonies from the tops of temples.

Flat terraces made more land usable for farming.

Maya temples were shaped like mountains, which the Maya considered sacred because they allowed people to approach the gods.

Maya buildings were covered with stucco and painted in bright colors.

Analyze Visuals
In what ways might Palenque's setting have helped the city? In what ways might it have hurt the city?

source of chocolate. But lowland crops did not grow well in the cool highlands. Instead, the highlands had valuable stones, such as jade and obsidian. People carried these and other products along trade routes.

Through trade, the Maya got supplies for construction. Maya cities had grand buildings, such as palaces decorated with carvings and paintings. The Maya also built stone pyramids topped with temples. Some temples honored local kings. For example, in the city of **Palenque** (pah-LENG-kay), the king Pacal (puh-KAHL) had a temple built to record his achievements.

In addition to palaces and temples, the Maya built canals and paved large plazas, or open squares, for public gatherings. Farmers used stone walls to shape hillsides into flat terraces so they could grow crops on them. Almost every Maya city also had a court for playing a special ball game. Using only their heads, shoulders, or hips, players tried to bounce a heavy rubber ball through rings attached high on the court walls. The winners of these games received jewels and clothing. The losers were often killed.

Volcanoes and volcanic activity influenced Maya civilization during the Classic Age. Volcanic ash fertilized fields but could also destroy them. Volcanic eruptions may have forced people to move from the south into Maya territory and altered trade routes. There was a period of time around AD 535 that historians call the Maya Hiatus. During that time, evidence suggests there wasn't as much activity in Maya cities. Historians have wondered what could cause a break in building and monument-making.

Reading Check
Summarize
How were Maya cities
connected?

Now, some scholars think giant volcanic explosions may have been responsible. In fact, volcanic activity in Central America may have even affected crops as far away as Rome and China.

Maya Culture

In Maya society, two main forces heavily influenced people's daily lives. One was the social structure and the other was religion.

Social Structure The king held the highest position in Maya society. The Maya believed their kings were related to the gods, so Maya kings had religious as well as political authority. Priests, rich merchants, and noble warriors were also part of the upper class. Together with the king, these people held all the power in Maya society.

Most Maya, though, belonged to the lower class. This group was made up of farming families who lived outside the cities. The women cared for the children, cooked, made yarn, and wove cloth. The men farmed, hunted, and crafted tools.

Lower-class Maya had to "pay" their rulers by giving the rulers part of their crops and goods such as cloth and salt. They also had to help

Historical Source

A Maya Ceremony

This carving comes from the palace at Yaxchilán (yahsh-chee-LAHN). The Maya recorded historical events on carvings like this one.

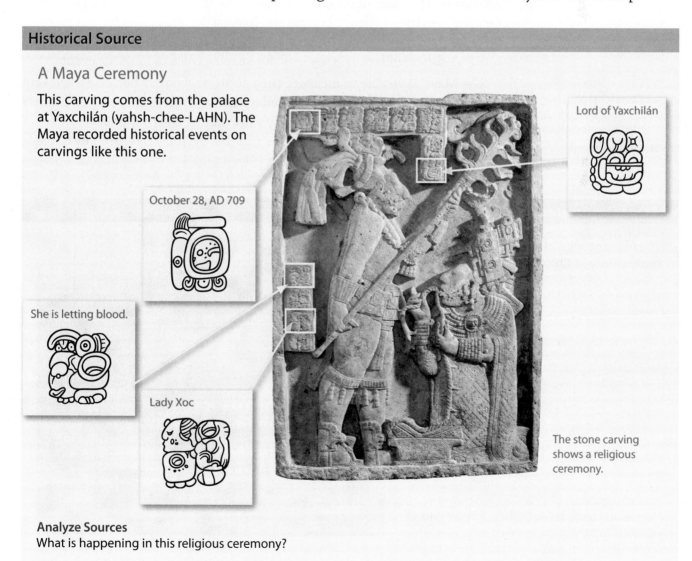

October 28, AD 709

Lord of Yaxchilán

She is letting blood.

Lady Xoc

The stone carving shows a religious ceremony.

Analyze Sources
What is happening in this religious ceremony?

construct temples and other public buildings. If their city went to war, Maya men had to serve in the army, and if captured in battle, they often became slaves. Slaves carried goods along trade routes or worked for upper-class Maya as servants or farmers.

Religion The Maya worshiped many gods, such as a creator, a sun god, a moon goddess, and a maize god. Each god was believed to control a different aspect of daily life.

According to Maya beliefs, the gods could be helpful or harmful, so people tried to please the gods to get their help. The Maya believed their gods needed blood to prevent disasters or the end of the world. Every person offered blood to the gods by piercing their tongue or skin. On special occasions, the Maya made human sacrifices. They usually used prisoners captured in battle, offering their hearts to stone carvings of the gods.

Achievements The Maya's religious beliefs led them to make impressive advances in science. They built large **observatories,** or buildings from which people could study the sky, so their priests could watch the stars and plan the best times for religious festivals. With the knowledge they gained about astronomy, the Maya developed two calendars. One, with 365 days, guided farming activities, such as planting and harvesting. This calendar was more accurate than the one used in Europe at that time. The Maya also had a separate 260-day calendar that they used for keeping track of religious events.

The Maya were able to measure time accurately partly because they were skilled mathematicians. They created a number system that helped them make complex calculations, and they were among the first people with a symbol for zero. The Maya used their number system to record key dates in their history.

A Maya Observatory

The Maya studied the stars from their observatory at Chichén Itzá.

Analyze Visuals
How would an observatory help someone to observe the stars?

Timelines and Number Lines

In math, you may have used a number line to visualize problems and solutions, especially for problems that use positive and negative numbers. A timeline is a special type of number line. Just like a number line can help you to understand the relationship between numbers, a timeline can help you see the relationship between events.

Instead of using positive and negative numbers on a timeline, historians use AD and BC. For BC dates, the bigger the number, the longer ago it took place. For dates that start with AD, bigger numbers mean more recent dates. CE and BCE are another way to say AD and BC.

Timeline: The Olmec and the Maya

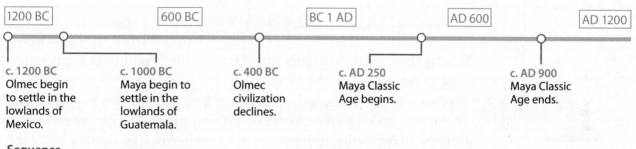

| 1200 BC | 600 BC | BC 1 AD | AD 600 | AD 1200 |

c. 1200 BC
Olmec begin to settle in the lowlands of Mexico.

c. 1000 BC
Maya begin to settle in the lowlands of Guatemala.

c. 400 BC
Olmec civilization declines.

c. AD 250
Maya Classic Age begins.

c. AD 900
Maya Classic Age ends.

Sequence
Which group settled in the lowlands first?

The Maya also developed a writing system. Anthropologists, or scholars who study people and cultures, have figured out that symbols used in Maya writing represented both objects and sounds. The Maya carved these symbols into large stone tablets to record their history. In some cases, the tablets were housed in shrines or temples. This method of record keeping has allowed scholars to learn more about the Maya. The Maya also wrote in bark-paper books and passed down stories and poems orally. Unfortunately, most Maya books were destroyed by the Spanish.

The Maya created amazing art and architecture as well. Their jade and gold jewelry was exceptional. Also, their huge temple-pyramids were masterfully built. The Maya had neither metal tools for cutting nor wheeled vehicles for carrying heavy supplies. Instead, workers used obsidian tools to cut limestone into blocks. Then workers rolled the giant blocks over logs and lifted them with ropes. The Maya decorated their buildings with paintings.

Reading Check
Evaluate
Which individuals do you think were most important to the Maya economy?

Decline of Maya Civilization

Maya civilization began to collapse in the AD 900s. People stopped building temples and other structures. They left the cities and moved back to the countryside. What caused this collapse? Historians are not sure, but they think that a combination of factors was probably responsible.

One factor could have been the burden on the common people. Maya kings forced their subjects to farm for them or work on building projects.

Academic Vocabulary
rebel to fight against authority

Perhaps people didn't want to work for the kings. They might have decided to **rebel** against their rulers' demands and abandon their cities.

Increased warfare between cities could also have caused the decline. Maya cities had always fought for power. But if battles became more widespread or destructive, they would have disrupted trade and cost many lives. People might have fled from the cities for their safety.

A related theory is that perhaps the Maya could not produce enough food to feed everyone. Growing the same crops year after year would have weakened the soil. In addition, as the population grew, the demand for food would have increased. To meet this demand, cities might have begun competing fiercely for new land. But the resulting battles would have hurt more crops, damaged more farmland, and caused even greater food shortages.

Climate change could have played a role, too. Scientists know that Mesoamerica suffered from droughts during the period when the Maya were leaving their cities. Droughts would have made it hard to grow enough food to feed people in the cities.

Whatever the reasons, the collapse of Maya civilization happened gradually. The Maya scattered after 900, but they did not disappear entirely. In fact, the Maya civilization later revived in the Yucatán Peninsula. By the time Spanish conquerors reached the Americas in the 1500s, though, Maya power had faded.

Reading Check
Summarize
What factors may have caused the end of Maya civilization?

Summary and Preview The Olmec were the first civilization in Mesoamerica and influenced later groups. The Maya built a civilization that peaked between about 250 and 900 but later collapsed for reasons still unknown. In the next lesson, you will learn about another people who lived in Mesoamerica, the Aztecs.

Lesson 1 Assessment

Review Ideas, Terms, and Places

1. a. Analyze How did Olmec trade affect other civilizations?

b. Make Inferences Why don't historians know more about the Olmec?

2. a. Recall What resources did the Maya get from the forest?

b. Elaborate How do you think Maya villages grew into large cities?

3. a. Describe What features did Maya cities include?

b. Make Inferences How did trade strengthen the Maya civilization?

4. a. Identify Who belonged to the upper class in Maya society?

b. Explain Why did the Maya build observatories?

c. Evaluate What do you think was the most impressive cultural achievement of the Maya? Why?

5. a. Describe What happened to the Maya after 900?

b. Evaluate What would you consider to be the key factor in the collapse of Maya civilization? Explain.

Critical Thinking

6. Compare and Contrast Create a Venn diagram like the one shown below. Use it to compare and contrast Maya and Olmec civilizations.

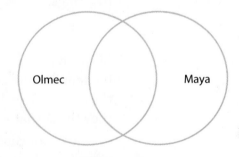

Olmec   Maya

The Aztecs

The Big Idea

The strong Aztec Empire, founded in central Mexico in 1325, lasted until the Spanish conquest in 1521.

Main Ideas

- The Aztecs built a rich and powerful empire in central Mexico.

- Social structure, religion, and warfare shaped life in the empire.

- Hernán Cortés conquered the Aztec Empire in 1521.

Key Terms and Places

Tenochtitlán
causeways
conquistadors

If YOU lived there . . .

You live in a village in southeastern Mexico that is ruled by the powerful Aztec Empire. Each year, your village must send the emperor many baskets of corn. You have to dig gold for him, too. One day, some pale, bearded strangers arrive by sea. They want to overthrow the emperor, and they ask for your help.

Should you help the strangers?
Why or why not?

The Aztecs Build an Empire

The first Aztecs were farmers who migrated from the north to central Mexico. Finding the good farmland already occupied, they settled on a swampy island in the middle of Lake Texcoco (tays-KOH-koh). There, in 1325, they began building their capital and conquering nearby towns.

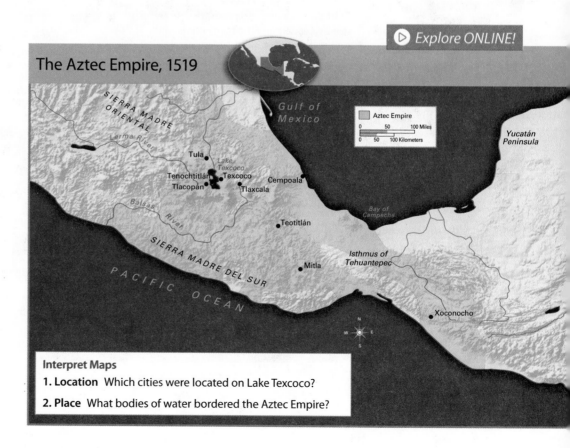

The Aztec Empire, 1519

▶ Explore ONLINE!

Interpret Maps

1. **Location** Which cities were located on Lake Texcoco?

2. **Place** What bodies of water bordered the Aztec Empire?

Tenochtitlán

The Aztecs turned a swampy, uninhabited island into one of the largest and grandest cities in the world. The first Europeans to visit Tenochtitlán were amazed. At the time, the Aztec capital was about five times bigger than London.

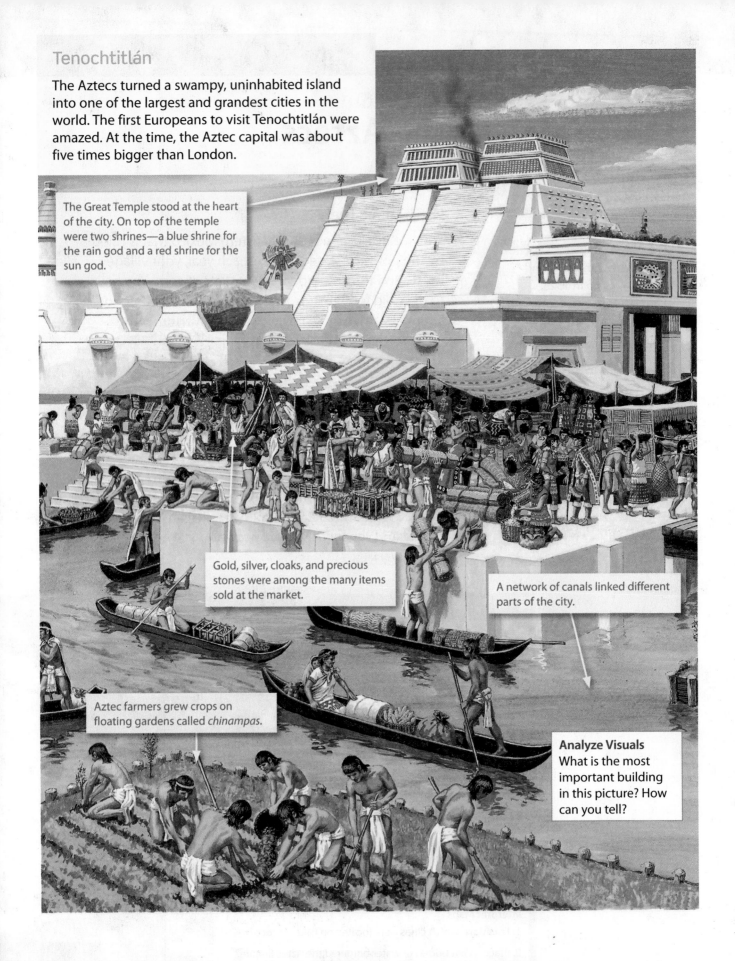

The Great Temple stood at the heart of the city. On top of the temple were two shrines—a blue shrine for the rain god and a red shrine for the sun god.

Gold, silver, cloaks, and precious stones were among the many items sold at the market.

A network of canals linked different parts of the city.

Aztec farmers grew crops on floating gardens called *chinampas*.

Analyze Visuals
What is the most important building in this picture? How can you tell?

War was a key factor in the Aztecs' rise to power. The Aztecs fought fiercely and demanded tribute payments from the people they conquered. The cotton, gold, and food that poured in as a result became vital to their economy. The Aztecs also controlled a huge trade network. Merchants carried goods to and from all parts of the empire. Many merchants doubled as spies, keeping the rulers informed about what was happening in their lands.

War, tribute, and trade made the Aztec Empire strong and rich. By the early 1400s the Aztecs ruled the most powerful state in Meso-america. By 1519 the Aztecs ruled much of central Mexico. Nowhere was the empire's greatness more visible than in its capital, **Tenochtitlán** (tay-nawch-teet-LAHN).

To build this amazing island city, the Aztecs first had to overcome many geographic challenges. One problem was the difficulty getting to and from the city. The Aztecs addressed this challenge by building three wide **causeways**—raised roads across water or wet ground—to connect the island to the lakeshore.

They also built canals that crisscrossed the city. The causeways and canals made travel and trade much easier.

Tenochtitlán's island location also limited the amount of land available for farming. To solve this problem, the Aztecs created floating gardens called *chinampas* (chee-NAHM-pahs). They piled soil on top of large rafts, which they anchored to trees that stood in the water. There they grew the corn, beans, and squash that most people ate.

The Aztecs made Tenochtitlán a truly magnificent city. Home to some 200,000 people at its height, it had huge temples, a busy market, and a grand palace.

Reading Check
Find Main Ideas
How did the Aztecs rise to power?

Link to Today

Solutions to Geographic Challenges

The Aztecs came up with innovative solutions to problems presented by the geography of where they settled. Today, we still use some of the solutions that the Aztecs used. Causeways connect islands to the mainland or go across bays and lakes. They make it easier for people to travel from place to place. The *chinampas* enabled farmers to grow food where land was scarce. Today, people are experimenting with floating island gardens. Some people are using them to grow food, and others are using them to help clean polluted water. These gardens are built on barges or large pieces of buoyant plastic. If populations continue to grow and oceans continue to rise, floating islands might be used more often.

Draw Conclusions
Why might floating islands be used more often in the future?

Life in the Empire

The Aztecs' way of life was as distinctive as their capital city. They had a complex social structure, a demanding religion, and a rich culture.

Aztec Society The Aztec emperor, like the Maya king, was the most important person in society. From his great palace, he attended to law, trade, tribute, and warfare. Trusted nobles helped him as tax collectors, judges, and other government officials. These noble positions were passed down from fathers to sons, and young nobles went to school to learn their responsibilities.

Just below the emperor and his nobles was a class of warriors and priests. Aztec warriors were highly respected and had many privileges, but priests were more influential. They led religious ceremonies and, as keepers of the calendars, decided when to plant and harvest.

The next level of Aztec society included merchants and artisans. Below them, in the lower class, were farmers and laborers, who made up the majority of the population. Many didn't own their land, and they paid so much in tribute that they often found it tough to survive. Only slaves, at the very bottom of society, struggled more.

Religion and Warfare Like the Maya, the Aztecs worshiped many gods, whom they believed controlled both nature and human activities. To please the gods, Aztec priests regularly made human sacrifices. Most victims were battle captives or slaves. In bloody ritual ceremonies, priests would slash open their victims' chests to "feed" human hearts and blood to the gods. The Aztecs sacrificed as many as 10,000 people a year. To supply enough victims, Aztec warriors often fought battles with neighboring peoples.

Cultural Achievements As warlike as the Aztecs were, they also appreciated art and beauty. Architects and sculptors created fine stone pyramids

Historical Source

An Aztec Marketplace

When Spanish conquistadors arrived in Tenochtitlán, they were amazed by the city. One explorer, Bernal Díaz del Castillo, wrote about his first visit to the market there. In his account, he described everything he saw and what people were selling and buying in detail.

Analyze Sources
Why might have Díaz del Castillo included details about the market in Tenochtitlán?

"When we arrived at the great market place, . . . we were astounded at the number of people and the quantity of merchandise that it contained, and at the good order and control that was maintained, for we had never seen such a thing before . . . . Each kind of merchandise was kept by itself and had its fixed place marked out. Let us begin with the dealers in gold, silver, and precious stones, feathers, mantles, and embroidered goods . . . . Next there were other traders who sold great pieces of cloth and cotton, and articles of twisted thread, and there were cacahuateros who sold cacao. In this way one could see every sort of merchandise that is to be found in the whole of New Spain."

—Bernal Díaz del Castillo,
from *The True History of the Conquest of New Spain*

Aztec artists were very skilled. They created detailed and brightly colored items. This double-headed serpent was probably worn during religious ceremonies. The man with the headdress is wearing it on his chest.

Analyze Visuals
What are some features of Aztec art that you can see in these pictures?

and statues. Artisans used gold, gems, and bright feathers to make jewelry and masks. Women embroidered colorful designs on the cloth they wove.

The Aztecs valued learning as well. They studied astronomy and devised a calendar much like the Maya had. They kept detailed written records of historical and cultural events. They also had a strong oral tradition. Stories about ancestors and the gods were passed from one generation to the next. The Aztecs also enjoyed fine speeches and riddles. Knowing the answers to riddles showed that one had paid attention in school.

Reading Check
Identify Cause and Effect How did Aztec religious practices influence warfare?

Cortés Conquers the Aztecs

In the late 1400s the Spanish arrived in the Americas, seeking adventure, riches, and converts to Catholicism. One group of **conquistadors** (kahn-KEES-tuh-dohrz), or Spanish conquerors, reached Mexico in 1519. Led by Hernán Cortés (er-NAHN kawr-TEZ), their motives were to find gold, claim land, and convert the native peoples to Christianity.

The Aztec emperor, Moctezuma II (MAWK-tay-SOO-mah), cautiously welcomed the strangers. He believed Cortés to be the god Quetzalcoatl (ket-suhl-kuh-WAH-tuhl), whom the Aztecs believed had left Mexico long ago. According to legend, the god had promised to return in 1519.

Moctezuma gave the Spanish gold and other gifts, but Cortés wanted more. He took the emperor prisoner, enraging the Aztecs, who attacked the Spanish. They managed to drive out the conquistadors, but Moctezuma was killed in the fighting.

Within a year, Cortés and his men came back. This time they had help from other peoples in the region who resented the Aztecs' harsh rule. In addition, the Spanish had better weapons, including armor, cannons, and swords. Furthermore, the Aztecs were terrified of the enemy's big horses—animals they had never seen before. The Spanish had also unknowingly brought diseases such as smallpox to the Americas. Diseases weakened or killed thousands of Aztecs. In 1521 the Aztec Empire came to an end.

Spanish Conquistadors and Aztec Warriors

Spanish conquistadors had stronger armor and more powerful weapons than Aztec warriors. The quilted leather armor of the Aztecs did not protect them from the guns of the Spanish.

An Aztec warrior

A Spanish conquistador

The Spanish, on the other hand, were there to stay. The diseases, plants, and animals they brought with them, as well as their culture and religion, left a lasting impact on the Americas.

Another effect of Spanish arrival in the Americas still impacts historians today. The Spanish destroyed most of the Aztec and Maya books they found, along with some religious artifacts. The information we have today about these cultures is filtered through the writings of Spanish writers. These writers had biases about the native people. Some wanted to prove that their actions in conquering the indigenous people were justified, some wanted to show the cruelty of the Spanish colonizers, and some aimed to document their experiences with less political motivation.

Summary and Preview The Aztec Empire, made strong by warfare and tribute, fell to the Spanish in 1521. In the next lesson, you will learn about civilizations in South America, including the Inca.

Reading Check
Analyze Causes
What factors helped the Spanish defeat the Aztecs?

Lesson 2 Assessment

Review Ideas, Terms, and Places

1. a. Recall Where and when did Aztec civilization develop?

   b. Explain How did the Aztecs in Tenochtitlán adapt to their island location?

   c. Elaborate How might Tenochtitlán's location have been both a benefit and a hindrance to the Aztecs?

2. a. Recall What did the Aztecs feed their gods?

   b. Explain Consider the roles of the emperor, warriors, priests, and others in Aztec society. Who do you think had the hardest role? Explain.

3. a. Identify Who was Moctezuma II?

   b. Form Generalizations Why did allies help Cortés defeat the Aztecs?

c. Describe What happened when the Spanish discovered the Aztec capital?

Critical Thinking

4. Evaluate Draw a diagram like the one shown. Identify three factors that contributed to the Aztecs' power. Put the factor you consider most important first and put the least important last. Explain your choices.

1.	2.	3.

Andean Civilizations

The Big Idea

After many smaller civilizations rose and fell, the Inca controlled a huge empire in South America, but it was conquered by the Spanish.

Main Ideas

■ Prior to the Inca Empire, several civilizations grew in the Andes and along the Pacific coast of South America.

■ The Inca created an empire with a strong central government in South America.

■ Life in the Inca Empire was influenced by social structure, religion, and the Inca's cultural achievements.

■ Francisco Pizarro conquered the Inca and took control of the region in 1537.

Key Terms and Places

Cuzco
Quechua
masonry

If YOU lived there . . .

You live in the Andes Mountains, where you raise llamas. You weave their wool into warm cloth. Last year, soldiers from the powerful Inca Empire took over your village. They brought in new leaders, who say you must all learn a new language and send much of your woven cloth to the Inca ruler. They also promise that the government will provide for you in times of trouble.

How do you feel about living in the Inca Empire?

Geography and Early Andean Civilizations

As the Olmec, the Maya, and the Aztecs developed in Mesoamerica, other civilizations developed in South America. A series of cultures rose and fell in the Andes Mountains and along the Pacific coast of South America. These cultures were influenced by the geography of the region in which they lived.

The Geography of the Andes The towering Andes Mountains run along the western side of South America. High plains, or *altiplano*, sit between mountain ridges. A narrow desert runs along the edge of rich fishing waters in the Pacific Ocean. Rivers run from the Andes to the Pacific through the dry region. Other rivers drain into the Amazon River system to the east. Climate varies with latitude and altitude. Higher altitudes are generally colder. Areas closer to the equator are generally warmer. Within this region, many civilizations grew, adapting to the land around them.

Many societies, including the Inca, lived in a region of high plains and mountains in western South America.

The Nazca created large designs in the desert. Scholars think this design depicts a hummingbird.

Early Societies The first major civilization in South America was the Chavín (chah-VEEN) culture, and it lasted from about 900 to 200 BC. This culture lived in what is now northern and central Peru. Its main city was a major religious and trading center in the highlands. In addition to growing maize, people in the Andes grew potatoes and other tubers. The Chavín culture is known for its woven textiles, carved stone monuments, and pottery shaped like animals and humans.

Later, in the first through the eighth centuries AD, the Moche (MOH-chay), or Mochica, lived in northern coastal Peru. River valleys provided water and fertile soil for farming. They used irrigation systems to grow corn and engineered pyramids out of adobe, or mud brick. Moche religion involved human sacrifice and drinking the blood of the sacrificed. Moche artwork, including pottery and metalwork, shows their artistic skill. Scholars are not sure why the Moche declined, though some think that drought was a factor.

Further south along the coast, the Nazca developed a collection of chiefdoms that lasted from around 200 BC to around AD 600. Nazca communities also had to use irrigation technology to farm the dry area in which they lived. In addition, they created cisterns, or large collection basins, to hold water. Nazca artifacts have been preserved by the dry climate. The artifacts include large figures carved into the desert called the Nazca lines. The designs, which are best seen from the air, depict animals, plants, and geometric shapes. Archaeologists are not sure of the meaning or purpose of these designs. Scholars think that the Nazca civilization was weakened by drought before being conquered.

The Chimú (chi-MOO) occupied the same area as the Moche but later in time. Since they lived in the same place, they dealt with the same geographic challenges of the Moche, including the scarcity of water. They were great engineers who built with adobe. They made irrigation systems, roads, and a large capital, Chan Chan. This organized city covered over 14 square miles (36.3 sq km). The layout of the city reflects the hierarchy of Chimú society with a clear class structure. Artists made complex metalwork and textiles. The Chimú were eventually conquered by the Inca around 1460. The Incas adopted many Chimú customs and technology.

Reading Check
Analyze Effects
How did the availability of water affect early Andean societies?

The Inca Create an Empire

The Inca began as a small tribe in the Andes in the 12th century. Their capital was **Cuzco** (KOO-skoh) in what is now Peru.

In the mid-1400s a ruler named Pachacuti (pah-chah-KOO-tee) began to expand Inca territory. Later leaders followed his example, and by the early 1500s the Inca Empire was huge. It stretched from what is now Ecuador south to central Chile. It included coastal deserts, snowy mountains, fertile valleys, and thick forests. About 12 million people lived in the empire. To rule effectively, the Inca formed a strong central government.

Central Rule Pachacuti did not want the people he conquered to have too much power. He began a policy of removing local leaders and replacing them with new officials whom he trusted. He also made the children of conquered leaders travel to Cuzco to learn about Inca government and religion. When the children were grown, they were sent back to govern their villages, where they taught their people about the Incas' history, traditions, and way of life.

As another way of unifying the empire, the Inca used an official Inca language, **Quechua** (KE-chuh-wuh). Although people spoke many other languages, all official business had to be done in Quechua. Even today, many people in Peru and the other former Inca lands still speak Quechua.

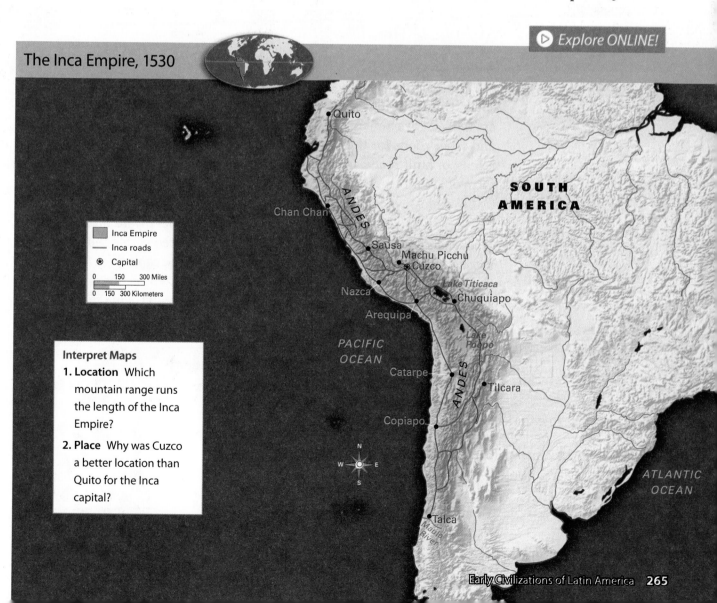

The Inca Empire, 1530

▷ *Explore ONLINE!*

Legend:
- Inca Empire
- Inca roads
- ⊛ Capital
- 0   150   300 Miles
- 0 150 300 Kilometers

Interpret Maps

1. **Location** Which mountain range runs the length of the Inca Empire?

2. **Place** Why was Cuzco a better location than Quito for the Inca capital?

Map labels: Quito, Chan Chan, ANDES, SOUTH AMERICA, Sausa, Machu Picchu, Cuzco, Nazca, Lake Titicaca, Chuquiapo, Arequipa, PACIFIC OCEAN, Lake Poopó, Catarpe, ANDES, Tilcara, Copiapo, ATLANTIC OCEAN, Talca, Maule River

The Inca System of Government

Conquistador Pedro de Cieza de León interviewed Inca about many aspects of daily life, including government. He later wrote a book about the Inca.

"Every district was as well regulated and governed as if the lord was actually present to chastise those who acted contrary to his rules. This fear arose from the known valor of the lords and their strict justice. It was felt to be certain that those who did evil would receive punishment without fail . . . . At the same time, the Incas always did good to those who were under their sway, and would not allow them to be ill-treated . . . . Many who dwelt in a sterile country where they and their ancestors had lived with difficulty, found that through the orders of the Inca their lands were made fertile and abundant . . . . In other districts, where there was scarcity of clothing, owing to the people having no flocks, orders were given that cloth should be abundantly provided. In short, it will be understood that as these lords knew how to enforce service and the payment of tribute, so they provided for the maintenance of the people, and took care that they should want for nothing."

—Pedro de Cieza de León, from
The Second Part of the Chronicle of Peru

Analyze Sources
According to Cieza de León, how did the Inca gain control over the people they conquered?

A Well-Organized Economy The Inca government strictly controlled the economy and told each household what work to do. Most Inca had to spend time working for the government as well as for themselves. Farmers tended government land in addition to their own. Villagers made cloth and other goods for the army. Some Inca served as soldiers, worked in mines, or built roads and bridges. In this way, the people paid taxes in the form of labor rather than money. This labor tax system was called the *mita* (MEE-tah).

Another feature of the Inca economy was that there were no merchants or markets. Instead, government officials distributed goods collected through the mita. Leftover goods were stored in the capital for emergencies. If a natural disaster struck, or if people simply could not care for themselves, the government provided supplies to help them.

Reading Check
Summarize
How did the Inca control their empire?

— BIOGRAPHY —

Pachacuti
Died 1471

Pachacuti became the Inca ruler in about 1438. Under his rule, the Inca Empire began a period of great expansion. Pachacuti, whose name means "he who remakes the world," had the Inca capital at Cuzco rebuilt. He also established an official Inca religion.

Analyze Effects
What effects did Pachacuti have on the Inca Empire?

Life in the Inca Empire

Because the rulers controlled Inca society so closely, the common people had little personal freedom. At the same time, the government protected the general welfare of all in the empire. But that did not mean everyone was treated equally.

Social Divisions Inca society had two main social classes. The emperor, government officials, and priests made up the upper class. Members of this class lived in stone houses in Cuzco and wore the best clothes. They did not have to pay the labor tax, and they enjoyed many other privileges. The Inca rulers, for example, could relax in luxury at Machu Picchu (MAH-choo PEEK-choo). This royal retreat lay nestled high in the Andes.

The people of the lower class in Inca society included farmers, artisans, and servants. There were no slaves, however, because the Incas did not practice slavery. Most Inca were farmers. In the warmer valleys, they grew crops such as maize and peanuts. In the cooler mountains, they carved terraces into the hillsides to create more space for farming and grew potatoes. High in the Andes, people raised llamas—South American animals related to camels—for wool and meat.

Lower-class Inca dressed in plain clothes and lived simply. By law, they could not own more goods than just what they needed to survive. Most of what they made went to the *mita* and the upper class.

Religion The Inca social structure was partly related to religion. For example, the Inca thought that their rulers were related to the sun god and never really died. As a result, priests brought mummies of former kings to many ceremonies. People gave these royal mummies food and gifts. In addition to the sun god, people worshiped other gods, including the rain god and the creator god.

Inca ceremonies included sacrifices. But unlike the Maya and the Aztecs, the Inca rarely sacrificed humans. They sacrificed llamas, cloth, or food instead.

In addition to practicing the official religion, people outside Cuzco worshiped other gods at local sacred places. The Inca believed certain mountaintops, rocks, and springs had magical powers. Many Inca performed sacrifices at these places as well as at the temple in Cuzco. Elements of Inca religion can still be found in rural areas of the Andes today.

Achievements Inca temples were grand buildings. The Inca were master builders, known for their expert **masonry,** or stonework. They cut stone blocks so precisely that they did not need cement to hold them together. The Inca also built a major network of roads. These were so well built that some of these stone buildings and roads have lasted until today.

The Inca produced works of art as well. Artisans made pottery as well as gold and silver jewelry. They even created a life-sized cornfield of gold and silver, crafting each cob, leaf, and stalk individually. Inca weavers also made some of the finest textiles in the Americas.

While such artifacts tell us much about the Inca, nothing was written about their empire until the Spanish arrived. Indeed, the Inca had no writing system. Instead, they kept records with knotted cords called *quipus* (KEE-pooz). Knots in the cords stood for numbers and, perhaps, sounds. Different colors represented information about crops, land, and other important topics. Today's scholars are just beginning to understand how to "read" *quipus*.

The Inca also passed down their stories and history orally. People sang songs and told stories about daily life and military victories. Official "memorizers" learned long poems about Inca legends and history. When the conquistadors arrived, the Inca records were written in Spanish and Quechua. We know about the Inca from these records and from the stories that survive in the songs and religious practices of the people in the region today. However, our knowledge of the Inca is limited by what the Spanish writers chose to include in their writings.

Reading Check
Contrast
How did daily life differ for upper- and lower-class Inca?

Inca Arts

Inca arts included beautiful textiles and gold and silver objects. Artists used materials that were available in the Inca Empire.

The Inca are famous for their textiles. Inca weavers made cloth from cotton and from the wool of llamas.

Inca artisans made many gold objects, such as this mask.

Inca artisans also made many silver offerings to the gods.

Analyze Visuals
What are some features of Inca art that you can see in these pictures?

Early Latin American Societies

Olmec	Maya	Aztecs	Inca
• worshiped many gods and influenced later religions • developed first urban civilization in Mesoamerica • created large-scale sculpture • developed first writing with symbols in the Americas • built large trade network	• worshiped many gods • ruled by kings who controlled cities; no central government • built grand buildings • created sophisticated 365-day calendar • studied astronomy • used writing and number system, including zero • built large trade network	• worshiped many gods • ruled by an emperor who collected tribute from conquered areas • built one of the world's largest cities • created highly layered society • used advanced writing and mathematical systems • built large trade network	• worshiped many gods • ruled by an emperor • created central government and language • built stone structures without using mortar • used advanced terrace agriculture • used the *mita,* a labor tax system • built advanced system of roads

Analyze Information
Which cultures' economies involved large trade networks?

Pizarro Conquers the Inca

The arrival of conquistadors changed more than how the Inca recorded history. In the late 1520s a civil war began in the Inca Empire after the death of the ruler. Two of the ruler's sons, Atahualpa (ah-tah-WAHL-pah) and Huáscar (WAHS-kahr), fought to claim the throne. Atahualpa won the war in 1532, but fierce fighting had weakened the Inca army.

On his way to be crowned as king, Atahualpa got news that a band of about 180 Spanish soldiers had arrived in the Inca Empire. They were conquistadors led by Francisco Pizarro. When Atahualpa came to meet the group, the Spanish attacked. They were greatly outnumbered, but they caught the unarmed Inca by surprise. They quickly captured Atahualpa and killed thousands of Inca soldiers.

To win his freedom, Atahualpa asked his people to fill a room with gold and silver for Pizarro. Inca brought jewelry, statues, and other valuable items from all parts of the empire. The precious metals would have been worth millions of dollars today. Despite this huge payment, the Spanish

BIOGRAPHY

Atahualpa 1502–1533

Atahualpa was the last Inca emperor. He was a popular ruler, but he didn't rule for long. At his first meeting with Pizarro, he was offered a religious book to convince him to accept Christianity. Atahualpa held the book to his ear and listened. When the book didn't speak, Atahualpa threw it on the ground. The Spanish considered this an insult and a reason to attack.

Identify Points of View
How do you think the Spanish viewed non-Christians?

Francisco Pizarro 1475–1541

Francisco Pizarro organized expeditions to explore the west coast of South America. His first two trips were mostly uneventful. But on his third trip, Pizarro met the Inca. With only about 180 men, he conquered the Inca Empire, which had been weakened by disease and civil war. In 1535 Pizarro founded Lima, the capital of modern Peru.

Predict
If Pizarro had not found the Inca Empire, what do you think might have happened?

killed Atahualpa. They knew that if they let the Inca ruler live, he might rally his people and defeat the smaller Spanish forces.

Some Inca did fight back after the emperor's death, but, in 1537, Pizarro defeated them. Spain took control over the entire empire.

The fall of the Inca Empire was similar to the fall of the Aztec Empire in several ways. Both empires had internal problems when the Spanish arrived and captured each empire's leaders. Also, guns and horses gave the Spanish a military advantage over disease-weakened native peoples.

Reading Check
Identify Cause and Effect
What events ended the Inca Empire?

The Spanish ruled the region for the next 300 years. Even though the Inca Empire was defeated, elements of the Inca culture, including language, religion, and food, remain important in the region today, especially in rural areas.

Summary After earlier Andean cultures thrived, the Inca built a huge empire in South America. But even with a strong central government, they could not withstand the Spanish conquest in 1537.

Lesson 3 Assessment

Review Ideas, Terms, and Places

1. **a. Recall** Which society most directly influenced the Inca?
   b. Summarize What types of artwork did each early Andean civilization make?

2. **a. Identify** Where was the Inca Empire located? What kinds of terrain did it include?
   b. Analyze How might a person who was conquered by the Incas describe being under their rule? Why might that description be different than how Pedro de Cieza de León described it?
   c. Evaluate Do you think the *mita* system was a good government policy? Why or why not?

3. **a. Describe** What was a unique feature of Inca masonry?
   b. Make Inferences How might the Inca road system have helped strengthen the empire?
   c. Analyze How did Inca art reflect where the Inca lived?

4. **a. Recall** When did the Spanish defeat the last of the Inca?
   b. Compare In what ways was the end of the Inca Empire like the end of the Aztec Empire?
   c. Analyze Why do you think Pizarro was able to defeat the much larger forces of the Inca? Name at least two possible reasons.

Critical Thinking

5. **Sequence** Create a timeline. Include dates given in the lesson for beginnings and endings of the civilizations mentioned.

6. **Analyze** Draw a diagram like the one below. Write a sentence in each box about how that topic influenced the next topic.

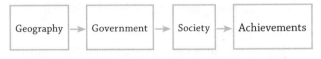

Geography → Government → Society → Achievements

Social Studies Skills

Analyze Information

Define the Skill

An important skill to learn is analyzing information presented in the text you read. One way to do this is to identify main ideas and supporting details. Everything in the paragraph should support the main idea.

After you identify the main idea, watch out for anything that is not relevant, or related to it, or necessary for its understanding. Don't let that extra information distract you from the most important material.

Sometimes you aren't given enough information to answer a question you might have. When you don't have adequate information, you can keep reading to see if your question is answered later in the text. If it isn't, you might do further research to find out more.

Learn the Skill

Look at the paragraph on this page about communication in the Maya civilization. Some unrelated and unnecessary information has been added so that you can learn to identify it. Use the paragraph to answer the questions here.

1. Which sentence expresses the main idea? What details support it?

2. What information is unnecessary, irrelevant, or unrelated to the main idea?

3. If you wanted to know what Maya books were made out of, would you have adequate information?

The Maya

Communication The Maya developed an advanced form of writing that used many symbols. Our writing system uses 26 letters. They recorded information on large stone monuments. Some early civilizations drew pictures on cave walls. The Maya also made books of paper made from the bark of fig trees. Fig trees need a lot of light.

Religion The Maya believed in many gods and goddesses. More than 160 gods and goddesses are named in a single Maya manuscript. Among the gods they worshiped were a corn god, a rain god, a sun god, and a moon goddess. The early Greeks also worshiped many gods and goddesses.

Practice the Skill

Use the passage on this page about Maya religion to answer the following questions.

1. What is the main idea of the paragraph?

2. What details support the main idea?

3. What information is unnecessary or irrelevant?

4. Do you have adequate information to explain how the Maya worshiped their gods?

Module 8 Assessment

Review Vocabulary, Terms, and Places

For each statement below, write T if it is true and F if it is false. If the statement is false, replace the underlined term with one that would make the sentence a true statement.

1. The main crops of the Olmec and Maya included <u>maize</u> and beans.
2. The <u>Quechua</u> came to the Americas to find land, gold, and converts to Catholicism.
3. <u>Palenque</u>, located on a swampy island, was the capital of the Aztec Empire.
4. Maya priests studied the sun, moon, and stars from stone <u>observatories</u>.
5. The official language of the Inca Empire was <u>Cuzco</u>.
6. The Aztecs built raised roads called <u>masonry</u> to cross from Tenochtitlán to the mainland.
7. <u>Tenochtitlán</u> was the Inca capital.
8. Many people in Mesoamerica died at the hands of the <u>conquistadors</u>.

Comprehension and Critical Thinking

Lesson 1

9. a. **Recall** Where and when did the Olmec live?

    b. **Categorize** What groups made up the different classes in Maya society?

    c. **Analyze** What was the connection between Maya religion and astronomy? How do you think this connection influenced Maya achievements?

    d. **Elaborate** Why did Maya cities trade with each other? Why did they fight?

Lesson 2

10. a. **Describe** What was Tenochtitlán like? Where was it located?

    b. **Make Inferences** Why do you think warriors had many privileges and were such respected members of Aztec society?

    c. **Compare** In what ways were Aztec and Maya societies similar?

    d. **Evaluate** What factor do you think played the biggest role in the Aztecs' defeat? Defend your answer.

Lesson 3

11. a. **Identify** Name two Inca leaders, and explain their roles in Inca history.

    b. **Draw Conclusions** What geographic and cultural problems did the Inca overcome to rule their empire?

    c. **Compare** What did Hernán Cortés and Francisco Pizarro have in common?

    d. **Elaborate** Do you think most people in the Inca Empire appreciated or resented the *mita* system? Explain your answer.

Reading Skills

Set a Purpose *Use the Reading Skills taught in this module to answer the questions about the reading selection below.*

Life in the Inca Empire

Because the rulers controlled Inca society so closely, the common people had little personal freedom. At the same time, the government protected the general welfare of all in the empire. But that did not mean everyone was treated equally.

12. After reading the beginning of the section, what are some questions you might ask before reading the rest of the section from Lesson 3?

13. State a purpose for reading this section in one or two sentences.

Social Studies Skills

Analyze Information *Use the Social Studies Skills taught in this module to answer the question about the passage below.*

Cacao beans had great value to the Maya. Cacao trees are evergreens. They were the source of chocolate, known as a favorite food of rulers and the gods. The Maya also used cacao beans as money.

14. In the passage, the first sentence expresses the main idea. One of the following sentences is nonessential to the main idea. Identify the nonessential sentence.

Map Activity

15. **Early History of the Americas** On a separate sheet of paper, match the letters on the map with their correct labels.

Palenque   **Tenochtitlán**

Cuzco

Focus on Writing

16. **Write an Article** Imagine you are a newspaper reporter. Write a article about three of the civilizations in this module. Your purpose is to inform readers about these civilizations. Write a headline or title and a short introduction to the civilizations. Then write a paragraph about one aspect of each civilization. You might discuss the religion, social structure, or scientific achievements of the societies. Use facts and details from the lessons to develop the body of your article. Include relevant vocabulary words. Write clearly and coherently so that your audience will fully understand you. Cite any sources that helped you to write your article. Use transition words as you switch topics. Then, write a conclusion for your article, summing up why you thought your topic was interesting or important and comparing and contrasting the civilizations with each other. Proofread your article to check it for correct spelling and grammar.

THE
Maya

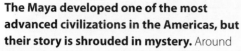
The Maya developed one of the most advanced civilizations in the Americas, but their story is shrouded in mystery. Around AD 250, the Maya began to build great cities in southern Mexico and Central America. They developed a writing system, practiced astronomy, and built magnificent palaces and pyramids with little more than stone tools. Around AD 900, however, the Maya abandoned their cities, leaving their monuments to be reclaimed by the jungle and, for a time, forgotten.

Explore some of the incredible monuments and cultural achievements of the ancient Maya online. You can find a wealth of information, video clips, primary sources, activities, and more through your online textbook.

Destroying the Maya's Past

Watch the video to learn how the actions of one Spanish missionary nearly destroyed the written record of the Maya world.

Finding the City of Palenque

Watch the video to learn about the great Maya city of Palenque and the European discovery of the site in the eighteenth century.

"Thus let it be done! Let the emptiness be filled! Let the water recede and make a void, let the earth appear and become solid; let it be done . . . "Earth!" they said, and instantly it was made."

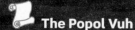

The Popol Vuh

Read the document to learn how the Maya believed the world was created.

Pakal's Tomb

Watch the video to explore how the discovery of the tomb of a great king helped archaeologists piece together the Maya past.

Mexico

Essential Question

Why is it important for Mexico and the United States to be good neighbors?

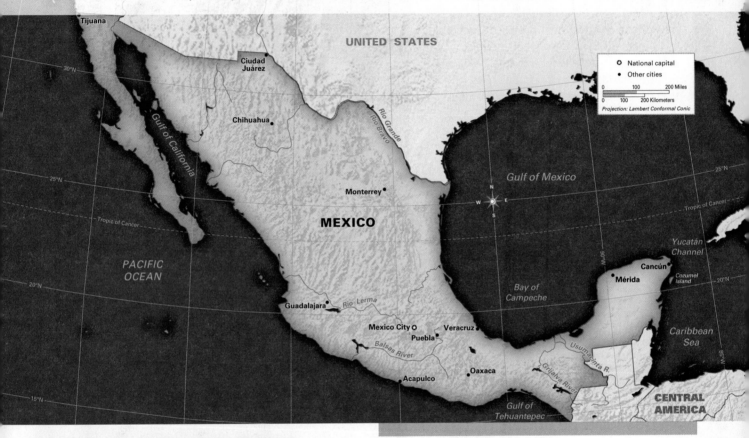

Explore ONLINE!

VIDEOS, including . . .
- The Peasant Revolution

HISTORY.

- ☑ Document-Based Investigations
- ☑ Graphic Organizers
- ☑ Interactive Games
- ☑ Channel One News Video: Geo Quiz: Mexico City
- ☑ Channel One News Video: Day of the Dead
- ☑ Compare Images: Trade vs. Tradition
- ☑ Interactive Map: Mexico's Culture Regions

In this module, you will learn about the major physical, cultural, and economic features of Mexico.

What You Will Learn

Culture Brightly costumed dancers perform a traditional dance or ballet folklórico in Cancún.

History The Spanish brought Christianity to Mexico and built churches like this one.

Geography Much of Mexico's landscape is dry, with high plateaus and mountains.

Reading Social Studies

Predict

READING FOCUS

Predicting is guessing what will happen next based on what you already know. In reading about geography, you can use what you know about the place you live to help you make predictions about other countries. Predicting helps you stay involved with your reading as you see whether your prediction was right. Your mind follows these four steps when you make predictions as you read:

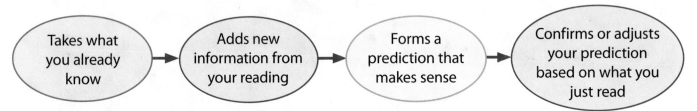

Takes what you already know → Adds new information from your reading → Forms a prediction that makes sense → Confirms or adjusts your prediction based on what you just read

See how you might make a prediction from the following text:

> *From snowcapped mountain peaks to warm, sunny beaches, Mexico has many different climates.*

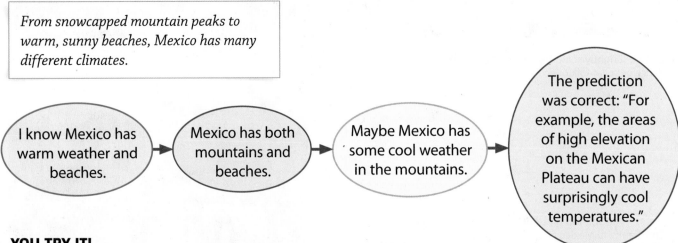

I know Mexico has warm weather and beaches. → Mexico has both mountains and beaches. → Maybe Mexico has some cool weather in the mountains. → The prediction was correct: "For example, the areas of high elevation on the Mexican Plateau can have surprisingly cool temperatures."

YOU TRY IT!

Read the following sentences. Then use a graphic organizer like the one below to help you predict what you will learn in your reading. Check the text in Lesson 3 to see if your prediction was correct.

> *Mexico has a democratic government. However, Mexico is not like the United States where different political parties have always competed for power.*

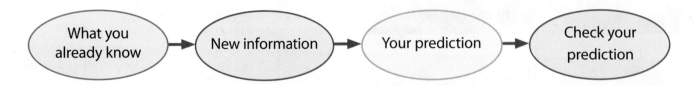

What you already know → New information → Your prediction → Check your prediction

Physical Geography

The Big Idea

Mexico is a large country with different natural environments in its northern, central, and southern regions.

Main Ideas

- Mexico's physical features include plateaus, mountains, and coastal lowlands.

- Mexico's climate and vegetation include deserts, tropical forests, and cool highlands.

- Key natural resources in Mexico include oil, silver, gold, and scenic landscapes.

Key Terms and Places

Río Bravo (Rio Grande)
peninsula
Baja California
Gulf of Mexico
Yucatán Peninsula
Sierra Madre

If YOU lived there . . .

You live on Mexico's Pacific coast. Sunny weather and good beaches bring tourists year-round. Now you are on your way to visit a cousin in Puebla, in the highlands. To get there, you will have to take a bus along the winding roads of the steep Sierra Madre Occidental. This rugged mountain range runs along the coast. You have never been to the interior of Mexico before.

What landscapes will you see on your trip?

Physical Features

Mexico, our neighbor to the south, shares a long border with the United States. Forming part of this border is one of Mexico's few major rivers, the **Río Bravo.** In the United States, this river is called the Rio Grande. At other places along the U.S.-Mexico border, it is impossible to tell where one country ends and the other country begins.

Bodies of Water Locate Mexico on the map and see that, except for its border with the United States, Mexico is mostly surrounded by water. Mexico's border in the west is the Pacific Ocean. Stretching south into the Pacific Ocean from northern Mexico is a narrow **peninsula,** or piece of land surrounded on three sides by water, called **Baja California.** To the east, Mexico's border is the **Gulf of Mexico.** The Gulf of Mexico is separated from the Caribbean Sea by a part of Mexico called the **Yucatán** (yoo-kah-TAHN) **Peninsula.**

Plateaus and Mountains Much of the interior landscape of Mexico consists of a high, mostly rugged region called the Mexican Plateau. The plateau's lowest point is more than a half mile above sea level. Its highest point is close to two miles above sea level. The entire plateau spreads between two mountain ranges that rise still higher. One range, the Sierra Madre Oriental, lies in the east. The other, the Sierra Madre Occidental, lies in the west. Together, these two mountain ranges and another shorter one in southern Mexico make up the **Sierra Madre** (SYER-rah MAH -dray), or "mother range."

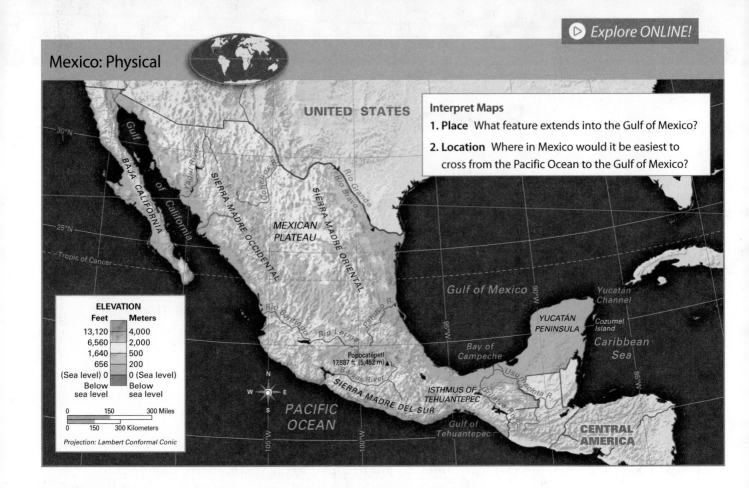

Mexico: Physical

UNITED STATES

Gulf of California

BAJA CALIFORNIA

30°N

25°N

Tropic of Cancer

Yaqui River

Conchos R.

SIERRA MADRE OCCIDENTAL

MEXICAN PLATEAU

Rio Grande

Rio Bravo

SIERRA MADRE ORIENTAL

Panuco R.

Rio Santiago

Rio Lerma

Balsas River

Popocatépetl
17,887 ft (5,452 m) ▲

SIERRA MADRE DEL SUR

ISTHMUS OF TEHUANTEPEC

Usumacinta R.

Grijalva River

Gulf of Mexico

YUCATÁN PENINSULA

Yucatán Channel

Cozumel Island

Caribbean Sea

Bay of Campeche

CENTRAL AMERICA

Gulf of Tehuantepec

PACIFIC OCEAN

90°W
96°W
86°W
100°W
105°W

Interpret Maps

1. Place What feature extends into the Gulf of Mexico?

2. Location Where in Mexico would it be easiest to cross from the Pacific Ocean to the Gulf of Mexico?

ELEVATION

Feet	Meters
13,120	4,000
6,560	2,000
1,640	500
656	200
(Sea level) 0	0 (Sea level)
Below sea level	Below sea level

0   150   300 Miles
0   150   300 Kilometers

Projection: Lambert Conformal Conic

Plateaus and mountains cover much of Mexico. Here, the volcano Popocatépetl rises above a mountain valley. Many people live and farm in the mountain valleys.

Between the two ranges in the south lies the Valley of Mexico. Mexico City, the country's capital, is located there. The mountains south of Mexico City include towering, snowcapped volcanoes. Volcanic eruptions, as well as earthquakes, are a threat there. The volcano Popocatépetl (poh-puh-cah-TE-pet-uhl) near Mexico City has been erupting from time to time since 1994.

Coastal Lowlands From the highlands in central Mexico, the land slopes down to the coasts. Beautiful, sunny beaches stretch all along Mexico's eastern and western coasts. The plain that runs along the west coast is fairly wide in the north. It becomes narrower in the south. On the east side of the country, the Gulf coastal plain is wide and flat. The soils and climate there are good for farming.

Locate Yucatán Peninsula on the *Mexico: Physical* map. As you can see, this region is also mostly flat. Limestone rock underlies much of the area. Erosion there has created caves and sinkholes, steep-sided depressions that form when the roof of a cave collapses. Many of these sinkholes are filled with water.

Reading Check
Summarize
What are Mexico's major physical features?

A tropical savanna climate supports lush vegetation along Mexico's southern beaches.

Climate and Vegetation

From snowcapped mountain peaks to warm, sunny beaches, Mexico has many different climates. You can see Mexico's climate regions on the map. This great variety of climates results in several different types of vegetation.

In some areas, changes in elevation cause climates to **vary** widely within a short distance. For example, the areas of high elevation on the Mexican Plateau can have surprisingly cool temperatures. At times, freezing temperatures reach as far south as Mexico City—even though it is located in the tropics. Mexico's mountain valleys generally have mild climates, and many people have settled there.

The valleys along Mexico's southern coastal areas also have pleasant climates. Warm temperatures and a summer rainy season support the forests that cover about 25 percent of Mexico's land area. Tropical rain forests provide a home for jaguars, monkeys, anteaters, and other animals.

Academic Vocabulary
vary to be different

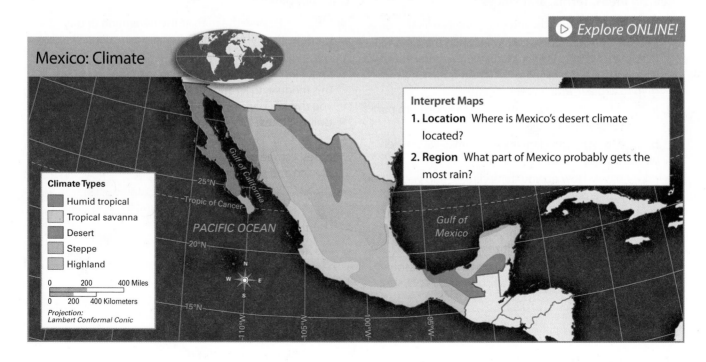

▷ *Explore ONLINE!*

Mexico: Climate

Climate Types
- Humid tropical
- Tropical savanna
- Desert
- Steppe
- Highland

0   200   400 Miles
0   200   400 Kilometers

Projection:
Lambert Conformal Conic

Gulf of California

PACIFIC OCEAN

Gulf of Mexico

25°N
Tropic of Cancer
20°N
15°N

Interpret Maps

1. **Location** Where is Mexico's desert climate located?

2. **Region** What part of Mexico probably gets the most rain?

Reading Check
Analyze Effects
Why does Mexico
City sometimes
experience freezing
temperatures even
though it is
in the tropics?

While most of southern Mexico is warm and humid, the climate in the northern part of the Yucatán Peninsula is hot and dry. The main vegetation there is scrub forest.

Like the Yucatán Peninsula in the south, most of northern Mexico is dry. The deserts in Baja California and the northern part of the plateau get little rainfall. Desert plants and dry grasslands are common in the north. Cougars, coyotes, and deer live in some areas of the desert.

Natural Resources

Mexico is rich in natural resources. One of its most important resources is petroleum, or oil. Oil reserves are found mainly under the southern and Gulf coastal plains as well as offshore in the Gulf of Mexico. Mexico sells much of its oil to the United States.

Before oil was discovered in Mexico, minerals were the country's most valuable resource. Some gold and silver mines that were begun many centuries ago are still in operation. In addition, new mines have been developed in Mexico's mountains. Today, Mexico's mines produce more silver than any other country in the world. Mexican mines also yield large amounts of copper, gold, lead, and zinc.

Reading Check
Find Main Ideas
What is one of
Mexico's most
important resources?

Another important resource is water. The refreshing water surrounding Mexico draws many tourists to the country's scenic beaches. Unfortunately, drinking water is limited in many parts of Mexico. Water scarcity is a serious issue.

Summary and Preview The natural environments of Mexico range from arid plateaus in the north to humid, forested mountains in the south. Next, you will study the history and culture of Mexico.

Lesson 1 Assessment

Review Ideas, Terms, and Places

1. a. **Describe** What is the interior of Mexico like?
   b. **Draw Conclusions** Locate Mexico on the climate map in this lesson. Do you think the Yucatán Peninsula is a good place for farming? Use your notes and the map to explain your answer.

2. a. **Recall** What is the climate like in the northern part of the Yucatán Peninsula?
   b. **Explain** Why can climates sometimes vary widely within a short distance?
   c. **Elaborate** How do you think climate and vegetation affect where people live in Mexico?

3. a. **Identify** Where are Mexico's oil reserves located?
   b. **Make Inferences** What problems might water scarcity cause for Mexican citizens?
   c. **Analyze** Look at the physical map in this lesson. Pose and answer a question about Mexico's physical features.

Critical Thinking

4. **Identify** Review the map at the beginning of this module, then answer the following question: What is the absolute location of Mexico's capital?

5. **Make Inferences** Review the map at the beginning of this module, then answer the following questions: Do you think Tijuana or Mérida is more influenced by the United States? Why?

6. **Categorize** Draw a chart like the one here. Using your notes, list the geographical features found in northern Mexico and southern Mexico.

Region	Geography
Northern Mexico	
Southern Mexico	

History and Culture

The Big Idea

Native American cultures and Spanish colonization shaped Mexican history and culture.

Main Ideas

- Early cultures of Mexico included the Olmec, the Maya, and the Aztecs.

- Mexico's period as a Spanish colony and its struggles since independence have shaped its culture.

- Spanish and native cultures have influenced Mexico's customs and traditions today.

Key Terms and Places

empire
conquistadors
mestizos
mulattoes
missions
haciendas

If YOU lived there . . .

You belong to one of the native Indian peoples in southern Mexico in the early 1500s. Years ago, the Aztec rulers went to war against your people. They took many captives. They have always treated you cruelly. Now some strangers have come from across the sea. They want your people to help them conquer the Aztecs.

Will you help the strangers fight the Aztecs? Why or why not?

Early Cultures

People first came to Mexico many thousands of years ago. As early as 5,000 years ago, they were growing beans, peppers, and squash. They also domesticated an early form of corn. Farming allowed these people to build the first permanent settlements in the Americas.

Olmec By about 1500 BC the Olmec people in Mexico were living in small villages. The Olmec lived on the humid southern coast of the Gulf of Mexico, where they built temples and giant statues. They also traded carved stones like jade and obsidian with other cultures in eastern Mexico.

Early Cultures of Mexico

Olmec
- The Olmec made sculptures of giant stone heads.
- The heads may have represented rulers or gods.

Maya
- The Maya had a trade network between cities.
- This Maya pyramid stands in Uxmal.

Aztecs
- The Aztecs built the first empire in the Americas.
- Aztec artisans made art like this turquoise mask.

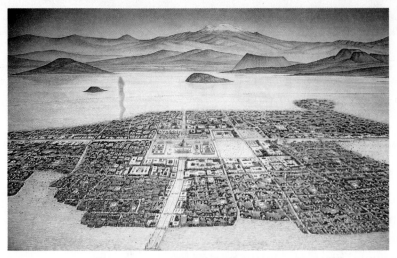

The Aztecs' magnificent capital, Tenochtitlán, was built on an island in Lake Texcoco. Mexico's capital today, Mexico City, is located where Tenochtitlán once stood.

Reading Check
Summarize What were some achievements of Mexico's early cultures?

Maya A few hundred years later, the Maya built on the achievements of the Olmec. Between about AD 250 and 900, the Maya built large cities in Mexico and Central America. They built stone temples to worship their gods. They studied the stars and developed a detailed calendar. They also kept written records that scholars still study to learn about Maya history. However, scholars do not fully understand why the Maya civilization suddenly collapsed sometime after 900.

Aztecs After the decline of the Maya civilization, people called the Aztecs moved to central Mexico from the north. In 1325 they built their capital on an island in a lake. Known as Tenochtitlán (tay-nawch-teet-LAHN), this capital grew into one of the largest and most impressive cities of its time.

The Aztecs also built a large, powerful empire. An **empire** is a land with different territories and peoples under a single ruler. The Aztecs built their empire through conquest. They defeated their neighboring tribes in war. Then they forced the other people to pay taxes and to provide war captives for sacrifice to the Aztec gods.

Colonial Mexico and Independence

In spite of its great size and power, the Aztec Empire did not last long after the first Europeans landed in Mexico. In 1519 Hernán Cortés, a Spanish soldier, arrived in Mexico with about 600 men. These **conquistadors** (kahn-KEES-tuh-dawrz), or conquerors, gained allies from other tribes in the region. They also had guns and horses, which the Aztecs had never seen before. The new weapons terrified the Aztecs and gave the Spanish an advantage.

The Spanish also unknowingly brought European diseases such as smallpox. The Aztecs had no resistance to these diseases, so many of them died. Greatly weakened by disease, the Aztecs were defeated. In 1521 Cortés claimed the land for Spain.

Colonial Times After the conquest, Spanish and American Indian peoples and cultures mixed. This mixing formed a new Mexican identity. Spaniards called people of mixed European and Indian ancestry **mestizos** (me-STEE-zohs). When Africans were brought to America as slaves, they added to this mix of peoples. The Spaniards called people of mixed European and African ancestry **mulattoes** (muh-LAH-tohs). Africans and American Indians also intermarried.

Life in colonial Mexico was greatly influenced by the Roman Catholic Church. Large areas of northern Mexico were left to the church to explore and to rule. Church outposts known as **missions** were scattered throughout the area. Priests at the missions learned native languages and taught the Indians Spanish. They also worked to convert the American Indians to Catholicism.

In addition to spreading Christianity, the Spaniards wanted to find gold and silver in Mexico. American Indians and enslaved Africans did most of the hard physical labor in the mines. As a result, many died from disease and overwork.

Like mining, agriculture became an important part of the colonial economy. After the conquest, the Spanish monarch granted **haciendas** (hah-see-EN-duhs), or huge expanses of farm or ranch land, to some favored people of Spanish ancestry. Peasants, usually Indians, lived and worked on these haciendas. The haciendas made their owners very wealthy.

Independence Spain ruled Mexico for almost 300 years before the people of Mexico demanded independence. The revolt against Spanish rule was led by a Catholic priest named Miguel Hidalgo. In 1810 he gave a famous speech calling for the common people to rise up against the Spanish. Hidalgo was killed in 1811, but fighting continued until Mexico won its independence in 1821.

Link to the Arts

Hidalgo Calls for Independence

Miguel Hidalgo (center, in black) calls for independence from Spain in 1810. The famous Mexican painter Juan O'Gorman painted this image.

Analyze Visuals
What kinds of people joined Hidalgo in his revolt?

Benito Juárez (1806–1872)

Benito Juárez was Mexico's first president of Indian heritage. A wise and passionate leader, Juárez stood up for the rights of all Mexicans. As the minister of justice, he got rid of special courts for members of the church and the military. As president, he passed reforms that laid the foundation for a democratic government. Today, he is considered a national hero in Mexico.

Draw Conclusions
How may Juárez's heritage have affected his efforts for Mexico's citizens?

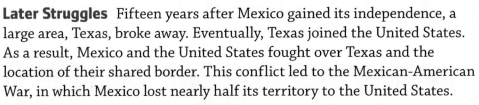

Later Struggles Fifteen years after Mexico gained its independence, a large area, Texas, broke away. Eventually, Texas joined the United States. As a result, Mexico and the United States fought over Texas and the location of their shared border. This conflict led to the Mexican-American War, in which Mexico lost nearly half its territory to the United States.

In the mid-1800s Mexico faced other challenges. During this time, the popular president Benito Juárez helped Mexico survive a French invasion. He also changed Mexican society by making reforms that reduced the privileges of the church and the army.

In spite of these reforms, in the early 1900s President Porfirio Diaz helped the hacienda owners take land from peasants. Also, foreign companies owned huge amounts of land in Mexico and, in turn, influenced Mexican politics. Many Mexicans thought the president gave these large landowners too many privileges.

As a result, the Mexican Revolution broke out in 1910. The fighting lasted ten years. One major result of the Mexican Revolution was land reform. The newly formed government took land from the large landowners and gave it back to the peasant villagers.

Reading Check
Sequence What events occurred after Mexico gained independence?

Academic Vocabulary
influence change or have an effect on

Culture

Mexico's history has **influenced** its culture. For example, one major influence from history is language. Most Mexicans speak Spanish because of the Spanish influence in colonial times. Another influence from Spain is religion. About 90 percent of all Mexicans are Roman Catholic.

However, Mexico's culture also reflects its American Indian heritage. For example, many people still speak American Indian languages. In Mexico, a person's language is tied to his or her ethnic group. Speaking an American Indian language identifies a person as Indian.

Mexicans also have some unique cultural practices that combine elements of Spanish influence with the influence of Mexican Indians. One example is a holiday called Day of the Dead. This holiday is a day to remember and honor dead ancestors.

Day of the Dead

Everyone is sad when a loved one dies. But during Day of the Dead, Mexicans celebrate death as part of life. This attitude comes from the Mexican Indian belief that the souls of the dead return every year to visit their living relatives. To prepare for this visit, Mexican families gather in graveyards. They clean up around their loved one's grave and decorate it with flowers and candles. They also set out food and drink for the celebration. Favorite foods often include sugar candy skulls, chocolate coffins, and sweet breads shaped like bones.

Summarize
Why do Mexicans celebrate Day of the Dead?

Reading Check
Categorize What aspects of Mexican culture show the influence of Spanish rule?

Mexicans celebrate Day of the Dead on November 1 and 2. These dates are similar to the dates that the Catholic Church honors the dead with All Saints' Day and All Souls' Day. The holiday also reflects native customs and beliefs about hopes of life after death.

Summary and Preview Mexico's early cultures formed great civilizations, but after the conquest of the Aztec Empire, power in Mexico shifted to Spain. Spain ruled Mexico for nearly 300 years before Mexico gained independence. Mexico's history and its mix of Indian and Spanish backgrounds have influenced the country's culture. In the next lesson, you will learn about life in Mexico today.

Lesson 2 Assessment

Review Ideas, Terms, and Places

1. a. **Recall** Where in Mexico did the Olmecs live?
   b. **Explain** How did the Aztecs build and rule their empire?
   c. **Elaborate** Why do you think scholars are not sure what caused the end of Maya civilization?

2. a. **Identify** Who began the revolt that led to Mexico's independence?
   b. **Evaluate** What social contributions did Benito Juárez make to Mexican society?
   c. **Predict** How might history have been different if the Aztecs had defeated the Spanish?

3. a. **Identify** What Mexican holiday honors dead ancestors?
   b. **Summarize** How did Mexico's colonial past shape its culture?

Critical Thinking

4. **Sequence** Draw a sequence diagram like the one below. Then, using your notes, list the major events in Mexico's history in the order they happened.

↓

↓

1821—Mexico wins independence from Spain

↓

↓

🌐
Mexico Today

The Big Idea

Mexico has four culture regions that all play a part in the country's government and economy.

Main Ideas

- Government has traditionally played a large role in Mexico's economy.
- Mexico has four distinct culture regions.

Key Terms and Places

inflation
indigenous
slash-and-burn agriculture
cash crop
Mexico City
smog
maquiladoras

Reading Check
Draw Conclusions
What might a negative effect be if Mexico always elects the same political party?

If YOU lived there . . .

For many years, your family has lived in a small village in southern Mexico. Jobs are scarce there. Your older brother and sisters talk about moving to a larger city. Big cities may provide some more opportunities, but they can be crowded and noisy. Many people from your village have already gone to the city.

How do you feel about moving to the city?

Government

Today people in Mexico can vote in certain elections for the first time. People can find jobs in cities and buy their families a home. More children are able to attend school. In recent years, changes in Mexico's government and economy have made improvements like these possible.

Mexico has a democratic government. However, Mexico is not like the United States where different political parties have always competed for power. In Mexico the same political party, the Institutional Revolutionary Party (PRI), controlled the government for 71 years. But this control ended in 2000 when Mexicans elected Vicente Fox their president. Fox represented a different political party. However, in 2012 the PRI regained the office of president when Mexicans elected Enrique Peña Nieto. As president, Peña Nieto worked to improve Mexico's economy and reduce drug-related violence.

Economy

Mexico is a developing country. It has struggled with debts to foreign banks, unemployment, and inflation. **Inflation** is a rise in prices that occurs when currency loses its buying power. When inflation occurs, the average person earns the same amount of money, but the price of goods—like food or gasoline—may cost much more. Therefore, they may not be able to afford to buy some things that they could before.

Although living standards in Mexico are lower than in many other countries, Mexico's economy is growing. The North American Free Trade Agreement (NAFTA), which took effect in 1994, has made trade among Mexico, the United States, and

Canada easier. Mexico's agricultural and industrial exports have increased since NAFTA went into effect.

However, not all Mexicans supported the NAFTA agreement. The same day it took effect, a rebellion by a group called the Zapatistas broke out in a rural area in southern Mexico. The Zapatistas believed the trade deal would not benefit the poor **indigenous** Indians who mostly farm on communal lands. The Zapatistas continue to support greater political and cultural power for the Indian people.

Agriculture Agriculture has long been a key part of the Mexican economy. This is true even though just 13 percent of the land is good for farming. Many farmers in southern Mexico practice **slash-and-burn agriculture,** which is the practice of burning forest in order to clear land for planting.

The high market demand for food in the United States has encouraged many farmers in Mexico to specialize by growing cash crops. A **cash crop** is a crop that farmers grow mainly to sell for a profit. Trucks bring cash crops like fruits and vegetables from Mexico to the United States.

Industry Oil is also an important export for Mexico. Many Mexicans work in the oil, mining, and manufacturing industries. These industries are growing.

The fastest-growing industrial centers in Mexico lie along the U.S. border. Because wages are relatively low in Mexico, many U.S. and foreign companies have built factories in Mexico. Mexican workers in these

Agricultural Fires in Southern Mexico

Many people in Mexico are subsistence farmers. They do not own much land and grow only enough food to feed their families. To gain more land, farmers in southern Mexico burn patches of forest. The fires clear the trees and kill weeds. The ash from the fires fertilizes the soil. The problem is that growing the same crops year after year drains valuable nutrients from the soil. So, farmers have to burn new forest land.

In this satellite image, agricultural fires appear as red dots. As you can see, the fires create a lot of smoke. The wind can blow the smoke great distances. Every few years, when the conditions are right, smoke from agricultural fires in Mexico reaches as far as the southern United States. The smoke can cause health problems for some people.

Analyze Effects
What direction is the wind blowing in this image?

factories assemble goods for export to the United States and other countries. Some Mexican workers also come to the United States to look for jobs that pay more than they can make at home.

Tourism Tourism is another important part of Mexico's economy. Many tourists visit old colonial cities and Maya and Aztec monuments. Coastal cities and resorts such as Cancún and Acapulco are also popular with tourists.

Reading Check
Summarize What effect has NAFTA had on Mexico's economy?

Mexico's Culture Regions

Although all Mexicans share some cultural characteristics, we can divide Mexico into four regions based on regional differences. These four culture regions differ from each other in their population, resources, climate, and other features.

Greater Mexico City Greater Mexico City includes the capital and about 50 smaller cities near it. With a population of about 20 million, **Mexico City** is one of the world's largest and most densely populated urban areas. Thousands of people move there every year looking for work.

While this region does provide job and educational opportunities not so easily found in the rest of the country, its huge population causes problems. For example, Mexico City is very polluted. Factories and cars release exhaust and other pollutants into the air. The surrounding mountains trap the resulting **smog**—a mixture of smoke, chemicals, and fog. Smog can cause health problems like eye irritation and breathing difficulties.

Another problem that comes from crowding is poverty. Wealth and poverty exist side by side in Mexico City. The city has large urban slums. The slums often exist right next to modern office buildings, apartments, museums, or universities.

Central Mexico North of greater Mexico City lies Mexico's central region. Many cities in this region were established as mining or ranching centers during the colonial period. Mexico's colonial heritage can still be seen today in these cities and towns. For example, small towns often have a colonial-style church near a main central square. The central square, or plaza, has served for hundreds of years as a community meeting spot and market area.

In addition to small colonial towns, central Mexico has many fertile valleys and small family farms. Farmers in this region grow vegetables, corn, and wheat for sale, mostly to cities in Mexico.

While central Mexico has always been a mining center, in recent years the region has also attracted new industries from overcrowded Mexico City. As a result, some cities in the region, such as Guadalajara, are growing rapidly.

Northern Mexico Northern Mexico has become one of the country's richest and most modern areas. Trade with the United States has helped the region's economy grow. Monterrey and Tijuana are now major cities there. Many U.S.- and foreign-owned factories called **maquiladoras** (mah-kee-lah-DORH-ahs) have been built along Mexico's long border with the United States.

Academic Vocabulary
affect to change or influence

Northern Mexico's closeness to the border has **affected** the region's culture as well as its economy. American television, music, and other forms of entertainment are popular there. Many Mexicans cross the border to shop, work, or live in the United States. While many people cross the border legally, the U.S. government tries to prevent Mexicans and others from crossing the border illegally.

Southern Mexico Southern Mexico is the least populated and industrialized region of the country. Many people in this region speak Indian languages and practice traditional ways of life. Subsistence farming and slash-and-burn agriculture are common.

▶ *Explore ONLINE!*

Mexico's Culture Regions

Northern Mexico
Northern Mexico's land is generally too dry to be much good for farming, but ranching is an important part of the region's economy.

Greater Mexico City
Traffic clogs Mexico City's busy streets. Taxis, buses, and private cars zoom past modern office buildings and old colonial government buildings.

Southern Mexico
While poverty is a problem in much of southern Mexico, some people make money selling traditional handicrafts to tourists.

Central Mexico
The architecture and cobblestone streets of many towns in central Mexico reflect the region's Spanish colonial heritage.

Interpret Maps
Location How does life in greater Mexico City differ from life in northern Mexico?

Mexico **289**

However, southern Mexico is vital to the country's economy. Sugarcane and coffee, two major export crops, grow well in the region's warm, humid climate. Also, oil production along the Gulf coast has increased in recent years. The oil business has brought more industry and population growth to this coastal area of southern Mexico.

Another place in southern Mexico that has grown in recent years is the Yucatán Peninsula. Maya ruins, beautiful sunny beaches, and clear blue water have made tourism a major industry in this area. Many cities that were just tiny fishing villages only 20 years ago are now booming with new construction for the tourist industry.

Mexico has a democratic government and a growing economy. Mexico will continue to change in the future. Changes are likely to bring more development. However, maintaining the country's unique regional cultures may be a challenge as those changes take place.

Summary and Preview Mexico has a democractic government and a growing economy. It also has distinct regions with different cultures, economies, and environments.

Reading Check
Compare and Contrast What similarities and differences exist between greater Mexico City and southern Mexico?

Lesson 3 Assessment

Review Ideas, Terms, and Places

1. a. Compare and Contrast How is Mexico's government similar to and different from the government of the United States?

   b. Identify Who is allowed to vote in Mexico?

2. Define What is the term for the practice of burning forest in order to clear land for planting?

3. a. Identify What is an environmental problem found in Mexico City?

   b. Make Inferences What conditions in Mexico lead some Mexicans to cross the border into the United States?

c. Develop If you were to start a business in Mexico, what type of business would you start and where would you start it? Explain your decisions.

Critical Thinking

4. Find Main Ideas Review your notes on Mexico's economy. Then use a chart like this one to identify the geographic factors responsible for the location of economic activities in each region of Mexico.

Greater Mexico City	Central Mexico	Northern Mexico	Southern Mexico

Social Studies Skills

Take Notes

Define the Skill

Taking notes can help you remember what you have learned from your textbook or in class. To be effective, your notes must be clear and organized. One good way to organize your notes is in a chart like the one here. Use the following steps to help you take useful notes:

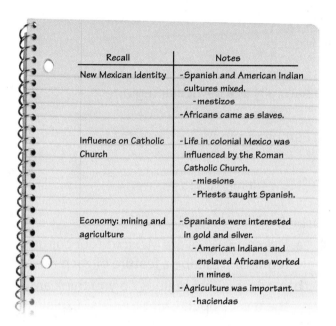

Before you read or listen:

- Divide a page in your notebook into two columns as shown.

While you read or listen:

- Write down your notes in phrases or sentences in the large column on the right.

After you read or listen:

- Review your notes. Then in the small column on the left, jot down ideas, key terms, or questions in your own words based on the notes you took.

Learn the Skill

Answer the following questions about taking notes.

1. Where should you write your notes while you read or listen in class?

2. How can jotting down key ideas, terms, and questions help you clarify your notes after you take them?

Practice the Skill

Look back at Lesson 1 of this module. Divide your paper into two columns and take notes on the lesson using the suggestions in the left column. Then answer the following questions.

1. What ideas or questions did you write in the Recall column on the left?

2. What are some advantages of taking notes?

Module 9 Assessment

Review Vocabulary, Terms, and Places

Unscramble each group of letters below to spell a term that matches the given definition.

1. **pmreie**—a land with different territories and peoples under a single ruler
2. **tflinnaoi**—a rise in prices that occurs when currency loses its buying power
3. **mogs**—a mixture of smoke, chemicals, and fog
4. **snipluane**—a piece of land surrounded on three sides by water
5. **ztosemsi**—people of mixed European and Indian ancestry
6. **hacs rpoc**—a crop that farmers grow mainly to sell for a profit
7. **ssnmiosi**—church outposts
8. **dqamiuarsloa**—U.S.- and foreign-owned factories in Mexico
9. **ndhceiasa**—expanses of farm or ranch land
10. **dingsounie**—produced, growing, living, or occurring naturally in a particular region or environment
11. **tulmato**—colonial Spanish term for a person of mixed European and African ancestry

Comprehension and Critical Thinking

Lesson 1

12. a. **Define** What is the Mexican Plateau? What forms its edges?

   b. **Contrast** How does the climate of Mexico City differ from the climate in the south?

   c. **Evaluate** What do you think would be Mexico's most important resource if it did not have oil? Explain your answer.

Lesson 2

13. a. **Recall** What early civilization did the Spanish conquer when they came to Mexico?

   b. **Analyze** How did Spanish rule influence Mexico's culture?

   c. **Evaluate** Which war—the war for independence, the Mexican War, or the Mexican Revolution—do you think changed Mexico the most? Explain your answer.

Lesson 3

14. a. **Describe** What are Mexico's four culture regions? Describe a feature of each.

   b. **Analyze** What regions do you think are the most popular with tourists? Explain your answer.

   c. **Evaluate** What are two major drawbacks of slash-and-burn agriculture?

Reading Skills

15. Predict Use the Reading Skills taught in this module to complete the following activity. Use your predicting skills to think about events that might happen in the future. Reread the text about Mexico's economy in Lesson 3. Write three or four sentences about how you think the economy might change in the future.

Social Studies Skills

16. Take Notes Use the Social Studies Skills taught in this module to complete the following activity. With a partner read aloud to each other about Mexico's government and economy in Lesson 3. As you listen to your partner, use a chart like the one below to take notes on the information in your book.

Recall	Notes

Map Activity 21st CENTURY

17. Mexico On a separate sheet of paper, match the letters on the map with their correct locations.

- Gulf of Mexico
- Baja California
- Río Bravo (Rio Grande)
- Tijuana
- Yucatán Peninsula
- Mexico City

Focus on Writing

18. Write an "I Am" Poem Countries have stories to tell, just like people do. Review what you have learned about Mexico. Then, write a poem. Title your poem "I Am Mexico" and make it six lines long. Use each line to give details about Mexico, such as "I have towering, snowcapped volcanoes." Make sure at least one line deals with physical geography, one line with history and culture, and one line with Mexico today. Your poem does not need to rhyme, but you should try to use vivid language. With a partner recite your poems to each other.

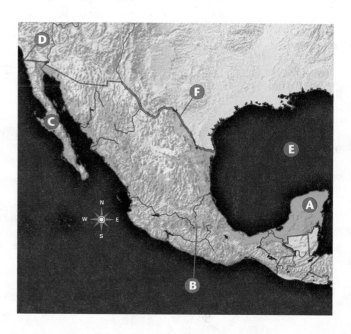

MEXICO

Teotihuacán, established around 200 BC, was the first great civilization of ancient Mexico. At its height around the middle of the first millennium AD, the "City of the Gods" was one of the largest cities in the world. It covered 12 square miles and was home to some 200,000 people. The Pyramid of the Sun, above, was the largest building in Teotihuacán.

For centuries after the fall of Teotihuacán, present-day Mexico was home to a number of great empires, including the highly sophisticated Aztec civilization. The arrival of the Spanish in the early 1500s forever changed life for Mexico's ancient peoples, and Mexican culture today is dominated by a blend of indigenous and Spanish cultures.

Explore the history of Mexico from ancient to modern times online. You can find a wealth of information, video clips, primary sources, activities, and more through your online textbook.

HISTORY Go online to view these and other **HISTORY**® resources.

The Arrival of the Spanish
Watch the video to learn how the arrival of the conquistadors led to the fall of the Aztec Empire.

Miguel Hidalgo's Call to Arms
Watch the video to learn about Miguel Hidalgo's path from priest to revolutionary leader.

Mexico in the Modern Era
Watch the video to learn about the role of oil in the industrialization of Mexico's economy.

Mexico's Ancient Civilizations
Watch the video to learn about the great civilizations that arose in ancient Mexico.

Central America and the Caribbean

Essential Question

What are the most important challenges for the nations of Central America and the Caribbean?

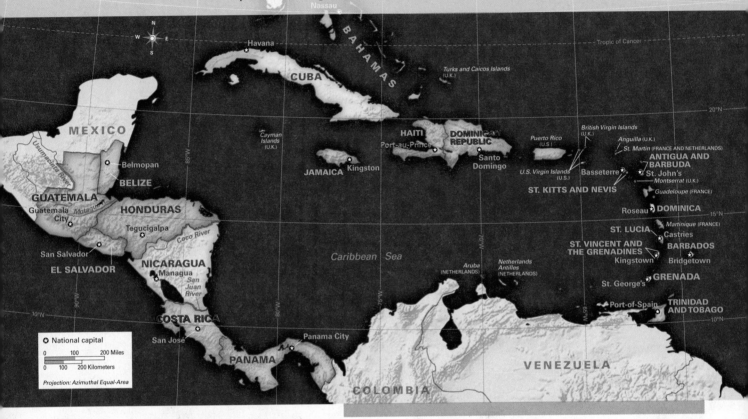

In this module, you will learn how geography, history, and challenges have shaped Central America and the Caribbean.

What You Will Learn

▶ *Explore ONLINE!*

VIDEOS, including . . .
• A Civilization Abandoned

HISTORY

☑ Document-Based Investigations

☑ Graphic Organizers

☑ Interactive Games

☑ Channel One News Video: Geo Week 2013: The Island of Enchantment

☑ Image with Hotspots: A Market in Guatemala

☑ Animation: How the Panama Canal Works

☑ Interactive Map: European Colonies in the Caribbean, 1763

Geography Beautiful, sandy beaches and tropical, forested plains are common in Central America and the Caribbean.

Culture Many people in the region maintain their traditional cultures. These Kuna women are from Panama.

History The Spanish built forts like this one in Puerto Rico to defend their islands and protect the harbors from pirates.

Reading Social Studies

Understand Comparison-Contrast

READING FOCUS

Comparing shows how things are alike. Contrasting shows how things are different. You can understand comparison-contrast by learning to recognize clue words and points of comparison. Clue words let you know whether to look for similarities or differences. Points of comparison are the main topics that are being compared or contrasted.

Many Caribbean islands share a similar history and culture. However, today the islands' different economies, governments, and cultural landscapes encourage many different ways of life in the Caribbean.

Underlined words are clue words.

Highlighted words are points of comparison.

Clue Words	
Comparison	**Contrast**
share, similar, like, also, both, in addition, besides	however, while, unlike, different, but, although

Haiti occupies the western part of the island of Hispaniola. Haiti's capital, Port-au-Prince, is the center of the nation's limited industry. Most Haitians farm small plots. Coffee and sugarcane are among Haiti's main exports.

The Dominican Republic occupies the eastern part of Hispaniola. The Dominican Republic is not a rich country. However, its economy, health care, education, and housing are more developed than Haiti's. Agriculture is the basis of the economy.

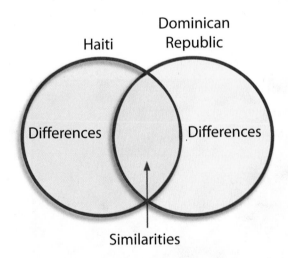

YOU TRY IT!

Read the passages above to see how Haiti and the Dominican Republic are alike and how they are different. Use a diagram like the one on this page to compare and contrast the two countries.

As you read this module, look for clue words that signal comparison or contrast.

Physical Geography

The Big Idea

The physical geography of Central America and the Caribbean islands includes warm coastal lowlands, cooler highlands, and tropical forests.

Main Ideas

- Physical features of the region include volcanic highlands and coastal plains.

- The climate and vegetation of the region include forested highlands, tropical forests, and humid lowlands.

- Key natural resources in the region include rich soils for agriculture, a few minerals, and beautiful beaches.

Key Terms and Places

isthmus
Caribbean Sea
archipelago
Greater Antilles
Lesser Antilles
cloud forest

If YOU lived there . . .

You live in San José, the capital of Costa Rica. But now you are visiting a tropical forest in one of the country's national parks. You make your way carefully along a swinging rope bridge in the forest canopy—40 feet above the forest floor! You see a huge green iguana making its way along a branch. A brilliantly colored parrot flies past you.

What other creatures might you see in the forest?

Physical Features

Sandy beaches, volcanic mountains, rain forests, clear blue water—these are images many people have of Central America and the Caribbean islands. The region's physical geography is beautiful. This beauty is one of the region's greatest resources.

Central America The region called Central America is actually the southern part of North America. Seven countries make up this region: Belize, Guatemala, Honduras, El Salvador, Nicaragua, Costa Rica, and Panama. As you can see on the map, Central America is an **isthmus,** or a narrow strip of land that connects two larger land areas. No place on this isthmus is more than about 125 miles (200 km) from either the Pacific Ocean or the **Caribbean Sea.**

A chain of mountains and volcanoes separates the Pacific and Caribbean coastal plains, and only a few short rivers flow through Central America. The ruggedness of the land and the lack of good water routes make travel in the region difficult.

Coastal plains, like this one in Cuba, are found in Central America and the Caribbean islands.

Explore ONLINE!

Gulf of Mexico

ATLANTIC OCEAN

Tropic of Cancer

Straits of Florida

BAHAMAS

20°N

Yucatán
Peninsula

CUBA

DOMINICAN
REPUBLIC

JAMAICA

HAITI

ANTIGUA
AND BARBUDA

BELIZE

Greater Antilles

Hispaniola

ST. KITTS AND NEVIS

DOMINICA

GUATEMALA

N
W   E
S

HONDURAS

Caribbean Sea

ST. LUCIA

EL SALVADOR

NICARAGUA

ST. VINCENT AND
THE GRENADINES

BARBADOS

GRENADA

Lesser Antilles

Lake
Nicaragua

Panama
Canal

TRINIDAD AND TOBAGO

PACIFIC OCEAN

COSTA
RICA

10°N

PANAMA

Gulf
of
Panama

ELEVATION

Feet		Meters
13,120		4,000
6,560		2,000
1,640		500
656		200
(Sea level) 0		0 (Sea level)
Below sea level		Below sea level

0   100   200 Miles

0   100   200 Kilometers

Projection: Azimuthal Equal-Area

Interpret Maps

1. **Location** On which island is Haiti located?

2. **Human-Environment Interaction** How do you think life in Honduras differs from life in the Bahamas?

The Caribbean Islands Across the Caribbean Sea from Central America lie hundreds of islands known as the Caribbean islands. They make up an **archipelago** (ahr-kuh-PE-luh-goh), or a large group of islands. Arranged in a long curve, the Caribbean islands stretch from the southern tip of Florida to northern South America. They divide the Caribbean Sea from the Atlantic Ocean.

There are two main island groups in the Caribbean. The four large islands of Cuba, Jamaica, Hispaniola, and Puerto Rico make up the **Greater Antilles** (an-TIL-eez). Many smaller islands form the **Lesser Antilles.** They stretch from the Virgin Islands to Trinidad and Tobago. A third island group, the Bahamas, lies in the Atlantic Ocean southeast of Florida. It includes nearly 700 islands and thousands of reefs.

Many Caribbean islands are actually the tops of underwater mountains and volcanoes. Others began as coral reefs that were gradually pushed up to become flat limestone islands. Colliding tectonic plates have pushed this region's land up out of the sea over several million years. You can see these tectonic plates on the map. Notice how the land follows the boundaries of the plates. Earthquakes and volcanic eruptions occur frequently as these plates shift. When such events do occur, they can cause great damage to the region and its people.

Reading Check
Compare What physical features do Central America and the Caribbean islands have in common?

Climate and Vegetation

Central America and the Caribbean islands are generally sunny and warm. Humid tropical and tropical savanna climates are common in the islands and on Central America's coastal plains. On the Pacific coast, much of the area's original savanna vegetation has been cleared. It has been replaced by plantations and ranches. The opposite coast, along the Caribbean Sea, has areas of tropical rain forest.

1 The Santa Ana volcano in El Salvador was formed by tectonic movements.

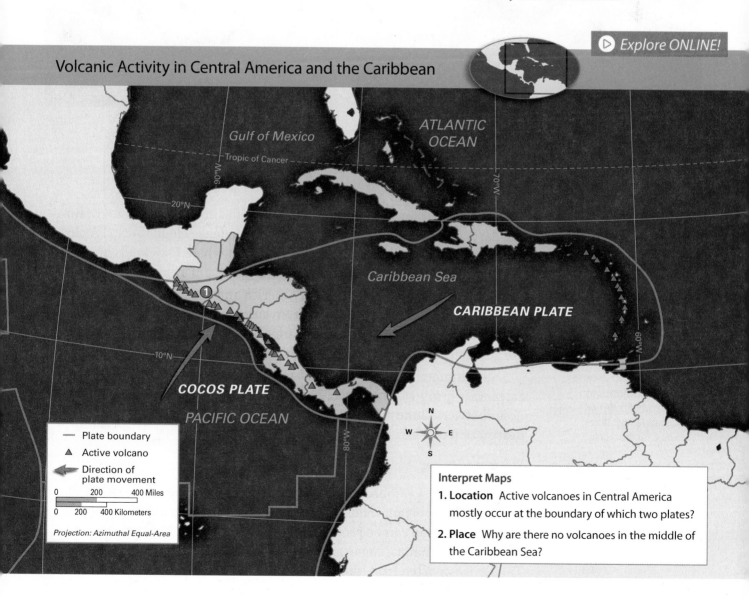

Volcanic Activity in Central America and the Caribbean

▷ Explore ONLINE!

Legend
- — Plate boundary
- ▲ Active volcano
- ← Direction of plate movement

0   200   400 Miles
0   200   400 Kilometers

Projection: Azimuthal Equal-Area

Interpret Maps

1. **Location** Active volcanoes in Central America mostly occur at the boundary of which two plates?

2. **Place** Why are there no volcanoes in the middle of the Caribbean Sea?

Hurricanes are rotating storms that bring heavy rain and winds that can reach speeds higher than 155 miles per hour (249 kph). This image shows a hurricane sweeping through the Caribbean Sea. Strong hurricanes like this one can shatter houses and hurl cars through the air.

Strong hurricane winds spin around a calm center point called the eye.

Analyze Visuals
How can you tell the storm is rotating?

Inland mountain areas contain cool, humid climates. Some mountainous parts of Central America are covered with dense cloud forests. A **cloud forest** is a moist, high-elevation tropical forest where low clouds are common. These forests are home to numerous plant and animal species.

Temperatures in most of Central America and the Caribbean do not change much from day to night or from summer to winter. Instead, the change in seasons is marked by a change in rainfall. Winters in the region are generally dry, while it rains nearly every day during the summers.

From summer to fall, hurricanes are a threat in the region. These tropical storms bring violent winds, heavy rain, and high seas. Most hurricanes occur between June and November. Their winds and flooding can cause destruction and loss of life.

Reading Check
Form Generalizations
Where would one find the coolest temperatures in the region?

Resources

The region's best resources are its land and climate. These factors make tourism an important industry. They also influence agriculture. Agriculture in the region can be profitable where volcanic ash has enriched the soil. Coffee, bananas, sugarcane, and cotton grow well and are major crops. Timber is exported from the rain forests.

Although its land and climate make good agricultural resources, the region has few mineral resources. Energy resources are also limited. Central America and the Caribbean islands must rely on energy imports, which limits their development.

Summary and Preview Central America and the Caribbean islands share volcanic physical features and a warm, tropical climate good for agriculture. In the next section, you will learn about the history and culture of Central America.

Lesson 1 Assessment

Review Ideas, Terms, and Places

1. a. **Define** What is an isthmus?

   b. **Explain** How has tectonic activity affected Central America and the Caribbean islands?

2. a. **Describe** What is a cloud forest?

   b. **Make Inferences** Why do temperatures in the region change little from summer to winter?

3. a. **Recall** What crops grow well in the region?

   b. **Evaluate** Do you think tourists who want to go to the beach are more likely to visit Guatemala or the Bahamas? Explain your answer.

Critical Thinking

4. **Categorize** Draw a two-column graphic organizer. Label the left column *Central America* and the right column *Caribbean Islands*. Using your notes, write descriptive phrases about the physical features, climate, and resources of both places.

Central America	Caribbean Islands

Central America

The Big Idea

Central America's native traditions and colonial history have created a mixed culture, unstable governments, and uncertain economies.

Main Ideas

- The history of Central America was mostly influenced by Spain.

- The culture of Central America is a mixture of Native American and European traditions.

- Today, the countries of Central America have challenges and opportunities.

Key Terms and Places

ecotourism
civil war
Panama Canal

If YOU lived there . . .

You live in El Salvador, in a town that is still living with the effects of a civil war 25 years ago. Your parents and your older neighbors still speak about those years with fear. One effect of the war was damage to the economy. Many people have gone to Mexico to try to make a better life. Now your parents are talking about going there to look for work. But you are not sure.

How do you feel about leaving your home?

History

Many countries of Central America have a shared history. This shared history has been influenced by the Maya, the Spanish, and the United States.

Early History In several Central American countries, the Maya were building large cities with pyramids and temples by about AD 250. The Maya abandoned most of their cities around 900, but the ruins of many ancient cities still stand in the region today. People of Maya descent still live in Guatemala and Belize. In fact, many ancient Maya customs still influence modern life there.

Hundreds of years later, in the early 1500s, most of Central America came under European control. Spain claimed most of the region. Britain claimed what is now Belize and also occupied part of Nicaragua's coast. The Spanish established large plantations in their colonies to grow crops like tobacco and sugarcane. They made Central American Indians work on the plantations or in gold mines elsewhere in the Americas. In addition, Europeans brought many enslaved Africans to the region to work on plantations and in mines.

Central America Since Independence The Spanish colonies of Central America declared independence from Spain in 1821, but much of the region remained joined together as the United Provinces of Central America. The countries of Costa Rica,

One-Crop Economies

The economies of many Central American countries relied on only one crop—bananas. The U.S.-based United Fruit Company was the biggest banana exporter and the largest employer in the region for many years. The old photo below shows the company's hiring hall in Guatemala.

Analyze Visuals
Why do workers place cushions between bananas?

Nicaragua, Honduras, El Salvador, and Guatemala separated from each other from 1838 to 1839. Panama remained part of Colombia until 1903. Belize did not gain independence from Britain until 1981.

For most countries in Central America, independence brought little change. The Spanish officials left, but wealthy landowners continued to run the countries and their economies. The plantation crops of bananas and coffee supported Central American economies.

In the early to mid-1900s, one landowner in particular, the U.S.-based United Fruit Company, controlled most of the banana production in Central America. To help its business, the company developed railroads and port facilities. This kind of development helped transportation and communications in the region.

Many people resented the role of foreign companies, however. They thought it was wrong that only a few people should own so much land while many people struggled to make a living. In the mid- to late 1900s, demands for reforms led to armed struggles in Guatemala, El Salvador, and Nicaragua. Only in recent years have these countries achieved peace.

Reading Check
Evaluate
How did Spain influence the region's history?

Culture

Central America's colonial history has influenced its culture. The region's people, languages, religion, and festivals reflect both Spanish and native practices.

People and Languages Most of the people in Central America are mestizos, or people of mixed European and Indian ancestry. Various Indian peoples descended from the ancient Maya live in places such as the Guatemalan Highlands. People of African ancestry also make up a significant minority in this region. They live mostly along the Caribbean coast.

In some countries in Central America, many people still speak the native Indian languages. In places that were colonized by England, English is spoken. For example, it is the official language of Belize. In most countries, however, Spanish is the official language. The Spanish colonization of Central America left this lasting mark on the region.

Religion, Festivals, and Food Many Central Americans practice a religion brought to the region by Europeans. Most people are Roman Catholic because Spanish missionaries taught the Indians about Catholicism.

A Market in Guatemala

Villages in Guatemala and all over Central America hold weekly markets. On market day, people come from all around to buy and sell food and other items. The market is also an important gathering spot for the community. Scenes like this one are typical in the region.

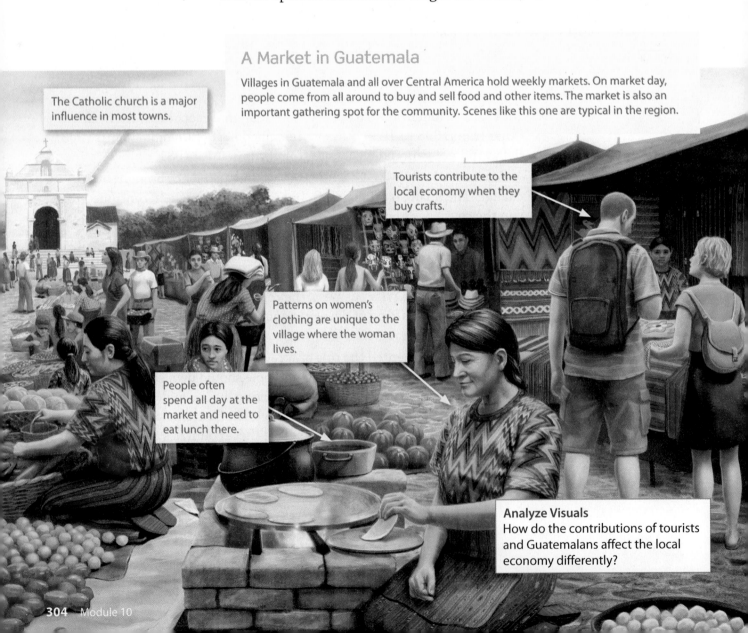

The Catholic church is a major influence in most towns.

Tourists contribute to the local economy when they buy crafts.

Patterns on women's clothing are unique to the village where the woman lives.

People often spend all day at the market and need to eat lunch there.

Analyze Visuals
How do the contributions of tourists and Guatemalans affect the local economy differently?

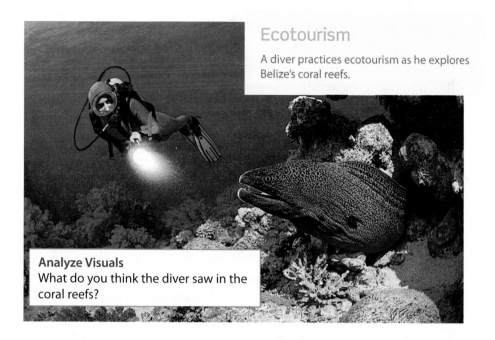

Ecotourism

A diver practices ecotourism as he explores Belize's coral reefs.

Analyze Visuals
What do you think the diver saw in the coral reefs?

Academic Vocabulary
traditional customary, time-honored

Reading Check
Contrast How is Belize culturally different from the rest of the region?

However, Indian traditions have influenced Catholicism in return. Also, Protestant Christians are becoming a large minority in places such as Belize.

Religion has influenced celebrations in towns throughout the region. For example, to celebrate special saints' feast days, some people carry images of the saint in parades through the streets. Easter is a particularly important holiday. Some towns decorate whole streets with designs made of flowers and colorful sawdust.

During festivals, people eat **traditional** foods. Central America shares some of its traditional foods, like corn, with Mexico. The region is also known for tomatoes, hot peppers, and cacao (kuh-KOW), which is the source of chocolate.

Central America Today

The countries of Central America share similar histories and cultures. However, they all face their own economic and political challenges today. In 2005 Costa Rica, the Dominican Republic, El Salvador, Guatemala, Honduras, and Nicaragua signed the Central American Free Trade Agreement (CAFTA) with the United States to help increase trade among the countries. This agreement was designed to create economic stability and jobs in Central America and the Dominican Republic. For example, the reduction of taxes on imports and exports resulted in economic growth. Farmers also received technical training to improve crop production.

Belize Belize has the smallest population in Central America. The country does not have much land for agriculture, either. But **ecotourism**—the practice of using an area's natural environment to attract tourists—has become popular lately. Tourists come to see the country's coral reefs, Maya ruins, and coastal resorts.

Guatemala Guatemala is the most populous country in Central America. More than 13 million people live there. About 60 percent of Guatemalans are mestizo and European. About 40 percent are Central American Indians. Many speak Maya languages.

Most people in Guatemala live in small villages in the highlands. Fighting between rebels and government forces there killed some 200,000 people between 1960 and 1996. Guatemalans are still recovering from this conflict.

Coffee, which grows well in the cool highlands, is Guatemala's most important crop. The country also is a major producer of cardamom, a spice used in Asian foods.

Honduras Honduras is a mountainous country. Most people live in mountain valleys and along the northern coast. The rugged land makes transportation difficult and provides little land where crops can grow. However, citrus fruits and bananas are important exports.

Honduras, Guatemala, and El Salvador make up Central America's Northern Triangle region. In recent years the area has experienced extreme levels of poverty, gang violence, and organized crime. Some cities in the Northern Triangle are among the most dangerous in the world. Many people have fled these nations to seek asylum from the violence.

El Salvador In El Salvador, a few rich families own much of the best land while most people live in poverty. These conditions were a reason behind a long civil war in the 1980s. A **civil war** is a conflict between two or more groups within a country. The war killed many people and hurt the economy.

El Salvador's people have been working to rebuild their country since the end of the war in 1992. One advantage they have in this rebuilding effort is the country's fertile soil. People are able to grow and export crops such as coffee and sugarcane.

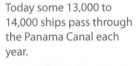

Today some 13,000 to 14,000 ships pass through the Panama Canal each year.

Nicaragua Nicaragua has also been rebuilding since the end of a civil war. In 1979 a group called the Sandinistas overthrew a dictator. Many Nicaraguans supported the Sandinistas, but rebel forces aided by the United States fought the Sandinistas for power. The civil war ended in 1990 when elections ended the rule of the Sandinistas. Nicaragua is now a democracy.

Costa Rica Unlike most other Central American countries, Costa Rica has a history of peace. It also has a stable, democratic government. The country does not even have an army. Peace has helped Costa Rica make progress in reducing poverty.

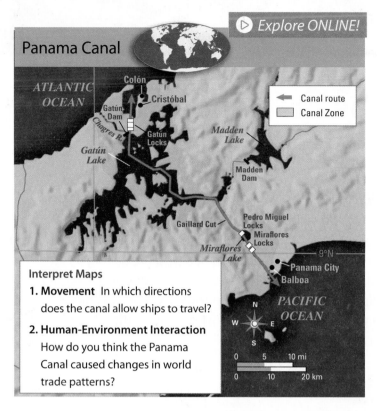

Panama Canal

▶ Explore ONLINE!

ATLANTIC OCEAN

Colón
Cristóbal
Gatún Dam
Chagres R.
Gatún Locks
Gatún Lake
Madden Lake
Madden Dam
Gaillard Cut
Pedro Miguel Locks
Miraflores Locks
Miraflores Lake
9°N
Panama City
Balboa
PACIFIC OCEAN

Canal route
Canal Zone

N W E S

0   5   10 mi
0   10   20 km

Interpret Maps

1. **Movement** In which directions does the canal allow ships to travel?

2. **Human-Environment Interaction** How do you think the Panama Canal caused changes in world trade patterns?

Agricultural products like coffee and bananas are important to Costa Rica's economy. Also, many tourists visit Costa Rica's rich tropical rain forests.

Panama Panama is the narrowest, southernmost country of Central America. Most people live in areas near the **Panama Canal.** Canal fees and local industries make the Canal Zone the country's most prosperous region.

The Panama Canal provides a link between the Pacific Ocean, the Caribbean Sea, and the Atlantic Ocean. The United States finished building the canal in 1914. For years, the Panama Canal played an important role in the economy and politics of the region. The United States controlled the canal until 1999. Then, as agreed to in a treaty, Panama finally gained full control of the canal.

Reading Check
Make Inferences Why do you think Panama wanted control of the canal?

Summary and Preview Native peoples, European colonizers, and the United States have influenced Central America's history and culture. Today most countries are developing stable governments. Their economies rely on tourism and agriculture. In the next section you will learn about the main influences on the Caribbean islands and life there today.

Lesson 2 Assessment

Review Ideas, Terms, and Places

1. a. **Recall** What parts of Central America did the British claim?

   b. **Analyze** How did independence affect most Central American countries?

   c. **Elaborate** What benefits and drawbacks might there be to the United Fruit Company's owning so much land?

2. a. **Identify** What language do most people in Central America speak?

   b. **Explain** How have native cultures influenced cultural practices in the region today?

3. a. **Define** What is a civil war, and where in Central America has a civil war been fought?

   b. **Explain** Why might some people practice ecotourism?

   c. **Elaborate** Why is the Panama Canal important to Panama? Why is it important to other countries?

Critical Thinking

4. **Summarize** Draw a two-column graphic organizer with seven rows. List the name of each Central American nation in the left column. Using your notes, write at least one important fact about each Central American country today.

Guatemala	
Belize	
Honduras	
El Salvador	
Nicaragua	
Costa Rica	
Panama	

The Caribbean Islands

The Big Idea

The Caribbean islands have a rich history and diverse cultures influenced by European colonization.

Main Ideas

- The history of the Caribbean islands includes European colonization followed by independence.

- The culture of the Caribbean islands shows signs of past colonialism and slavery.

- Today, the Caribbean islands have distinctive governments with economies that depend on agriculture and tourism.

Key Terms and Places

Columbian Exchange
dialect
commonwealth
refugee
Havana
cooperative

If YOU lived there . . .

You are a young sailor on Christopher Columbus's second voyage to the New World. The year is 1493. Now that your ship is in the Caribbean Sea, you are sailing from island to island. You have seen volcanoes and waterfalls. You have met native peoples. Columbus has decided to establish a trading post on one of the islands. You are part of the crew who will stay there.

What do you expect in your new home?

History

When Christopher Columbus sailed to America in 1492, he actually arrived in the Caribbean islands. These islands now include 13 independent countries. The countries themselves show the influence of those first European explorers.

Early History Christopher Columbus first sailed into the Caribbean Sea from Spain in 1492. He thought he had reached the Indies, or the islands near India. Therefore, he called the Caribbean islands the West Indies and the people who lived there Indians.

Columbus's fleet sails toward the New World.

Spain had little interest in the smaller Caribbean islands, but the English, French, Dutch, and Danish did. In the 1600s and 1700s these countries established colonies on the islands. They built huge sugarcane plantations that required many workers. Most Caribbean Indians, who had been forced to work on the plantations, had died from diseases spread by European settlers. So, enslaved Africans were brought to the islands and forced to work. Soon Africans and people of African descent outnumbered Europeans on many islands.

Much of the sugar grown in this area was exported to Europe, along with other crops. Colonists then imported products, foods, and even animals from Europe. This movement of people, animals, plants, ideas, and diseases between Europe and the Americas came to be known as the **Columbian Exchange.**

Independence A slave revolt led by Toussaint Louverture (too-SAN loo-vehr-TOOR) eventually helped Haiti win independence from France in

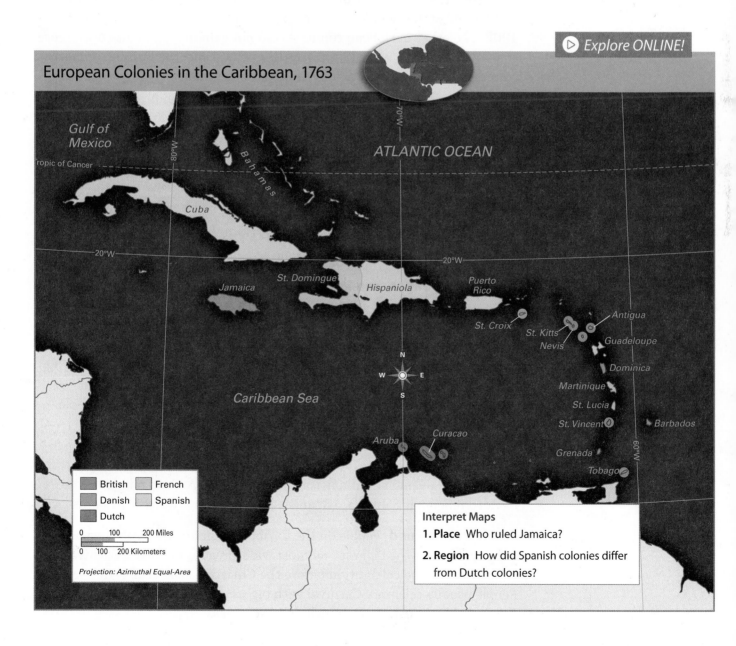

▶ *Explore ONLINE!*

European Colonies in the Caribbean, 1763

Gulf of Mexico

ATLANTIC OCEAN

Tropic of Cancer

Bahamas

Cuba

Jamaica

St. Domingue

Hispaniola

Puerto Rico

St. Croix

St. Kitts

Nevis

Antigua

Guadeloupe

Dominica

Martinique

St. Lucia

St. Vincent

Barbados

Caribbean Sea

Grenada

Aruba

Curacao

Tobago

British
Danish
Dutch
French
Spanish

0   100   200 Miles
0   100   200 Kilometers

Projection: Azimuthal Equal-Area

Interpret Maps

1. **Place** Who ruled Jamaica?

2. **Region** How did Spanish colonies differ from Dutch colonies?

Toussaint Louverture
(c. 1743–1803)

Toussaint Louverture was born a slave. A few years after he gained his freedom, a slave revolt broke out in Haiti. Toussaint soon realized the rebels did not have very good leaders, so he went on to form an army of his own. He proved to be an excellent army general. He later became a popular governor of Haiti, gaining the respect of both black and white people on the island.

Reading Check
Identify Points of View Why might an island's people not be interested in gaining independence?

1804. Along with independence came freedom for the people enslaved in Haiti. Ideas of independence then spread throughout the region.

By the mid-1800s the Dominican Republic had gained independence. The United States won Cuba from Spain, but Cuba gained independence in 1902. The other Caribbean countries did not gain independence until more than 40 years later, after World War II. At that time, the Europeans transferred political power peacefully to most of the islands.

Many Caribbean islands still are not independent countries. For example, the islands of Martinique and Guadeloupe are still French possessions. Each has its own elected government and is also represented in the French government. Most people on these islands seem not to wish for independence from their ruling countries.

Culture

Today, nearly all Caribbean islands show signs of past colonialism and slavery. These signs can be seen in the region's culture.

People, Languages, and Religion Most islanders today are descended either from Europeans or from Africans who came to the region as slaves, or from a mixture of the two. Some Asians also live on the islands. They came to work on plantations after slavery ended in the region.

Languages spoken in the region reflect a colonial heritage. Spanish, English, and French, as well as mixtures of European and African languages, are spoken on many islands. For example, Haitians speak French Creole. Creole is a **dialect,** or a regional variety of a language.

The region's past is also reflected in the religions people practice. Former French and Spanish territories have large numbers of Catholics. People also practice a blend of Catholicism and traditional African religions. One blended religion is Santería, a Spanish word meaning "worship of saints."

Festivals and Food People on the Caribbean islands celebrate a variety of holidays. One of the biggest and most widespread is Carnival. Carnival is a time of feasts and celebration before the Christian season of Lent begins. People usually celebrate Carnival with big parades and fancy costumes. Festivals like Carnival often include great music.

Caribbean food and cooking also reflect the region's past. For example, slave ships carried foods as well as people to the Caribbean. Now foods from Africa, such as yams and okra, are popular there. Also, in Barbados, people eat a dish called souse, which is made of pigs' tails, ears, and snouts. This dish was developed among slaves because slaveholders ate the best parts of the pig and gave slaves the leftovers. Another popular flavor on the islands, curry, was brought to the region by people from India who came as plantation workers after slavery ended.

Reading Check
Form Generalizations
How does Caribbean culture reflect African influences?

The Caribbean Islands Today

Many Caribbean islands share a similar history. Still, each island has its own economy, government, and culture. In 2008 nations of the Caribbean signed an Economic Partnership Agreement with the European Union. This free trade agreement was created to simplify processes for investment and trading between the two regions. The plan also was designed to promote opportunities for economic growth and job creation in Caribbean countries.

Puerto Rico Once a Spanish colony, Puerto Rico today is a U.S. commonwealth. A **commonwealth** is a self-governing territory associated with another country. Puerto Ricans are U.S. citizens, but they do not have voting representation in Congress.

Overall, Puerto Rico's economy has benefitted from U.S. aid and investment. Still, wages are lower and unemployment is higher on the island than in the United States. Many Puerto Ricans have moved to the United States for better paying jobs. Today, Puerto Ricans debate whether their island should remain a U.S. commonwealth, become an American state, or become an independent nation.

Haiti Haiti occupies the western part of the island of Hispaniola. Haiti's capital, Port-au-Prince, is the center of the nation's limited industry. Most Haitians farm small plots. Coffee and sugarcane are among Haiti's main exports.

Languages of the Caribbean

Language	Countries
English	Antigua and Barbuda, Barbados, Trinidad and Tobago
Creole English	Saint Kitts and Nevis, Grenada, Jamaica, Bahamas
Creole French	Haiti, Dominica, Saint Lucia
Spanish	Cuba, Puerto Rico, Dominican Republic

Interpret Charts
What language do people speak in Barbados?

Caribbean Music

The Caribbean islands have produced many unique styles of music. For example, Jamaica is famous as the birthplace of reggae. Merengue is the national music and dance of the Dominican Republic. Trinidad and Tobago is the home of steel-drum and calypso music.

In this photo, a band in the Grenadines performs on steel drums. Steel-drum bands can include as few as 4 or as many as 100 musicians. The instruments are actually metal barrels like the kind used for shipping oil. The end of each drum is hammered into a curved shape with multiple grooves and bumps. Hitting different-sized bumps results in different notes.

Make Inferences
What role might trade have played in the development of steel-drum music?

Haiti is the poorest country in the Americas. Its people have suffered under a string of corrupt governments during the last two centuries. Violence, political unrest, and poverty have created many political refugees. A **refugee** is someone who flees to another country, usually for political or economic reasons. Many Haitian refugees have come to the United States.

On January, 12, 2010, a catastrophic earthquake struck close to Port-au-Prince. The quake devastated Haiti, leaving about 230,000 Haitians dead, 300,000 injured, and over a million homeless. Today, many Haitians continue working to rebuild their lives and nation.

Dominican Republic The Dominican Republic occupies the eastern part of Hispaniola. The capital is Santo Domingo. Santo Domingo was the first permanent European settlement in the Western Hemisphere.

The Dominican Republic is not a rich country. However, its economy, health care, education, and housing are more developed than Haiti's. Agriculture is the basis of the economy in the Dominican Republic. The country's tourism industry also has grown in recent years. Beach resorts along the coast are popular with many tourists from Central and South America as well as from the United States.

Even though they share possession of Hispaniola, the relationship between the Dominican Republic and Haiti has a long history of conflict. The struggles date back to colonial times when there was a dispute over control of the island. In 2015 the Dominican government asked for all Haitians without legal papers to leave the country. Some were even threatened with violence. Many people from Haiti had migrated into the Dominican Republic to find work in a better economy. Despite the orders and potential risks, Haitian people continue to cross the border in search of economic opportunities.

Cuba Cuba is the largest and most populous country in the Caribbean. It is located just 92 miles (148 km) south of Florida. **Havana,** the capital, is the country's largest and most important city. Twenty percent of Cubans live in Havana and most of the population resides in urban areas. There are several major seaports for the export of goods. Easy ocean access is the backbone of the nation's fishing industry, which provides food and a livelihood for many Cuban people.

Cuba's tropical climate makes it warm to hot all year long. Residents can enjoy the beaches and landscape of the country. Tourism is a growing industry that provides jobs for people and encourages economic growth. The climate allows Cuba to grow a variety of crops that can be traded with other nations.

Cuba has been run by a Communist government since Fidel Castro came to power at the end of the Cuban Revolution in 1959. The revolution was an armed revolt that began in 1953. Its goal was to remove President Fulgencio Batista and the authoritarian government. On January 1, 1959, Batista was finally overthrown and a new government was put into place.

Communism promotes control by a central government over all aspects of smaller units of government. Cuba is a dictatorship, and legislative authority lies with the National Assembly of People's Power. Citizens may vote for members of this group. The National Assembly elects the president from among its members. They also appoint a 31-member Council of State which is headed by the president.

Fidel Castro came to power at the end of the Cuban Revolution in 1959.

Cubans Divided

Government-sponsored rallies are a part of Cuban life. Meanwhile, some Cubans try to flee their country on tiny rafts.

Analyze Visuals
How can you tell that the people in the raft are trying to flee Cuba?

When Fidel Castro assumed power, the government took over banks, large sugarcane plantations, and other businesses. Many of these businesses were owned by U.S. companies. Because of the takeovers, the U.S. government banned trade with Cuba and restricted travel there by U.S. citizens. In December 2014 U.S. president Barack Obama and Cuban president Raúl Castro formed an agreement to mend relations between the countries. Embassies were reopened, many travel restrictions from the United States to Cuba were lifted, and some trade was reestablished between the two countries. Since Donald Trump took office as U.S. president in 2017, some restrictions have been reinstated. In April 2018 Miguel Díaz-Canel was officially named as the new leader of Cuba, ending nearly six decades of Castro family rule.

Today, the government still controls the economy. Most of Cuba's farms are organized as cooperatives or government-owned plantations. A **cooperative** is an organization owned by its members and operated for their mutual benefit.

Besides controlling the economy, Cuba's government also controls all newspapers and television and radio stations. While many Cubans support these policies, others oppose them. Some people who oppose the government have become refugees in the United States. Many Cuban refugees have become U.S. citizens.

Other Islands The rest of the Caribbean islands are small countries. Jamaica is the largest of the remaining Caribbean countries. The smallest country is Saint Kitts and Nevis. It is not even one-tenth the size of Rhode Island, the smallest U.S. state!

Curacao was once the center of the Caribbean slave trade. The island's economy was drastically affected by the abolition of slavery in 1863. Construction of oil refineries in the early 20th century helped Curacao and neighboring Aruba regain economic strength. Both islands are just off the coast of Venezuela. Venezuela's oil industry has provided economic opportunities for Curacao and Aruba.

A number of Caribbean islands are not independent countries but territories of other countries. These territories include the U.S. and British Virgin Islands. The Netherlands and France also still have some Caribbean territories.

Caribbean Tourism

Tourism has helped Caribbean economies. New developments, like this hotel in Saint Martin, have also changed many islands' landscapes.

Island homes in Barbados feature an array of bright Caribbean colors.

Reading Check
Contrast How are the governments of Puerto Rico and Cuba different?

Some of these islands have enough land to grow some coffee, sugarcane, or spices. However, most islands' economies are based on tourism. Hundreds of people on the islands work in restaurants and hotels visited by tourists. While tourism has provided jobs and helped economies, not all of its effects have been positive. For example, new construction sometimes harms the same natural environment tourists come to the islands to enjoy.

Summary The Caribbean islands were colonized by European countries, which influenced the culture of the islands. Today, the islands have different types of governments but similar economies.

Lesson 3 Assessment

Review Ideas, Terms, and Places

1. a. Describe What crop was the basis of the colonial economy on the Caribbean islands?

b. Make Inferences Why do you think most smaller Caribbean countries were able to gain independence peacefully?

2. a. Define What is a dialect?

b. Explain In what ways have African influences shaped Caribbean culture?

3. a. Recall What is a refugee, and from what Caribbean countries have refugees come?

b. Make Inferences Why do you think many Cubans support their government's policies?

c. Evaluate What would be the benefits and drawbacks for Puerto Rico if it became a U.S. state?

Critical Thinking

4. Summarize Look over your notes. Create a web diagram to note specific influences on the region and where they came from in each oval. Start with a horizontal oval in the center of the diagram and label it *Caribbean Islands*. Draw four horizontal ovals around the center oval, using arrows to connect and point to the center. You may add more ovals if you need to.

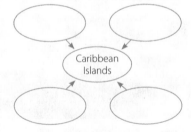

Social Studies Skills

Create a Thematic Map

Define the Skill

Thematic maps show specific information, or a theme, of a particular geographic area. When you draw a thematic map, it is easiest to use an existing map as a guide. On the map you draw, you can show geographical information. You can also draw other kinds of information, such as data on climates, population, disease, and economic activities. This data often comes from a graph or a chart.

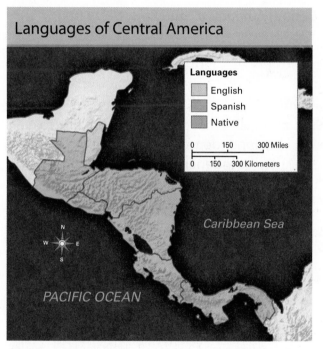

Languages of Central America

Languages
- English
- Spanish
- Native

0   150   300 Miles
0   150   300 Kilometers

Caribbean Sea

PACIFIC OCEAN

Learn the Skill

The first step in creating a thematic map is to decide the theme or subject. Once you have the theme, you will need to find facts and data about that theme. Formulate appropriate questions to guide your research. You should reference primary and secondary sources. Collect information from print and digital sources. Use non-print sources such as maps and charts. Then use your research to create the map. The thematic map on this page shows the languages people speak in Central America. Follow these steps to create your own thematic map:

1. Decide what your thematic map will be about.

2. Conduct research at the library or on the Internet to find facts and details about your theme. You may also want to find related maps to use as a guide.

3. Create a title that shows the purpose of the map.

4. Create a legend to explain any colors or symbols used.

Practice the Skill

Create your own map. Turn to the chart titled "Languages of the Caribbean" in Lesson 3. Use the steps and the map on this page as a guide to help you draw a thematic map of the languages people speak in the Caribbean.

Module 10 Assessment

Review Vocabulary, Terms, and Places

Complete each sentence by filling in the blank with the correct term from the word pair.

1. An _____ is a narrow strip of land that connects two larger land areas. (**archipelago/isthmus**)

2. A _____ is a self-governing territory associated with another country. (**commonwealth/cooperative**)

3. A _____ is someone who flees to another country, usually for political or economic reasons. (**traditional/refugee**)

4. The United States controlled the _____ until 1999. (**Caribbean Sea/Panama Canal**)

5. The large islands of Cuba, Jamaica, Hispaniola, and Puerto Rico make up the _____. (**Greater Antilles/Lesser Antilles**)

6. _____ is found in the mountainous part of Central America. (**Cloud forest/Havana**)

Comprehension and Critical Thinking

Lesson 1

7. a. Describe What process has formed many of the Caribbean islands? Describe the effect this process has on the region today.

    b. Compare and Contrast How are summer and winter similar in Central America and the Caribbean? How are the seasons different?

    c. Elaborate What kinds of damage might hurricanes cause? What damage might earthquakes and volcanic eruptions cause?

Lesson 2

8. a. Identify In what Central American country is English the official language?

    b. Make Inferences Why do you think people of African ancestry live mainly along the coast?

    c. Elaborate How might recent political conflict have affected development in some countries?

Lesson 3

9. a. Recall What country was the first to gain independence? Who led the revolt that led to independence?

    b. Analyze Look at the Caribbean Music feature in Lesson 3. What is the relationship between some Caribbean cultures and their music?

Module 10 Assessment, continued

Reading Skills

10. Understand Comparison-Contrast *Use the Reading Skills taught in this module to answer a question about the reading selection below.*

The Caribbean countries are islands in an archipelago, while Central America is an isthmus. Both areas have generally warm, sunny climates, although the more elevated areas of Central America are cool and humid. In both areas, mineral and energy resources are limited, but the soil is rich. Both areas are similar in that climate is their best resource, as it brings tourists, but the political unrest in Central America limits tourism.

What clue words in the paragraph signal comparison? Contrast?

Social Studies Skills

Create a Thematic Map *Use the Social Studies Skills taught in this module to answer questions about the Lesson 1 map titled Volcanic Activity in Central America and the Caribbean.*

11. What information, or theme, does the map show?

12. How does this map differ from a political map of the Caribbean?

13. Using information you learned in this module, decide on a theme for a map. Create a thematic map depicting aspects of Central America and the Caribbean. Make sure to include a title and a legend on your map.

Map Activity

14. Central America and the Caribbean On a separate sheet of paper, match the letters on the map with their correct labels.

Guatemala

Panama

Havana, Cuba

Caribbean Sea

Puerto Rico

Lesser Antilles

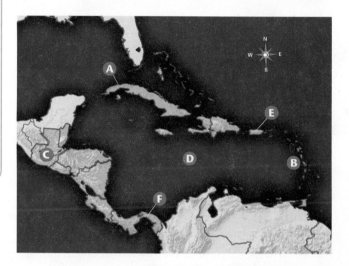

Focus on Writing

15. **Create a Travel Guide** Choose one place in this region to be the subject of a travel guide. Use the module, your notes, and other primary and secondary resources to find facts to interest your reader. Formulate appropriate questions to guide your research. You should use both print and digital sources. Collect information from non-print sources such as maps and photographs. Begin your guide with a paragraph describing the outstanding physical features of the place. Your second paragraph should identify interesting details about its history and culture. End with a sentence that might encourage your readers to visit. Include two images in your guide to show off the features of the place you have chosen. Be sure to apply key terms acquired from the module in your writing. Your travel guide should be focused and organized. Check for errors in spelling, grammar, capitalization, and punctuation.

Module 11

South America

Are the biggest challenges South American countries face economic, political, or environmental?

Cartagena
Caracas
VENEZUELA
Georgetown
Paramaribo
10°N
Bogotá
GUYANA
French Guiana
(FRANCE)
PACIFIC
OCEAN
COLOMBIA
SURINAME
Quito
0° Equator
ECUADOR
Manaus
Galápagos
Islands
Guayaquil
Amazon River
PERU
BRAZIL
10°S
Lima
N
W   E
S
La Paz
Brasília
Salvador
BOLIVIA
ATLANTIC
OCEAN
Sucre
20°S
Paraná River
Rio de
Janeiro
Tropic of Capricorn
CHILE
PARAGUAY
São Paulo
Asunción
30°S
Córdoba
Santiago
URUGUAY
Buenos Aires
Montevideo
ARGENTINA
40°S
50°S
Falkland
Islands
South Georgia
Island

National capital
0   300   600 Miles
0   300   600 Kilometers
Projection:
Lambert Azimuthal Equal-Area

Explore ONLINE!

- ✓ Document-Based Investigations
- ✓ Graphic Organizers
- ✓ Interactive Games
- ✓ Image Carousel: Venezuela's Canaima National Park
- ✓ Channel One News Video: Oil Exploration in Ecuador
- ✓ Image with Hotspots: The Amazon Rain Forest
- ✓ Image with Hotspots: Climate Zones in the Andes
- ✓ Compare Images: El Niño

In this module, you will learn about the varied physical geography of South America. You'll read about the different people who have shaped its history and developed the continent's many and diverse cultures.

What You Will Learn

Geography The Amazon Basin covers a
huge forested region in northern Brazil.

History Early cultures in Peru made beautiful
gold and silver objects, like this mask.

Culture Cowboys called *llaneros* work on the plains
of Venezuela.

Reading Social Studies

Identify Supporting Details

READING FOCUS

Why believe what you read? One reason is because of details that support or prove the main idea. These details might be facts, statistics, examples, or definitions. In the example below, notice what kind of proof or supporting details help you believe the main idea.

> Colombia's economy relies on several valuable resources. Rich soil, steep slopes, and tall shade trees produce world-famous Colombian coffee. Other major export crops include bananas, sugarcane, and cotton. Many farms in Colombia produce flowers that are exported around the world. In fact, 80 percent of the country's flowers are shipped to the United States.

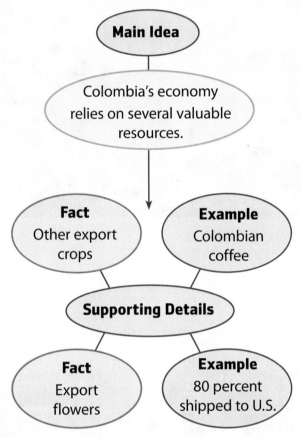

YOU TRY IT!

Read the following sentences. Then identify the supporting details in a graphic organizer like the one above.

> Caribbean South America is home to some remarkable wildlife. For example, hundreds of bird species, meat-eating fish called piranhas, and crocodiles live in or around the Orinoco River. Colombia has one of the world's highest concentrations of plant and animal species. The country's wildlife includes jaguars, ocelots, and several species of monkeys.

As you read this module, identify supporting details to help add to your understanding of the text.

Physical Geography

The Big Idea

South America is a continent made up of diverse physical features, wildlife, climates, and resources.

Main Ideas

- Coastal lowlands, mountains and highlands, and river systems shape much of Caribbean South America.

- Atlantic South America's rain forests are its major source of natural resources.

- The Andes mountains are Pacific South America's main physical feature.

Key Terms and Places

Andes
cordillera
Llanos
Orinoco River
Amazon River
Río de la Plata
estuary
Pampas
deforestation
soil exhaustion
altiplano
El Niño

If YOU lived there . . .

You live on the coast of Brazil, near the mouth of the Amazon River. Now you are taking your first trip up the river deep into the rain forest. The river is amazingly wide and calm. Trees on the riverbanks seem to soar to the sky. Your boat slows as you pass a small village. You notice that all the houses rest on poles that lift them eight to ten feet out of the water.

What would it be like to live in the rain forest?

Caribbean South America

Look at the map of Caribbean South America on the next page. As you can see, this region features rugged mountains, highlands, and plains drained by huge river systems. Caribbean South America also has one of the world's highest concentrations of plant and animal species.

Physical Features The highest point in the region is in Colombia, a country larger than California and Texas combined. On the western side of Colombia, the **Andes** (AN-deez) mountains reach 18,000 feet (5,490 m). The Andes form a **cordillera** (kawr-duhl-YER-uh), a mountain system made up of roughly parallel ranges. Some of the Andes' snowcapped peaks are active volcanoes. Eruptions and earthquakes shake these mountains frequently.

Lying on the Caribbean coast, Venezuela is located in the middle of the other countries in the region. Venezuela's highest elevation is in the Guiana Highlands, which stretch into Guyana and Suriname. For millions of years, wind and rain have eroded these highlands' plateaus. However, some of the steep-sided plateaus are capped by sandstone layers that have resisted erosion. These unusual flat-topped formations are sometimes called *tepuís* (tay-PWEEZ). The *tepuís* create a dramatic landscape as they rise about 3,000 to 6,000 feet (900 to 1,800 m) above the surrounding plains.

As you look at the map, notice how much the elevation drops between the highlands and the Andes. This region of plains is known as the **Llanos** (YAH-nohs). The Llanos is mostly grassland with few trees. At a low elevation and without much vegetation, these plains flood easily.

Flowing for about 1,600 miles (2,575 km), the **Orinoco** (OHR-ee-NOH-koh) **River** is the region's longest river. Snaking its way through Venezuela to the Atlantic Ocean, the Orinoco and its tributaries drain the plains and highlands. Two other important rivers, the Cauca and the Magdalena, drain the Andean region.

Climate and Vegetation Caribbean South America's location near the equator means that most of the region has warm temperatures year-round. However, temperatures do vary with elevation. For example, in the Andes, as you go up in elevation, the temperature can drop rapidly—about four degrees Fahrenheit (two degrees Celsius) every 1,000 feet (305 m).

In contrast, the vast, flat landscape of the Llanos region has a tropical savanna climate. Here, both the wet and dry seasons provide favorable conditions for grasslands to grow.

Rain forests, another type of landscape, thrive in the humid tropical climate of southern Colombia. This area is a part of the Amazon Basin. Here, rain falls throughout the year, watering the forest's huge trees. These trees form a canopy where the vegetation is so dense that sunlight barely shines through to the jungle floor.

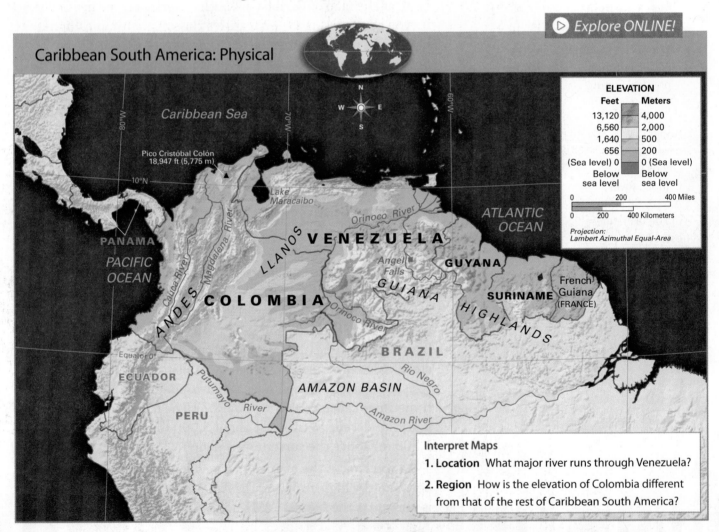

▶ *Explore ONLINE!*

Caribbean South America: Physical

ELEVATION

Feet	Meters
13,120	4,000
6,560	2,000
1,640	500
656	200
(Sea level) 0	0 (Sea level)
Below sea level	Below sea level

Projection: Lambert Azimuthal Equal-Area

Interpret Maps

1. **Location** What major river runs through Venezuela?

2. **Region** How is the elevation of Colombia different from that of the rest of Caribbean South America?

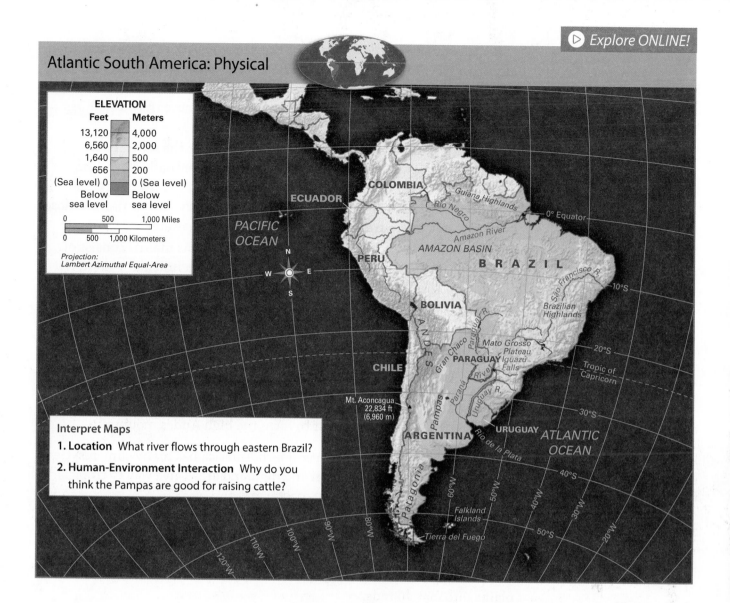

Explore ONLINE!

ELEVATION

Feet		Meters
13,120		4,000
6,560		2,000
1,640		500
656		200
(Sea level) 0		0 (Sea level)
Below sea level		Below sea level

0   500   1,000 Miles
0   500   1,000 Kilometers

Projection:
Lambert Azimuthal Equal-Area

Interpret Maps

1. **Location** What river flows through eastern Brazil?

2. **Human-Environment Interaction** Why do you think the Pampas are good for raising cattle?

Natural Resources Good soil and moderate climates help make most of Caribbean South America a rich agricultural region. Major crops include rice, coffee, bananas, and sugarcane.

In addition, the region has other valuable resources, such as oil, iron ore, and coal. Both Venezuela and Colombia have large oil-rich areas. Forests throughout the region provide timber. While the seas provide plentiful fish and shrimp, the region's major rivers are used to generate hydro-electric power.

Reading Check
Summarize
What are the region's major physical features?

Atlantic South America

The region of Atlantic South America includes four countries: Brazil, Argentina, Uruguay, and Paraguay. This large region covers about two-thirds of South America.

Physical Features The world's largest river system, the Amazon, flows eastward across northern Brazil. The **Amazon River** is about 4,000 miles (6,440 km) long. It extends from the Andes mountains in Peru to the Atlantic Ocean. Hundreds of tributaries flow into it, draining an area that includes parts of most South American countries.

Because of its huge drainage area, the Amazon carries more water than any other river in the world. About 20 percent of the water that runs off Earth's surface flows down the Amazon. Where it meets the Atlantic, this freshwater lowers the salt level of the Atlantic for more than 100 miles (160 km) from shore.

The Paraná (pah-rah-NAH) River drains much of the central part of South America. Water from the Paraná River eventually flows into the **Río de la Plata** (REE-oh day lah PLAH-tah) and the Atlantic Ocean beyond. The Río de la Plata is an estuary. An **estuary** is a partially enclosed body of water where freshwater mixes with salty seawater.

As you can see on the map, this region's landforms mainly consist of plains and plateaus. The Amazon Basin in northern Brazil is a giant, flat floodplain. South of the Amazon Basin are the Brazilian Highlands, a rugged region of old, eroded mountains, and another area of high plains called the Mato Grosso Plateau.

Farther south, a low plains region known as the Gran Chaco (grahn CHAH-koh) stretches across parts of Paraguay and northern Argentina. In central Argentina are the wide, grassy plains of the **Pampas.** South of the Pampas is Patagonia—a region of dry plains and plateaus. All of these southern plains rise in the west to form the high Andes mountains.

Climate and Vegetation Atlantic South America has many climates. Generally, cool climates in southern and highland areas give way to tropical, moist climates in northern and coastal areas.

In southern Argentina, Patagonia has a cool, desert climate. North of Patagonia, rich soils and a humid subtropical climate make parts of the Pampas good for farming. Farther north in Argentina, the Gran Chaco has a humid tropical climate. There, summer rains can turn some parts of the plains into marshlands.

North of Argentina in Brazil, a large part of the central region has a tropical savanna climate with warm grasslands. The northeastern part of the country has a hot, dry climate, while the southeast is cooler and more humid.

In northern Brazil the Amazon Basin's humid tropical climate supports the world's largest tropical rain forest. Rain falls almost every day in this region. The Amazon rain forest contains the world's greatest variety of plant and animal life.

Natural Resources The Amazon rain forest is one of the region's greatest natural resources. It provides food, wood, rubber, plants for medicines, and other products. In recent years **deforestation,** or the clearing of trees, has become an issue in the forest.

The region's land is also a resource for commercial farming, which is found near coastal areas of Atlantic South America. In some areas, however, planting the same crop every year has caused **soil exhaustion,** which means the soil is infertile because it has lost nutrients needed by plants.

Atlantic South America also has good mineral and energy resources such as gold, silver, copper, iron, and oil. Dams on some of the region's large rivers also provide hydroelectric power.

Reading Check
Summarize What resources does the rain forest provide?

Pacific South America

The countries of Pacific South America stretch along the Pacific coast from the equator south almost to the Antarctic Circle. All of the countries in this region share one major physical feature—the high Andes mountains.

Physical Features The Andes run through Ecuador, Peru, Bolivia, and Chile. Some ridges and volcanic peaks in the Andes rise more than 20,000 feet (6,800 m) above sea level. Because two tectonic plates meet at the region's edge, earthquakes and volcanoes are a constant threat. Sometimes these earthquakes disturb Andean glaciers, sending ice and mud rushing down mountain slopes.

Landscapes in the Andes differ from south to north. In southern Chile, rugged mountain peaks are covered by ice caps. In the north, the Andes are more rounded than rugged, and there the range splits into two ridges. In southern Peru and Bolivia these ridges are quite far apart. A broad, high plateau called the **altiplano** lies between the ridges of the Andes.

Andean glaciers are the source for many tributaries of the Amazon River. Other than the Amazon tributaries, the region has few major rivers. Rivers on the altiplano have no outlet to the sea. Water collects in two

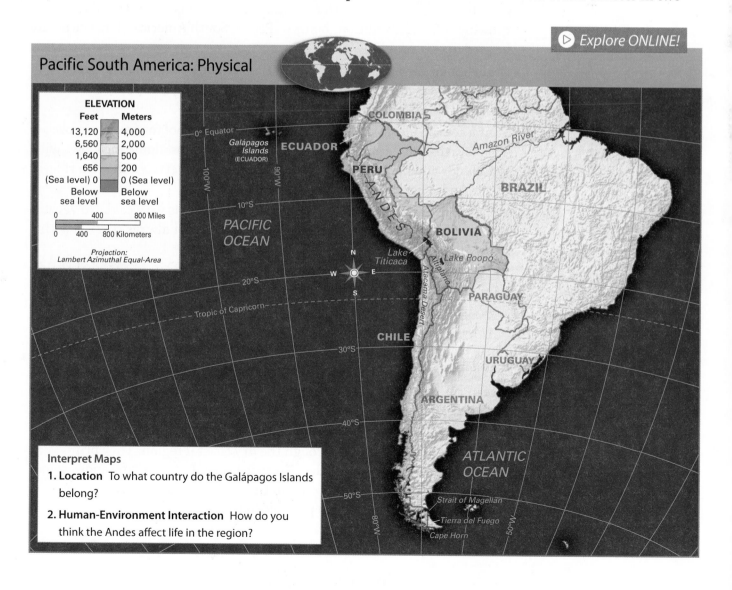

Pacific South America: Physical

Explore ONLINE!

ELEVATION

Feet	Meters
13,120	4,000
6,560	2,000
1,640	500
656	200
(Sea level) 0	0 (Sea level)
Below sea level	Below sea level

0   400   800 Miles
0   400   800 Kilometers

Projection:
Lambert Azimuthal Equal-Area

Interpret Maps

1. **Location** To what country do the Galápagos Islands belong?

2. **Human-Environment Interaction** How do you think the Andes affect life in the region?

large lakes. One of these, Lake Titicaca, is the highest lake in the world that large ships can cross.

At the southern tip of the continent, the Strait of Magellan links the Atlantic and Pacific Oceans. A strait is a narrow body of water connecting two larger bodies of water. The large island south of the strait is Tierra del Fuego, or "land of fire."

Climate and Vegetation Climate, vegetation, and landscapes all vary widely in Pacific South America. We usually think of latitude as the major factor that affects climate. However, in Pacific South America, elevation has the biggest effect on climate and vegetation.

Mountain environments change with elevation. For this reason, we can identify five different climate zones in the Andes.

The lowest zone includes the hot and humid lower elevations near sea level. Crops such as sugarcane and bananas grow well there. This first zone is often found along the coast, but it is also found inland in eastern Ecuador and Peru and northern Bolivia. These regions are part of the Amazon basin. They have a humid tropical climate with thick, tropical rain forests.

As elevation increases, the air becomes cooler. The second elevation zone has moist climates with mountain forests. This zone is good for growing coffee. In addition, many of Pacific South America's large cities are located in this zone.

Higher up the mountains is a third, cooler zone of forests and grasslands. Farmers grow potatoes and wheat there. Many people in Pacific South America live and farm in this climate zone.

At a certain elevation, the climate becomes too cool for trees to grow. This fourth climate zone above the tree line contains alpine meadows with grasslands and hardy shrubs. The altiplano region between the two ridges of the Andes lies mostly in this climate zone.

The fifth climate zone, in the highest elevations, is very cold. No vegetation grows in this zone because the ground is almost always covered with snow and ice.

Pacific South America also has some climates that are not typical of any of the five climate zones. Instead of hot and humid climates, some coastal regions have desert climates.

Northern Chile contains the Atacama Desert. This desert is about 600 miles (965 km) long. Rain falls there less than five times a century, but fog and low clouds are common. They form when a cold current in the Pacific Ocean chills the warmer air above the ocean's surface. Cloud cover keeps the air near the ground from being warmed by the sun. As a result, coastal Chile is one of the cloudiest—and driest—places on Earth.

In Peru, some rivers cut through the dry coastal region. They bring snowmelt down from the Andes. Because they rely on melting snow, some of these rivers only appear at certain times of the year. The rivers have made some small settlements possible in these dry areas.

About every two to seven years, this dry region experiences **El Niño,** an ocean and weather pattern that affects the Pacific coast. During an El Niño year, cool Pacific water near the coast warms. This change may cause extreme ocean and weather events that can have global effects.

As El Niño warms ocean waters, fish leave what is usually a rich fishing area. This change affects fishers. Also, El Niño <u>causes</u> heavy rains, and areas along the coast sometimes experience flooding. Some scientists think that air pollutants have made El Niño last longer and have more damaging effects.

Natural Resources The landscapes of Pacific South America provide many valuable natural resources. For example, forests in southern Chile and in eastern Peru and Ecuador provide lumber. Also, as you have read, the coastal waters of the Pacific Ocean are rich in fish.

In addition, the region has valuable oil and minerals. Ecuador in particular has large oil and gas reserves, and oil is the country's main export. Bolivia has some deposits of tin, gold, silver, lead, and zinc. Chile has copper deposits. In fact, Chile exports more copper than any other country in the world. Chile is also the site of South America's deepest open pit mine.

Academic
Vocabulary
cause to make something happen

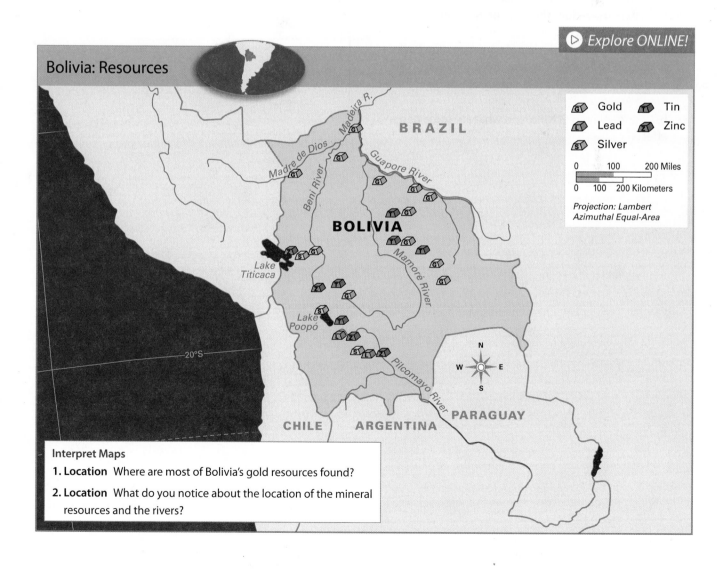

Bolivia: Resources

▷ *Explore ONLINE!*

Gold   Tin
Lead   Zinc
Silver

0   100   200 Miles
0   100   200 Kilometers

Projection: Lambert Azimuthal Equal-Area

BRAZIL

Madre de Dios   *Madeira R.*

Beni River   *Guapore River*

BOLIVIA

Lake Titicaca   *Mamoré River*

Lake Poopó

Pilcomayo River

PARAGUAY

CHILE   ARGENTINA

—20°S

Interpret Maps

1. Location Where are most of Bolivia's gold resources found?

2. Location What do you notice about the location of the mineral resources and the rivers?

Reading Check
Contrast How do
the Andes differ from
north to south?

Although the countries of Pacific South America have many valuable resources, one resource they do not have much of is good farmland. Many people farm, but the region's mostly cool, arid lands make it difficult to produce large amounts of crops for export.

Summary and Preview In this lesson, you learned that the physical geography of Caribbean South America includes mountains, highlands, plains, and rivers. Physical features of Atlantic South America include great river systems and plains. A huge part of the region is the Amazon rain forest. Finally, you learned that the Andes mountains are the main physical feature of Pacific South America. Next you will learn about Brazil, the country of the Amazon.

Lesson 1 Assessment

Review Ideas, Terms, and Places

1. a. **Elaborate** Why do the Llanos in Colombia and Venezuela flood easily?

   b. **Make Inferences** How does Caribbean South America's location near the equator affect its climate?

2. a. **Explain** How does the Amazon River affect the Atlantic Ocean at the river's mouth?

   b. **Analyze** What is one benefit and one drawback of practicing commercial agriculture in the rain forest?

3. a. **Identify** What is the main physical feature of Pacific South America?

   b. **Define** What is El Niño, and what are some of its effects?

Critical Thinking

4. **Categorize** Review your notes on the Andes. Then use a diagram like this one to describe the climate and vegetation in each of the five climate zones in the Andes.

Brazil

The Big Idea

The influence of Brazil's history can be seen all over the country in its people and culture.

Main Ideas

- Brazil's history has been affected by Brazilian Indians, Portuguese settlers, and enslaved Africans.
- Brazil's society reflects a mix of people and cultures.
- Brazil today is experiencing population growth in its cities and new development in rain forest areas.

Key Terms and Places

São Paulo
megacity
Rio de Janeiro
favelas
Brasília
Manaus

If YOU lived there . . .

You live in Rio de Janeiro, Brazil's second-largest city. For months your friends have been preparing for Carnival, the year's biggest holiday. During Carnival, people perform in glittery costumes and there is dancing all day and all night in the streets. The city is packed with tourists. It can be fun, but it is hectic! Your family is thinking of leaving Rio during Carnival so they can get some peace and quiet, but you may stay in Rio with a friend if you like.

**Would you stay for Carnival?
Why or why not?**

History

Brazil is the largest country in South America. Its population of about 211 million people is larger than the population of all of the other South American countries combined. Most Brazilians are descended from three diverse groups of people whose experiences have contributed in different ways throughout Brazil's history.

Colonial Brazil The area that is now Brazil was originally home to different groups of native peoples. They arrived in the region many thousands of years ago and developed a way of life based on hunting, fishing, and small-scale farming.

In 1500 Portuguese explorers became the first Europeans to arrive in Brazil. Soon Portuguese settlers began to move there. Good climates and soils, particularly in the northeast, made Brazil a large sugar-growing colony. Colonists brought a third group of people—Africans—to work as slaves on the plantations. Sugar plantations made Portugal rich, but they also eventually replaced forests along the Atlantic coast.

Other parts of Brazil also contributed to the colonial economy. Inland, many Portuguese settlers created cattle ranches. In the late 1600s and early 1700s, people discovered gold and precious gems in the southeast. A mining boom drew people to Brazil from around the world. Finally, in the late 1800s southeastern Brazil became a major coffee-producing region.

Brazil Since Independence Brazil gained independence from Portugal without a fight in 1822. However, independence did not change Brazil's economy much. For example, Brazil was the last country in the Americas to end slavery.

Since the end of Portuguese rule, Brazil has been governed at times by dictators and at other times by elected officials. Today the country has an elected president and legislature. Brazilians can participate in politics through voting.

Reading Check
Summarize
What was Brazil's
colonial economy like?

People and Culture

More than half of Brazilians consider themselves of European descent. These people include descendants of original Portuguese settlers along with descendants of more recent immigrants from Spain, Germany, Italy, and Poland. Nearly 40 percent of Brazil's people are of mixed African and European descent. Brazil also has the largest Japanese population outside of Japan.

Because of its colonial heritage, Brazil's official language is Portuguese. In fact, since Brazil's population is so huge, there are more Portuguese-speakers in South America than there are Spanish-speakers, even though Spanish is spoken in almost every other country on the continent. Other Brazilians speak Spanish, English, French, Japanese, or native languages.

Religion Brazil has the largest population of Roman Catholics of any country in the world. About 75 percent of Brazilians are Catholic. In recent years Protestantism has grown in popularity, particularly among the urban poor. Some Brazilians practice macumba (mah-KOOM-bah), a religion that combines beliefs and practices of African and Indian religions with Christianity.

Academic
Vocabulary
aspects parts

Festivals Other **aspects** of Brazilian life also reflect the country's mix of cultures. For example, Brazilians celebrate Carnival before the Christian season of Lent. The celebration mixes traditions from Africa, Brazil, and Europe. During Carnival, Brazilians dance the samba, which was adapted from an African dance.

Reading Check
Analyze Effects How
has cultural borrowing
affected Brazilian
culture?

Brazil Today

Brazil's large size creates opportunities and challenges for the country. For example, Brazil has the largest economy in South America and has modern and wealthy areas. However, many Brazilians are poor.

While some of the same issues and characteristics can be found throughout Brazil, other characteristics are unique to a particular region of the country. Brazil can be divided into four regions, based on their people, economies, and landscapes.

The Southeast Most people in Brazil live in the southeast. **São Paulo** is located there. About 21 million people live in and around São Paulo. It is the largest urban area in South America and the fourth largest in the world. São Paulo is considered a **megacity,** or a giant urban area that includes surrounding cities and suburbs.

Rio de Janeiro, Brazil's second-largest city, lies northeast of São Paulo. About 12 million people live there. The city was the capital of Brazil from 1822 until 1960. Today Rio de Janeiro remains a major port city. Its spectacular setting and exciting culture are popular with tourists.

In addition to having the largest cities, the southeast is also Brazil's richest region. It is rich in natural resources and has most of the country's industries and productive farmland. It is one of the major coffee-growing regions of the world.

Although the southeast has a strong economy, it also has poverty. Cities in the region have huge slums called **favelas** (fah-VE-lahz). Many people who live in favelas have come to cities of the southeast from other regions of Brazil in search of jobs.

Regions of Brazil

Brazil's regions differ from each other in their people, climates, economies, and landscapes.

Rivers provide resources and transportation for people living in the Amazon region.

About one-third of Brazilians live in the dry northeast, the nation's poorest region.

Interior

The southeast has the country's largest cities, such as Rio de Janeiro.

Analyze Visuals
Which region appears to be the wealthiest?

Soccer in Brazil

To Brazilians, soccer is more than a game. It is part of being Brazilian. Professional stars are national heroes. The national team often plays in the Maracanã Stadium in Rio de Janeiro. Some fans beat drums all through the games. But it is not just professional soccer that is popular. People all over Brazil play soccer—in cleared fields, on the beach, or in the street. Here, boys in Rio practice their skills.

Analyze Causes
Why do you think soccer is so popular in Brazil?

The Northeast The northeast is Brazil's poorest region. Many people there cannot read, and health care is poor. The region often suffers from droughts, which make farming and raising livestock difficult. The northeast has little industry. However, the region's beautiful beaches do attract tourists.

Other tourist attractions in northeastern Brazil are the region's many old colonial cities. These cities were built during the days of the sugar industry. They have brightly painted buildings, cobblestone streets, and elaborate Catholic churches.

The Interior The interior region of Brazil is a frontier land. Few people live there, except for those who reside in the country's capital, **Brasília.**

In the mid-1950s government officials hoped that building a new capital city in the Brazilian interior would help develop the region. Brasília has modern buildings and busy highways.

The Amazon The Amazon region covers the northern part of Brazil. **Manaus,** which lies 1,000 miles (1,600 km) from the mouth of the Amazon, is a major port and industrial city. About 2 million people live there. They rely on the river for transportation and communication.

Isolated Indian villages are scattered throughout the region's dense rain forest. Some of Brazil's Indians had little contact with outsiders until recently. Now, logging, mining, and new roads are bringing more people and development to this region.

Reading Check
Contrast How does
the northeast of
Brazil differ from the
southeast?

This new development provides needed income for some people. For example, people need wood for building and making paper. Also, farmers, loggers, and miners need to make a living. But new development destroys large areas of the rain forest. This deforestation in the Amazon also threatens the survival of many plant and animal species. Deforestation threatens hundreds of unique ecosystems. It also creates tensions among the Brazilian Indians, new settlers, miners, and the government.

Summary and Preview In this lesson you read about Brazil—a huge country of many contrasts. Brazil reflects the mixing of people and cultures from its history. In the next lesson, you will learn about Brazil's neighbors—Argentina, Uruguay, and Paraguay.

Lesson 2 Assessment

Review Ideas, Terms, and Places

1. a. Recall What European country colonized Brazil?

   b. Analyze What diverse groups have contributed to Brazil's society? What were some of the experiences of these groups?

2. a. Identify What religion is most common in Brazil?

   b. Explain Why is so much of Brazil's culture influenced by African traditions?

3. a. Define What is a megacity, and what is an example of a megacity in Brazil?

   b. Make Inferences Why might development in the Amazon cause tensions between Brazilian Indians and new settlers?

Critical Thinking

4. Compare and Contrast Review your notes on Brazil. Write a statement about the economy of each region. Use a graphic organizer like this one.

	Economy
The Southeast	
The Northeast	
The Interior	
The Amazon	

Argentina, Uruguay, and Paraguay

The Big Idea

Argentina, Uruguay, and Paraguay have been influenced by European immigration and a tradition of ranching.

Main Ideas

- European immigrants have dominated the history and culture of Argentina.

- Argentina's capital, Buenos Aires, plays a large role in the country's government and economy today.

- Uruguay has been influenced by its neighbors.

- Paraguay is the most rural country in the region.

Key Terms and Places

gauchos
Buenos Aires
Mercosur
informal economy
landlocked

If YOU lived there . . .

You live in Montevideo, the capital of Uruguay. On weekends you like to visit the old part of the city and admire its beautiful buildings. You also enjoy walking along the banks of the Río de la Plata and watching fishers bring in their catch. Sometimes you visit the parks and beaches along the banks of the river.

How do you think the river has influenced Montevideo?

Argentina's History and Culture

Like most of South America, Argentina was originally home to groups of Indians. Groups living on the Pampas hunted wild game, while farther north Indians built irrigation systems for farming. However, unlike most of South America, Argentina has very few native peoples remaining. Instead, Argentina's culture has been mostly influenced by Europeans.

Early History The first Europeans to come to Argentina were the Spanish. In the 1500s Spanish conquerors spread from the northern part of the continent into southern South America in search of silver and gold. They named the region Argentina. *Argentina* means "land of silver" or "silvery one."

The Spanish soon built settlements in Argentina. The Spanish monarch granted land to the colonists, who in turn built the settlements. These landowners were also given the right to force the Indians living there to work.

During the colonial era, the Pampas became an important agricultural region. Argentine cowboys, called **gauchos** (GOW-chohz), herded cattle and horses on the open grasslands. Although agriculture is still important on the Pampas, very few people in Argentina live as gauchos today.

In the early 1800s Argentina fought for independence from Spain. A period of violence and instability followed during this time. Many Indians were killed or driven away by fighting.

Modern Argentina As the Indians were being killed off, more European influences dominated the region. New immigrants

Gauchos were a popular subject in Argentine art. In this painting from 1820, gauchos gather to watch a horse race.

arrived from Italy, Germany, and Spain. Also, the British helped build railroads across the country. Railroads made it easier for Argentina to transport agricultural products for export to Europe. Beef exports, in particular, made the country rich.

Argentina remained one of South America's richest countries throughout the 1900s. However, the country also struggled under dictators and military governments during those years.

Some political leaders, like Eva Perón, were popular. But many leaders abused human rights. During the "Dirty War" in the 1970s, they tortured and killed many accused of disagreeing with the government. Both the country's people and its economy suffered. Finally, in the 1980s, Argentina's last military government gave up power to an elected government.

BIOGRAPHY

Eva Perón (1919–1952)

Known affectionately as Evita, Eva Perón helped improve the living conditions of people in Argentina, particularly the poor. As the wife of Argentina's president, Juan Perón, Evita established thousands of hospitals and schools throughout Argentina. She also helped women gain the right to vote. After years of battling cancer, Evita died at age 33. All of Argentina mourned her death for weeks.

Analyze Effects
Why was Eva Perón able to help many people?

Reading Check
Form Generalizations
What kind of governments did Argentina have in the 1900s?

People and Culture Argentina's historical ties to Europe still affect its culture. Most of Argentina's roughly 44 million people are descended from Spanish, Italian, or other European settlers. Argentine Indians and mestizos make up only about 3 percent of the population. Most Argentines are Roman Catholic.

Beef is still a part of Argentina's culture. A popular dish is parrilla (pah-REE-yah), which includes grilled sausage and steak. Supper is generally eaten late.

Argentina Today

Today many more of Argentina's people live in **Buenos Aires** (BWAY-nohs EYE-rayz) than in any other city. Buenos Aires is the country's capital. It is also the second-largest urban area in South America. Several geographic factors are responsible for the dense pattern of population in and around Buenos Aires. These factors include the location of most of Argentina's industry in and around the city, and its location on the coast and near the Pampas.

The Pampas are the country's most developed agricultural region. About 11 percent of Argentina's labor force works in agriculture. Large ranches and farms there produce beef, wheat, and corn for export to other countries.

Argentina's economy has always been affected by government policies. In the 1990s government leaders made economic reforms to help businesses grow. Argentina joined **Mercosur**—an organization that promotes trade and economic cooperation among the southern and eastern countries of South America. One of the goals of Mercosur and other trade organizations is to move toward global free trade. To reach this goal, they are removing trade barriers such as quotas, tariffs, and embargos. A quota is a limit on the amount of a product that can be brought into a country. A tariff is a fee on goods brought into a country. An embargo is a law that cuts off trade with a specific country.

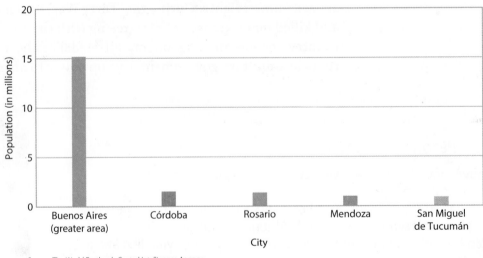

Argentina's Largest Cities

Source: The World Factbook, Central Intelligence Agency

Interpret Graphs
How many times bigger is the greater Buenos Aires area than Argentina's second-largest city?

Reading Check
Compare and Contrast
What are some similarities and differences between Buenos Aires and the Pampas?

However, in Argentina, heavy debt and government spending brought the country into an economic crisis in the late 1900s and early 2000s. This economic crisis caused a political crisis. As a result, during 2001, Argentina's government changed hands four times as its leaders tried to solve the problems. By 2003 the economy had stabilized somewhat, but thousands of people's lives had changed forever. The crisis caused many people who once had professional careers to lose their jobs and join the informal economy. The **informal economy** is a part of the economy based on odd jobs that people perform without government regulation through taxes. Today, many Argentines are still searching for ways to improve their economy.

Uruguay

Tucked between Argentina and Brazil lies Uruguay. Its capital, Montevideo (mawn-tay-vee-DAY-oh), is located on the north shore of the Río de la Plata, not far from Buenos Aires. Uruguay has always been influenced by its larger neighbors.

Portugal claimed Uruguay during the colonial era, but the Spanish took over in the 1770s. By that time, few Uruguayan Indians remained. A few years later, in 1825, Uruguay declared independence from Spain. Since then, military governments have ruled Uruguay off and on. In general, however, the country has a strong tradition of respect for political freedom. Today Uruguay is a democracy.

People As in Argentina, people of European descent make up the majority of Uruguay's population. Only about 12 percent of the population is mestizo, Indian, or of African descent. Roman Catholicism is the main religion in the country. Spanish is the official language, but many people also speak Portuguese because of Uruguay's location near Brazil.

More than 90 percent of Uruguay's people live in urban areas. More than a third of Uruguayans live in or near Montevideo. The country has a high literacy rate. In addition, many people there have good jobs and can afford a wide range of consumer goods and travel to Europe. However, many young people leave Uruguay to explore better economic opportunities elsewhere.

Buenos Aires is a huge modern city. Its main street is said to be the widest avenue in the world.

Economy Just as Uruguay's culture is tied to its neighbors, its economy is tied to the economies of Brazil and Argentina. In fact, more than half of Uruguay's foreign trade is with these two Mercosur partners. Beef is an important export. As in Argentina, ranchers graze livestock on inland plains.

Agriculture, along with some limited manufacturing, is the basis of Uruguay's economy. Uruguay has few mineral resources. One important source of energy is hydroelectric power. Developing poor rural areas in the interior, where resources are in short supply, is a big challenge.

Reading Check
Compare
In what ways is Uruguay similar to Argentina?

Paraguay

Paraguay shares borders with Bolivia, Brazil, and Argentina. It is a landlocked country. **Landlocked** means completely surrounded by land with no direct access to the ocean. The Paraguay River divides the country into two regions. East of the river is the country's most productive farmland. Ranchers also graze livestock in some parts of western Paraguay.

Paraguay was claimed by Spanish settlers in the mid-1530s. It remained a Spanish colony until 1811, when it won independence. From independence until 1989, Paraguay was ruled off and on by dictators. Today, the country has elected leaders and a democratic government.

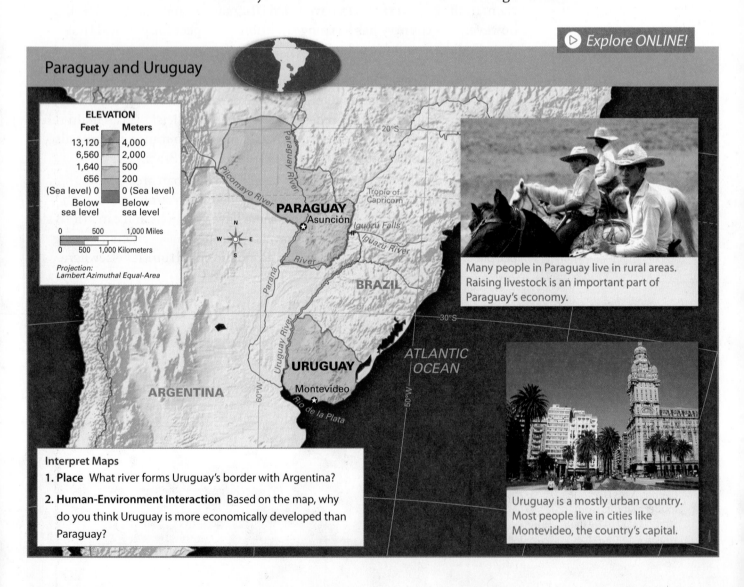

▶ Explore ONLINE!

Paraguay and Uruguay

ELEVATION

Feet	Meters
13,120	4,000
6,560	2,000
1,640	500
656	200
(Sea level) 0	0 (Sea level)
Below sea level	Below sea level

0   500   1,000 Miles
0   500   1,000 Kilometers

Projection: Lambert Azimuthal Equal-Area

Many people in Paraguay live in rural areas. Raising livestock is an important part of Paraguay's economy.

Uruguay is a mostly urban country. Most people live in cities like Montevideo, the country's capital.

Interpret Maps

1. **Place** What river forms Uruguay's border with Argentina?

2. **Human-Environment Interaction** Based on the map, why do you think Uruguay is more economically developed than Paraguay?

People A great majority—about 95 percent—of Paraguayans are mestizos. Indians and people of mostly European descent make up the rest of the population. Paraguay has two official languages. Almost all people in Paraguay speak both Spanish and Guarani (gwah-ruh-NEE), an Indian language. As in Uruguay, most people are Roman Catholic.

Paraguay's capital and largest city is Asunción (ah-soon-SYOHN). The city is located along the Paraguay River near the border with Argentina.

Economy Much of Paraguay's wealth is controlled by a few rich families and companies. These families and companies have tremendous influence over the country's government.

Agriculture is an important part of the economy. In fact, nearly half of the country's workers are farmers. Many of these farmers grow just enough food to feed themselves and their families. They grow crops such as corn, cotton, soybeans, and sugarcane. Paraguay also has many small businesses but not much industry.

Paraguay's future may be promising as the country learns how to use its resources more effectively. For example, the country has built large hydroelectric dams on the Paraná River. These dams provide more power than Paraguay needs, so Paraguay is able to sell the surplus electricity to Brazil and Argentina.

Summary and Preview In this lesson you learned that the people of Paraguay, Argentina, and Uruguay share some aspects of their European heritage. Their economies are also closely tied. In the next lesson, you will learn about Colombia, Venezuela, and the Guianas.

Lesson 3 Assessment

Review Ideas, Terms, and Places

1. **a. Define** What is a gaucho?

   b. Explain Why is Argentina's population mostly of European descent?

2. **a. Identify** What is Argentina's biggest city?

   b. Make Inferences What benefits do you think being part of Mercosur brings to Argentina and Uruguay?

   c. Elaborate What are some benefits the informal economy provides, and what are some of its drawbacks?

3. **a. Recall** Where is Uruguay's capital located?

   b. Summarize How has Uruguay's location influenced its culture?

4. **a. Define** What does it mean to say a country is landlocked?

   b. Explain What is Paraguay's economy like?

   c. Predict What are some possible ways Paraguay may be able to improve its economy in the future?

Critical Thinking

5. **Compare and Contrast** Look over your notes on Uruguay and Paraguay. Then draw a diagram like the one here and use it to show similarities and differences between the two countries.

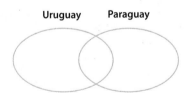

Colombia, Venezuela, and the Guianas

The Big Idea

Spanish conquest and valuable natural resources have shaped the histories, cultures, and economies of Colombia, Venezuela, and the Guianas.

Main Ideas

- Native cultures, Spanish conquest, and independence shaped Colombia's history.

- In Colombia today, the benefits of a rich culture and many natural resources contrast with the effects of a long period of civil war.

- Spanish settlement shaped the history and culture of Venezuela.

- Oil production plays a large role in Venezuela's economy and government today.

- The Guianas have diverse cultures and plentiful resources.

Key Terms and Places

Cartagena
Bogotá
guerrillas
Caracas
llaneros
Lake Maracaibo
strike

If YOU lived there . . .

You live in the beautiful colonial city of Cartagena, on the coast of the Caribbean. Your family runs a small restaurant there. You're used to the city's wide beaches and old colonial buildings with wooden balconies that overhang the street. Now you are on your way to visit your cousins. They live on a cattle ranch on the inland plains region called the Llanos.

How do you think life on the ranch is different from yours?

Colombia's History

Giant mounds of earth, mysterious statues, and tombs—these are marks of the people who lived in Colombia more than 1,500 years ago. Colombia's history begins with these people. It also includes conquest by Spain and, later, independence.

The Chibcha In ancient times, the Chibcha Indians in Colombia inspired legends of a land rich in gold. A well-developed civilization, they practiced pottery making, weaving, and metalworking. Their gold objects were among the finest in ancient America.

Spanish Conquest In about 1500 Spanish explorers arrived on the Caribbean coast of South America. The Spaniards wanted to expand Spain's new empire. In doing so, the Spanish conquered the Chibcha and seized much of their treasure. Soon after claiming land for themselves, the Spaniards founded a colony and cities along the Caribbean coast.

This gold Chibcha artifact represents the ceremonial raft used by their king.

Cartagena's Spanish Fort

Cartagena, Colombia, lies on the Caribbean coast. In the 1600s, the city was attacked by English pirates several times. They stole tons of silver and gold that were waiting shipment to Spain. In response, Spanish colonists built a huge fort to protect Cartegena. Today this fort still stands on a peninsula outside the city. A statue commemorates one of the heroes that defended the city from attack.

Draw Conclusions
Why did the Spanish want to defend Cartagena from the pirates?

One colonial city, **Cartagena,** was a major naval base and commercial port in the Spanish empire. By the 1600s Spaniards and their descendants had set up large estates in Colombia. Spanish estate owners forced South American Indians and enslaved Africans to work the land.

Independence In the late 1700s people in Central and South America began struggling for independence from Spain. After independence was achieved, the republic of Gran Colombia was created. It included Colombia, Ecuador, Panama, and Venezuela. In 1830 the republic dissolved, and New Granada, which included Colombia and Panama, was created.

After independence, two different groups of Colombians debated over how Colombia should be run. One group wanted the Roman Catholic Church to participate in government and education. Another group did not want the church involved in their lives.

Outbreaks of violence throughout the 1800s and 1900s killed thousands of people. Part of the problem had to do with the country's rugged geography, which isolated people in one region from those in another region. As a result, they developed separate economies and identities. Uniting these different groups into one country was hard.

Reading Check
Draw Conclusions
How did Spanish conquest shape Colombia's history and culture?

Colombia Today

Colombia is Caribbean South America's most populous country. The national capital is **Bogotá,** a city located high in the eastern Andes.

People and Culture Most Colombians live in the fertile valleys and river basins among the mountain ranges, where the climate is moderate and good for farming. Rivers, such as the Cauca and the Magdalena, flow down

from the Andes to the Caribbean Sea. These rivers provide water and help connect settlements located between the mountains and the coast. Other Colombians live on cattle ranches scattered throughout the Llanos. Few people live in the tropical rain forest regions in the south.

Because the physical geography of Colombia isolates some regions of the country, the people of Colombia are often known by the region where they live. For example, those who live along the Caribbean coast are known for songs and dances influenced by African traditions.

Colombian culture is an interesting mix of influences:
- Music: traditional African songs and dances on the Caribbean coast and South American Indian music in remote areas of the Andes
- Sports: soccer, as well as a traditional Chibcha ring-toss game called *tejo*
- Religion: primarily Roman Catholicism
- Official language: Spanish
- Ethnic groups: 58 percent mestizo; also Spanish, African, and Indian descent

Economy and Natural Resources Colombia's economy relies on several valuable resources. Rich soil, steep slopes, and tall shade trees produce world-famous Colombian coffee. Other major export crops include bananas, sugarcane, and cotton. Many farms in Colombia produce flowers that are exported around the world. In fact, 80 percent of the country's flowers are shipped to the United States.

Colombia's economy also depends on the country's natural resources. Recently oil has become Colombia's major export. Other natural resources include iron ore, gold, and coal. Most of the world's emeralds also come from Colombia.

Civil War Civil war is a major problem in Colombia today. Many different groups have waged war with each other and with Colombia's government. For more than 40 years, these heavily armed militant groups have controlled large areas of the country.

Reading Check
Draw Conclusions
How do you think civil war affects daily life in Colombia?

One of these groups is an army of **guerrillas,** or members of an irregular military force. These guerrillas want to overthrow the government. The guerrillas, as well as other militant groups, have forced farmers off their land and have caused thousands of Colombians to flee the country. All of these groups are also involved in growing crops of the illegal coca plant. This plant is used to make cocaine, a dangerous drug.

Because of the instability caused by civil war, the future of Colombia is uncertain. However, the Colombian government has passed new laws that make it harder for the guerrillas and other militant groups to operate freely.

Venezuela's History

Venezuela was originally the home of many small tribes of South American Indians. Those groups were conquered by the Spanish in the early 1500s. Though Venezuela became independent from Spain in the early 1800s, the three centuries of Spanish rule shaped the country's history and culture.

Spanish Settlement and Colonial Rule The Spanish came to Venezuela hoping to find gold and pearls. They forced the Indians to search for these treasures but finally realized there was little gold to be found. The Spanish turned to agriculture, once again forcing the Indians to do the work. They grew indigo (IN-di-goh), a plant used to make a deep blue dye. Because the work was very hard, many of the Indians died. Then the Spanish began bringing enslaved Africans to take the Indians' places. Eventually, some of the slaves escaped, settling in remote areas of the country.

Independence and Self-Rule Partly because the colony was so poor, some people in Venezuela revolted against Spain. Simon Bolívar helped lead the fight against Spanish rule. Bolívar is considered a hero in many South American countries because he led wars of independence throughout the region. Bolívar helped win Venezuelan independence from Spain by 1821. However, Venezuela did not officially become independent until 1830.

BIOGRAPHY

Simon Bolívar (1783–1830)

Known as the "George Washington of South America," Simon Bolívar was a revolutionary general. In the early 1800s he led the liberation of several South American countries from Spanish rule.

Beginning in 1811 Bolívar helped free his native Venezuela. He was president of Gran Colombia (present-day Venezuela, Colombia, Panama, and Ecuador) and then Peru. Because Bolívar also helped free Bolivia, the country was named in his honor. People across South America admire Bolívar for his determination in achieving independence for the former Spanish colonies. Today in both Venezuela and Bolivia, Bolívar's birthday is a national holiday.

Make Inferences
Why do you think Bolívar is often compared to George Washington?

Reading Check
Summarize How did
the Spanish contribute
to Venezuela's history?

Throughout the 1800s Venezuelans suffered from dictatorships and civil wars. Venezuela's military leaders ran the country. After oil was discovered in the early 1900s, some leaders kept the country's oil money for themselves. As a result, the people of Venezuela did not benefit from their country's oil wealth.

Venezuela Today

Caracas (kah-RAH-kahs) is Venezuela's capital and the economic and cultural center of the country. Caracas has a population of more than 4 million people. It is a large city with a modern subway system, busy expressways, and tall office buildings.

People and Culture The people of Venezuela are descended from native peoples, Europeans, and Africans. The majority of Venezuelans are of mixed Indian and European descent. Indians make up only about 2 percent of the population. People of European descent tend to live in the large cities. People of African descent tend to live along the coast. Most Venezuelans are Spanish-speaking Roman Catholics, but the country's Indians speak 25 different languages and follow the religious practices of their ancestors.

Venezuelan culture includes dancing and sports. Venezuela's national dance, the *joropo*, is a lively foot-stomping couples' dance. Large crowds of Venezuelans attend rodeo events. Baseball and soccer are also popular throughout Venezuela.

Many Venezuelans make a living by farming and ranching. Northern Venezuela has some small family farms as well as large commercial farms. **Llaneros** (yah-NAY-rohs)—or Venezuelan cowboys—herd cattle on the many ranches of the Llanos region. However, some small communities of Indians practice traditional agriculture.

Economy and Natural Resources In the 1960s Venezuela began earning huge sums of money from oil production. This wealth allowed part of the population to buy luxuries. However, the vast majority of the population still lived in poverty. Many of Venezuela's poor people moved to the cities to try to find work. Some settled on the outskirts in communities of shacks. They had no running water, sewers, or electricity.

Venezuela's wealth attracted many immigrants from Europe and other South American countries. These immigrants, like most other Venezuelans, suffered in the 1980s when the price of oil dropped sharply. Without the money provided by high oil prices, the economy couldn't support the people. Oil prices recovered in the 1990s, and the Venezuelan economy continues to be based on oil production.

As you can see on the map, the Orinoco River basin and **Lake Maracaibo** (mah-rah-KY-boh) are rich in oil. Venezuela is the only South American member of the Organization of Petroleum Exporting Countries (OPEC). The member countries in this organization attempt to control world oil production and keep oil prices from falling too low.

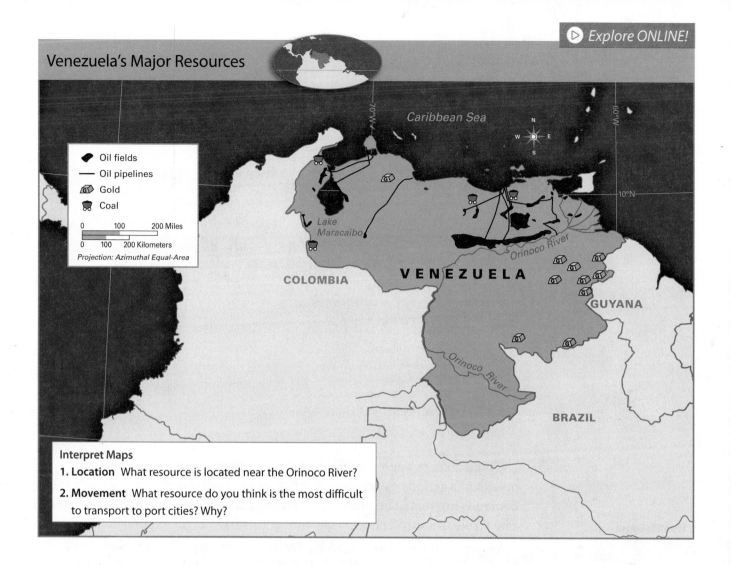

Venezuela's Major Resources

Explore ONLINE!

Legend:
- Oil fields
- Oil pipelines
- Gold
- Coal

0   100   200 Miles
0   100   200 Kilometers
Projection: Azimuthal Equal-Area

Caribbean Sea

Lake Maracaibo

COLOMBIA

VENEZUELA

Orinoco River

GUYANA

Orinoco River

BRAZIL

Interpret Maps

1. **Location** What resource is located near the Orinoco River?

2. **Movement** What resource do you think is the most difficult to transport to port cities? Why?

Oil-related pollution is a problem in Venezuela. Pits collect oil that spills from oil wells. Sometimes the oil in these pits seeps into underground water sources and pollutes the water supply. To prevent this, Venezuela's state oil company now has procedures to clean out the oil pits.

The Guiana Highlands in the southeast are rich in other minerals, such as iron ore for making steel. Gold is also mined in remote areas of the highlands. Dams on tributaries of the Orinoco River produce hydroelectricity.

Neither Caracas nor other parts of Venezuela have escaped poverty. Caracas is encircled by slums, and many Venezuelans living in the rural areas of the country are also poor.

Government After years of suffering under military dictatorships, the people of Venezuela elected their first president in 1959. Since then, Venezuela's government has dealt with economic and political turmoil.

In 2002 Venezuela's president, Hugo Chavez, started to distribute the country's oil income equally among all Venezuelans. Before Chavez's presidency, only a small percentage of wealthy Venezuelans benefited from the country's oil income.

World's Top Oil Exporters

	Country	Oil Exports (million barrels per day)
1	Saudi Arabia	7.4
2	Russia	4.9
3	Canada	3.2
4	United Arab Emirates	2.6
5	Iraq	2.5
6	Nigeria	2.2
7	Angola	1.8
8	Kuwait	1.7
9	Venezuela	1.5

Source: *The World Factbook*, Central Intelligence Agency.

Reading Check
Identify Cause and Effect What effect did the workers' strike have on Venezuela's economy?

Thousands of Venezuelan oil workers went on strike to protest the president's actions. A **strike** is a group of workers stopping work until their demands are met. The protestors wanted Chavez to resign, but he refused. The strike caused Venezuela's economy to suffer as oil exports fell.

Chavez continued as president until his death in 2013. Nicolas Maduro then became president and continued many of Chavez's policies. Venezuela's economy has continued to struggle.

The Guianas

The countries of Guyana, Suriname, and French Guiana are together known as the Guianas (gee-AH-nuhz). Dense tropical rain forests cover much of this region, which lies east of Venezuela.

Guyana Guyana (gy-AH-nuh) comes from a South American Indian word that means "land of waters." About one-third of the country's population lives in Georgetown, the capital. Nearly all of Guyana's agricultural lands are located on the flat, fertile plains along the coast. Guyana's most important agricultural products are rice and sugar.

Guyana's population is diverse. About half of its people are descended from people who migrated to Guyana from India. These immigrants came to Guyana to work on the country's sugar plantations. Today, most Guyanese farm small plots of land or run small businesses. About one-third of the population is descended from former African slaves. These people operate large businesses and hold most of the government positions.

Suriname The resources and economy of Suriname (soohr-uh-NAHM) are similar to those of Guyana. Like Guyana, Suriname has a diverse population. The country's population includes South Asians, Africans, Chinese, Indonesians, and Creoles. The capital, Paramaribo (pah-rah-MAH-ree-boh), is home to nearly half of the country's people.

French Guiana French Guiana (gee-A-nuh) is a territory of France and sends representatives to the government in Paris. French Guiana's roughly 200,000 people live mostly in coastal areas. About two-thirds of the people are of African descent. Other groups include Europeans, Asians, and South American Indians. The country depends heavily on imports for its food and energy.

Reading Check
Contrast How is French Guiana different from the rest of the Guianas?

Summary and Preview In this lesson you learned that Colombia's history includes the Chibcha, Spanish conquest, and independence. Today, Colombia's people are dealing with a long civil war. You also found out that Venezuela's history was largely shaped by Spanish settlement. Today Venezuela's economy is based on oil. Also, to the east, the Guianas are home to a diverse population. In the next lesson, you will learn about Ecuador, Bolivia, Peru, and Chile.

Lesson 4 Assessment

Review Ideas, Terms, and Places

1. a. Recall Who were the Chibcha?

b. Draw Conclusions Why did Spain want land in Colombia?

2. a. Describe What factors make Colombia ideal for growing coffee?

b. Predict How might Colombia solve the problem of guerrillas trying to control the country?

3. a. Recall What did Spanish settlers hope to find in Venezuela?

b. Explain Who led Venezuela's revolt against Spain?

4. a. Describe What does the landscape of Caracas include?

b. Elaborate Why did some Venezuelans go on strike?

5. a. Describe What are Guyana's agricultural lands and products like?

b. Contrast How is the population of the Guianas different from that of Colombia and Venezuela?

Critical Thinking

6. Analyze Using your notes, write a sentence about the topic of each box in a diagram like this one.

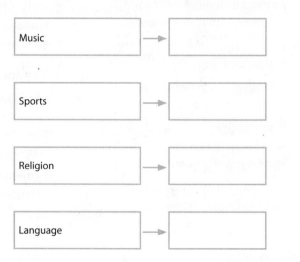

Ecuador, Bolivia, Peru, and Chile

The Big Idea

Native cultures and Spanish colonization have shaped the history of Pacific South America, and today people of the region are working to overcome poverty and political instability.

Main Ideas

- The countries of Pacific South America share a history influenced by the Inca civilization and Spanish colonization.
- The culture of Pacific South America includes American Indian and Spanish influences.
- Ecuador struggles with poverty and political instability.
- Bolivia's government is trying to gain stability and improve the economy.
- Peru has made progress against poverty and violence.
- Chile has a stable government and a strong economy.

Key Terms and Places

viceroy
Creoles
Quito
La Paz
Lima
coup
Santiago

If YOU lived there . . .

You live in Cuzco, the capital of the Inca Empire. You are required to contribute labor to the empire, and you have been chosen to work on a construction project. Hauling the huge stones will be difficult, but the work will be rewarding. You can either choose to help build a magnificent temple to the sun god or you can help build a road from Cuzco to the far end of the empire.

Which project will you choose? Why?

Pacific South America's History

Thousands of years ago, people in Pacific South America learned how to adapt to and modify their environments. They built stone terraces into the steep mountainsides so they could raise crops. In coastal areas, people created irrigation systems to store water and control flooding.

The Inca Empire Eventually, one culture came to rule most of the region. By the early 1500s, these people, the Incas, controlled an area that stretched from northern Ecuador to central Chile. The Inca Empire was home to as many as 12 million people.

The huge Inca Empire was highly organized. Irrigation projects turned deserts into rich farmland. Thousands of miles of stone-paved roads connected the empire. Rope suspension bridges helped the Incas cross the steep Andean valleys.

As advanced as their civilization was, the Incas had no wheeled vehicles or horses. Instead, relay teams of runners carried messages from one end of the empire to the other. Working together, a team of runners could carry a message up to 150 miles (240 km) in one day. The runners did not carry any letters, however, because the Incas did not have a written language.

Spanish Rule In spite of its great organization, however, the Inca Empire did not last long. A new Inca ruler, on his way to be crowned king, met the Spanish explorer Francisco Pizarro. Pizarro captured the Inca king, who ordered his people to bring enough gold and silver to fill a whole room. These riches were supposed to be a ransom for the king's freedom. Instead,

Pizarro ordered the Inca king killed. Fighting broke out, and by 1537 the Spaniards controlled all of the Inca Empire.

The new Spanish rulers often dealt harshly with the South American Indians of the fallen Inca Empire. Many Indians had to work in gold or silver mines or on the Spaniards' plantations. A Spanish **viceroy,** or governor, was appointed by the king of Spain to make sure the Indians followed the Spanish laws and customs that had replaced native traditions.

Independence By the early 1800s, people in Pacific South America began to want independence. They began to revolt against Spanish rule. **Creoles,** South American-born descendants of Europeans, were the main leaders of the revolts. The success of the revolts led to independence for Chile, Ecuador, Peru, and Bolivia by 1825.

Reading Check
Evaluate How did Inca civilization influence the history of the region?

Pacific South America's Culture

Spanish and native cultures have both left their marks on Pacific South America. Most people in the region speak Spanish, and Spanish is the official language in all of the countries of the region.

However, people in many parts of the region also maintain much of their native culture. Millions of South American Indians speak native languages in addition to or instead of Spanish. In Bolivia, two native languages are official languages in addition to Spanish.

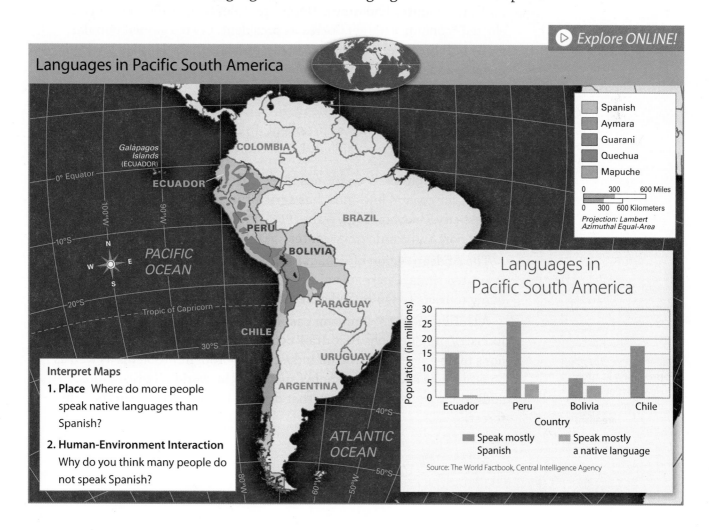

▶ Explore ONLINE!

Languages in Pacific South America

Legend: Spanish, Aymara, Guarani, Quechua, Mapuche

Projection: Lambert Azimuthal Equal-Area

Languages in Pacific South America

Chart: Population (in millions) by Country — Ecuador, Peru, Bolivia, Chile. Speak mostly Spanish / Speak mostly a native language.

Source: The World Factbook, Central Intelligence Agency

Interpret Maps

1. **Place** Where do more people speak native languages than Spanish?

2. **Human-Environment Interaction** Why do you think many people do not speak Spanish?

The people and customs of Pacific South America also reflect the region's Spanish and Indian heritage. For example, Bolivia's population has the highest percentage of South American Indians of any country on the continent. Many Bolivian Indians follow customs and lifestyles that have existed for many centuries. They often dress in traditional styles—full skirts and derby hats for the women and colorful, striped ponchos for the men.

Another part of the region's culture that reflects Spanish and Indian influences is religion. Most people in Pacific South America practice the religion of the Spanish—Roman Catholicism. Some people in the Andes, however, also still practice ancient religious customs. Every June, for example, people participate in a festival to worship the sun that was celebrated by the Incas. During festivals people wear traditional costumes, sometimes with wooden masks. They also play traditional instruments, such as wooden flutes.

Reading Check
Find Main Ideas
What traditional customs do people in the region still practice today?

Ecuador Today

In recent decades, the countries of Pacific South America have all experienced periods of political instability. Widespread poverty has been a constant threat to stable government in Ecuador, for example.

Government Ecuador has been a democracy since 1979. From 1996 to 2007, the country had nine different presidents. In 2006 Ecuadorians elected economist Rafael Correa as president. Correa gained popularity by building roads, bridges, schools, and hospitals. He also lowered poverty and unemployment levels.

Correa often clashed with journalists, and some government officials found working with him difficult. Still, Correa's achievements helped him win two more terms as president. In 2016 Ecuadorians elected Correa's former vice-president, Lenín Moreno, president.

Economic Regions Ecuador has three different economic regions. One region, the coastal lowlands, has agriculture and industry. The country's largest city, Guayaquil (gwy-ah-KEEL), is located there. It is Ecuador's major port and commercial center.

The Andean region of Ecuador is poorer. **Quito,** the national capital, is located there. Open-air markets and Spanish colonial buildings attract many tourists to Quito and other towns in the region.

A third region, the Amazon basin, has valuable oil deposits. The oil industry provides jobs that draw people to the region. Oil is also Ecuador's main export. But the oil industry has brought problems as well as benefits. The country's economy suffers if the world oil price drops. In addition, some citizens worry that drilling for oil could harm the rain forest.

Reading Check
Form Generalizations
How was Correa able to win three terms as president?

The Informal Economy

Many people in the countries of Pacific South America are part of the informal economy. Street vendors, like the ones shown here in Quito, are common sights in the region's cities. People visit street vendors to buy items like snacks, small electronics, or clothing. The informal economy provides jobs for many people. However, it does not help the national economy because the participants do not pay taxes. Without income from taxes, the government cannot pay for services.

Analyze Effects
How does the informal economy affect taxes?

Bolivia Today

Like Ecuador, Bolivia is a poor country. Poverty has been a cause of political unrest in recent years.

Government After years of military rule, Bolivia is now a democracy. Bolivia's government is divided between two capital cities. The supreme court meets in Sucre (SOO-kray), but the congress meets in **La Paz.** Located at about 12,000 feet (3,660 m), La Paz is the highest capital city in the world. It is also Bolivia's main industrial center.

In the early 2000s, many Bolivians disagreed with their government's plans for fighting poverty. National protests forced several presidents to resign. Then in 2005 Bolivians elected an indigenous leader, Evo Morales, as president. Morales was reelected president in 2009 and 2014.

Economy Bolivia is the poorest country in South America. In the plains of eastern Bolivia there are few roads and little money for investment. However, foreign aid has provided funds for some development. In addition, the country has valuable resources, including metals and natural gas.

Reading Check
Analyze Issues Why might political revolts slow development?

Peru Today

Peru is the largest and most populous country in Pacific South America. Today, it is making some progress against political violence and poverty.

Lima Peru's capital, **Lima** (LEE-muh), is the largest city in the region. Nearly one-third of all Peruvians live in Lima or the nearby port city of Callao (kah-YAH-oh). Lima has industry, universities, and government jobs, which attract many people from the countryside to Lima.

Lima was the colonial capital of Peru, and the city still contains many beautiful old buildings from the colonial era. It has high-rise apartments and wide, tree-lined boulevards. However, as in many big urban areas, many people there live in poverty.

In spite of the poverty, central Lima has few slum areas. This is because most poor people prefer to claim land on the outskirts of the city and build their own houses. Often they can get only poor building materials. They also have a hard time getting water and electricity from the city.

Settlements of new self-built houses are called "young towns" in Lima. Over time, as people improve and add to their houses, the new settlements develop into large, permanent suburbs. Many of the people in Lima's young towns are migrants from the highlands. Some came to Lima to escape violence in their home villages.

Settlements around Lima

Lima has three main types of settlements. The wealthier people tend to live in houses and apartments in town. Poor people live mostly in slums or in recently built "young towns."

Young Towns

In recent years, many poor people have taken over land on the outskirts of Lima and have built their own shelters.

Houses and Apartments

Most housing in Lima is made up of high-rise apartments and private houses, some of which are from the colonial era.

Slums

Just outside downtown and near the port area, many people live in slum housing. These buildings are permanent but run down.

Government In the 1980s and 1990s, a terrorist group called the Shining Path was active. This group carried out deadly attacks because it opposed government policies. Some 70,000 people died in violence between the Shining Path and government forces, and Peru's economy suffered. However, after the arrest of the group's leaders, Peru's government began making progress against political violence and poverty. The country has an elected president and congress.

Resources Peru's resources are key factors in its economic progress. Some mineral deposits are located near the coast, and hydroelectric projects on rivers provide energy. Peru's highlands are less developed than the coastal areas. However, many Peruvian Indians grow potatoes and corn there.

Chile Today

Like Peru, Chile has ended a long violent period. Chile now has a stable government and a growing economy.

Government In 1970 Chileans elected a president who had some ideas influenced by communism. A few years later he was overthrown and died in a U.S.-backed military coup (KOO). A **coup** is a sudden overthrow of a government by a small group of people.

In the years after the coup, military rulers tried to crush their political enemies. Chile's military government was harsh and often violent. It imprisoned or killed thousands of people.

In the late 1980s Chile's military dictatorship weakened and Chileans created a new, democratic government. In 2006 Chileans elected their first female president, Michelle Bachelet, and in 2010 they elected business leader Sebastián Piñera president. Michelle Bachelet was elected president again in 2013.

Resources and Economy Chile's economy is the strongest in the region. Poverty rates have decreased, and Chile's prospects for the future seem bright. Small businesses and factories are growing quickly. More Chileans are finding work, and wages are rising.

About one-third of all Chileans live in central Chile. This region includes the capital, **Santiago,** and a nearby seaport, Valparaíso (bahl-pah-rah-EE-soh). Its mild Mediterranean climate enables farmers to grow many crops. For example, grapes grow well there, and Chilean fruit and wine are exported around the world.

Farming, fishing, forestry, and mining form the basis of Chile's economy. Copper mining is especially important. It accounts for more than one-third of Chile's exports.

Chile's economic stability was rocked by a massive earthquake that struck on February 27, 2010. The quake killed about 500 Chileans and caused about $30 billion of damage to buildings, homes, and streets. Today, Chile's people and government continue to rebuild their nation.

Reading Check
Identify Cause and Effect How did the Shining Path affect Peru?

Reading Check
Identify Points of View Why might Chile want to join a free trade group?

A man in Chile harvests grapes to be made into wine for export.

Summary In this lesson you learned that Pacific South America was home to one of the greatest ancient civilizations in the Americas—the Inca. The Spanish conquered the Incas. Today, the region's culture still reflects Inca and Spanish influences. In recent years Ecuador, Peru, Bolivia, and Chile have struggled with political violence and poverty. However, Peru and Chile are recovering.

Lesson 5 Assessment

Review Ideas, Terms, and Places

1. **a. Recall** What ancient empire built paved roads through the Andes?

   b. Explain What role did Creoles play in the history of Pacific South America?

   c. Identify How did the early Peruvians adapt to their physical environment?

2. **a. Recall** What country has the highest percentage of South American Indians in its population?

   b. Make Generalizations What aspects of culture in Pacific South America reflect Spanish influence, and what aspects reflect Indian heritage?

3. **a. Identify** What is Ecuador's largest city?

   b. Make Generalizations Why have Ecuadorians been unhappy with their government in recent years?

4. **a. Identify** What are Bolivia's two capital cities?

   b. Analyze Why might Bolivia's economy improve in the future?

5. **a. Recall** Why did many Peruvians move to Lima from the highlands in the 1980s?

   b. Elaborate What challenges do you think people who move to Lima from the highlands face?

6. **a. Define** What is a coup?

   b. Make Inferences What might happen to Chile's economy if the world price of copper drops?

Critical Thinking

7. **Solve Problems** Review your notes. Then, in a diagram like the one here, write one sentence about each country, explaining how that country is dealing with poverty or government instability.

Ecuador	
Bolivia	
Peru	
Chile	

Social Studies Skills

Interpret an Elevation Profile

Define the Skill

An elevation profile is a diagram that shows a side view of an area. This kind of diagram shows the physical features that lie along a line from Point A to Point B. Keep in mind that an elevation profile typically exaggerates vertical distances because vertical and horizontal distances are measured differently on elevation profiles. If they were not, even tall mountains would appear as tiny bumps.

Learn the Skill

Use the elevation profile below to answer the following questions.

1. What place does this elevation profile measure?

2. What is the highest point, and what is its elevation?

3. How can you tell that the vertical distance is exaggerated?

Practice the Skill

Look at the physical map of Pacific South America in Lesson 1 of this module. Choose a latitude line and create your own elevation profile for the land at that latitude. Be sure to pay attention to the scale and the legend so that you use correct measurements.

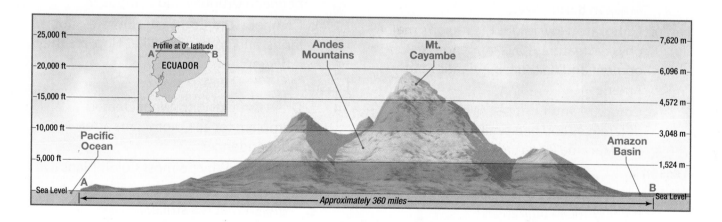

Module 11 Assessment

Review Vocabulary, Terms, and Places

For each statement below, write T *if it is true and* F *if it is false.*

1. The Andes is a river system.
2. Caribbean South America's location near the equator means that the region is very cold.
3. Huge slums in Brazilian cities are called favelas.
4. Deforestation in the Amazon region threatens the survival of many plant and animal species.
5. Most Argentines today work as gauchos, herding cattle and horses on grasslands.
6. Paraguay is a landlocked country.
7. Colombian culture includes traditional African songs and dances.
8. Venezuela's economy depends on oil production.
9. La Paz, Bolivia, is the capital city with the lowest elevation in the world.
10. Today Chile has a stable government and a growing economy.

Comprehension and Critical Thinking

Lesson 1

11. a. Recall What is the region's longest river?
    b. Analyze How does the temperature vary in the Andes?
    c. Recall What kind of climate does the Amazon Basin have?
    d. Elaborate How might the region's major physical features have influenced development and daily life in Atlantic South America?
    e. Compare and Contrast What are two differences and one similarity between the Atacama Desert and the altiplano?

Lesson 2

12. a. Identify What parts of Brazilian culture reflect African influences?
    b. Analyze What factors cause people from the northeast of Brazil to move to the southeast?
    c. Evaluate Is deforestation of the Amazon rain forest necessary? Explain your answer. What arguments might someone with a different opinion use?

Lesson 3

13. a. Describe How is Argentina's culture different from other South American countries?
    b. Contrast What is one difference between Uruguay and Paraguay?
    c. Compare and Contrast How are quotas, tariffs, and embargos alike? How are they different?

Lesson 4

14. a. Draw Conclusions What created a problem for all Colombians after independence?
    b. Elaborate Why do most Colombians live in fertile valleys and river basins?
    c. Define What is a strike?
    d. Draw Conclusions Why did people from India immigrate to Guyana?

Lesson 5

15. **a. Describe** How did the Incas organize their huge empire?

b. Analyze How have Spanish and native cultures left their marks on culture in Pacific South America?

c. Analyze What problems in Ecuador and Bolivia cause political unrest?

d. Evaluate What would be some benefits and drawbacks of moving from the highlands to one of Lima's "young towns"?

Reading Skills 21ST CENTURY

16. **Identify Supporting Details** Look back over the first part of Lesson 1 about the physical geography of Caribbean South America. Then make a list of details you find to support that part of the lesson's main ideas. Make sure you include details about physical features, climate, vegetation, and natural resources.

Social Studies Skills

Interpret an Elevation Profile *Use the elevation profile from the Social Studies Skills activity in this module to answer the questions below.*

17. Which view of the area does this diagram give you, from above or from the side?

18. What information does the locator map give you?

19. What is located at the lowest point, and what is its elevation?

20. How much area is covered between Points A and B?

Map Skills 21ST CENTURY

21. **Atlantic South America** On a separate sheet of paper, match the letters on the map with their correct labels.

São Paulo   Pampas   Patagonia

Paraná River   Río de la Plata   Amazon River

Focus on Writing

22. **Write a Letter** Imagine that you live in a specific South American country. Your pen pal in the United States has asked you to write a letter telling her about life in your region. Begin a letter to your pen pal by describing the most interesting physical and cultural features of the whole region in which you live: Caribbean South America, Atlantic South America, or Pacific South America. Then write a second paragraph telling your pen pal about the special physical and cultural features of the country in which you live. Try to keep your pen pal interested in reading by including fascinating details and descriptions.

Europe before the 1700s

Essential Question

What are the major political, social, and cultural legacies from Europe's early history?

About the Photo: Eilean Donan castle was built in the Highlands of Scotland during the 13th century. The castle protected the lands of Kintail against Viking raids.

In this module, you will learn about the early history of Europe, from prehistoric cultures through the Reformation, and how political, social, and cultural developments changed Europe and still influence our world today.

Explore ONLINE!

HISTORY

VIDEOS, including . . .
- Origins of Western Culture
- Rome Falls
- Battle of Hastings

☑ Document-Based Investigations

☑ Graphic Organizers

☑ Interactive Games

☑ Interactive Map: Greek City-States and Colonies, c. 600 BC

☑ Image with Hotspots: Roman Engineering

☑ Image Carousel: The Renaissance

What You Will Learn

Society In 1517 Martin Luther, a German monk, posted problems he saw in the Catholic Church.

Politics Warriors called knights were key to the political system of Europe in the Middle Ages. Knights wore suits of armor like this one into battle.

Culture The ancient Greeks were known for their artwork. This vase shows Greek soldiers tending to horses.

Reading Social Studies

Understand Implied Main Ideas

READING FOCUS

Do you ever "read between the lines" when people say things? You understand what people mean even when they don't come right out and say it. You can do the same thing with writing. Writers don't always state the main idea directly, but you can find clues to the main idea in the details. To understand an implied main idea, first read the text carefully and think about the topic. Next, look at the facts and details and ask yourself what the paragraph is saying. Then create a statement that sums up the main idea. Notice the way this process works with the paragraph below.

> 1. What is the topic?
> Jesus as a young man

As a young man Jesus lived in the town of Nazareth and probably studied with Joseph to become a carpenter. Like many young Jewish men of the time, Jesus also studied the laws and teachings of Judaism. By the time he was about 30, Jesus had begun to travel and teach.

> 2. What are the facts and details?
> • lived in Nazareth
> • studied to be a carpenter
> • learned about Judaism

> 3. What is the main idea?
> Jesus lived the typical life of a young Jewish man.

YOU TRY IT!

Read the following sentences. Notice the main idea is not stated. Using the three steps described above, develop a statement that expresses the main idea of the paragraph.

Justinian was stopped from leaving by his wife, Theodora. She convinced Justinian to stay in the city. Smart and powerful, Theodora helped her husband rule effectively. With her advice, he found a way to end the riots. Justinian's soldiers killed all the rioters—some 30,000 people—and saved the emperor's throne.

As you read this module, practice understanding the implied main ideas.

Prehistoric Cultures

The Big Idea

Prehistoric people adapted to their environment and developed agriculture.

Main Ideas

- Scientists study the remains of early humans to learn about prehistory.
- Early humans moved out of Africa and migrated all over the world.
- People adapted to new environments by making clothing and new types of tools.
- The first farmers learned to grow plants and raise animals in the New Stone Age.
- Farming changed societies and the way people lived.

Key Terms

prehistory
tool
Paleolithic Era
society
hunter-gatherers
migrate
ice ages
land bridge
Mesolithic Era
Neolithic Era
domestication
agriculture
megaliths

If YOU lived there . . .

You are a hunter-gatherer in Europe about 34,000 years ago. Your tribe has just arrived to this new land, which is much colder than your old home. You wrap yourself in animal hides, but it is difficult to keep them on while you hunt. Strange tall plants with pale flowers fill the land around you. You notice a few have been ripped out of the ground. When you examine them, you see long, strong fibers inside their stalks.

How can you use these plants to help you stay warm?

Prehistoric Humans

Although humans have lived on Earth for more than a million years, writing was not invented until about five thousand years ago. Historians call the time before there was writing **prehistory.** To study prehistory, historians rely on the work of archaeologists and anthropologists. Historic time periods, on the other hand, are those for which information has been recorded with letters, words, or numbers.

The earliest human ancestors, or hominids, may have first appeared in Africa about 4–5 million years ago. These hominids walked upright and had brains about one-third the size of modern humans. Over time, hominids developed larger brains, and each group of hominids was more advanced than the one before it.

Scientists are not exactly sure when or where the first modern humans lived. Many think that they first appeared in Africa about two hundred thousand years ago. Scientists call these people *Homo sapiens*, or "wise man." Every person alive today belongs to this group.

Early Hominids

Four major groups of hominids appeared in Africa between about two hundred thousand and 5 million years ago. Each group was more advanced than the one before it and could use better tools.

Australopithecus
- Name means "southern ape"
- Appeared in Africa about 4–5 million years ago
- Stood upright and walked on two legs
- Brain was about one-third the size of modern humans

Homo habilis
- Name means "handy man"
- Appeared in Africa about 2.4 million years ago
- Used early stone tools for chopping and scraping
- Brain was about half the size of modern humans

Homo erectus
- Name means "upright man"
- Appeared in Africa about 1.5–2 million years ago
- Used early stone tools like the hand ax
- Learned to control fire
- Migrated out of Africa to Asia and Europe

Homo sapiens
- Name means "wise man"
- Appeared in Africa about 200,000 years ago
- Migrated around the world
- Same species as modern human beings
- Learned to create fire and use a wide variety of tools
- Developed language

The First Tools The first humans and their ancestors lived during a long period of time called the Stone Age. To help in their studies, archaeologists divide the Stone Age into three periods based on the kinds of tools used at the time. To archaeologists, a **tool** is any handheld object that has been modified to help a person accomplish a task.

The first part of the Stone Age is called the **Paleolithic** (pay-lee-uh-LI-thik) **Era,** or Old Stone Age. It lasted until about ten thousand years ago. During this time, people used stone tools.

Scientists have found the oldest tools in Tanzania, a country in East Africa. These sharpened stones, about the size of an adult's fist, are about 2.6 million years old. Each stone had been struck with another rock to

Early people worked together and used spears to hunt large animals.

Hunter-gatherers

Early people were hunter-gatherers. They hunted animals and gathered wild plants to survive. Life for these hunter-gatherers was difficult and dangerous. Still, people learned how to make tools, use fire, and even create art.

Analyze Visuals
What tools are people using in this picture?

create a sharp, jagged edge along one side. This process left one unsharpened side that could be used as a handle.

Scientists think that these first tools were mostly used to process food. The sharp edge could be used to cut, chop, or scrape roots, bones, or meat. Tools like these were used for about 2 million years.

Later Tools Over time, people learned to make better tools. For example, they developed the hand ax. They often made this tool out of a mineral called flint. Flint is easy to shape, and tools made from it can be very sharp. People used hand axes to break tree limbs, to dig, and to cut animal hides.

People also learned to attach wooden handles to tools. By attaching a wooden shaft to a stone point, for example, they invented the spear. Because a spear could be thrown, hunters no longer had to stand close to animals they were hunting. As a result, people could hunt larger animals. Among the animals hunted by Stone Age people were deer, horses, bison, and elephant-like creatures called mammoths.

Society As early humans developed tools and new hunting techniques, they formed societies. A **society** is a community of people who share a common culture. These societies developed cultures with languages, religions, and art.

The early humans of the Stone Age were **hunter-gatherers**—people who hunt animals and gather wild plants, seeds, fruits, and nuts to survive. Anthropologists believe they lived in small groups. In bad weather, they might have taken shelter in a cave if there were one nearby. When food or water became hard to find, groups of people would have to move to new areas.

Each person in a hunter-gatherer society did tasks to help meet the needs of the community. Anthropologists believe that most Stone Age hunters were men and that women gathered plants to eat. Women likely stayed near camps and took care of children. The first pets may also have appeared at this time. People kept dogs to help them hunt and for protection.

Language, Art, and Religion The most important development of early Stone Age culture was language. Scientists have many theories about why language first developed. Some think it was to make hunting in groups easier. Others think it developed as a way for people to form relationships. Still others think language made it easier for people to resolve issues like how to **distribute** food.

Language wasn't the only way early people expressed themselves. They also created art. People carved figures out of stone, ivory, and bone. They carved beads for personal ornamentation. They painted and carved images of people and animals on cave walls. Scientists still aren't sure why people made art. Perhaps the cave paintings were used to teach people how to hunt, or maybe they had religious meanings. Scholars know little about the religious beliefs of early people. Archaeologists have found graves that included food and artifacts. Many scientists think these discoveries are proof that the first human religions developed during the Stone Age.

Academic
Vocabulary
distribute to divide among a group of people

Reading Check
Make Inferences What information about early humans might be missing from prehistoric sources?

Thousands of years ago, early people decorated cave walls with paintings, like this one in France. No one knows for sure why people created cave paintings, but many historians think they were related to hunting.

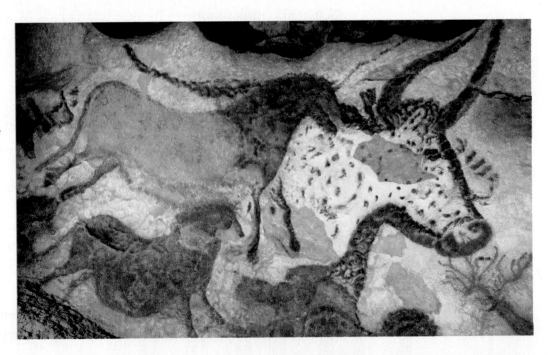

Early Human Migration

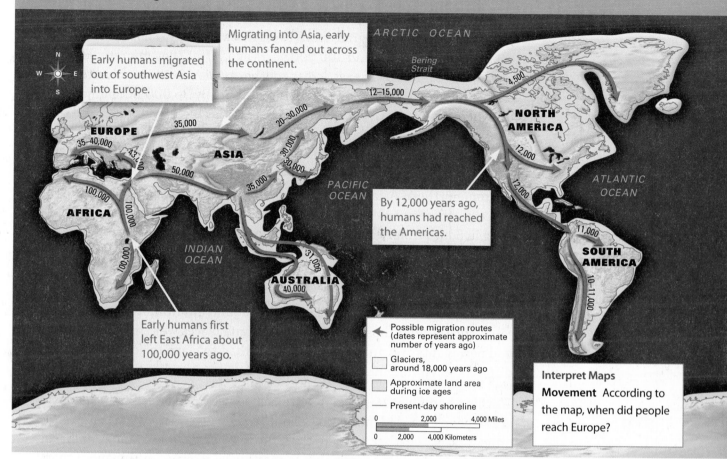

Early humans migrated out of southwest Asia into Europe.

Migrating into Asia, early humans fanned out across the continent.

ARCTIC OCEAN

Bering Strait

12–15,000

4,500

NORTH AMERICA

12,000

EUROPE

35,000

35–40,000

43,000

50,000

ASIA

20–30,000

30,000

30,000

30,000

100,000

100,000

AFRICA

100,000

35,000

PACIFIC OCEAN

12,000

12,000

ATLANTIC OCEAN

11,000

SOUTH AMERICA

10–11,000

INDIAN OCEAN

31,000

AUSTRALIA

40,000

By 12,000 years ago, humans had reached the Americas.

Early humans first left East Africa about 100,000 years ago.

← Possible migration routes (dates represent approximate number of years ago)

☐ Glaciers, around 18,000 years ago

☐ Approximate land area during ice ages

— Present-day shoreline

0   2,000   4,000 Miles
0 2,000   4,000 Kilometers

Interpret Maps
Movement According to the map, when did people reach Europe?

People Move Out of Africa

During the Old Stone Age, climate patterns around the world changed, transforming Earth's geography. In response to these changes, people began to **migrate,** or move, to new places.

The Ice Ages Most scientists believe that about 1.6 million years ago, many places around the world began to experience long periods of freezing weather. These freezing times are called the **ice ages.** The ice ages ended about ten thousand years ago.

During the ice ages, huge sheets of ice covered much of Earth's land. These ice sheets were formed from ocean water, leaving ocean levels lower than they are now. Many areas that are now underwater were dry land then. For example, a narrow body of water now separates Asia and North America. But scientists think that during the ice ages, the ocean level dropped and exposed a **land bridge,** a strip of land connecting two continents. Land bridges allowed Stone Age people to migrate around the world.

Settling New Lands Scientists agree that migration around the world took hundreds of thousands of years. Early hominids migrated from Africa to Asia as early as 2 million years ago. Some early hominids reached Europe around 730,000 BC, and some also spread to Southeast Asia.

Reading Check
Make Inferences
Why do you think it took humans hundreds of thousands of years to migrate around the world?

Later, humans also began to migrate around the world, and earlier hominids died out. Look at the map to see the dates and routes of early human migration.

Humans began to migrate from East Africa to southern Africa and southwestern Asia around 100,000 years ago. After they migrated out of Africa, people moved east across southern Asia. From southwestern Asia, humans also migrated north into Europe. By 35,000 BC, humans lived across Europe. Geographic features such as high mountains and cold temperatures delayed migration northward into northern Asia. Eventually, however, people from both Europe and southern Asia moved into that region.

From northern Asia, people moved into North America. Once in North America, these people moved south, following herds of animals and settling in South America. By 9000 BC, humans lived on all continents of the world except Antarctica.

People Adapt to New Environments

As early people moved to new lands, they found environments that differed greatly from those in East Africa. Many places were much colder and had new plants and animals. Early people had to learn to adapt to these different environments.

Clothing and Shelter Although fire helped keep people warm in very cold areas, people needed more protection. To keep warm, they learned to sew animal skins together to make clothing. In Georgia, for example, archaeologists discovered flax fibers that humans used to sew clothing more than 34,000 years ago.

In addition to clothing, people needed shelter to survive. Some took shelter in caves. Another early type of human-made shelter was the pit house. They were pits in the ground with roofs of branches and leaves.

Early people encountered new environments and colder climates as they migrated away from East Africa.

Some early people lived in tents made of animal skins. Others built more permanent structures of wood, stone, clay, or other materials. Even bones from large animals such as mammoths were used in building shelters.

New Tools and Technologies People also adapted to new environments with new types of tools. These tools were smaller and more complex than tools from the Old Stone Age. They defined the **Mesolithic** (me-zuh-LI-thik) **Era,** or the Middle Stone Age. This period began more than ten thousand years ago and lasted to about five thousand years ago in some places.

During this time period, people found new uses for bone and stone tools. People who lived near water invented hooks and fishing spears. Other groups invented the bow and arrow.

In addition to tools, people developed new technologies to improve their lives. For example, some learned to make canoes by hollowing out logs. They used the canoes to travel on rivers and lakes. People also began to make pottery. Developments like these, in addition to clothing and shelter, allowed people to adapt to new environments.

Reading Check
Find Main Ideas What were two ways people adapted to new environments?

The First Farmers

After the Middle Stone Age came a period of time that scientists call the **Neolithic** (nee-uh-LI-thik) **Era,** or New Stone Age. It began as early as ten thousand years ago in Southwest Asia and reached parts of Europe as early as 7000 BC.

During the New Stone Age, people learned to polish stones to make tools like saws and drills. People also learned how to make fire. Before, they could only use fire that had been started by natural causes such as lightning. But tools and fire weren't the only major changes that occurred during the Neolithic Era. In fact, the biggest changes came in how people produced food.

Plants and Animals After a warming trend brought an end to the ice ages, new plants began to grow in some areas. For example, wild barley and wheat plants started to spread throughout Southwest Asia. Over time, people came to depend on these wild plants for food. They began to settle where grains grew.

People soon learned that they could plant seeds themselves to grow their own crops. Historians call the shift from food gathering to food producing the Neolithic Revolution. Most experts believe that this revolution, or change, first occurred in the societies of Southwest Asia.

Eventually, people learned to change plants to make them more useful. They planted only the largest grains or the sweetest fruits. They found new ways to use animals. They kept sheep or goats for milk, food, and wool. They used larger animals to carry or pull heavy loads or tools. The process of changing plants or animals to make them more useful to humans is called **domestication.**

Academic Vocabulary
development growth

The domestication of plants and animals led to the **development** of **agriculture,** or farming. For the first time, people could produce their own food. This development changed human society forever.

Reading Check
Analyze Effects What was one effect of domestication?

Farming Changes Societies

The Neolithic Revolution brought huge changes to people's lives. With survival more certain, people could focus on activities other than finding food.

Domestication of plants and animals enabled people to use plant fibers to make cloth. The domestication of animals made it possible to use wool from goats and sheep and skins from horses for clothes.

People also began to build permanent settlements. As they started raising crops and animals, they needed to stay in one place instead of continuing to travel on nomadic journeys to other areas of the world. Then, once people were able to control their own food production, the world's population grew. In some areas, farming communities developed into towns.

Early Economies In Neolithic communities, people used primitive tools and methods to grow, harvest, and hunt sources of food. They created large pits for storage of food. This meant that farmers could increase their productivity by harvesting large amounts of food and storing it after harvest. Having a surplus, or an extra amount, made trade possible, since farmers had a supply of food that others might want to purchase or gain through barter. A barter system is a form of exchange where goods and services are traded for other goods and services.

Social Order Farming and trade led to the growth of wealth in Neolithic communities. As Neolithic societies grew wealthy, they started to divide people into classes, or social groups based on wealth. Remains of societies can sometimes give clues about these social structures. In Europe, for example, archaeologists have found luxury goods such as jewelry in the graves of women. This evidence might show that women had high positions in some early European societies. They also found weapons in graves, which might mean that warriors became important to early European societies.

Early farmers harvest and process the food they grew while domesticated sheep and goats graze.

Stonehenge was built about five thousand years ago in what is now Wiltshire, England. Scholars think Neolithic humans may have constructed Stonehenge as a burial site, a site for religious ceremonies, or as an astronomical observatory.

Reading Check
Compare
What are the common ways Paleolithic, Mesolithic, and Neolithic people used tools?

Religious Practices As populations of towns grew, groups of people gathered to perform religious ceremonies. Some put up megaliths. **Megaliths** are huge stones used as monuments or as the sites for religious gatherings.

Early people probably believed in gods and goddesses associated with the four elements—air, water, fire, and earth—or with animals. For example, one early European group honored a thunder god, while another group worshiped bulls. Some scholars also believe that many prehistoric people prayed to their ancestors. People in some societies today still hold many of these same beliefs.

Summary and Preview Stone Age people adapted to new environments by domesticating plants and animals. These changes led to the development of religion and the growth of towns. In the next lesson, you will learn about ancient Greece, Europe's first great civilization.

Lesson 1 Assessment

Review Ideas, Terms, and Places

1. **a. Explain** Why do historians need archaeologists and anthropologists to study prehistory?

   b. Recall What kinds of tools did people use during the Paleolithic Era?

2. **a. Define** What is a land bridge?

   b. Explain How do scientists estimate when humans reached a new area?

3. **a. Recall** What did people use to make tools in the Mesolithic Era?

   b. Summarize Why did people have to learn to make clothes and build shelters?

4. **a. Define** What is domestication of a plant or animal?

   b. Form Generalizations How did early people use domesticated animals?

5. **a. Explain** How did farming allow people to create settlements and become less nomadic?

   b. Summarize How did early people express their religious beliefs?

Critical Thinking

6. **Analyze Causes and Effects** Draw a three-box chart to list the cause and effects of the development of agriculture. Use this graphic organizer to show one cause and three effects of the development of agriculture.

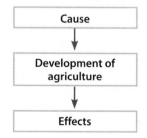

Ancient Greece

The Big Idea

Greek culture spread in Europe and Asia through colonization, trade, and conquest.

Main Ideas

- Early Greek culture saw the rise of the city-state and the creation of colonies.

- The golden age of Greece saw advances in government, art, and philosophy.

- Alexander the Great formed a huge empire and spread Greek culture into new areas.

Key Terms and Places

city-states
golden age
Athens
Sparta
Hellenistic

If YOU lived there . . .

You live in the ancient city of Athens, one of the largest cities in Greece. Your brother, just two years older than you, is excited. He is finally old enough to take part in the city's government. He and your father, along with the other free men in the city, will meet to vote on the city's laws and leaders. Your mother and your sisters, however, cannot take part in the process.

Why is your brother excited about voting?

Early Greek Culture

Suppose you and some friends wanted to go to the movies, but you could not decide which movie to see. Some of you might want to see the latest action thriller, while others are more in the mood for a comedy. How could you decide which movie you would go to see? One way to decide would be to take a vote. Whichever movie got more votes would be the one you saw.

Did you know that by voting you would be taking part in a process invented some 2,500 years ago? It is true. One of the earliest peoples to use voting to make major decisions was the ancient Greeks. Voting was only one of the many contributions the Greeks made to our culture, though. In fact, many people call ancient Greece the birthplace of modern civilization.

City-States Early Greece could be a dangerous place. Waves of invaders swept through the land, and violence was common. Eventually, people began to band together in groups for protection. Over time, these groups developed into **city-states,** or political units made up of a city and all the surrounding lands.

In the center of most city-states was a fortress on a hill. This hill was called the acropolis (uh-KRAH-puh-luhs), which is Greek for "highest city." In addition to the fortress, many city-states built temples and other public buildings on the acropolis.

Around the acropolis was the rest of the city, including houses and markets. High walls usually surrounded the city for protection. In wartime, farmers who lived outside the walls could seek safety inside.

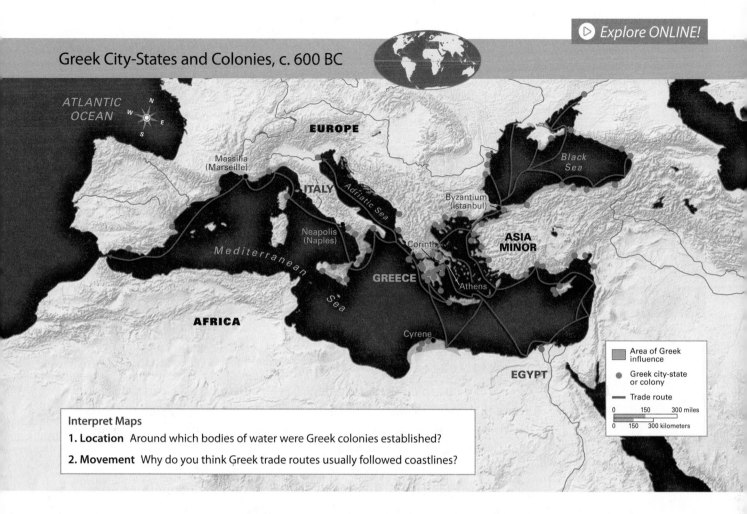

Explore ONLINE!

ATLANTIC
OCEAN

EUROPE

Massilia
(Marseille)

ITALY

Adriatic Sea

Byzantium
(Istanbul)

*Black
Sea*

Neapolis
(Naples)

Corinth

ASIA
MINOR

Mediterranean

GREECE

Athens

Sea

AFRICA

Cyrene

EGYPT

Area of Greek
influence

Greek city-state
or colony

Trade route

| 0 | 150 | 300 miles |
| 0 | 150 | 300 kilometers |

Interpret Maps

1. **Location** Around which bodies of water were Greek colonies established?

2. **Movement** Why do you think Greek trade routes usually followed coastlines?

Life in the city often focused on the marketplace, or *agora* (A-guh-ruh) in Greek. Farmers brought their crops to the market to trade for goods made by craftspeople in the town. Because it was a large open space, the market also served as a meeting place. People held both political and religious assemblies in the market. It often contained shops as well.

The city-state became the foundation of Greek civilization. In addition to providing its people with security and a marketplace, the city-state gave people a new sense of identity. People thought of themselves as residents of a particular city-state, not as Greeks.

Colonies In time, some Greeks became curious about neighboring lands around the Mediterranean and Black Seas. Some city-states established new outposts, or colonies, around these seas. You can see these colonies on the map. Some of them still exist today as modern cities, such as Naples, Italy, and Marseille, France.

Although they were independent, most colonies kept ties with the older cities of Greece. They traded goods and shared ideas. These ties helped strengthen the economies of both cities and colonies, and they kept Greek culture strong. Because they stayed in contact, Greek cities all over Europe shared a common culture.

Reading Check
Summarize Where did the ancient Greeks establish colonies?

The agora of Athens was located below the Acropolis. It was the center of commercial and political life.

The Golden Age of Greece

When most people think of ancient Greek culture today, certain images come to mind. They think of the ruins of stately temples and of realistic statues. They also think of great writers, philosophers, and scientists whose ideas changed the world.

These images represent some of the many contributions the Greeks made to world history. Remarkably, most of these contributions were developed during a relatively short time, between 500 and 300 BC. For that reason, this period is often called a **golden age,** a period in a society's history marked by great achievements.

The Growth of Greek Power Early in Greece's history, city-states remained fiercely independent. Each city-state focused on its own concerns and did not interfere in the others' affairs.

Around 500 BC, however, an invading army caused the Greeks to band together against a common enemy. That invasion came from Persia, a powerful empire in central Asia. The Persian army was huge, well trained, and experienced. Greece, on the other hand, had no single army. Each city-state had an army, but none was as large as Persia's. As a result, the Persians expected a quick victory.

Nevertheless, the Greeks took up arms against the Persians. Led by **Athens,** a city-state in eastern Greece, the Greeks were able to defeat the Persians and keep Greece from being conquered. When the Persians invaded again ten years later, the Athenians once again helped defeat them.

The victory over the Persians increased the confidence of people all over Greece. They realized that they were capable of great achievements. In the period after the Persian invasion, the people of Greece made amazing advances in art, writing, and thinking. Many of these advances were made by the people of Athens.

Pericles (c. 495–429 BC)

Pericles, the most famous leader in all of Athenian history, wanted the city's people to be proud of their city. In his speeches, he emphasized the greatness of Athenian democracy and encouraged everyone to take part. He also worked to make the city beautiful. He hired the city's best architects to build monuments, such as the Parthenon, and hired great artists to decorate them. He also supported the work of writers and poets in order to make Athens the cultural center of all Greece.

Athenian Culture In the century after the defeat of Persia, Athens was the cultural center of Greece. Some of history's most famous politicians, artists, and thinkers lived in Athens during this time.

One reason for the great advances the Athenians made during this time was their city's leadership. Leaders such as Pericles (PER-uh-kleez), who ruled Athens in the 400s BC, supported the arts and encouraged the creation of great works.

Athens became prosperous, or successful and wealthy, under Pericles's leadership. Because of this wealth, Pericles was able to hire great architects and artists to construct and decorate the Parthenon, ancient Greece's most famous temple.

Athenian Democracy Leaders like Pericles had great power in Athens, but they did not rule alone. The city of Athens was a democracy, and its leaders

Athenian Democracy

Athens was governed as a democracy. Once a month, all adult men in the city gathered together in an assembly to make the city's laws.

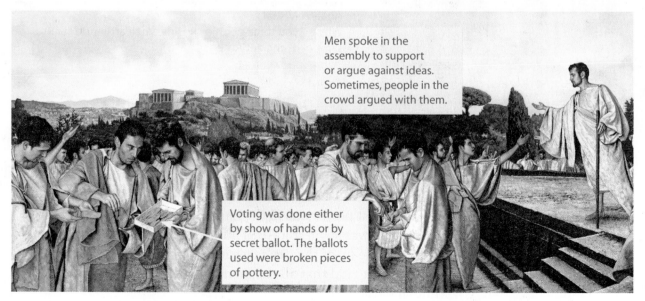

Men spoke in the assembly to support or argue against ideas. Sometimes, people in the crowd argued with them.

Voting was done either by show of hands or by secret ballot. The ballots used were broken pieces of pottery.

The Parthenon

The Parthenon is often seen as a symbol of ancient Athens. It was a temple to the goddess Athena, whom the people of Athens considered their protector. The temple is now in ruins, but this illustration shows how it may have looked when it was built around 440 BC.

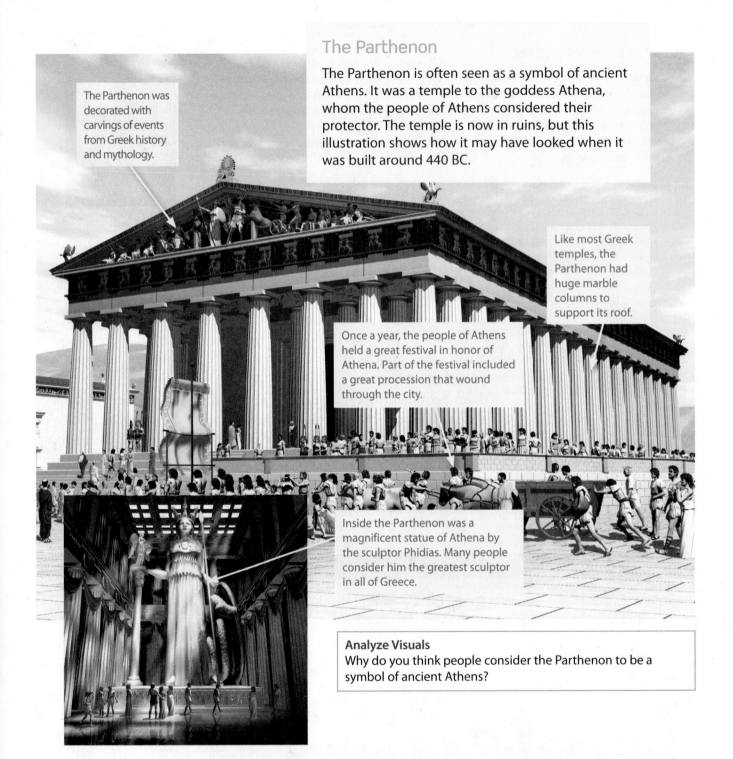

The Parthenon was decorated with carvings of events from Greek history and mythology.

Like most Greek temples, the Parthenon had huge marble columns to support its roof.

Once a year, the people of Athens held a great festival in honor of Athena. Part of the festival included a great procession that wound through the city.

Inside the Parthenon was a magnificent statue of Athena by the sculptor Phidias. Many people consider him the greatest sculptor in all of Greece.

Analyze Visuals
Why do you think people consider the Parthenon to be a symbol of ancient Athens?

were elected. In fact, Athens was the world's first democracy. No one else in history had created a government in which people ruled themselves.

In Athens, most power was in the hands of the people. All the city's leaders could do was suggest ideas. Those ideas had to be approved by an assembly made up of the city's free men before they were enacted. As a result, it was vital that all the men of Athens took part in making government decisions.

The people of Athens were very proud of their democracy and also of their city in general. This pride was reflected in their city's buildings and art.

Look at the picture of the Parthenon again. Why do you think the temple was so large and so elaborately decorated? Like many Greek buildings, it was designed to be a symbol of the city. It was supposed to make people see Athens as a great and glorious city.

Architecture and Art The Parthenon may be the most famous building from ancient Greece, but it is only one of many magnificent structures built by the Greeks. All over Greece, builders created beautiful marble temples. These temples were symbols of the glory of the cities in which they were built.

Greek temples and other buildings were often decorated with statues and carvings. These works by Greek artists are still admired by people today.

Greek art is so admired because of the skill and careful preparation of ancient Greek artists. These artists wanted their works to look realistic. To achieve their goals, they watched people as they stood and moved. They wanted to learn exactly what the human body looked like while it was in motion. The artists then used what they learned from their observations to make their statues as lifelike as possible.

Science, Philosophy, and Literature Artists were not the only people in ancient Greece to study other people. Scientists, for example, studied people to learn how the body worked. Through these studies, the Greeks learned a great deal about medicine and biology. Other Greek scholars made great advances in math, astronomy, and other areas of science.

Greek philosophers, or thinkers, also studied people. They wanted to figure out how people could be happy. Three of the world's most influential philosophers—Socrates, Plato, and Aristotle—lived and taught in Athens during this time. Their ideas continue to shape how we live and think even today.

Greek Art

The ancient Greeks were master artists. Their paintings and statues have been admired for hundreds of years. Greek statues are so admired because the sculptors who made them tried to make them look perfect. They took great care to make their art lifelike. Because of this, artists from later civilizations admired and imitated the works of Greek artists. This Roman sculpture is of Pallas, the Roman equivalent of the goddess Athena. It is similar to a sculpture of Athena by the Greek artist Phidias that once stood in the Acropolis.

Analyze Visuals
What details make this statue lifelike?

The ancient Greeks also made huge contributions to world literature. Some of the world's timeless classics were written in ancient Greece. They include stories of Greek heroes and their daring adventures, poems about love and friendship, and myths meant to teach lessons about life.

Among the earliest Greek writings are two great epic poems, the *Iliad* and the *Odyssey*, by a poet named Homer. Like most epics, both poems describe the deeds of great heroes. The heroes in Homer's poems fought in the Trojan War. In this war, the Mycenaean Greeks fought the Trojans, people of the city called Troy.

Chances are that you have read a book, seen a film, or watched a play inspired by—or even written by—the ancient Greeks. Actually, if you have ever seen a play at all, then you have the Greeks to thank. The ancient Greeks were the first people to write and perform drama, or plays. Once a part of certain religious ceremonies, plays became one of the most popular forms of entertainment in Greece.

The Decline of the City-States As great as it was, the Greek golden age could not last forever. In the end, Greece was torn apart by a war between Athens and its rival city-state, **Sparta.**

Historical Source

The *Odyssey* takes place after the Trojan War has ended. It describes the adventures of another hero, Odysseus, as he makes his way home to his kingdom of Ithaca. His voyage is full of obstacles—including the two sea monsters described in this passage. The idea for these monsters probably came from an actual strait in the Mediterranean Sea, where a jagged cliff rose on one side and dangerous whirlpools churned on the other.

Analyze Sources
The Greeks used myths to explain the natural world. How does the passage from the *Odyssey* illustrate this?

And all this time, in travail [pain], sobbing, gaining on the current, we rowed into the strait—Scylla to port and on our starboard beam Charybdis, dire gorge [terrible throat] of the salt sea tide. By heaven! when she vomited, all the sea was like a cauldron seething over intense fire, when the mixture suddenly heaves and rises. The shot spume [foam] soared to the landside heights, and fell like rain. But when she swallowed the sea water down we saw the funnel of the maelstrom [whirlpool], heard the rock bellowing all around, and dark sand raged on the bottom far below. My men all blanched [grew pale] against the gloom, our eyes were fixed upon that yawning mouth in fear of being devoured.

—Homer from the *Odyssey*,
translated by Robert Fitzgerald

A Greek Theater

The ancient Greeks built their theaters into hillsides so that everyone in the audience had a good view. Actors wore masks with exaggerated faces so that the audience could identify characters and emotions from a distance.

To represent Greek gods appearing from the sky, stage workers used a crane to lower actors who played the roles of gods to the stage.

Actors performed the plays on stage.

All plays had a chorus who helped explain what was happening on stage.

Background scenery made the play appear more realistic.

Analyze Visuals
In what ways are modern-day plays similar to those held in ancient Greece?

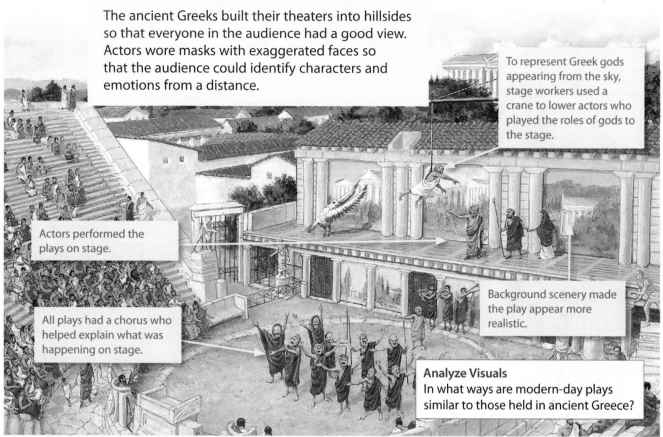

Sparta was a military city with one of the strongest armies in Greece. Jealous of the influence Athens had over other city-states, the Spartans attacked Athens.

The war between these two powerful city-states devastated Greece. Other city-states joined the war, supporting one side or the other. For years, the war went on. In the end, Sparta won, but Greece was in shambles. Thousands of people had been killed, and whole cities had been destroyed. Weakened, Greece lay open for a foreign conqueror to swoop in and take over.

Reading Check
Find Main Ideas
Why is the period between 500 and 300 BC called a golden age in Greece?

The Empire of Alexander

In fact, a conqueror did take over all of Greece in the 330s BC. For the first time in its history, all of Greece was unified under a single ruler. He was from an area called Macedonia just north of Greece, an area that many Greeks considered uncivilized. He was known as Alexander the Great.

Alexander's Conquests Alexander swept into Greece with a strong, well-trained army in 336 BC. In just a few years, he had conquered all of Greece.

Alexander, however, was not satisfied to rule only Greece. He wanted to create a huge empire. In 334 BC he set out to do just that. As you can see on the map, he was quite successful.

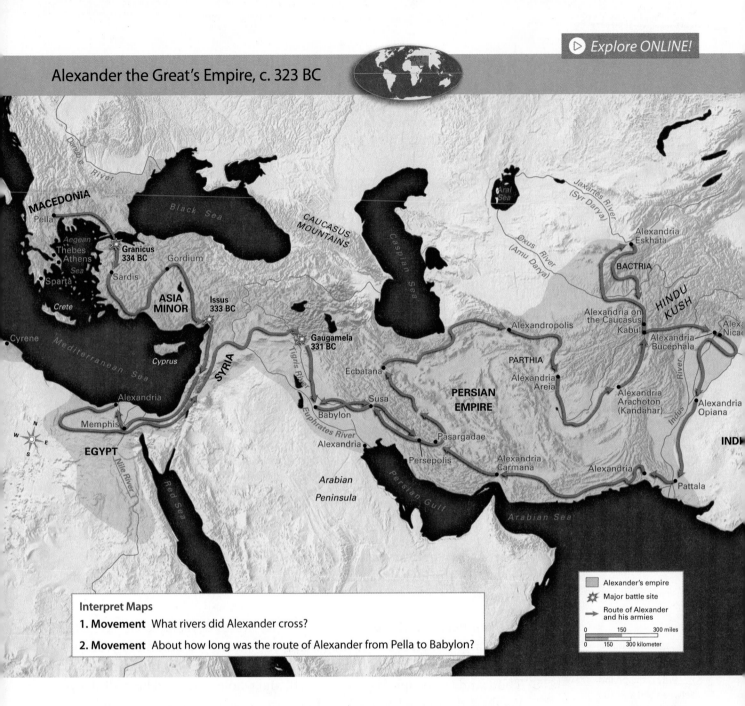

Alexander the Great's Empire, c. 323 BC

MACEDONIA
Pella
Black Sea
Aegean
Thebes
Athens
Sea
Sparta
Crete
Granicus
334 BC
Gordium
Sardis
ASIA
MINOR
Issus
333 BC
SYRIA
Cyprus
Cyrene
Mediterranean Sea
Alexandria
Memphis
EGYPT
Nile River
Red Sea
Danube River
CAUCASUS
MOUNTAINS
Caspian Sea
Tigris River
Euphrates River
Gaugamela
331 BC
Ecbatana
Susa
Babylon
Alexandria
Pasargadae
Persepolis
Arabian
Peninsula
Persian Gulf
Arabian Sea
PERSIAN
EMPIRE
PARTHIA
Alexandria
Areia
Alexandria
Carmana
Aral
Sea
Jaxartes River
(Syr Darya)
Oxus River
(Amu Darya)
Alexandropolis
Alexandria on
the Caucasus
Kabul
BACTRIA
Alexandria
Eskhata
HINDU
KUSH
Alexandria
Bucephala
Indus River
Alexandria
Arachoton
(Kandahar)
Alex
Nica
Alexandria
Opiana
INDI
Alexandria
Pattala

Alexander's empire
Major battle site
Route of Alexander
and his armies

0   150   300 miles
0   150   300 kilometer

Interpret Maps

1. **Movement** What rivers did Alexander cross?

2. **Movement** About how long was the route of Alexander from Pella to Babylon?

At its greatest extent, Alexander's empire stretched from Greece in the west all the way to India in the east. It included nearly all of central Asia—including what had been the Persian Empire—and Egypt.

Alexander had dreams of extending his empire even farther east, but his troops refused to keep fighting. Tired and far from home, they demanded that Alexander turn back. He did, turning back toward home in 325 BC. On his way back home, however, Alexander became ill and died. He was 33.

The Spread of Greek Culture During his life, Alexander wanted Greek culture to spread throughout his empire. To help the culture spread, he built cities in the lands he conquered and urged Greek people to move there. He named many of the cities Alexandria after himself.

As Greek people moved to these cities, however, they mingled with the people and cultures in the area. As a result, Greek culture blended with other cultures. The result was a new type of culture that mixed elements from many people and places.

Because the Greek word for *Greek* is "Hellenic," historians often refer to these blended cultures as **Hellenistic,** or Greek-like. Hellenistic culture helped shape life in Egypt, central Asia, and other parts of the world for many years.

Summary and Preview Greece was the location of the first great civilization in Europe. In the next lesson, you will learn about the powerful civilization that defeated Greece, the Roman Empire.

Reading Check
Find Main Ideas
What lands were included in Alexander's empire?

Lesson 2 Assessment

Review Ideas, Terms, and Places

1. **a. Describe** What did an ancient Greek city-state include?

   b. Explain Why did the Greeks form city-states?

2. **a. Identify** What were some major achievements in Greece between 500 and 300 BC?

   b. Summarize What was the government of ancient Athens like?

   c. Evaluate Would you have liked living in ancient Greece? Why or why not?

3. **a. Describe** How did Alexander the Great try to spread Greek culture in his empire?

   b. Draw Conclusions How might Greek history have been different if Alexander had not existed?

Critical Thinking

4. **Analyze Events** Using your notes, draw a timeline of major events in Greek history. For each event you list on your timeline, write a sentence explaining why it was important.

The Roman World

The Big Idea

The Romans created one of the ancient world's greatest civilizations.

Main Ideas

- The Roman Republic was governed by elected leaders.

- The Roman Empire was a time of great achievements.

- The spread of Christianity began during the empire.

- Various factors helped bring about the decline of Rome.

Key Terms and Places

Rome
republic
Senate
citizens
Carthage
empire
aqueducts

If YOU lived there . . .

You live in Rome in about 50 BC. Times are difficult for ordinary Romans. Bread is scarce in the city, and you are finding it hard to find work. Now a popular general is mounting a campaign to cross the mountains into a territory called Gaul. He wants to try to conquer the barbarians who live there. It might be dangerous, but being a soldier guarantees work and a chance to make money.

Will you join the army? Why or why not?

The Roman Republic

"All roads lead to Rome." "Rome was not built in a day." "When in Rome, do as the Romans do." Have you heard these sayings before? All of them were inspired by the civilization of ancient Rome, a civilization that collapsed more than 1,500 years ago.

Why would people today use sayings that relate to so old a culture? They refer to Rome because it was one of the greatest and most influential civilizations in history. In fact, we can still see the influence of ancient Rome in our lives.

Rome's Early History Rome was not always so influential, however. At first, it was just a small city in Italy. According to legend, the city of **Rome** was established in the year 753 BC by a group called the Latins.

Not much of Italy is flat. Most of the land that isn't mountainous is covered with hills. Throughout history, people have built cities on these hills for defense. As a result, many of the ancient cities of Italy, such as Rome, sat atop hills. Rome was built on seven hills.

For many years, the Romans were ruled by kings. Not all of these kings were Latin, though. For many years, the Romans were ruled by a group called the Etruscans. The Romans learned a great deal from the Etruscans. For example, they learned about written language and how to build paved roads and sewers. Building on what they learned from the Etruscans, the Romans made Rome into a large and successful city.

The ancient Romans adapted to their environment. In an effort to defend the city, Rome was built atop seven hills.

The Beginning of the Republic Not all of Rome's kings were good leaders or good people. Some were cruel, harsh, and unfair. The last king of Rome was so unpopular that he was overthrown. In 509 BC a group of Roman nobles forced the king to flee the city.

In place of the king, the people of Rome created a new type of government. They formed a **republic,** a type of government in which people elect leaders to make laws for them. Once elected, these leaders made all government decisions.

To help make some decisions, Rome's leaders looked to the **Senate,** a council of rich and powerful Romans who helped run the city. By advising the city's leaders, the Senate gained much influence in Rome.

For Rome's republican government to succeed, **citizens,** or people who could take part in the government, needed to be active. Rome's leaders encouraged citizens to vote and to run for office. As a result, speeches and debates were common in the city. One popular place for these activities was in the Forum, the city's public square.

Link to Civics

The Roman Forum

The Forum was a large public square that stood in the center of the city. Government buildings and temples stood on the hills around the Forum.

Many people met in the Forum to discuss politics, current events, and other issues. Citizens, or people who could vote, often met in the forum to discuss city affairs and politics. Citizens wore togas to show their rank in the city.

Analyze Visuals
What are some places in your local community that serve the same function as the Forum did?

Growth and Conquest After the creation of the republic, the Romans began to expand their territory. They started this expansion in Italy. As the map shows, however, the republic kept growing. By 100 BC the Romans ruled much of the Mediterranean world.

The Romans were able to take so much land because of their strong, organized army. They used this army to conquer their rivals. For example, the Romans fought the people of **Carthage,** a city in North Africa, and took over their lands.

Rome's expansion did not stop in 100 BC. In the 40s BC a general named Julius Caesar conquered many new lands for Rome. Caesar's conquests made him powerful and popular in Rome. Afraid of Caesar's power, a group of senators decided to put an end to it. They banded together and killed Caesar in 44 BC.

Reading Check
Summarize How did the Romans expand their territory?

The Roman Empire

The murder of Julius Caesar changed Roman society completely. The Romans were shocked and horrified by his death, and they wanted Caesar's murderers to be punished. One of the people they called on to punish the murderers was Caesar's adopted son, Octavian. Octavian's actions would reshape the Roman world. Under his leadership, Rome changed from a republic to an **empire,** a government that includes many different peoples and lands under a single rule.

The First Emperor Octavian moved quickly to punish his great-uncle's murderers. He led an army against them and defeated them all.

After defeating his enemies, Octavian became more powerful. One by one, he eliminated his rivals for power. Eventually, Octavian alone ruled the entire Roman world as Rome's first emperor.

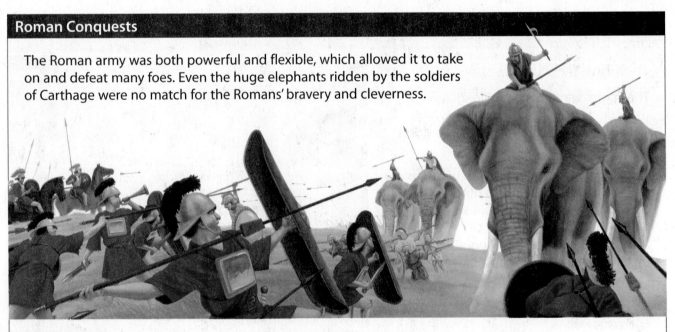

Roman Conquests

The Roman army was both powerful and flexible, which allowed it to take on and defeat many foes. Even the huge elephants ridden by the soldiers of Carthage were no match for the Romans' bravery and cleverness.

Analyze Visuals
What kind of equipment did the Roman army use?

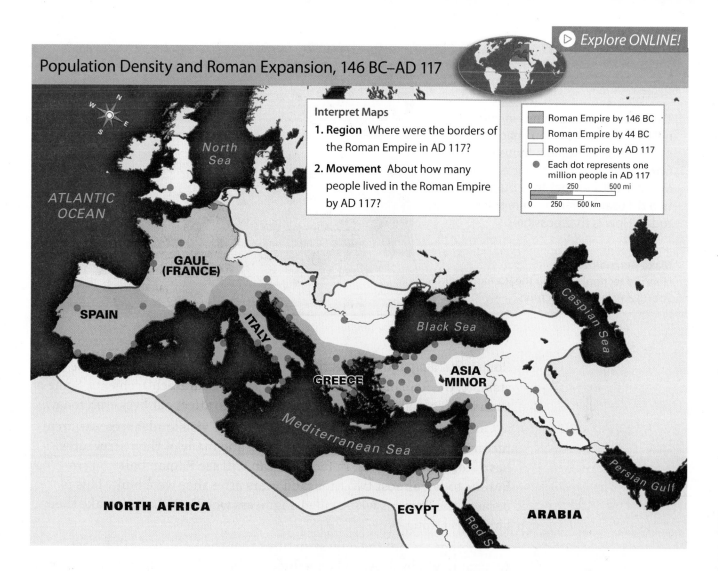

Population Density and Roman Expansion, 146 BC–AD 117

Explore ONLINE!

Interpret Maps

1. **Region** Where were the borders of the Roman Empire in AD 117?

2. **Movement** About how many people lived in the Roman Empire by AD 117?

Roman Empire by 146 BC
Roman Empire by 44 BC
Roman Empire by AD 117
Each dot represents one million people in AD 117

0   250   500 mi
0   250   500 km

ATLANTIC OCEAN

North Sea

GAUL (FRANCE)

SPAIN

ITALY

GREECE

Black Sea

ASIA MINOR

Caspian Sea

Mediterranean Sea

Persian Gulf

NORTH AFRICA

EGYPT

Red Sea

ARABIA

Academic Vocabulary
facilitate (fuh-SI-luh-tayt) to make easier

As emperor, Octavian was given a new name, Augustus, which means "honored one." The people of Rome respected and admired Augustus. This respect was mainly the result of his many accomplishments. As the map shows, Augustus added a great deal of territory to the empire. He also made many improvements to lands already in the empire. For example, he built monuments and public buildings in the city of Rome. He also improved and expanded Rome's network of roads, which **facilitated** travel, trade, and the spread of Roman culture and ideas to its new territories.

The Pax Romana The emperors who ruled after Augustus tried to follow his example. Some of them worked to add even more land to the empire. Others focused their attentions on improving Roman society.

Because of these emperors' efforts, Rome experienced a long period of peace and achievement. There were no major wars or rebellions within the empire, and trade increased. This period, which lasted for about 200 years, was called the Pax Romana, or the Roman Peace.

The Romans knew many techniques for building strong, long-lasting structures. Look at the Colosseum, pictured below. Notice how many arches were used in its design. Arches are one of the strongest shapes you can use in construction, a fact the Romans knew well. They also invented materials like cement to make their buildings stronger.

Built to Last

Think about the buildings in your neighborhood. Can you imagine any of them still standing a thousand years from now? The ancient Romans could. Many structures that they built nearly two thousand years ago are still standing today. How is that possible?

Make Generalizations
How did technology help the Romans build strong and lasting structures?

Roman Building and Engineering Because the Pax Romana was a time of stability, the Romans were able to make great cultural achievements. Some of the advances made during this time continue to affect our lives even today.

One of the areas in which the Romans made visible advances was architecture. The Romans were great builders, and many of their structures have stood for centuries. In fact, you can still see Roman buildings in Europe today, almost two thousand years after they were built. This is because the Romans were skilled engineers who knew how to make their buildings strong.

Buildings are not the only structures that the Romans built to last. Ancient roads, bridges, and **aqueducts**—channels used to carry water over long distances—are still seen all over Europe. Planned by skilled Roman engineers, many of these structures are still in use.

Roman Language and Law Not all Roman achievements are as easy to see as buildings, however. For example, the Romans greatly influenced how we speak, write, and think even today. Many of the languages spoken in Europe today, such as Spanish, French, and Italian, are based on Latin, the Romans' language. English, too, has adopted many words from Latin.

The Romans used the Latin language to create great works of literature. Among these works were some of the world's most famous plays, poems, and stories. Many of them are read and enjoyed by millions of people around the world today.

Even more important to the world than their literary achievements, however, were the Romans' political contributions. All around the world, people use legal systems based on ancient Roman law. In some countries, the entire government is based largely on the ancient Roman system.

One such country is the United States. The founders of our country admired the Roman government and used it as a model for our government. Like ancient Rome, the United States is a republic. We elect our

Reading Check
Identify Which Roman achievements continue to shape our world today?

leaders and trust them to make our laws. Also like the Romans, we require all people to obey a set of basic written laws. In ancient Rome, these laws were carved on stone tablets and kept on display. In the United States, they are written down in a document, the Constitution.

The Spread of Christianity

In addition to art and law, the ancient Romans also had a tremendous influence on religion. One of the world's major religions, Christianity, first appeared and spread in the Roman world.

The Beginnings of Christianity Christianity is based on the life, actions, and teachings of Jesus of Nazareth. He and his early followers lived in the Roman territory of Judea in southwest Asia. They converted many people in Jerusalem and other cities in Judea to Christianity.

However, Christianity quickly spread far beyond the borders of Judea. Jesus's followers traveled widely, preaching and spreading his teachings. Through their efforts, communities of Christians began to appear in cities throughout the Roman world. Christian ideas spread quickly through these cities, as more and more people converted to Christianity.

Persecution and Acceptance The rapid spread of Christianity worried some Roman leaders. They feared that Christianity would soon grow larger than all other religions in the empire. If that ever happened, they feared the Christians might rebel and take over Rome.

To prevent a rebellion, some emperors began to persecute, or punish, Christians. They arrested, fined, or even killed any Christians they found.

The persecution did not cause people to abandon Christianity, however. Instead, Christians began to meet in secret, hiding their religion from the government.

Eventually, the persecution was ended. In the 300s a powerful emperor named Constantine became a Christian himself. Once the emperor had converted, the Christian faith was openly accepted even more widely in the empire. Look at the map to see how Christianity spread between 300 and 400.

Official Religion Even after Constantine became a Christian, many people in the Roman Empire did not convert. Romans continued to practice many different religions.

Over time, however, Rome's leaders supported Christianity more and more. By the 380s support for Christianity had grown so much that an emperor chose to ban all other religions. With that ban, Christianity was the only religion allowed in the Roman Empire.

By the end of the 300s the Christian Church had grown into one of the most influential forces in the Roman world. As the church was growing, however, many other parts of Roman society were falling apart. The Roman Empire was ending.

Reading Check
Sequence How did the Christian church gain influence in Rome?

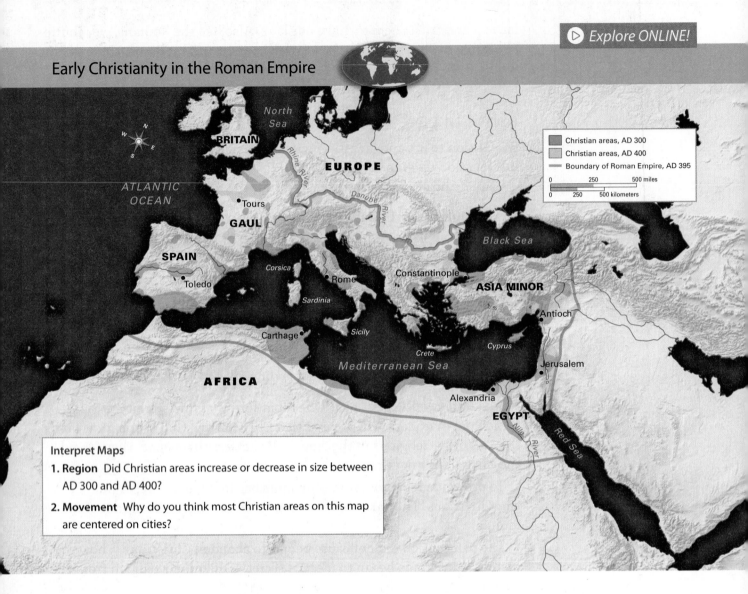

Explore ONLINE!

Interpret Maps

1. **Region** Did Christian areas increase or decrease in size between AD 300 and AD 400?

2. **Movement** Why do you think most Christian areas on this map are centered on cities?

The Decline of Rome

Rome's problems had actually started long before 300. For about a century, crime rates had been rising and poverty had been increasing. In addition, the Roman systems of education and government had begun breaking down, and many people no longer felt loyal to Rome. What could have happened to cause these problems?

Problems in the Government Many of Rome's problems were the result of poor government and overexpansion. After about 200, Rome was ruled by a series of bad emperors. Most of these emperors were more interested in their own happiness than in ruling well. Some simply ignored the needs of the Roman people. Others raised taxes to pay for new buildings or wars, driving many Romans into poverty.

Frustrated by these bad emperors, some military leaders tried to take over and rule Rome in their place. In most cases, though, these military leaders were no better than the emperors they replaced. Most of them were poor leaders, and fighting between rival military leaders almost led to civil war on many occasions. In addition, the Roman Empire became too large to control. Communication between the various Roman territories became difficult, even with Rome's road systems. Leaders could not quickly coordinate attacks against rebellions or get resources to Rome's frontiers.

Rome did have a few good emperors who worked to save the empire. One emperor saw that the empire had grown too large for one person to rule. To correct this problem, he divided the empire in half and named a co-ruler to help govern. Later, the emperor Constantine built a new capital, Constantinople, in what is now Turkey, nearer to the center of the Roman Empire. He thought that ruling from a central location would help keep the empire together. These measures helped restore order for a time, but they were not enough to save the Roman Empire.

Invasions Although internal problems weakened the empire, they alone probably would not have destroyed it. However, as the empire was getting weaker from within, invaders from outside also began to attack in the late 300s and the 400s. Already suffering from their own problems, the Romans could not fight off these invasions.

Most Romans considered the various groups who invaded their empire barbarians and uncivilized. In truth, however, some of these so-called barbarian groups had their own complex societies and strong, capable leaders. As a result, they were able to defeat Roman armies and take lands away from the empire. In the end, the barbarians were able to attack and destroy the city of Rome itself. In 476 the last emperor of Rome was overthrown and replaced by the leader of an invading group.

Even with a large and organized military, the Roman Empire began to have trouble defending itself from the multiple threats to the empire.

The Decline of Rome

Beginning around 200 the once-mighty Roman Empire began to weaken. Factors from inside and outside the empire caused many problems for Rome's leaders and led to the empire's collapse in the late 400s.

Reasons for the Decline of Rome

- Poor leaders cared less for the people of Rome than they did for their own happiness.
- Taxes and prices rose, increasing poverty.
- People became less loyal to Rome.
- Military leaders fought each other for power.
- The empire was too large for a single person to govern well.
- Barbarians invaded the empire from outside.

Analyze Visuals
Which factors in Rome's decline were internal? Which came from outside the empire?

Barbarian invaders

Reading Check
Form Generalizations
Why did the Roman Empire decline?

Most historians consider the capture of the Roman emperor in 476 the end of the Roman Empire in western Europe. Although people continued to think of themselves as Romans, there was no empire to tie them together. As a result, European society slowly broke apart.

Summary and Preview In this lesson you learned that the Romans brought a vast territory under one government. Next, you will learn what happened after that government collapsed in western Europe and how the Roman Empire continued in Constantinople.

Lesson 3 Assessment

Review Ideas, Terms, and Places

1. a. **Describe** What was the government of the Roman Republic like?
   b. **Contrast** How was Rome's government in the republic unlike the government under kings?

2. a. **Identify** Who was Augustus?
   b. **Explain** How did the Pax Romana help the Romans make great achievements?

3. **Form Generalizations** How did Rome's emperors affect the spread of Christianity?

4. a. **Identify** What threats to the Roman Empire appeared in the 200s, 300s, and 400s?
   b. **Contrast** Do you think internal problems or invasions were more responsible for Rome's fall? Why?

Critical Thinking

5. **Identify Causes** Draw a side-by-side graph. On the left side, list the main causes of Rome's growth. On the right side, list the main causes of its decline.

Growth	Decline

The Byzantine Empire

The Big Idea

The eastern Roman Empire prospered long after the western empire fell.

Main Ideas

- Eastern emperors ruled from Constantinople and tried but failed to reunite the whole Roman Empire.

- The people of the eastern empire created a new society that was very different from society in the west.

- Byzantine Christianity was different from religion in the west.

Key Terms and Places

Constantinople
Byzantine Empire
mosaics

If YOU lived there . . .

You are a trader visiting Constantinople. You have traveled to many cities but have never seen anything so magnificent. The city has huge palaces and stadiums for horse races. In the city center, you enter a church and stop, speechless with amazement. Above you is a vast, gold dome lit by hundreds of candles.

How does the city make you feel about its rulers?

Emperors Rule from Constantinople

In the late 200s the emperor Diocletian divided the Roman Empire into two parts—east and west—hoping to make the empire easier to rule. In spite of his efforts, years of invasions and economic instability eventually led to the fall of the western Roman Empire in 476.

▷ *Explore ONLINE!*

The Byzantine Empire, 1025

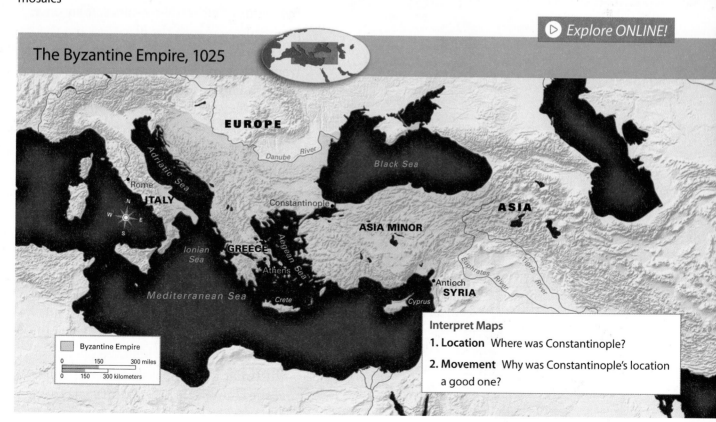

Interpret Maps

1. **Location** Where was Constantinople?

2. **Movement** Why was Constantinople's location a good one?

Constantinople was strategically located where Europe and Asia meet. As a result, the city was in a perfect location to control trade routes between the two continents.

Even before the fall of Rome, power had begun to shift to the richer, more stable east. The Roman Empire continued in the east, and the people of the eastern Roman Empire considered themselves Romans. The culture, however, was also very different from that of Rome itself.

The center of the eastern Roman Empire was the city of **Constantinople.** Constantinople was built on the site of an ancient Greek trading city called Byzantium (buh-ZAN-tee-uhm). It lay on a peninsula near both the Black Sea and the Mediterranean Sea, which protected the city from attack and let the city control trade between Europe and Asia. This protection allowed Constantinople to continue Rome's legacy, and the city became a magnificent city filled with great buildings, palaces, and churches.

Justinian and Theodora

Justinian After Rome fell, the emperors of the eastern Roman Empire dreamed of taking it back and reuniting the old Roman Empire. For Justinian (juh-STIN-ee-uhn), an emperor who ruled from 527 to 565, reuniting the empire was a passion. He sent his army to retake Italy. In the end, this army conquered not only Italy but also much land around the Mediterranean.

Justinian's other passions were the law and the church. He ordered officials to remove any out-of-date or unchristian laws. He then organized the laws into a legal system called Justinian's Code. By preserving and then simplifying Roman law, the code helped guarantee fairer treatment for all.

Despite his achievements, Justinian made many enemies. Two groups of these enemies joined together and tried to overthrow him in 532. These groups led riots in the streets. Scared for his life, Justinian prepared to leave Constantinople.

Justinian was stopped from leaving by his wife, Theodora (thee-uh-DOHR-uh). She convinced Justinian to stay in the city. Smart and powerful, Theodora helped her husband rule effectively. With her advice, he found a way to end the riots. Justinian's soldiers killed all the rioters—some 30,000 people—and saved the emperor's throne.

The Empire after Justinian After the death of Justinian in 565, the eastern empire began to decline. Faced with invasions by barbarians, Persians, and Muslims, later emperors lost all the land Justinian had gained. The eastern empire remained a major power in the world for hundreds of years, but it never regained its former strength.

The eastern Roman Empire finally ended nearly 900 years after the death of Justinian. In 1453 a group called the Ottoman Turks swept in and captured Constantinople. With this defeat, the thousand-year history of the eastern Roman Empire came to an end.

Reading Check

Compare What common event led to the fall of Rome and the decline of Constantinople?

The Glory of Constantinople

Constantinople was a crossroads for traders, a center of Christianity, and the capital of an empire. It was a magnificent city filled with great buildings, palaces, and churches. The city's rulers led processions, or ceremonial walks, to show their wealth and power. This procession went from the church to the royal palace. It showed the power and importance of the emperor as head of the church.

Analyze Visuals
Where did the procession begin and end? What was the significance of this beginning and ending?

A New Society

In many ways, Justinian was the last Roman emperor of the eastern empire. After he died, non-Roman influences took hold throughout the empire. People began to speak Greek, the language of the eastern empire, rather than Latin. Scholars studied Greek, not Roman, philosophy. Gradually, the empire lost its ties to the old Roman Empire, and a new society developed.

The people who lived in this society never stopped thinking of themselves as Romans. In addition to living under a Roman legal system, they preserved other elements of the Roman Empire. For example, their army descended from the Roman army. But modern historians have given their society a new name. They call the society that developed in the eastern Roman Empire after the west fell the **Byzantine** (BI-zuhn-teen) **Empire,** named for Byzantium.

Outside Influence One reason eastern and western Roman societies were different was the Byzantines' interaction with other groups. This interaction was largely a result of trade. Because Constantinople's location was ideal for trading between Europe and Asia, it became the greatest trading city in Europe.

Merchants from all around Europe, Asia, and Africa traveled to Constantinople to trade. Over time, Byzantine society began to reflect these outside influences as well as its Roman and Greek roots.

Government The forms of government in the two empires were also different. Byzantine emperors had more power than western emperors did. Eastern emperors also liked to show off their great power. For example, people could not stand while they were in the presence of the eastern emperor. They had to crawl on their hands and knees to talk to him.

The power of an eastern emperor was greater, in part, because the emperor was considered the head of the church as well as the political ruler. The Byzantines thought the emperor had been chosen by God to lead both the empire and the church. In contrast, the emperor in the west was limited to political power. Popes and other bishops were the leaders of the church.

Reading Check
Contrast What were two ways in which eastern and western Roman societies were different?

Byzantine Christianity

Christianity was central to the Byzantines' lives, just as it was to the lives of people in the west. Nearly everyone who lived in the Byzantine Empire was Christian.

To show their devotion to God and the Christian Church, Byzantine artists created beautiful works of religious art. Among the grandest works were **mosaics,** pictures made with pieces of colored stone or glass. Some mosaics sparkled with gold, silver, and jewels.

Even more magnificent than their mosaics were Byzantine churches, especially Hagia Sophia (HAH-juh soh-FEE-uh). Built by Justinian in the 530s, its huge domes rose high above Constantinople. According to legend, when Justinian saw the church, he exclaimed in delight:

Byzantine mosaics were often placed on walls, not floors, as was customary. They also inserted glass and metal to help reflect light and create a "heavenly" appearance around certain figures.

> **"Glory to God, who has judged me worthy of accomplishing this work! Solomon! I have outdone thee!"**
>
> —Justinian, quoted in *Sancta Sophia and Troitza*

As time passed, people in the east and west began to interpret and practice Christianity differently. For example, eastern priests could get married, while priests in the west could not. Religious services were performed in Greek in the east. In the west, they were held in Latin.

For hundreds of years, church leaders from the east and west worked together peacefully despite their differences. However, the differences between their ideas continued to grow. In time, the differences led to divisions within the Christian Church. In the 1000s the split between east and west became official. Eastern Christians formed what became known as the Orthodox Church and developed Orthodox Christianity. As a result, eastern and western Europe were divided by religion.

Summary and Preview In this lesson you learned that the Orthodox Church became a major force in the Byzantine Empire. In the next lesson, you will learn about the changes western Europe went through after the Roman Empire fell.

Reading Check
Summarize
What led to a split in the Christian Church?

Lesson 4 Assessment

Review Ideas, Terms, and Places

1. a. Explain How did Constantinople's location help the Roman Empire continue in the east?

b. Summarize What were two of Justinian's major accomplishments?

c. Elaborate What do you think Theodora's role in the government says about women in the eastern empire?

2. a. Identify What was one major difference between the powers of emperors in the east and the west?

b. Explain How did contact with other cultures help change the Byzantine Empire?

3. a. Define What is a mosaic?

b. Form Generalizations What led to the creation of two different Christian societies in Europe?

Critical Thinking

4. Compare and Contrast Draw a Venn diagram by creating two large overlapping circles. Using your notes and the diagram, compare and contrast Christianity in the western Roman Empire with Christianity in the Byzantine Empire.

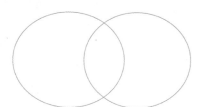

The Middle Ages

The Big Idea
Christianity and social systems influenced life in Europe in the Middle Ages.

Main Ideas
- The Christian Church influenced nearly every aspect of society in the Middle Ages.
- Complicated political and economic systems governed life in the Middle Ages.
- The period after 1000 was a time of great changes in medieval society.

Key Terms and Places
Middle Ages
pope
Crusade
Holy Land
Gothic architecture
feudal system
manor
nation-state

If YOU lived there . . .

You are the youngest child of a noble family in medieval France. One day your father tells you that you are being sent to the court of another noble family. There you will learn fine manners and proper behavior. You will also learn music and drawing. You know it is a great honor, but you will miss your own home.

How do you feel about this change in your life?

The Christian Church and Society

When historians talk about the past, they often divide it into three long periods. The first period is the ancient world, the time of the world's earliest civilizations, such as Egypt, China, Greece, and Rome. The last period historians call the modern world, the world since about 1500. Since that time, new ideas and contacts between civilizations changed the world completely.

What happened between ancient and modern times? We call this period, which lasted from about 500 until about 1500, the **Middle Ages.** We also call it the medieval (mee-DEE-vuhl) period. The word *medieval* comes from two Latin words that mean "middle age." It was a time of great changes in Europe, many of them inspired by the Christian Church.

The Importance of the Church When the Roman Empire fell apart in the late 400s, the people of Europe were left without a single dominant government to unite them. In the absence of strong leaders, Europe broke into many small kingdoms. Each of these kingdoms had its own laws, customs, and language. Europe was no longer the same place it had been under the Romans.

One factor, however, continued to tie the people of Europe together—religion. Nearly everyone in Europe was Christian, and so most Europeans felt tied together by their beliefs. Over time, the number of Christians in Europe increased. People came to feel more and more like part of a single religious community.

Because Christianity was so important in Europe, the Christian Church gained a great deal of influence. In time, the church began to influence the politics, art, and daily lives of people all over the continent. In fact, almost no part of life in Europe in the Middle Ages was unaffected by the church and its teachings.

The Crusades As the Christian Church gained influence in Europe, some church leaders became powerful. They gained political power in addition to their religious authority.

The most powerful religious leader was the **pope,** the head of the Roman Catholic Church. The pope's decisions could have huge effects on people's lives. For example, one pope helped start a religious war, or **Crusade,** against the Muslims in Southwest Asia.

For many years, Palestine had been in the hands of Muslims. In general, the Muslims did not bother Christians who visited the region. In the late 1000s, though, a group of Turkish Muslims entered the area and captured the city of Jerusalem. Pilgrims returning to Europe said that these Turks had attacked them in the **Holy Land,** the region where Jesus lived, preached, and died, which was no longer safe for Christians.

Before long, the Turks began to raid the Byzantine Empire. The Byzantine emperor, fearing an attack on Constantinople, asked Pope Urban II of the Roman Catholic Church for help. The pope agreed to the request. He called on Christians from all over Europe to retake the Holy Land from the Muslim Turks.

About five thousand Crusaders left Europe for the Holy Land in 1096 and arrived in 1099. As the map shows, they traveled thousands of miles to fight. After about a month of fighting, the Crusaders took Jerusalem. After the Europeans took Jerusalem, they set up four small kingdoms in the Holy Land.

The kingdoms the Christians created in the Holy Land didn't last, though. Within 50 years the Muslims had started taking land back from the Christians. In response, the Europeans launched more Crusades, but none were successful. By 1291 the Muslim armies had taken back all of the Holy Land and the Crusades had ended.

Crusades Change Europe Although the Crusades failed, they changed Europe forever. More trade routes between Europe and Asia were established. Europeans who went to the Holy Land learned about products such as apricots, rice, and cotton cloth. Crusaders also brought ideas of Muslim thinkers back with them. In both these ways, Islamic achievements in math, science, and other subjects were introduced to Europe.

The greatest changes occurred with Christian and Muslim relationships. Each group learned about the other's religion and culture. Sometimes this led to mutual respect. In general, though, the Crusaders saw Muslims as unbelievers who threatened innocent Christians. Most Muslims viewed the Crusaders as vicious invaders. Some historians think the distrust that began during the Crusades still affects Christian and Muslim relationships today.

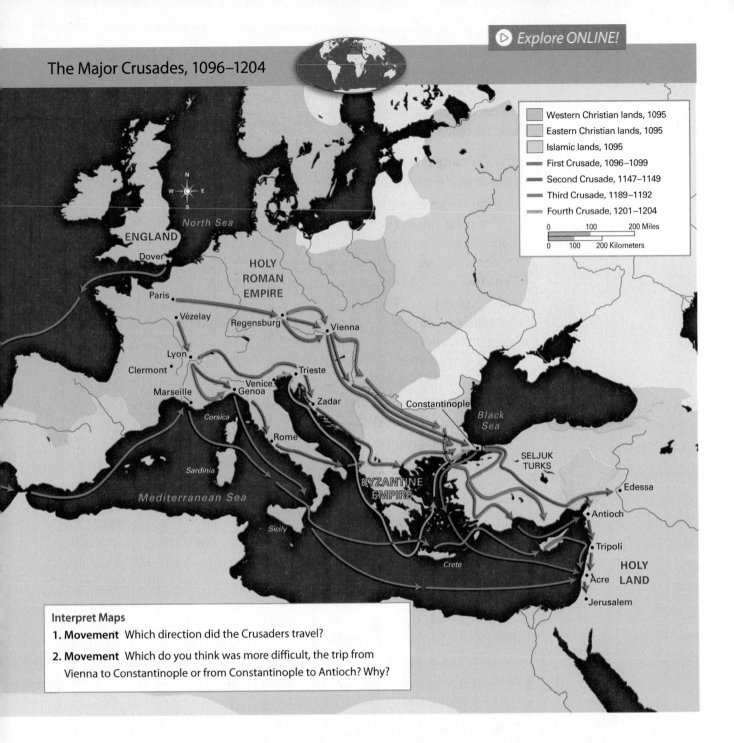

The Major Crusades, 1096–1204

ENGLAND
Dover
North Sea
HOLY
ROMAN
EMPIRE
Paris
Vézelay
Regensburg
Vienna
Lyon
Clermont
Trieste
Marseille
Venice
Genoa
Zadar
Constantinople
Black
Sea
Corsica
Rome
Sardinia
SELJUK
TURKS
Mediterranean Sea
Edessa
BYZANTINE
EMPIRE
Antioch
Sicily
Tripoli
Crete
HOLY
Acre
LAND
Jerusalem

Western Christian lands, 1095
Eastern Christian lands, 1095
Islamic lands, 1095
First Crusade, 1096–1099
Second Crusade, 1147–1149
Third Crusade, 1189–1192
Fourth Crusade, 1201–1204

0   100   200 Miles
0   100   200 Kilometers

Interpret Maps

1. **Movement** Which direction did the Crusaders travel?

2. **Movement** Which do you think was more difficult, the trip from Vienna to Constantinople or from Constantinople to Antioch? Why?

The Church and Art Politics was not the only area in which the church had great influence. Most art of the Middle Ages was also influenced by the church. Medieval painters and sculptors, for example, used religious subjects in their works. Most music and literature from the period is centered on religious themes.

The greatest examples of religious art from the Middle Ages are church buildings. Huge churches were built all over Europe. Many of them are examples of **Gothic architecture,** a style known for its high pointed ceilings, tall towers, and stained glass windows. People built Gothic churches as symbols of their faith. They believed that building these amazing structures would show their love for God. The insides of such churches are as elaborate and ornate as the outsides.

Gothic Architecture

Many of Europe's churches were incredible works of art. The grandest of these churches were cathedrals, large churches in which bishops led religious services. Beginning in the 1100s, Europeans built their cathedrals using a dramatic new style called Gothic architecture.

Gothic churches were designed to tower over medieval cities as symbols of the church's greatness. As a result, they were towering works of majesty and glory. This cathedral, Westminster Abbey, stands in London, England.

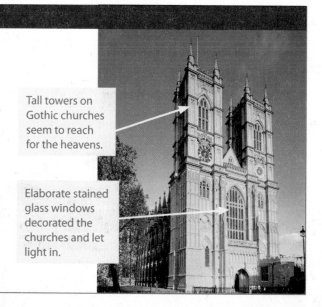

Tall towers on Gothic churches seem to reach for the heavens.

Elaborate stained glass windows decorated the churches and let light in.

Reading Check
Summarize
How did the Christian Church shape life in the Middle Ages?

The Church and Daily Life Most people in Europe never saw a Gothic church, especially not the inside. Instead, they worshiped at small local churches. In fact, people's lives often centered around their local church. Markets, festivals, and religious ceremonies all took place there. Local priests advised people on how to live and act. In addition, because most people could not read or write, they depended on the church to keep records for them.

Life in the Middle Ages

Christianity was a major influence on people's lives in the Middle Ages, but it was not the only one. Much of European society was controlled by two systems of relationships. They were the feudal (FYOO-duhl) system and the manor system.

The Feudal System When Rome fell, western Europe lost its central political authority. Medieval Europe was divided into many small kingdoms. In most kingdoms, the king owned all the land. Sometimes,

Feudal Relationships

Europe's feudal system was based on relationships between knights and nobles. Each had certain duties that he had to perform.

Noble's Duties

- Provide knight with land
- Treat knights fairly and honestly

Knight's Duties

- Provide military service
- Supply food and shelter for noble during visits

Analyze Visuals
Who had to provide military service as one of his duties?

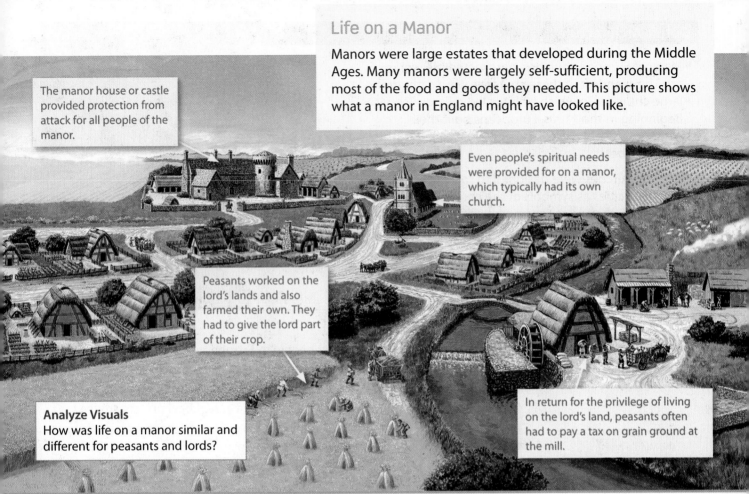

Life on a Manor

Manors were large estates that developed during the Middle Ages. Many manors were largely self-sufficient, producing most of the food and goods they needed. This picture shows what a manor in England might have looked like.

The manor house or castle provided protection from attack for all people of the manor.

Even people's spiritual needs were provided for on a manor, which typically had its own church.

Peasants worked on the lord's lands and also farmed their own. They had to give the lord part of their crop.

Analyze Visuals
How was life on a manor similar and different for peasants and lords?

In return for the privilege of living on the lord's land, peasants often had to pay a tax on grain ground at the mill.

kings gave parts of their land to nobles—people born into wealthy, powerful families. In turn, these nobles gave land to knights, or trained warriors, who promised to help them defend both their lands and the king. This system of exchanging land for military service is called the **feudal system,** or feudalism (FYOO-duh-li-zuhm).

Everyone involved in the feudal system had certain duties to perform. The kings and nobles provided land and promised to protect the people who served them and to treat everyone fairly. In return, the knights who received land promised to serve the nobles dutifully, especially in times of war. The set of relationships between knights and nobles was the heart of Europe's feudal system.

The feudal system was very complex. Its rules varied from kingdom to kingdom and changed constantly. Feudal duties in France, for example, were not the same as those in Germany or England. Also, it was possible for one knight to owe service to more than one noble. If the two nobles he served went to war, the poor knight would be torn between them. In such situations, feudal relationships could be confusing or even dangerous.

The Manor System The feudal system was only one set of guidelines that governed life in the Middle Ages. Another system, the manor system, controlled most economic activities in Europe during this period.

Merchants traveled from all over to sell their goods at trade fairs. Here, they bought and sold goods from other merchants to sell in their local markets.

At the center of the manor system was the **manor,** a large estate owned by a noble or knight. Every manor was different, but most included a large house or castle, fields, pastures, and forests. A manor also had a village where workers lived. They traveled back and forth to the fields each day.

The owner of a manor did not farm his own land. Instead, he had workers to farm it for him. Most of the crops grown on the manor went to the owner. In exchange for their work, the workers got a place to live and a small piece of land on which they could grow their own food.

The workers on most manors included either free peasants or serfs. Peasants were free farmers. Serfs, on the other hand, were not free. Although they were not slaves, they were not allowed to leave the land on which they worked.

Towns and Trade Not everyone in the Middle Ages lived on manors. Some people chose to live in towns and cities like Paris or London. Compared to our cities today, most of these medieval cities were small, dirty, and dark.

Many of the people who lived in cities were traders. They bought and sold goods from all over Europe and other parts of the world. Most of their goods were sold at trade fairs. Every year, merchants from many places in Europe would meet at these large fairs to sell their wares.

Before the year 1000, trade was not very common in Europe. After that year, however, trade increased. As it did, more people began to move to cities. Once small, these cities began to grow. As cities grew, trade increased even more, and the people who lived in them became wealthier. By the end of the Middle Ages, cities had become the centers of European culture and wealth.

Reading Check
Find Main Ideas
What were two systems that governed life in Europe during the Middle Ages? How did they differ?

Magna Carta

Magna Carta was one of the first documents to protect the rights of the people. Magna Carta was so influential that the British still consider it part of their constitution. Some of its ideas are also in the U.S. Constitution. Included in Magna Carta were 63 demands that English nobles made King John agree to follow. A few of these demands are listed here. Demand number 31, for example, defended people's right to property, while number 38 guaranteed that free men had the right to a fair trial.

Demand 31 defended people's right to own any property, not just wood.

Magna Carta guaranteed that everyone had the right to a fair trial.

"We have also granted to all freeman of our kingdom, for us and our heirs forever, all the underwritten liberties. . . .

(9) Neither we nor our bailiffs shall seize any land or rent for any debt, so long as the chattels [belongings] of the debtor are sufficient to repay the debt. . . .

(31) Neither we nor our bailiffs shall take, for our castles or for any other work of ours, wood which is not ours, against the will of the owner of that wood.

(38) No bailiff for the future shall, upon his own unsupported complaint, put any one to his 'law,' [on trial] without credible [believable] witnesses brought for this purpose."

—from *Magna Carta*

Analyze Sources
In what ways do you think the demands listed on the right influenced modern democracy?

Changes in Medieval Society

Life in the Middle Ages changed greatly after the year 1000. You have already seen how cities grew and trade increased. Even as these changes were taking place, bigger changes were sweeping through Europe.

Political Changes in England One of the countries most affected by change in the Middle Ages was England. In the year 1066 a noble from northern France, William the Conqueror, sailed to England and overthrew the old king. He declared himself the new king of England.

William built a strong government in England, something the English had not had before. Later kings of England built on William's example. For more than a century, these kings increased their power. By the late 1100s England's king was one of the most powerful men in Europe.

When William's descendant John took the throne, however, he angered many nobles by raising taxes. John believed that the king had the right to do whatever he wanted. England's nobles disagreed.

In 1215 a group of nobles forced King John to sign Magna Carta, one of the most important documents in English history. Magna Carta stated that the law, not the king, was the supreme power in England. The king had to obey the law. He could not raise taxes without the nobles' permission.

Many people consider Magna Carta to be one of the first steps toward democracy in modern Europe and one of history's most important documents. By stating that the king was not above the law, Magna Carta set limits on his power. In addition, it gave a council of nobles the power to advise the king. In time, that council developed into Parliament (PAHR-luh-muhnt), the elected body that governs England today.

The Black Death Not all of the changes that struck medieval Europe had such positive results. In 1347 a disease called the Black Death swept through Europe. Up to a third of Europe's people died from the disease. Even such a disaster, however, had some positive effects. With the decrease in population came a labor shortage. As a result, people could demand higher wages for their work.

The Black Death

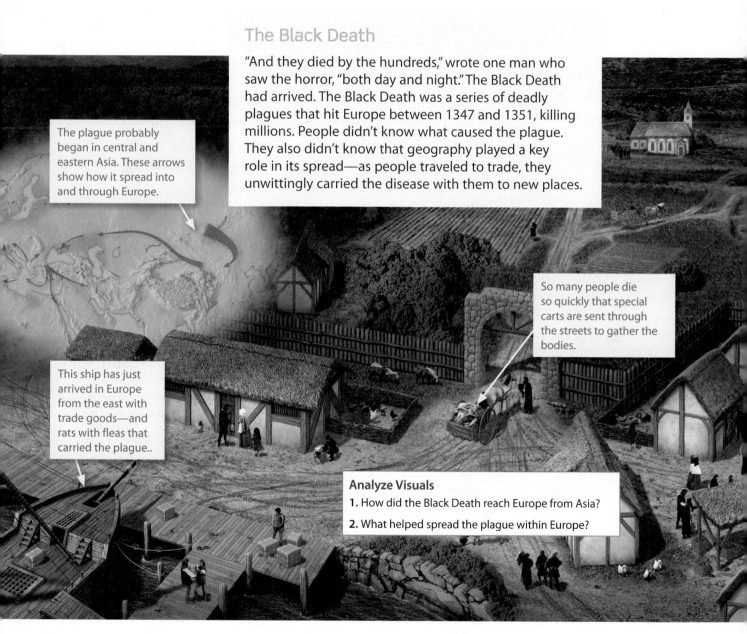

"And they died by the hundreds," wrote one man who saw the horror, "both day and night." The Black Death had arrived. The Black Death was a series of deadly plagues that hit Europe between 1347 and 1351, killing millions. People didn't know what caused the plague. They also didn't know that geography played a key role in its spread—as people traveled to trade, they unwittingly carried the disease with them to new places.

The plague probably began in central and eastern Asia. These arrows show how it spread into and through Europe.

So many people die so quickly that special carts are sent through the streets to gather the bodies.

This ship has just arrived in Europe from the east with trade goods—and rats with fleas that carried the plague..

Analyze Visuals

1. How did the Black Death reach Europe from Asia?

2. What helped spread the plague within Europe?

Joan of Arc c. 1412–1431

One of the most famous war leaders in all of European history was a teenage girl. Joan of Arc, a leader of French troops during the Hundred Years' War, was only 16 when she first led troops into battle. She won many battles against the English but was captured in battle in 1430, tried, and executed. Nevertheless, her courage inspired the French, who went on to win the war. Today, Joan is considered a national hero in France.

Make Inferences
Why do you think Joan is considered a hero in France?

The Fight for Power Even as the Black Death was sweeping across Europe, kings fought for power. In 1337 the Hundred Years' War broke out between England and France. As its name suggests, the war lasted more than a hundred years. In the end, the French won.

Inspired by the victory, France's kings worked to increase their power. They took land away from nobles to rule themselves. France became a **nation-state,** a country united under a single strong government.

Around Europe, other rulers followed France's example. As nation-states arose around Europe, feudalism disappeared, and the Middle Ages came to an end.

Summary and Preview In this lesson you read about early Europe, a time that still influences how we live today. From the earliest civilizations of Greece and Rome to the Middle Ages, the people of Europe helped shape Western society. Next, you will learn how new ideas influenced the arts, science, and attitudes toward religion in Europe.

Reading Check
Find Main Ideas
What changes occurred in Europe after 1000?

Lesson 5 Assessment

Review Ideas, Terms, and Places

1. **a. Recall** Why did the pope call for a Crusade?
   b. Form Generalizations How did the Christian Church affect art in the Middle Ages?
2. **a. Define** What was the feudal system?
   b. Explain How did the manor system work?
   c. Elaborate What made the feudal system so complex?
3. **a. Describe** How did the Black Death affect Europe?
   b. Explain How did England's government change after 1000?

Critical Thinking

4. **Analyze** Use your notes to complete a graphic organizer like the one shown. List ways the church shaped medieval politics, life, and art.

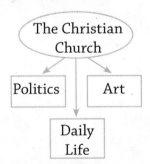

The Renaissance and Reformation

The Big Idea

The periods of the Renaissance and the Reformation introduced new ideas and new ways of thinking into Europe.

Main Ideas

- The Renaissance was a period of new learning, new ideas, and new advances in art, literature, and science.
- The Reformation changed the religious map of Europe.

Key Terms and Places

Renaissance
Florence
Venice
humanism
Reformation
Protestants
Catholic Reformation

If YOU lived there . . .

You live in Florence, Italy, in the 1400s. Your father, a merchant, has just hired a tutor from Asia Minor to teach you and your sisters and brothers. Your new teacher starts by stating, "Nothing good has been written in a thousand years." He insists that you learn to read Latin and Greek so that you can study Roman and Greek books that were written long ago.

What can you learn from these ancient books?

The Renaissance

Do you ever get the urge to do something creative? If so, how do you express your creativity? Do you like to draw or paint? Maybe you prefer to write stories or poems or create music.

At the end of the Middle Ages, people across Europe found the urge to be creative. Their creativity was sparked by new ideas and discoveries that were sweeping through Europe at the time. This period of creativity, of new ideas and inspirations, is called the **Renaissance** (REN-uh-sahns). It lasted from about 1350 through the 1500s. *Renaissance* is French for "rebirth." The people who named this period believed it represented a new beginning, or rebirth, in Europe's history and culture.

New Ideas The Renaissance started in Italy. During and after the Crusades, Italian cities such as **Florence** and **Venice** became rich through trade. Goods from faraway Asia moved through these cities.

These goods made the people who lived there curious about the larger world. At the same time, scholars from other parts of the world came to Italy. They brought books written by ancient Greeks and Romans.

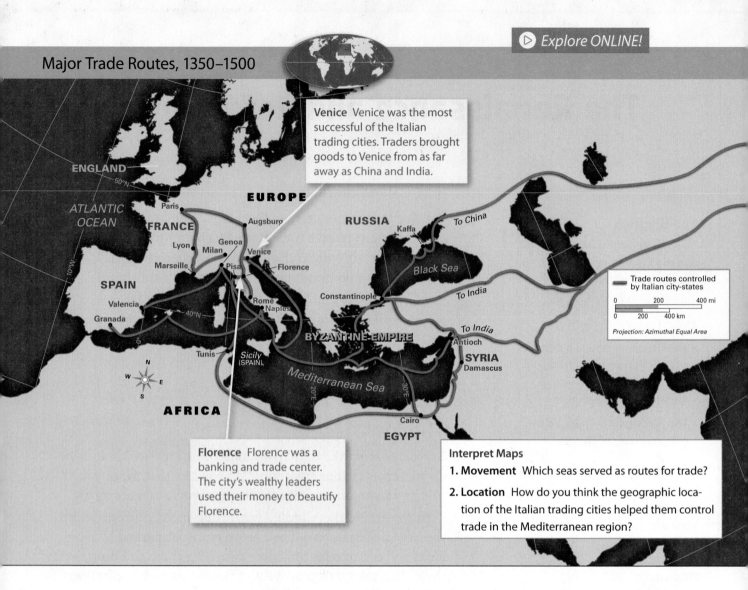

Major Trade Routes, 1350–1500

Explore ONLINE!

Venice Venice was the most successful of the Italian trading cities. Traders brought goods to Venice from as far away as China and India.

ENGLAND
50°N
ATLANTIC OCEAN
Paris
EUROPE
FRANCE
Augsburg
RUSSIA
Kaffa
To China
Lyon
Genoa
Milan
Venice
Marseille
Pisa
Florence
Black Sea
SPAIN
Valencia
40°N
Rome
Naples
Constantinople
To India
Granada
Tunis
Sicily (SPAIN)
BYZANTINE EMPIRE
To India
Antioch
SYRIA
Damascus
Mediterranean Sea
AFRICA
Cairo
EGYPT

Trade routes controlled by Italian city-states
0   200   400 mi
0   200   400 km
Projection: Azimuthal Equal Area

Florence Florence was a banking and trade center. The city's wealthy leaders used their money to beautify Florence.

Interpret Maps

1. **Movement** Which seas served as routes for trade?

2. **Location** How do you think the geographic location of the Italian trading cities helped them control trade in the Mediterranean region?

Inspired by these books and by the ancient ruins around them, some people in Italy became interested in ancient cultures. These people began reading works in Greek and Latin and studying subjects that had been taught in Greek and Roman schools. These subjects, known as the humanities, included history, poetry, and grammar. Increased study of the humanities led to a new way of thinking and learning known as humanism.

Humanism emphasized the abilities and accomplishments of human beings. The humanists believed that people were capable of great things. As a result, they admired artists, architects, leaders, writers, scientists, and other talented individuals.

Renaissance Art The Renaissance was a period of talented artistic achievements. Artists of the period created new techniques to improve their work. For example, they developed the technique of perspective, a method of showing a three-dimensional scene on a flat surface so that it looks real.

Many Renaissance artists were also humanists. Humanist artists valued the achievements of individuals. These artists wanted their paintings and sculptures to show people's unique personalities. One of the artists best able to show this sense of personality in his works was the Italian Michelangelo (mee-kay-LAHN-jay-loh). He was both a great painter and sculptor. His statues, like the one of King David below, seem almost to be alive.

Another famous Renaissance artist was Leonardo da Vinci. Leonardo achieved the Renaissance goal of excelling in many areas. He was not only a great painter and sculptor but also an architect, scientist, and engineer. He sketched plants and animals as well as inventions such as a submarine. He collected knowledge about the human body. Both Leonardo and Michelangelo are examples of what we call Renaissance people—people who can do practically anything well.

The Renaissance

The Renaissance was a period of great creativity and advances in art, literature, and science.

Leonardo da Vinci drew sketches of many devices that were not invented until centuries after his death. This model of a type of helicopter was based on a sketch by Leonardo.

Painters like Pieter Bruegel the Younger wanted to show what real life was like for people in Europe.

William Shakespeare is considered the greatest of all Renaissance writers. His plays are still read and performed today.

Renaissance sculptors were careful to show the tiniest details in their works. This statue by Michelangelo is of David, a king of ancient Israel.

Analyze Visuals
Based on the sculpture of David and on the Holbein painting, how would you describe Renaissance art?

Renaissance Literature Like artists, Renaissance writers expressed the attitudes of the time. The most famous Renaissance writer is probably the English dramatist William Shakespeare. He wrote excellent poetry, but Shakespeare is best known for his plays. They include more than 30 comedies, histories, and tragedies. In his plays, Shakespeare turned popular stories into great drama. His writing shows a deep understanding of human nature and skillfully expresses the thoughts and feelings of his characters. For these reasons, Shakespeare's plays are still highly popular in many parts of the world.

Renaissance writings were read and enjoyed by a larger audience than earlier writings had been. This change was largely due to advances in science and technology, such as the printing press.

Renaissance Science Some of the ancient works rediscovered during the Renaissance dealt with science. For the first time in centuries, Europeans could read about early Greek and Roman scientific advances. Inspired by what they read, some people began to study math, astronomy, and other fields of science.

Using this new scientific knowledge, Europeans developed new inventions and techniques. For example, they learned how to build enormous domes that could rise higher than earlier buildings.

Another invention of the Renaissance was the movable type printing press. A German named Johann Gutenberg built the first movable type printing press in the mid-1400s. This type of printing press could print books quickly and cheaply. For the first time, people could easily share ideas with others in distant areas. The printing press helped the ideas of the Renaissance spread beyond Italy.

Reading Check
Summarize How did life in Europe change during the Renaissance?

Link to Technology

The Printing Press

Printing was not a new idea in Renaissance Europe. What was new was the method of printing. Johann Gutenberg designed a printing system called movable type. It used a set of tiny lead blocks, each carved with a letter of the alphabet. These blocks could then be used to spell out an entire page of text for printing. Once copies of the page were made, the printer could reuse the blocks to spell out another page. This was much faster and easier than earlier systems had been.

Form Generalizations
How did movable type improve printing?

Religion in Europe, 1600

Regions By the Reformation's end, parts of Europe were still Catholic, while others had become mostly Protestant.

Legend:
- Protestant
- Roman Catholic
- Roman Catholic with Protestant minorities
- Eastern Orthodox
- Muslim
- Boundary of the Holy Roman Empire

0   250   500 Miles
0   250   500 Kilometers

ICELAND
SWEDEN
NORWAY
SCOTLAND
North Sea
IRELAND
DENMARK
Baltic Sea
ENGLAND
London
RUSSIA
ATLANTIC OCEAN
Wittenberg
POLAND
Paris
FRANCE
Geneva
HUNGARY
PORTUGAL
Madrid
SPAIN
PAPAL STATES
Rome
OTTOMAN EMPIRE
Mediterranean Sea
OTTOMAN EMPIRE

Interpret Maps

1. **Place** In which part of Europe were most people Protestant?

2. **Movement** How were religious areas spread across the Holy Roman Empire?

The Reformation

By the early 1500s some Europeans had begun to complain about problems they saw in the Roman Catholic Church. For example, they thought the church had become corrupt. In time, their complaints led to a religious reform movement called the **Reformation** (re-fuhr-MAY-shuhn).

The Protestant Reformation Although people called for church reform in other places, the Reformation began in what is now Germany. This area was part of the Holy Roman Empire. Some people there thought church officials were too focused on their own power and had lost sight of their religious duties. They thought the church should focus more on spiritual matters.

One of the first people to express protests against the Catholic Church was a German monk named Martin Luther. In 1517 Luther nailed a list of complaints to a church door in the town of Wittenberg. Luther's protests angered church officials, who soon expelled him from the church. In response, Luther's followers formed a separate church. They became the first **Protestants,** Christians who broke from the Catholic Church over religious issues.

Other reformers who followed Luther began creating churches of their own as well. The Roman Catholic Church was no longer the only church in Western Europe. As you can see on the map, many areas of Europe had become Protestant by 1600.

The Catholic Reformation Protestants were not the only ones who called for reform in the Roman Catholic Church. Many Catholic officials wanted to reform the church as well. Even as the first Protestants were breaking away from the church, Catholic officials were launching a series of reforms that became known as the **Catholic Reformation.**

As part of the Catholic Reformation, church leaders began focusing more on spiritual concerns and less on political power. They also worked to make church teachings easier for people to understand. To tell people about the changes, church leaders sent priests and teachers all over Europe. Church leaders also worked to spread Catholic teachings into Asia, Africa, and other parts of the world.

Religious Wars The Reformation caused major changes to the religious map of Europe. Catholicism, once the main religion in most of Europe, was no longer so dominant. In many areas, especially in the north, Protestants now outnumbered Catholics.

In some parts of Europe, Catholics and Protestants lived together in peace. In some other places, however, this was not the case. Bloody religious wars broke out in France, Germany, the Netherlands, and Switzerland. Wars between religious groups left parts of Europe in ruins.

These religious wars led to political and social changes in Europe. For example, many people began relying less on what church leaders and other authority figures told them. Instead, people raised questions and began looking to science for answers.

Summary In the 1300s through the 1500s, new ideas changed Europe. The making of paper, the printing press, and new universities helped spread the Renaissance beyond Italy into lands where its ideas changed. The Reformation caused great changes in Europe.

Reading Check
Find Main Ideas How did Europe change after the Reformation?

Lesson 6 Assessment

Review Ideas, Terms, and Places

1. a. Define What was the Renaissance?

b. Summarize What were some changes made in art during the Renaissance?

c. Elaborate How did the printing press help spread Renaissance ideas?

2. a. Describe What led to the Reformation?

b. Explain Why did church leaders launch the series of reforms known as the Catholic Reformation?

c. Compare How did Protestants and Catholic Reformation both influence changes in the Catholic Church?

Critical Thinking

3. Find Main Ideas Draw a two-column chart. Use your notes to describe new ideas of the Renaissance and the Reformation. Add rows as needed.

Idea	Description

Social Studies Skills

Interpret a Historical Map

Western Europe, 1000
Define the Skill

History and geography are closely related. You cannot truly understand the history of a place without knowing where it is and what it is like. For that reason, historical maps are important in the study of history. A historical map is a map that shows what a place was like at a particular time in the past.

Like other maps, historical maps use colors and symbols to represent information. One color, for example, might represent the lands controlled by a certain kingdom or the areas in which a particular religion or type of government was common. Symbols might identify key cities, battle sites, or other major locations.

Learn the Skill

Use the map on this page to answer the following questions.

1. Read the map's title. What area does this map show? What time period?

2. Check the map's legend. What does the color purple represent on this map?

3. According to the map, what territory lay between France and the Holy Roman Empire at this time?

4. What parts of Europe were Muslim in the year 1000?

Practice the Skill

Look back at the map called Early Christianity in the Roman Empire in Lesson 3 of this module. Study the map, and then write five questions that you might see about such a map on a test. Make sure that the questions you ask can be answered with just the information on the map.

Module 12 Assessment

Review Vocabulary, Terms, and Places

For each group of terms below, write the letter of the term that does not relate to the others. Then write a sentence that explains how the other two terms are related.

1. **a.** Paleolithic Era   **b.** agriculture   **c.** domestication
2. **a.** Athens   **b.** Sparta   **c.** Rome
3. **a.** feudal system   **b.** republic   **c.** citizens
4. **a.** Constantinople   **b.** Byzantine Empire   **c.** Protestants
5. **a.** Senate   **b.** Crusade   **c.** Holy Land
6. **a.** Renaissance   **b.** pope   **c.** humanism

Comprehension and Critical Thinking

Lesson 1

7. **a. Categorize** Identify each of the following as either prehistoric or historic: Stone Age tool; map with writing on it; stone tablet engraved with pictures and symbols.

   b. Evaluate About 15,000 years ago, where do you think life would have been more difficult—in eastern Africa or northern Europe? Why?

   c. Analyze Effects Explain the impact that agriculture had on the movement and settlement of early civilizations.

Lesson 2

8. **a. Identify** What was the basic political unit in ancient Greece? What is one example?

   b. Contrast How was life in Greece different under Alexander than it had been during the golden age?

   c. Evaluate What do you think was the greatest achievement of the ancient Greeks? Why?

Lesson 3

9. **a. Define** What was the Pax Romana? What happened during that time?

   b. Summarize How did Rome's government change after the republic fell apart?

   c. Elaborate What role did Rome's leaders play in the spread of Christianity?

Lesson 4

10. **a. Identify** Who were Justinian and Theodora, and what did they accomplish?

    b. Contrast In what ways was the Byzantine Empire different from the western Roman Empire?

    c. Explain What influenced the split between the western and eastern Church in the 1000s?

Lesson 5

11. **a. Describe** What were three events that changed Europe during the late Middle Ages?

    b. Explain What duties did knights have under the feudal system?

    c. Develop Why do you think so much of the art created in the Middle Ages was religious?

Lesson 6

12. **a. Describe** What was the Reformation?

    b. Summarize How did the Renaissance affect art, literature, and science?

    c. Sequence Describe how the church continued to remain influential throughout early European history, from the Roman Empire to the Reformation.

Reading Skills

13. Understand Implied Main Ideas *Use the Reading Skills taught in this module to complete this activity*. Look back at the beginning of Lesson 4 of this module. For each paragraph under the heading "Justinian," write a statement that you think is the implied main idea of the paragraph.

Social Studies Skills

Interpret a Historical Map *Use the Population Density and Roman Expansion map in Lesson 3 of this module to answer the following questions.*

14. What time period is shown on this map?

15. What does the yellow color on this map represent?

16. About how many people lived in Spain by AD 117?

17. What large bodies of water border the Roman Empire by 44 BC?

18. What continents were part of the entire Roman Empire by AD 117?

Map Skills

19. Europe, 2000 BC–AD 1500 On a separate sheet of paper, match the letters on the map with their correct labels.

Athens	Carthage	Rome
Gaul	Holy Land	Alexandria

Focus on Writing

20. Persuasion During the Renaissance, humanist artists and writers spread new ideas about the world. Choose a Renaissance artist or writer from your textbook, and learn more about his or her life. Then, write an essay to persuade your reader that this person was important to European history. Be sure to analyze primary sources, like a work of art or literature by the person. In addition, use secondary sources, such as your textbook or historical websites, to find more evidence to support your opinion. Your paper should have an introduction that states your opinion on why he or she is important. The body of the essay should discuss your reasons using the evidence you found from primary and secondary sources. Your last paragraph should restate your opinion and summarize your reasons.

ANCIENT GREECE

The Acropolis of Athens symbolizes the city and represents the architectural and artistic legacy of ancient Greece. *Acropolis* means "highest city" in Greek, and there are many such sites in Greece. Historically, an acropolis provided shelter and defense against a city's enemies. The Acropolis of Athens—the best known of them all—contained temples, monuments, and artwork dedicated to the Greek gods. Archaeological evidence indicates that the Acropolis was an important place to inhabitants from much earlier eras. However, the structures that we see today on the site were largely conceived by the statesman Pericles during the Golden Age of Athens in the 5th century BC.

Explore the Acropolis of ancient Greece and learn about the legacy of Greek civilization. You can find a wealth of information, video clips, primary sources, activities, and more through your online textbook.

HISTORY. Go online to view these and other **HISTORY**® resources.

The Parthenon

Watch the video to see what the Parthenon, one of the most important temples on the Acropolis, might have looked like after it was completed.

The Persian Wars

Watch the video to find out how Athens emerged as the principal Greek city-state at the conclusion of the Persian Wars.

The Goddess Athena

Watch the video to learn how, according to Greek mythology, Athena became the protector of Athens.

Legacy of Greece

Watch the video to analyze The School of Athens, a painting by the Italian Renaissance artist Raphael, which pays tribute to the legacy of ancient Greece in philosophy and science.

History of Modern Europe

Essential Question

Has Modern Europe's influence on the rest of the world been positive or negative?

About the Photo: The Discovery Monument in Lisbon honors Portuguese explorers. At the top, Prince Henry looks out to sea.

▶ *Explore ONLINE!*

VIDEOS, including . . .
• Industrial Revolution

HISTORY.

☑ Document-Based Investigations

☑ Graphic Organizers

☑ Interactive Games

☑ Channel One News Video: World War I Anniversary

☑ Image with Hotspots: Trench Warfare

☑ Interactive Chart: Benefits of Membership in the European Union

In this module, you will learn how from the 1400s to the present day new ideas, inventions, explorations, and wars changed life and expanded knowledge across Europe and throughout the world.

What You Will Learn

World War I Soldiers from Europe's most powerful countries engaged in trench warfare during World War I.

World War II The rise of strong dictators, like Germany's Adolf Hitler, led to the outbreak of the Second World War.

The Industrial Revolution During the 1700s and 1800s, the invention of the steam engine powered factories, trains, and ships and helped change life in Europe.

Reading Social Studies

Use Context Clues—Contrast

READING FOCUS

Did you play this game as a young child: "Which of these things is not like the others?" This same game can help you understand new words as you read. Sometimes the words or sentences around a new word will show contrast, or how the word is not like something else. These contrast clues can help you figure out the new word's meaning. Look at how the following passage indicates that *persevered* means something different from *give in*.

> The German air force repeatedly attacked British cities and military targets. Hitler hoped the British would surrender. Rather than give in, however, the British *persevered*.

Contrast Clues:

1. Look for words or sentences that signal contrast. Words that signal contrast include *however, rather than, instead of,* and *not.* In this paragraph, the words *rather than* signal the contrast clues for the unfamiliar word *persevered.*

2. Check the definition by substituting a word or phrase that fits. *Persevere* likely means to keep on trying. *Rather than give in, however, the British kept on trying.*

YOU TRY IT!

Read the following paragraph. Then, use the graphic organizer below to develop a definition for the word *compete*.

> Some people believed that creating a feeling of community in Europe would make countries less likely to go to war. Leaders like Great Britain's Winston Churchill believed the countries of Europe should cooperate rather than *compete*.

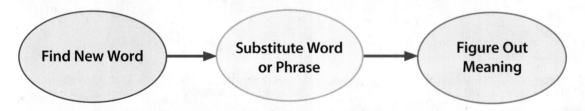

Find New Word → Substitute Word or Phrase → Figure Out Meaning

As you read this module, use contrast clues to help you understand the meaning of the text.

Science and Exploration

The Big Idea

New inventions and knowledge led to European exploration and empires around the world.

Main Ideas

- During the Scientific Revolution, discoveries and inventions expanded knowledge and changed life in Europe.

- In the 1400s and 1500s, Europeans led voyages of discovery and exploration.

- As Europeans discovered new lands, they created colonies and new empires all over the world.

- As Europeans interacted with new lands and peoples, mew plants and animals, and ideas were exchanged that changed the world.

Key Terms and Places

Scientific Revolution
New World
circumnavigate
Columbian Exchange

If YOU lived there . . .

You are an adviser to a European king in the 1500s. The rulers of several other countries have sent explorers to search for new trade routes. Your king does not want to fall behind. Now a young sea captain has come to the royal court with a daring plan. The king is interested, but funding such a voyage could be costly.

What will you advise the king to do?

The Scientific Revolution

Can you imagine what your life would be like without science? Think of all the things that science has provided in our daily lives. Without it, we would have no electricity, no automobiles, no plastic. Our lives would be totally different.

Did you know that there was a time when people lived without the benefits of modern science? In fact, it was not until the 1500s and 1600s that most people in Europe began to appreciate what science and technology could do to improve life.

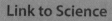

Link to Science

Scientific Advances and Exploration

Several inventions and technical advances enabled people to explore the world and to study the heavens.

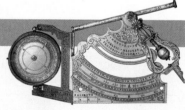

Compass
The compass, which always points north, helped sailors find their way at sea.

Astrolabe
With an astrolabe, sailors could use the stars to calculate a ship's exact location.

Telescope
With the telescope, scientists could study the heavens like never before.

Analyze Visuals
Why do you think these inventions and advances contributed to increased exploration of the world?

A New View of Science Before the 1500s most educated people who studied the world relied on authorities such as ancient Greek writers and church officials. People thought these authorities could tell them all they needed to know. Europeans had little need for science.

Between about 1540 and 1700, though, European views about how to study the world changed. This widespread change in views was part of the **Scientific Revolution,** the series of events that led to the birth of modern science. People began placing more importance on what they observed and less on what they were told. They used their observations to come up with **logical** explanations for how the world worked. This new focus on observation marked the start of modern science. In fact, the scientific method developed during this time. This step-by-step process is used to test an idea, or hypothesis, through observation and data collection. Our knowledge of science and technology has increased greatly since then. But, today's scientists use the same principles of the scientific method.

Why is the birth of modern science called a revolution? The new approach to science was a radical idea. In the same way a political revolution changes a country, this new view of science changed society.

Science and Religion Not everyone was happy with the new role of science in society. Some people feared that scientific ideas would eventually lead to the breakdown of European society.

Many of the people who most feared the increasing influence of science were church officials. They tended to oppose science when it went against the teachings of the church. For example, the church taught that Earth was at the center of the universe. Some scientists, though, had observed through telescopes that Earth orbited the sun. This observation went against the church's teaching.

This growing tension between religion and science came to a head in 1632. That year, an Italian scientist named Galileo (gal-uh-LAY-oh) published a book in which he stated that Earth orbited the sun. He was arrested and put on trial. Afraid that the church would expel him, Galileo publicly stated that his writings were wrong. Privately, though, he held to his beliefs.

Despite conflicts such as these, science and religion were able to exist together in Europe. In fact, many scientists saw a connection between science and religion. These scientists believed that science could better explain church teachings. Science continued developing rapidly as a result.

Discoveries and Inventions The Scientific Revolution was a period of great advances in many fields of science. With increased interest in science came discoveries in astronomy, biology, physics, and other fields. For example, astronomers discovered how the stars and the planets move in the sky. Biologists learned how blood circulates throughout the human body. Physicists figured out how mirrors and pendulums worked.

Some of the greatest advances of the Scientific Revolution were made by one man, Sir Isaac Newton. He made exciting contributions to both math

Academic Vocabulary
logical reasoned, well thought out

A Caravel

Many of the explorers who set out from Europe in the 1400s and 1500s did so in a new type of ship, the caravel. These ships could sail across huge distances because of some important advances in shipbuilding technology.

Triangular sails enabled the caravel to sail into the wind.

The smooth, rounded hull, or frame, handled rough seas well.

A large center rudder made quick turns possible.

Analyze Visuals
What features made the caravel an excellent sailing ship?

and physics. Newton is probably best known today for his observations about gravity, the force that attracts objects to each other. Before his observations, scientists knew very little about how gravity works.

Many of the discoveries of the Scientific Revolution were possible because of new inventions. These devices—the microscope, the thermometer, the telescope, and the barometer—are very common today. In fact, you have probably used at least one of them yourself. But when they were invented, they were dramatic advances in technology. They gave scientists the tools they needed to make more accurate observations of the world and to conduct experiments. They were the tools of the Scientific Revolution. Some of these new inventions helped contribute to another exciting time—the Age of Exploration.

Reading Check
Summarize What happened during the Scientific Revolution?

The Voyages of Discovery

Some advances in science and technology enabled people to make longer, safer sea voyages. New compasses and astrolabes helped sailors figure out where they were even when far from land. Improvements in mapmaking helped people plan safer routes for their journeys. In addition, new ships, such as the caravel, made sea travel safer. The caravel could sail farther than earlier ships could.

Equipped with these new advances, many Europeans set out on great voyages of discovery. They sailed into unknown waters, hoping to find new trade routes to faraway places. They would succeed in their quest, and their discoveries would change the world.

The Drive to Discover Why were Europeans so eager to explore? They had many reasons. Some explorers were curious about the unknown. They hoped to find out what lay beyond the horizon. Others sought adventure and the excitement of life at sea. Still others had religious reasons. These explorers wanted to spread the Christian faith.

Another reason to explore was the desire to get rich. Some explorers wanted to find new lands that had products they could sell in Europe. The explorers hoped to sell these goods for lots of money and to become rich. Others looked for new markets to sell European goods.

In addition, some European leaders promoted exploration in hope it would benefit their countries. Prince Henry, a member of the Portuguese royal family, encouraged explorers to find a route to India's rich spice trade. Queen Isabella of Spain also promoted exploration. She paid for explorers to seek out new lands and claim them for Spain. She hoped these lands would bring Spain wealth.

BIOGRAPHY

Queen Isabella 1451–1504

Christopher Columbus's voyage to the Americas would not have been possible without the support of Queen Isabella of Spain. In 1492 Columbus approached the queen in search of money to pay for his voyage. He had already been turned down by the king of Portugal, who thought Columbus's plan was foolhardy. Isabella liked his plan, however. She gave Columbus money and ships to help make his voyage. With the support of the queen and others, he was able to complete his journey. It would change the history of Europe, the Americas, and the world forever.

Analyze
How did Isabella make Columbus's voyage possible?

Voyages to the East In the mid-1400s, explorers from Europe began searching for an all-water route to Asia. They wanted to reach Asia to get goods from China and India. During the Middle Ages, Europeans had discovered the exotic goods available in Asia. Many of them, such as silk and spices, were not found in Europe. These Asian goods were costly, because traders had to bring them long distances over land. Further, Italian traders controlled the sale of such goods in Europe—and these Italian traders had become very rich.

Other European countries wanted to break the hold the Italians had on trade with Asia. The Italians controlled all the trade routes in the eastern Mediterranean. If other countries could find an all-water route to Asia, they would not have to pay Italian traders to get exotic Asian goods. During the 1400s and 1500s, explorers set sail upon the ocean from many countries in Europe. Their voyages carried them to places all around the world.

▶ *Explore ONLINE!*

European Exploration, 1487–1580

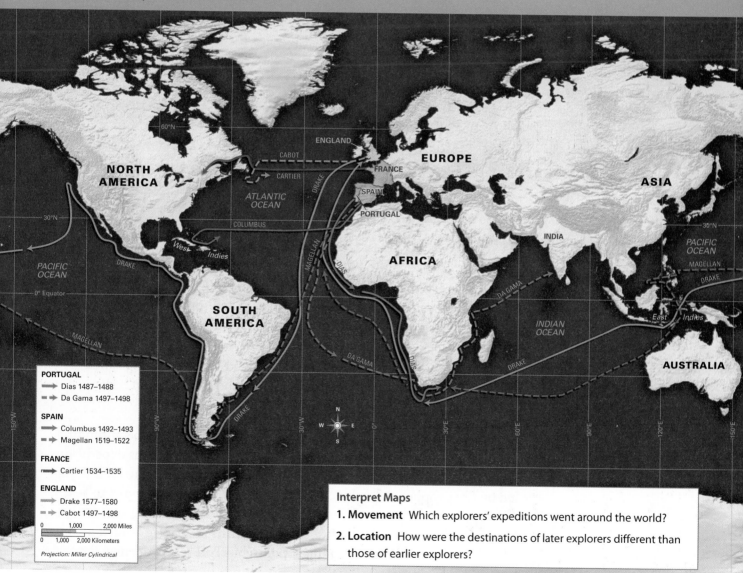

Interpret Maps

1. **Movement** Which explorers' expeditions went around the world?

2. **Location** How were the destinations of later explorers different than those of earlier explorers?

Europeans in the East, 1487–1700

Explore ONLINE!

European territories
- ☐ Dutch
- ☐ English
- ☐ French
- ☐ Portuguese
- ☐ Spanish

European trading posts
- ⚓ Dutch
- ⚓ English
- ⚓ French
- ⚓ Portuguese
- ⚓ Spanish

Interpret Maps

1. **Location** Which European countries had territories in Africa?

2. **Location** Which European country had the largest territory in Asia?

The first explorers to search for a sea route to Asia were from Portugal. Under the direction of Prince Henry, they sailed south along Africa's west coast. As they went, they set up trading posts along the Atlantic coast of Africa. In time, explorers sailed farther south.

In 1497–1498 a Portuguese explorer named Vasco da Gama sailed around the southern tip of Africa and on to the west coast of India. Portugal had found a new sea route to Asia.

Voyages to America Meanwhile, other countries had also been sending explorers out to find new routes to Asia. The most important expedition came from Spain. In 1492 Queen Isabella of Spain helped pay for a voyage led by Christopher Columbus, an Italian sailor. Columbus hoped to reach Asia by sailing west across the Atlantic. The voyage was long and difficult, but he finally reached land after several months at sea. He landed on an island in what is now the Bahamas. Columbus had reached a new land.

Columbus thought he had found a route to Asia, which Europeans called the Indies. Europeans came to realize that he had reached a land unknown to them. They called this land, which in time came to be known as America, the **New World.**

Excited by the new discovery, explorers set out from Europe to learn more about the new land. Led by Spain, explorers from Portugal, France, England, and the Netherlands set sail for North and South America. Before long, little of the Americas would remain unexplored.

This wave of European exploration of the Americas had many different causes. Some explorers were still looking for the best water route to Asia. They hoped to find a passage through the Americas by which ships could sail to India or China.

Other explorers led voyages in search of riches. These explorers had heard that the native people of the Americas had lots of gold—more gold than most Europeans had ever seen. These explorers dreamed of the glory and riches they hoped to gain from conquering the lands and people of the Americas.

Voyages around the World For some Europeans, their new knowledge of the Americas made them more curious about the world. Since they had not known about the Americas, they wondered what else about the world they did not know. One way to learn more about the world, they decided, would be to **circumnavigate,** or travel all the way around, Earth.

The first person to try such a journey was Ferdinand Magellan (MUH-JEHL-UHN), a Portuguese sailor. Magellan sailed west from Spain around the southern tip of South America. From there he continued into the Pacific Ocean, where no European had sailed before. Magellan made it as far as the Philippines, where he was killed in a conflict with natives. His crew pushed on, however, and finally reached Spain to complete their trip around the world.

Reading Check
Identify Cause and Effect What were two causes of exploration?

The voyages of explorers like Magellan taught Europeans much about the world. In time, they even achieved the goal of Christopher Columbus— to reach Asia by sailing west from Europe. In addition, they paved the way for European settlement and colonization of the Americas.

New Empires

As European explorers discovered new lands in the Americas, Africa, and Asia, they claimed these lands for their countries. These land claims started new European empires and trading outposts that stretched across the sea into lands far from Europe. Portugal was the first European country to establish trading outposts along the west coast of Africa. By 1498 the Portuguese had explored the east coast of Africa and reached India. The Portuguese merchants loaded their ships with spices and other goods from Asia. It cost less to ship the goods by sea than it did to ship them overland. As a result, more Europeans could afford these items. Soon, other European countries were looking for new territories and trading partners.

Conquests and Empires The Spanish, who were the first Europeans to reach the Americas, claimed large areas of land there. In some places, the Spanish met powerful native empires. These native people fought to defend their lands.

Before long, though, the Spanish had defeated the two most powerful empires in the Americas. These empires were the Aztecs in what is now Mexico and the Incas in what is now Peru. The Spanish had steel swords, firearms, and horses—all unknown in the Americas. This advantage helped the Spanish defeat the Aztec and Inca armies. In addition, diseases that the Spanish carried killed many thousands of Native Americans. By the mid-1500s, Spain ruled a huge area in the Americas.

One of Spain's central goals in the Americas was to gain wealth. The Spanish wanted the gold and silver that could be found in Mexico and some other places. To get these riches, the Spanish enslaved Native

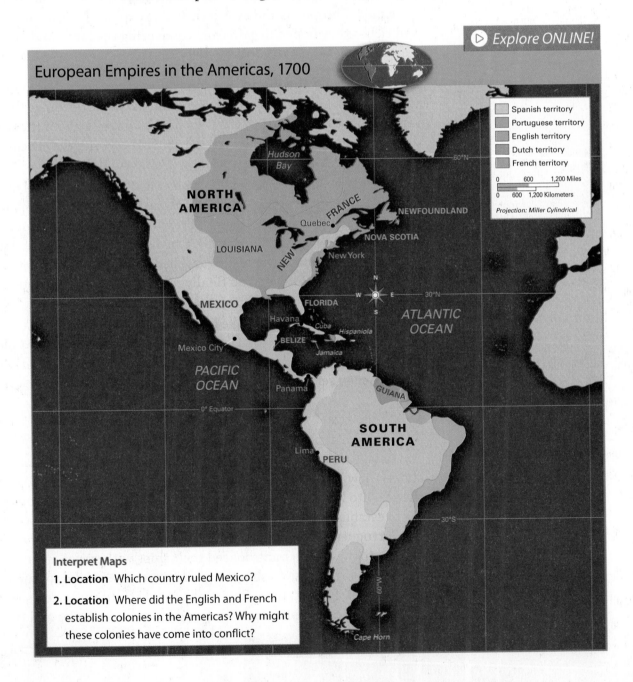

> Explore ONLINE!

European Empires in the Americas, 1700

Legend:
- Spanish territory
- Portuguese territory
- English territory
- Dutch territory
- French territory

0   600   1,200 Miles
0   600 1,200 Kilometers

Projection: Miller Cylindrical

Interpret Maps

1. **Location** Which country ruled Mexico?

2. **Location** Where did the English and French establish colonies in the Americas? Why might these colonies have come into conflict?

Americans and forced them to work in mines. In addition, the Spanish brought African slaves to the Americas to work in the mines. Soon, ships full of gold and silver from these mines were crossing the Atlantic Ocean back to Spain.

Riches from the Americas made Spain the wealthiest country in Europe. Spain's rulers used this money to buy equipment for its armies and to produce ships for its navy. With this powerful military, Spain became Europe's mightiest country, the center of a huge empire.

Other Colonies Other European countries envied Spain's wealth and power. They wanted a share of the wealth that Spain was finding in the Americas. In hope of finding similar wealth, these countries began to establish colonies in the lands they explored. As the map shows, colonists from England, France, the Netherlands, and Portugal had settled in the Americas by 1700.

Like the Spanish, these colonists found Native Americans living in the places they settled. In some cases, new colonists lived peacefully with Native Americans. In other cases, conflict occurred, and colonists and Native Americans fought bloody wars.

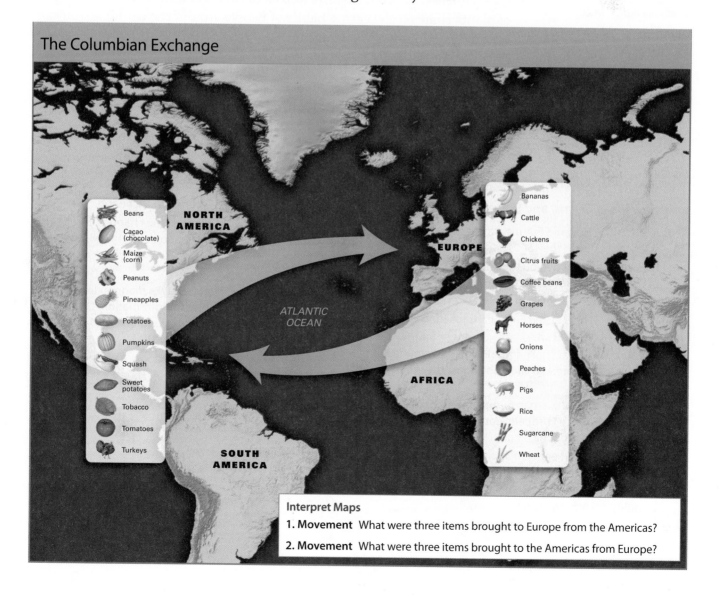

The Columbian Exchange

Beans
Cacao (chocolate)
Maize (corn)
Peanuts
Pineapples
Potatoes
Pumpkins
Squash
Sweet potatoes
Tobacco
Tomatoes
Turkeys

NORTH AMERICA

EUROPE

ATLANTIC OCEAN

AFRICA

SOUTH AMERICA

Bananas
Cattle
Chickens
Citrus fruits
Coffee beans
Grapes
Horses
Onions
Peaches
Pigs
Rice
Sugarcane
Wheat

Interpret Maps

1. **Movement** What were three items brought to Europe from the Americas?

2. **Movement** What were three items brought to the Americas from Europe?

Unlike the Spanish, other European colonists in the Americas did not find huge deposits of gold or silver. They did find other valuable resources, though. Among these resources were wood, furs, rich soil, and different foods. These resources helped the countries of England, France, Portugal, and the Netherlands grow wealthy.

The Columbian Exchange

As Europeans interacted with new lands and new people, one unexpected effect occurred. This effect was the **Columbian Exchange,** when plants, animals, and ideas exchanged between the New World and the Old World. For example, when Europeans took seeds to plant crops, they brought new plants to the Americas. They also brought new domesticated animals, like the horse. In addition, Europeans introduced their ideas, religions, language, and technology to the places they conquered. And, explorers unknowingly carried germs for diseases such as measles and smallpox for which the native peoples had no immunities.

While Europeans introduced plants and animals to the New World, they also found plants and animals there they had never seen before. They took samples back to Europe as well as to Africa and Asia. This exchange of plants changed the eating habits of people around the world, as you can see on the Columbian Exchange map.

Summary and Preview The Scientific Revolution and the Age of Exploration expanded knowledge and led to changes around the world. Next, you will read about another time of great change. Called the Enlightenment, this period led to major political changes in Europe.

Lesson 1 Assessment

Review Ideas, Terms, and Places

1. a. Describe How did European attitudes toward science change in the 1500s and 1600s?

   b. Evaluate What do you think is the greatest advance of the Scientific Revolution? Why?

2. a. Identify Who was Christopher Columbus?

   b. Explain What caused Europeans to launch the voyages of discovery?

   c. Elaborate What challenges do you think made it difficult for explorers to circumnavigate the world for the first time?

3. a. Identify Study the map Europeans in the East, 1487–1700. Which European countries had territories in Africa and Asia? Which had trading outposts?

   b. Describe What enabled Spain to create a huge, powerful empire in the Americas?

   c. Contrast How did other countries' American colonies differ from Spain's?

4. a. Define What is the Columbian Exchange?

   b. Explain What were some of the changes European explorers brought to native peoples in the New World?

Critical Thinking

5. Identify Cause and Effect Draw a diagram like the one shown. Use your notes for information. On the left, list the causes of European exploration. On the right, list the effects of that exploration.

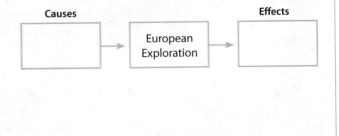

Causes | European Exploration | Effects

Political Change in Europe

The Big Idea

Ideas of the Enlightenment inspired revolutions and new governments in Europe.

Main Ideas

- During the Enlightenment, new ideas about government took hold in Europe.

- The 1600s and 1700s were an Age of Revolution in Europe.

- Napoleon Bonaparte conquered much of Europe after the French Revolution.

Key Terms and Places

Enlightenment
English Bill of Rights
Magna Carta
Declaration of Independence
Declaration of the Rights of Man and of the Citizen
Reign of Terror

If YOU lived there . . .

You live in a village in northern France in the 1700s. Your father is a baker, and your mother is a seamstress. Like most people in your village, your family struggles to make ends meet. All your life you have been taught that the nobility has a right to rule over you. Today, though, a man made an angry speech in the village market. He said that the common people should demand more rights.

How do you think your village will react?

The Enlightenment

Think about the last time you faced a problem that required careful thought. Perhaps you were working a complex math problem or trying to figure out how to win a game. Whatever the problem, when you thought carefully about how to solve it, you were using your power to reason, or to think logically.

The Age of Reason During the 1600s and 1700s, a number of people began to put great importance on reason, or logical thought. They started using reason to challenge long-held beliefs about education, government, law, and religion. By using reason, these people hoped to solve problems such as poverty and war. They believed the use of reason could achieve three great goals—knowledge, freedom, and happiness—and thereby improve society. The use of reason in shaping people's ideas about society and politics defined a period called the **Enlightenment.** Because of its focus on reason, this period is also known as the Age of Reason.

New Ideas about Government During the Enlightenment, some people used reason to examine government. They questioned how governments worked and what the purpose of government should be. In doing so, these people developed completely new ideas about government. These ideas would help lead to the creation of modern democracy.

At the time of the Enlightenment, monarchs, or kings and queens, ruled in most of Europe. Many of these monarchs believed they ruled through divine right. That is, they thought God gave them the right to rule however they chose.

The Enlightenment

Key Enlightenment Ideas

- The ability to reason is unique to humans.
- Reason can be used to solve problems and to improve people's lives.
- Reason can free people from ignorance.
- The natural world is governed by laws that can be discovered through reason.
- Natural laws also govern human behavior.
- Governments should reflect natural laws and encourage education and debate.

Find Main Ideas
What were the key Enlightenment ideas about natural laws?

During the Enlightenment, people went to social gatherings called *salons* to meet and to discuss Enlightenment ideas. These social organizations and the technology of the printing press helped spread new ideas that would impact world history over time.

Academic Vocabulary
contract a binding legal agreement

Reading Check
Contrast
How did Enlightenment ideas about government differ from the views of most monarchs?

Some people challenged rule by divine right. They thought rulers' powers should be limited to protect people's freedoms. These people said government's purpose was to protect and to serve the people.

John Locke, an English philosopher, had a major influence on Enlightenment thinking about the role of government. Locke thought government should be a **contract** between a ruler and the people. A contract binds both sides, so it would limit the ruler's power. Locke also believed that all people had certain natural rights, such as life, liberty, and property. If a ruler did not protect these natural rights, people had the right to change rulers.

Other scholars built on Locke's ideas. One was Jean-Jacques Rousseau (roo-SOH). He said government should express the will, or desire, of the people. According to Rousseau, citizens give the government the power to make and enforce laws. But if these laws do not serve the people, the government should give up its power.

These Enlightenment ideas spread far and wide. In time, they would inspire some Europeans to rise up against their rulers.

The Age of Revolution

The 1600s and 1700s were a time of great change in Europe. Some changes were peaceful, such as those in science. Other changes were more violent. In England, North America, and France, new ideas about government led to war and the Age of Revolution.

Civil War and Reform in England In England, Enlightenment ideas led to conflict between the monarchs, or rulers, and Parliament, the lawmaking body. For many years, England's rulers had shared power with Parliament.

Over time, these key documents greatly influenced the growth of modern democracy and impacted future politics and government in the world.

Magna Carta (1215)
- Limited the power of the monarchy
- Identified people's rights to property
- Established people's rights to trial by a jury

The English Bill of Rights (1689)
- Outlawed cruel and unusual punishment
- Guaranteed free speech for members of Parliament

The U.S. Declaration of Independence (1776)
- Declared that people have natural rights that governments must protect
- Argued that people have the right to replace their governments

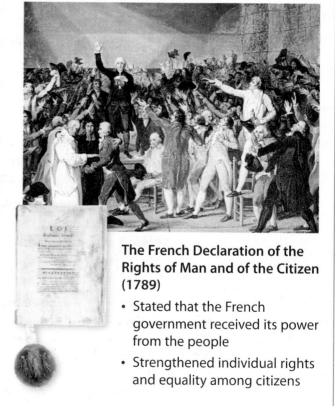

The French Declaration of the Rights of Man and of the Citizen (1789)
- Stated that the French government received its power from the people
- Strengthened individual rights and equality among citizens

Analyze Visuals
Which two of the documents contain some of John Locke's ideas?

But the relationship was an uneasy one. As rulers and Parliament fought for power, the situation grew worse.

In 1642 the power struggle erupted in civil war. Supporters of Parliament forced King Charles I from power. He was later tried and beheaded. A new government formed, but it was unstable.

By 1660 many of the English were tired of instability. They wanted to restore the monarchy. They asked the former king's son to rule England as Charles II. However, Charles had to agree to let Parliament keep powers it had gained during the civil war.

In 1689 Parliament further limited the monarch's power. That year, it approved the **English Bill of Rights.** This document listed rights for Parliament and the English people. For example, it gave Parliament the power to pass laws and to raise taxes.

In addition, Parliament made the king promise to honor **Magna Carta.** In 1215 the English nobles forced King John to sign this document. It limited the English ruler's power and protected some rights of the people. However, few monarchs had honored it during the previous 400 years. Parliament wanted to be sure future rulers honored Magna Carta.

By 1700 Parliament held most of the political power in England. Divine right to rule had ended for England's monarchy.

The American Revolution In time, Enlightenment ideas spread to the British colonies in North America. There, the British ruler's power was not limited as it was in England. The colonies were located in an area with abundant natural resources. Therefore, the British government mainly viewed the colonies as exporters of raw materials for British manufacturing, and as importers to buy England's finished products. In addition, England levied or charged the colonists taxes on legal papers, newspapers, pamphlets, tea, and other daily products in order to raise money for its government. And, since London's Parliament did not allow the colonists to have representatives, the colonists had no power to change things. For this reason, many colonists had grown unhappy with British rule. These colonists began to protest the British laws that they thought were unfair.

In 1775 the protests turned to violence, starting the Revolutionary War. Colonial leaders, influenced by the ideas of Locke and Rousseau, claimed Great Britain had denied their rights. In July 1776 they signed the **Declaration of Independence.** Mostly written by Thomas Jefferson, this document declared the American colonies' independence from Britain. A new nation, the United States of America, was born.

In 1783 the United States officially won its independence. The colonists had successfully put Enlightenment ideas into practice. Their success would inspire many other people, particularly in France.

The French Revolution The people of France closely watched the events of the American Revolution. Soon, they grew inspired to fight for their own rights in the French Revolution.

A major cause of the French Revolution was anger over the differences between social classes. In France, the king ruled over a society split into three classes called estates. The Catholic clergy made up the First Estate. They enjoyed many benefits. Nobles belonged to the Second Estate. These people held important positions in military, government, and the courts. The majority of the French people were members of the Third Estate. This group included peasants, craftworkers, and shopkeepers.

Many Third Estate members thought France's classes were unfair. These people were poor and often hungry. Yet, they paid the highest taxes. While they suffered, King Louis XVI held fancy parties, and Queen Marie-Antoinette wore costly clothes.

Meanwhile, France's government was deeply in debt. To raise money, Louis XVI wanted to tax the wealthy. He called a meeting of the representatives of the three estates to discuss a tax increase.

The meeting did not go smoothly. Some members of the Third Estate were familiar with Enlightenment ideas. These members demanded a greater voice in the meeting's decisions. Eventually, the Third Estate members formed a separate group called the National Assembly. This group demanded that the French king accept a constitution limiting his powers.

Louis XVI refused, which angered the common people of Paris. On July 14, 1789, this anger led a mob to storm the Bastille, a prison in Paris. The mob released the prisoners and destroyed the building. The French Revolution had begun.

The Storming of the Bastille

On July 14, 1789, a mob stormed and destroyed the Bastille, a prison in Paris. To many French people, this prison symbolized the king's harsh rule.

Analyze Visuals
What were some weapons used in the French Revolution?

The French Revolution quickly spread to the countryside. In events called the Great Fear, peasants took revenge on landlords and other nobles for long years of poor treatment. In their rage, the peasants burned down houses and monasteries.

At the same time, other leaders of the revolution were taking peaceful steps. The National Assembly wrote and approved the **Declaration of the Rights of Man and of the Citizen.** This 1789 French constitution guaranteed French citizens some rights and made taxes fairer. Among the freedoms the constitution supported were the freedoms of speech, of the press, and of religion.

The French Republic In time, revolutionary leaders created a French republic. The new republic did not end France's many growing problems, however. Unrest soon returned.

In 1793 the revolutionaries executed Louis XVI. His execution was the first of many, as the government began arresting anyone who questioned its rule. The result was the **Reign of Terror,** a bloody period of the French Revolution during which the government executed thousands of its opponents and others at the guillotine (GEE-uh-teen). This device beheaded victims with a large, heavy blade. The Reign of Terror finally ended when one of its own leaders was executed in 1794.

Although a violent period, the French Revolution did achieve some of its goals. French peasants and workers gained new political rights. The government opened new schools and improved wages. In addition, it ended slavery in France's colonies.

The French republic's leaders struggled, though. As problems grew worse, a strong leader rose up to take control.

Reading Check
Analyze Motives
Why did many members of the Third Estate support the revolution?

Napoleon Bonaparte

Jacques-Louis David painted this scene of Napoleon crowning his wife, Josephine, empress after crowning himself emperor. The coronation took place in 1804 in Notre Dame Cathedral in Paris, France.

Napoleonic Empire, 1812

Analyze Visuals
How does the event show Napoleon's power?

Napoleon Bonaparte

In 1799 France was ripe for a change in leadership. That year, Napoleon Bonaparte, a 30-year-old general, took control. Many French people welcomed him because he seemed to support the Revolution's goals. His popularity grew quickly, and in 1804 Napoleon crowned himself emperor.

Military Conquests and Rule Napoleon was a brilliant military leader. Under his command, the French army won a series of dazzling victories. By 1810 France's empire stretched across Europe.

In France, Napoleon restored order. He created an efficient government, made taxes fairer, and formed a system of public education. Perhaps his most important accomplishment was the creation of a new French legal system, the Napoleonic Code. This legal code reflected the ideals of the French Revolution, such as equality before the law and equal civil rights.

With these many accomplishments, Napoleon sounds like a perfect leader. But he was not. He harshly punished anyone who opposed or questioned his rule.

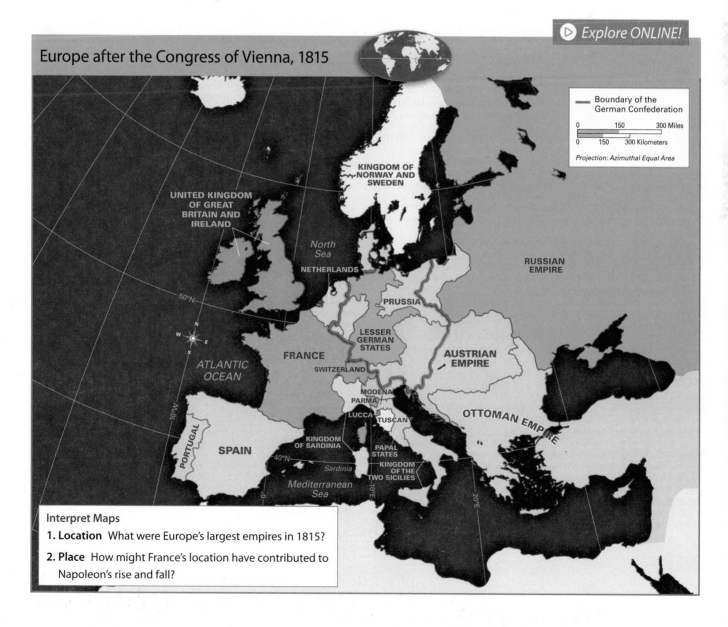

▷ Explore ONLINE!

Europe after the Congress of Vienna, 1815

— Boundary of the German Confederation

0   150   300 Miles
0   150   300 Kilometers

Projection: Azimuthal Equal Area

KINGDOM OF NORWAY AND SWEDEN

UNITED KINGDOM OF GREAT BRITAIN AND IRELAND

North Sea

NETHERLANDS

RUSSIAN EMPIRE

PRUSSIA

LESSER GERMAN STATES

FRANCE

SWITZERLAND

AUSTRIAN EMPIRE

ATLANTIC OCEAN

MODENA
PARMA
LUCCA
TUSCANY

OTTOMAN EMPIRE

PORTUGAL

SPAIN

KINGDOM OF SARDINIA

PAPAL STATES

KINGDOM OF THE TWO SICILIES

Sardinia

Mediterranean Sea

Interpret Maps

1. **Location** What were Europe's largest empires in 1815?

2. **Place** How might France's location have contributed to Napoleon's rise and fall?

Napoleon's Defeat In the end, bad weather contributed to Napoleon's downfall. In 1812 he led an invasion of Russia. The invasion was a disaster. Bitterly cold weather and smart Russian tactics forced Napoleon's army to retreat. Many French soldiers died.

Great Britain, Prussia, and Russia then joined forces and in 1814 defeated Napoleon's weakened army. He returned a year later with a new army, but was again defeated. The British then exiled him to an island, where he died in 1821.

After the defeat of Napoleon in 1814, European leaders met at the Congress of Vienna to reorganize Europe. There, they redrew the map of Europe. Their goal was to keep any country from ever becoming powerful enough to threaten Europe again.

Summary and Preview You have read how new ideas about government arose out of the Enlightenment. These ideas led to revolutions and political change in Europe and elsewhere. Next, you will read about the growth of industry and how it changed European society.

Reading Check
Make Inferences
Why did other
countries want to
defeat Napoleon?

Lesson 2 Assessment

Review Ideas, Terms, and Places

1. a. **Define** What does divine right mean?

   b. **Explain** What did Enlightenment thinkers believe the purpose of government should be?

2. a. **Describe** What was the significance of the English Bill of Rights?

   b. **Make Inferences** Why do you think many Americans consider Thomas Jefferson a hero?

   c. **Evaluate** How successful do you think the French Revolution was? Explain your answer.

3. a. **Identify** Who was Napoleon Bonaparte, and what were his main accomplishments?

   b. **Analyze** How were Napoleon's forces weakened and then defeated?

Critical Thinking

4. **Compare** In what ways did Thomas Jefferson and Napoleon change political development throughout the world?

5. **Sequence** Review your notes. Then make a timeline like the one here to list the main events of the Age of Revolution. List the events in the order in which they occurred.

The Industrial Revolution

The Big Idea

Driven by new ideas and technologies, much of Europe developed industrial societies in the 1700s and 1800s.

Main Ideas

- Britain's large labor force, raw materials, and money to invest led to the start of the Industrial Revolution.

- Industrial growth began in Great Britain and then spread to other parts of Europe.

- The Industrial Revolution led to both positive and negative changes in society.

Key Terms

Industrial Revolution
textiles
capitalism
suffragettes

If YOU lived there . . .

You live in Lancashire, England, in 1815. You and your family are weavers. You spin sheep's wool into thread. Then you weave the thread into fine woolen cloth to sell to local merchants. Now a mill is being built nearby. It will have large machines that weave cloth. The mill owner is looking for workers to run the machines. Some of your friends are going to work in the mill to earn more money.

What do you think about working in the mill?

Start of the Industrial Revolution

Each day, machines from alarm clocks to dishwashers perform many jobs for us. In the early 1700s, however, people had to do most work themselves. They made most of the items they needed by hand. For power, they used animals or water or their own muscles. Then around the mid-1700s, everything changed. People began inventing machines to make goods and supply power. These machines completely changed the way people across Europe worked and lived. We call this period of rapid growth in machine-made goods the **Industrial Revolution.**

From Farmworker to Industrial Laborer Changes in farming helped pave the way for industrial growth. Since the Middle Ages, farming in Europe had been changing. Wealthy farmers had started buying up land and creating larger farms. These large farms were more efficient. For this reason, many people who owned small farms lost their land. They then had to work for other farmers or move to cities.

At the same time, Europe's growing population was creating a need for more food. To meet this need, farmers began looking for ways to grow more and better crops. Farmers began to experiment with new methods. They also began improving farm technology. English farmer Jethro Tull, for example, invented a seed drill. This device made it possible to plant seeds in straight rows and at certain depths. As a result, more seeds grew into plants.

Better farming methods and technology had several effects. First, farmers could grow more crops with less labor. Second, with more crops available for food, the population grew even more. However, with less need for labor, many farmworkers lost their jobs. As a result, these workers moved to cities to look for work. There, they created a large labor force for the coming industrial growth.

Great Britain's Resources Great Britain provided the setting for the Industrial Revolution's start. Britain and its colonies had the resources needed for industrial growth. These resources included labor, raw materials, and money to invest. For example, Britain had a large workforce, rich supplies of coal, and many rivers for waterpower.

In addition, Great Britain's colonial markets and its growing population were increasing the demand for manufactured goods. Increased demand led people to look for ways to make goods faster or more easily. In Britain, all these things came together to start the Industrial Revolution.

Reading Check
Identify Cause and Effect How did new technology and better farming methods affect agriculture in Europe?

Inventions of the Industrial Revolution

Starting in the mid-1700s, inventions changed the way goods were made. James Hargreaves's spinning jenny made thread quickly. The Bessemer furnace was an invention of the late Industrial Revolution. The furnace made steel from molten iron.

Analyze Visuals
What do you think operating a Bessemer furnace was like?

Industrial Growth

Industrial growth began with **textiles,** or cloth products. In the early 1700s people made cloth by hand. They used spinning wheels to make thread and looms to weave it into cloth. Given the time and effort this took, it is not surprising that people would want a way to make cloth quickly.

The Textile Industry A big step toward manufactured clothing came in 1769. That year, an English inventor and industrialist Richard Arkwright invented a water-powered spinning machine. Called a water frame, this machine could produce dozens of threads at one time. In contrast, a person using a traditional spinning wheel could produce only one thread at a time.

Other machines sped up production even more. With these new machines, workers could produce large amounts of cloth quickly. As a result, the price of cloth fell. Soon, the British were using machines to make many types of goods. People housed these machines in buildings called factories, and the factories needed power.

Other Inventions Most early machines ran on waterpower. Thus, factories had to be located by rivers. Although Britain had many rivers, they were not always in desirable locations.

Steam power provided a solution. In the 1760s James Watt, a Scot, built the first modern steam engine. Soon, steam powered most machines. Factories could now be built in better places, such as in cities.

Steam power increased the demand for coal and iron, which were needed to make machinery. Iron can be a brittle metal, though, and iron parts often broke. In 1855 English inventor Henry Bessemer developed a cheap way to convert iron into steel, which is stronger. This invention led to the growth of the steel industry, which helped expand the railroad business.

In addition, new inventions improved transportation and communication. Steam engines powered riverboats and trains, speeding up transportation. The telegraph made communication faster. Instead of sending a note by boat or train, people could go to a telegraph office and instantly send a message over a long distance. These advancements in communication and transportation made it easier for people to do business over greater distances. For example, manufactured goods could be shipped by train from city to city. These improvements also helped spread ideas and culture more quickly.

The Factory System Industrial growth led to major changes in the way people worked and lived. Before, most people had worked on farms or in their homes. Now, more people were going to work in factories. Many of these workers were young women and children, whom owners paid lower wages.

Factory work was long, tiring, and dangerous. Factory workers did the same tasks for 12 hours or more a day, six days a week. Breaks were few, and rules were strict. Although people made more than on farms, wages were still low.

A British Textile Factory

In early textile factories, workers ran machines in a large room. A supervisor kept a watchful eye. Conditions in factories were poor, and the work was long, tiring, and dangerous. Even so, young women and children as young as six worked in many early factories.

Factory owners keep windows shut to prevent air from blowing the threads. This creates a hot, stuffy room.

Dust and cotton fibers fill the air, causing breathing problems.

Machines are loud. Workers must shout to be heard over the deafening roar.

To avoid being injured or killed, girls must tie back their hair to keep it from getting caught in the machines.

One task is to straighten threads as they come out of the machines. This task can cut workers' hands.

Analyze Visuals
Why do you think the machines in early textile factories caused so many injuries?

To add to the toil, factory conditions were miserable and unsafe. Year-round, the air was thick with dust, which could harm workers' lungs. In addition, the large machines were dangerous and caused many injuries. Even so, factory jobs were desirable to people with few alternatives.

Spread of Industry In time, the Industrial Revolution spread from Great Britain to other parts of Europe. By the late 1800s, factories were making goods across much of Western Europe.

The growth of industry helped lead to a new economic system, **capitalism.** In this system, individuals own most businesses and resources. People invest money in businesses in the hope of making a profit.

Changes in Society

The Industrial Revolution improved life in Europe in many ways. Manufactured goods became cheaper and more available. Inventions made life easier. More people grew wealthier and joined the middle class. These people could afford to live well.

At the same time, industrial growth made life worse in other ways. Cities grew rapidly. They became dirty, noisy, and crowded. Many workers remained poor. They often had to live crammed together in shabby, unsafe apartments. In these conditions, diseases spread rapidly as well.

Reading Check
Evaluate If you had lived at this time, would you have left a farm to work in a factory for more money? Why or why not?

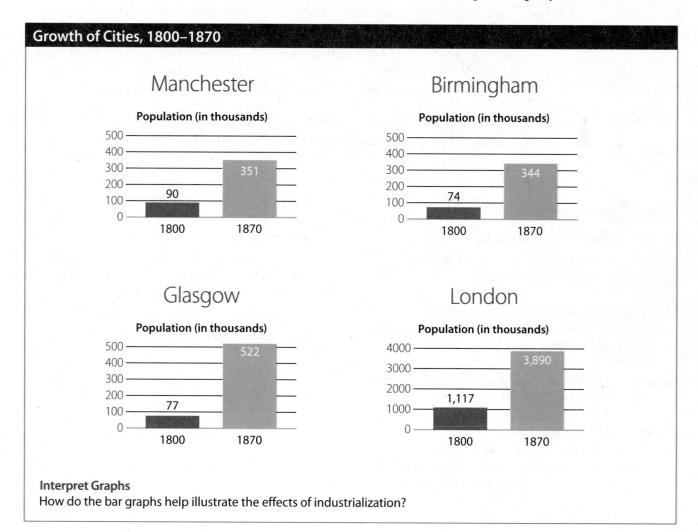

Growth of Cities, 1800–1870

Interpret Graphs
How do the bar graphs help illustrate the effects of industrialization?

Reading Check
Summarize
How did the
Industrial Revolution
affect cities in Europe?

Reform efforts addressed the workplace, society, and government. Here, British suffragettes campaign for the right to vote.

Such problems led to efforts to reform society and politics. People worked to have laws passed improving wages and factory conditions. Others worked to make cities cleaner and safer. Efforts to gain political power were led by **suffragettes,** women who campaigned to gain the right to vote. In 1928 British suffragettes won the right to vote for women in Great Britain. Changes like these helped usher in the modern age.

Summary and Preview As you have read, industrial growth greatly changed how many Europeans lived and worked. In the next lesson, you will learn about how European growth and prosperity led to world war.

Lesson 3 Assessment

Review Ideas, Terms, and Places

1. **a. Recall** In which country did the start of the Industrial Revolution take place?

   b. Draw Conclusions How did changes in farming help pave the way for industrial growth?

   c. Develop Write a few sentences defending the idea that Great Britain was ready for industrial growth in the early 1700s.

2. **a. Identify** What were two inventions that contributed to industrial growth during this period?

   b. Make Inferences How do you think work in a factory differed from that on a farm?

3. **a. Recall** What did the suffragettes achieve?

   b. Summarize What problems did industry create? How did people work to solve these problems?

Critical Thinking

4. **Identify Cause and Effect** Review your notes. Then make a diagram like the one shown to explain how each change in society led to the next.

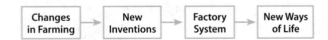

| Changes in Farming | → | New Inventions | → | Factory System | → | New Ways of Life |

🌐 World War I

If YOU lived there . . .

It is 1914, and you live in London. For years you have heard about an important alliance between Great Britain, France, and Russia. Each country has promised to protect the others. Just days ago, you learned that war has broken out in Eastern Europe. Russia and France are preparing for war. People are saying that Britain will fight to protect its allies. If that happens, Europe's most powerful countries will be at war.

How do you feel about the possibility of war?

The Outbreak of War

In the early 1900s Europe was on the brink of war. Rivalries were building among Europe's strongest nations. One small spark would be enough to start World War I.

Causes of the War During the 1800s nationalism changed Europe. **Nationalism** is devotion and loyalty to one's country. Some groups that were ruled by powerful empires wanted to build their own nation-states. For example, nationalism led some people in Bosnia and Herzegovina, a region in southeastern Europe, to demand their independence from the Austro-Hungarian Empire. Nationalism also created rivalries among many nations. By the early 1900s nationalism had grown so strong that countries were willing to go to war to prove their superiority over their rivals. A fierce competition emerged among the countries of Europe.

Another force that helped set the stage for war in Europe was **imperialism.** The nations of Europe competed fiercely for colonies in Africa and Asia. The quest for colonies sometimes pushed European nations to the brink of war. As European countries continued to compete for overseas empires, their rivalry and mistrust of one another deepened.

This competition for land, resources, and power drove many European countries to strengthen their armed forces. They built powerful armies and created stockpiles of new weapons. Each country wanted to show its strength and intimidate its rivals.

The Big Idea

World War I and the peace treaty that followed brought tremendous change to Europe.

Main Ideas

- Rivalries in Europe led to the outbreak of World War I.
- After a long, devastating war, the Allies claimed victory.
- The war's end brought great political and territorial changes to Europe.

Key Terms

nationalism
imperialism
alliance
trench warfare
Treaty of Versailles
communism

European Alliances, 1914

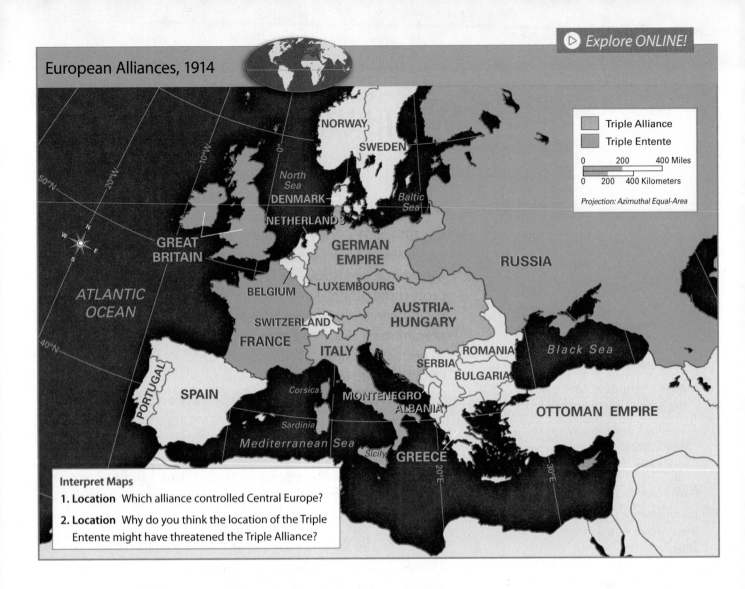

Explore ONLINE!

Interpret Maps

1. **Location** Which alliance controlled Central Europe?

2. **Location** Why do you think the location of the Triple Entente might have threatened the Triple Alliance?

Both Great Britain and Germany, for example, competed to build strong navies and powerful new battleships.

As tensions and suspicions grew, some European leaders hoped to protect their countries by creating alliances. An **alliance** is an agreement between countries. If one country is attacked, its allies—members of the alliance—help defend it. Soon, these rivalries split Europe into two powerful, opposing alliances. In 1882 Italy, Germany, and Austria-Hungary formed the Triple Alliance. In response, France, Great Britain, and Russia created their own alliance in 1907, the Triple Entente (ahn-TAHNT).

The Spark for War By the summer of 1914, war in Europe seemed certain. Tensions between Austria-Hungary and Serbia arose over the control of Bosnia and Herzegovina, a province of Austria-Hungary and Serbia's neighbor. On June 28, 1914, a Serbian assassin shot and killed Archduke Franz Ferdinand, the heir to the throne of Austria-Hungary. Seeking revenge, Austria-Hungary declared war on Serbia. After Serbia turned to Russia for help, the alliance system quickly split Europe into two warring sides. On one side was Austria-Hungary and Germany, known as the Central Powers. The Allied Powers—Serbia, Russia, Great Britain, and France—were on the other side.

Reading Check
Find Main Ideas What were the causes of World War I?

War and Victory

Germany struck the first blow in the war, sending a large army into Belgium and France. Allied troops, however, managed to stop the Germans just outside Paris. In the east, Russia attacked Germany and Austria-Hungary, forcing Germany to fight on two fronts. Hopes on both sides for a quick victory soon disappeared.

A New Kind of War A new military **strategy**, trench warfare, was largely responsible for preventing a quick victory. Early in the war, both sides turned to trench warfare. **Trench warfare** is a style of fighting in which each side fights from deep ditches, or trenches, dug into the ground.

Both the Allies and the Central Powers dug hundreds of miles of trenches along the front lines. Soldiers in the trenches faced great suffering. Not only did they live in constant danger of attack, but cold, hunger, and disease also plagued them. Sometimes, soldiers would "go over the top" of their trenches and fight for a few hours, only to retreat to the same position. Trench warfare cost millions of lives, but neither side could win the war.

To gain an advantage in the trenches, each side developed deadly new weapons. Machine guns cut down soldiers as they tried to move forward. Poison gas, first used by the Germans, blinded soldiers in the trenches. It was later used by both sides. The British introduced another weapon, the tank, to break through enemy lines.

At sea, Britain used its powerful navy to block supplies from reaching Germany. Germany responded by using submarines, called U-boats. German U-boats tried to break the British blockade and sink ships carrying supplies to Great Britain.

Academic Vocabulary
strategy a plan for fighting a battle or war

Trench Warfare

Both the Allied Powers and the Central Powers relied on trenches for defense during World War I. As a result, the war dragged on for years with no clear victor. Each side developed new weapons and technology to try to gain an advantage in the trenches.

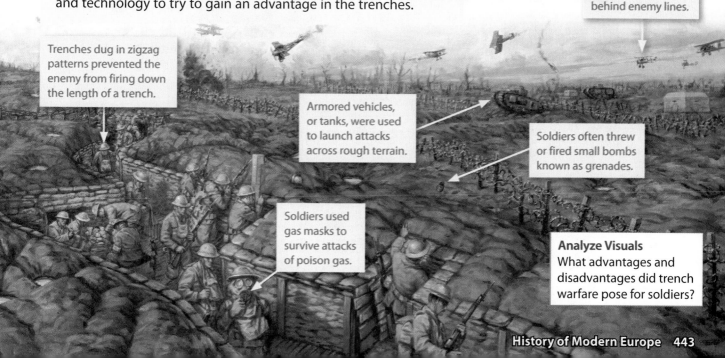

Each side used airplanes to observe troop movements and other actions behind enemy lines.

Trenches dug in zigzag patterns prevented the enemy from firing down the length of a trench.

Armored vehicles, or tanks, were used to launch attacks across rough terrain.

Soldiers often threw or fired small bombs known as grenades.

Soldiers used gas masks to survive attacks of poison gas.

Analyze Visuals
What advantages and disadvantages did trench warfare pose for soldiers?

The Allies Win For three years, the war was a stalemate—neither side could defeat the other. Slowly, however, the war turned in favor of the Allies. In early 1917 German U-boats began attacking American ships carrying supplies to Britain. When Germany ignored U.S. warnings to stop, the United States entered the war on the side of the Allies.

Help from American forces gave the Allies a fresh advantage. Soon afterward, however, the exhausted Russians pulled out of the war. Germany quickly attacked the Allies, hoping to put an end to the war. Allied troops, however, stopped Germany's attack. The Central Powers had suffered a great blow. In the fall of 1918, the Central Powers surrendered. The Allied Powers were victorious.

Reading Check
Sequence What events led to the end of World War I?

The War's End

After more than four years of fighting, the war came to an end on November 11, 1918. More than 8.5 million soldiers had been killed, and at least 20 million more were wounded. Millions of civilians had lost their lives as well. The war brought tremendous change to Europe.

Making Peace Shortly after the end of the war, leaders from the Allied nations met at Versailles (ver-SY), near Paris. There, they debated the terms of peace for the Central Powers.

Quick Facts

World War I Statistics

Total Number of Troops Mobilized

Allied Powers:
42 million

Central Powers:
23 million

Battlefield Deaths of Major Combatants

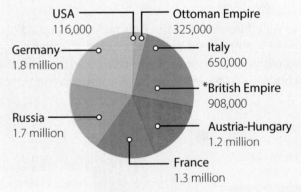

USA
116,000

Germany
1.8 million

Russia
1.7 million

France
1.3 million

Ottoman Empire
325,000

Italy
650,000

*British Empire
908,000

Austria-Hungary
1.2 million

Source:
Encyclopaedia Britannica

* Includes troops from Britain, Canada, Australia, New Zealand, India, and South Africa

Interpret Graphs

1. Which Allied nation suffered the greatest number of battlefield deaths?

2. Which four nations accounted for about 75 percent of all battlefield deaths?

World War I flying aces fought each other in aerial dogfights.

The United States, led by President Woodrow Wilson, wanted a just peace after the war. He did not want harsh peace terms that might anger the losing countries and lead to future conflict.

Other Allied leaders, however, wanted to punish Germany. They believed that Germany had started the war and should pay for it. They believed that weakening Germany would prevent future wars.

In the end, the Allies forced Germany to sign a treaty. The **Treaty of Versailles** was the final peace settlement of World War I. It forced Germany to accept the blame for starting the war. Germany also had to slash the size of its army and give up its overseas colonies. Additionally, Germany had to pay billions of dollars for damages caused during the war.

A New Europe World War I had a tremendous effect on the countries of Europe. It changed the governments of some European countries and the borders of others. For example, in Russia, the war had caused great hardship for the people. A revolution then forced the Russian czar, or emperor, to give up power. Shortly after, Vladimir Lenin took over Russia's government and established a Communist government. **Communism** is a political system in which the government owns all property and controls all aspects of life in a country. An uprising toward the end of the war also forced the German emperor from power. A fragile republic replaced the German Empire.

World War I also altered the borders of many European countries. Austria and Hungary became separate countries. Poland and Czechoslovakia each gained their independence. Serbia, Bosnia and Herzegovina,

Vladimir Lenin encouraged Russian workers to support his new Communist government.

Reading Check

Summarize
How did World War I change Europe?

and other Balkan states were combined to create Yugoslavia. Finland, Estonia, Latvia, and Lithuania, which had been part of Russia, became independent.

Summary and Preview Intense rivalries among the countries of Europe led to World War I, one of the most devastating wars in history. However, at the end of the war, the harsh terms of the Treaty of Versailles changed the map of Europe and created resentment. This resentment, along with other factors, would soon lead to more conflict. Next, you will learn about problems that plagued Europe and led to World War II.

Lesson 4 Assessment

Review Ideas, Terms, and Places

1. **a. Identify** What event triggered World War I?

   b. Analyze How did nationalism cause rivalries between some European countries?

   c. Evaluate How did conflict and cooperation among the alliances help or hurt most countries? Explain your answer.

2. **a. Describe** What was trench warfare like?

   b. Draw Conclusions What difficulties did soldiers face as a result of trench warfare?

   c. Predict How might the war have been different if the United States had not entered it?

3. **a. Recall** How did the Treaty of Versailles punish Germany for its role in the war?

   b. Contrast How did the Allied leaders' ideas for peace with Germany differ?

   c. Elaborate Why do you think the war caused changes in government in Russia and Germany?

Critical Thinking

4. **Categorize** Draw a chart like the one here. Use your notes to list the results of World War I in the appropriate category. Then answer the following question. How did the rise of nationalist groups change world history?

Political	Economic

🌐
World War II

The Big Idea

Problems in Europe led to World War II, the deadliest war in history.

Main Ideas

- Economic and political problems troubled Europe in the years after World War I.

- World War II broke out when Germany invaded Poland.

- Nazi Germany targeted the Jews during the Holocaust.

- Allied victories in Europe and Japan brought the end of World War II.

Key Terms

Great Depression
dictator
Axis Powers
Allies
Holocaust

If YOU lived there . . .

It is 1922, and you are part of a huge crowd in one of Rome's public squares. Everyone is listening to the fiery speech of a dynamic new leader. He promises to make Italy great again, as it was in the days of ancient Rome. You know that your parents and some of your teachers are excited about his ideas. Others are concerned that he may be too forceful.

What do you think of this new leader's message?

Problems Trouble Europe

After World War I, Europeans began rebuilding their countries. Just as they had started to recover, however, many economic and political problems emerged. These problems threatened the peace and security of Europe.

The Great Depression World War I left much of Europe in shambles. Factories and farmland had been destroyed, and economies were in ruins. Countries that had lost the war, like Germany and Austria, owed billions in war damages. Many countries turned to the United States for help. During the 1920s the U.S. economy was booming. Loans from American banks and businesses helped many European nations recover and rebuild after World War I.

In 1929, however, the recovery fell apart. A stock market crash in the United States triggered a global economic crisis in the 1930s known as the **Great Depression.** As the U.S. economy faltered, American banks stopped lending to Europe. Without U.S. loans and investments, European economies declined. Unemployment skyrocketed as businesses and farms, as well as banks, went bankrupt.

The Rise of Dictators The Great Depression added to Europe's problems. Blaming weak governments for the hard times, some Europeans turned to dictators to strengthen their countries and improve their lives. A **dictator** is a ruler who has total control. Dictators rose to power in Russia, Italy, and Germany.

Popular dictators rose to power in Europe in the 1920s and 1930s. Adolf Hitler in Germany and Benito Mussolini in Italy gained public support with promises to make life better and to strengthen their countries.

One of the first dictators in Europe was Russia's Vladimir Lenin. Lenin gained power as a result of a 1917 revolution. He formed the first Communist government and took control of businesses and private property. He also united Russia and other republics to create the Soviet Union. After Lenin's death in 1924, Joseph Stalin took power. As dictator, he made all economic decisions, restricted religious worship, and used secret police to spy on citizens.

Benito Mussolini of Italy was another powerful dictator during this period. In the 1920s Mussolini won control of the Italian government and made himself dictator. He promised to make Italy stronger and to revive the economy. He even spoke of restoring the glory of the former Roman Empire. As dictator, however, Mussolini suspended basic rights like freedom of speech and trial by jury.

By the 1930s many Germans had lost faith in their government. They turned to a new political party, the Nazi Party. The party's leader, Adolf Hitler, promised to strengthen Germany. He vowed to rebuild Germany's military and economy. After years of struggle, many Germans listened eagerly to his message. In 1933 Hitler rose to power and soon became dictator. He banned all parties except the Nazi Party. He also began discriminating against so-called inferior races, particularly Germany's Jews.

Reading Check
Summarize
Why did some people support the rise of dictators?

War Breaks Out

As dictators, Hitler and Mussolini were determined to strengthen their countries at any cost. Their actions led to history's deadliest war—World War II.

Academic Vocabulary

aggression
forceful action intended to dominate or master

Threats to Peace After World War I, European countries wanted peace. Many countries hoped to prevent another deadly war. By the late 1930s, however, attempts at peace had failed. Instead of peace, Italian and German **aggression** forced Europe into a second world war.

In 1935 Benito Mussolini ordered his Italian troops to invade Ethiopia, a country in East Africa. Other nations were shocked by his actions, but none tried to turn back the invasion. Meanwhile, the Italian leader and Germany's Adolf Hitler joined together to form an alliance known as the Rome-Berlin Axis.

Hitler was next to act. In 1938 he broke the Treaty of Versailles when he annexed, or added, Austria to Germany's territory. Although Britain and France protested, they did not attempt to stop Germany.

Later that year, Hitler announced his plan to take part of Czechoslovakia as well. Many European leaders were worried, but they still hoped to avoid a war. They allowed Hitler to annex part of Czechoslovakia in return for his promise of peace. By the spring of 1939, however, Germany had conquered the rest of Czechoslovakia. Italy quickly moved to occupy Albania in the Balkans. Attempts to keep the peace had failed.

Eventually, Great Britain and France realized they could not ignore Hitler's actions. When Germany threatened to take Polish territory, the Allies vowed to protect Poland at all costs. On September 1, 1939, German forces launched an all-out attack on Poland. Two days later, Great Britain and France responded by declaring war on Germany. World War II had begun.

Allies Lose Ground Germany's invasion of Poland triggered the Second World War. Germany, Italy, and Japan formed an alliance called the **Axis Powers.** Against them stood the **Allies**—France, Great Britain, and other countries that opposed the Axis.

Germany struck first. After defeating Poland, Germany moved on to a series of quick victories in Western Europe. One by one, countries fell to German forces. In June 1940 Germany invaded and quickly defeated one of Europe's greatest powers, France. In less than a year, Hitler had gained control of almost all of Western Europe.

Next, Germany set its sights on Britain. The German air force repeatedly attacked British cities and military targets. Hitler hoped the British would surrender. Rather than give in, however, the British persevered.

Reading Check
Make Inferences
Why do you think the Axis Powers easily gained the advantage in the early years of the war?

Unable to defeat Great Britain, the Axis Powers turned their attention elsewhere. As German troops marched into Eastern Europe, Italian forces invaded North Africa. By the end of 1941, Germany had invaded the Soviet Union and Japan had attacked the United States at Pearl Harbor, Hawaii. The Axis Powers controlled much of Europe. The Allies were losing ground in the war.

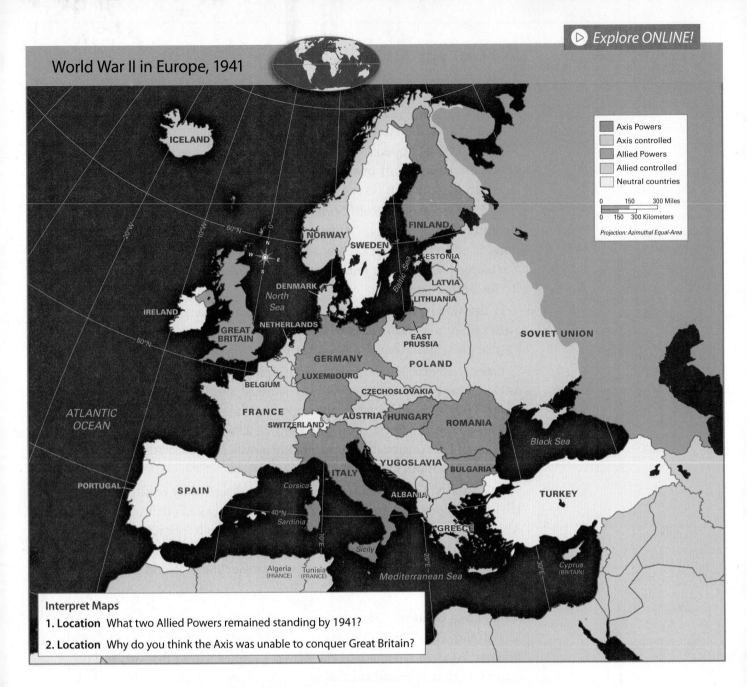

World War II in Europe, 1941

▷ Explore ONLINE!

Axis Powers
Axis controlled
Allied Powers
Allied controlled
Neutral countries

0   150   300 Miles
0   150   300 Kilometers

Projection: Azimuthal Equal-Area

ICELAND

NORWAY
SWEDEN
FINLAND
ESTONIA
LATVIA
LITHUANIA
DENMARK
North
Sea
Baltic Sea
IRELAND
GREAT
BRITAIN
NETHERLANDS
EAST
PRUSSIA
SOVIET UNION
GERMANY
POLAND
LUXEMBOURG
BELGIUM
CZECHOSLOVAKIA
FRANCE
AUSTRIA HUNGARY
SWITZERLAND
ROMANIA
Black Sea
ATLANTIC
OCEAN
YUGOSLAVIA
BULGARIA
ITALY
PORTUGAL
SPAIN
Corsica
ALBANIA
TURKEY
Sardinia
GREECE
Sicily
Cyprus
(BRITAIN)
Algeria
(FRANCE)
Tunisia
(FRANCE)
Mediterranean Sea

Interpret Maps
1. **Location** What two Allied Powers remained standing by 1941?
2. **Location** Why do you think the Axis was unable to conquer Great Britain?

The Holocaust

One of the most horrifying aspects of the war was the Holocaust (HAWL-uh-kawst). The **Holocaust** was the attempt by the Nazi government during World War II to eliminate Europe's Jews. Believing that the Germans were a superior race, the Nazis tried to destroy people who they believed were inferior, especially the Jews.

Even before the war began, the Nazi government began restricting the rights of Jews and others in Germany. For example, laws restricted Jews from holding government jobs or attending German schools. Nazis imprisoned countless Jews in camps.

Thousands of Jews fled Germany to escape persecution, but many had to remain behind because they were not allowed into other countries.

Germany's expansion into Eastern Europe brought millions more Jews under Hitler's control. In 1942 the Nazi government ordered the

Anne Frank (1929–1945)

Anne Frank was a Jewish teenager living in Frankfurt, Germany, when Hitler came to power. When the Nazis' treatment of German Jews became too aggressive, Anne and her family moved to Amsterdam in the Netherlands. However, soon afterward, the Nazis began rounding up Jews there. So the Franks were forced to hide in a friend's home.

Anne could bring only a few items with her. She brought pictures of movie stars, books, and a diary her parents had given her on her 13th birthday. While in hiding, Anne wrote in her diary. Her diary became an important record of the Franks' years in hiding.

For two years, the Franks lived in constant fear of being caught by the Nazis. On August 4, 1944, they were discovered. For the next seven months, Anne and her family were moved from one concentration camp to another. Her mother died at Auschwitz, in Poland. Anne and her sister were moved to Bergen-Belsen in Germany, where they died of disease in March 1945. Anne Frank's father was the only family member to survive the war. Later, he published her diary.

Make Inferences
Why do you think Anne Frank's diary became an important record of this time period?

destruction of Europe's entire Jewish population. The Nazis used mass executions and concentration camps, like Auschwitz in Poland, to murder about 6 million Jews.

The Nazis did face resistance. Some Jews fought back. For example, Jews in Warsaw, Poland, staged an uprising. Some non-Jewish Europeans tried to save Jews from the Nazis. German factory owner Oskar Schindler, for example, saved Jews by employing them in his factories. By the time the Nazis were defeated, they had killed about two-thirds of Europe's Jews and several million non-Jews.

Reading Check
Analyze Causes
Why did Hitler's Nazi government attempt to destroy the Jews?

End of the War

The Allies did not fare well in the early years of the war. Victories in 1943 and 1944, though, helped them end World War II.

Allies Are Victorious In early 1943 U.S. and British forces gained control of North Africa. Next, they invaded Italy, forcing Mussolini to surrender. That same year, the Allies defeated the Japanese in several key battles. In the east, Soviet troops forced Germany to retreat.

In June 1944 Allied forces landed on the beaches of Normandy, France. The invasion, or D-Day as it was called, dealt a serious blow to the Axis. It paved the way for Allied forces to advance on Germany.

By the spring of 1945, Allied troops had crossed into German territory. In May 1945 Germany surrendered. In August 1945 the United States used

Timeline: World War II

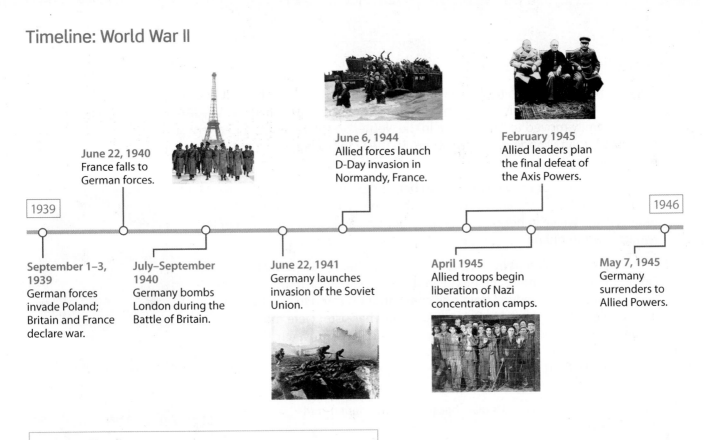

June 22, 1940
France falls to German forces.

June 6, 1944
Allied forces launch D-Day invasion in Normandy, France.

February 1945
Allied leaders plan the final defeat of the Axis Powers.

1939

1946

September 1–3, 1939
German forces invade Poland; Britain and France declare war.

July–September 1940
Germany bombs London during the Battle of Britain.

June 22, 1941
Germany launches invasion of the Soviet Union.

April 1945
Allied troops begin liberation of Nazi concentration camps.

May 7, 1945
Germany surrenders to Allied Powers.

Interpret Timelines
About how long after the beginning of the war did Germany invade the Soviet Union?

a powerful new weapon, the atomic bomb, to bring the war with Japan to an end. After almost six years of fighting, World War II was over.

Results of the War The war had a huge impact on the world. It resulted in millions of deaths, tensions between the Allies, and the creation of the United Nations.

World War II was the deadliest conflict in history. More than 50 million people lost their lives. Millions more were wounded.

The United States did not want to repeat the mistakes of the Treaty of Versailles, which left Germany in hopeless debt after World War I. Therefore, the United States created the European Recovery Program, or Marshall Plan, that provided money and other assistance to help rebuild 16 European countries after World War II.

Japan also was left devastated by World War II. With the end of the war, U.S. forces under General Douglas MacArthur occupied Japan and began a series of reforms to help rebuild the country and to keep communism from taking hold. As part of the reform, Japan's emperor lost most of his authority. Instead, power was given to an elected parliament. The Americans also helped strengthen and modernize the Japanese economy.

Costs of World War II	
Military deaths	22,000,000
Military wounded	34,000,000
Civilian deaths	30,000,000
Financial cost to governments	$1,000,000,000,000

Analyze Visuals
What does the high number of civilian deaths tell you about where the fighting took place?

Sources: The National WWII Museum, New Orleans; TIME magazine; Encyclopaedia Britannica

Causes and Effects of World War II

Causes

- Germany invades neighboring countries in an effort to build a new German empire under Nazi rule.
- Japan invades countries in Asia.

Effects

- More than 50 million people are killed.
- The Jewish population in Europe is almost completely wiped out by the Holocaust.
- The United States and the Soviet Union emerge as the world's strongest powers.
- Japan loses all acquired territory and is occupied by the Allies until 1952.

Reading Check
Summarize What were the main results of World War II?

The United States and the Soviet Union emerged from the war as the most powerful countries in the world. An intense rivalry developed between the two countries.

After the war, people hoped to prevent another deadly conflict. In 1945 some 50 nations formed the United Nations, an international peacekeeping organization.

Summary and Preview World War II was the deadliest war in history. Next, you will learn about developments in Europe during the postwar period.

Lesson 5 Assessment

Review Ideas, Terms, and Places

1. a. Define What was the Great Depression?

b. Explain How did economic problems in the United States lead to the Great Depression?

2. a. Describe What led to the outbreak of World War II?

b. Predict What might have happened if Great Britain had fallen to Germany?

3. a. Identify What was the Holocaust?

b. Make Inferences Why did the Nazis target certain groups for elimination?

4. a. Recall What events led to Germany's surrender?

b. Analyze How did World War II change Europe?

Critical Thinking

5. Sequence Draw a timeline like this one. Use your notes on important events to place the main events and their dates on the timeline.

Europe since 1945

The Big Idea

After years of division during the Cold War, today Europe is working toward unity.

Main Ideas

- The Cold War divided Europe between democratic and Communist nations.

- Many Eastern European countries changed boundaries and forms of government at the end of the Cold War.

- European cooperation has brought economic and political change to Europe.

Key Terms

superpowers
Cold War
arms race
common market
European Union (EU)
refugee
asylum
migrant

If YOU lived there . . .

It is November 1989, and you live on the East German side of Berlin. For years the Berlin Wall has divided your city in two. The government has carefully controlled who could cross the border. One night, you hear an exciting rumor—the gate through the wall is open. People in East and West Berlin can now travel back and forth freely. Young Berliners are celebrating in the streets.

What will this change mean for your country?

The Cold War

Although Europeans were relieved when World War II ended, new problems soon arose. Countries whose governments and economies had been weakened during the war had to work to strengthen them. Entire cities had to be rebuilt. Most importantly, postwar tensions between the Allies divided Europe.

Superpowers Face Off The United States and the Soviet Union emerged from World War II as the world's most powerful nations. Allies during the war, the two **superpowers,** or strong and influential countries, now distrusted each other. Growing hostility between these superpowers led to the **Cold War,** a period of tense rivalry between the United States and the Soviet Union.

Much of the hostility between the Soviet Union and the United States focused on political and economic differences. The United States is a democracy, with an economy based on free enterprise. The Soviet Union was a Communist country, in which individual freedoms were limited. Its leaders exerted strict control over the political system and the economy. These basic differences separated the two countries.

A Divided Europe The Cold War divided Europe into non-Communist and Communist countries. Most of Western Europe supported democracy and the United States. Much of Eastern Europe practiced Soviet-style communism.

Within this divided Europe was a divided Germany. After World War II, the Allies had separated Germany into four zones. By 1948 the Western Allies were ready to reunite their

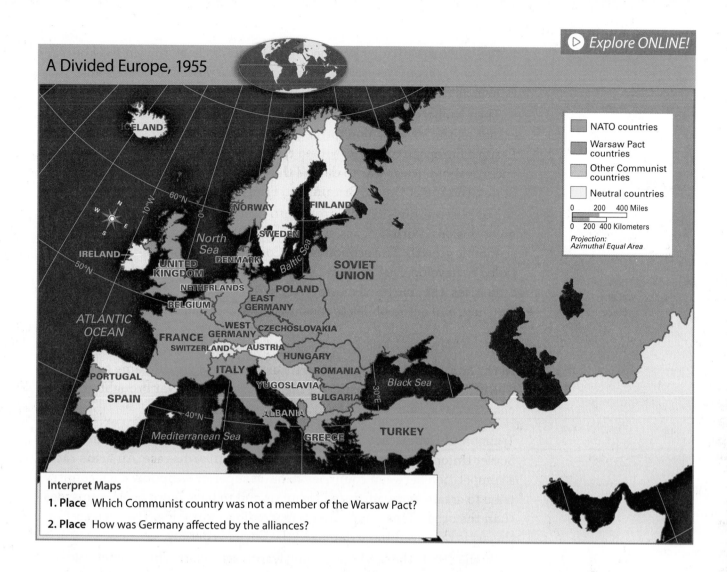

A Divided Europe, 1955

Explore ONLINE!

Legend:
- NATO countries
- Warsaw Pact countries
- Other Communist countries
- Neutral countries

0   200   400 Miles
0 200 400 Kilometers

Projection:
Azimuthal Equal Area

Interpret Maps

1. **Place** Which Communist country was not a member of the Warsaw Pact?

2. **Place** How was Germany affected by the alliances?

zones. However, the Soviet government feared the threat that a united Germany might pose. The next year, the Western zones were joined to form the Federal Republic of Germany, or West Germany. The Soviets helped to establish the German Democratic Republic, or East Germany. The city of Berlin, located within East Germany, was itself divided into East and West. In 1961 Communist leaders built the Berlin Wall to prevent any East Germans from fleeing to the West.

Causes and Effects of the Cold War

Causes	Effects
• Rivalry develops between the United States and the Soviet Union after World War II.	• Alliances divide Europe between Communist and non-Communist countries.
• Hostilities increase between democratic and Communist governments.	• Germany is divided into two separate countries.
• The superpowers dispute the division of Germany after World War II.	• The United States and the Soviet Union engage in a nuclear arms race.
• The superpowers compete to win the loyalty of non-European countries by providing aid, military equipment, advisers, food, etc.	• The political and economic development of many developing countries becomes more dependent on superpower approval.

New alliances divided Europe even further. In 1949 the United States joined with several Western nations to create a powerful new alliance known as NATO, or the North Atlantic Treaty Organization.

The members of NATO agreed to protect each other if attacked. In response, the Soviet Union formed its own alliance, the Warsaw Pact. Most Eastern European countries joined the Warsaw Pact. The two alliances used the threat of nuclear war to defend themselves. By the 1960s the United States, the Soviet Union, Britain, and France all had nuclear weapons.

The postwar division of Europe into East and West had a lasting effect on both sides. With U.S. assistance, many Western countries experienced economic growth. The economies of Communist Eastern Europe, however, failed to develop. Due to their lack of a market economy and strong industries, they suffered many shortages. They often lacked enough food, clothing, and automobiles to meet demand.

Reading Check
Summarize How did the Cold War affect Europe?

The End of the Cold War

In the late 1980s tensions between East and West finally came to an end. The collapse of communism and the end of the Cold War brought great changes to Europe.

Triumph of Democracy During the Cold War, the United States and the Soviet Union competed against each other in an arms race. An **arms race** is a competition between countries to build superior weapons. Each country tried to create more-advanced weapons and to have more nuclear missiles than the other. This arms race was incredibly expensive. The high cost of the arms race eventually damaged the Soviet economy.

By the 1980s the Soviet economy was in serious trouble. Soviet leader Mikhail Gorbachev (GAWR-buh-chawf) hoped to solve the many problems his country faced. He reduced government control of the economy and introduced democratic elections. He improved relations with the United States. Along with U.S. president Ronald Reagan, Gorbachev took steps to slow the arms race.

—— BIOGRAPHY ——

Mikhail Gorbachev

(1931–)

Mikhail Gorbachev was a key figure in bringing the Cold War to an end. In 1985 Communist officials appointed Gorbachev the leader of the Soviet Union. He quickly enacted reforms to modernize his country. He expanded basic freedoms, such as freedom of speech and freedom of the press. His democratic reforms helped bring an end to communism in the Soviet Union. In 1990 Mikhail Gorbachev won the Nobel Peace Prize for his efforts to end the Cold War and promote peace.

Evaluate
Do you think Gorbachev was a popular ruler? Why or why not?

In part because of these new policies, reform movements soon spread. Beginning in 1989, democratic movements swept through the East. For example, Poland and Czechoslovakia threw off Communist rule. Joyful Germans tore down the Berlin Wall that separated East and West. Several Soviet republics began to demand their independence. Finally, in December 1991 the Soviet Union broke apart.

Changes in Eastern Europe The end of the Cold War brought many changes to Eastern Europe. These changes resulted from Germany's reunification, the creation of new countries, and rising ethnic tensions in southeastern Europe.

The reunification of East and West Germany was one of many changes in Eastern Europe that marked the end of the Cold War. After the fall of the Berlin Wall in 1989, thousands of East Germans began demanding change. In early 1990 the Communist government crumbled. A few months later, the governments of East and West Germany agreed to reunite. After 45 years of division, Germany was reunited.

Other important changes occurred in Eastern Europe after the Cold War. The breakup of the Soviet Union created more than a dozen independent nations. The Russian Federation is the largest and most powerful of these new countries. Ukraine, Lithuania, Belarus, and others also emerged from the former Soviet Union.

Ethnic conflicts have also transformed Eastern Europe since the end of the Cold War. For example, tensions between ethnic groups in Czechoslovakia and Yugoslavia led to the breakup of both countries.

The Fall of Communism

Reforms in the Soviet Union in the 1980s encouraged support for democracy throughout Eastern Europe.

Fall of the Berlin Wall

East and West Germans celebrate the fall of the Berlin Wall.

Democracy in Czechoslovakia

In 1989 pro-democracy demonstrations swept Czechoslovakia. Rallies like this one led to the collapse of Czechoslovakia's Communist government.

Analyze Visuals
What role did the people play in communism's collapse?

Academic
Vocabulary
advocate to plead
in favor of

Reading Check
Draw Conclusions
How did the end
of the Cold War
affect Europe?

In Czechoslovakia, ethnic tensions divided the country. Disputes between the country's two main ethnic groups emerged in the early 1990s. Both the Czechs and the Slovaks <u>advocated</u> separate governments. In January 1993 Czechoslovakia peacefully divided into two countries—the Czech Republic and Slovakia.

While ethnic problems in the former Czechoslovakia were peaceful, ethnic tension in Yugoslavia triggered violence. After the collapse of communism, several Yugoslav republics declared their independence. Different ethnic groups fought each other for control of territory. Yugoslavia's civil wars resulted in years of fighting and thousands of deaths. By 1994 Yugoslavia had split into six countries—Bosnia and Herzegovina, Croatia, Macedonia, Serbia, Montenegro, and Slovenia.

European Cooperation

Many changes shaped postwar Europe. One of the most important of those changes was the creation of an organization that now joins together most of the countries of Europe.

A European Community Two world wars tore Europe apart in the 1900s. After World War II, many of Europe's leaders began to look for ways to prevent another deadly war. Some people believed that creating a feeling of community in Europe would make countries less likely to go to war. Leaders like Great Britain's Winston Churchill believed the countries of Europe should cooperate rather than compete. They believed strong economic and political ties were the key.

Six countries—Belgium, France, Italy, Luxembourg, the Netherlands, and West Germany—took the first steps toward European unity. In the early 1950s these six countries joined to create a united economic community. The organization's goal was to form a **common market,** a group of nations that cooperate to make trade among members easier. This European common market, created in 1957, made trade easier among member countries. Over time, other nations joined. Europeans had begun to create a new sense of unity.

The European Union Since its beginning in the 1950s, many new nations have become members of this European community, now known as the European Union. The **European Union (EU)** is an organization that promotes political and economic cooperation in Europe. Today, the European Union has 28 members. Together, they deal with a wide range of issues, including trade, the environment, and migration. The EU also protects the common good and individual rights of its members by enforcing international rules and laws.

The European Union has executive, legislative, and judicial branches. The EU is run by a commission made up of one representative from each member nation. Two legislative groups, the Council of the European Union and the European Parliament, debate and make laws. Finally, the Court of Justice resolves disputes and enforces EU laws.

The European Union

Country	Year Admitted	Monetary Unit	Representatives in the European Parliament
Austria	1995	Euro	18
Belgium	1958	Euro	21
Bulgaria	2007	Lev	17
Croatia	2013	Kuna	11
Cyprus	2004	Euro	6
Czech Republic (Czechia)	2004	Koruna	21
Denmark	1973	Krone	13
Estonia	2004	Euro	6
Finland	1995	Euro	13
France	1958	Euro	74
Germany	1958	Euro	96
Greece	1981	Euro	21
Hungary	2004	Forint	21
Ireland	1973	Euro	11
Italy	1958	Euro	73
Latvia	2004	Euro	8
Lithuania	2004	Euro	11
Luxembourg	1958	Euro	6
Malta	2004	Euro	6
The Netherlands	1958	Euro	26
Poland	2004	Zloty	51
Portugal	1986	Euro	21
Romania	2007	Leu	32
Slovakia	2004	Euro	13
Slovenia	2004	Euro	8
Spain	1986	Euro	54
Sweden	1995	Krona	20
United Kingdom*	1973	Pound	73

* The United Kingdom plans to leave the EU in 2019.

Source: European Union, 2017

Draw Conclusions
What are the most powerful countries in the European Parliament?

Benefits of Membership in the European Union

Trade	Before	After
	• European countries had to pay customs duties, or taxes, on goods they traded with other European countries. • Many European countries' economies were small compared to those of larger nations such as the United States.	• EU countries are part of a common market. They can trade freely with each other without paying duties. • EU countries create a combined economy that is one of the largest in the world.
Currency	**Before**	**After**
	• Each European country had its own separate currency, or form of money. • European countries and their citizens had to exchange currencies to buy goods from other European countries.	• Most EU countries share one currency, the euro. • EU countries and their citizens can use the euro to buy goods and trade throughout the EU.
Work and Travel	**Before**	**After**
	• Europeans had to have passports or other special permits to travel from one European country to another. • Europeans had to obtain permission to live and work in other countries in Europe.	• Citizens of EU countries do not need passports or special permits to travel throughout most of the EU. • Citizens of EU countries can live and work anywhere in the EU without having to obtain permission.

Interpret Charts
Based on the chart, what are two benefits of EU membership?

Through the European Union, the countries of Europe work together toward common economic goals. The EU helps its member nations compete with economic powers like the United States and Japan. In 1999 the EU introduced a common currency, the euro, which many member countries now use. The euro has made trade much easier.

The European Union has helped unify Europe. In recent years, many countries from Eastern Europe have joined the EU. Other countries hope to join in the future. However, the EU has experienced some turmoil in recent times because some members disagree with specific policies.

Link to Economics

The Euro

The front sides of the euro coins all have the same image, but the backs feature a unique symbol for each country. Euro bills show symbols of unity.

In September 2016 Brexit supporters who want the United Kingdom to leave the European Union hold a rally outside the British Parliament.

For example, the long, bloody civil war in Syria has created a refugee crisis. A **refugee** is someone who has been forced to flee his or her country because of persecution, war, or violence. For several years, over a thousand children a day fled Syria, alone or with family members. They face an uncertain future. Many refugees want **asylum,** or protection, in Europe to start new lives. Others, called **migrants,** have fled violence and poverty in Africa, the Middle East, and other regions. More than a million migrants and refugees crossed into Europe in 2015. Some traveled overland. Many others braved the Mediterranean Sea on overcrowded boats. Some were not so lucky. In April 2015 approximately 800 migrants drowned when their boat capsized.

European countries struggled to figure out what to do with their new arrivals. The crisis caused divisions in the European Union about how best to resettle so many people. Many Europeans welcomed the refugees and helped them find homes, jobs, and schools for their children. Others believed the newcomers might take their jobs or not adapt to a different way of life. These fears helped create a new spirit of nationalism in Europe. Some people believed that their own country might be better off both politically and economically outside the European Union.

In June 2016 the United Kingdom voted to leave the European Union. British citizens approved the Brexit vote (for "British Exit") by a narrow margin. It is the first time a member country has decided to leave the EU. Both sides have two years to work out an exit agreement. Despite difficulties, EU leaders hope to continue their goal to bring the nations of Europe closer together.

Summary The establishment of the European Union helped unify much of Europe after years of division during the Cold War.

Reading Check
Find Main Ideas
How has cooperation in Europe affected the region?

Lesson 6 Assessment

Review Ideas, Terms, and Places

1. **a. Recall** What was the Cold War?

   b. Analyze Why was Europe divided during the Cold War?

2. **a. Identify** What new countries were formed after the end of the Cold War?

   b. Compare and Contrast How were ethnic tensions in Czechoslovakia and Yugoslavia similar and different?

   c. Compare How did the roles that the United States and the Soviet Union played after World War II change the political and economic development of other countries in the world?

3. **a. Define** What is a common market?

   b. Make Inferences Why did some Europeans believe stronger economic and political ties could prevent war in Europe?

Critical Thinking

4. **Summarize** Use your notes and the chart below to summarize the effect that each event had on the different regions of Europe. Write a sentence that summarizes the effect of each event.

	Cold War	End of Cold War	European Union
Western Europe			
Eastern Europe			

Social Studies Skills

Interpret Political Cartoons

Define the Skill

Political cartoons are drawings that express views on important political or social issues. The ability to interpret political cartoons will help you understand issues and people's attitudes about them.

Political cartoons use images and words to convey a message about a particular event, person, or issue in the news. Most political cartoons use symbols to represent those ideas. For example, political cartoonists often use Uncle Sam to represent the United States. They also use titles and captions to express their point of view.

Soviet leader Mikhail Gorbachev examines a broken hammer and sickle.

Learn the Skill

Examine the cartoon. Then, answer the following questions to interpret its message.

1. Read any title, labels, or captions to identify the subject of the cartoon. What information does the caption for this cartoon give you? To what event does this cartoon refer?

2. Identify the people and symbols in the cartoon. What person is pictured in this cartoon? What does the crushed hammer and sickle represent?

3. What message is the cartoonist trying to convey?

Practice the Skill

Use your new skills to interpret a recent political cartoon. Locate a political cartoon that deals with an issue or event that has been in the news recently. Then, answer the questions below.

1. What issue or event does the cartoon address?

2. What people or symbols are represented in the cartoon?

3. What point is the cartoon attempting to make?

Module 13 Assessment

Review Vocabulary, Terms, and Places

Match the words or names with their definitions or descriptions.

1. arms race

2. Enlightenment

3. Axis Powers

4. dictator

5. suffragettes

6. nationalism

7. circumnavigate

8. strategy

9. Treaty of Versailles

10. trench warfare

a. a powerful ruler who exerts complete control and often rules by force

b. a period during which people used reason to examine society and politics

c. a style of fighting in which each side fights from deep ditches dug into the ground

d. British women who campaigned for the right to vote

e. a plan for fighting a battle or war

f. Magellan led a voyage that was the first to do this to Earth

g. the alliance of Germany, Italy, and Japan in World War II

h. devotion and loyalty to one's country

i. a competition between countries for superior weapons

j. its harsh terms ended World War I and led to World War II

Comprehension and Critical Thinking

Lesson 1

11. a. Identify What did Christopher Columbus and Ferdinand Magellan achieve?

b. Identify Cause and Effect How did the Scientific Revolution help contribute to the Age of Exploration?

c. Elaborate How did European colonization of the Americas affect European society?

Lesson 2

12. a. Recall What three goals did the Enlightenment thinkers believe the use of reason could achieve?

b. Compare What ideas did John Locke and Jean-Jacques Rousseau share?

c. Elaborate How did the English Bill of Rights and the Declaration of the Rights of Man and of the Citizen change the power of monarchs?

Lesson 3

13. a. Recall In which country did the Industrial Revolution start?

b. Identify Cause and Effect How did industrial growth lead to improvements in society?

c. Evaluate Which Industrial Revolution invention do you think was most significant? Why?

Lesson 4

14. a. Recall What causes led to the outbreak of World War I?

b. Draw Conclusions How did the U.S. entry into World War I affect the war's outcome?

c. Elaborate Why do you think World War I led to revolutions in some countries?

Module 13 Assessment, continued

Lesson 5

15. **a. Identify** What two alliances fought in World War II? What countries belonged to each?

 b. Compare In what ways were Joseph Stalin, Benito Mussolini, and Adolf Hitler similar?

 c. Elaborate In your opinion, how were the Allies able to win World War II?

Lesson 6

16. **a. Identify** Into what alliances was Europe divided during the Cold War?

 b. Analyze How did the Cold War come to an end?

 c. Predict Do you think that the European Union will hurt or help Europe? Explain.

Reading Skills

Use Context Clues—Contrast Use the Reading Skills taught in this module to complete the following activity.

Use context clues to determine the meaning of the underlined words in the sentences below.

17. During World War II, people who aided Jews were often underlined detained rather than set free.

18. Many celebrations at the end of the Cold War were underlined frenzied, not calm and orderly.

19. European dictators who rose to power were underlined ruthless as opposed to kind.

Social Studies Skills

Interpret Political Cartoons *Examine the political cartoon, then answer the following questions.*

20. What event does the cartoon depict?

21. What symbols does the cartoon use? To what do those symbols refer?

22. What point is the artist trying to make?

Map Activity

23. **Europe, 1989** On a separate sheet of paper, match the letters on the map with their correct labels.

Berlin	Poland	West Germany
London	Moscow	Yugoslavia
Paris		

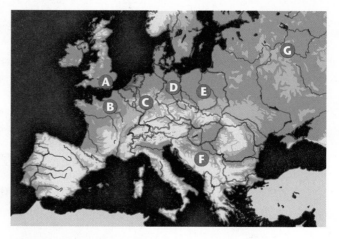

Focus on Writing

24. **Write a Diary Entry** Imagine you are a person who has witnessed the events of the 20th century. Review your notes to organize the diary of your imaginary person. Divide your diary into three periods—World War I, World War II, and 1945–today. Describe the events your imaginary person experienced from his or her point of view. Remember to describe his or her thoughts and feelings about each event.

Dear home: LETTERS FROM WWI

When U.S. troops arrived in Europe in 1917 to fight in World War I, the war had been dragging on for nearly three years. The American soldiers suddenly found themselves in the midst of chaos. Each day, they faced the threats of machine-gun fire, poison gas, and aerial attacks. Still, the arrival of American reinforcements had sparked a new zeal among the Allies, who believed the new forces could finally turn the tide in their favor. The letters soldiers wrote to their families back home reveal the many emotions they felt on the battlefield: confusion about their surroundings, fear for their own safety, concern for friends and loved ones, and hope that the war would soon be over.

Explore World War I online through the eyes of the soldiers who fought in it. You can find a wealth of information, video clips, primary sources, activities, and more through your online textbook.

"I have been on every front in France. You can't imagine how torn up this country really is. Every where there are wire entanglements and trenches and dugouts. Even out of the war zone there are entanglements and dugouts to protect the civilians from air raids."

—Corp. Albert Smith, U.S. soldier

Letter from France
Read the document to learn about one soldier's observations of wartime life.

Over There
Watch the video to learn about the experiences of American soldiers on the way to Europe and upon their arrival.

War on the Western Front
Watch the video to hear one soldier's vivid account of battle and its aftermath.

Surrender!
Watch the video to experience soldiers' reactions to the news that the war was finally over.

Southern Europe

Essential Question

How has climate influenced the land and people of Southern Europe?

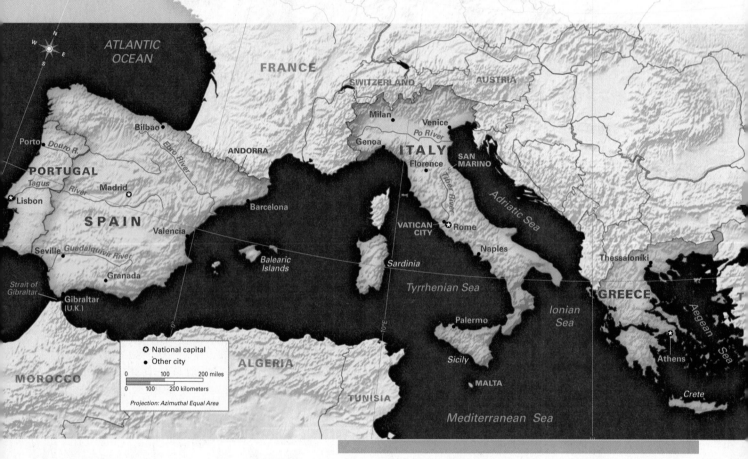

In this module, you will learn about the mild climates of Southern Europe and the influential civilizations that have developed there.

What You Will Learn

▶ Explore ONLINE!

HISTORY.

VIDEOS, including . . .
• Pompeii

☑ Document-Based Investigations

☑ Graphic Organizers

☑ Interactive Games

☑ Interactive Map: Southern Europe: Physical

☑ Image Carousel: Mediterranean Climate

☑ Interactive Chart: Eras in Italian History

Geography Mountains cover large areas of Southern Europe. The Dolomites, shown here, are in northern Italy.

Culture Bullfights are popular events in parts of Spain. Bullfighters, called matadors, are honored members of society.

History Greece was the home of Europe's first great civilization. The ruins in Delphi are more than 2,300 years old.

Reading Social Studies

Ask Questions

READING FOCUS

Reading is one place where asking questions will never get you in trouble. The five *W* questions can help you be sure you understand the material you read. After you read a section, ask yourself the 5 *W*s: *Who* was this section about? *What* did they do? *Where* and *when* did they live? *Why* did they do what they did? See the example below to learn how this reading strategy can help you identify the main points of a passage.

> Many Greeks were not happy under Turkish rule. They wanted to be free of foreign influences. In the early 1800s, they rose up against the Turks. The rebellion seemed likely to fail, but the Greeks received help from other European countries and drove the Turks out. After the rebellion, Greece became a monarchy.

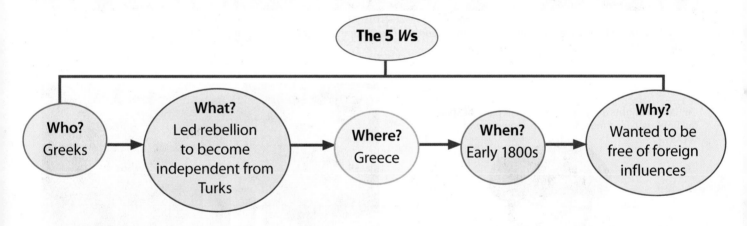

YOU TRY IT!

With a partner, read the following passage to each other and answer the 5 *W*s to check your understanding of it.

> Italy remained divided into small states until the mid-1800s. At that time, a rise in nationalism, or strong patriotic feelings for a country, led people across Italy to fight for unification. As a result of their efforts, Italy became a unified kingdom in 1861.

As you read this module, ask questions to help you understand the text.

Physical Geography

The Big Idea

The peninsulas of Southern Europe have rocky terrains and sunny, mild climates.

Main Ideas

- Southern Europe's physical features include rugged mountains and narrow coastal plains.
- The region's climate and resources support such industries as agriculture, fishing, and tourism.

Key Terms and Places

Mediterranean Sea
Pyrenees
Apennines
Alps
Mediterranean climate

If YOU lived there . . .

You are in a busy fish market in a small town on the coast of Italy, near the Mediterranean Sea. It is early morning. Colorful fishing boats have just pulled into shore with their catch of fresh fish and seafood. They unload their nets of slippery octopus and wriggling shrimp. Others bring silvery sea bass. You are looking forward to lunch—perhaps a tasty fish soup or pasta dish.

How does the Mediterranean affect your life?

Physical Features

The continent of Europe has often been called a "peninsula of peninsulas." Europe juts out from Asia like one big peninsula. From that one big peninsula, smaller peninsulas extend into the many bodies of water that surround the continent.

Look at the map of Southern Europe on the first page of this module. Do you see the three large peninsulas that extend south from Europe? From west to east, these are the Iberian Peninsula, the Italian Peninsula, and the Balkan Peninsula. Together with some large islands, they form the region of Southern Europe. Greece, Italy, Spain, and Portugal are countries in Southern Europe.

Southern Europe is also known as Mediterranean Europe. Many of the countries of Southern Europe have long coastlines on the **Mediterranean Sea.** In addition to this common location on the Mediterranean, the countries of Southern Europe share many common physical features.

Landforms The three peninsulas of Southern Europe are largely covered with rugged mountains. In Greece, for example, about three-fourths of the land is mountainous. Because much of the land is so rugged, farming and travel in Southern Europe can be a challenge.

The mountains of Southern Europe form several large ranges. On the Iberian Peninsula, the **Pyrenees** (PIR-uh-neez) form a boundary between Spain and France to the north. Italy

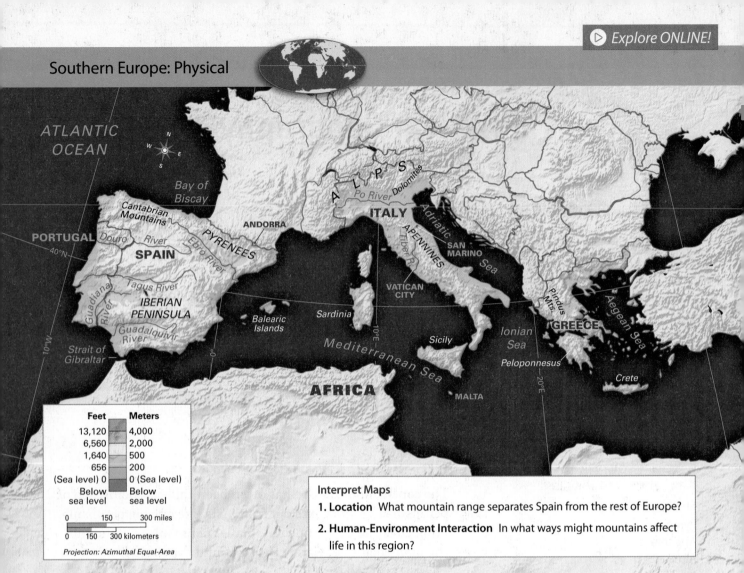

Explore ONLINE!

Interpret Maps

1. **Location** What mountain range separates Spain from the rest of Europe?

2. **Human-Environment Interaction** In what ways might mountains affect life in this region?

has two major ranges. The **Apennines** (A-puh-nynz) run along the whole peninsula, and the **Alps**—Europe's highest mountains—are in the north. The Pindus Mountains cover much of Greece.

Southern Europe's mountains extend into the sea as well, where they rise above the water to form islands. Southern Europe is known for its mountains and seas. The Aegean Sea east of Greece is home to more than 2,000 islands. Southern Europe also has many larger islands formed by undersea mountains. These include Crete, which is south of Greece; Sicily, at the southern tip of Italy; and many others.

Not all of Southern Europe is rocky and mountainous, though. Some flat plains lie in the region. Most of these plains are along the coast and in the valleys of major rivers. It is here that most farming in Southern Europe takes place. It is also here that most of the region's people live.

Water Features Since Southern Europe is mostly peninsulas and islands, water is central to the region's geography. No place in Southern Europe is very far from a major body of water. The largest of these bodies of water is the Mediterranean, but the Adriatic, Aegean, and Ionian seas are also important to the region. For many centuries, these seas have given the people of Southern Europe food and a relatively easy way to travel around the region.

Only a few large rivers run through Southern Europe. The region's longest river is the Tagus (TAY-guhs), which flows across the Iberian Peninsula. In northern Italy, the Po runs through one of Southern Europe's most fertile and densely populated areas. Other rivers run out of the mountains and into the many surrounding seas.

Reading Check
Find Main Ideas
What are the region's major features?

Mediterranean Climate

Southern Europe is known for its Mediterranean climate, which features warm, dry summers and mild, wet winters. This climate affects nearly every aspect of life in the region.

Agriculture The climate of Southern Europe is ideal for growing many crops. Here, Portuguese farmers harvest grapes.

Tourism The region's mild and sunny climate draws millions of tourists to places like this beach in Ibiza, Spain.

Vegetation This field in Tuscany, a region of Italy, shows the variety of plants that thrive in Southern Europe's climate.

Architecture Climate also affects architecture in Southern Europe. Buildings, like these in Greece, are airy and made of light materials to reflect sunlight and heat.

Analyze Visuals
What are four ways in which the Mediterranean climate affects life in Southern Europe?

On Greece's coast, mountains and sea come together to create a dramatic landscape.

Climate and Resources

Southern Europe is famous for its pleasant climate. Most of the region enjoys warm, sunny days and mild nights for most of the year. Little rain falls in the summer, falling instead during the mild winter. In fact, the type of climate found across Southern Europe is called a **Mediterranean climate** because it is common in this region.

The region's climate is also one of its most valuable resources. The mild climate is ideal for growing a variety of crops, from citrus fruits and grapes to olives and wheat. These crops are important products traded with other countries. In addition, millions of tourists are drawn to the region each year by its climate, beaches, and breathtaking scenery.

The sea is also an important resource in Southern Europe. Many of the region's largest cities are ports from which goods are shipped all over the world. This trade supports the economies of Southern European countries. In addition, the nearby seas are full of fish and shellfish, which provide the basis for profitable fishing industries.

Reading Check
Form Generalizations
How is a mild climate important to Southern Europe?

Summary and Preview In this lesson, you learned about the physical features of Southern Europe. In the next lesson, you will learn how those features affect life in two countries—Greece and Italy.

Lesson 1 Assessment

Review Ideas, Terms, and Places

1. **a. Recall** Which three peninsulas are in Southern Europe?

   b. Explain Why is the sea important to Southern Europe?

   c. Elaborate Why do you think most people in Southern Europe live on coastal plains or in river valleys?

2. **a. Describe** What is the Mediterranean climate like?

   b. Generalize How is climate an important resource for the region?

Critical Thinking

3. **Find Main Ideas** Draw a diagram like the one shown here. In the left oval, use your notes to explain how landforms affect life in Southern Europe. In the right oval, explain how climate affects life in the region.

Landforms   Climate

Greece and Italy

The Big Idea

Greece and Italy are home to two of the Western world's oldest and most influential civilizations.

Main Ideas

- Early in its history, Greece was the home of a great civilization, but it was later ruled by foreign powers.

- The Greek language, the Orthodox Church, and varied customs have helped shape Greece's culture.

- In Greece today, many people are looking for new economic opportunities.

- Italian history can be divided into three periods: ancient Rome, the Renaissance, and unified Italy.

- Religion and local traditions have helped shape Italy's culture.

- Italy today has two distinct economic regions—northern Italy and southern Italy.

Key Terms and Places

Orthodox Church
Athens
Christianity
Catholicism
pope
Vatican City
Sicily
Naples
Milan
Rome

If YOU lived there . . .

You live in a small town on one of the many Greek islands. White houses perch on steep streets leading down to the sea. Many tourists come here by boat after visiting the busy capital city of Athens. They tell you about the beautiful ancient buildings they saw there. But your island has ancient statues and temple sites, too. Still, some of your friends talk about moving to the city.

What might make people move to the city?

Greece's History

Greece is a country steeped in history. Home to one of the world's oldest civilizations, it has been called the birthplace of Western culture. Even today, remnants of ancient Greece can be found all over the country, and ideas from ancient thinkers continue to affect people's lives today.

Ancient Greece Theater, philosophy, democracy—these are just a few of the ideas that the modern world owes to ancient

An ancient Greek jar

Greece. The Greeks were pioneers in many fields, and their contributions still affect how we live and think.

In art, the Greeks created lifelike paintings and statues that served as examples for later artists to imitate. In architecture, they built temples of marble that continue to inspire architects around the world. The Greeks invented new forms of literature, including history and drama, and made advances in geometry and other branches of math that we still study. In philosophy, they created a system of reasoning that is the foundation for modern science. In government, Greeks created democracy, which inspired the government embraced by most people around the world today.

Proportion

The ancient Greeks were great admirers of mathematics. They thought math could be used in many areas of their lives. For example, they used it to design temples and other buildings.

Greek builders believed in a concept called the Golden Mean. This concept said that the height of a building should be a particular fraction of the building's width. If the building were too tall, they thought it would look flimsy. If it were too wide, it would look squat and ugly. As a result, these builders were very careful in planning their buildings. The Parthenon, the temple pictured here, was built using the Golden Mean. Many consider it to be the greatest of all Greek temples.

Make Generalizations
How did mathematical ideas influence ancient Greek architecture?

No ancient civilization lasted forever, though. In the 300s BC Greece became a part of Alexander the Great's empire, which also included Egypt and much of Southwest Asia. Under Alexander, Greek culture spread throughout his empire.

The Romans and the Turks Alexander's empire did not last very long. When it broke up, Greece became part of another empire, the Roman Empire. For about 300 years, the Greeks lived under Roman rule.

After about AD 400 the Roman Empire was divided into two parts. Greece became part of the Eastern, or Byzantine, Empire. The rulers of the Byzantine Empire admired Greek culture and encouraged people to adopt the Greek language and customs. They also encouraged people to adopt their religion, Christianity.

Greece was part of the Byzantine Empire for about 1,000 years. In the 1300s and 1400s, however, Greece was taken over by the Ottoman Turks from central Asia. The Turks were Muslim, but they allowed the people of Greece to remain Christian. Some elements of Greek culture, though, began to fade. For example, many people began speaking Turkish instead of Greek.

Independent Greece Many Greeks were not happy under Turkish rule. They wanted to be free of foreign influences. In the early 1800s they rose up against the Turks. The rebellion seemed likely to fail, but the Greeks received help from other European countries and drove the Turks out. After the rebellion, Greece became a monarchy.

Greece's government has changed many times since independence. The country's first kings took steps toward restoring democracy, but for most

Reading Check
Sequence What groups have ruled Greece throughout history?

of the 1900s the nation experienced instability. A military dictatorship ruled from 1967 to 1974. After its decline, democracy once again took root in the country where it was born nearly 2,500 years ago.

Greece's Culture

Over the course of its history, many factors have combined to shape Greece's culture. These factors include the Greek language, Christianity, and customs adopted from the many groups who have ruled Greece.

Language and Religion The people of Greece today speak a form of the same language their ancestors spoke long ago. In fact, Greek is one of the oldest languages still spoken in Europe today. The language has changed greatly over time, but it was never lost.

Although the Greeks maintained their language, their ancient religions have long since disappeared. Today, nearly everyone in Greece belongs to the **Orthodox Church,** a branch of Christianity that dates to the Byzantine Empire. Religion is important to the Greeks, and holidays such as Easter are popular times for celebration.

Customs Greek customs reflect the country's long history and its physical geography. Greek food, for example, is influenced both by products native to Greece and by groups who have ruled Greece over time.

Ingredients such as lamb, olives, and vegetables are easily available in Greece because they grow well there. As a result, the Greeks use lots of these ingredients in their cooking. Greek cuisine was later enhanced with ideas borrowed from other people. From the Turks, the Greeks learned to cook with yogurt and honey, and from the Italians they learned about pasta.

Greek meals are often eaten at family gatherings. For centuries, family has been central to Greek culture. Even as Greece is becoming more modernized, the family has remained the cornerstone of society.

Reading Check
Summarize What are two dominant elements of Greek culture?

Easter in Greece

Easter is one of the most sacred days of the year for Orthodox Christians. All over Greece, people celebrate Easter with festivals, feasts, and special rituals.

Analyze Visuals
What evidence in this photo suggests that Easter is a major celebration?

The priests carry containers of holy water. Later, they will sprinkle this holy water on crowds as part of a blessing.

Many Easter ceremonies are led by an archbishop, a high-ranking official in the Orthodox Church.

Priests wear richly decorated robes as part of their Easter celebration.

Greece Today

When many people think of Greece now, they think about the country's history. In fact, Greece's past often overshadows its present. Today, though, Greece is a largely urbanized society with a diverse economy.

Urban and Rural Greece About three-fifths of all people in Greece today live in cities. Of these cities, **Athens**—the nation's capital—is by far the largest. In fact, almost one-third of the country's entire population lives in or around the city of Athens.

Athens is a huge city where old and new mix. Modern skyscrapers rise high above the ancient ruins of Greek temples. Most of the country's industry is centered there. However, this industry has resulted in air pollution, which damages the ancient ruins and causes health problems.

Outside of the city, Greek life is very different. People in rural areas still live largely as people have lived for centuries. Many live in isolated mountain villages, where they grow crops and raise sheep and goats. Village life often centers around the village square. People meet there to discuss local events and make decisions.

Greece's Economy One industry in which Greece excels is shipping. Greece has one of the largest shipping fleets in the world. Greek ships can be found in ports all around the world, loaded with cargo from countries in Europe and other parts of the world.

Another profitable industry in Greece is tourism. Millions of people from around the world visit every year. Some are drawn to ancient ruins in Athens and other parts of the country. Others prefer the sunny, sandy beaches of Greece's many islands. Despite the boost that tourism provides, Greece has in recent years experienced severe economic troubles.

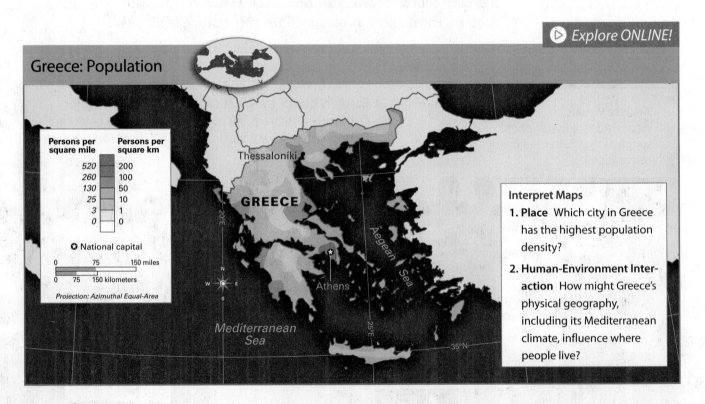

Explore ONLINE!

Greece: Population

Persons per square mile	Persons per square km
520	200
260	100
130	50
25	10
3	1
0	0

✪ National capital

0   75   150 miles
0   75   150 kilometers

Projection: Azimuthal Equal-Area

Thessaloníki

GREECE

Athens

Aegean Sea

Mediterranean Sea

Interpret Maps

1. **Place** Which city in Greece has the highest population density?

2. **Human-Environment Interaction** How might Greece's physical geography, including its Mediterranean climate, influence where people live?

In 2009 an international economic crisis exposed the Greek government's huge debt. To avoid bankruptcy, Greek leaders in 2012 agreed to accept billions of dollars in loans from the International Money Fund and the European Union. In addition, Greece's parliament approved government spending cuts, which led to violent protests.

Greece's gross domestic product (GDP) has steeply dropped. The GDP of a country is the market value of all final goods and services produced within that country during a given time period. It is a key indicator of economic growth. Greece's GDP in 2016 was 44 percent less than it was in 2008. This means that Greece's economic growth currently lags behind most other European nations.

A country's education system is another key factor in its economic success. Educated citizens are more likely to rise above poverty. Currently, Greece's education system ranks lower than other Southern European countries' systems.

Reading Check
Find Main Ideas What are the most important industries in Greece?

Italy's History

Locate Italy on the political map at the beginning of this module. As you can see on the map, Italy is located on the Mediterranean Sea near Greece. For centuries, Italy was the heart of one of the largest and most powerful states the world has ever seen. Even after that state collapsed, Italy remained a major influence on Europe and other parts of the world.

Ancient Rome The great civilization that developed in Italy was Rome. Built in the 700s BC as a tiny village, Rome grew to control nearly all the land around the Mediterranean Sea. At the height of the Roman Empire, the Romans controlled a huge empire that stretched from Britain in the northwest to the Persian Gulf. It included most of Europe as well as parts of southwest Asia and northern Africa.

Roman influences in the world can still be seen today. The Romans' art, architecture, and literature are still admired. Their laws and political ideas have influenced the governments and legal systems of many countries. In addition, the Romans helped spread **Christianity,** a major world religion based on the life and teachings of Jesus of Nazareth.

The Renaissance The Roman Empire collapsed in the AD 400s, largely due to weak leadership and invasions from outside. With no central government to unite them, Italy's cities formed their own states. Each had its own laws, its own government, and its own army. Wars between them were common.

The head of the Christian church was the pope, a Roman Catholic. A long series of popes governed the Papal States, which occupied most of central Italy, from 754 to 1870. Popes were powerful political figures with much influence over Europe's monarchs.

As time passed, the cities of Italy became major centers of trade. Merchants from these cities traveled to far-off places like China to bring goods back to Europe.

Many Italian merchants became very rich from this trade. With the money they made, these merchants sponsored artists and architects. Their support of the arts helped lead to the Renaissance, a period of great creativity in Europe. It lasted from about 1350 through the 1500s. During the Renaissance, artists and writers—many of them Italian—created some of the world's greatest works of art, architecture, and literature.

Unified Italy Italy remained divided into small states until the mid-1800s. At that time, a rise in nationalism, or strong patriotic feelings for a country, led people across Italy to fight for unification. As a result of their efforts, Italy became a unified kingdom in 1861.

In the 1920s a new government came to power. Under Benito Mussolini, Italy became a dictatorship. That dictatorship was short-lived, however. Mussolini joined Hitler to fight other countries of Europe in World War II. In 1945 Italy was defeated.

After World War II, Italy became a democracy. Since that time, power has rested in an elected parliament and prime minister. Also since the end of the war, Italy has developed one of the strongest economies in Europe.

Reading Check
Summarize What are some key periods in the history of Italy?

———BIOGRAPHY———

Giuseppe Garibaldi (1807–1882)

Italy's fight for unification was led by Italian revolutionary Giuseppe Garibaldi. When young, he served as a sailor and became a merchant captain. Eventually, Garibaldi served in the navy of the kingdom of Piedmont-Sardinia. While in the navy, he became an Italian nationalist.

Garibaldi took part in a mutiny intended to start a revolution in Piedmont. The mutiny failed. Garibaldi escaped punishment by fleeing to South America. Fighting against a dictator in Uruguay, he became a famous military leader. Garibaldi became known as a rebel leader for hire, based on his military experience and his strong drive to fight for freedom.

In 1848 Garibaldi took his Italian legion back to Italy and continued fighting for independence, this time for Italy. His determination to never surrender became an inspiration to Italians. He became a popular folk hero in his country.

Garibaldi joined the fight for the unification of Italy. In 1860 he led 30,000 men in the largest battle of his career. This army successfully unified southern and northern Italy.

In his old age, Giuseppe Garibaldi became a pacifist, believing that wars seldom achieved their goals. He worked for women's emancipation, racial equality, labor rights, and the abolition of capital punishment.

Summarize
Why did many Italians see Garibaldi as a folk hero?

Italy's Culture

For centuries, people around the world have admired and borrowed from Italian culture. Italy's culture has been shaped by many factors. Among these factors are the Roman Catholic Church, local traditions, and regional geography.

Religion Most Italians belong to the Roman Catholic Church. Historically, **Catholicism,** the largest branch of Christianity, has been the single strongest influence on Italian culture and politics. This influence is strong in part because the **pope,** the spiritual head of the Roman Catholic Church, lives on the Italian Peninsula. He resides in **Vatican City,** an independent state located within the city of Rome. The pope heads Vatican City's government, as well as the Roman Catholic Church. After he is elected by church officials, the pope is the absolute ruler until his death, with only a few exceptions. This means that the religious traditions of Roman Catholicism have had a huge political and social impact on Vatican City, Italy, and the rest of Southern Europe for many centuries.

The lasting importance of the church can be seen in many ways in Italy. For example, the city of Rome alone is home to hundreds of Catholic churches from all periods of history. In addition, religious holidays and festivals are major events.

Local Traditions In addition to religion, local traditions have influenced Italian culture. Italian food, for example, varies widely from region to region. These variations are based on local preferences and products. All over Italy, people eat many of the same foods—olives, tomatoes, rice, pasta. However, the ways in which people prepare this food differ. In the south, for example, people often serve pasta with tomato sauces. In the north, creamy sauces are much more common.

Other traditions reflect Italy's past. For example, Italy has always been known as a center of the arts. The people of Italy have long been trendsetters, shaping styles that are later adopted by other people. As a result, the Italians are leaders in many <u>contemporary</u> art forms. For example, Italy has produced some of the world's greatest painters, sculptors, authors, composers, fashion designers, and filmmakers.

Italy Today

A shared language, the Roman Catholic Church, and strong family ties help bind Italians together. At the same time, though, major differences exist in the northern and southern parts of the country.

Italy, like other Southern European countries, has a high literacy rate. A literacy rate is the percentage of citizens who can read and write. The high literacy rate helps Italy make products that people want to buy, supporting the country's economy. A good economy helps people enjoy a high standard of living.

Southern Italy Southern Italy is the country's poorer half. Its economy has less industry than the north and depends heavily on agriculture. Farming

Academic Vocabulary
contemporary
modern

Reading Check
Find Main Ideas What are two major influences on Italian culture?

Rome, Milan, and Naples are the three largest cities in Italy. Because of their varied histories and locations, each city has a distinct landscape and culture.

Milan Milan, the largest city in northern Italy, is a global fashion capital. The clothes created there influence fashion designers around the world.

Naples Naples is the most important city in southern Italy. Less glamorous than many northern cities, it is a port and manufacturing center.

Rome Rome, the capital of Italy, is in the central part of the country. A major center of banking and industry, Rome is also one of the world's most popular tourist sites.

Analyze Visuals
Which city would you most like to visit?

Academic Vocabulary
incentive something that leads people to follow a certain course of action

is especially important in **Sicily,** an island at the peninsula's tip. Tourism is also vital to the south's economy. Among the region's attractions are its dazzling beaches and ancient Roman ruins.

In recent decades, Italy's government has tried to promote industry in the south. It has offered **incentives**, such as lower taxes, to private companies that will build factories there. Many of these government efforts center on the city of **Naples,** a busy port and the largest city in southern Italy. Thanks to government programs, Naples is now also an industrial center.

Northern Italy In contrast to southern Italy, the northern part of the country has a strong economy. The geographic factors responsible for the location of the region's economic activities include Italy's most fertile farmlands, its major trade centers, and its most popular tourist destinations.

For decades, the Po River valley has been called the breadbasket of Italy because most of the country's crops are grown there. Despite its fertile soils, farmers cannot grow enough to support Italy's population. Italy has to import much of its food.

The north is also home to Italy's major industrial centers. Busy factories in such cities as Turin and Genoa make appliances, automobiles, and other goods for export. **Milan** is also a major industrial center as well as a worldwide center for fashion design. The location of these cities near central Europe helps companies sell their goods to foreign customers. Railroads, highways, and tunnels make the shipment of goods through the Alps easy.

Tens of millions of tourists visit the cities of northern Italy every year. They are drawn by the cities' rich histories and unique cultural features. Florence, for example, is a center of Italian art and culture. It was there that the Renaissance began in the 1300s. To the west of Florence is Pisa, famous for its Leaning Tower—the bell tower of the city's cathedral. On the coast of the Adriatic Sea lies the city of Venice. Tourists are lured there by the romantic canals that serve as roads through the city.

The Duomo is a cathedral in Florence, Italy. Its tall dome rises above the city. Construction on the cathedral started in the late 13th century. It took about two centuries to complete it.

Venice

Venice, in northeastern Italy, is one of the country's most visited tourist attractions. Look at the image of Venice here, taken by an orbiting satellite. Does it look like other cities you have seen? What may not be obvious is that the paths that wind their way through the city are not roads but canals. In fact, Venice has very few roads. This is because the city was built on islands—118 of them! People move about the city on boats that navigate along the canals. Every year, millions of tourists travel to Venice to see the sights as they are rowed along the scenic waterways.

Contrast
How is Venice unlike other cities you have studied?

Reading Check
Contrast How are northern and southern Italy different?

Nestled in the center of the country is Italy's capital, **Rome.** With ties to both north and south, Rome does not fully belong to either region. From there, the country's leaders attempt to bring all the people of Italy together as one nation.

Summary and Preview In this lesson, you learned about Greece and Italy, countries with long and varied histories that still shape their cultures and economies today. Next you will study two other countries whose pasts still affect life there—Spain and Portugal.

Lesson 2 Assessment

Review Ideas, Terms, and Places

1. **a. Identify** What were two major achievements of the ancient Greeks?
   b. Sequence What steps did the Greeks take to gain their independence?
2. **a. Define** What is the Orthodox Church?
   b. Generalize What is one way in which Greece's history affects its culture today?
3. **a. Describe** What is life like in Athens today?
   b. Explain Why is Greece's economic growth slower than most other European nations?
4. **a. Describe** What was Renaissance Italy like?
   b. Interpret How did nationalism influence Italian history?
5. **a. Identify** What religion has had a major impact on Italian culture?
   b. Explain How have local traditions helped shape Italian culture?

6. **a. Recall** What is the main economic activity of southern Italy?
   b. Contrast How are the economies of Milan, Rome, and Naples different?

Critical Thinking

7. **Categorize** Draw a table like the one here. Ancient Greece and Rome made important contributions to the world today. Use the table to prioritize the importance and relevance of these contributions.

Prioritizing Contributions		
	Most Important/ Relevant	Least Important/ Relevant
Ancient Greece		
Ancient Rome		

Spain and Portugal

The Big Idea

Spain and Portugal have rich cultures, stable governments, and struggling economies.

Main Ideas

- Over the centuries, Spain and Portugal have been part of many large and powerful empires.

- The cultures of Spain and Portugal reflect their long histories.

- Having been both rich and poor in the past, Spain and Portugal today have struggling economies.

Key Terms and Places

Iberia
parliamentary monarchy
Madrid
Barcelona
Lisbon

If YOU lived there . . .

You have just moved to southern Spain from a town in the far north. You cannot help noticing that many of the buildings here look different from those in your hometown. Many of the buildings here have rounded arches over the doorways and tall towers in front of them. In addition, some are decorated with ornate tiles.

Why do you think the buildings look different?

History

Locate Spain and Portugal on the physical map in Lesson 1. As you can see, the two countries share the Iberian Peninsula, or **Iberia,** the westernmost peninsula in Europe. Although the two are different in many ways, they share a common history.

Across the centuries, several powerful empires controlled all or part of the Iberian Peninsula. By 700 BC the Phoenicians, from the eastern Mediterranean, had colonized coastal areas of what is now Spain. After the Phoenicians came the Greeks. A few centuries later, all of Iberia became part of the Roman Empire.

After the Roman Empire fell apart, Iberia was invaded by the Moors, a group of Muslims from North Africa. For about 600 years, much of the Iberian Peninsula was under Muslim rule.

By the end of the 1400s, however, the Muslims were driven out of Iberia. The rulers of the Christian kingdoms of Spain and Portugal banded together to force non-Christians to leave Iberia. Those who refused to leave were made to convert or face severe punishments.

Moorish structures, such as this tower outside of Lisbon, Portugal, can still be seen all over Iberia.

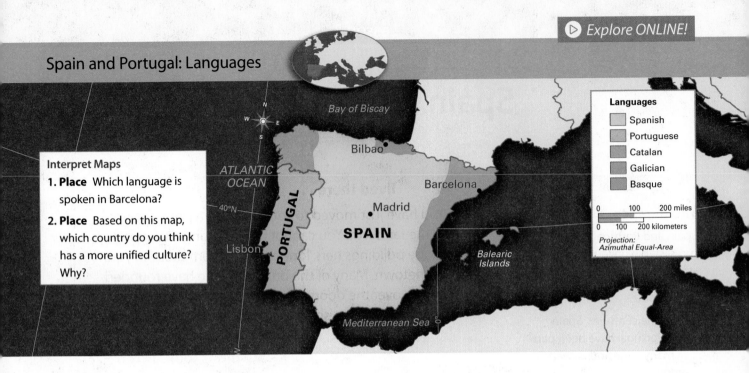

Explore ONLINE!

Interpret Maps

1. **Place** Which language is spoken in Barcelona?

2. **Place** Based on this map, which country do you think has a more unified culture? Why?

Languages
- Spanish
- Portuguese
- Catalan
- Galician
- Basque

0   100   200 miles
0   100   200 kilometers
Projection:
Azimuthal Equal-Area

Bay of Biscay
ATLANTIC OCEAN
Bilbao
40°N
Barcelona
Madrid
SPAIN
PORTUGAL
Lisbon
Balearic Islands
Mediterranean Sea

Reading Check
Summarize
What empires have ruled Spain and Portugal?

Spain and Portugal went on to build large empires that spanned the oceans. Both countries ruled huge territories in the Americas as well as smaller areas in Africa and Asia. These territories made the two kingdoms rich and powerful until most of their colonies broke away and became independent in the 1800s and 1900s.

Culture

In some ways, the cultures of Spain and Portugal are like those of other Southern European countries. For example, the Spanish, Portuguese, Greeks, and Italians all cook with many of the same ingredients. The Catholic Church is very influential in Italy as well as Spain and Portugal. In other ways, Iberian cultures are unique.

Language The most spoken languages in Iberia are, of course, Spanish and Portuguese. Various dialects of these languages are spoken in different parts of the peninsula. In addition, other languages are also spoken by many people in Iberia. The Catalan language of eastern Spain is similar to Spanish. Galician, which is spoken in northwest Spain, is more closely related to Portuguese.

In addition, the Basque (BASK) people of the Pyrenees have their own language, which is not related to either Spanish or Portuguese. The Basques also have their own customs and traditions, unlike those of the rest of Spain. As a result, many Basques have long wanted to form their own independent country.

Religion Most people in both Spain and Portugal are Roman Catholic. People in both countries celebrate Christian holidays like Christmas and Easter. In addition, many towns hold fiestas, or festivals, in honor of their patron saints. At these festivals, people may gather to dance or to watch a bullfight.

Reading Check
Compare
What is one culture element that Spain and Portugal share?

Music and Art Music and art have been central to Iberian culture for centuries. The Portuguese are famous for sad folk songs called fados. The Spanish are known for a style of song and dance called flamenco.

Many elements of Iberia's art and architecture reflect its Muslim past. Many buildings in the peninsula have elements of Muslim design, such as round arches and elaborate tilework.

Spain and Portugal Today

Compared to most other countries in Western Europe, Spain's and Portugal's economies are struggling. Their economic problems were caused by recent hardships and by past events.

Challenge of the Past Spain and Portugal were once Europe's richest countries. Their wealth came from gold and silver found in their colonies. When other countries in Europe began to build industrial economies, Spain and Portugal continued to rely on gold from their colonies. As those colonies became independent, that source of income was lost. As a result, Spain and Portugal were late in developing manufacturing.

All Southern European countries are now members of the European Union (EU). The EU is an organization formed to increase economic and political cooperation among its members. One of the EU's actions was to get rid of trade barriers. This action supported the expansion of global markets. By joining the EU, Spain and Portugal aimed to increase their trade and improve their economies. However, Spain and Portugal are still poorer than other countries in Western Europe. Despite recent economic growth and vibrant industries such as tourism, their economies are struggling.

Focus on Culture

Flamenco

Complex guitar rhythms, a heavy beat, and whirling dancers—these are all part of the traditional Spanish art form known as flamenco. The word *flamenco* refers both to a style of music and a style of dance. The most important instrument in the music is the guitar, which was itself a Spanish invention. Most of the time, the guitar is accompanied by other musical instruments and by singers.

When most people think of flamenco, however, they picture dancers. Flamenco dancers perform alone, in pairs, or in large groups. They wear brightly colored costumes as they perform complex steps. It is not unusual for dancers to clap their hands or snap their fingers to the beat or to play castanets as they dance. Castanets are small, hinged wooden instruments. The dancers clap the castanets together to make a clicking noise.

Find Main Ideas
What are the major elements of flamenco music and dancing?

Spanish culture blends old and new ideas. Here, modern vehicles drive by historic buildings in Barcelona.

Spain Today The people of Spain have kept many aspects of their history alive. For example, Spain is still governed by a king, a descendant of the kings who ruled the country long ago. Unlike in the past, however, Spain today is a **parliamentary monarchy,** which means that the king shares power with an elected parliament and a prime minister.

In other ways, Spain has become a more modern country. Agriculture was once the major economic activity, but factories now create automobiles and other high-tech products. Cities such as **Madrid**—the capital—and **Barcelona** are centers of industry, tourism, and culture.

Portugal Today Unlike Spain, Portugal is not a monarchy. It is a republic with elected leaders. As in Spain, the economy is based largely on industries centered in large cities, especially **Lisbon.** In many rural areas, though, people depend on agriculture. Farmers there grow many crops but are most famous for grapes and cork. Farmers harvest cork from the bark of a particular type of oak tree. Once it is dried, the cork is used to make bottle stoppers and other products.

Reading Check
Contrast
How are Spain's and Portugal's governments different?

Summary In this lesson, you have learned about the countries of Spain and Portugal in Southern Europe. You have explored their rich cultures, stable governments, and struggling economies.

Lesson 3 Assessment

Review Ideas, Terms, and Places

1. a. **Recall** What is Iberia? What two countries are located there?

   b. **Sequence** What people have ruled Iberia, and in what order did they rule it?

2. a. **Identify** What is the most common religion in Spain and Portugal?

   b. **Generalize** How is Spain's history reflected in its architecture?

   c. **Elaborate** Why do you think many Basques want to become independent from Spain?

3. a. **Identify** What are two crops grown in Portugal?

   b. **Analyze** What is Spain's government like?

Critical Thinking

4. **Categorizing** Draw a table like the one here. Using your notes, record information about the cultures and economies of Spain and Portugal.

	Spain	Portugal
Culture		
Economy		

Social Studies Skills

Read a Climate Map

Define the Skill

Geographers use many different types of maps to study a region. One type that can be very useful is a climate map. Because climate affects so many aspects of people's lives, it is important to know which climates are found in a region.

Learn the Skill

Use the climate map of Europe below to answer the following questions.

1. What does orange mean on this map?

2. What city has a highland climate?

3. What is the dominant climate in the countries of Southern Europe?

Practice the Skill

Choose one of the cities shown on the map below. Imagine that you are planning a trip to that city and need to know what the climate is like so you can prepare. Use the map to identify the type of climate found in your chosen city. Then use the library or the Internet to find out more about that type of climate. Write a short description of the climate and how you could prepare for it.

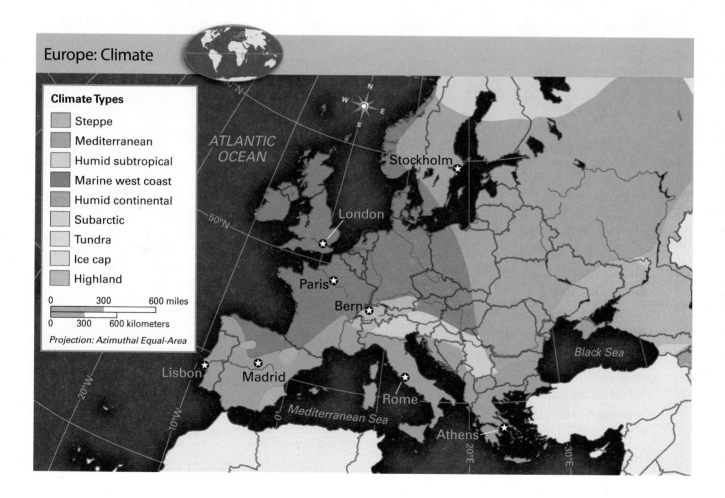

Europe: Climate

Climate Types
- Steppe
- Mediterranean
- Humid subtropical
- Marine west coast
- Humid continental
- Subarctic
- Tundra
- Ice cap
- Highland

0   300   600 miles
0   300   600 kilometers

Projection: Azimuthal Equal-Area

ATLANTIC OCEAN

Stockholm

London

Paris

Bern

Lisbon

Madrid

Rome

Athens

Black Sea

Mediterranean Sea

Module 14 Assessment

Review Vocabulary, Terms, and Places

Fill in the blanks with the correct term or location from this module.

1. The climate found in most of Southern Europe is the _____.
2. The _____ is the head of the Roman Catholic Church.
3. The highest mountains in Europe are the _____.
4. _____ is the capital of Greece.
5. A _____ is a government in which a king rules with the help of an elected body.
6. Italy's capital, _____, was the birthplace of an ancient civilization.
7. _____ is an independent state located within the city of Rome.
8. Spain and Portugal are located on a peninsula known as _____.

Comprehension and Critical Thinking

Lesson 1

9. a. Describe What are two physical features that all the countries of Southern Europe have in common?
    b. Draw Conclusions Why has Southern Europe's climate been called its most valuable resource?
    c. Predict How would daily life in Southern Europe be different if it were not a coastal region?

Lesson 2

10. a. Identify What is the largest city in Greece? How would you describe the city?
    b. Generalize How has Greece's economy changed in the last decade? What is largely responsible for this change?
    c. Elaborate How does Greek history still affect the country today?
    d. Identify Study the Greece: Population map and the Social Studies Skills page. What geographic factors do you think are responsible for the location of economic activities and high populations in Greece? Explain.

11. a. Recall Which region of Italy has the stronger economy? Why?
    b. Sequence What periods followed the Roman Empire in Italy? What happened during those periods?
    c. Elaborate What are some ways in which the Italians have influenced world culture?

Lesson 3

12. a. Identify Who are the Basques?
    b. Compare and Contrast How are Spain and Portugal alike? How are they different?
    c. Elaborate How do you think Iberia's history makes it different from other places in Europe?

Module 14 Assessment, continued

Reading Skills

Ask Questions *Read the passage below. After you read it, answer the questions below to be sure you have understood what you read.*

> Spain is a democracy, but it has not always been. From 1939 to 1975, a dictator named Francisco Franco ruled the country. He came to power as a result of a bloody civil war and was unpopular with the Spanish people.

13. Who is this paragraph about?

14. What did the people in this passage do?

15. When did the events described take place?

16. Where did the events described take place?

17. Why did the events happen?

Social Studies Skills

Read a Climate Map *Use the climate map from the Social Studies Skills lesson of this module to answer the following questions.*

18. What type of climate does London have?

19. What climate is found only in the far north?

20. Where in Europe would you find a humid subtropical climate?

Map Activity

21. **Southern Europe** On a separate sheet of paper, match the letters on the map with their correct labels.

    Mediterranean Sea   Lisbon, Portugal
    Athens, Greece   Po River
    Sicily   Rome, Italy
    Spain   Aegean Sea

Focus on Writing

22. **Write a News Report** Select a topic for a news report. Create a plan for your report by answering these questions: What is the scene or setting of the event? Who is there? Why is it important enough to include in the news? What happened? Start your news report with a dateline—your location and today's date. Begin your first paragraph with an interesting observation or detail. Explain the event in two or three short paragraphs. Close with an important piece of information or interesting detail.

Western Europe

Essential Question

Which Western European country has most benefited from its physical geography?

▷ Explore ONLINE!

VIDEOS, including . . .
- The Vikings
- Gothic Cathedrals
- The Celts

HISTORY.

✓ Document-Based Investigations

✓ Graphic Organizers

✓ Interactive Games

✓ Animation: Polders

✓ Image with Hotspots: The Berlin Wall

✓ Channel One©Video: Brexit

In this module, you will learn about the diverse region of Western Europe, its cultures, governments, and history.

What You Will Learn

History The Palace of Westminster in London has been home to the British Parliament for over 600 years.

Culture Skiing, snowboarding, and other forms of outdoor recreation are popular throughout much of Scandinavia and the Alpine Countries.

Geography The Netherlands is famous for its fields of brightly colored tulips.

Reading Social Studies

Recognize Word Origins

READING FOCUS

English is a language that loves to borrow words from other languages and cultures. The diversity of European languages that arose from the array of cultures across Europe has influenced the English language as it has developed. From French, English speakers took *façon* and changed it to *fashion*. From German, we took *strollen* and changed it to *stroll*. From Dutch, we took *koekje* and changed it to *cookie*. Below is a list of examples of other words that come from other languages.

English Words from French	English Words from German	English Words from Latin
conquer	muffin	culture
brilliant	dollar	defeat
restaurant	rocket	general
republic	kindergarten	forces
fashion	hamburger	join
parliament	noodle	president
several	pretzel	elect
power	snorkel	control
exiled	hex	territory

YOU TRY IT!

Read the following sentences. Refer to the above word lists and make a list of the words in the passage below that originally came from other languages. After each word, list the original language.

A few years later a brilliant general named Napoleon took power. In time, he conquered much of Europe. Then in 1815 several European powers joined forces and defeated Napoleon. They exiled him and chose a new king to rule France. . . . France is now a republic with a parliament and an elected president. France still controls several overseas territories, such as Martinique in the West Indies.

As you read this module, look for words that originally came from other languages.

Physical Geography

The Big Idea

Western Europe has a range of landscapes, diverse climates, and rich resources including farmland.

Main Ideas

- West-Central Europe includes many types of physical features and a mild climate that supports agriculture, energy production, and tourism.

- Northern Europe contains low mountains, jagged coastlines, a variety of natural resources, and a range of climates.

Key Terms and Places

Northern European Plain
North Sea
English Channel
Danube River
Rhine River
navigable river
North Atlantic Drift
British Isles
Scandinavia
fjord
geothermal energy

If YOU lived there . . .

You are a photographer planning a book about the landscapes of Western Europe. You are trying to decide where to find the best pictures of all the varied landscapes including rich farmland, forested plateaus, and rocky coastlines. So far, you are planning to show the colorful tulip fields of the Netherlands, the hilly Black Forest region of Germany, and the rocky fjords of Norway.

What other places might you want to show?

West-Central Europe

Western Europe can be thought of as two separate regions, Northern Europe and West-Central Europe. From fields of tulips, to sunny beaches, to icy mountain peaks, West-Central Europe offers a wide range of landscapes. Its climate supports farming and tourism.

Physical Features Even though the region of West-Central Europe is small, it includes three major types of landforms—plains, uplands, and mountains. These landforms extend in wide bands across the region.

Look at the physical map of West-Central Europe. Picture West-Central Europe as an open fan, with Italy as the handle. The outer edge of this imaginary fan is a broad coastal plain called the **Northern European Plain.** This plain stretches from the Atlantic coast into Eastern Europe.

Most of this plain is flat or rolling and lies less than 500 feet (150 m) above sea level. In the Netherlands, parts of the plain dip below sea level. There, people must build walls to hold back the sea.

The Northern European Plain provides the region's best farmland. Many people live on the plain, and the region's largest cities are located there.

The Central Uplands extend across the center of our imaginary fan. This area has many rounded hills, small plateaus, and valleys. In France, the uplands include the Massif Central (ma-SEEF sahn-TRAHL), a plateau region, and the Jura Mountains.

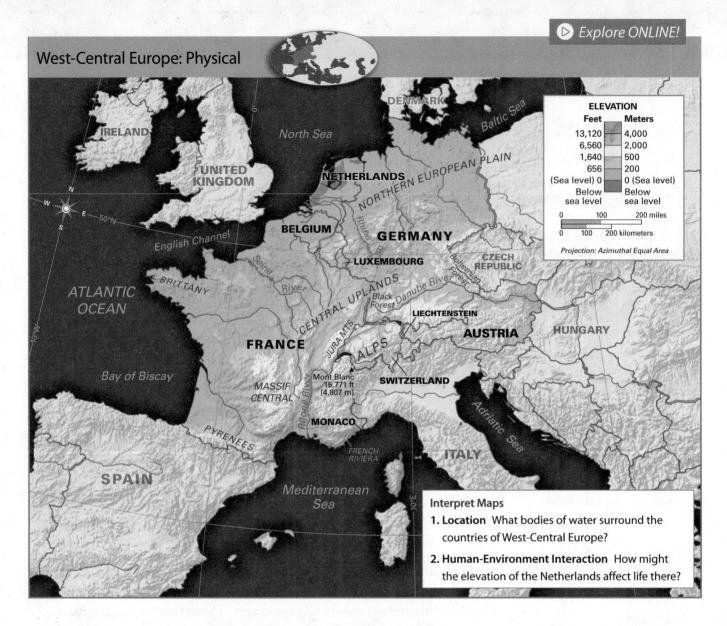

Explore ONLINE!

ELEVATION

Feet		Meters
13,120		4,000
6,560		2,000
1,640		500
656		200
(Sea level) 0		0 (Sea level)
Below sea level		Below sea level

0   100   200 miles
0   100   200 kilometers

Projection: Azimuthal Equal Area

Interpret Maps

1. **Location** What bodies of water surround the countries of West-Central Europe?

2. **Human-Environment Interaction** How might the elevation of the Netherlands affect life there?

This range is on the French-Swiss border. In Germany, uplands cover much of the southern two-thirds of the country. Dense woodlands, such as the Black Forest, blanket many of the hills in this area.

The Central Uplands have many productive coalfields. As a result, the area is important for mining and industry. Some valleys provide fertile soil for farming, but most of the area is too rocky to farm.

Along the inner part of our imaginary fan, the land rises dramatically to form the alpine mountain system. This system includes the Alps and the Pyrenees.

The Alps are Europe's highest mountain range. They stretch from southern France to the Balkan Peninsula. Several of the jagged peaks in the Alps soar to more than 14,000 feet (4,270 m). Because of the height of the Alps, large snowfields coat some peaks.

Several bodies of water are important to West-Central Europe's physical geography. The **North Sea** and **English Channel** lie to the north. The Bay of Biscay and Atlantic Ocean lie to the west. The Mediterranean Sea borders France to the south.

At high elevations in the Alps, snow does not melt. For this reason, the snow builds up over time. As the snow builds up, it turns to ice and eventually forms glaciers. A glacier is a large, slow-moving sheet or river of ice. This satellite image shows glaciers in the Swiss Alps. The white regions are the glaciers, and the blue areas are alpine lakes. As the climate changes, glaciers in the Alps are receding, or shrinking, at increasing rates.

The buildup of snow and ice in the Alps can cause avalanches at lower elevations. An avalanche is a large mass of snow or other material that suddenly rushes down a mountainside. Avalanches pose a serious danger to people. It seems that climate changes have also increased avalanche activity.

Analyze Information
Why do glaciers sometimes form at higher elevations in the Alps?

High in the Swiss Alps, snow builds up to form glaciers, like the one shown here.

Several rivers cross the region as well. Look at the physical map of West-Central Europe to identify them. Two important rivers are the **Danube** (DAN-yoob) and the **Rhine** (RYN). For centuries, people and goods have traveled these rivers, and many cities, farms, and industrial areas line their banks.

Several of West-Central Europe's rivers are navigable. A **navigable river** is one that is deep and wide enough for ships to use. These rivers and a system of canals link the region's interior to the seas. These waterways are important for trade and travel.

Climate and Resources A warm ocean current, the **North Atlantic Drift,** flows along Europe's northwestern coast. This ocean current brings warm, moist air across the Atlantic Ocean and creates a marine west coast climate in most of West-Central Europe. This climate makes much of the area a pleasant place to live. Though winters can get cold, summers are mild. Rain and storms occur often, though.

At higher elevations, such as in the Alps, the climate is colder and wetter. In contrast, southern France has a warm Mediterranean climate. Summers are dry and hot, and winters are mild and wet.

West-Central Europe's mild climate is a valuable natural resource. Mild temperatures, plenty of rain, and rich soil have made the region's farmlands highly productive. Farm crops include grapes, grains, and vegetables. In the uplands and Alps, pastures and valleys support livestock.

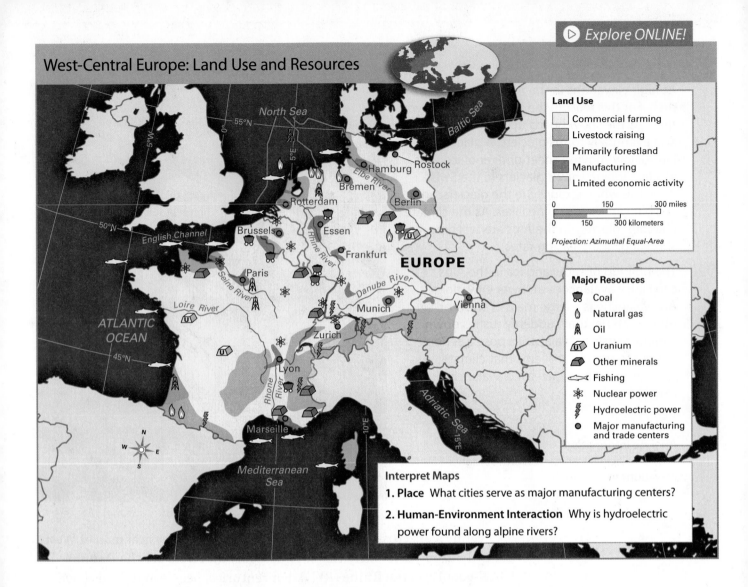

Explore ONLINE!

Land Use

- Commercial farming
- Livestock raising
- Primarily forestland
- Manufacturing
- Limited economic activity

0   150   300 miles
0   150   300 kilometers

Projection: Azimuthal Equal-Area

EUROPE

Major Resources

- Coal
- Natural gas
- Oil
- Uranium
- Other minerals
- Fishing
- Nuclear power
- Hydroelectric power
- Major manufacturing and trade centers

North Sea · Baltic Sea · Hamburg · Rostock · Elbe River · Bremen · Berlin · Rotterdam · Brussels · Essen · Rhine River · Frankfurt · Paris · Seine River · Danube River · Munich · Vienna · Loire River · Zurich · ATLANTIC OCEAN · Lyon · Rhône River · Marseille · Adriatic Sea · Mediterranean Sea · English Channel

Interpret Maps

1. **Place** What cities serve as major manufacturing centers?

2. **Human-Environment Interaction** Why is hydroelectric power found along alpine rivers?

As the land use and resources map shows, energy and mineral resources are not evenly distributed across the region. France has coal and iron ore, Germany also has coal, and the Netherlands has natural gas. Fast-flowing alpine rivers provide hydroelectric power. Even so, many countries must import fuels.

Another valuable natural resource is found in the breathtaking beauty of the Alps. Each year, tourists flock to the Alps to enjoy the scenery and to hike and ski.

Reading Check
Find Main Ideas
What are the region's three major landform areas? What natural resources do they hold?

Northern Europe

Two regions—the British Isles and Scandinavia—make up Northern Europe. To the southwest lie the **British Isles,** a group of islands located across the English Channel from the rest of Europe. Northeast of the British Isles is **Scandinavia,** a region of islands and peninsulas in far northern Europe. The island of Iceland, to the west, is often considered part of Scandinavia.

From Ireland's gently rolling hills to Iceland's icy glaciers and fiery volcanoes, Northern Europe is a land of great variety. The physical geography of Northern Europe differs greatly from one location to another.

Physical Features Rough, rocky hills and low mountains cover much of Northern Europe. Rugged hills stretch across much of Iceland, northern Scotland, and Scandinavia. The jagged Kjolen (CHUH-luhn) Mountains on the Scandinavian Peninsula divide Norway from Sweden. The rocky soil and uneven terrain in these parts of Northern Europe make farming there difficult. As a result, fewer people live there than in the rest of Northern Europe.

Farming is easier in other parts of the region. Fertile farmland and flat plains stretch across the southern parts of the British Isles and Scandinavia. Ireland's rolling, green hills provide rich farmland. Wide valleys in England and Denmark also have plenty of fertile soil.

Glaciers have left their mark on Northern Europe's coastlines and lakes. As you can see on the physical map of Northern Europe, Norway's western coastline is very jagged. Millions of years ago, glaciers cut deep valleys into Norway's coastal mountains. As the glaciers melted, these valleys filled with water, creating deep fjords. A **fjord** (fee-AWRD) is a narrow inlet of the sea set between high, rocky cliffs. Many fjords are very long and deep.

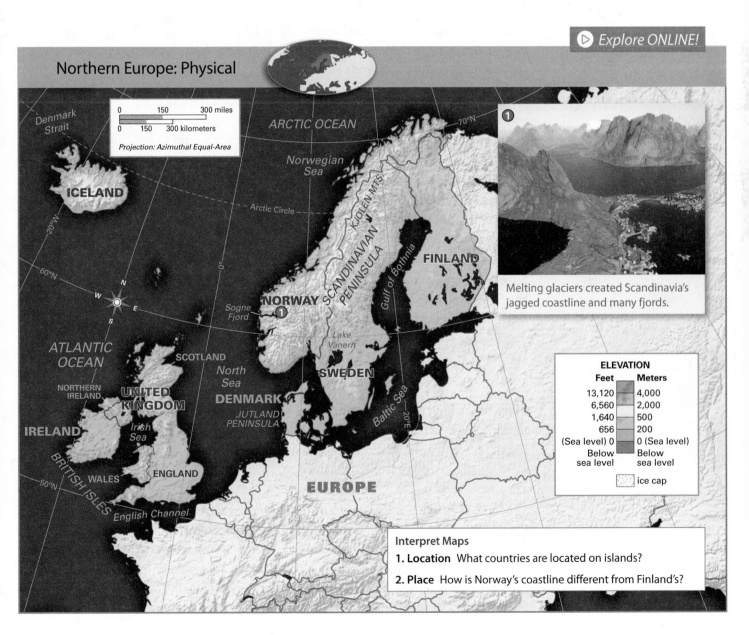

Explore ONLINE!

Northern Europe: Physical

Melting glaciers created Scandinavia's jagged coastline and many fjords.

ELEVATION

Feet		Meters
13,120		4,000
6,560		2,000
1,640		500
656		200
(Sea level) 0		0 (Sea level)
Below sea level		Below sea level

ice cap

Interpret Maps

1. **Location** What countries are located on islands?

2. **Place** How is Norway's coastline different from Finland's?

Norway's Fjords

Millions of years ago, much of Norway was covered with glaciers. As the glaciers flowed slowly downhill, they carved long, winding channels, or fjords, into Norway's coastline.

As you can see in this satellite image, fjords cut many miles into Norway's interior, bringing warm waters from the North and Norwegian seas. As warm waters penetrate inland, they keep temperatures relatively mild. In fact, people have used these unfrozen fjords to travel during the winter when ice and snow made travel over land difficult.

Analyze Information
How do fjords benefit life in Norway?

Academic Vocabulary
primary main, most important

Melting glaciers also carved thousands of lakes in Northern Europe. Sweden's Lake Vanern, along with many of the lakes in the British Isles, were carved by glaciers thousands of years ago.

Natural Resources Natural resources have helped to make Northern Europe one of the wealthiest regions in the world. Northern Europe's **primary** resources are its energy resources, forests and soils, and surrounding seas.

Northern Europe has a variety of energy resources. Norway and the United Kingdom benefit from oil and natural gas deposits under the North Sea. Hydroelectric energy is produced by the region's many lakes and rivers. In Iceland, steam from hot springs produces **geothermal energy,** or energy from the heat of Earth's interior.

Forests and soils are two other important natural resources in Northern Europe. Large areas of timber-producing forests stretch across Finland and the Scandinavian Peninsula. Fertile soils provide rich farmland for crops, such as wheat and potatoes. Livestock like sheep and dairy cattle are also common.

The seas that surround Northern Europe are another important natural resource. For centuries, these seas have provided rich stocks of fish. Today, fishing is a key industry in Norway, Denmark, and Iceland.

Climates Much of Northern Europe lies near the Arctic Circle. Due to the region's high latitude, you might imagine that it would be quite cold during much of the year. In reality, however, the climates there are remarkably mild. Just like in West-Central Europe, Northern Europe's mild climates are a result of the North Atlantic Drift.

Much of Northern Europe has a marine west coast climate. Denmark, the British Isles, and western Norway benefit from mild summers and frequent rainfall. Snow and frost may occur in winter but do not usually last long. Along with the rich soils, the climate allows farming in Northern Europe. The North Atlantic Drift also keeps many ports from being frozen for much of the winter, allowing trade to happen year-round.

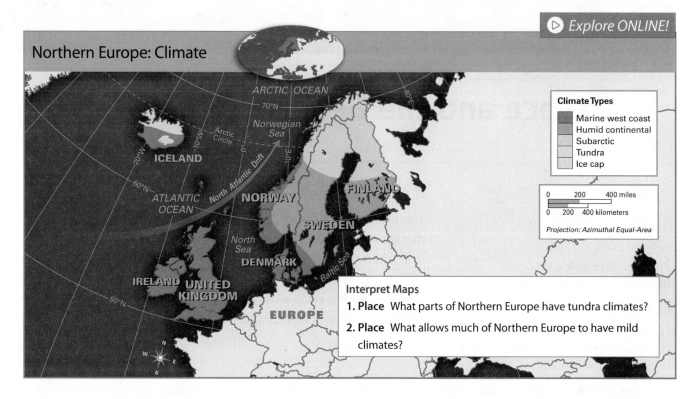

Northern Europe: Climate

ARCTIC OCEAN
70°N
Norwegian Sea
Arctic Circle
ICELAND
ATLANTIC OCEAN
North Atlantic Drift
60°N
NORWAY
FINLAND
SWEDEN
North Sea
DENMARK
Baltic Sea
IRELAND
UNITED KINGDOM
50°N
EUROPE

Climate Types
Marine west coast
Humid continental
Subarctic
Tundra
Ice cap

| 0 | 200 | 400 miles |
| 0 | 200 | 400 kilometers |

Projection: Azimuthal Equal-Area

Interpret Maps

1. **Place** What parts of Northern Europe have tundra climates?

2. **Place** What allows much of Northern Europe to have mild climates?

Central Norway, Sweden, and southern Finland have a humid continental climate. This area has four true seasons with cold, snowy winters and mild summers.

Far to the north are colder climates. Subarctic regions, like those in Northern Scandinavia, have long, cold winters and short summers. Iceland's tundra and ice cap climates produce extremely cold temperatures all year. Most people in Northern Europe live in urban areas, and few live in the far north, where the climate makes life more difficult.

Reading Check
Summarize
What are some physical features of Northern Europe?

Summary and Preview Western Europe includes West-Central Europe and Northern Europe. The varied climate, rich resources, and wide variety of physical features support farming, industry, fishing, and tourism. Next, you will read about France and the Benelux Countries.

Lesson 1 Assessment

Review Ideas, Terms, and Places

1. **a. Describe** What are the main physical features of the Northern European Plain?

   b. Analyze How does having many navigable rivers benefit West-Central Europe?

   c. Recall What is the region's main climate?

   d. Make Inferences How might an uneven distribution of mineral resources affect the region?

   e. Analyze How does the pattern of where manufacturing areas are in West-Central Europe differ from the pattern of where livestock raising occurs?

2. **a. Describe** What are the physical features of Northern Europe?

   b. Analyze What role did glaciers play in shaping the physical geography of Northern Europe?

   c. Make Inferences How do people in Northern Europe benefit from the surrounding seas?

   d. Identify What climates exist in Northern Europe?

Critical Thinking

3. **Categorize** Draw a fan like this one. Label each band with the landform area in West-Central Europe it represents. Identify each area's physical features, climate, and resources.

France and the Benelux Countries

The Big Idea
France and the Benelux Countries have strong economies and rich cultural traditions.

Main Ideas
- During its history, France has been a kingdom, empire, colonial power, and republic.
- The culture of France has contributed to the world's arts and ideas.
- France today is a farming and manufacturing center.
- The Benelux Countries have strong economies and high standards of living.

Key Terms and Places
Paris
Amsterdam
The Hague
Brussels
cosmopolitan

If YOU lived there . . .
You are strolling through one of the many open-air markets in a Paris neighborhood. You stop to buy some fruit, then go into a bakery to buy bread, cheese, and lemonade. You sit on a park bench to eat lunch. You end your day with a stroll along the banks of the Seine River, where you look at books and postcards.

Why do you think people enjoy living in Paris?

History of France

In southwest France, Lascaux (lah-SKOH) Cave holds a treasure from the past. Inside, prehistoric paintings of bulls run and jump along the stone walls. More than 15,000 years old, these paintings show how long people have lived in what is now France.

Early History In ancient times, France was part of a region called Gaul (GAWL). Centuries ago, Celtic peoples from eastern Europe settled in Gaul. In the 50s BC, the Romans conquered the region. They introduced Roman law. The Romans also established a Latin-based language that in time developed into French.

Roman rule in Gaul lasted until the AD 400s. The Franks, a Germanic people, then conquered much of Gaul. It is from the Franks that France gets its name. The Franks' greatest ruler was Charlemagne (SHAHR-luh-mayn), who built a powerful Christian empire. After he had conquered much of the old Roman Empire, the pope crowned him emperor of the Romans in 800.

After Charlemagne's death, many invaders attacked the Franks. One such group, the Normans, settled in northwestern France. This area is called Normandy.

In 1066 the Normans conquered England. William the Conqueror, the Duke of Normandy, became king of England. He now ruled England as well as part of France. In the 1300s England's king tried to claim the French throne to gain control of the rest of France. This event led to the Hundred Years' War (1337–1453). The French eventually drove out the English.

Charlemagne built a powerful empire that included most of France.

The Arc de Triomphe celebrates the victories of Napoleon and his army.

Revolution and Empire From the 1500s to the 1700s, France built a colonial empire. The French established colonies in the Americas, Africa, and Asia. At this time, most French people lived in poverty and had few rights. For these reasons, in 1789 the French people overthrew their king in the French Revolution.

A few years later, a brilliant general named Napoleon took power. In time, he conquered much of Europe. Then in 1815 several European powers joined forces and defeated Napoleon. They exiled him and chose a new king to rule France.

Modern History During both World War I and World War II, German forces invaded France. After each war, France worked to rebuild its economy. In the 1950s it experienced rapid growth.

During the 1950s and 1960s, many of the French colonies gained their independence. Some people from these former colonies then moved to France.

France is now a democratic republic with a parliament and an elected president. France still controls several overseas territories, such as Martinique in the West Indies.

Reading Check
Summarize Which foreign groups have affected France's history?

Historical Source

Germany Occupies France

During World War II, German forces controlled France. Here, German tanks roll down a street in Toulouse.

Analyze Sources
How might the French people standing along the street have felt the moment this photo was taken?

The Culture of France

During their long history, the French have developed a strong cultural identity. Today, French culture is admired worldwide.

Language and Religion A common heritage unites many of the French. Most people speak French and are Catholic. Over time, many immigrants have settled in France. These immigrants have their own languages, religions, and customs. For example, many Algerian Muslims have moved to France. There are also small Jewish and Buddhist populations. This immigration is making France more culturally diverse.

While most of France is Catholic, the French take the idea of maintaining a secular, or non-religious, society very seriously. This is seen in schools, where religious symbols are not allowed. Unlike in most other European countries, there is no religious education given in public schools. The government is secular, and there is no state religion.

Customs The French have a phrase that describes their attitude toward life—*joie de vivre* (zhwah duh VEEV-ruh), meaning "enjoyment of life." The French enjoy good food, good company, and good conversation.

An enjoyment of food has helped make French cooking some of the best in the world. French chefs and cooking schools have worldwide reputations. The French have also contributed to the language of food. Terms such as *café*, *cuisine* (cooking), and *menu* all come from the French.

The French also enjoy their festivals. The major national festival is Bastille Day, held on July 14. On that date in 1789, a mob destroyed the Bastille, a Paris prison symbolizing the French king's harsh rule. The event began the French Revolution.

Ideas and the Arts The French have made major contributions to the arts and ideas. In the Middle Ages, the French built majestic cathedrals in the Gothic style. This style has high pointed ceilings, stained-glass windows, and tall towers that reach heavenward. Notre Dame Cathedral in Paris is an example.

In the 1700s France was a center of the Enlightenment, a period in which people used reason to improve society. French Enlightenment ideas about government inspired the American Revolution and the development of modern democracy.

In the 1800s France was the center of one of the most famous art movements of the modern age—impressionism. This style of painting uses rippling light to create an impression of a scene. During the same period, French authors wrote classics such as *The Three Musketeers* by Alexandre Dumas (doo-MAH). Novels like Dumas's and impressionism have become well-known around the world, transmitting French culture across the world and over time. Today, France is known for art and its fashion and film industries.

The Eiffel Tower in Paris, France, was completed in 1889. It was the world's tallest structure until 1930.

Reading Check
Summarize What are some main features of French culture?

France Today

France is now Western Europe's largest country. Locate France on the political map at the beginning of this module.

Today, about 75 percent of the French live in cities. **Paris,** the capital, is by far the largest city, with over 10 million people in the metropolitan area.

Fashionable with a quick pace, Paris is a center of business, finance, learning, and culture. It boasts world-class museums, art galleries, and restaurants, as well as famous landmarks such as the Eiffel Tower and Notre Dame Cathedral. Paris is also known for its many sidewalk cafés, where people meet to eat, socialize, and relax.

Other major cities include Marseille (mar-SAY), a Mediterranean seaport, and Lyon (LYAWN), located on the Rhone River. A modern system of highways, canals, and high-speed trains links France's cities.

France has a strong economy. It is the European Union's top agricultural producer, and its major crops include wheat and grapes. French workers are also highly productive. Rich soil and efficient workers have made France a major exporter of goods, such as its famous perfumes and wines.

Tourism is also vital to the economy. Each year, millions of people visit Paris, the French Alps, and the sunny French Riviera, a resort area on the Mediterranean coast.

Reading Check
Draw Conclusions
Why do you think tourists might want to visit Paris?

Paris

Some two thousand years old, Paris grew up along the banks of the Seine (SEN) River. Known as "the City of Light" for its gleaming beauty, Paris shines as one of Europe's most cultured cities. Wide tree-lined avenues, historic squares, and lovely gardens and parks grace the city center.

The Seine River winds through the heart of Paris. Beautiful bridges cross the river, and in places booksellers line its banks.

Notre Dame is France's most famous cathedral. It is a masterpiece of Gothic architecture.

The Paris Métro, or subway, is known for its decorative wrought-iron entrances built in the early 1900s.

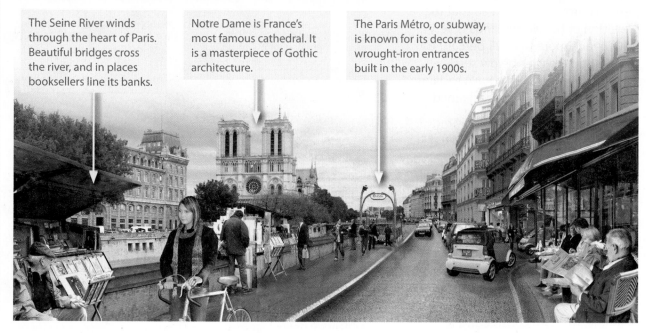

Analyze Visuals
What examples do you see of the mixing of the new and the old in Paris?

The Benelux Countries

Belgium, the Netherlands, and Luxembourg are called the Benelux Countries. *Benelux* combines the first letters of each country's name. They are also called the Low Countries because of their elevation.

History Many nations and empires dominated the Benelux region. In 1648 the Netherlands gained its independence. It ruled Belgium until 1830, and Luxembourg until 1867, when they gained independence.

In World War II, Germany occupied the Benelux Countries. After the war, they joined the North Atlantic Treaty Organization (NATO) for protection. NATO is an alliance of nations. In the 1950s the Benelux Countries joined the group of nations now known as the EU. The EU allows these small countries a larger market for free trade and allies in solving mutual problems, like environmental issues.

Today, the Benelux Countries each have a parliament and ceremonial monarch. The tiny, densely populated countries lie between larger, stronger countries. This location has led to invasions but has also promoted trade. The Benelux Countries now have wealthy economies.

The Netherlands Bordering the North Sea, the Netherlands is low and flat. Some of the land lies below sea level. The Netherlands includes the historical region of Holland and is sometimes called Holland. The people here are the Dutch, and the language they speak is also called Dutch.

Link to Technology

Dutch Polders

If you look on the physical map of West-Central Europe, you can see that the elevation of the Netherlands is very low. In fact, more than 25 percent of the Netherlands lies below sea level. For centuries, the Dutch have reclaimed land from the sea. These reclaimed lands are called polders.

To create polders, the Dutch build dikes, or earthen walls, near the shoreline. They then use pumps to remove the water behind the dikes. A national system of dikes, dams, floodgates, and storm barriers now holds back the sea.

Unfortunately, creating polders has caused sinking lowlands and other environmental damage. The Dutch are working to address these problems. For example, they are considering restoring some of the polders to wetlands, lakes, and the seas.

Find Main Ideas
How have the Dutch modified their environment to live in a region that lies below sea level?

Excellent harbors on the North Sea have made the Netherlands a center of international trade. The city of Rotterdam is one of the world's busiest seaports. It is also part of a highly industrial and urban, or city-based, area. This area includes **Amsterdam,** the capital, and **The Hague** (HAYG), the seat of government. Agriculture is also important to the Dutch economy, and Dutch cheese and tulips are world famous.

Belgium Belgium is a highly urban country. More than 95 percent of the people of Belgium live in cities. The capital city, **Brussels,** serves as the headquarters for many international organizations, including the EU and NATO. The city of Brussels is as a result highly **cosmopolitan,** or characterized by many foreign influences.

Language divides Belgium. The coast and the north are called Flanders. The people there speak Flemish. The southern interior is called Wallonia. The people there speak French and are called Walloons. These cultural differences have caused tensions.

Belgium is known for its cheeses, chocolate, cocoa, and lace. The city of Antwerp is a key port and diamond-cutting center.

Luxembourg Luxembourg is a forested, hilly country. Although smaller than Rhode Island, it has one of the world's highest standards of living. Most of the people in Luxembourg are Roman Catholic and speak either French or German.

Luxembourg earns much of its income from services such as banking. The region also produces steel and chemicals. Its small cities are cosmopolitan centers of international business and government.

Summary and Preview As you have learned, France and the Benelux Countries are modern and urban, with strong economies. Next, you will read about Germany and the Alpine Countries.

Reading Check
Compare and Contrast What do the Benelux Countries have in common? How do they differ?

Lesson 2 Assessment

Review Ideas, Terms, and Places

1. **a. Identify** Who was Charlemagne?
   b. Explain Why is Napoleon considered a significant figure in French history?
   c. Synthesize Why might the French be proud of their long history?
2. **a. Define** What is impressionism?
   b. Summarize What are some major contributions of French culture?
   c. Elaborate How has immigration influenced French culture?
3. **a. Describe** Why is Paris an important city?
   b. Summarize What is the French economy like?
4. **a. Describe** How does language divide Belgium?
   b. Draw Conclusions Why might Brussels be such a cosmopolitan city?

c. Elaborate What are some ways in which technology influences human interactions with the environment in the Netherlands?

Critical Thinking

5. **Categorize** Draw a circle chart like the one here. Enter relevant information from the lesson into each category. Within each category, organize the information by country.

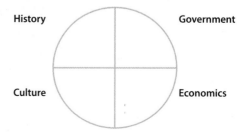

Germany and the Alpine Countries

The Big Idea

Germany and the Alpine Countries are prosperous countries with similar cultures.

Main Ideas

- After a history of division and two world wars, Germany is now a unified country.

- German culture, known for its contributions to music, literature, and science, is growing more diverse.

- Germany today has Europe's largest economy, but eastern Germany faces challenges.

- The Alpine Countries reflect German culture and have strong economies based on tourism and services.

Key Terms and Places

Berlin
Protestants
chancellor
Vienna
cantons
neutral
Bern

If YOU lived there . . .

You are walking with your grandfather through Berlin, Germany. He begins telling you about a time when Germany was divided into two countries—one democratic and one communist. A large wall even divided the city of Berlin. Germans could not pass freely through the wall. You think of your friends who live in eastern Berlin. They would have been on the other side of the wall back then.

What do you think life in Berlin was like then?

History of Germany

Some countries have had a strong influence on world events. Germany is one of these countries. Locate Germany on the political map. From its location in the heart of Europe, Germany has shaped events across Europe and the world—for both good and bad.

Growth of a Nation In ancient times, tribes from northern Europe settled in the land that is now Germany. The Romans called this region Germania, after the name of one of the tribes. Over time, many small German states developed in the region. Princes ruled these states. With the support of the Roman Catholic Church, these states became part of the Holy Roman Empire.

For hundreds of years, Germany remained a loose association of small states. Then in 1871, Prussia, the strongest state, united Germany into one nation. As a unified nation, Germany developed into an industrial and military world power.

War and Division From 1914 until 1918, Germany fought and lost World War I. Payments for war damages and a major worldwide depression severely hurt the German economy. Looking for a strong leader, Germans found Adolf Hitler and his Nazi Party. Hitler promised the Germans to restore their country to its former glory. Yet, Hitler ruled ruthlessly and Germany became a dictatorship.

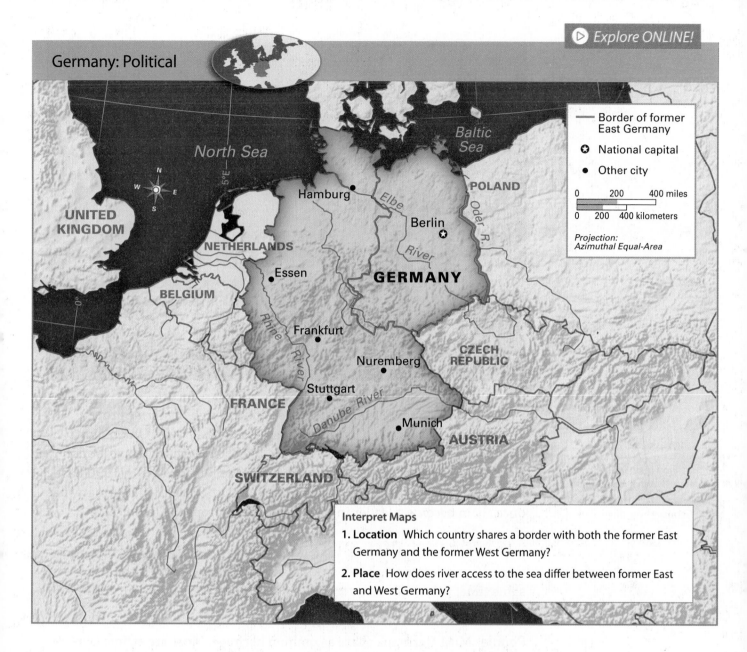

Germany: Political

UNITED KINGDOM

North Sea

Baltic Sea

NETHERLANDS

BELGIUM

Hamburg

Elbe River

POLAND

Oder R.

Berlin

GERMANY

Essen

FRANCE

Rhine River

Frankfurt

Nuremberg

Stuttgart

Danube River

CZECH REPUBLIC

Munich

AUSTRIA

SWITZERLAND

Border of former East Germany

⊗ National capital

● Other city

0   200   400 miles

0   200   400 kilometers

Projection: Azimuthal Equal-Area

Interpret Maps

1. **Location** Which country shares a border with both the former East Germany and the former West Germany?

2. **Place** How does river access to the sea differ between former East and West Germany?

In 1939 Germany attacked Poland, starting World War II. Soon, Germany had conquered much of Europe. The Nazis also sought to kill all European Jews in what is called the Holocaust. Germany lost the war, though. By 1945 it lay in ruins, defeated.

After the war, British, French, and U.S. troops occupied West Germany. The Soviet Union's troops occupied East Germany. Over time, two countries emerged.

The city of **Berlin** was in communist East Germany. Even so, West Germany kept control of the western part of the city. In 1961 communist leaders built the Berlin Wall. The Wall's **purpose** was to prevent East Germans from fleeing to West Berlin.

A Reunited Germany After World War II, U.S. aid helped West Germany rebuild rapidly. It soon became an economic power. East Germany rebuilt as well, but its economy lagged. In addition, its people had limited freedoms.

Academic Vocabulary
purpose the reason something is done

The Brandenburg Gate connects eastern and western Berlin. For 28 years, the Berlin Wall blocked the gate. It reopened in 1989.

Reading Check
Find Main Ideas
What major challenges has Germany overcome?

In 1989 movements for democracy swept through Eastern Europe. Communist governments began collapsing, and the Soviet Union didn't have as much control over the countries, like East Germany, that it once dominated. Joyful East Germans tore down the Berlin Wall. In 1990 East and West Germany reunited to form one country. Since then, Germany has once again become a leader in Europe and the European Union (EU).

Culture of Germany

Germans are known as hardworking and efficient people. At the same time, they enjoy their traditions and celebrating their cultural achievements.

People Most Germans share a common heritage. Most are ethnic Germans, and most speak German. Due to a shortage in skilled labor and an aging population, Germany has tried to attract highly skilled workers from diverse groups to immigrate to Germany. As a result, the influence of these immigrants is making Germany more multicultural. The arrival of many refugees and migrants from the Middle East, Europe, and Asia has also made Germany more diverse.

Religion In 1517 the ideas of Martin Luther, a German monk, led to a religious protest movement called the Reformation. Those who protested against the Catholic Church became known as **Protestants.** Protestant churches arose in many Germanic states. Today, in north and central Germany, most people are Protestant. In the south, most are Catholic. In eastern Germany, fewer Germans have religious ties, reflecting the area's communist past. As more people immigrate to Germany, the number of Muslims in Germany is rising, but Muslims still only account for a small percentage of the population. There are also small Jewish and Hindu populations, along with other smaller religious minorities.

Germany's long history has enriched its culture. Historic castles dot the landscape, and long-held traditions continue. Blending with this history is a modern culture that includes a love of sports.

A Bavarian Castle King Ludwig II of Bavaria had the fairy-tale Neuschwanstein (noy-SHVAHN- shtyn) Castle built in the mid-1800s. The castle sits amid the Bavarian Alps in southern Germany.

Soccer Fans German soccer fans celebrate a victory. Soccer is the most popular sport in Germany. The country hosted the soccer World Cup in 2006.

Christmas Markets German Christmas markets and fairs, like this one, have been popular for centuries. Booths sell trees, crafts, and food. Rides and music provide entertainment.

Cow Festivals A German teen participates in a traditional Bavarian cow festival. These autumn festivals in the Alps celebrate the cows coming back to the village after spending the summer in mountain pastures.

Analyze Visuals
Which of these images shows long-held traditions?

Customs Festivals and holidays tell us much about German culture. Religious festivals are very popular. For example, many areas hold festivals before the Christian season of Lent. In addition, Christmas is a major family event. The tradition of the Christmas tree even began in Germany.

Each region has local festivals as well. The best known is Oktoberfest in Bavaria, the region of southeast Germany. This festival is held each fall in Munich (MYOO-nik) to celebrate the region's food and drink.

Reading Check
Summarize
What contributions
have Germans made
to world culture?

The Arts and Sciences Germany's contributions to the arts and sciences are widely admired. In music, Germany has produced famed classical composers, such as Johann Sebastian Bach and Ludwig van Beethoven. In literature, author Johann Wolfgang von Goethe (GOOH-tuh) ranks among Europe's most important writers. In science, Germans have made contributions in chemistry, engineering, medicine, and physics.

Germany Today

Despite a stormy history, Germany has endured. Today, the country is a leading power in Europe and the world.

Government and Economy Germany is a federal republic. Citizens of Germany can vote in German elections. Citizens vote for a representative and a party to represent them in the lower house of the German parliament. The members of the upper house are selected by the Land, or state, governments. The parliament chooses a **chancellor,** or prime minister, to run the government. The parliament also helps elect a president, whose duties are largely ceremonial. On the world stage, Germany belongs to the EU and NATO (North Atlantic Treaty Organization). EU citizens living in Germany may vote in some local elections.

The German constitution was ratified in 1949 and protects many basic rights of Germans. These rights include the freedom of religion and of expression. However, German law places some limits on the freedom of expression by banning Holocaust denial and the use of Nazi symbols.

Germany's market economy has helped the country become an economic giant. It is Europe's largest economy, producing about one-fifth of all goods and services in the EU. The nation exports a wide range of products. Most of its exports go to other European countries, its closest trade partners. With EU trade partners, there are also no barriers to trade, like tariffs, embargoes, or quotas. However, some exports go to Asia and the Americas. You may be familiar with German cars, such as BMWs or Volkswagens. German exports are influenced by its natural resources, including iron. Trade has helped the German economy thrive.

The German economy is based on industry, such as chemicals, engineering, and steel. The main industrial district is the Ruhr, located in western Germany. Fewer Germans farm than in the past, but agriculture remains important. Major crops that grow well in its climate include grain, potatoes, and grapes. Timber is harvested in the south.

Pollution from all this industry and from vehicle exhaust started having a noticeable impact on the Black Forest and other areas of Germany in the early 1980s. When rain fell and mixed with the pollutants, it became acidic. This acid rain damaged and killed many of the trees in Germany's forests. After figuring out that acid rain was a problem, Germany and other countries around the world reduced pollutants from factories and cars. This change has lessened the impact of acid rain, but the soil in the Black Forest is still acidic and impacts the plants that grow there.

Germany's population is slowly aging because Germans are living longer and families are becoming smaller.

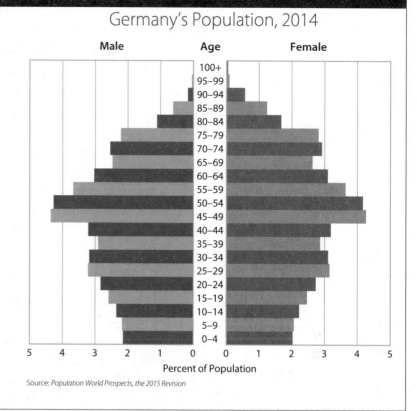

Germany's Population, 2014

Source: *Population World Prospects, the 2015 Revision*

Interpret Graphs
Which age group in Germany was the largest in 2014?

The economy of former East Germany continues to lag behind that of the former West Germany. The region also suffers higher unemployment. Germany's government is working to solve these problems.

Cities Most Germans live in cities. The largest city is Berlin, the capital. During World War II, Berlin suffered major destruction. Today, Germans have restored their capital to its former splendor. A historic city, it has wide boulevards and many parks.

Other major German cities include Hamburg, a key port city on the North Sea, and Munich, a cultural and manufacturing center. After reunification, many people in East Germany moved to West German cities for better economic opportunities.

Like France, Germany has an excellent transportation system that links its cities. Germany's highway system, the Autobahn, is one of the best in the world.

Reading Check
Analyze Effects
How did the success of the German economy affect the environment?

The Alpine Countries

The beauty of the Alps draws many tourists to Austria and Switzerland. These countries are called the Alpine Countries after the Alps, which cover much of them.

Austria and Switzerland have many similarities. Both are landlocked. Both are heavily influenced by German culture and were once part of the Holy Roman Empire. Yet, the countries have their differences.

Austria Austria was once the center of one of the most powerful empires in Europe. The royal Habsburg family came to control this empire. At its height, the Habsburg line ruled the Netherlands, Spain, and much of Germany, Italy, and Eastern Europe.

In 1918, however, the Habsburgs were on the losing side of World War I. After the war, Austria became a republic. Since then, Austria has grown into a modern, industrialized nation. Today, it is a federal republic and EU member.

Most Austrians speak German and are Roman Catholic. The city of **Vienna** is Austria's capital and largest city. Located on the banks of the Danube, Vienna was once the center of Habsburg rule. Today, historic palaces grace the city, which is a center of music and the fine arts.

Austria has a prosperous economy with low unemployment. Service industries, such as banking, are important and employ more than half of Austria's workforce. Tourism is important as well.

Switzerland Since the 1600s Switzerland has been an independent country. Today, it is a federal republic with 26 districts called **cantons.** Citizens are active in local government. In addition, all male citizens serve for a period in the militia, a citizen army.

Switzerland's location in the Alps has helped it remain **neutral** for centuries. Neutral means not taking sides in international conflict. To stay neutral, Switzerland has not joined the EU or NATO. However, the Swiss are active in other international organizations.

As the map shows, the Swiss speak several languages. The main languages are German and French. Romansh and Italian are the two

The Alpine Countries

Austria and Switzerland draw millions of tourists each year. On the right, tourists ride through Vienna, Austria, famous for its history and culture. At left, a mountain village shows the beauty of the Swiss Alps.

Analyze Visuals
How are Vienna and the village in the Swiss Alps alike?
How are they different?

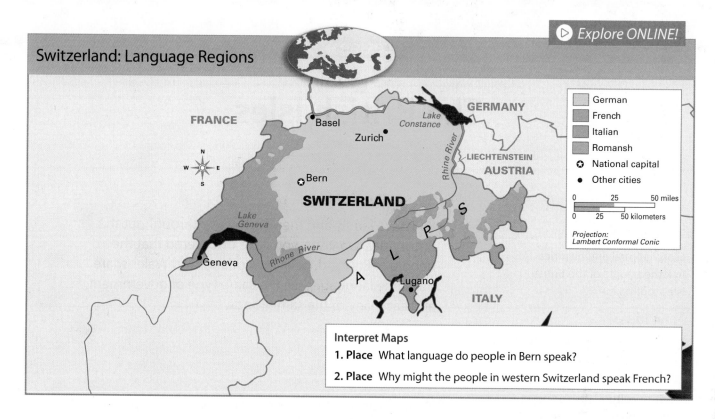

Switzerland: Language Regions

FRANCE

Basel

Zurich

Lake Constance

GERMANY

Rhine River

LIECHTENSTEIN

AUSTRIA

Bern

SWITZERLAND

Lake Geneva

Rhone River

Geneva

A L P S

Lugano

ITALY

German

French

Italian

Romansh

National capital

Other cities

0   25   50 miles

0   25   50 kilometers

Projection:
Lambert Conformal Conic

Interpret Maps

1. **Place** What language do people in Bern speak?

2. **Place** Why might the people in western Switzerland speak French?

other official languages. Each canton of Switzerland chooses its official language. Switzerland's capital, **Bern,** is centrally located to be near both German- and French-speaking regions. Unlike in Austria, only a little over a third of Switzerland's population is Catholic, and about a quarter identify as Protestant.

Switzerland has one of the world's highest standards of living. It is famous for its banks, watches and other precision devices, and chocolate and cheese.

Reading Check
Contrast
How are the countries of Austria and Switzerland different?

Summary and Preview You have read that Germany is an economic power with a rich culture, while the Alpine Countries are prosperous with beautiful mountain scenery. In the next lesson, you will learn about the British Isles.

Lesson 3 Assessment

Review Ideas, Terms, and Places

1. **a. Identify** Why is Adolf Hitler significant in history?

   b. Sequence What events led to German reunification?

2. **a. Recall** What are some popular festivals in Germany?

   b. Evaluate What contributions are diverse groups making to Germany?

3. **a. Describe** What is the role of Germany's chancellor?

   b. Explain Why has Germany's economy slowed?

   c. Analyze Compare how Germany's climate, location, and natural resources affect its economy and trade with how another country you've learned about is affected by those factors.

4. **a. Define** What are cantons, and where are they found?

   b. Analyze How are the Alps a valuable resource?

Critical Thinking

5. **Compare and Contrast** Draw a Venn diagram like this one. List the differences and similarities between Germany and the Alpine Countries.

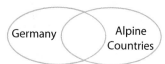

Germany   Alpine Countries

The British Isles

The Big Idea

The Big Idea

Close cultural and historical ties link the people of the British Isles today.

Main Ideas

- Invaders and a global empire have shaped the history of the British Isles.

- British culture, such as government and music, has influenced much of the world.

- Efforts to bring peace to Northern Ireland and maintain strong economies are important issues in the British Isles today.

Key Terms and Places

constitutional monarchy
Magna Carta
London
Dublin
disarm

If YOU lived there . . .

You have family and friends who live throughout the British Isles. On visits, you have discovered that the people of England, Ireland, Scotland, and Wales share the same language, use the same type of government, and eat many of the same foods.

Why might culture in the British Isles be similar?

History

Two independent countries—the Republic of Ireland and the United Kingdom—make up the British Isles. Locate the United Kingdom on the British Isles map in this lesson. As you can see, the countries of England, Scotland, Wales, and Northern Ireland make up the United Kingdom.

Early History The history of the British Isles dates back thousands of years. Early settlers built Stonehenge, an ancient monument, some five thousand years ago. Around 450 BC, the Celts (KELTS) arrived in the British Isles and settled Scotland, Wales, and Ireland. Britain was even part of the ancient Roman Empire.

In the Middle Ages, a series of invaders ruled the British Isles. The Angles, Saxons, and Vikings all established small kingdoms in Britain. Finally, in 1066, the Normans from northern France conquered England and established a strong kingdom there.

Over time, England grew in strength and power. It soon overshadowed its neighbors in the British Isles. By the 1500s strong rulers like Queen Elizabeth I had turned England into a world power.

Rise of the British Empire A strong economy and mighty navy helped England build a vast empire. Over time, England joined with Wales and Scotland to create the United Kingdom of Great Britain. Eventually, Ireland was annexed, too. England also launched an overseas empire. By the 1800s Britain had colonies in the Americas, India, and Australia.

The United Kingdom's economy soared in the 1700s and 1800s, thanks to the Industrial Revolution. Industries like iron, steel, and textiles, or cloth products, helped make the United Kingdom one of the world's richest countries.

Timeline: History of the British Isles

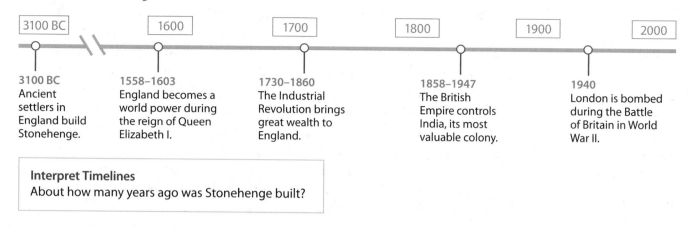

| 3100 BC | 1600 | 1700 | 1800 | 1900 | 2000 |

3100 BC
Ancient settlers in England build Stonehenge.

1558–1603
England becomes a world power during the reign of Queen Elizabeth I.

1730–1860
The Industrial Revolution brings great wealth to England.

1858–1947
The British Empire controls India, its most valuable colony.

1940
London is bombed during the Battle of Britain in World War II.

Interpret Timelines
About how many years ago was Stonehenge built?

Not everyone benefited, however. In the 1840s a severe food shortage devastated Ireland. Lack of support from the English government during the famine increased tensions between the two countries.

By the late 1800s the British Empire spanned the globe. Africa, Asia, Australia, and the Americas were all home to British colonies. At its height, the British Empire was the largest empire in history.

Decline of Empire In the 1900s the British Empire began to fall apart. Both World War I and the Great Depression hurt the British economy. Rebellions in Ireland forced Britain to grant self-rule to all but the northern part of Ireland. In 1949 the Republic of Ireland gained full independence. Movements for independence also emerged in Britain's overseas colonies. After World War II, Great Britain gave up most of its colonies. The British Empire was no more.

Culture

For years, the British ruled much of the world. As a result, the government, people, and popular culture of the British Isles have influenced people all around the globe.

Government The government of the United Kingdom is a **constitutional monarchy.** In this type of democracy, a monarch, or a king or queen, serves as head of state. However, a legislature, often a parliament, makes the laws.

Reading Check
Sequence
What major events mark the history of the British Isles?

BIOGRAPHY

Sir Winston Churchill 1874–1965

Sir Winston Churchill guided the United Kingdom through the dark days of World War II. Churchill was appointed prime minister shortly after the beginning of World War II. He inspired the British to continue fighting despite Germany's defeat of much of Europe. He encouraged British citizens to "never surrender." His creation of an alliance with the Soviet Union and the United States led to Germany's eventual defeat. Churchill's determination helped the Allies win the war.

Evaluate
Do you think Churchill was important to British history? Why or why not?

The English first limited the power of monarchs in the Middle Ages. A document known as **Magna Carta,** or Great Charter, limited the powers of kings. It also required everyone to obey the law, including kings. Today, Magna Carta's influence still can be seen in the governments of many countries, including the United Kingdom and the United States. In these governments, government is limited and everyone must obey the laws.

Today, a prime minister leads the British government. Most members of Britain's legislative body, known as Parliament, are elected. British and Irish citizens living in the United Kingdom can vote in all elections for the area in which they live. Unlike in Germany, where only citizens can vote in all elections, citizens of Commonwealth countries who live in the United Kingdom can vote in elections. Commonwealth countries include many countries that are or were controlled by the United Kingdom, like Australia and India. While people vote for members of Parliament, the leader of the controlling party of Parliament is appointed as prime minister.

The Republic of Ireland has a president as head of state. The president, who has limited powers, appoints a prime minister. Together with the Irish parliament, the prime minister runs the government.

People For hundreds of years, the countries of the British Isles have had close ties. As a result, the countries share many culture traits. One similarity is their common heritage. Many people in the British Isles can trace their heritage to the region's early settlers, such as the Celts, Angles, and Saxons. Sports like soccer and rugby are another shared trait among the people of Britain. English is spoken throughout the British Isles, though people in Wales, Scotland, and Ireland also speak Celtic languages.

Although people in the British Isles share many culture traits, each region still maintains its own unique identity. This is particularly true in Ireland and Scotland. Unlike the rest of the British Isles where most people are either Protestant or not religious, most Irish are Roman Catholic.

People in different regions of the British Isles hold fast to regional traditions and customs. Here, Scots proudly display two symbols of Scottish culture—bagpipes and kilts.

Additionally, Irish Gaelic, a Celtic language, is one of the Ireland's official languages. The people of Scotland have also maintained their unique culture. It is not unusual in Scotland to see people wearing kilts and playing bagpipes on special occasions.

Immigrants from all corners of the world have settled in Britain. Many immigrants from former British colonies, such as India and Jamaica, add to the rich culture of the British Isles.

Popular Culture Popular culture of the British Isles influences people all around the globe. For example, English is the language of business, education, and the Internet in many places. British and Irish music and literature are also popular. Millions of people around the globe listen to music by bands like Ireland's U2 and England's the Beatles and read works by British authors like William Shakespeare and J.K. Rowling.

British Isles Today

The British Isles face some challenges. Efforts to maintain a powerful economy, the United Kingdom's relationship with the EU, and challenges to peace in Northern Ireland are key issues in the British Isles today.

The Economy The economies of both the United Kingdom and the Republic of Ireland are among the strongest in Europe. North Sea energy reserves have made the United Kingdom a major producer of oil

Reading Check
Summarize
What parts of British culture have spread around the world?

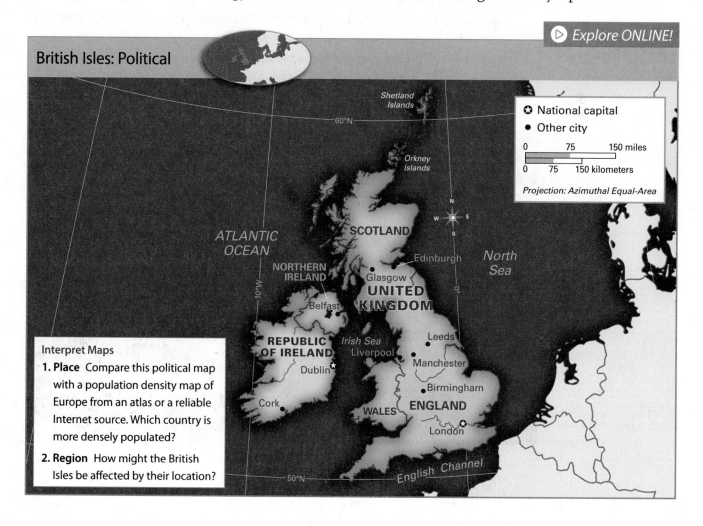

British Isles: Political

▷ *Explore ONLINE!*

✪ National capital
● Other city

0   75   150 miles
0   75   150 kilometers

Projection: Azimuthal Equal-Area

Shetland Islands

Orkney Islands

ATLANTIC OCEAN

SCOTLAND

Edinburgh

North Sea

NORTHERN IRELAND

Glasgow

UNITED KINGDOM

Belfast

Leeds

REPUBLIC OF IRELAND

Irish Sea

Liverpool

Manchester

Dublin

Birmingham

Cork

WALES   ENGLAND

London

English Channel

Interpret Maps

1. **Place** Compare this political map with a population density map of Europe from an atlas or a reliable Internet source. Which country is more densely populated?

2. **Region** How might the British Isles be affected by their location?

and natural gas. The economy of the United Kingdom also relies on service industries like banking, tourism, and insurance. Such industries are centered in cities. As a result, most people in the United Kingdom live in urban areas. For example, **London,** the capital of the United Kingdom, is a center for world trade, finance, and industry. Liverpool and Manchester are also centers of industry and trade. Both cities are also near coal mines. Initially, Manchester grew because it had rivers to power textile mills. Liverpool was a port city.

Since the United Kingdom is an island nation, its trade is dependent on shipping and its ports are important. The United Kingdom's location on the Atlantic Ocean and its historical ties to the United States have made the United States an important trade partner.

In Ireland, computer equipment and software have become major industries, especially near **Dublin,** Ireland's capital. High literacy rates, good infrastructure, and favorable tax laws enabled this growth. The Irish economy's recovery after the 2008 global recession has been strong. Like the United Kingdom, the Republic of Ireland is reliant on the service sector.

Brexit The United Kingdom joined the European Union in 1973. In June 2016 there was a referendum, or a yes or no vote on one issue, about whether or not the citizens of the UK wanted to leave the EU. This departure has been nicknamed Brexit, a combination of the words *British* and *exit*. Many people who voted for Brexit were concerned about the number of immigrants from EU countries and the amount of money the United Kingdom pays to be a part of the EU. Many people who voted to remain a part of the EU thought the trade benefits and ability to travel and move freely within Europe outweighed the downsides of membership. The majority of people voted that they did want to leave the EU.

London is the largest city in the British Isles and serves as one of Europe's major financial centers. In the past, London was affected by air pollution from burning coal, and its skyline was hazy at times. Now, the traffic in the city produces high levels of air pollution.

On March 29, 2017, British prime minister Theresa May formally asked the European Council to withdraw from the EU. From that date, the EU and the United Kingdom have two years to work out all the details of what Brexit will look like and what new treaties and trade deals the United Kingdom will have with the EU. The United Kingdom may now face trade quotas and tariffs from some of their closest trading partners.

Northern Ireland One of the toughest problems facing the British Isles today is conflict in Northern Ireland. Disputes between the people of Northern Ireland have a long history.

In the 1500s Protestants from England and Scotland began settling in Northern Ireland. Over time, they outnumbered Irish Catholics in the area. When Ireland became a separate state, Northern Ireland's Protestant majority chose to remain part of the United Kingdom.

Since then, many Catholics in Northern Ireland believe they have not been treated fairly by Protestants. Some Catholics hope to unite with the Republic of Ireland. For years, the two sides waged a bitter and violent struggle. In the late 1990s peace talks began between the two warring sides. An **agreement** eventually led to a cease-fire and the creation of a national Assembly in Northern Ireland that takes care of much of the local governing. However, the refusal of some groups to **disarm,** or give up all weapons, delayed the peace process. Hopes are high that peaceful relations between the groups will continue. However, a scandal in the Assembly, difficulty finding compromises within the power-sharing agreement, and concern over how Brexit will affect Northern Ireland mean that Northern Ireland is once again in a difficult time.

Summary and Preview You have learned about the rich history and culture of the British Isles. Next, you will learn about the countries of Scandinavia.

Academic Vocabulary
agreement a decision reached by two or more people or groups

Reading Check
Summarize
What is Brexit?

Lesson 4 Assessment

Review Ideas, Terms, and Places

1. **a. Identify** What peoples invaded the British Isles?
   b. Make Inferences How did the Industrial Revolution strengthen the British Empire?

2. **a. Describe** What elements of British culture are found around the world?
   b. Explain How did Magna Carta affect British government?

3. **a. Define** What does *disarm* mean?
   b. Analyze What are the causes of the continuing conflict in Northern Ireland?
   c. Explain How has the status of Northern Ireland changed over time?
   d. Elaborate Why do you think the economy of the British Isles is so strong?

Critical Thinking

4. **Summarize** Using a graphic organizer like the one here, summarize the history and culture of the British Isles in your own words.

History

Culture

Scandinavia

The Big Idea

Scandinavia has developed into one of the most stable and prosperous regions in Europe.

Main Ideas

- The history of Scandinavia dates back to the time of the Vikings.

- Scandinavia today is known for its peaceful and prosperous countries.

Key Terms and Places

Vikings
Stockholm
uninhabitable
Oslo
Helsinki
geysers

If YOU lived there . . .

You live in Copenhagen, the picturesque capital of Denmark. One of your favorite walks is along the waterfront, which is lined with colorful medieval buildings. Sailing boats of all sizes are anchored here. A famous statue in the harbor shows the *Little Mermaid*. But your favorite place of all is the huge amusement park called Tivoli Gardens, where you can enjoy fun and good food.

What sights would you show to a visitor?

History

Hundreds of years ago, Scandinavia was home to warlike Vikings. The **Vikings** were Scandinavian warriors who raided Europe and the Mediterranean in the early Middle Ages. Excellent sailors, the Vikings used quick and powerful longboats to attack villages along coasts or rivers. The Vikings conquered the British Isles, Finland, and parts of France, Germany, and Russia. They were some of the most feared warriors of their time.

The Vikings were also great explorers. They established the first settlements in Iceland in the 800s and in Greenland in the 900s. A short time later, Vikings led by Leif Eriksson became the first Europeans to reach North America. The ruins of a Viking colony have been found in present-day Newfoundland, off the southeast coast of Canada.

In the 1100s the Viking raids ended. Powerful Scandinavian chiefs instead concentrated on strengthening their kingdoms. During the Middle Ages, three kingdoms—Norway, Sweden, and Denmark—competed for power in the region.

Denmark was the first of these kingdoms to gain the upper hand. By the late 1300s Denmark ruled a union of all the Scandinavian kingdoms and territories. Eventually, Sweden challenged Denmark's power. In time, Sweden left the Danish-led union, taking Finland with it. Many years later, Sweden won control of Norway as well.

By the 1900s Scandinavian countries wanted their independence. Norway won its independence from Sweden in the early 1900s. Soon after, Finland became independent after centuries

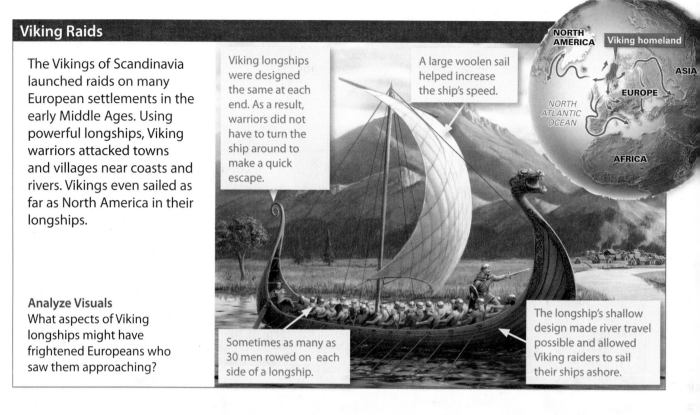

The Vikings of Scandinavia launched raids on many European settlements in the early Middle Ages. Using powerful longships, Viking warriors attacked towns and villages near coasts and rivers. Vikings even sailed as far as North America in their longships.

Viking longships were designed the same at each end. As a result, warriors did not have to turn the ship around to make a quick escape.

A large woolen sail helped increase the ship's speed.

Analyze Visuals
What aspects of Viking longships might have frightened Europeans who saw them approaching?

Sometimes as many as 30 men rowed on each side of a longship.

The longship's shallow design made river travel possible and allowed Viking raiders to sail their ships ashore.

NORTH AMERICA · Viking homeland · ASIA · EUROPE · NORTH ATLANTIC OCEAN · AFRICA

Reading Check
Draw Conclusions
What historical ties do the countries of Scandinavia have?

of foreign domination, or control, by Sweden and later by Russia. Iceland, then a Danish territory, declared its independence in 1944. To this day, however, Greenland remains a part of Denmark as a self-ruling territory.

Scandinavia Today

Today, the countries of Scandinavia have much in common. Similar political views, languages, and religion unite the region. Most people in the region are Protestant, but many people are not very religious. Scandinavian countries have, historically, had official state churches. Recently, Sweden and Norway have separated church and state. Many of the holidays celebrated by both religious people and non-religious people have religious roots.

The countries of Scandinavia have large, wealthy cities, strong economies, and well-educated workers. Scandinavian countries provide early childhood education, as well as elementary and secondary education for all students. Public universities are also mostly state-funded. The literacy rates in Scandinavia are high, and Scandinavians enjoy some of the world's highest standards of living. Each country provides its citizens with excellent social programs and services, such as free health care. Sweden, Denmark, Norway, Finland, and Iceland are among the world's most peaceful, stable, and prosperous nations.

Sweden Sweden is Scandinavia's largest and most populous country. Most Swedes live in the southern part of the country in large towns and cities. In fact, more than 85 percent of Swedes live in urban areas. **Stockholm,** Sweden's capital and largest city, is located on the east coast near the Baltic Sea. Often called a floating city, Stockholm is built on 14 islands and part of the mainland.

Like most Scandinavians, the people of Oslo, Norway, enjoy one of the highest standards of living in the world. High per capita GDPs are one reason why.

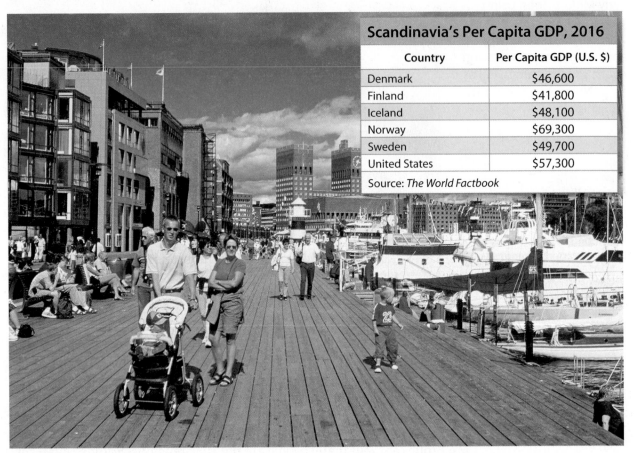

Scandinavia's Per Capita GDP, 2016	
Country	Per Capita GDP (U.S. $)
Denmark	$46,600
Finland	$41,800
Iceland	$48,100
Norway	$69,300
Sweden	$49,700
United States	$57,300

Source: *The World Factbook*

Analyze Visuals
What elements in the photograph indicate a high standard of living?

For almost two hundred years, Sweden has been a neutral country, like Switzerland. Sweden does, however, play an active role in the United Nations as well as the European Union.

Denmark Denmark, once the most powerful country in Scandinavia, is also the smallest. It is Scandinavia's most densely populated country, with some 338 people per square mile (131 per square km).

About 50 percent of Denmark's land is good for farming. Farm goods, especially meat and dairy products, are important Danish exports. Denmark also has modern industries, including iron, steel, textiles, and electronics industries.

Greenland The island of Greenland is geographically part of North America. However, it is a territory of Denmark. A thick ice sheet covers about 80 percent of the island. Because of this, much of Greenland is **uninhabitable,** or not able to support human settlement. Most people have adapted to living on the island's southwest coast, where the climate is warmest. Most of Greenland's population is Inuit. The Inuit are an indigenous cultural group who live in Greenland and in Arctic regions of Canada and the United States.

Recently, a movement for complete independence from Denmark has gained popularity. However, economic problems make independence unlikely, as Greenland relies heavily on imports and economic aid from Denmark.

Norway With one of the longest coastlines in the world, Norway has adapted to its access to the sea. Fjords shelter Norway's many harbors. Its fishing and shipping fleets are among the largest in the world. **Oslo,** Norway's capital, is the country's leading seaport as well as its industrial center.

Norway has other valuable resources as well. Oil and natural gas provide Norway with the highest per capita GDP in Scandinavia. However, North Sea oil fields are expected to run dry over the next century. Despite strong economic ties to the rest of Europe, Norway's citizens have voted to not join the European Union.

Finland Finland is Scandinavia's easternmost country. It lies between Sweden and Russia. The capital and largest city is **Helsinki,** which is located on the southern coast.

As with other countries in the region, trade is important to Finland. Paper and other forest products are major exports. Shipbuilding and electronics are also important industries in Finland.

Focus on Culture

The Sami

The Sami (SAH-me) people are a unique culture group who live in far northern Norway, Sweden, Finland, and parts of Russia. They are descendants of Scandinavia's earliest settlers. Traditionally, the Sami have earned a living herding reindeer, farming, and fishing. While today's Sami often work and live in modern cities and towns, they try to preserve many traditional Sami culture traits. The Sami language is taught in public schools, traditional reindeer grazing land is protected, and organizations promote Sami customs.

Make Inferences
Why do you think the Sami are trying to preserve their traditions and customs?

Iceland's geysers and hot springs produce great amounts of energy. Geothermal plants provide heat for buildings and homes throughout the country. The geothermal plant in the photo on the right is near Blue Lagoon hot spring.

Analyze Visuals
How are the hot springs being used?

Reading Check
Compare and Contrast
In what ways are the countries of Scandinavia similar and different?

Iceland Iceland is much greener than its name implies. Fertile farmland along the island's coast produces potatoes and vegetables and supports cattle and sheep.

Icelanders also make good use of their other natural resources. Fish from the rich waters of the Atlantic Ocean account for about 70 percent of Iceland's exports. Icelanders have adapted to their physical environment by using steam from hot springs and geysers to produce geothermal energy. **Geysers** are springs that shoot hot water and steam into the air. Geothermal energy heats many of Iceland's buildings. Each year, thousands of tourists flock to see Iceland's geysers, volcanoes, and glaciers.

Summary Scandinavia today is a region of relative peace and stability. A common history and culture link the people of the region. Today, Scandinavia is one of the wealthiest regions in Europe and in the world.

Lesson 5 Assessment

Review Ideas, Terms, and Places

1. **a.** Identify Who were the Vikings?

   b. Analyze What effect did the Vikings have on Scandinavian history?

   c. Evaluate Do you think the Vikings helped or hurt the future of Scandinavia? Explain your answer.

   d. Sequence List who controlled Scandinavia before the 1900s in sequential order.

2. **a.** Recall Which Scandinavian country has remained neutral?

   b. Analyze How have some people in Scandinavia adapted to their physical environment?

   c. Elaborate In which Scandinavian country would you prefer to live? Why?

Critical Thinking

3. **Find Main Ideas** Create a chart like this one, and use it to identify two main ideas about Scandinavia's history and two about its culture today.

History	Today

Social Studies Skills

Analyze Graphs

Define the Skill

Graphs can be used to explain relationships. They visually represent data or statistics. The many types of graphs include bar graphs, line graphs, and circle graphs.

Circle graphs, also called pie charts, represent all the parts that make up something. Each piece of the circle, or "pie," shows what proportion that part is of the whole.

Use the following guidelines to analyze graphs.

- Read the title to identify the graph's subject. The circle graph to the right shows the sources of electricity in Finland.

- Read the graph's other labels. For a graph with axes, note what each axis is labeled. For a circle graph, note what each part, or slice, of the circle graph represents. In Finland's Electricity Sources, 2012, each slice represents a different energy source.

- Analyze the data by comparing the size of parts of the graph. Think about what the differences mean or imply.

Learn the Skill

1. Based on the circle graph titled Finland's Electricity Sources, 2012, what type of power provides over half of the electricity there?

2. What are Finland's other two main sources of power?

3. What percentage of electricity comes from other renewable sources?

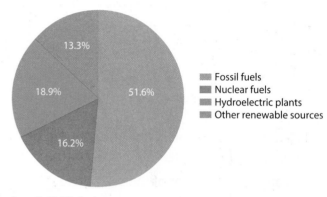

Finland's Electricity Sources, 2012

- Fossil fuels
- Nuclear fuels
- Hydroelectric plants
- Other renewable sources

Source: *The World Factbook*

Practice the Skill

To answer the following questions, use the circle graph titled France's Export Partners, 2015.

1. To which country does France send the highest percentage of its exports?

2. How many of France's main export partners belong to the European Union?

3. What percentage of French exports go to the United States?

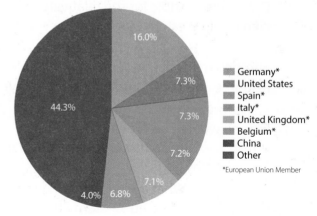

France's Export Partners, 2015

- Germany*
- United States
- Spain*
- Italy*
- United Kingdom*
- Belgium*
- China
- Other

*European Union Member

Source: The World Bank

Module 15 Assessment

Review Vocabulary, Terms, and Places

Match each "I" statement below with the person, place, or thing that might have made the statement.

a. Berlin   **f.** Danube River

b. Paris   **g.** cosmopolitan city

c. canton   **h.** navigable river

d. chancellor   **i.** Dublin

e. fjord   **j.** North Sea

1. "I am the capital of France and a center of business, finance, learning, and culture."

2. "I am a narrow inlet of the sea between high, rocky cliffs."

3. "I am an important waterway in the region of West-Central Europe."

4. "I am a prime minister in Germany."

5. "I am the capital of the Republic of Ireland."

6. "I am a type of river that is wide and deep enough for ships to use."

7. "I am a district in Switzerland."

8. "I am a city that has many foreign influences."

9. "I am a large body of water located to the north of the Benelux Countries and Germany and between the British Isles and Scandinavia."

10. "I was divided into two parts after World War II and am now the capital of Germany."

Comprehension and Critical Thinking

Lesson 1

11. **a. Analyze** How have geographic features supported trade and travel across the region of West-Central Europe?

     b. Analyze Explain how the North Atlantic Drift is responsible for the relatively mild climates in Western Europe.

     c. Elaborate How does West-Central Europe's mild climate serve as a valuable resource and contribute to the economy?

     d. Elaborate In which region of Western Europe would you prefer to live—the British Isles, Scandinavia, or West-Central Europe? Why?

     e. Summarize What are two ways in which glaciers have affected Western Europe?

Lesson 2

12. **a. Identify** Where is the busiest seaport in the Netherlands located?

     b. Summarize What are some products and cultural features for which France is famous?

     c. Analyze How does France's physical geography affect its economy?

Lesson 3

13. **a. Recall** What were three major events in German history, and when did each one occur?

     b. Analyze How is Switzerland's position in European affairs unique?

     c. Elaborate How has the royal Habsburg family shaped Austria's history?

Lesson 4

14. **a. Describe** What culture traits do the people of the British Isles share?

     b. Summarize Study the timeline of the history of the British Isles in this lesson. Then, organize the information from the timeline into a written summary.

     c. Predict How might Brexit affect the future of the United Kingdom?

Lesson 5

15. **a. Recall** What countries make up Scandinavia?

b. Compare and Contrast In what ways are the countries of Scandinavia similar and different?

c. Elaborate Why do you think Scandinavian countries today are so prosperous and stable?

Reading Skills

Recognize Word Origins *Use the Reading Skills taught in this module to answer the question below.*

16. Find the word *cosmopolitan* in Lesson 2. Write its definition. Then use a good dictionary to research the word's origins. Explain how the word's origins relate to its definition.

Social Studies Skills

Analyze Graphs *Use the Social Studies Skills taught in this module to answer the questions about the graphs on the Social Studies Skills page.*

17. What percentage of Finland's electricity comes from hydroelectric plants?

18. What percentage of goods went to France's top three export partners?

Map Activity

19. **West-Central Europe** On a separate sheet of paper, match the letters on the map with their correct labels.
    Alps
    Berlin
    English Channel
    North Sea
    Northern European Plain
    Paris
    Pyrenees
    Vienna

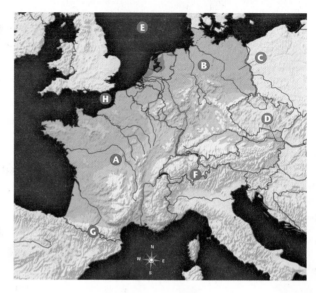

Focus on Writing

20. **Write a Persuasive Speech** Create a list of issues affecting Western Europe. Issues are topics that people disagree about. Perhaps coal mining or having one national language would be some of the issues you would identify. Choose one of the issues to focus on for your speech. Identify what you already know about the issue. Write down some questions that you would like to answer and questions your audience might have. Through research, try to answer these questions. Use the module and other digital and print sources to find information. You could read opinion pieces in newspapers or listen to news broadcasts. Read sources that support both sides of the issue. Be sure to assess the credibility and accuracy of each source. After learning some more about the issue, write a clear opinion statement. Next, list at least three facts or examples that support your opinion. Then use the list of effective supporting evidence to write your short persuasive speech. Apply the vocabulary you acquired while reading. Make sure you conclude your speech with a strong and convincing closing sentence. When you give your speech, speak formally and confidently and in an appropriate tone of voice. After you present your speech, respond to any questions your audience may have.

Eastern Europe

Essential Question

How can Eastern Europe overcome the challenges presented since the breakup of the Soviet Union?

In this module, you will learn about the geography and history of Eastern Europe. You will also learn how these nations have changed since the collapse of the Soviet Union.

What You Will Learn

▶ *Explore ONLINE!*

VIDEOS, including . . .
- Poland
- Fall of Constantinople

HISTORY

☑ Document-Based Investigations

☑ Graphic Organizers

☑ Interactive Games

☑ Channel One News Video: Geo Quiz: The Baltics

☑ Interactive Map: Eastern Europe under Soviet Influence, 1988

☑ Image with Hotspots: Budapest

Geography Like the Danube River shown here, many rivers flow through the mountains and plains of Eastern Europe.

Culture Eastern Europe is home to dozens of cultures, each with its own unique customs.

History Buildings in cities like Prague, Czech Republic, are symbols of Eastern Europe's long history.

Reading Social Studies

Understand Problems and Solutions

READING FOCUS

Throughout history, people have faced problems and found solutions to them. As a result, writers who describe historical events often structure their writing by identifying a problem and then describing its solution. The ability to identify this pattern of writing will help you understand what you read. Notice how the following passage presents one problem with a two-pronged solution.

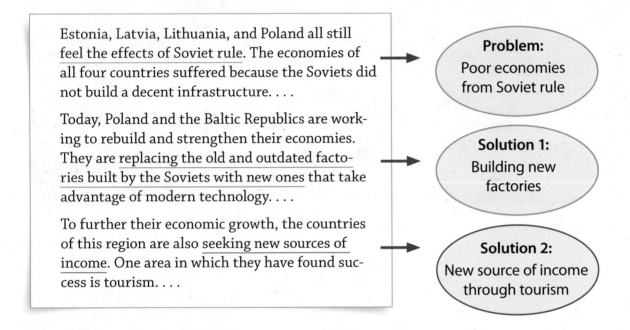

Estonia, Latvia, Lithuania, and Poland all still feel the effects of Soviet rule. The economies of all four countries suffered because the Soviets did not build a decent infrastructure. . . .

Today, Poland and the Baltic Republics are working to rebuild and strengthen their economies. They are replacing the old and outdated factories built by the Soviets with new ones that take advantage of modern technology. . . .

To further their economic growth, the countries of this region are also seeking new sources of income. One area in which they have found success is tourism. . . .

Problem: Poor economies from Soviet rule

Solution 1: Building new factories

Solution 2: New source of income through tourism

YOU TRY IT!

Read the following passage, and then use the process on this page to identify the problems and solutions the writer presents. Create as many circles as you need.

Many Eastern Europeans opposed Communist rule, and eventually the Communist governments in the region fell. Poland rejected Communism and elected new leaders in 1989. The Baltic Republics broke away from the Soviet Union in 1991 and became independent once more.

As you read this module, look for writing structure that identifies a problem and describes its solution.

Physical Geography

The Big Idea

The physical geography of Eastern Europe varies greatly from place to place.

Main Ideas

- The physical features of Eastern Europe include wide open plains, rugged mountain ranges, and many rivers.

- The climate and vegetation of Eastern Europe differ widely in the north and the south.

Key Terms and Places

Carpathians
Balkan Peninsula
Chernobyl

If YOU lived there . . .

You are traveling on a boat down the Danube River, one of the longest in Europe. As you float downstream, you pass through dozens of towns and cities. Outside of the cities, the banks are lined with huge castles, soaring churches, and busy farms. From time to time, other boats pass you, some loaded with passengers and some with goods.

Why do you think the Danube is so busy?

Physical Features

Eastern Europe is a land of amazing contrasts. The northern parts of the region lie along the cold, often stormy shores of the Baltic Sea. In the south, however, are warm, sunny beaches along the Adriatic and Black seas. Jagged mountain peaks jut high into the sky in some places, while wildflowers dot the gently rolling hills of other parts of the region. These contrasts stem from the region's wide variety of landforms, water features, and climates.

Landforms As you can see on the map, the landforms of Eastern Europe are arranged in a series of broad bands. In the north is the Northern European Plain. As you have already learned, this large plain stretches across most of Northern Europe.

South of the Northern European Plain is a low mountain range called the **Carpathians** (kahr-PAY-thee-uhnz). These rugged mountains are an extension of the Alps of West-Central Europe. They stretch in a long arc from the Alps to the Black Sea area.

South and west of the Carpathians is another plain, the Great Hungarian Plain. As its name suggests, this fertile area is located mostly within Hungary.

South of the plain are more mountains, the Dinaric (duh-NAR-ik) Alps and Balkan Mountains. These two ranges together cover most of the **Balkan Peninsula,** one of the largest peninsulas in Europe. It extends south into the Mediterranean Sea.

Academic Vocabulary
function use or purpose

Water Features Like the rest of the continent, Eastern Europe has many bodies of water that affect how people live. To the southwest is the Adriatic Sea, an important route for transportation and trade. To the east, the Black Sea serves the same <u>function</u>. In the far north is the Baltic Sea. It is another important trade route, though parts of the sea freeze over in the winter.

In addition to these seas, Eastern Europe has several rivers that are vital paths for transportation and trade. The longest of these rivers, the Danube, begins in Germany and flows east across the Great Hungarian Plain. The river winds its way through nine countries before it finally empties into the Black Sea.

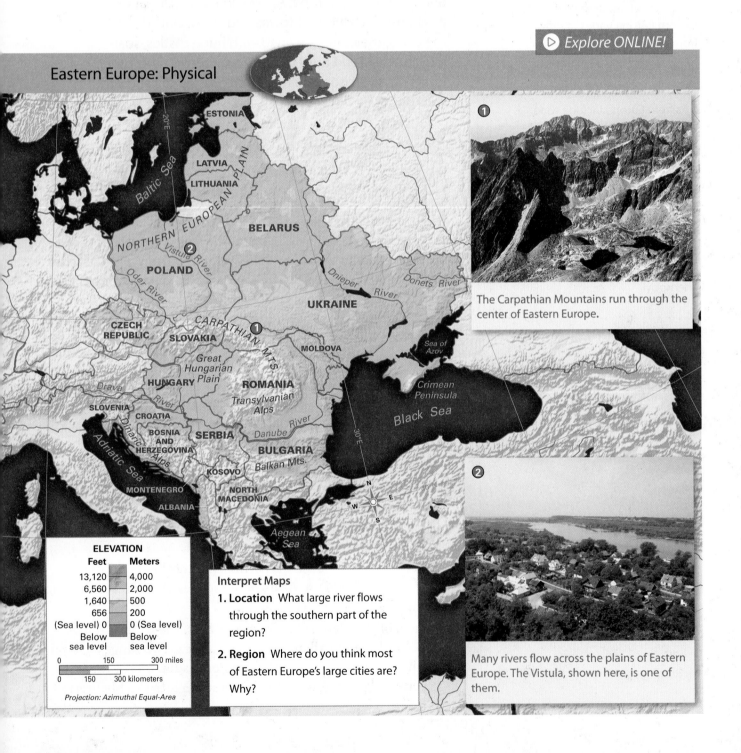

▷ *Explore ONLINE!*

Eastern Europe: Physical

The Carpathian Mountains run through the center of Eastern Europe.

ELEVATION

Feet	Meters
13,120	4,000
6,560	2,000
1,640	500
656	200
(Sea level) 0	0 (Sea level)
Below sea level	Below sea level

0   150   300 miles
0   150   300 kilometers

Projection: Azimuthal Equal-Area

Interpret Maps

1. **Location** What large river flows through the southern part of the region?

2. **Region** Where do you think most of Eastern Europe's large cities are? Why?

Many rivers flow across the plains of Eastern Europe. The Vistula, shown here, is one of them.

The Plains of Ukraine

One of Russia's greatest novelists, Nikolai Gogol (GAW-guhl), was actually born in what is now Ukraine. Very fond of his homeland, he frequently wrote about its great beauty. In this passage from the short story "Taras Bulba," he describes a man's passage across the wide open fields of Ukraine.

Analyze Sources
What features does Gogol describe on the plains of Ukraine?

"No plough had ever passed over the immeasurable waves of wild growth; horses alone, hidden in it as in a forest, trod it down. Nothing in nature could be finer. The whole surface resembled a golden-green ocean, upon which were sprinkled millions of different flowers. Through the tall, slender stems of the grass peeped light-blue, dark-blue, and lilac star-thistles; the yellow broom thrust up its pyramidal head; the parasol-shaped white flower of the false flax shimmered on high. A wheat-ear, brought God knows whence, was filling out to ripening. Amongst the roots of this luxuriant vegetation ran partridges with outstretched necks. The air was filled with the notes of a thousand different birds."

—from "Taras Bulba," by Nikolai Gogol

Reading Check
Find Main Ideas What are the main bodies of water in Eastern Europe?

As you might expect, the Danube is central to the Eastern European economy. Some of the region's largest cities lie on the Danube's banks. Thousands of ships travel up and down the river every year, loaded with both goods and people. In addition, dams on the western parts of the river generate much of the region's electricity. Unfortunately, the high level of activity on the Danube has left it heavily polluted.

Climate and Vegetation

Like its landforms, the climates and natural vegetation of Eastern Europe vary widely. In fact, the climates and landscapes found across Eastern Europe determine which plants will grow there.

The Baltic Coast The shores of the Baltic Sea are the coldest location in Eastern Europe. Winters there are long, cold, and harsh. This northern part of Eastern Europe receives less rain than other areas, but fog is common. In fact, some parts of the area have as few as 30 sunny days each year. The climate allows huge forests to grow there.

The Interior Plains The interior plains of Eastern Europe are much milder than the far north. Winters there can be very cold, but summers are generally pleasant and mild. The western parts of these plains receive much more rain than those areas farther east.

A nuclear accident in 1986 leaked dangerous amounts of radiation into Eastern Europe's soil. Ukraine's government and scientists are still working to repair the damage.

Analyze Visuals
What precautions are the scientists taking to protect themselves from radiation in the environment?

Because of this variation in climate, the plains of Eastern Europe have many types of vegetation. Huge forests cover much of the north. South of these forests are open grassy plains.

Unfortunately, Eastern Europe's forests were greatly damaged by a terrible accident in 1986. A faulty reactor at the **Chernobyl** (chuhr-NOH-buhl) nuclear power plant in Ukraine exploded, releasing huge amounts of radiation into the air. This radiation poisoned millions of acres of forest and ruined soil across much of the region.

The Balkan Coast Along the Adriatic Sea, the Balkan coast has a Mediterranean climate, with warm summers and mild winters. As a result, its beaches are popular tourist destinations.

Because a Mediterranean climate does not bring much rain, the Balkan coast does not have many forests. Instead, the land there is covered by shrubs and hardy trees that do not need much water.

Summary and Preview The landforms of Eastern Europe vary widely, as do its cultures. Next you will study the cultures of the northernmost parts of the region.

Reading Check
Contrast How do the climates and vegetation of Eastern Europe vary?

Lesson 1 Assessment

Review Ideas, Terms, and Places

1. a. **Identify** What are the major mountain ranges of Eastern Europe?

   b. **Make Inferences** How do you think the physical features of Eastern Europe influence where people live?

   c. **Elaborate** Why is the Danube so important to the people of Eastern Europe?

2. a. **Describe** What is the climate of the Balkan Peninsula like?

   b. **Explain** Why are there few trees in the far southern areas of Eastern Europe?

   c. **Predict** How do you think the lingering effects of the Chernobyl accident affect the plant life of Eastern Europe?

Critical Thinking

3. **Categorize** Draw a chart and for each column, identify the landforms, climates, and vegetation of the specific area in Eastern Europe.

	Landforms	Climates	Vegetation
Baltic coast			
Interior plains			
Balkan coast			

Poland and the Baltic Republics

The Big Idea

The histories of Poland and the Baltic Republics, both as free states and as areas dominated by the Soviet Union, still shape life there.

Main Ideas

- History ties Poland and the Baltic Republics together.

- The cultures of Poland and the Baltic Republics differ in language and religion but share common customs.

- Economic growth is a major issue in the region today.

Key Terms and Places

infrastructure
Warsaw

If YOU lived there . . .

You live in the beautiful and historic city of Krakow, Poland. Over the centuries, terrible wars have damaged many Polish cities, but Krakow is filled with cobblestone streets, romantic castles, and elaborate churches. The city is home to one of Europe's oldest shopping malls, the 500-year-old Cloth Hall. Glorious old Catholic churches also rise high above many parts of the city.

What does the city suggest about Polish history?

History

The area around the Baltic Sea was settled in ancient times by many different groups. In time, these groups developed into the people who live in the region today. One group became the Estonians, one became the Latvians and Lithuanians, and one became the Polish. Each of these groups had its own language and culture. Over the centuries, however, shared historical events have helped tie all these people together.

Early History By the Middle Ages, the people of the Baltics had formed many independent kingdoms. The kingdoms of Lithuania and Poland were large and strong. Together they ruled much of Eastern and Northern Europe. The smaller kingdoms of Latvia and Estonia, on the other hand, were not strong. In fact, they were often invaded by their more powerful neighbors. These invasions continued through the 1800s.

—— BIOGRAPHY ——

Pope John Paul II (1920–2005)

Karol Wojtyła, later called Pope John Paul II, was born in Poland. Raised a Roman Catholic, he became a priest shortly after the Soviets took over the country. After becoming pope in 1978, he encouraged the Polish people to protest against their Communist government. The pope's efforts played a role in Poland breaking away from the Soviet Union in 1989.

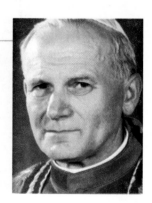

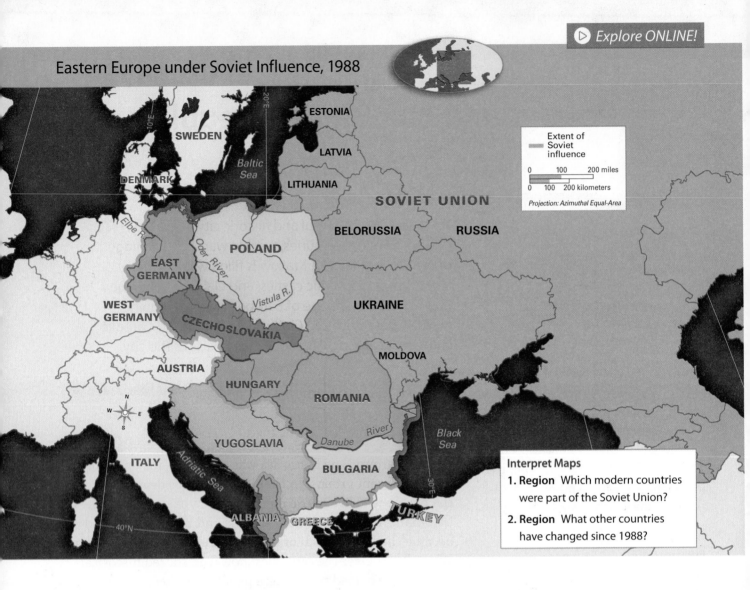

Eastern Europe under Soviet Influence, 1988

Explore ONLINE!

Extent of Soviet influence

0   100   200 miles
0   100   200 kilometers

Projection: Azimuthal Equal-Area

SWEDEN

DENMARK

Baltic Sea

ESTONIA

LATVIA

LITHUANIA

SOVIET UNION

BELORUSSIA   RUSSIA

POLAND

Elbe R.

EAST GERMANY

Oder River

WEST GERMANY

CZECHOSLOVAKIA

Vistula R.

UKRAINE

AUSTRIA

MOLDOVA

HUNGARY

ROMANIA

YUGOSLAVIA

Danube   River

Black Sea

ITALY

Adriatic Sea

BULGARIA

ALBANIA   GREECE

TURKEY

Interpret Maps

1. **Region** Which modern countries were part of the Soviet Union?

2. **Region** What other countries have changed since 1988?

The World Wars Both World War I and World War II were devastating for the Baltic people. Much of the fighting in World War I took place in Poland. As a result, millions of Poles—both soldiers and civilians—died. Thousands more were killed in the Baltic countries.

World War II began when the Germans invaded Poland from the west. As the Germans pushed through Poland from the west, the army of the Soviet Union invaded Poland from the east. Once again, Poland suffered tremendously. Millions of people were killed, and property all over Poland was destroyed. Estonia, Latvia, and Lithuania also suffered. All three countries were occupied by the Soviet army.

Soviet Domination As the map shows, the Soviet Union totally dominated Eastern Europe after World War II. Estonia, Latvia, and Lithuania became parts of the Soviet Union. Poland remained free, but the Soviets forced the Poles to accept a Communist government.

Many Eastern Europeans opposed Communist rule, and the Communist governments in the region eventually fell. Poland rejected Communism and elected new leaders in 1989. The Baltic Republics broke away from the Soviet Union in 1991 and became independent once more.

Reading Check
Analyze Effects
How did the Soviet Union influence the region's history?

Culture

In some ways, the cultures of Poland and the Baltic Republics are very different from each other. For example, people in the area speak different languages and practice different religions. In other ways, however, their cultures are actually quite similar. Because the four countries lie near each other, common customs have taken root in all of them. People cook similar foods and enjoy the same types of entertainment.

Cultural Differences The most obvious differences between the cultures of the Baltic countries are their languages and religions. Because the countries were first settled by different groups, each has its own language today. Of these languages, only Latvian and Lithuanian are similar to each other. Polish is related to the languages of countries farther south. Estonian is similar to Finnish.

Trade patterns and invasions have affected religion in the area. Poland and Lithuania traded mostly with Roman Catholic countries, and so most people there are Catholic. Latvia and Estonia, on the other hand, were ruled for a long time by Sweden. Because the Swedish are mostly Lutheran, most people in Latvia and Estonia are Lutheran as well.

Cultural Similarities Unlike language and religion, many of the customs practiced in the Baltic countries cross national boundaries. For example, people in these countries eat many of the same types of foods. Potatoes and sausage are very popular, as is seafood.

Other shared customs tie the Baltic countries together as well. For example, people in all three countries practice many of the same crafts. Among these crafts are pottery, painting, and embroidery.

Link to the Arts

Baltic Embroidery

One of the crafts for which the people of the Baltic region are best known is embroidery. This type of decorative sewing lets people create beautiful designs. They use these designs on their clothing, tablecloths, and other cloth goods.

For centuries, people in the Baltic countries—both men and women—have embroidered the clothing they wear on special occasions, such as weddings. They use many colors of thread to sew intricate patterns of flowers, hearts, and geometric designs. Because the embroidery is done by hand, it can take hours of work to create a single garment.

Draw Conclusions
Why do you think people embroider only clothing for special occasions?

Reading Check
Compare
How are the
cultures of the Baltic
countries similar?

Also common to the countries of the Baltic Sea area is a love of music and dance. For centuries, people of the Baltics have been famous for their musical abilities. Frédéric Chopin (1810–1849), for example, was a famous Polish pianist and composer. Today, people throughout Poland and the Baltic Republics gather at music festivals to hear popular and traditional tunes.

The Region Today

Estonia, Latvia, Lithuania, and Poland all still feel the effects of decades of Soviet rule. The economies of all four countries suffered because the Soviets did not build a decent infrastructure. An **infrastructure** is the set of resources, like roads, airports, and factories, that a country needs in order to support economic activities. The many factories built by the Soviets in Poland and the Baltics could not produce as many goods as those in Western Europe.

Today, Poland and the Baltic Republics are working to rebuild and strengthen their economies. They are replacing the old and outdated factories built by the Soviets with new ones that take advantage of modern technology. As a result, cities like **Warsaw,** the capital of Poland, have become major industrial centers.

Reading Check
Form
Generalizations
How has the
region changed in
recent years?

To further their economic growth, the countries of this region are also seeking new sources of income. One area in which they have found some success is tourism. Since the collapse of the Soviet Union in 1991, many Americans and Western Europeans have begun visiting. Polish cities like Warsaw and Krakow have long attracted tourists with their rich history and famous sites. Vilnius, Lithuania; Tallinn, Estonia; and Riga, Latvia, have also become tourist attractions. People are drawn to these cities by their fascinating cultures, cool summer climates, and historic sites.

Summary and Preview Poland and the Baltic Republics are still feeling the effects of decades of Soviet rule. In the next section, you will learn about more countries that feel the same effects.

Lesson 2 Assessment

Review Ideas, Terms, and Places

1. **a. Identify** What country ran the area after World War II?

   b. Draw Conclusions How do you think the two world wars affected the people of Poland?

2. **a. Describe** How do the languages spoken in Poland and the Baltic Republics reflect the region's history?

   b. Elaborate Why do you think that people across the region practice many of the same customs?

3. **a. Recall** What is one industry that has grown in the region since the fall of the Soviet Union?

   b. Explain How did Soviet rule hurt the area's economy?

Critical Thinking

4. **Analyze Effects** Draw a two-column chart with three rows. List major events for the region in the left column. For each box on the right, explain how the event affected the cultures or economies of the region.

Event	Effect
Soviet rule	
Breakup of the Soviet Union	
Growth of tourism	

Inland Eastern Europe

The Big Idea

The countries of inland Eastern Europe have varied histories and cultures but face many of the same issues today.

Main Ideas

- The histories and cultures of inland Eastern Europe vary from country to country.

- Most of inland Eastern Europe today has stable governments, strong economies, and influential cities.

Key Terms and Places

Prague
Kiev
Commonwealth of Independent
    States
Budapest

If YOU lived there . . .

You are a tourist visiting Budapest, the capital of Hungary. One morning, you stand on a bridge over the glittering water of the Danube River. You read in a guidebook that the two banks of the river were once separate cities. On the bank to your right, you see huge castles and churches standing on a tall hill. To your left is the Parliament building, obviously a much newer building.

What might have brought the cities together?

History and Culture

Located on the Northern European and Hungarian plains, inland Eastern Europe consists of six countries. They are the Czech Republic—also known as Czechia (che-kee-uh), Slovakia, Hungary, Ukraine, Belarus, and Moldova. Throughout history, many different peoples ruled these countries. Each ruling group influenced the culture and customs of the area.

Czech Republic and Slovakia The area that now includes the Czech Republic and Slovakia was once home to many small kingdoms. People called the Slavs founded these kingdoms. The Slavs were people from Asia who moved into Europe by AD 1000. Eventually, strong neighbors such as Austria conquered the Slavic kingdoms.

After World War I, the victorious Allies took land away from Austria to form a new nation, Czechoslovakia. About 50 years later, in 1993, it split into the Czech Republic and Slovakia.

Because of their location, these two countries have long had ties with Western Europe. As a result, Western influences are common. For example, many people in the two countries are Roman Catholic. The architecture of cities like **Prague** (PRAHG), the capital of the Czech Republic, also reflects Western influences.

Hungary In the 900s, a group of fierce invaders called the Magyars swept into what is now Hungary. Although they were conquered by the Austrians, the Magyars continued to shape Hungarian culture. The Hungarian language is based on the language spoken by the Magyars. In fact, people in Hungary today still refer to themselves as Magyars.

Ukraine, Belarus, and Moldova The Slavs also settled Ukraine, Belarus, and Moldova. Later other groups, including the Vikings of Scandinavia, invaded and conquered the Slavs.

A group called the Rus (RUHS) built a settlement in what is now **Kiev** (KEE-ev)—also known as Kyiv, Ukraine, in the 800s. The rulers of Kiev eventually created a huge empire.

In the late 1700s, that empire became part of Russia. When the Soviet Union was formed in 1922, Ukraine and Belarus were made Soviet republics. Moldova became a republic two years later. They did not become independent until the breakup of the Soviet Union in 1991.

The long history of Russian influence in the region is reflected in the countries' cultures. For example, most people in these countries are Orthodox Christians, like the people of Russia. In addition, Ukrainian and Belarusian languages are written in the Cyrillic, or Russian, alphabet.

Reading Check
Analyze Events
Which groups have influenced the history of the region?

The Kievan Empire

Kiev, now the capital of Ukraine, was once the capital of a large and powerful empire. At its height, the Kievan Empire stretched across much of Eastern Europe and Central Asia.

According to an old legend, the city of Kiev was built by three brothers and their sister. This monument built in the 1980s honors the city's legendary founders.

The people of Kiev built Saint Sophia Cathedral in the 1000s. By that time, nearly everyone who lived in the Kievan Empire was Orthodox Christian.

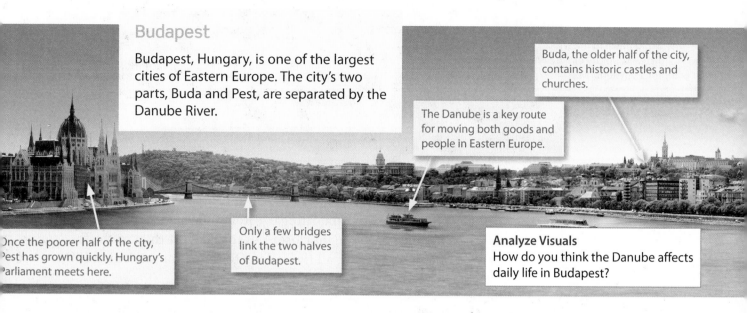

Budapest

Budapest, Hungary, is one of the largest cities of Eastern Europe. The city's two parts, Buda and Pest, are separated by the Danube River.

Buda, the older half of the city, contains historic castles and churches.

The Danube is a key route for moving both goods and people in Eastern Europe.

Once the poorer half of the city, Pest has grown quickly. Hungary's Parliament meets here.

Only a few bridges link the two halves of Budapest.

Analyze Visuals
How do you think the Danube affects daily life in Budapest?

Inland Eastern Europe Today

All of the countries of inland Eastern Europe were either part of the Soviet Union or run by Soviet-influenced governments. Since the end of Soviet domination, the people of inland Eastern Europe have largely overcome the problems created by the Soviets. Still, a few issues remain for the region's governments and economies.

Government During the Soviet era, the countries of inland Eastern Europe had Communist governments. Under the Communists, people had few freedoms. In addition, the Soviets were poor economic planners, and their policies caused many hardships.

Since the collapse of the Soviet Union, the governments of inland Eastern Europe have changed. Hungary, Slovakia, the Czech Republic, Ukraine, and Moldova are now republics in which the people elect their leaders. Belarus also claims to be a republic, but it is really a dictatorship.

One example of a change in government occurred when Ukraine's first free elections were held in 1994. This event indicated that democracy was taking root. However, the country faced deep divisions. The eastern part of Ukraine had more in common culturally and politically with Russia, while western Ukraine was more similar to Europe. These differences led to armed conflict over which group should control the nation.

Conflict continued over whether Ukraine should have a closer connection with Western democracies or with Russia. In 2014, Russian troops marched into the eastern region of Ukraine known as Crimea. Eventually, Russia annexed, or took over, Crimea as well as other parts of eastern Ukraine. Many consider the annexation to be a violation of international law and do not recognize Russia's claim.

The countries of inland Eastern Europe belong to several international alliances. One such alliance, the **Commonwealth of Independent States,** or CIS, meets to discuss issues such as trade and immigration that affect former Soviet republics. The CIS is based in Minsk, the capital of Belarus. Ukraine and Moldova are also members, as are many countries in Asia.

Tourists from all over the world travel to the picturesque city of Prague, Czech Republic.

The Czech Republic, Slovakia, Hungary, Romania, and Bulgaria are not part of the CIS. They have sought closer ties to the West than to the former Soviet Union. As a result, all five belong to the European Union (EU).

Economy Economic development has been a major challenge for these countries since the collapse of the Soviet Union. The Czech Republic, Slovakia, Hungary, and Ukraine have been most successful. All four are thriving industrial centers. Ukraine, with rich, productive farmlands, grows grains, potatoes, and sugar beets. Although some factors for a strengthening economy are present, such as high literacy rates and industry, the nations still face many challenges.

Cities Life in inland Eastern Europe is centered around cities, especially national capitals. In each country, the capital is both a key economic center and a cultural one.

Three cities in the region are especially important—Prague, Kiev, and **Budapest,** the capital of Hungary. They are the most prosperous cities in the region and home to influential leaders and universities. In addition, the cities are popular tourist destinations. People from all over the world visit Eastern Europe to see these cities' architectural and cultural sites.

Summary and Preview Inland Eastern Europe has been successful in facing the challenges left by Soviet influence. Next, you will learn about a region that has faced more challenges, the Balkans.

Reading Check
Form Generalizations
What are the countries of inland Eastern Europe like today?

Lesson 3 Assessment

Review Ideas, Terms, and Places

1. a. Recall In what country is Prague located?

b. Sequence List the groups that ruled Kiev and the surrounding area in chronological order.

c. Elaborate How has Hungary's history helped set it apart from other countries in inland Eastern Europe?

2. a. Identify What is the Commonwealth of Independent States? Which countries in this region are members?

b. Draw Conclusions How have the economies of the region changed since the collapse of the Soviet Union?

c. Explain Why do you think life is largely centered around cities in inland Eastern Europe?

Critical Thinking

3. Form Generalizations Draw a diagram to show how the government of Eastern Europe has changed. In the left oval, describe the government and economy of inland Eastern Europe under the Soviet Union. In the right oval, describe them since the Soviet Union's collapse.

Russia Today

The Balkan Countries

The Big Idea

Life in the Balkans reflects the region's troubled past and its varied ethnic makeup.

Main Ideas

- The history of the Balkan countries is one of conquest and conflict.

- The cultures of the Balkan countries are shaped by the many ethnic groups who live there.

- Civil wars and weak economies are major challenges to the region today.

Key Terms and Places

ethnocentrism
ethnic cleansing

If YOU lived there . . .

As part of your summer vacation, you are hiking across the Balkan Peninsula. As you hike through villages in the rugged mountains, you are amazed at the different churches you see. There are small Roman Catholic churches, huge Orthodox churches with onion-shaped domes, and Muslim mosques with tall minarets.

Why are there so many types of churches here?

History

Like the rest of Eastern Europe, the Balkan Peninsula has been conquered and ruled by many different groups. The presence of these many groups continues to shape life in the area today.

Early History By the 600s BC the ancient Greeks had founded colonies on the northern Black Sea coast. The area they settled is now part of Bulgaria and Romania. Later, the Romans conquered most of the area from the Adriatic Sea to the Danube River.

When the Roman Empire divided into west and east in the late AD 300s, the Balkan Peninsula became part of the Eastern, or Byzantine, Empire. Under Byzantine rule, many people of the Balkans became Orthodox Christians. More than a thousand years later, Muslim Ottoman Turks conquered the Byzantine Empire. Under the Ottomans, many people became Muslim.

The Ottomans ruled the Balkan Peninsula until the 1800s. At that time, the people of the region rose up and drove the Ottomans out. They then created their own kingdoms.

World War I and After Trouble between the Balkan kingdoms and their neighbors led to World War I. In the late 1800s the Austro-Hungarian Empire, which lay north of the Balkans, took over part of the peninsula. In protest, a man from Serbia shot the heir to the Austro-Hungarian throne, sparking the war.

Reading Check
Summarize
How did
World War I
affect the
Balkan Peninsula?

After World War I, the Balkans changed dramatically. Europe's leaders divided the peninsula into new countries. Among these new countries was Yugoslavia, which combined many formerly independent countries under one government.

The nation of Yugoslavia lasted until the 1990s. The country eventually broke up, however, because of conflict between ethnic and religious groups.

Culture

Culturally, the Balkans are the most diverse area of Europe. This diversity is reflected in the large number of religions practiced and languages spoken there.

Religion Most of the people of the Balkans, like most Europeans, are Christian. However, three types of Christianity are practiced in the area. Most Balkan Christians belong to the Orthodox Church. In the western part of the peninsula, there are many Roman Catholics. In addition, many countries also have large Protestant communities.

Christianity is not the only religion in the Balkans. Because of the Ottomans' long rule, Islam is also common. In fact, Albania is the only country in Europe in which most people are Muslim.

Language People in the Balkans speak languages from three major groups. Most languages in the region belong to the Slavic family and are related to Russian. In Romania, though, people speak a language that developed from Latin. It is more closely related to French, Italian, and Spanish than to Slavic languages. In addition, some people in Romania speak Germanic languages.

Reading Check
Draw Conclusions
Why is Balkan
culture so
diverse?

Some languages of the Balkans are not related to these groups. For example, Albanian is unlike any other language in the world. In addition, a group called the Roma have a language of their own.

Religion in the Balkans

Buildings from many religions can be found around the Balkans. This Orthodox church is in Bulgaria.

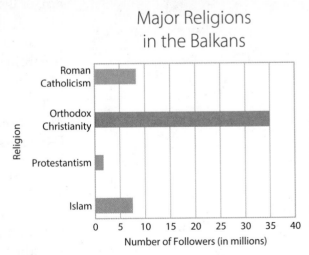

Major Religions in the Balkans

Analyze Graphs
What is the largest religion in the Balkans?

The Roma

The Roma are a nomadic people. For centuries, they have roamed from place to place in horse-drawn wagons, working as blacksmiths, animal trainers, and musicians. Although Roma live all over the world, the largest concentration of them is in southeastern Europe.

For centuries, many other Europeans did not trust the Roma. They were suspicious of the Roma's nomadic lifestyle and could not understand their language. As a result, many Roma have been subject to prejudice and discrimination.

Summarize
What is traditional Roma life like?

The Balkans Today

The countries of the Balkan Peninsula, like most of Eastern Europe, were once run by Communist governments. Weak economic planning has left most of them poor and struggling to improve their economies. This area is still the poorest in Europe today.

Relations among religious and ethnic groups have had serious **implications** for the Balkans. When Yugoslavia broke apart, violence broke out among groups in some of the newly formed countries. There were feelings of **ethnocentrism,** or the belief that one's own culture or ethnic group is superior. Members of the largest religious or ethnic group in each country tried to get rid of all other groups who lived there. They threatened those who refused to leave with punishments or death. This kind of effort to remove all members of a group from a country or region is called **ethnic cleansing.**

The violence in the former Yugoslavia was so terrible that other countries stepped in to put an end to it. In 1995 countries around the world sent troops to Bosnia and Herzegovina to help bring an end to the fighting. The fighting between groups eventually ended, and in 2008, ten countries shared the Balkan Peninsula:

- **Albania** Albania struggled with high unemployment rates and crime after the end of the Soviet period. The country's economy has shown great improvement in recent years.
- **North Macedonia** Once a part of Yugoslavia, North Macedonia broke away in 1991. It was the first country to do so peacefully.
- **Slovenia** Slovenia also broke from Yugoslavia in 1991. In 2004 it became the first Balkan country to join the EU.
- **Croatia** When Croatia broke away from Yugoslavia, fighting broke out within the country. Ethnic Croats and Serbs fought over land for many years. In the end, many Serbs left Croatia, and peace was restored.
- **Bosnia and Herzegovina** Since the end of ethnic and religious

Academic Vocabulary
implications
consequences

Fighting between ethnic groups left the city of Mostar in Bosnia and Herzegovina in ruins. After the war, the people of Mostar had to rebuild their city.

violence, peace has returned to Bosnia and Herzegovina. The people there are working to rebuild.

- **Serbia** Serbia is the largest nation to emerge from the former Yugoslavia. Like other Balkan countries, Serbia has seen fighting among ethnic groups.
- **Kosovo** Formerly a province of Serbia, Kosovo declared independence in 2008. Its population is mostly ethnic Albanian.
- **Montenegro** The mountainous country of Montenegro separated peacefully from Serbia in June 2006.
- **Romania** Romania, the largest of the Balkan states, is working to recover from years of bad government. Poor leaders have left its government and economy in ruins.
- **Bulgaria** Since the fall of the Soviet Union, Bulgaria has changed dramatically. People there are working to develop a capitalist economy based on industry and tourism.

Reading Check
Form Generalizations
What issues does the Balkan region face today?

Summary The Soviet Union had a huge impact on Eastern Europe. The nations of this region are still working to overcome many challenges today.

Lesson 4 Assessment

Review Ideas, Terms, and Places

1. **a. Describe** What was Yugoslavia? When did it break apart?
   b. Explain What role did the Balkan countries play in starting World War I?
2. **a. Identify** What are the four most common religions in the Balkans?
   b. Analyze Why are so many different languages spoken in the Balkans?
3. **a. Define** What is ethnic cleansing?
   b. Elaborate Why do you think other countries sent troops to Bosnia and Herzegovina? How has the country changed since the war ended?

Critical Thinking

4. **Summarize** Draw a chart like this one. Use your notes to write a sentence about how each topic listed in the left column affected life in the Balkans after the breakup of Yugoslavia.

The Balkans Today

Soviet influence	
Ethnic diversity	
Religion	

Social Studies Skills

Create a Benefits-and-Costs Chart

Define the Skill

Decisions can be tough to make. A seemingly simple choice can have both positive effects, or benefits, and negative effects, or costs. Before you make a decision, it can be helpful to analyze all the possible benefits and costs that will result.

One way to analyze benefits and costs is to create a chart. On one side, list all the benefits that will result from your decision. On the other side, list the costs. Not all costs involve money. You must also consider opportunity costs, or the things that you might lose as a result of your decision. For example, going to a movie might mean that you have to miss a baseball game.

Learn the Skill

The chart on this page could have been written by an official considering whether to develop a tourism industry in Croatia. Decide whether each of the numbered items listed should be added to the Benefits column or the Costs column. Once you have determined that, use the chart to decide whether the benefits of tourism outweigh the costs. Write a short paragraph to support your decision.

1. Would mean that tourist areas were not available for farming or industry

2. Would improve Croatia's image to people in other parts of the world

Tourism in Dalmatia, Croatia	
Benefits	Costs
• Would create much needed income for towns in the region	• Would require building of hotels, airports, and roads
• Would not require much new investment, since tourists are drawn to region's beaches and climate	• Increase in tourism could lead to damaging of local environments
•	•
•	•

Practice the Skill

Imagine that city leaders in your area are trying to decide whether to build a new school. They cannot make a decision and have asked you to help analyze the benefits and costs of building the school. Gather information and prioritize the facts according to importance. Create a chart to list those benefits and costs. Then write a brief paragraph stating whether the benefits of the plan outweigh its costs.

The Breakup of Yugoslavia

Essential Elements

The World in Spatial Terms

Places and Regions

Physical Systems

Human Systems

Environment and Society

The Uses of Geography

Background

A school playground has a limited amount of space. If many students want to use the playground at the same time, they have to work together and consider each other's feelings. Otherwise, conflict could break out.

Space on Earth is also limited. As a result, people are sometimes forced to live near people with whom they disagree. Like students on a playground, they must learn to work together to live in peace.

Yugoslavia

The country of Yugoslavia was created after World War I. As a result, people from many ethnic groups—Serbs, Montenegrins, Bosnians, Croats, Slovenes, and Macedonians—lived together in one country. Each group had its own republic, or self-governed area, in the new country.

For decades, the republics of Yugoslavia worked together peacefully. People from various ethnic groups mixed within each republic. Then in 1991 Croatia, Macedonia, and Slovenia declared independence. The republic of Bosnia and Herzegovina did the same a year later. These republics were afraid Serbia wanted to take over Yugoslavia.

It appeared that they were right. Serbia's leader, Slobodan Milosevic (sloh-BOH-dahn mee-LOH-suhvich), wanted to increase Serbia's power. He took land from other ethnic groups. He also called on Serbs who lived in other republics to vote to give Serbia more influence in the country.

Refugees Violence between ethnic groups led many people in Yugoslavia to leave their homes. The people in this photo are fleeing Bosnia to seek refuge in a safer area.

When the other republics broke away from Yugoslavia, Milosevic called on Serbs who lived there to rise up and demand that they rejoin the country. He also provided aid to Serbian military groups in these republics. In Bosnia and Herzegovina, Serbian rebels fought for three years against the Bosnian army in a destructive civil war.

Milosevic's ethnocentric actions caused other ethnic groups in Yugoslavia to resent the Serbs. As a result, additional violence broke out. In Croatia, for example, the army violently expelled all Serbs from their country. War raged in the area until 1995, when a peace accord was signed. As a result of that accord, Yugoslavia was dissolved. In its place were five countries that had once been Yugoslav republics.

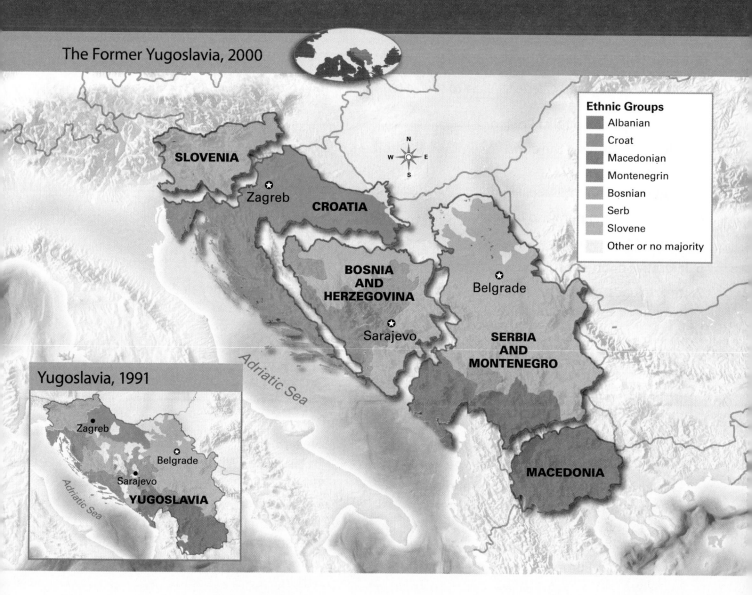

The Former Yugoslavia, 2000

SLOVENIA

Zagreb

CROATIA

BOSNIA
AND
HERZEGOVINA

Sarajevo

Belgrade

SERBIA
AND
MONTENEGRO

Adriatic Sea

MACEDONIA

Ethnic Groups

- Albanian
- Croat
- Macedonian
- Montenegrin
- Bosnian
- Serb
- Slovene
- Other or no majority

Yugoslavia, 1991

Zagreb

Belgrade

Sarajevo

YUGOSLAVIA

Adriatic Sea

What It Means

The violent breakup of Yugoslavia has taught other countries some valuable lessons. First, it reinforced the idea that national borders are not permanent. Borders can and do change.

More importantly, however, the struggles in Yugoslavia have made some countries more aware of their people's needs. People want to feel that they have some say in their lives. When they feel as though another group is trying to take that say from them, as many in Yugoslavia felt the Serbs were doing, then trouble will often follow.

Geography for Life Activity

1. **Analyze Causes** What led to the breakup of Yugoslavia?

2. **Analyze Events** Look at the maps on this page. Identify the changes based on human activities. What trends do you notice among ethnic groups in Yugoslavia between 1991 and 2000? Why do you think this is so?

Review Vocabulary, Terms, and Places

Unscramble each group of letters below to spell a term that matches the given definition.

1. **arwswa**—the capital of Poland
2. **neicht glncaenis**—the effort to remove all members of a group from a country or region
3. **subdatep**—the capital of Hungary
4. **ageurp**—the capital and largest city of the Czech Republic
5. **ncimlaitpiso**—consequences
6. **laknab**—the peninsula on which much of Eastern Europe is located
7. **ufrnrtriuacste**—the set of resources, like roads and factories, that a country needs to support economic activities
8. **nrhatcapias**—a mountain range in Eastern Europe

Comprehension and Critical Thinking

Lesson 1

9. **a.** Identify Name two major bodies of water that border Eastern Europe.
   b. Explain How do the Danube and other rivers affect life for people in Eastern Europe?
   c. Evaluate If you could live in any region of Eastern Europe, where would it be? Why?

Lesson 2

10. **a.** Identify What are the three Baltic Republics? Why are they called that?
    b. Compare and Contrast What are two cultural features that Poland and the Baltic Republics have in common? What are two features that are different in those countries?
    c. Elaborate How did the collapse of the Soviet Union affect people in Poland and the Baltic Republics?

Lesson 3

11. **a.** Describe What is the government of Belarus like? What type of government do the other countries of inland Eastern Europe have?
    b. Draw Conclusions Why do you think that some countries in inland Eastern Europe have stronger economies than others?
    c. Elaborate How has its location influenced the culture of the Czech Republic?

Lesson 4

12. **a.** Identify What religions are common in the Balkan countries?
    b. Explain Why did countries from around the world send troops to Kosovo?
    c. Predict How do you think peace will affect life in the Balkans?

Module 16 Assessment, continued

Reading Skills

13. Understand Problems and Solutions *Use the Reading Skills taught in this module to answer a question about the reading selection below.*

> Estonia, Latvia, Lithuania, and Poland all still feel the effects of decades of Soviet rule. The economies of all four countries suffered because the Soviets did not build a decent infrastructure. An infrastructure is the set of resources, like roads, airports, and factories, that a country needs in order to support economic activities. The many factories built by the Soviets in Poland and the Baltics could not produce as many goods as those in Western Europe.

Write a short paragraph that explains the main problem facing Poland and the Baltics today. End your paragraph by suggesting a solution their governments might use to address the problem.

Social Studies Skills

14. Create a Benefits-and-Costs Chart *Use the Social Studies Skills taught in this module to complete the following activity.*

Imagine that you are a government official in Ukraine. Your country cannot produce enough energy to meet its needs and has to buy energy from Russia. A company in Kiev has expressed interest in building nuclear power plants, but many people are leery of nuclear power since the Chernobyl incident. Create a chart that lists the costs and benefits of nuclear power. Then write a statement that either supports or argues against the plan.

Map Activity

15. Eastern Europe On a separate sheet of paper, match the letters on the map with their correct labels.

Great Hungarian Plain	Kiev, Ukraine
Latvia	Warsaw, Poland
Albania	Danube River

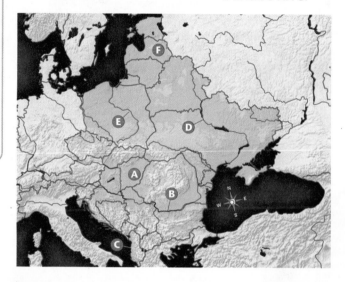

Focus on Writing

16. Write a Report For centuries the Balkans have been an arena of conflict. Use Lesson 4 and other primary and secondary sources to learn about the history and cultures of the Balkans and investigate recent conflicts there. Formulate appropriate questions to guide your research. You should gather relevant information from multiple print and digital sources. Collect information from non-print sources such as photographs and maps. Write a report on what you find. Be sure to apply key terms acquired from the lesson in your writing. Include at least one visual that presents information related to the topic. Your report should be focused and organized, with a clear introduction, supporting paragraphs, and conclusion. Check your report for spelling, grammar, capitalization, and punctuation. Present your report to the class. Speak clearly and keep eye contact with your audience.

Russia and the Caucasus

Essential Question

Are the challenges faced by Russia and the Caucasus countries in establishing and maintaining their democracies greater than those faced by the United States after it won the American Revolution?

In this module, you will learn about Russia's geography, history, and challenges. You will also learn about Georgia, Armenia, and Azerbaijan, the three countries located south of Russia in the Caucasus region.

Explore ONLINE!

VIDEOS, including . . .
- The Romanovs
- Peter the Great: The Tyrant Reformer
- Military Blunders: Stalin's Purges
- The Trans-Siberian Railroad

HISTORY

✓ Document-Based Investigations

✓ Graphic Organizers

✓ Interactive Games

✓ Interactive Map: History of Russian Expansion, 1500–1800

✓ Image with Hotspots: St. Basil's Cathedral

✓ Interactive Graph: Russia's Population Decline

What You Will Learn

Geography A volcano created Crater Bay in the Kuril Islands off the east coast of Russia. The islands have several active volcanoes.

Culture The Bolshoi Ballet in Moscow, Russia, is famous throughout the world. Above, dancers perform *Swan Lake*.

History The Kremlin complex houses Russia's government as well as gold-domed churches and beautiful, historical palaces.

Reading Social Studies

Use Context Clues

READING FOCUS

One way to figure out the meaning of an unfamiliar word or phrase is by finding clues in its context, the words or sentences surrounding it. A common context clue is a restatement. Restatements simply define the new word using ordinary words you already know. Notice how the following passage uses a restatement to define *Bolsheviks*.

> Later that year the **Bolsheviks**, a radical Russian Communist group, seized power in the Russian Revolution. They then killed the czar and his family. In 1922 the Bolsheviks formed a new country, the Union of Soviet Socialist Republics (USSR), or the Soviet Union.

Restatement:

a radical Russian Communist group

YOU TRY IT!

Read the following sentences, and identify the restatement for each underlined term.

> Stalin had anyone who spoke out against the government jailed, exiled, or killed. Millions of people were sent to **gulags**, harsh Soviet labor camps often located in Siberia.

> During World War I (1914–1918), the Turks forced all Armenians to leave. Hundreds of thousands of Armenians died during this **ethnic cleansing**, or attempt to remove an ethnic group.

As you read this module, look for context clues that restate the meanings of words you may not have encountered before.

Physical Geography

The Big Idea

Russia is big and cold with vast plains and forests, while the Caucasus features rugged mountains with seas to the east and west.

Main Ideas

- The physical features of Russia and the Caucasus include plains, mountains, and rivers.

- Russia's cold climate contrasts sharply with the warmer Caucasus.

- Russia has a wealth of natural resources, but many are hard to access.

Key Terms and Places

Ural Mountains
Caspian Sea
Caucasus Mountains
Moscow
Siberia
Volga River
taiga

If YOU lived there . . .

You are making a documentary about the Trans-Siberian Railway, a famous train that crosses the vast country of Russia. The train travels more than 5,700 miles across plains and mountains and through thick forests. As the train leaves the city of Moscow, you look out the window and see wheat fields and white birch trees.

What scenes might you include in your film?

Physical Features

Have you ever stood on two continents at once? In Russia's **Ural (YOOHR-uhl) Mountains,** the continents of Europe and Asia meet. Europe lies to the west, Asia to the east. Together, Europe and Asia form the large landmass of Eurasia. On the map, you can see that a large chunk of Eurasia is the country of Russia. In fact, Russia is the world's largest country. Compared to the United States, Russia is almost twice as big.

Georgia, Armenia (ahr-MEE-nee-uh), and Azerbaijan (a-zuhr-by-JAHN) lie south of Russia in the Caucasus (KAW-kuh-suhs), the area between the Black Sea and the **Caspian Sea.** This area, which includes part of southern Russia, is named for the **Caucasus Mountains.**

Landforms Locate Russia on the physical map. As the map shows, Russia's landforms vary from west to east. The Northern European Plain stretches across western, or European, Russia. This fertile plain forms Russia's heartland, where most Russians live. **Moscow,** Russia's capital, is located there.

To the east, the plain rises to form the Ural Mountains. These low mountains are worn down

The Caucasus includes both tiny villages and sprawling cities, such as Baku, the capital of Azerbaijan, on the Caspian Sea.

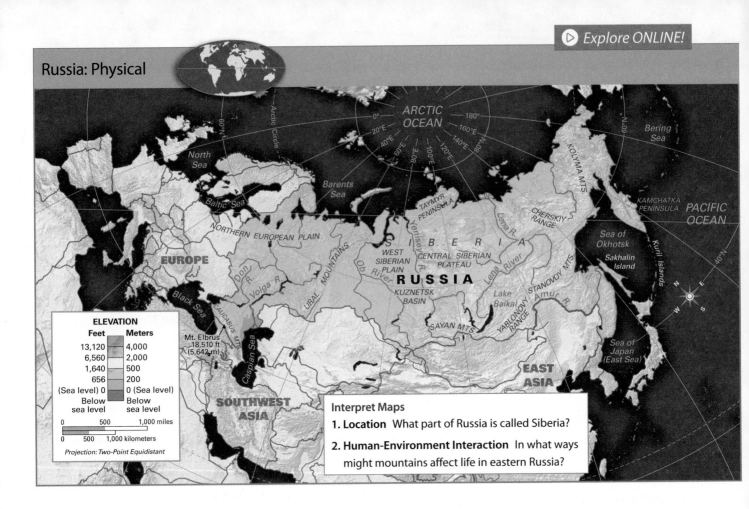

Explore ONLINE!

ARCTIC OCEAN

Bering Sea

North Sea

Barents Sea

Baltic Sea

KOLYMA MTS.

KAMCHATKA PENINSULA

PACIFIC OCEAN

NORTHERN EUROPEAN PLAIN

EUROPE

TAYMYR PENINSULA

CHERSKIY RANGE

Sea of Okhotsk

Sakhalin Island

S I B E R I A

WEST SIBERIAN PLAIN

CENTRAL SIBERIAN PLATEAU

Yenisey R.

Lena R.

RUSSIA

Kuril Islands

Don R.

Volga R.

URAL MOUNTAINS

Ob River

Lena River

KUZNETSK BASIN

Lake Baikal

STANOVOY MTS.

Amur R.

Black Sea

CAUCASUS MTS.

SAYAN MTS.

YABLONOVY RANGE

Sea of Japan (East Sea)

Mt. Elbrus 18,510 ft (5,642 m)

Caspian Sea

EAST ASIA

SOUTHWEST ASIA

ELEVATION

Feet		Meters
13,120		4,000
6,560		2,000
1,640		500
656		200
(Sea level) 0		0 (Sea level)
Below sea level		Below sea level

0   500   1,000 miles
0   500   1,000 kilometers

Projection: Two-Point Equidistant

Interpret Maps

1. Location What part of Russia is called Siberia?

2. Human-Environment Interaction In what ways might mountains affect life in eastern Russia?

and rounded from erosion. The vast area between the Urals and the Pacific Ocean is **Siberia.** This area includes several landforms.

The West Siberian Plain lies between the Urals and the Yenisey River and between the shores of the Arctic Ocean and the foothills of the Altay Mountains. Because the plain tilts northward, its rivers flow toward the Arctic Ocean. The West Siberian Plain is a flat, marshy area. It is one of the largest plains in the world.

East of this plain lies the Central Siberian Plateau. Mountain ranges run through southern and eastern Siberia.

Eastern Siberia is called the Russian Far East. This area includes the Kamchatka (kuhm-CHAHT-kuh) Peninsula and several islands. The Russian Far East is part of the Ring of Fire, the area circling the Pacific.

The Kamchatka Peninsula on Russia's east coast has many old and active volcanoes.

The snow-capped peaks of the Caucasus Mountains rise above a mountain village and the remains of a fortress built in the 900s.

The Ring of Fire is known for its volcanoes and earthquakes, and the Russian Far East is no exception. The Kamchatka Peninsula alone contains 120 volcanoes, 20 of which are still active. In some areas, steam from within Earth breaks free to form geysers and hot springs. The Sakhalin and Kuril islands lie south of the peninsula. Russia seized the islands from Japan after World War II. Japan still claims ownership of the Kuril Islands.

The Caucasus countries consist largely of rugged uplands. The Caucasus Mountains cover much of Georgia and extend into Armenia and Azerbaijan. These soaring mountains include Mount Elbrus (el-BROOS). At 18,510 feet (5,642 m), it is the highest peak in Europe.

South of the Caucasus Mountains, a plateau covers much of Armenia. Gorges cut through this plateau, and earthquakes are common there.

Bodies of Water Some of the longest rivers in the world flow through the region. One of the most important is the **Volga (VAHL-guh) River** in western Russia. The longest river in Europe, the Volga winds southward to the Caspian Sea. The Volga has long formed the core of Russia's river network. Canals link the Volga to the nearby Don River and to the Baltic Sea.

Even longer rivers than the Volga flow through Siberia in the Asian part of Russia. The Ob (AWB), Yenisey (yi-ni-SAY), and Lena rivers flow northward to the Arctic Ocean. Like many of Russia's rivers, they are frozen for much of the year. The ice often hinders shipping and trade and closes some of Russia's ports for part of the year.

In addition to its rivers, Russia has some 200,000 lakes. Lake Baikal (by-KAHL), in south-central Siberia, is the world's deepest lake. Although not that large in surface area, Lake Baikal is deep enough to hold all the water in all five of the Great Lakes. Because of its beauty, Lake Baikal is called the Jewel of Siberia. Logging and factories have polluted the water, but Russians are now working to clean up the lake.

Reading Check
Summarize
What are the major landforms in Russia and the Caucasus?

In the Caucasus, lowlands lie along the Black and Caspian seas. The Black Sea forms the region's western border. This sea connects to the Mediterranean Sea and is important for trade.

To the east, the region is bordered by the Caspian Sea, which is actually a salt-water lake that stretches for nearly 750 miles (1,207 km) from north to south. It is the largest inland sea in the world.

Climate and Plant Life

Russians sometimes joke that winter lasts for 12 months and then summer begins. Russia is a cold country. The reason is its northern location partly within the Arctic Circle. In general, Russia has short summers and long, snowy winters. The climate is milder west of the Urals and grows colder and harsher as one goes north and east. Because of the climate, the majority of Russia's population lives west of the Urals and is more concentrated in the south than the north.

Russia's northern coast is tundra. Winters are dark and bitterly cold, and the brief summers are cool. Much of the ground is permafrost, or permanently frozen soil. Only small plants such as mosses grow.

Distance from the sea affects the amount of precipitation the region gets, as well as its temperatures. Most of the region's moisture comes from the Atlantic Ocean. The air coming from the ocean loses its moisture as it travels farther and farther inland.

Russia's Climate and Plant Life

In the photo on the left, Russians bundled up in furs hurry through the snow and cold of Moscow, the capital. In the photo above, evergreen forest called taiga blankets a Russian plain. In the distance, the low Ural Mountains mark the division between Europe and Asia.

South of the tundra is a vast forest of evergreen trees called **taiga** (TY-guh). This huge forest covers about half of Russia. In Siberia, snow covers the taiga much of the year. South of the taiga is a flat grassland called the steppe (STEP). With rich, black soil and a warmer climate, the steppe is Russia's most important farming area.

Climate in the Caucasus, on the other hand, ranges from warm and wet along the Black Sea, to cooler in the uplands, to hot and dry in much of Azerbaijan. Moist air from the Mediterranean Sea contributes to a humid subtropical climate zone. The region's health resorts were a favorite destination of tourists until ethnic conflict made traveling there dangerous.

Like Russia, the Caucasus boasts some impressive forests, including oak, beech, pine, birch, and aspen trees, at various elevations in the mountains. Wildflowers blanket the mountains. In fact, many experts consider the Caucasus to be one of the most biologically diverse regions on Earth. The climate and soil also make the region a good area for farming and commercial agriculture.

Reading Check
Find Main Ideas
How does Russia's location affect its climate?

Natural Resources

Russia has a wealth of resources. The Northern European Plain and the steppe provide fertile soil for farming. The taiga provides wood for building and paper products. Metals such as copper and gold and precious gems such as diamonds provide useful raw materials.

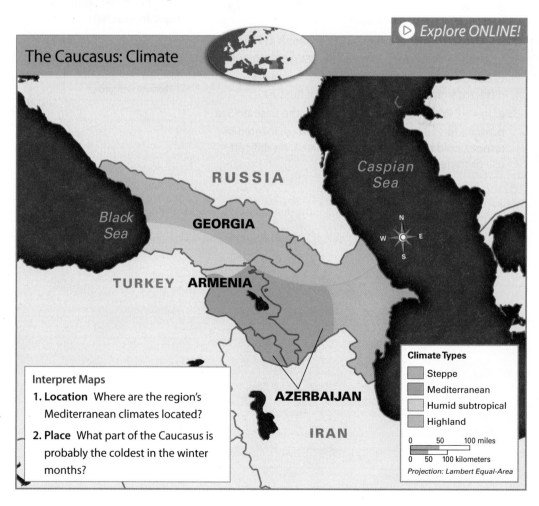

> Explore ONLINE!

The Caucasus: Climate

Interpret Maps
1. **Location** Where are the region's Mediterranean climates located?
2. **Place** What part of the Caucasus is probably the coldest in the winter months?

Climate Types
- Steppe
- Mediterranean
- Humid subtropical
- Highland

0   50   100 miles
0   50   100 kilometers
Projection: Lambert Equal-Area

Russia's main energy resources are coal, hydroelectricity, natural gas, and oil. Russia has large oil and gas fields. Oil also lies beneath the Caspian Sea. As a result, oil, natural gas, and coal are among Russia's largest exports.

Russia's natural resources have been poorly managed, however. Until the early 1990s this region was part of the Soviet Union. The Soviet government put more importance on industry than on managing its resources.

In Russia, many people chose to live in the south and west not only for the climate but because resources in this part of the country were easier to reach. However, many of the resources that were easy to access are gone. For example, most of the timber in western Russia has been cut down. Many remaining resources are in remote Siberia.

Summary and Preview Russia is big and cold, with vast plains, forests, and many natural resources. The Caucasus features rugged mountains and a varied climate. Next, you will read about Russia's history and culture.

Reading Check
Analyze Causes
Why are some of Russia's natural resources difficult to obtain?

Lesson 1 Assessment

Review Ideas, Terms, and Places

1. a. Describe Why are the Ural Mountains significant?
   b. Draw Conclusions Why might the Russian Far East be a dangerous place to live?

2. a. Describe What are winters like in much of Russia?
   b. Analyze How does climate affect Russia's plant life?
   c. Contrast How is the climate in the Caucasus different from the climate in much of Russia?

3. a. Recall What valuable resource is in the Caspian Sea?
   b. Make Inferences Why might resources located in remote, cold areas, as they are in Russia, be difficult to use or trade?

Critical Thinking

4. Generalize Draw a chart for Russia, like the one here. Use your notes, and enter one general idea for each topic in the chart.

Physical Features	
Climate and Plants	
Natural Resources	

Russia

If YOU lived there . . .

It is 1992, an exciting time in your hometown of Moscow. At the end of 1991 the Soviet Union fell apart. Russia became independent. You watched on TV as people pulled down the red Soviet flag and knocked down statues of former leaders. Everyone is talking about new freedoms and a new kind of government.

What new freedoms do you hope to have?

The Russian Empire

Russia's roots lie in the grassy, windswept plains of the steppe. For thousands of years, people from Asia moved across the steppe. These groups of people included the Slavs. As you may have read, the Slavs settled in Eastern Europe, including what is now Ukraine and western Russia.

Early History and Empire The Slavs developed towns and began trading with people from other areas. In the AD 800s, Viking traders from Scandinavia invaded the Slavs. These Vikings were called Rus (ROOS), and the word *Russia* probably comes from their name. The Vikings shaped the first Russian state among the Slavs. This Russian state, called Kievan (KEE-e-fuhn) Rus, centered around the city of **Kiev.** This city is now the capital of Ukraine.

Over time, missionaries introduced the Orthodox Christian faith to Kiev. In addition, the missionaries introduced a form of the Greek alphabet called **Cyrillic** (suh-RI-lik). The Russians adopted this Cyrillic alphabet and still use it today.

The alphabet is one of several factors that separate Russian, a Slavic language, from languages spoken in Europe such as French and Italian, which came from Latin. The Slavs came from Asia and moved to Europe by AD 1000. They founded a number of small kingdoms in the area now known as the Czech Republic and Slovakia. In the 1200s fierce Mongol invaders called Tatars (TAH-ters) swept out of Central Asia and conquered Kiev. The Mongols let Russian princes rule over local states. In time, Muscovy became the strongest state. Its main city was Moscow.

The Big Idea

Strict rule, unrest, and ethnic diversity have shaped Russia's history and culture. Today, it faces many challenges.

Main Ideas

- The Russian Empire grew under powerful leaders, but unrest and war led to its end.
- The Soviet Union emerged as a Communist superpower, with rigid government control.
- Russia's history and diversity have influenced its culture.
- The Russian Federation is working to develop democracy and a market economy.
- Russia's physical geography, cities, and economy define its many culture regions.
- Russia faces a number of serious challenges.

Key Terms and Places

Kiev
Cyrillic
czar
Bolsheviks
gulags
dachas
St. Petersburg
smelters
Trans-Siberian Railway
Chechnya

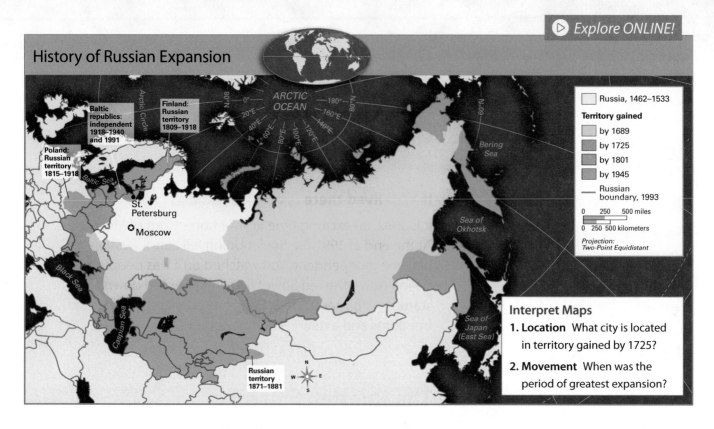

History of Russian Expansion

Baltic republics: independent 1918–1940 and 1991

Finland: Russian territory 1809–1918

Poland: Russian territory 1815–1918

St. Petersburg

✪ Moscow

Russian territory 1871–1881

ARCTIC OCEAN

Bering Sea

Sea of Okhotsk

Sea of Japan (East Sea)

Black Sea

Caspian Sea

Baltic Sea

Arctic Circle

	Russia, 1462–1533

Territory gained
- by 1689
- by 1725
- by 1801
- by 1945
- Russian boundary, 1993

0   250   500 miles
0 250 500 kilometers

Projection: Two-Point Equidistant

Interpret Maps

1. **Location** What city is located in territory gained by 1725?

2. **Movement** When was the period of greatest expansion?

After about 200 years, Muscovy's prince, Ivan III, seized control from the Mongols. In the 1540s his grandson, Ivan IV, crowned himself **czar** (ZAHR). *Czar* is Russian for "caesar." As czar, Ivan IV had total power. A cruel and savage ruler, he became known as Ivan the Terrible.

Muscovy developed into Russia. Strong czars such as Peter the Great (1682–1725) and Catherine the Great (1762–1796) built Russia into a huge empire and a world power. This empire included many conquered peoples.

At this time, Russia built a series of fortresses across the steppe called the Orenburg Line. These fortresses served to support trade that came in from the Indian Ocean and traveled the Silk Roads from east to west. They protected caravans from steppe tribes, letting merchants as far away as India and the Ottoman Empire send spices, teas, cotton, silk, and many other commodities to Moscow, St. Petersburg, and European cities.

Along with these welcome trade goods came an unwelcome traveler: disease. Illnesses such as the Black Death found their way into Russia via these trade routes as early as 1351. The spread of other contagious illnesses and parasites have also been traced to these trade routes.

Still, by the 19th century, a north-south trans-Eurasian "Cotton Road" arose. With the spread of the Industrial Revolution, technologies such as textile mills demanded cotton. Cotton could not be produced in Russia due to the climate. Still, Russian industrialists could keep their textile mills humming thanks to merchants who transported it both overland and across the ocean from India, Egypt, and the United States. Many Central Asian farmers grew cotton as a cash crop to export to Russia.

But Russia remained a country of poor farmers. The czars and nobles had most of the wealth. In the early 1900s Russians demanded improvements. The czar agreed to some changes, but unrest continued to grow.

War and Revolution In 1914 Russia entered World War I. The country suffered huge losses in the war. In addition, the Russian people experienced severe food shortages. When the czar seemed to ignore the people's hardship, they rose up against him. He was forced to give up his throne in 1917.

Later that year, the **Bolsheviks,** a radical Russian Communist group, seized power in the Russian Revolution. They then killed the czar and his family. In 1922 the Bolsheviks formed a new country, the Union of Soviet Socialist Republics (USSR), or the Soviet Union. It soon included 15 republics, the strongest of which was Russia. The first leader was Vladimir Lenin.

Reading Check
Sequence
What series of events led to the creation of the Soviet Union?

The Soviet Union

The Soviet Union adopted communism. In this political system, the government owns all property and controls all aspects of life. In 1924 Lenin died. Joseph Stalin took power, ruling as a brutal and paranoid dictator.

The Soviet Union under Stalin Under Stalin, the Soviet Union set up a command economy. In this system, the government owns all businesses and farms and makes all decisions. People were told what to make and how much to charge. Without competition, though, efficiency and the quality of goods fell over time.

The Soviet Union strictly controlled its people as well as its economy. Stalin had anyone who spoke out against the government jailed, exiled, or killed. Millions of people were sent to **gulags,** harsh Soviet labor camps often located in Siberia.

Academic Vocabulary
reaction a response to something

Cold War and Collapse During World War II, the Soviet Union fought with the Allies against Germany. Millions of Soviet citizens died in the war. Stalin's **reaction** to the war was to build a buffer around the

---

Communist-Era Poster

The Soviet Union used posters as propaganda. Propaganda is information designed to promote a specific cause or idea by influencing people's thoughts and beliefs. For example, Soviet posters often promoted the greatness and power of the Soviet state, its leaders, and their Communist policies.

The message of this 1924 poster reads, "Long live the Young Communist League! The young are taking over the older generation's torch!"

The color red in this poster symbolizes communism and the Russian Revolution.

Analyze Sources
How do you think the poster's images and message influenced Soviet teens at the time?

Soviet Union to protect it from invasion. To do so, he set up Communist governments in Eastern Europe.

The United States opposed communism and saw its spread as a threat to democracy. This opposition led to the Cold War, a period of tense rivalry between the Soviet Union and the United States. The two rival countries became superpowers as they competed to have superior weapons.

Partly because of the high costs of weapons, the Soviet economy neared collapse by the 1980s. Mikhail Gorbachev (GAWR-buh-chawf), the Soviet leader, reduced government control and introduced some democracy.

Still, the Soviet republics pushed for independence. In 1991 the Soviet Union broke into 15 independent countries, including Russia.

Reading Check
Analyze Causes
How did the Cold War help lead to the Soviet Union's collapse?

Russia's Culture Today

In the Soviet Union, the government had controlled culture just like everything else. Today, Russian culture is once again alive and vibrant.

People and Religion Russia is big and diverse, with more than 140 million people. About 80 percent are ethnic Russians, or Slavs, but Russia also has many other ethnic groups. The largest are the Tatars and Ukrainians. Russia's many ethnic groups once again take great pride in their cultures.

Like ethnic culture, religious worship has revived. The Soviet government opposed religion and closed many houses of worship. Today, many have reopened, including historic Russian cathedrals with their onion-shaped domes. The main faith is Russian Orthodox Christian. Other religions include other forms of Christianity, Islam, Judaism, and Buddhism.

Customs Russian history has shaped its customs, such as holidays. Religious holidays, like Easter, Christmas, and the Islamic holiday Eid al-Adha, are popular. The main family holiday is New Year's Eve. To celebrate this holiday, families decorate a tree where, according to Russian folklore, Grandfather Frost and his helper the Snow Maiden leave gifts. Russian Independence Day marks the end of the Soviet Union on June 12.

The Arts and Sciences Russia has made great contributions in the arts and sciences. Russia's ballet companies are world famous for their skill. Peter Tchaikovsky (chy-KAWF-skee) is Russia's most famous composer. His many works include *The Nutcracker* ballet and the *1812 Overture*.

In the material arts, Russia's Fabergé eggs are priceless. Gifts for the czars, these eggs are made of precious metals and covered with gems such as emeralds and rubies. Each egg opens to reveal a tiny surprise.

In the sciences, Russia has contributed to space research. In 1957 the Soviet Union launched Sputnik, the first artificial satellite in space. Russian scientists now help work on the International Space Station.

Reading Check
Generalize
How did the end of the Soviet Union affect Russian culture?

The Russian Federation Today

For decades, the Soviet Union reigned as a superpower, with Russia as its strongest republic. In 1991 the Soviet Union broke apart. Russia's leaders struggled to change its government from communism to democracy.

Government The Russian Federation is a federal republic, a system in which power is divided between national and local governments. The voters elect a president to serve as the country's chief executive, Russia's most powerful official. The president appoints a prime minister to serve as the head of the government. A legislature, called the Federal Assembly, makes the country's laws.

Increased democracy led to more freedom for Russians. Voters can choose from several political parties. Information flows more freely. The government no longer controls every aspect of life. The move toward democracy improved relations between Russia and Western nations.

Russia's current government system is similar in some ways to both the parliamentary system of the UK and the federal system of Germany. In all three systems, a parliament or legislature is elected by the citizens. In Germany and the UK, the prime minister is chosen by the parliament rather than by the president, unlike in Russia, where the president chooses.

Changing to a democracy has been difficult. Problems such as government corruption, or dishonesty, have slowed the development of a free society. Time will tell whether Russia will continue to grow as a democracy.

Economy With the move to democracy, Russia began shifting to a market economy. This type of economy is based on free trade and competition. The Russian government greatly reduced its control of the economy. Most businesses and farms are now privately owned. These changes brought economic growth, improving daily life for many of Russia's citizens. Still, most of Russia's wealth remains in the hands of a small number of people.

Today, Russia produces and exports oil, natural gas, timber, metals, and chemicals. Heavy industry, such as machinery, is still important. But light industry, such as clothing and electronics, has grown, and service industries now make up the largest part of Russia's economy.

In agriculture, Russia is now a major grower and exporter of grains. Other major crops are fruits, potatoes, and sugar beets.

Kaliningrad

The small region of Kaliningrad—only slightly bigger than Connecticut—is more than 200 miles (322 km) from the rest of Russia. So why would Russia want this area? The reason has to do with the country's cold climate. Kaliningrad is Russia's only Baltic seaport that is free of ice all year. This important port provides Russia with year-round access to profitable European markets and trade. Railroads connect the port to Russia's major cities, as the map to the right shows.

Draw Conclusions
How do you think Russia's economy benefits from a Baltic seaport that is free of ice all year?

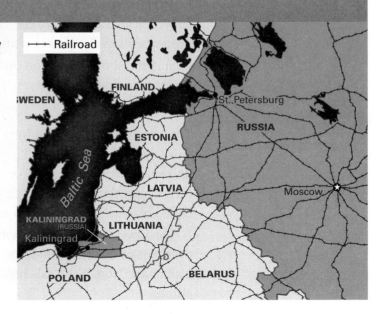

City and Rural Life Cities show the changes sweeping Russia, with more restaurants and shopping centers available. Stores offer a wider range of consumer goods, such as TVs. Some wealthy Russians can afford luxuries. However, the average Russian's standard of living remains low.

About 75 percent of all Russians live in cities. Most live in small apartments in high-rise buildings. In rural areas, more people live in houses.

Russians living in cities can enjoy nature. Cities often have large parks and wooded areas in and around them. Many richer Russians own **dachas,** or Russian country houses, where they can garden and enjoy the fresh air.

Culture Regions

Russia is vast and diverse. Therefore, we divide it into several culture regions, as the map on the next page shows. These regions differ in **features** such as population, natural resources, and economic activity.

The four western culture regions make up Russia's heartland. Most of Russia's people live here, where the country's capital and largest cities are. The fertile plains here are the country's most productive farming area.

The Moscow Region Moscow is Russia's capital and largest city. The modern city has wide boulevards and large public squares. Its many cultural attractions include the world-famous Bolshoi Ballet and Moscow Circus.

At Moscow's heart is the Kremlin, the center of Russia's government. In Russian, *kremlin* means "fortress." The Kremlin consists of several buildings surrounded by a wall and towers. The buildings include not only government offices but also palaces, museums, and gold-domed churches.

Next to the Kremlin is Red Square, an immense plaza. It is lined by many famous landmarks, such as St. Basil's Cathedral.

The Moscow region is Russia's most important economic area. Its factories produce a wide range of goods. The city is also a transportation center and links by road, rail, and plane to all parts of Russia.

The St. Petersburg Region **St. Petersburg**, founded by Peter the Great, was styled after cities in Western Europe. For 200 years, it served as Russia's capital and home to the czars. It has wide avenues, grand palaces, and numerous canals. Theaters and museums enrich the city's cultural life.

St. Petersburg's location on the Gulf of Finland has made the city a major port and trade center. This northern location produces "White Nights," a period during summer when it never gets totally dark.

The Volga and Urals Regions The Volga River and Ural Mountains are the third and fourth regions. The Volga is a major shipping route. Dams along its course form lakes and give hydroelectric power. Factories here process oil and gas. A site on the Caspian Sea gives sturgeon, a fish that lays eggs called black caviar. The eggs are a costly delicacy, or rare and valued food.

The Ural Mountains are an important mining region and produce nearly every major mineral. **Smelters,** factories that process metal ores, process copper and iron. The Urals region is also known for gems and semiprecious stones.

Reading Check
Summarize
How has Russia changed since it became independent?

Academic Vocabulary
features
characteristics

Siberia East of the Urals lies Siberia. In the Tatar language, *Siberia* means "Sleeping Land." Long, severe Siberian winters mean that much of the land lies frozen or buried under snow for most or all of the year. Its harsh climate makes its many valuable resources difficult to access.

Siberia's main industries are lumber, mining, and oil production. Large coal deposits are mined in southwest Siberia. Rivers produce hydroelectric power. The warmer southern steppes are Siberia's main farmlands.

Because of Siberia's harsh climate, jobs there pay high wages. Even so, few people choose to live in Siberia. Most towns and cities are in the western and southern parts of the region. These cities tend to follow the

Russia: Culture Regions

Russia's culture regions show tremendous diversity. They include, among others, the Western-looking St. Petersburg region (1), the politically focused Moscow region (2), and the harsh but resource-rich Siberia region (3).

St. Petersburg's State Hermitage Museum, once the Winter Palace of the czars, now houses priceless works of art.

Moscow is Russia's capital and largest city. It is a political, cultural, and transportation center.

In Siberia, a Nenets woman leads a group of decorated reindeer as part of a village festival.

Cultural Regions
- Moscow
- St. Petersburg
- Volga
- Ural
- Siberia
- Far East

0   300   600 miles
0   300   600 kilometers

Projection:
Two-point equidistant

Interpret Maps

1. **Regions** What are the six culture regions?

2. **Place** Which geographic feature separates the Urals culture region from regions farther west?

Trans-Siberian Railway. This rail line runs from Moscow to Vladivostok on the east coast and is the longest single rail line in the world.

The Russian Far East Russia's long coastline on the Pacific Ocean is the Russian Far East. Much land remains heavily forested. In the few cities, factories process forest and mineral resources. Farming occurs in the Amur River valley. The city of Vladivostok is a naval base and the area's main seaport. Islands off the coast provide oil, minerals, and commercial fishing.

Reading Check
Find Main Ideas
What areas make up Russia's culture regions?

Russia's Challenges

Russia has made great progress since 1991, but challenges remain. First, Russia's shift to a market economy has brought problems. Prices and unemployment have risen. The gap between rich and poor has widened.

Second, Russia's population is falling. More Russians are dying than are being born, in part because many Russians cannot afford good health care.

Third, the Soviet government did not prevent environmental problems. Pollution, such as industrial chemicals, has seriously harmed Russia's environment. The government must now repair the damage. Yet, because much of Russia's wealth comes from selling natural resources such as fossil fuels, many in both Russia's government and private sectors hesitate. They may fear that tackling these problems will weaken the country's economy.

Also, deforestation due to illegal logging in Russia's northwest and far east regions caused higher levels of both erosion and carbon dioxide, and harmed the plants and animals that live in those forests. In late 2013, Russia's president Vladimir Putin stated that environmental conditions in a significant percentage of the country were unsatisfactory and that the country must change its policies.

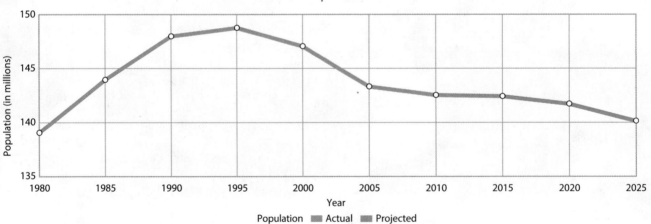

Russia's Population Decline

Source: United States Census Bureau International Database.

Interpret Graphs
Approximately how much did Russia's population decline between 2000 and 2010?

Fourth, there is tension between Russia and Ukraine over the status of Crimea. In 2013 the Ukrainian president said that he would be abandoning an agreement with Europe in order to seek closer ties to Russia. Many in Ukraine protested this move, and the president was forced to flee.

Crimea, however, is ethnically 60 percent Russian. Protesters in this region sought to secede from Ukraine. Violent protests included assault troops taking over the Crimean parliament. A referendum was held in which Crimean citizens supposedly voted overwhelmingly to leave Ukraine and join the Russian Federation. Russia annexed Crimea in an aggressive act that Ukraine and most other countries insist was a violation of international law.

Last, Russia faces ethnic conflicts, such as those in the Russian republic of **Chechnya** (CHECH-nyah) in the Caucasus Mountains. Some in this Muslim area want independence. Fighting and terrorism there have caused many deaths.

Reading Check
Categorize
What social, economic, and political challenges face Russia?

Summary and Preview In this lesson you learned that Russia had a long, contentious history and is now a federal republic with a market economy. In the next lesson, you will read about the Caucasus, three republics that were part of the Soviet Union until gaining their independence in 1991.

Lesson 2 Assessment

Review Ideas, Terms, and Places

1. **a. Define** Who were the czars?
   b. Analyze What role did the city of Kiev play in Russian history?
   c. Elaborate What problems and events caused the Russian Empire to decline?

2. **a. Identify** Why are Vladimir Lenin and Joseph Stalin significant in Russian history?
   b. Evaluate Do you think life in the Soviet Union was an improvement over life in the Russian Empire? Why or why not?

3. **a. Recall** What is the main religion in Russia?
   b. Summarize How has Russian culture changed since the collapse of the Soviet Union in 1991?

4. **a. Recall** What type of government does Russia now have?
   b. Explain How is Russia's economy changing?
   c. Analyze What are the roles of the president, prime minister, and Federal Assembly in Russia?

5. **a. Recall** From west to east, what are Russia's major culture regions?

   b. Draw Conclusions Why do you think most Siberian towns and cities are located along the Trans-Siberian Railway?
   c. Rate Which of Russia's culture regions would you most want to live in, and why?

6. **a. Identify** What are the main challenges that face Russia today?
   b. Elaborate What difficulties does Chechnya pose for Russia's leaders?

Critical Thinking

7. Use what you have learned about Russia, and what you know of the United Kingdom, to fill out the following chart. Then answer the question below.

	Russia	United Kingdom
Location		
Climate		
Natural Resources		

Compare How do the location, climate, and natural resources of the UK and Russia affect where people live and how they trade?

The Caucasus

The Big Idea

In an area long ruled by outside groups, the Caucasus republics are struggling to strengthen their economies and to deal with ethnic unrest.

Main Ideas

- Many groups have ruled and influenced the Caucasus during its long history.

- Today, the Caucasus republics are working to improve their economies, but they struggle with ethnic unrest and conflict.

Key Terms and Places

Tbilisi
Yerevan
Baku

Reading Check
Find Main Ideas
Why do the countries in the Caucasus reflect a range of cultural influences?

If YOU lived there . . .

You live in Tbilisi, the capital of the country of Georgia. Several years ago, your sister and her college friends joined the Rose Revolution, a political protest that forced a corrupt president to resign. The protesters' symbol was a red rose. Since the protest, you have become more interested in politics.

What kind of government do you want?

History

The Caucasus lies in the rugged Caucasus Mountains between the Black and Caspian seas. Located where Europe blends into Asia, it reflects a range of cultural influences. Persians, Greeks, Romans, Arabs, Turks, and Mongols have all ruled or invaded the area. The Russians took control in the early 1800s.

Russian control in the Caucasus did not include what is now western Armenia. The Ottoman Turks held this area. Over time, the Turks grew to distrust the Armenians, however, and in the late 1800s began abusing and killing them. During World War I (1914–1918), the Turks forced all Armenians to leave. Hundreds of thousands of Armenians died during this ethnic cleansing, or attempt to remove an ethnic group. The Turks lost World War I, though, and had to give up western Armenia.

After World War I, Armenia, Azerbaijan, and Georgia gained independence—but not for long. By the early 1920s they were part of the vast Soviet Union. Finally, in 1991, when the Soviet Union fell, the Caucasus republics achieved true independence.

The Caucasus Today

The Caucasus may have a long history, but the Caucasus countries do not. Like other former Soviet republics, these young countries have had to create new governments and economies. Meanwhile, ethnic unrest and conflicts have slowed progress.

The Caucasus republics have similar governments. An elected president governs each nation, and an appointed prime minister runs each government. An elected parliament, or legislature, makes the laws.

The Caucasus: Political

Explore ONLINE!

Mount Elbrus
18,510 ft
(5,642 m)

RUSSIA

CAUCASUS MOUNTAINS

Ingur R.

Black Sea

GEORGIA

Tbilisi

Kür River

ARMENIA

Lake Sevan

AZERBAIJAN

TURKEY

Baku

Yerevan

Aras River

40°N

Caspian Sea

IRAN

National capital

0   50   100 miles

0   50   100 kilometers

Projection: Lambert Equal-Area

1. **Location** What two seas border the Caucasus?

2. **Place** Based on the map, how does Armenia differ from Azerbaijan and Georgia?

Georgia The country of Georgia lies in the Caucasus Mountains east of the Black Sea. **Tbilisi** is the capital. About 70 percent of the people are ethnic Georgians, and most belong to the Georgian Orthodox Church. The official language is Georgian, a unique language with its own alphabet. However, many other languages are also spoken.

Since 1991 Georgia has struggled with unrest and civil war. In 2003 Georgians forced out their president in the peaceful Rose Revolution. Meanwhile, ethnic groups in northern Georgia were fighting for independence. Because these groups now hold parts of northern Georgia, division and unrest continue.

There is hope for the future, however. In 2012 and 2016 the country saw democratic elections and a peaceful government transition of power. The government, and the people, tend to look to the West. Two major foreign policy goals involve joining the European Union and NATO.

Palm trees thrive in Batumi, Georgia, a seaside city on the Black Sea. Located in a humid subtropical climate zone, Batumi is the wettest city in the Caucasus.

Although unrest has hurt Georgia's economy, international aid is helping it improve. Georgia's economy is based on services and farming. Major crops include citrus fruits, grapes, and tea. In addition, Georgia produces steel and mines copper and manganese. Georgia is also famous for its wines. The Black Sea is a resort area, and tourism contributes to the economy, too.

Armenia South of Georgia is the small, landlocked country of Armenia. The tiny country is slightly larger than the state of Maryland. **Yerevan** (yer-uh-VAHN) is the capital. Almost all the people are ethnic Armenian. Armenia prides itself as being the first country to adopt Christianity, and most people belong to the Armenian Orthodox Church.

In the early 1990s Armenia fought a bitter war with its neighbor Azerbaijan. The war involved an area of Azerbaijan where most people are ethnic Armenian. Armenia wanted this area to become part of its country. Although a cease-fire stopped the fighting in 1994, Armenian armed forces remained in control of the area for years afterward.

This conflict has greatly hurt Armenia's economy. However, international aid is helping Armenia's economy recover and expand. For example, diamond processing is now a growing industry in Armenia.

Azerbaijan East of Armenia is Azerbaijan. In contrast to the other Caucasus republics, Azerbaijan is largely Muslim. The Azeri (uh-ZE-ree) make up 90 percent of the population.

Azerbaijan's economy is based on oil, which is found along and under the Caspian Sea. **Baku,** the capital, is the center of a large oil-refining industry. This industry has led to strong economic growth. Corruption is high, though, and many of the country's people are poor. In addition, Azerbaijan has many Azeri refugees who were forced to leave homes in Armenia.

Summary In this lesson you learned about the geography and culture of the Caucasus.

Reading Check
Summarize
What challenges do the Caucasus republics face?

Lesson 3 Assessment

Review Ideas, Terms, and Places

1. **a. Identify** Which country controlled much of the Caucasus for most of the 1800s?
   b. Identify Cause and Effect How did Turkish rule affect Armenians in the Ottoman Empire?
   c. Elaborate How has location affected the history and culture of the Caucasus area?
2. **a. Recall** How does Baku contribute to the economy of Azerbaijan?
   b. Compare and Contrast How is religion in Georgia and Armenia similar? How does religion in these countries differ from that in Azerbaijan?
   c. Elaborate How did the war between Armenia and Azerbaijan affect each country?

Critical Thinking

3. **Compare and Contrast** Draw a Venn diagram like the one here. Use your notes to identify the ways in which Georgia, Armenia, and Azerbaijan are similar and different.

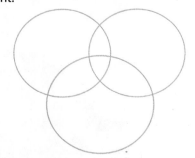

Social Studies Skills

Interpret a Population Map

Define the Skill

Population maps give you a snapshot of the distribution of people in a region or country. Each color on a population map represents an average number of people living within a square mile or square kilometer. Sometimes, symbols identify the cities with populations of a certain size. The map's legend identifies what the colors and symbols in the map mean.

Learn the Skill

1. Based on the map below, in which region of Russia do most of the country's people live?

2. Which two cities in Russia have the largest population?

3. How many Russian cities have more than 1 million people?

Practice the Skill

Use an atlas to locate a current population map of the United States. Using the map, identify where the most and the least populated regions of the United States are. Then identify the number of U.S. cities or metropolitan areas with more than 2 million people.

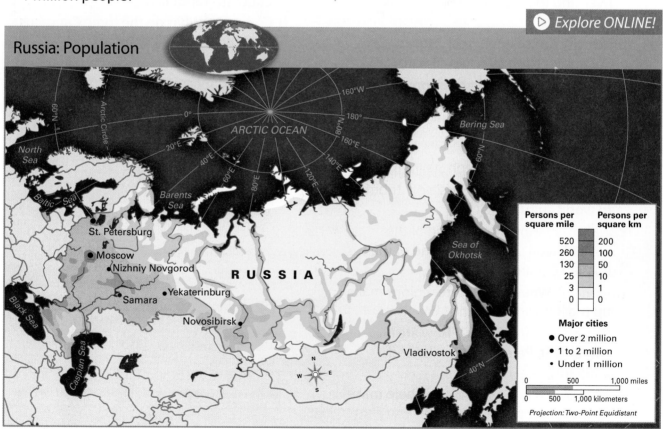

Russia: Population

Explore ONLINE!

Russia and the Caucasus   573

Module 17 Assessment

Review Vocabulary, Terms, and Places

For each statement below, write T *if it is true and* F *if it is false. If the statement is false, replace the boldfaced term with one that makes the sentence a true statement.*

1. The **Caucasus Mountains** separate European Russia from Asian Russia.
2. Russia's capital and largest city is **St. Petersburg**.
3. Under the rule of the **Bolsheviks**, the Russian Empire expanded in size and power.
4. Many wealthier Russians have country houses, which are called **gulags**.
5. Russia's main government buildings are located in the **Kremlin** in Moscow.
6. Russia's culture regions differ in **features** such as cities, natural resources, and economic activity.
7. **Moscow** is a major port and was once home to Russia's czars.
8. Armenia is the only one of the three countries in the Caucasus that is **landlocked**.

Comprehension and Critical Thinking

Lesson 1

9. **a. Recall** What is Russia's most important river, and to what major bodies of water does it link?

   b. Identify Cause and Effect How does Russia's location affect its climate?

   c. Elaborate Why might developing the many natural resources in Siberia be difficult?

Lesson 2

10. **a. Identify** Who was Joseph Stalin?

   b. Summarize How has Russia contributed to world culture?

   c. Elaborate How was the end of the Soviet Union similar to the end of the Russian Empire?

   d. Identify What four culture regions make up the Russian heartland?

   e. Compare and Contrast How are Moscow and St. Petersburg similar and different?

   f. Elaborate How might Siberia help make Russia an economic success?

Lesson 3

11. **a. Recall** What is the capital of each of the Caucasus republics?

   b. Compare What do the three Caucasus countries have in common?

   c. Elaborate What issues and challenges do the Caucasus countries need to address to improve their economies?

Module 17 Assessment, continued

Reading Skills

Use Context Clues *Use the Reading Skills taught in this module to answer a question about the reading selection below.*

> Russia's northern coast is tundra. Winters are dark and bitterly cold, and the brief summers are cool. Most of the ground is permafrost, or permanently frozen soil. Only small plants such as mosses grow.

12. What is permafrost?

Social Studies Skills

Interpret a Population Map *Use the Social Studies Skills taught in this module to answer the questions below. Use a good atlas to find a population density map of Europe. The map does not need to include Russia. Use the map to answer the following questions. Do not include the country of Russia when answering the questions.*

13. Not including the cities of Russia, how many cities or metropolitan areas in Europe have more than 2 million people?

14. Not including Russia, which regions of Europe are the most populated? Which regions of Europe are the least populated?

Map Activity

15. **Using Physical and Population Density Maps** Examine the physical map of Russia in Lesson 1 of this module, and compare it with the population density map of Russia in the Social Studies Skills section of this module.

    a. Do you see a pattern to human settlement on this map? If so, what?

    b. Using what you have learned in this module, what are some reasons people have chosen to settle where they did in Russia?

Focus on Writing

16. Using what you have learned about locations in Russia, pretend you are a real estate agent. Choose one location for a piece of real estate you will sell. What are its best features? How would you describe the land and climate? What are the benefits of living there? If it is a building, what does it look like? What is nearby? Gather information from both print and online sources about the area to bolster your information. Remember to include details that will make the property attractive to possible buyers.

References

References

Mount Rainier
14,410 ft
(4,392 m)

ROCKY

CASCADE RANGE

COAST RANGES

COAST Ranges

SIERRA NEVADA

GREAT
BASIN

Central Valley

Mount Whitney
14,494 ft
(4,419 m)

Death Valley

Mojave
Desert

PACIFIC
OCEAN

Channel
Islands

Monterey
Bay

San Francisco Bay

Cape
Mendocino

Puget
Sound

Juan de Fuca

Columbia River

Columbia Plateau

Snake
River

Salmon
River
Mts.

Sawtooth
Mts.

Bitterroot
Range

Salmon River
Range

CONTINENTAL

Lewis
Range

Flathead Lake

Flathead River

Pend
Oreille
River

Clark Fork

Franklin D.
Roosevelt Lake

Milk River

Missouri River

Fort Peck
Lake

Yellowstone River

Lake
Sakakawea

Lake
Oahe

GREAT

Grand
Tetons

Gannett Peak
13,804 ft
(4,207 m)

Wind
River
Range

Yellowstone
Lake

Wind
River

Bighorn Mts.

Bighorn River

Powder
River

Black
Hills

Cheyenne
River

White
River

North Platte River

Niobrara - River

INTER

Wasatch Range

Great
Salt
Lake

Utah
Lake

Uinta
Mts.

Green River

Colorado River

Lake
Powell

COLORADO

PLATEAU

Painted Desert

San Juan River

DIVIDE

Front Range

South Platte River

Platte River

Republican River

Smoky Hill River

Mount Elbert
14,433 ft
(4,400 m)

Pikes Peak
14,110 ft
(4,301 m)

Sangre De Cristo Mts.

San Luis
Valley

M O U N T A I N S

PLAINS

Klamath
River

Shasta
Lake

Pyramid
Lake

Goose
Lake

Lake Tahoe

Sacramento River

San Joaquin River

Grand
Canyon

Lake
Mead

Colorado River

Salton
Sea

Imperial
Valley

Gila River

Sonoran
Desert

Gulf of
California

DIVIDE

Rio Grande

CONTINENTAL

Canadian
River

River

Pecos River

Colorado

Amistad
Reservoir

Rio

Grande

Nueces

MEXICO

To understand the relative locations of Alaska and
Hawaii, as well as the vast distances separating them
from the rest of the United States, see the world map.

Kauai

Niihau

Oahu

Molokai

HAWAII

PACIFIC
OCEAN

Lanai

Maui

Kahoolawe

Mauna Kea
13,796 ft
(4,206 m)

Hawaii

22°N

19°N

0   75   150 Miles
0   75   150 Kilometers
Projection: Mercator

N
W   E
S

RUSSIA

ARCTIC OCEAN

Arctic Circle

Bering
Strait

BROOKS RANGE

Yukon River

Tanana River

ALASKA

RANGE

Mount McKinley
20,320 ft
(6,194 m)

CANADA

St. Lawrence
Island

St. Matthew
Island

Nunivak
Island

Kuskokwim River

Bering Sea

Attu Island

55°N

50°N

PACIFIC
OCEAN

ALEUTIAN
ISLANDS

Kodiak Island

Gulf of Alaska

Alexander
Archipelago

55°N

0   250   500 Miles
0   250   500 Kilometers
Projection: Albers Equal Area

N
W   E
S

45°N

40°N

35°N

30°N

125°W

120°W

170°E

180°

170°W

160°W

150°W

155°W

160°W

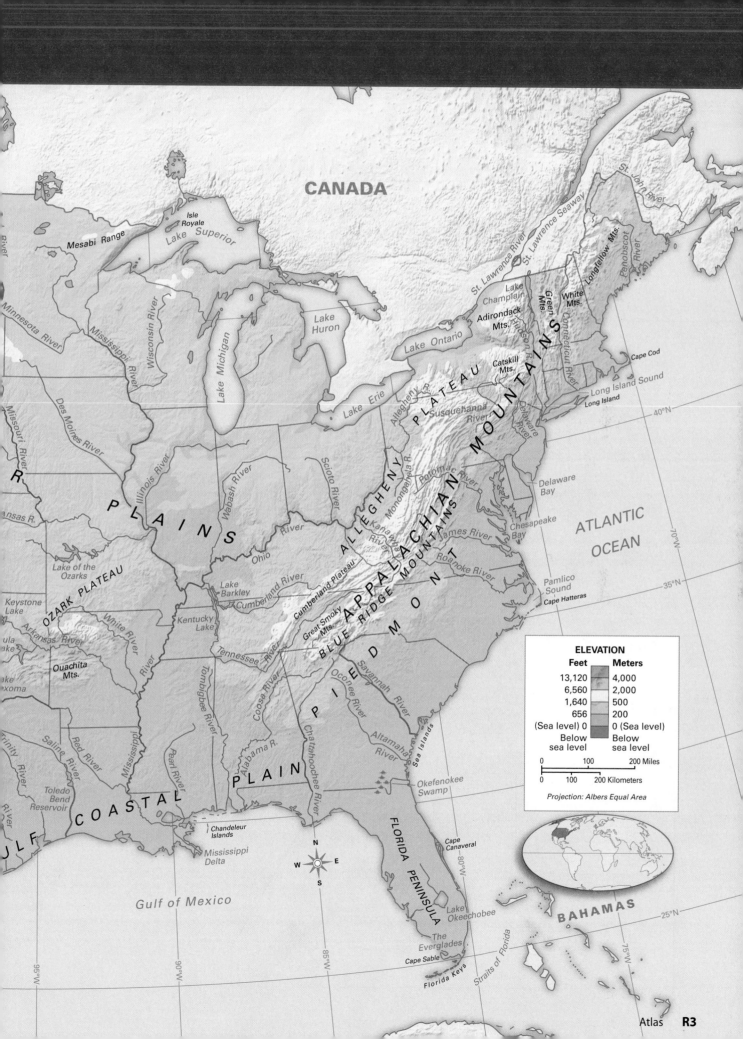

CANADA

Isle
Royale

Mesabi Range

Lake Superior

St. John River

Longfellow Mts.

Penobscot River

St. Lawrence Seaway

St. Lawrence River

Lake Champlain

White Mts.

Green Mts.

Adirondack Mts.

Connecticut River

Hudson R.

Cape Cod

Lake Ontario

Catskill Mts.

Long Island Sound

Long Island

Minnesota River

Mississippi River

Wisconsin River

Lake Huron

Lake Michigan

Lake Erie

ALLEGHENY PLATEAU

Susquehanna River

Delaware River

40°N

70°W

Des Moines River

Illinois River

Wabash River

Scioto River

River

Ohio

Monongahela R.

Potomac River

Delaware Bay

Chesapeake Bay

ATLANTIC OCEAN

Missouri River

P L A I N S

A P P A L A C H I A N   M O U N T A I N S

Kanawha River

James River

ansas R.

Lake of the Ozarks

OZARK PLATEAU

Lake Barkley

Cumberland River

Cumberland Plateau

BLUE RIDGE MOUNTAINS

Roanoke River

Pamlico Sound

35°N

Keystone Lake

Kentucky Lake

Great Smoky Mts.

P I E D M O N T

Cape Hatteras

ula ake xoma

Arkansas River

White River

Ouachita Mts.

Tennessee River

River

Coosa River

Oconee River

Savannah River

Trinity River

Saline River

Red River

Mississippi River

Pearl River

Tombigbee River

Alabama R.

Chattahoochee River

Altamaha River

Sea Islands

Toledo Bend Reservoir

River

G U L F   C O A S T A L   P L A I N

Okefenokee Swamp

Chandeleur Islands

Mississippi Delta

N

W   E

S

Cape Canaveral

80°W

FLORIDA PENINSULA

Gulf of Mexico

BAHAMAS

25°N

Lake Okeechobee

85°W

The Everglades

75°W

Cape Sable

Florida Keys

Straits of Florida

95°W

90°W

ELEVATION

Feet		Meters
13,120		4,000
6,560		2,000
1,640		500
656		200
(Sea level) 0		0 (Sea level)
Below sea level		Below sea level

0   100   200 Miles

0   100   200 Kilometers

Projection: Albers Equal Area

United States: Political

Seattle
Olympia
Tacoma
Spokane
WASHINGTON
Puget Sound
Strait of Juan de Fuca
Franklin D. Roosevelt Lake
Pend Oreille
Flathead Lake
Portland
Salem
Columbia River
Eugene
OREGON
Great Falls
Helena
MONTANA
Fort Peck Lake
Missouri River
Yellowstone River
Billings
NORTH DAKO
Lake Sakakawea
Bismarc
IDAHO
Boise
Sun Valley
Snake River
Pocatello
Yellowstone Lake
WYOMING
Lake Oahe
SOUTH DAKOT
Pierre
Rapid City
Cape Mendocino
Goose Lake
Shasta Lake
Sacramento River
Pyramid Lake
NEVADA
Great Salt Lake
Ogden
Salt Lake City
Provo
Utah Lake
Green River
Cheyenne
NEBRAS
Platte
Berkeley
Oakland
San Francisco
San Francisco Bay
San Jose
Reno
Carson City
Lake Tahoe
Sacramento
San Joaquin River
Monterey Bay
Fresno
CALIFORNIA
UTAH
Boulder
Vail
Denver
Aspen
Colorado Springs
COLORADO
Pueblo
Arkansas River
KAN
Lake Powell
Las Vegas
Lake Mead
Colorado River
Santa Barbara
Ventura
Los Angeles
Long Beach
Anaheim
Santa Ana
Riverside
Palm Springs
Salton Sea
Channel Islands
San Diego
PACIFIC OCEAN
Flagstaff
ARIZONA
Taos
Santa Fe
Albuquerque
NEW MEXICO
OKLAH
Canadian River
Oklahom
L
Amarillo
Phoenix
Gila River
Casa Grande
Tucson
Las Cruces
El Paso
Lubbock
Brazos Rive
Abilene
For
Midland
Odessa
TEX
Colorad
Gulf of California
Pecos River
Rio
Amistad Reservoir
San Antonio
Rio Grande
Corpus
Laredo
MEXICO

To understand the relative locations of Alaska and Hawaii, as well as the vast distances separating them from the rest of the United States, see the world map.

Kauai
Niihau
Oahu
Honolulu
HAWAII
Molokai
Lanai
Maui
Kahoolawe
PACIFIC OCEAN
0   75   150 Miles
0   75   150 Kilometers
Projection: Mercator
Hilo
Hawaii
22°N
155°W
19°N

ARCTIC OCEAN
RUSSIA
Bering Strait
Arctic Circle
St. Lawrence Island
St. Matthew Island
Nunivak Island
Nome
Yukon River
Fairbanks
CANADA
ALASKA
Anchorage
Valdez
Skagway
Juneau
Gulf of Alaska
Kodiak Island
Alexander Archipelago
Bering Sea
Attu Island
ALEUTIAN ISLANDS
PACIFIC OCEAN
0   250   500 Miles
0   250   500 Kilometers
Projection: Albers Equal Area
55°N
50°N

CANADA

MINNESOTA
Grand Forks
Fargo
Duluth
Superior
Marquette
Sault Ste. Marie

Red River
Minnesota River

WISCONSIN
Minneapolis
St. Paul
Green Bay
Madison
Milwaukee

Lake Superior

MICHIGAN
Grand Rapids
Saginaw
Lansing
Detroit
Ann Arbor

Lake Michigan
Lake Huron

Sioux Falls
Sioux City

IOWA
Cedar Rapids
Davenport
Des Moines
Rockford
Chicago
Gary
South Bend
Fort Wayne

Omaha
Lincoln

Mississippi River
Missouri River
Illinois River

MISSOURI
Kansas City
Kansas City
Jefferson City
Springfield

ILLINOIS
Peoria
Springfield
St. Louis
East St. Louis

INDIANA
Indianapolis
Dayton

OHIO
Columbus
Cincinnati
Cleveland
Youngstown
Akron
Toledo
Pittsburgh

Lake Erie

NEW YORK
Buffalo
Rochester
Syracuse
Albany

Lake Ontario

PENNSYLVANIA
Allentown
Harrisburg
Philadelphia
Baltimore

Susquehanna River

Hudson R.
St. Lawrence River

MAINE
Augusta
Portland

Lake Champlain
Burlington
Montpelier

VT
NH
Concord
Manchester

Connecticut R.

MA
Boston
Worcester
Providence
Springfield
Hartford
CT
RI
New Haven
Bridgeport
Jersey City
Newark
Yonkers
New York City
Trenton
NJ
Camden
DE
Dover
MD
Annapolis
Washington, D.C.
Atlantic City

Long Island Sound
Long Island
Cape Cod

Topeka
Wichita

Lake of the Ozarks

Keystone Lake
Tulsa
Fayetteville

Eufaula Lake

Lake Texoma

ARKANSAS
Little Rock
Pine Bluff

Springfield

KENTUCKY
Frankfort
Lexington
Louisville
Evansville

Lake Barkley
Kentucky Lake
Ohio River
Mississippi River
Kentucky River

WEST VIRGINIA
Charleston

VIRGINIA
Richmond
Newport News
Norfolk
Virginia Beach

Delaware Bay
Chesapeake Bay
Cape Hatteras

ATLANTIC OCEAN

TENNESSEE
Nashville
Knoxville
Chattanooga
Memphis
Huntsville
Asheville

NORTH CAROLINA
Winston-Salem
Greensboro
Durham
Raleigh
Charlotte
Greenville

SOUTH CAROLINA
Columbia
Charleston

Savannah River

MISSISSIPPI
Vicksburg
Jackson
Meridian

ALABAMA
Birmingham
Montgomery

GEORGIA
Atlanta
Macon
Columbus
Savannah

Chattahoochee R.
Sea Islands

Dallas
Waco

Toledo Bend Reservoir

LOUISIANA
Shreveport
Baton Rouge
New Orleans
Beaumont
Houston
Galveston

Red River

Mobile
Pensacola
Biloxi
Chandeleur Islands

Tallahassee
Jacksonville
Gainesville

FLORIDA
Orlando
Tampa
St. Petersburg
Fort Myers
Fort Lauderdale
Miami

Lake Okeechobee
Cape Canaveral
Cape Sable
Florida Keys
Straits of Florida

Gulf of Mexico

BAHAMAS

N
W   E
S

⊛ National capital
★ State capitals
• Other cities

0   100   200 Miles
0   100   200 Kilometers

Projection: Albers Equal Area

40°N
35°N
25°N
70°W
80°W
85°W
90°W
95°W
75°W

Atlas

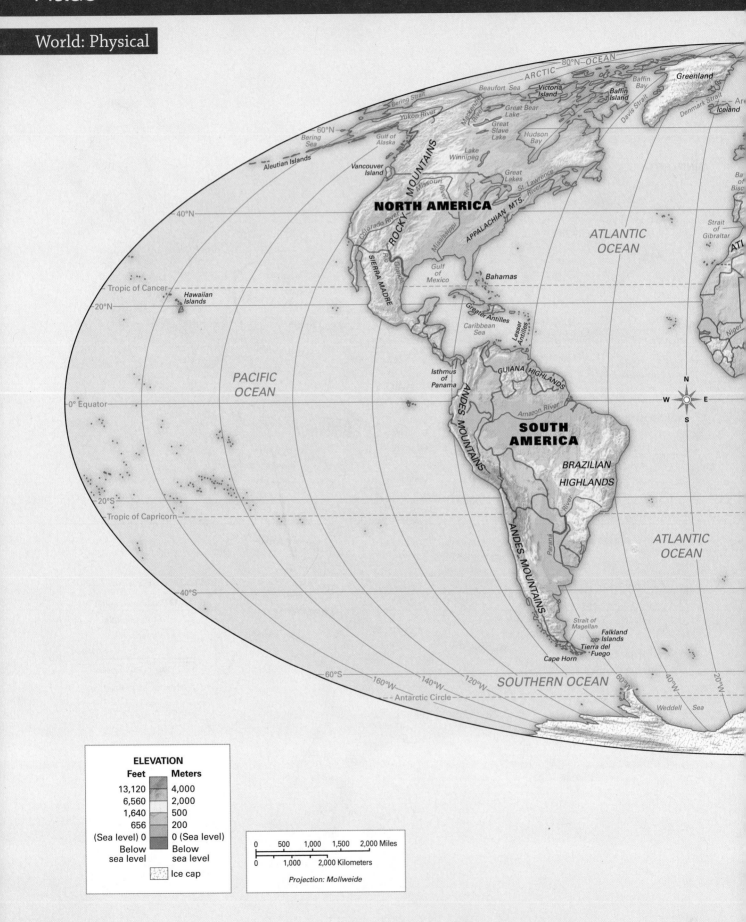

ELEVATION

Feet		Meters
13,120		4,000
6,560		2,000
1,640		500
656		200
(Sea level) 0		0 (Sea level)
Below sea level		Below sea level

Ice cap

0   500   1,000   1,500   2,000 Miles

0   1,000   2,000 Kilometers

Projection: Mollweide

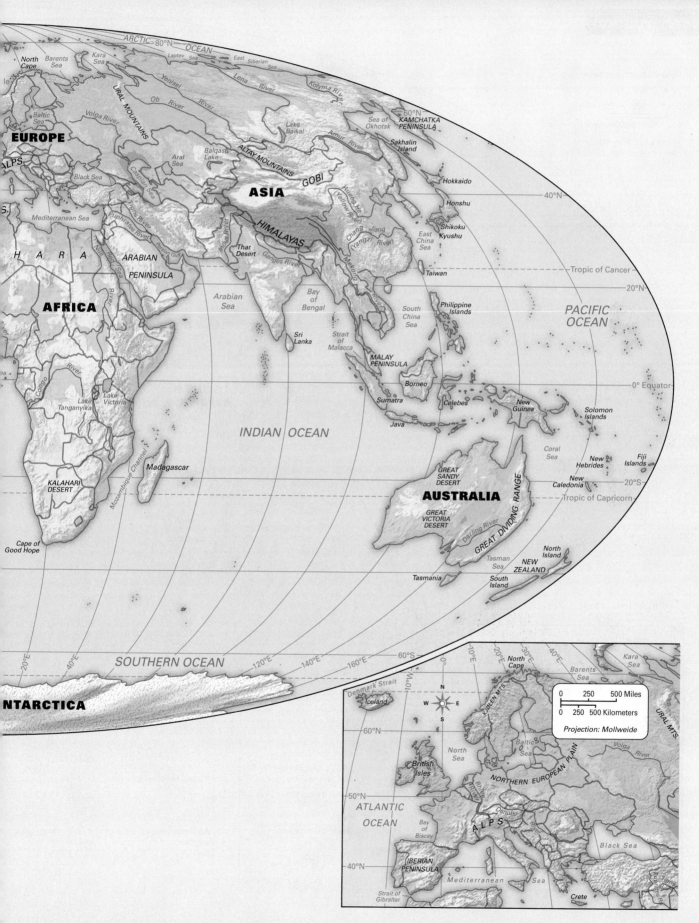

ARCTIC 80°N OCEAN

North Cape
Barents Sea
Kara Sea
Laptev Sea
East Siberian Sea

EUROPE

Baltic Sea
Black Sea
ALPS
S,

URAL MOUNTAINS
Volga River
Ob River
Yenisei River
Lena River
Kolyma River

Aral Sea
Balqash Lake
ALTAY MOUNTAINS
Lake Baikal
Amur River

60°N
Sea of Okhotsk
KAMCHATKA PENINSULA

Sakhalin Island
Hokkaido

Caspian Sea
ASIA
GOBI
Honshu
40°N

Mediterranean Sea
Tigris River
Euphrates River
Persian Gulf
HIMALAYAS
Chang Jiang (Yangzi) River
Huang He (Yellow River)
Mekong River
Shikoku
Kyushu
East China Sea
Taiwan

H A R A

ARABIAN PENINSULA
Thar Desert
Indus River
Ganges River
Tropic of Cancer

AFRICA

Nile River
Red Sea
Arabian Sea
Bay of Bengal
20°N
South China Sea
Philippine Islands
PACIFIC OCEAN

Sri Lanka
Strait of Malacca
MALAY PENINSULA
Borneo
Celebes
New Guinea
Solomon Islands

Congo River
Lake Tanganyika
Lake Victoria
0° Equator
Sumatra
Java

INDIAN OCEAN

Coral Sea
New Hebrides
Fiji Islands

Mozambique Channel
Madagascar
GREAT SANDY DESERT
AUSTRALIA
GREAT DIVIDING RANGE
New Caledonia
20°S

KALAHARI DESERT
GREAT VICTORIA DESERT
Darling River
Tropic of Capricorn

Cape of Good Hope
North Island
Tasman Sea
NEW ZEALAND

Tasmania
South Island

20°E 40°E
SOUTHERN OCEAN
120°E 140°E 160°E 60°S

NTARCTICA

Inset map:

Denmark Strait
North Cape
Kara Sea
Barents Sea
URAL MTS.

N W E S

Iceland
60°N
KJØLEN MTS.
Baltic Sea
Volga River

| 0 | 250 | 500 Miles |
| 0 | 250 | 500 Kilometers |

Projection: Mollweide

British Isles
North Sea
NORTHERN EUROPEAN PLAIN

50°N
Rhine
Danube

ATLANTIC OCEAN
Bay of Biscay
ALPS
Black Sea

40°N
IBERIAN PENINSULA
Mediterranean Sea

Strait of Gibraltar
Crete

Atlas

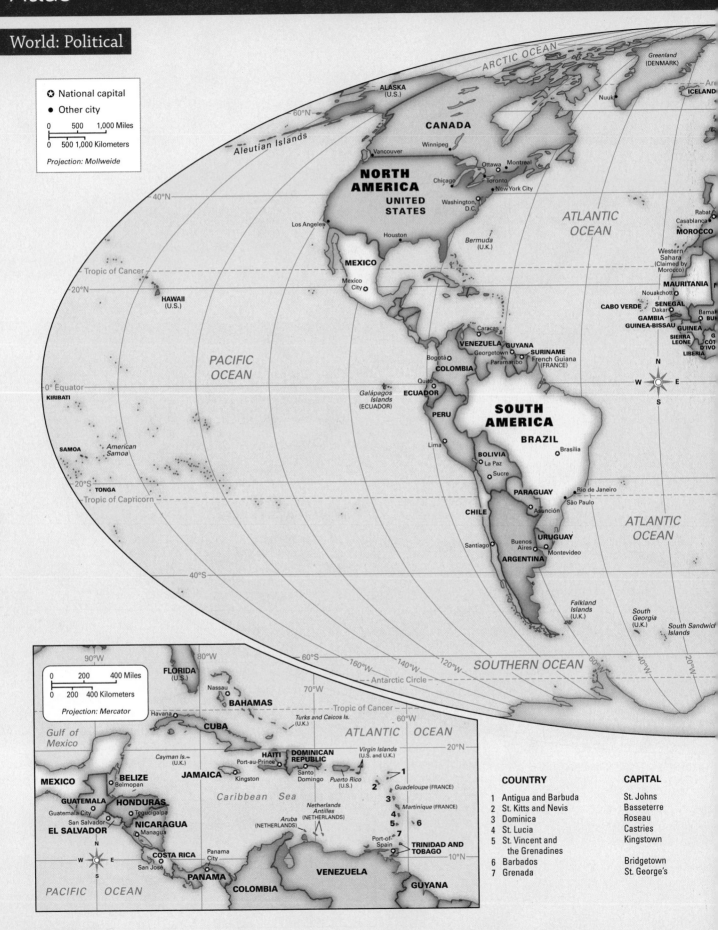

National capital
Other city

0   500   1,000 Miles
0   500 1,000 Kilometers

Projection: Mollweide

ARCTIC OCEAN

Greenland
(DENMARK)

ICELAND

ALASKA
(U.S.)

60°N

CANADA

Nuuk

Winnipeg

Vancouver

Ottawa   Montreal

**NORTH
AMERICA**

Chicago

Toronto

New York City

40°N

**UNITED
STATES**

Washington,
D.C.

ATLANTIC
OCEAN

Rabat
Casablanca
MOROCCO

Los Angeles

Houston

Bermuda
(U.K.)

Western
Sahara
(Claimed by
Morocco)

Tropic of Cancer

MEXICO

20°N

Nouakchott
MAURITANIA

HAWAII
(U.S.)

Mexico
City

CABO VERDE

SENEGAL
Dakar

Bama
BU

GAMBIA
GUINEA-BISSAU

GUINEA

G
CÔT
D'IVO

Caracas

VENEZUELA   **GUYANA**
SURINAME

**SIERRA
LEONE**

Georgetown   Paramaribo

French Guiana
(FRANCE)

LIBERIA

Bogotá

**PACIFIC
OCEAN**

COLOMBIA

Quito

N

0° Equator

KIRIBATI

Galápagos
Islands
(ECUADOR)

ECUADOR

W   E

S

PERU

**SOUTH
AMERICA**

SAMOA

American
Samoa

Lima

BRAZIL

Brasília

BOLIVIA
La Paz

20°S

TONGA

Sucre

Rio de Janeiro

Tropic of Capricorn

PARAGUAY

São Paulo

Asunción

CHILE

ATLANTIC
OCEAN

URUGUAY

Santiago

Buenos
Aires

Montevideo

ARGENTINA

40°S

Falkland
Islands
(U.K.)

South
Georgia
(U.K.)

South Sandwich
Islands

60°S   160°W   140°W   120°W   **SOUTHERN OCEAN**   60°   40°W   20°

Antarctic Circle

90°W   80°W

0   200   400 Miles
0   200   400 Kilometers

Projection: Mercator

FLORIDA
(U.S.)

70°W

Tropic of Cancer

60°W

Nassau

BAHAMAS

ATLANTIC   OCEAN

20°N

Havana

Turks and Caicos Is.
(U.K.)

Virgin Islands
(U.S. and U.K.)

Gulf of
Mexico

CUBA

HAITI   **DOMINICAN
REPUBLIC**

1

MEXICO

Cayman Is.
(U.K.)

Port-au-Prince

Santo
Domingo

2

Guadeloupe (FRANCE)

BELIZE
Belmopan

JAMAICA

Kingston

Puerto Rico
(U.S.)

3

Martinique (FRANCE)

GUATEMALA

HONDURAS

Caribbean Sea

Netherlands
Antilles
(NETHERLANDS)

4
5   6

Guatemala City

Tegucigalpa

Aruba
(NETHERLANDS)

7

San Salvador
EL SALVADOR

NICARAGUA
Managua

Port-of-
Spain

**TRINIDAD AND
TOBAGO**

COSTA RICA

N

Panama
City

10°N

W   E

San José

S

PANAMA

VENEZUELA

GUYANA

PACIFIC   OCEAN

COLOMBIA

COUNTRY	CAPITAL
1 Antigua and Barbuda	St. Johns
2 St. Kitts and Nevis	Basseterre
3 Dominica	Roseau
4 St. Lucia	Castries
5 St. Vincent and the Grenadines	Kingstown
6 Barbados	Bridgetown
7 Grenada	St. George's

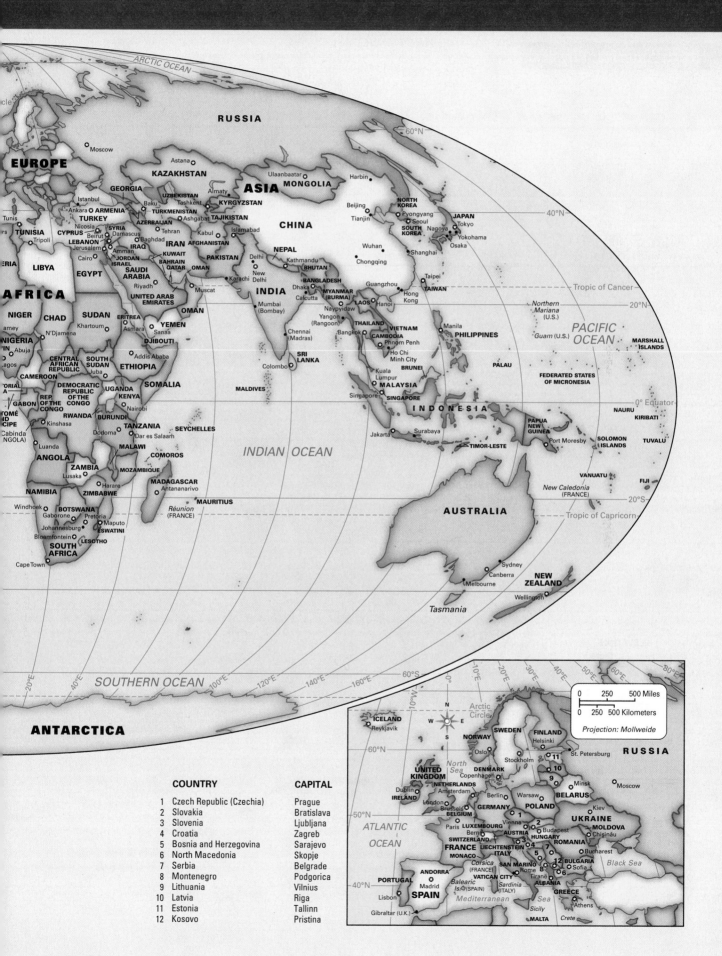

COUNTRY

1 Czech Republic (Czechia)
2 Slovakia
3 Slovenia
4 Croatia
5 Bosnia and Herzegovina
6 North Macedonia
7 Serbia
8 Montenegro
9 Lithuania
10 Latvia
11 Estonia
12 Kosovo

CAPITAL

Prague
Bratislava
Ljubljana
Zagreb
Sarajevo
Skopje
Belgrade
Podgorica
Vilnius
Riga
Tallinn
Pristina

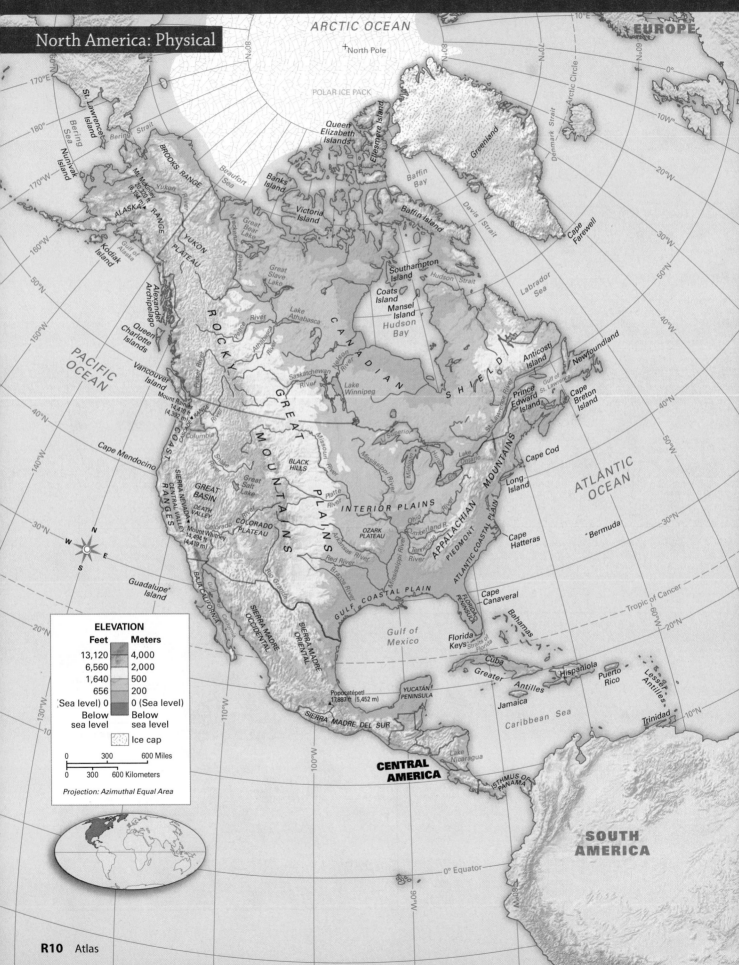

ARCTIC OCEAN

+ North Pole

EUROPE

POLAR ICE PACK

Queen
Elizabeth
Islands

Ellesmere Island

Greenland

Denmark Strait

Arctic Circle

Bering Strait

Beaufort
Sea

Banks
Island

Victoria
Island

Baffin
Bay

Baffin Island

Davis Strait

Cape
Farewell

St. Lawrence
Island

Nunivak
Island

BROOKS RANGE

Mt. McKinley
20,320 ft
(6,194 m)

ALASKA

RANGE

Yukon River

YUKON
PLATEAU

Mackenzie River

Great
Bear
Lake

Great
Slave
Lake

Southampton
Island

Coats
Island

Mansel
Island

Hudson Strait

Labrador
Sea

Kodiak
Island

Gulf of
Alaska

ROCKY

Peace River

Lake
Athabasca

CANADIAN

Hudson
Bay

Alexander
Archipelago

Queen
Charlotte
Islands

Athabasca River

Anticosti
Island

Newfoundland

Vancouver
Island

GREAT

Saskatchewan
River

Nelson River

SHIELD

Prince
Edward
Island

Gulf of
St. Lawrence

Cape
Breton
Island

PACIFIC
OCEAN

Mount Rainier
14,410 ft
(4,392 m)

CASCADE RANGE

Fraser River

Lake
Winnipeg

MOUNTAINS

Columbia River

Lake
Superior

Lake
Huron

St. Lawrence River

APPALACHIAN

Cape Cod

Long
Island

ATLANTIC
OCEAN

Cape Mendocino

COAST

Snake River

PLAINS

Missouri River

Lake
Michigan

Lake
Ontario

Lake
Erie

MOUNTAINS

SIERRA NEVADA

GREAT
BASIN

Great
Salt
Lake

BLACK
HILLS

Mississippi River

RANGES

CENTRAL VALLEY

DEATH
VALLEY

COLORADO
PLATEAU

Colorado River

Platte River

INTERIOR PLAINS

Ohio River

PIEDMONT

Cape
Hatteras

Bermuda

Mount Whitney
14,494 ft
(4,419 m)

Arkansas River

OZARK
PLATEAU

Cumberland R.

Tennessee River

ATLANTIC COASTAL PLAIN

Red River

Mississippi River

Guadalupe
Island

BAJA CALIFORNIA

Gulf of California

Rio Grande

Brazos River

GULF COASTAL PLAIN

FLORIDA
PENINSULA

Cape
Canaveral

Tropic of Cancer

SIERRA MADRE
OCCIDENTAL

SIERRA MADRE
ORIENTAL

Gulf of
Mexico

Florida
Keys

Straits of
Florida

Bahamas

Cuba

Jamaica

Greater
Antilles

Hispaniola

Puerto
Rico

Lesser
Antilles

Popocatépetl
17,887 ft (5,452 m)

YUCATÁN
PENINSULA

Caribbean Sea

Trinidad

SIERRA MADRE DEL SUR

Lake
Nicaragua

CENTRAL
AMERICA

ISTHMUS OF
PANAMA

SOUTH
AMERICA

ELEVATION

Feet	Meters
13,120	4,000
6,560	2,000
1,640	500
656	200
(Sea level) 0	0 (Sea level)
Below sea level	Below sea level

Ice cap

0   300   600 Miles

0   300   600 Kilometers

Projection: Azimuthal Equal Area

ARCTIC OCEAN

EUROPE

+ North Pole

CANADA

ALASKA
(U.S.)

Anchorage

Juneau

UNITED STATES

PACIFIC
OCEAN

ATLANTIC
OCEAN

Greenland
(DENMARK)

ICELAND

MEXICO

Gulf of
Mexico

BAHAMAS

CUBA

HAITI

**DOMINICAN
REPUBLIC**

Caribbean Sea

JAMAICA

BELIZE

GUATEMALA

HONDURAS

EL SALVADOR

NICARAGUA

**COSTA
RICA**

PANAMA

SOUTH
AMERICA

⊛ National capital
• Other city

| 0 | 300 | 600 Miles |
| 0 | 300 | 600 Kilometers |

Projection: Azimuthal Equal-Area

Atlas

ELEVATION

Feet	Meters
13,120	4,000
6,560	2,000
1,640	500
656	200
(Sea level) 0	0 (Sea level)
Below sea level	Below sea level

0   250   500 Miles

0   250   500 Kilometers

Projection: Azimuthal Equal Area

Labels on map:

CENTRAL AMERICA

Caribbean Sea

Panama Canal

Gulf of Panama

Lake Maracaibo

Margarita Island · Tobago · Trinidad

Orinoco River Delta

LLANOS

Meta River · Orinoco River

Angel Falls

GUIANA HIGHLANGS

Devil's Island · Cape Orange

Malpelo Island

Mount Tolima 18,425 ft (5,616 m)

Magdalena River · Cauca River

Caqueta River · Orinoco River

Amazon River Delta

ATLANTIC OCEAN

0° Equator

Galápagos Islands

Gulf of Guayaquil

Mount Chimborazo 20,561 ft (6,267 m)

Japurá River · Rio Negro · AMAZON BASIN · Amazon River

Marañón River · Amazon River · Juruá River · Purus · Madeira River · Tapajós River · Xingu River · Tocantins River · Parnaiba River

ANDES

Ucayali River

Mount Huascarán 22,205 ft (6,768 m)

PACIFIC OCEAN

Beni River · Mamoré River

MATO GROSSO PLATEAU

BRAZILIAN HIGHLANDS

São Francisco River · Araguaia River

Lake Titicaca · Ancohuma Peak 20,958 ft (6,388 m)

Lake Poopó · Pilcomayo River

CHACO

BRAZILIAN PLATEAU

Tropic of Capricorn

ATACAMA DESERT

San Ambrosio Island · San Félix Island

ANDES · Salado River · Paraguay River · Paraná River · Uruguay River

Juan Fernández Islands

Mount Aconcagua 22,834 ft (6,960 m)

PAMPAS · Rio de la Plata

Colorado River · Salado River

ATLANTIC OCEAN

Chiloé Island

Chonos Archipelago

PATAGONIA

Gulf of San Matias

Gulf of San Jorge · Cape Tres Puntas

Bahia Grande · Strait of Magellan · Falkland Islands

South Georgia Islands

Tierra del Fuego · Cape Horn

CENTRAL AMERICA

Caribbean Sea

Barranquilla
Cartagena
Caracas

VENEZUELA

Lake Maracaibo

Georgetown
Paramaribo
Cayenne

GUYANA

SURINAME

French Guiana (FRANCE)

Medellín

Bogotá

COLOMBIA

Cali

ATLANTIC OCEAN

Malpelo Island* (COLOMBIA)

Quito

ECUADOR

Guayaquil

Galápagos Islands (ECUADOR)

0° Equator

Belém

PERU

BRAZIL

Recife

Trujillo

Callao Lima

Lake Titicaca

Salvador

PACIFIC OCEAN

Arequipa

La Paz

Lake Poopó

BOLIVIA

Brasília

Sucre

Belo Horizonte

PARAGUAY

Campinas
São Paulo

Rio de Janeiro

Asunción

Curitiba

San Ambrosio Island (CHILE)

San Félix Island (CHILE)

CHILE

Pôrto Alegre

Juan Fernández Islands (CHILE)

Córdoba

Valparaíso
Santiago

Rosario

URUGUAY

ARGENTINA

Buenos Aires

Montevideo

ATLANTIC OCEAN

Tropic of Capricorn

○ National capital
● Other city

0   250   500 Miles
0   250   500 Kilometers

Projection: Azimuthal Equal-Area

Strait of Magellan

Falkland Islands (U.K.)

Tierra del Fuego

South Georgia Island (U.K.)

Atlas

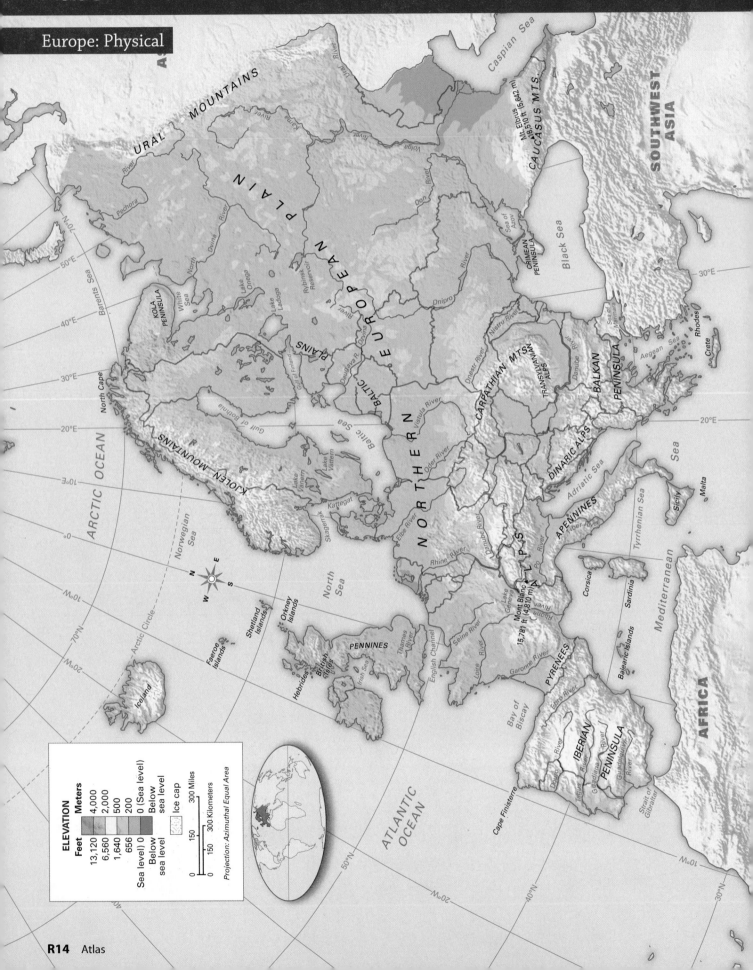

URAL MOUNTAINS

Caspian Sea

Mt. Elbrus
18,510 ft (5,642 m)

CAUCASUS MTS.

SOUTHWEST
ASIA

Pechora River

NORTHERN EUROPEAN PLAIN

Kama River

Volga River

Don River

Sea of Azov

CRIMEAN PENINSULA

Black Sea

Barents Sea

North Dvina River

White Sea

Lake Onega

Rybinsk Reservoir

Lake Ladoga

Dnipro River

30°E

KOLA PENINSULA

Gulf of Finland

Daugava R.

Dvina R.

Dniester River

Nistru River

Sea of Marmara

Aegean Sea

Rhodes

Crete

40°E

BALTIC PLAINS

Vistula River

CARPATHIAN MTS.

TRANSYLVANIAN ALPS

BALKAN PENINSULA

North Cape

Gulf of Bothnia

Baltic Sea

Oder River

Danube River

DINARIC ALPS

Adriatic Sea

Ionian Sea

Malta

30°E

KJOLEN MOUNTAINS

Lake Vänern

Lake Vättern

Elbe River

Rhine River

Danube River

Po River

APENNINES

Tiber River

Sicily

Tyrrhenian Sea

20°E

ARCTIC OCEAN

North Cape

Kattegat

Skagerrak

A L P S

Corsica

Sardinia

Balearic Islands

Mediterranean Sea

10°E

Norwegian Sea

N
W   E
S

North Sea

Mont Blanc
15,781 ft (4,810 m)

Lake Geneva

Rhône River

PYRENEES

AFRICA

Iceland

Arctic Circle

Shetland Islands

Orkney Islands

Faeroe Islands

Hebrides

British Isles

Irish Sea

PENNINES

Thames River

English Channel

Seine River

Loire River

Garonne River

Ebro River

Bay of Biscay

IBERIAN PENINSULA

Douro River

Tagus River

Guadiana River

Guadalquivir River

70°N

70°N

50°N

40°N

30°N

ATLANTIC OCEAN

Cape Finisterre

Strait of Gibraltar

60°N

50°N

40°N

ELEVATION

Feet	Meters
13,120	4,000
6,560	2,000
1,640	500
656	200
Sea level) 0	0 (Sea level)
Below sea level	Below sea level

Ice cap

300 Miles
0   150   300

300 Kilometers
0   150   300

Projection: Azimuthal Equal Area

ASIA

URAL MOUNTAINS

RUSSIA

Caspian Sea

SOUTHWEST ASIA

Nizhny Novgorod

Moscow

Barents Sea

White Sea

St. Petersburg

Black Sea

FINLAND

Minsk

BELARUS

Kiev

UKRAINE

MOLDOVA

Chișinău

Bucharest

ROMANIA

BULGARIA

Sofia

Rhodes

Aegean Sea

Crete

Tallinn

ESTONIA

LATVIA

Riga

Gulf of Finland

Helsinki

LITHUANIA

Vilnius

RUSSIA

POLAND

Warsaw

Krakow

SLOVAKIA

Bratislava

HUNGARY

Budapest

SERBIA

Belgrade

KOSOVO

Pristina

NORTH MACEDONIA

Skopje

ALBANIA

Tirana

GREECE

Athens

Sea

NORTH CAPE

North Cape

ARCTIC OCEAN

SWEDEN

Stockholm

Göteborg

Gulf of Bothnia

Baltic Sea

NORWAY

Oslo

Bergen

DENMARK

Copenhagen

Hamburg

Berlin

Dresden

GERMANY

Cologne

Bonn

CZECH REPUBLIC

Prague

AUSTRIA

Vienna

SLOVENIA

Ljubljana

CROATIA

Zagreb

BOSNIA AND HERZEGOVINA

Sarajevo

MONTENEGRO

Podgorica

SAN MARINO

San Marino

ITALY

Rome

VATICAN CITY

Naples

Adriatic Sea

MALTA

Valletta

Sicily

Mediterranean Sea

Sardinia (ITALY)

Corsica (FRANCE)

MONACO

Monaco

LIECHTENSTEIN

Vaduz

Milan

Lake Geneva

Bern

SWITZERLAND

ALPS

Munich

Luxembourg

LUXEMBOURG

Amsterdam

THE NETHERLANDS

Brussels

BELGIUM

Paris

Lyon

FRANCE

Marseille

PYRENEES

ANDORRA

Andorra la Vella

Barcelona

Balearic Islands (SPAIN)

SPAIN

Madrid

Valencia

Seville

Gibraltar (U.K.)

Strait of Gibraltar

PORTUGAL

Lisbon

Bay of Biscay

English Channel

Channel Islands (U.K.)

UNITED KINGDOM

SCOTLAND

Edinburgh

Belfast

NORTHERN IRELAND

IRELAND

Dublin

WALES

ENGLAND

Liverpool

London

British Isles

Shetland Islands

Faeroe Islands (DENMARK)

North Sea

ICELAND

Reykjavik

ATLANTIC OCEAN

AFRICA

Arctic Circle

70°N

60°N

50°N

40°N

70°E

60°E

50°E

40°E

30°E

20°E

10°E

0°

10°W

20°W

30°W

30°E

20°E

0°

N
E
S
W

✪ National capital
• Other city

300 Miles
150
0

300 Kilometers
150
0

Projection: Azimuthal Equal-Area

Asia: Physical

ELEVATION

Feet	Meters
13,120	4,000
6,560	2,000
1,640	500
656	200
(Sea level) 0	0 (Sea level)
Below sea level	Below sea level

Ice cap

750 Miles
0   250   500   750 Kilometers

Projection: Two-Point Equidistant

National capitals
Other cities

750 Miles
250 500 750 Kilometers

Projection: Two-Point Equidistant

PACIFIC OCEAN

AUSTRALIA

New Guinea

Arafura Sea

TIMOR-LESTE

Dili

INDONESIA

Ujung Pandang

Java Sea

Surabaya

Jakarta

Bandung

Celebes Sea

PHILIPPINES

Manila

South China Sea

BRUNEI

Bandar Seri Begawan

MALAYSIA

Kuala Lumpur

SINGAPORE

Singapore

Medan

Andaman Sea

Nicobar Islands (INDIA)

Andaman Islands (INDIA)

INDIAN OCEAN

MALDIVES

Male

SRI LANKA

Colombo

Chennai (Madras)

Bay of Bengal

Bangalore

Lakshadweep Islands (INDIA)

Mumbai (Bombay)

Arabian Sea

Socotra (YEMEN)

Gulf of Aden

AFRICA

Red Sea

YEMEN

Sanaa

Mecca

Jidda

SAUDI ARABIA

Riyadh

OMAN

Masqat (Muscat)

UNITED ARAB EMIRATES

Abu Dhabi

QATAR

Doha

BAHRAIN

Manama

Kuwait City

KUWAIT

Basra

Persian Gulf

IRAQ

Baghdad

Mosul

Damascus

SYRIA

Amman

JORDAN

ISRAEL

Tel Aviv

Jerusalem

LEBANON

Beirut

CYPRUS

Nicosia

Izmir

TURKEY

Ankara

Istanbul

Mediterranean Sea

Black Sea

ARMENIA

Yerevan

GEORGIA

Tbilisi

AZERBAIJAN

Baku

Caspian Sea

IRAN

Tehran

Shiraz

Ural Mountains

TURKMENISTAN

Ashgabat

AFGHANISTAN

Kabul

PAKISTAN

Karachi

Lahore

Islamabad

UZBEKISTAN

Tashkent

TAJIKISTAN

Dushanbe

KYRGYZSTAN

Bishkek

Almaty

KAZAKHSTAN

Astana

Aral Sea

Lake Balkhash

INDIA

Ahmadabad

Jaipur

New Delhi

Delhi

NEPAL

Kathmandu

BHUTAN

Thimphu

BANGLADESH

Dhaka

Kolkata (Calcutta)

MYANMAR (BURMA)

Naypyidaw

Yangon (Rangoon)

THAILAND

Bangkok

LAOS

Vientiane

CAMBODIA

Phnom Penh

Gulf of Thailand

VIETNAM

Hanoi

Ho Chi Minh City

CHINA

Chengdu

Chongqing

Wuhan

Nanjing

Beijing

Shanghai

Guangzhou

Hong Kong

Macao

Hainan (CHINA)

TAIWAN

Taipei

East China Sea

Yellow Sea

Qingdao

Dalian

Fushun

Harbin

MONGOLIA

Ulaanbaatar

Irkutsk

Lake Baykal

Novosibirsk

Omsk

Yekaterinburg

Chelyabinsk

Moscow

EUROPE

RUSSIA

Barents Sea

Kara Sea

Arctic Circle

North Pole

Aleutian Islands

Bering Sea

Sea of Okhotsk

Sakhalin

Kuril Islands (RUSSIA)

JAPAN

Sapporo

Vladivostok

Tokyo

Yokohama

Kyoto

Osaka

Hiroshima

Fukuoka

Nagasaki

Pusan

NORTH KOREA

Pyongyang

SOUTH KOREA

Seoul

Ryukyu Islands (JAPAN)

Tropic of Cancer

Equator

RUSSIA

Atlas

Africa: Physical

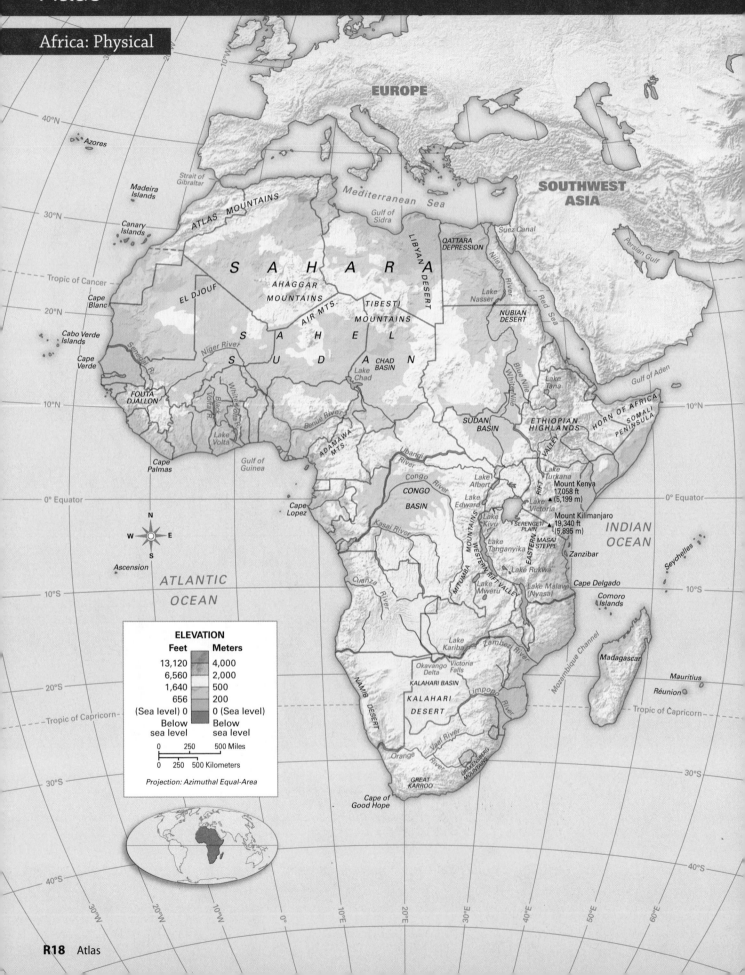

EUROPE

SOUTHWEST ASIA

Mediterranean Sea

Strait of Gibraltar

ATLAS MOUNTAINS

Gulf of Sidra

LIBYAN DESERT

QATTARA DEPRESSION

Suez Canal

Persian Gulf

Azores

Madeira Islands

Canary Islands

Tropic of Cancer

Cape Blanc

40°N

30°N

20°N

SAHARA

AHAGGAR MOUNTAINS

EL DJOUF

AIR MTS.

TIBESTI MOUNTAINS

Nile River

Lake Nasser

NUBIAN DESERT

Red Sea

Cabo Verde Islands

Cape Verde

SAHEL

Niger River

Senegal R.

SUDAN

CHAD BASIN

Lake Chad

Blue Nile

White Nile

Lake Tana

Gulf of Aden

10°N

FOUTA DJALLON

White Volta R.

Black Volta R.

Benue River

ADAMAWA MTS.

SUDAN BASIN

ETHIOPIAN HIGHLANDS

HORN OF AFRICA

SOMALI PENINSULA

Cape Palmas

Lake Volta

Gulf of Guinea

Ubangi River

Congo River

Lake Albert

Lake Edward

RIFT VALLEY

Lake Turkana

Mount Kenya
17,058 ft
▲ (5,199 m)

0° Equator

Cape Lopez

CONGO BASIN

Kasai River

Lake Kivu

Lake Victoria

SERENGETI PLAIN

Mount Kilimanjaro
19,340 ft
▲ (5,895 m)

INDIAN OCEAN

Seychelles

MITUMBA MOUNTAINS

WESTERN RIFT VALLEY

EASTERN RIFT VALLEY

MASAI STEPPE

Zanzibar

ATLANTIC OCEAN

Ascension

Cuanza River

Lake Tanganyika

Lake Rukwa

10°S

Lake Mweru

Lake Malawi (Nyasa)

Cape Delgado

Comoro Islands

Madagascar

Mauritius

Réunion

Lake Kariba

Zambezi River

Okavango Delta

Victoria Falls

KALAHARI BASIN

NAMIB DESERT

KALAHARI DESERT

Limpopo River

Mozambique Channel

Tropic of Capricorn

20°S

30°S

Vaal River

Orange River

DRAKENSBERG MOUNTAINS

GREAT KARROO

Cape of Good Hope

ELEVATION

Feet	Meters
13,120	4,000
6,560	2,000
1,640	500
656	200
(Sea level) 0	0 (Sea level)
Below sea level	Below sea level

0   250   500 Miles

0   250   500 Kilometers

Projection: Azimuthal Equal-Area

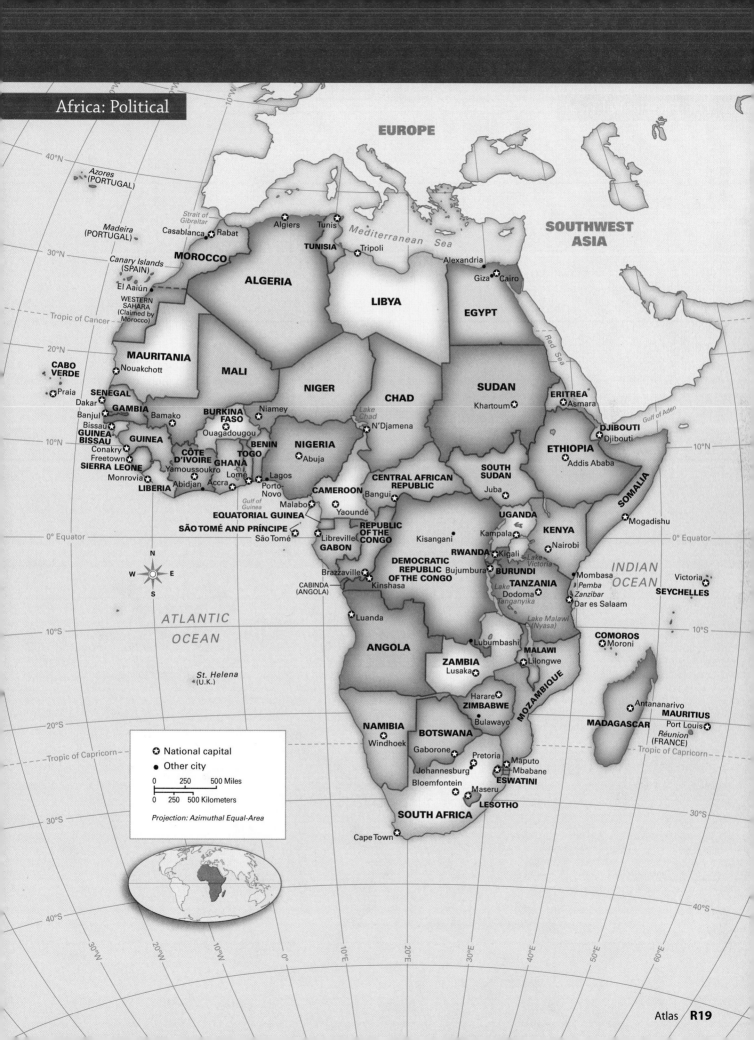

Africa: Political

EUROPE

SOUTHWEST ASIA

Azores (PORTUGAL)

Madeira (PORTUGAL)

Strait of Gibraltar

Casablanca • Rabat ✪
Algiers ✪ ✪ Tunis

MOROCCO

Canary Islands (SPAIN)

El Aaiún •

WESTERN SAHARA (Claimed by Morocco)

Mediterranean Sea

TUNISIA
✪ Tripoli

Alexandria •

Giza • ✪ Cairo

ALGERIA

LIBYA

EGYPT

Red Sea

Tropic of Cancer

MAURITANIA

CABO VERDE

• Praia ✪

SENEGAL

Dakar ✪

GAMBIA

Banjul ✪

Bissau ✪

GUINEA BISSAU

Conakry ✪

Freetown ✪

SIERRA LEONE

Monrovia ✪

LIBERIA

Nouakchott ✪

MALI

Bamako ✪

BURKINA FASO

Ouagadougou ✪

GUINEA

CÔTE D'IVOIRE

Yamoussoukro ✪

GHANA

Abidjan • Accra ✪

Niamey ✪

NIGER

BENIN

TOGO

Lomé ✪

Porto-Novo ✪

NIGERIA

Abuja ✪

Lagos •

N'Djamena ✪

CHAD

Lake Chad

Khartoum ✪

SUDAN

ERITREA

Asmara ✪

Gulf of Aden

DJIBOUTI

Djibouti ✪

ETHIOPIA

Addis Ababa ✪

Gulf of Guinea

CAMEROON

Malabo ✪

EQUATORIAL GUINEA

SÃO TOMÉ AND PRÍNCIPE

São Tomé ✪

Yaoundé ✪

CENTRAL AFRICAN REPUBLIC

Bangui ✪

SOUTH SUDAN

Juba ✪

REPUBLIC OF THE CONGO

GABON

Libreville ✪

Brazzaville ✪

CABINDA (ANGOLA)

Kinshasa ✪

Kisangani •

DEMOCRATIC REPUBLIC OF THE CONGO

Bujumbura ✪

UGANDA

Kampala ✪

RWANDA

Kigali ✪

BURUNDI

Lake Victoria

KENYA

Nairobi ✪

SOMALIA

Mogadishu ✪

INDIAN OCEAN

Victoria ✪

SEYCHELLES

Mombasa •

Pemba

Zanzibar

Dar es Salaam •

TANZANIA

Dodoma ✪

Lake Tanganyika

Lake Malawi (Nyasa)

N
W   E
S

ATLANTIC OCEAN

Luanda ✪

St. Helena (U.K.)

ANGOLA

Lubumbashi •

ZAMBIA

Lusaka ✪

MALAWI

Lilongwe ✪

COMOROS

Moroni ✪

Harare ✪

ZIMBABWE

Bulawayo •

MOZAMBIQUE

Antananarivo ✪

MADAGASCAR

MAURITIUS

Port Louis ✪

Réunion (FRANCE)

Tropic of Capricorn

NAMIBIA

Windhoek ✪

BOTSWANA

Gaborone ✪

Pretoria ✪

Johannesburg •

Bloemfontein ✪

Maputo ✪

Mbabane ✪

ESWATINI

Maseru ✪

LESOTHO

SOUTH AFRICA

Cape Town ✪

Legend

✪ National capital
• Other city

0   250   500 Miles
0   250   500 Kilometers

Projection: Azimuthal Equal-Area

The Pacific: Political

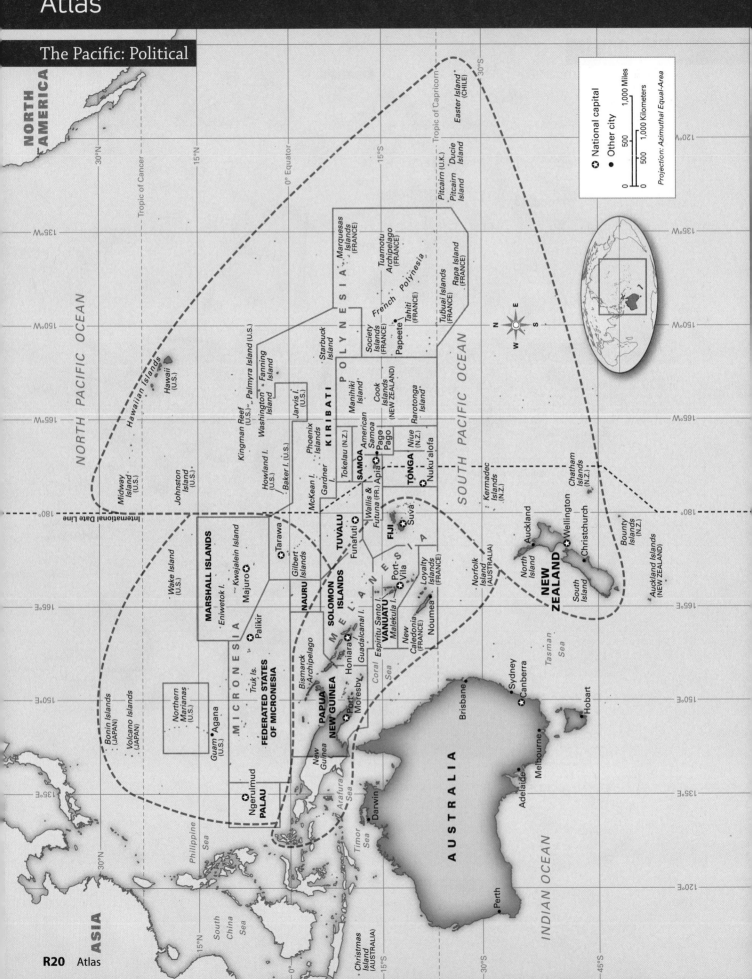

NORTH AMERICA

ASIA

NORTH PACIFIC OCEAN

SOUTH PACIFIC OCEAN

INDIAN OCEAN

- National capital
- Other city

Projection: Azimuthal Equal-Area

1,000 Miles
1,000 Kilometers
500
500

Tropic of Cancer

0° Equator

Tropic of Capricorn

International Date Line

30°N
15°N
15°S
30°S
45°S

135°W
150°W
165°W
180°
165°E
150°E
135°E
120°E

Easter Island (CHILE)

Pitcairn (U.K.)
Ducie Island
Pitcairn Island

Marquesas Islands (FRANCE)

Tuamotu Archipelago (FRANCE)

POLYNESIA

French Polynesia

Rapa Island (FRANCE)

Society Islands (FRANCE)

Tahiti (FRANCE)
Papeete

Tubuai Islands (FRANCE)

Starbuck Island

Manihiki

Cook Islands (NEW ZEALAND)

Rarotonga Island

KIRIBATI

Hawaiian Islands
Hawaii (U.S.)

Kingman Reef (U.S.)
Palmyra Island (U.S.)
Washington Island
Fanning Island

Jarvis I. (U.S.)

Phoenix Islands

Tokelau (N.Z.)

American Samoa
Pago Pago

Niue (N.Z.)

SAMOA
Apia

Howland I. (U.S.)
Baker I. (U.S.)

McKean I.
Gardner I.

Wallis & Futuna (FR.)

TONGA
Nuku'alofa

Kermadec Islands (N.Z.)

Midway Island (U.S.)

Johnston Island (U.S.)

NORTH PACIFIC OCEAN

Wake Island (U.S.)

MARSHALL ISLANDS
Eniwetok I.
Kwajalein Island
Majuro

Tarawa

Gilbert Islands

TUVALU
Funafuti

FIJI
Suva

Chatham Islands (N.Z.)

Wellington
Auckland
North Island
Christchurch
South Island

NEW ZEALAND

Bounty Islands (N.Z.)

Auckland Islands (NEW ZEALAND)

Bonin Islands (JAPAN)

Volcano Islands (JAPAN)

Northern Marianas (U.S.)

Guam (U.S.)
Agana

MICRONESIA

Truk Is.

FEDERATED STATES OF MICRONESIA

Palikir

NAURU

SOLOMON ISLANDS
Honiara

Guadalcanal I.

Bismarck Archipelago

PAPUA NEW GUINEA
Port Moresby

New Guinea

Espiritu Santo I.
Malekula I.

VANUATU
Port-Vila

New Caledonia (FRANCE)
Noumea

Loyalty Islands (FRANCE)

MELANESIA

Norfolk Island (AUSTRALIA)

Coral Sea

Ngerulmud
PALAU

Arafura Sea

Timor Sea

Darwin

AUSTRALIA

Brisbane
Sydney
Canberra
Melbourne
Adelaide
Hobart

Perth

Tasman Sea

South China Sea

Philippine Sea

Christmas Island (AUSTRALIA)

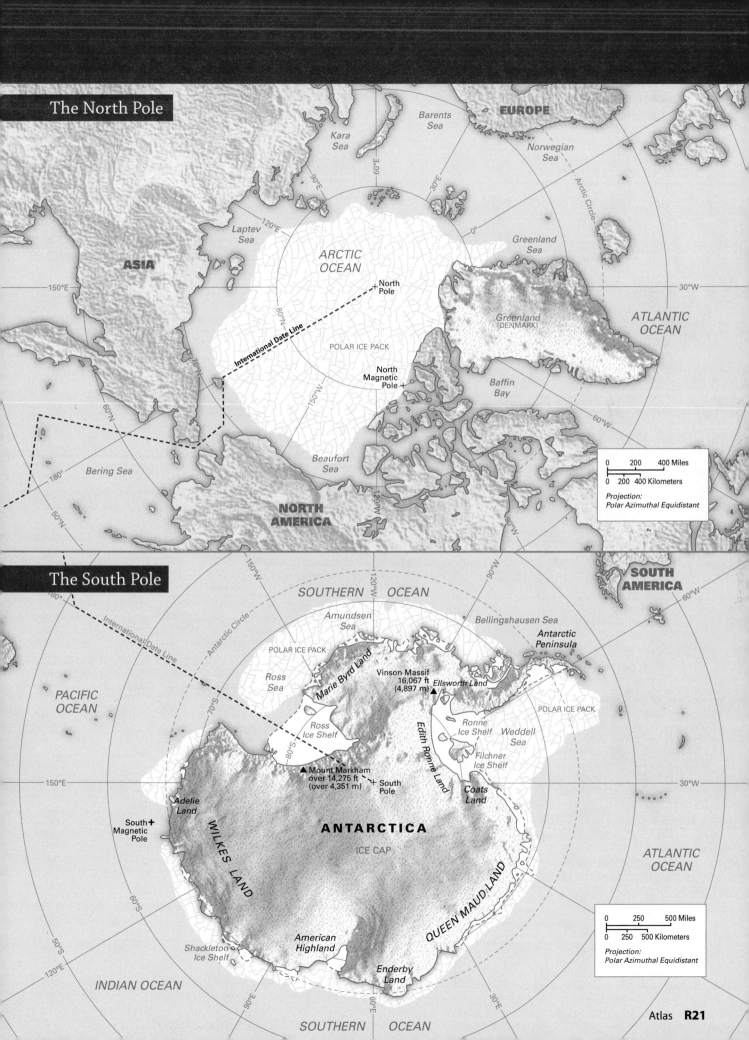

EUROPE

Barents
Sea

Kara
Sea

Norwegian
Sea

60°E

90°E

Greenland
Sea

Arctic Circle

0°

30°E

Laptev
Sea

120°E

ARCTIC
OCEAN

+ North
Pole

Greenland
(DENMARK)

ATLANTIC
OCEAN

30°W

ASIA

150°E

80°N

International Date Line

70°N

POLAR ICE PACK

North
Magnetic
Pole +

Baffin
Bay

60°W

150°W

Beaufort
Sea

60°N

180°

Bering Sea

90°W

120°W

NORTH
AMERICA

50°N

| 0 | 200 | 400 Miles |
| 0 | 200 | 400 Kilometers |

Projection:
Polar Azimuthal Equidistant

SOUTH
AMERICA

SOUTHERN OCEAN

150°W

120°W

90°W

60°W

Antarctic Circle

Amundsen
Sea

Bellingshausen Sea

Antarctic
Peninsula

POLAR ICE PACK

PACIFIC
OCEAN

Ross
Sea

Marie Byrd Land

Vinson Massif
16,067 ft
(4,897 m) ▲

Ellsworth Land

POLAR ICE PACK

70°S

Ross
Ice Shelf

Ronne
Ice Shelf

Weddell
Sea

80°S

Edith Ronne Land

Filchner
Ice Shelf

150°E

▲ Mount Markham
over 14,275 ft
(over 4,351 m)

+ South
Pole

Coats
Land

30°W

South +
Magnetic
Pole

Adelie
Land

WILKES LAND

ANTARCTICA

ICE CAP

ATLANTIC
OCEAN

QUEEN MAUD LAND

60°E

Shackleton
Ice Shelf

American
Highland

Enderby
Land

90°E

50°S

International Date Line

180°

120°E

30°E

INDIAN OCEAN

SOUTHERN OCEAN

| 0 | 250 | 500 Miles |
| 0 | 250 | 500 Kilometers |

Projection:
Polar Azimuthal Equidistant

The Americas: Physical

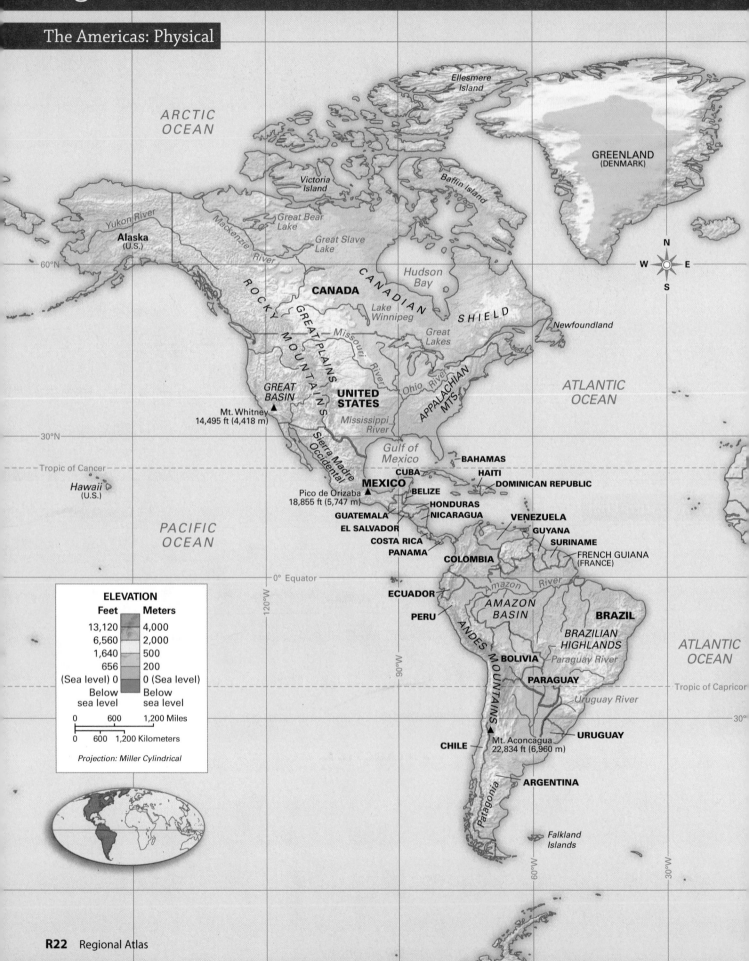

ELEVATION

Feet		Meters
13,120		4,000
6,560		2,000
1,640		500
656		200
(Sea level) 0		0 (Sea level)
Below sea level		Below sea level

0   600   1,200 Miles

0   600   1,200 Kilometers

Projection: Miller Cylindrical

The Americas

Geographical Extremes: The Americas

Longest River	Amazon River, Brazil/Peru: 4,000 miles (6,435 km)
Highest Point	Mt. Aconcagua, Argentina: 22,834 feet (6,960 m)
Lowest Point	Death Valley, United States: 282 feet (86 m) below sea level
Highest Recorded Temperature	Death Valley, United States: 134°F (56.6°C)
Lowest Recorded Temperature	Snag, Canada: -81.4°F (-63°C)
Wettest Place	Lloro, Colombia: 523.6 inches (1,329.9 cm) average precipitation per year
Driest Place	Arica, Chile: .03 inches (.08 cm) average precipitation per year
Highest Waterfall	Angel Falls, Venezuela: 3,212 feet (979 m)
Most Tornadoes	United States: More than 1,000 per year

Death Valley, United States

Size Comparison: The United States and the Americas

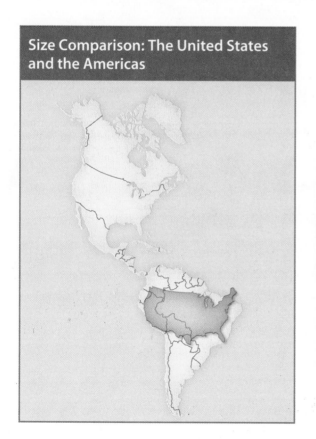

Workers harvest coffee beans in Costa Rica.

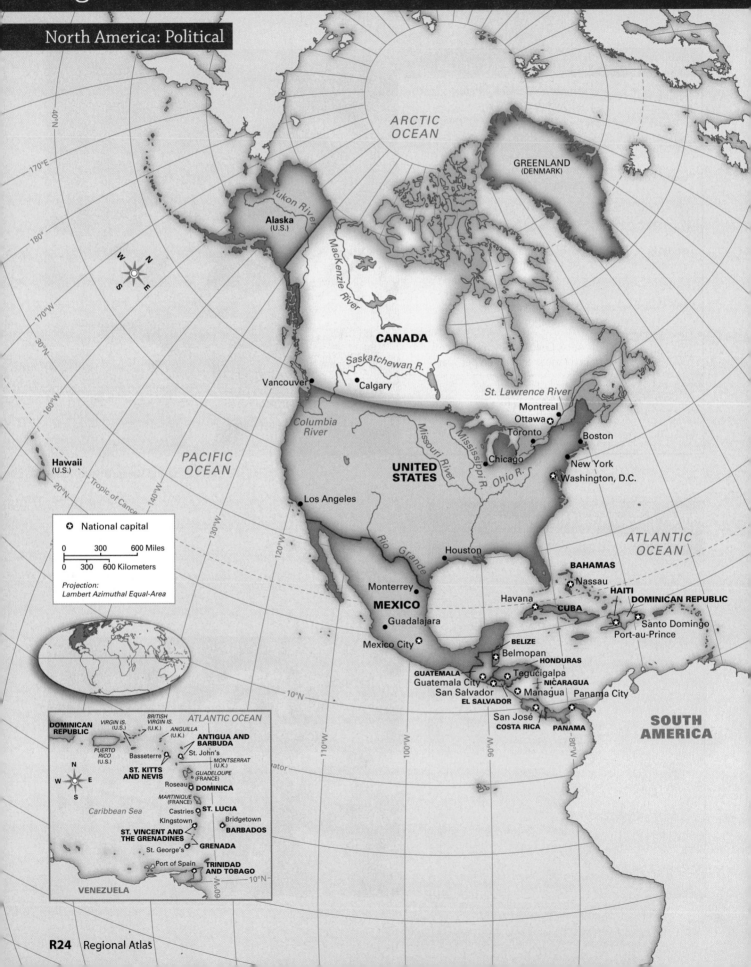

- National capital

0   300   600 Miles
0   300   600 Kilometers

Projection:
Lambert Azimuthal Equal-Area

ARCTIC OCEAN

GREENLAND (DENMARK)

Yukon River

Alaska (U.S.)

MacKenzie River

CANADA

Saskatchewan R.

St. Lawrence River

Vancouver   Calgary

Columbia River

Montreal
Ottawa
Toronto
Boston

Missouri River

Chicago

New York
Washington, D.C.

Mississippi R.

Ohio R.

UNITED STATES

Hawaii (U.S.)

PACIFIC OCEAN

Los Angeles

Rio Grande

ATLANTIC OCEAN

Houston

BAHAMAS
Nassau

Monterrey

MEXICO

Guadalajara

Havana

HAITI
DOMINICAN REPUBLIC

CUBA

Santo Domingo
Port-au-Prince

Mexico City

BELIZE
Belmopan
HONDURAS

GUATEMALA
Guatemala City

Tegucigalpa
NICARAGUA

San Salvador
EL SALVADOR

Managua

Panama City

San José
COSTA RICA

PANAMA

SOUTH AMERICA

Tropic of Cancer

40°N
30°N
20°N
10°N

170°E
180°
170°W
160°W
150°W
140°W
130°W
120°W
110°W
100°W
90°W
80°W

Caribbean inset

DOMINICAN REPUBLIC

VIRGIN IS. (U.S.)

BRITISH VIRGIN IS. (U.K.)

ANGUILLA (U.K.)

ATLANTIC OCEAN

ANTIGUA AND BARBUDA

PUERTO RICO (U.S.)

St. John's

MONTSERRAT (U.K.)

Basseterre

ST. KITTS AND NEVIS

GUADELOUPE (FRANCE)

DOMINICA

Roseau

MARTINIQUE (FRANCE)

Caribbean Sea

ST. LUCIA

Castries

Kingstown

Bridgetown

ST. VINCENT AND THE GRENADINES

BARBADOS

St. George's

GRENADA

Port of Spain

TRINIDAD AND TOBAGO

VENEZUELA

Equator

10°N

70°W
60°W

South America: Political

Cartagena
Caracas
VENEZUELA
Bogotá
GUYANA
Georgetown
Paramaribo
COLOMBIA
SURINAME
French Guiana
(FRANCE)

0° Equator
Quito
ECUADOR
Galápagos Islands
Guayaquil
Manaus
Amazon River

PACIFIC OCEAN

PERU
BRAZIL

10°N
10°S
Lima

N
W   E
S

La Paz
Salvador
BOLIVIA
Brasília
Sucre
ATLANTIC OCEAN

20°S
Paraná River
PARAGUAY
Rio de Janeiro
Tropic of Capricorn
CHILE
Asunción
São Paulo

30°S
Córdoba
Santiago
URUGUAY
Buenos Aires
Montevideo
ARGENTINA

✪ National capital

0   300   600 Miles

0   300   600 Kilometers

*Projection:
Lambert Azimuthal Equal-Area*

40°S

Falkland Islands

50°S

South Georgia Island

100°W 90°W 80°W 70°W 60°W 50°W 40°W 30°W 20°W

Regional Atlas

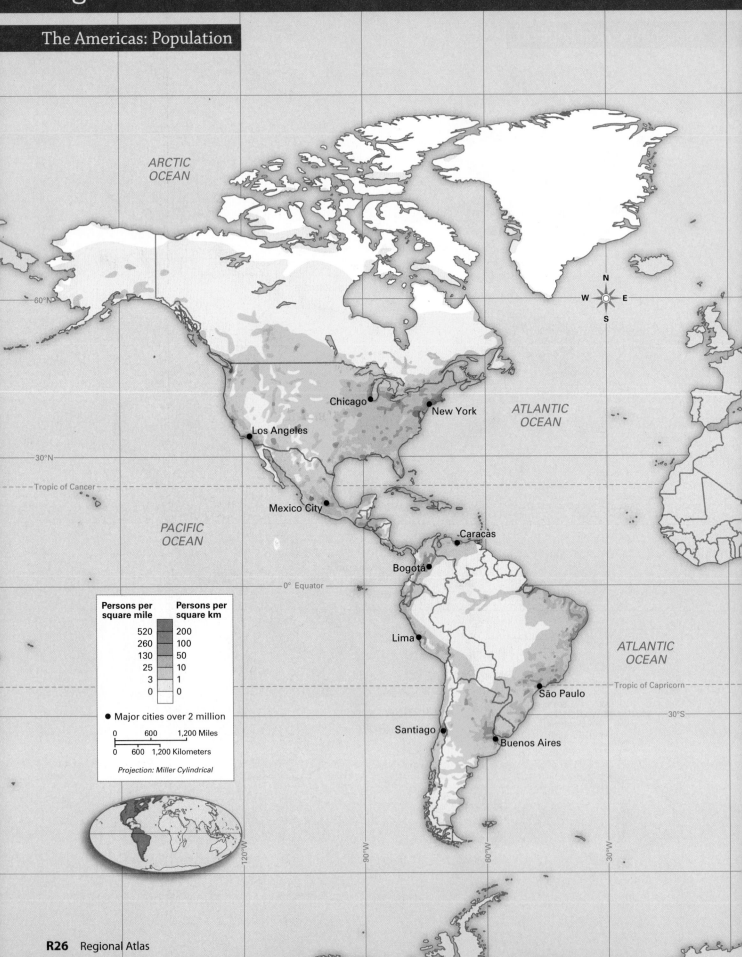

ARCTIC
OCEAN

60°N

ATLANTIC
OCEAN

Chicago
New York
Los Angeles

30°N

Tropic of Cancer

Mexico City

PACIFIC
OCEAN

Caracas

Bogotá

0° Equator

Lima

ATLANTIC
OCEAN

São Paulo

Tropic of Capricorn

30°S

Santiago

Buenos Aires

Persons per square mile / **Persons per square km**

Persons per square mile	Persons per square km
520	200
260	100
130	50
25	10
3	1
0	0

● Major cities over 2 million

0   600   1,200 Miles

0   600   1,200 Kilometers

Projection: Miller Cylindrical

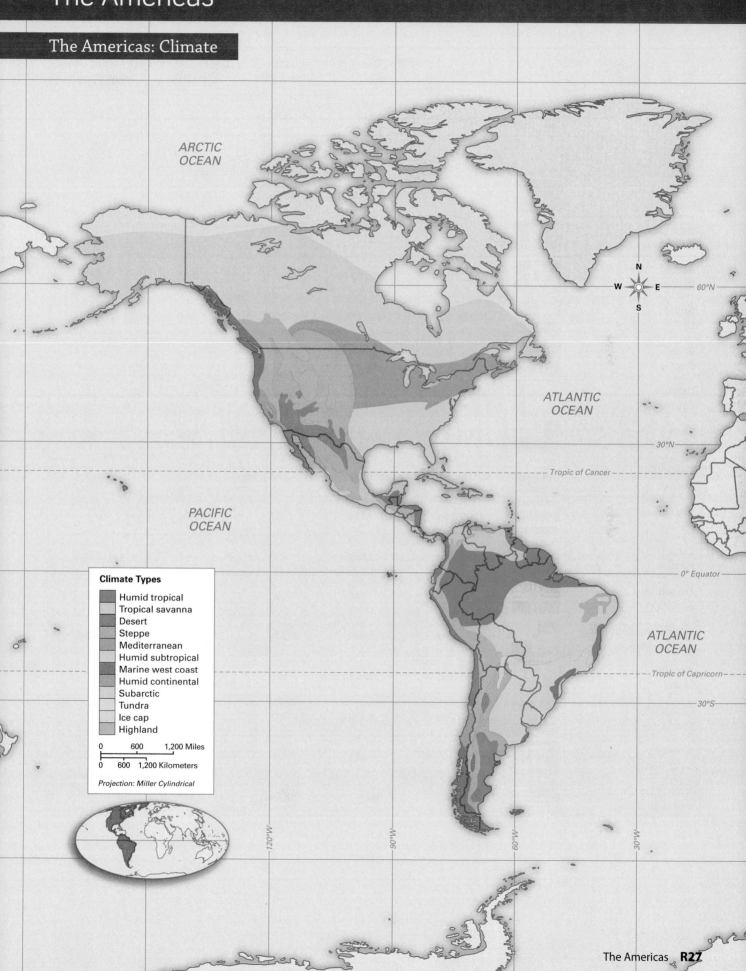

The Americas

ARCTIC
OCEAN

ATLANTIC
OCEAN

PACIFIC
OCEAN

ATLANTIC
OCEAN

60°N

30°N

Tropic of Cancer

0° Equator

Tropic of Capricorn

30°S

N
W   E
S

120°W

90°W

60°W

30°W

Climate Types

Humid tropical
Tropical savanna
Desert
Steppe
Mediterranean
Humid subtropical
Marine west coast
Humid continental
Subarctic
Tundra
Ice cap
Highland

0   600   1,200 Miles

0   600   1,200 Kilometers

Projection: Miller Cylindrical

Country Capital	Flag	Population	Area (sq mi)	GDP (billions $ U.S.)	Life Expectancy at Birth	Internet Users (per 1,000 pop.)
Antigua and Barbuda St. John's		93,581	171	1.3	76.5	650
Argentina Buenos Aires		43.8 million	1,068,302	630.4	77.1	690
The Bahamas Nassau		327,316	5,382	8.9	72.4	780
Barbados Bridgetown		291,495	166	4.4	75.3	760
Belize Belmopan		353,858	8,867	1.8	68.7	420
Bolivia La Paz, Sucre		10.9 million	424,164	33.2	69.2	450
Brazil Brasília		205.8 million	3,286,488	1,773	73.8	590
Canada Ottawa		35.8 million	3,855,103	1,553	82.1	890
Chile Santiago		17.6 million	292,260	240	78.8	640
Colombia Bogotá		47.2 million	439,736	292	75.7	560
Costa Rica San José		4.8 million	19,730	53	78.6	600
Cuba Havana		11.2 million	42,803	77	78.7	310
Dominica Roseau		73,757	291	0.5	77	680
Dominican Republic Santo Domingo		10.6 million	18,815	67	78.1	520
Ecuador Quito		16 million	109,483	101	76.8	490
El Salvador San Salvador		6.2 million	8,124	26	74.7	270
Grenada Saint George's		111,219	133	1.4	74.3	540
United States Washington, DC		324 million	3,794,083	18,040	79.8	750

Country / Capital	Flag	Population	Area (sq mi)	GDP (billions $ U.S.)	Life Expectancy at Birth	Internet Users (per 1,000 pop.)
Guatemala Guatemala City		15.2 million	42,043	64	72.3	270
Guyana Georgetown		735,909	83,000	3.2	68.4	380
Haiti Port-au-Prince		10.5 million	10,714	8.7	63.8	120
Honduras Tegucigalpa		8.9 million	43,278	20.5	71.1	200
Jamaica Kingston		2.9 million	4,244	14.2	73.6	430
Mexico Mexico City		123.1 million	761,606	1,144	75.9	570
Nicaragua Managua		5.9 million	49,998	12.7	73.2	200
Panama Panama City		3.7 million	30,193	52.1	78.6	510
Paraguay Asunción		6.8 million	157,047	27.7	77.2	440
Peru Lima		30.7 million	496,226	192	73.7	410
Saint Kitts and Nevis Basseterre		52,329	101	0.9	75.7	760
Saint Lucia Castries		164,464	238	1.4	77.8	520
Saint Vincent and the Grenadines; Kingstown		102,350	150	0.7	75.3	520
Suriname Paramaribo		585,824	63,039	5.2	72.2	430
Trinidad and Tobago Port-of-Spain		1.2 million	1,980	24.6	72.9	690
Uruguay Montevideo		3.4 million	68,039	53.1	77.2	650
Venezuela Caracas		30.9 million	352,144	260.1	75.8	620
United States Washington, DC		324 million	3,794,083	18,040	79.8	750

Europe, Russia, and the Eurasian Republics: Physical

ICELAND

Norwegian Sea

Arctic Circle

Kjölen Mountains

Kola Peninsula

Ob River

West Siberian Plain

ATLANTIC OCEAN

BRITISH ISLES

Highlands

North Sea

Scandinavian Peninsula

NORWAY

SWEDEN

FINLAND

Lake Onega

Lake Ladoga

Volga

Irtysh River

Jutland Peninsula

DENMARK

Baltic Sea

ESTONIA

LATVIA

LITHUANIA

RUSSIA

EUROPEAN PLAIN

Kama River

URAL MOUNTAINS

Ob River

IRELAND

UNITED KINGDOM

NETHERLANDS

NORTHERN

BELARUS

RUSSIA

Esil River

BELGIUM

GERMANY

POLAND

Ural River

KAZAKHSTAN

LUXEMBOURG

CZECH REPUBLIC

Rhine

Danube

AUSTRIA

SLOVAKIA

Carpathian Mts.

UKRAINE

Donets Basin

Caspian Depression

Aral Sea

Syr Darya

Kazakh Upland

Ile R.

Lake Ball

FRANCE

SWITZERLAND

ALPS

SLOVENIA

HUNGARY

ROMANIA

MOLDOVA

Don R.

Zhayyk R.

Bay of Biscay

Mont Blanc
15,771 ft
(4,807 m)

ITALY

Apennines

CROATIA

BOSNIA AND HERZEGOVINA

SERBIA

KOSOVO

Dinaric Alps

Mt. Elbrus
18,510 ft
(5,642 m)

Caucasus Mts.

Caspian Sea

UZBEKISTAN

KYRGYZSTAN

Tien

Pyrenees

BULGARIA

NORTH MACEDONIA

Black Sea

GEORGIA

ARMENIA

Ismail Peak
24,590
(7,495)

PORTUGAL

SPAIN

Iberian Peninsula

MONTENEGRO

ALBANIA

Balkan Peninsula

GREECE

AZERBAIJAN

TURKMENISTAN

Amu Darya

TAJIKISTAN

Pamirs

Mediterranean Sea

SOUTHWEST ASIA

AFGHANISTAN

Hindu Kush

Khyber Pass

AFRICA

ELEVATION

Feet		Meters
13,120		4,000
6,560		2,000
1,640		500
656		200
(Sea level) 0		0 (Sea level)
Below sea level		Below sea level

0   300   600 Miles

0   30   600 Kilometers

Projection: Robinson

Size Comparison: The United States and Europe, Russia, and the Eurasian Republics

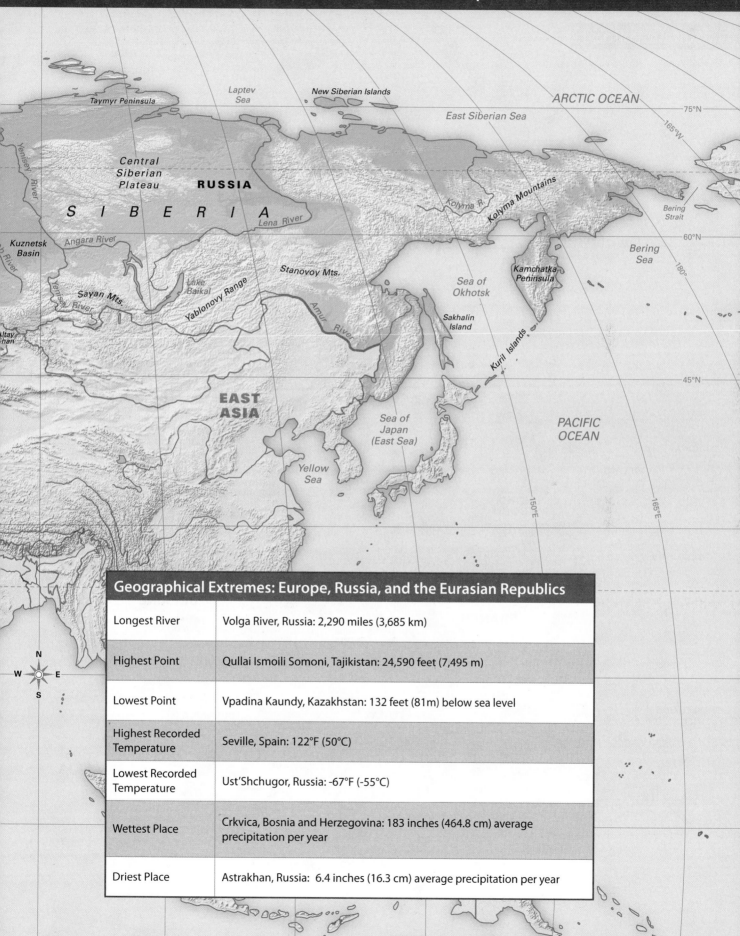

Geographical Extremes: Europe, Russia, and the Eurasian Republics	
Longest River	Volga River, Russia: 2,290 miles (3,685 km)
Highest Point	Qullai Ismoili Somoni, Tajikistan: 24,590 feet (7,495 m)
Lowest Point	Vpadina Kaundy, Kazakhstan: 132 feet (81m) below sea level
Highest Recorded Temperature	Seville, Spain: 122°F (50°C)
Lowest Recorded Temperature	Ust'Shchugor, Russia: -67°F (-55°C)
Wettest Place	Crkvica, Bosnia and Herzegovina: 183 inches (464.8 cm) average precipitation per year
Driest Place	Astrakhan, Russia: 6.4 inches (16.3 cm) average precipitation per year

Europe: Political

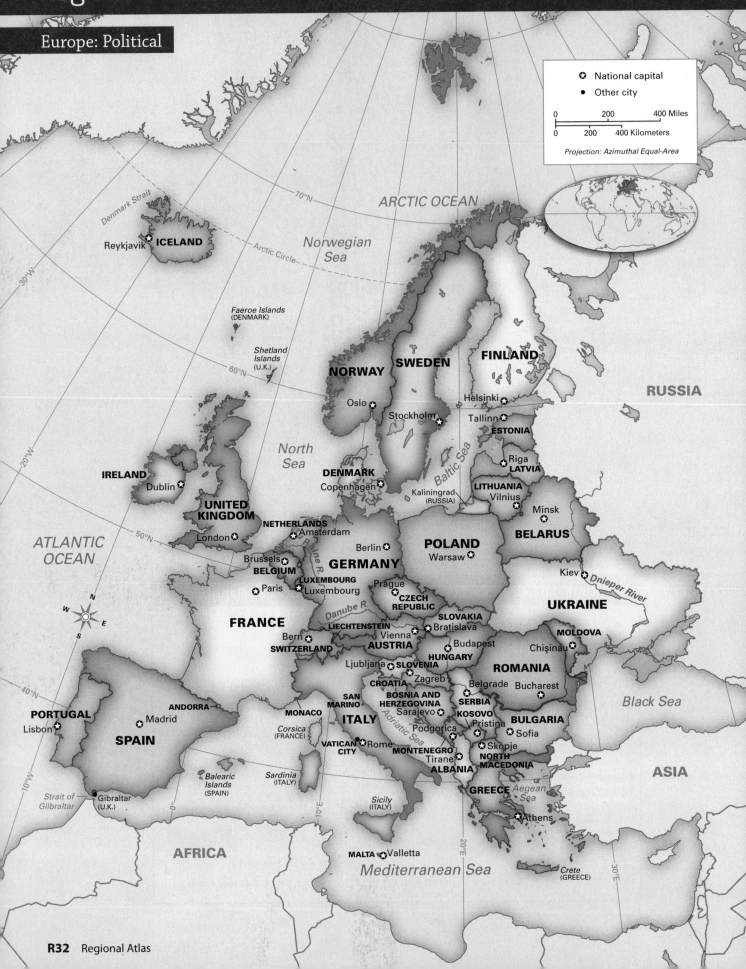

National capital
Other city

0   200   400 Miles
0 200 400 Kilometers

Projection: Azimuthal Equal-Area

ARCTIC OCEAN

Denmark Strait

Arctic Circle

Norwegian Sea

70°N

Reykjavik ICELAND

30°W

Faeroe Islands (DENMARK)

Shetland Islands (U.K.)

60°N

NORWAY   SWEDEN   FINLAND

Oslo   Stockholm   Helsinki   RUSSIA

North Sea

Tallinn   ESTONIA

20°W

IRELAND

Dublin

DENMARK   Baltic Sea   Riga   LATVIA

Copenhagen   Kaliningrad (RUSSIA)   LITHUANIA   Vilnius

UNITED KINGDOM

NETHERLANDS   Minsk

50°N   London   Amsterdam   Berlin   POLAND   BELARUS

ATLANTIC OCEAN

Brussels   GERMANY   Warsaw

BELGIUM   Rhine R.

LUXEMBOURG   Kiev   Dnieper River

Paris   Luxembourg   Prague

CZECH   UKRAINE

REPUBLIC

Danube R.   SLOVAKIA

FRANCE   LIECHTENSTEIN   Bratislava   MOLDOVA

Bern   Vienna   Budapest   Chișinău

SWITZERLAND   AUSTRIA

HUNGARY   ROMANIA

Ljubljana   SLOVENIA

40°N   CROATIA   Zagreb   Belgrade   Bucharest   Black Sea

PORTUGAL   ANDORRA   Madrid

SAN   BOSNIA AND   SERBIA

MARINO   HERZEGOVINA   KOSOVO   BULGARIA

Lisbon   MONACO   ITALY   Sarajevo   Pristina

SPAIN   Corsica (FRANCE)   Adriatic Sea   Podgorica   Sofia

10°W   VATICAN   Rome   Skopje

CITY   MONTENEGRO   NORTH

Balearic   Tirane   MACEDONIA

Islands   Sardinia   ALBANIA

(SPAIN)   (ITALY)

Strait of   Gibraltar   GREECE   Aegean Sea   ASIA

Gibraltar   (U.K.)

AFRICA   Sicily   Athens

(ITALY)

MALTA   Valletta

Mediterranean Sea   Crete (GREECE)

20°E   30°E

National capital
Other city

0   300   600 Miles
0   300   600 Kilometers

Projection: Two-Point Equidistant

Europe: Population

Persons per square mile / **Persons per square km**

Persons per square mile	Persons per square km
520	200
260	100
130	50
25	10
3	1
0	0

● Major cities over 2 million

0   150   300 Miles
0   150   300 Kilometers

Projection: Azimuthal Equal-Area

ARCTIC OCEAN

70°N

Denmark Strait

Arctic Circle

Norwegian Sea

60°N

North Sea

Baltic Sea

RUSSIA

Kaliningrad (RUSSIA)

50°N

London ●

Berlin ●

Warsaw ●

Kiev ●

ATLANTIC OCEAN

Paris ●

Vienna ●

N
W   E
S

40°N

Madrid ●

Barcelona ●

Rome ●

Adriatic Sea

Bucharest ●

Black Sea

ASIA

Aegean Sea

10°W

Strait of Gibraltar

0°

10°E

20°E

30°E

AFRICA

Mediterranean Sea

30°W

20°W

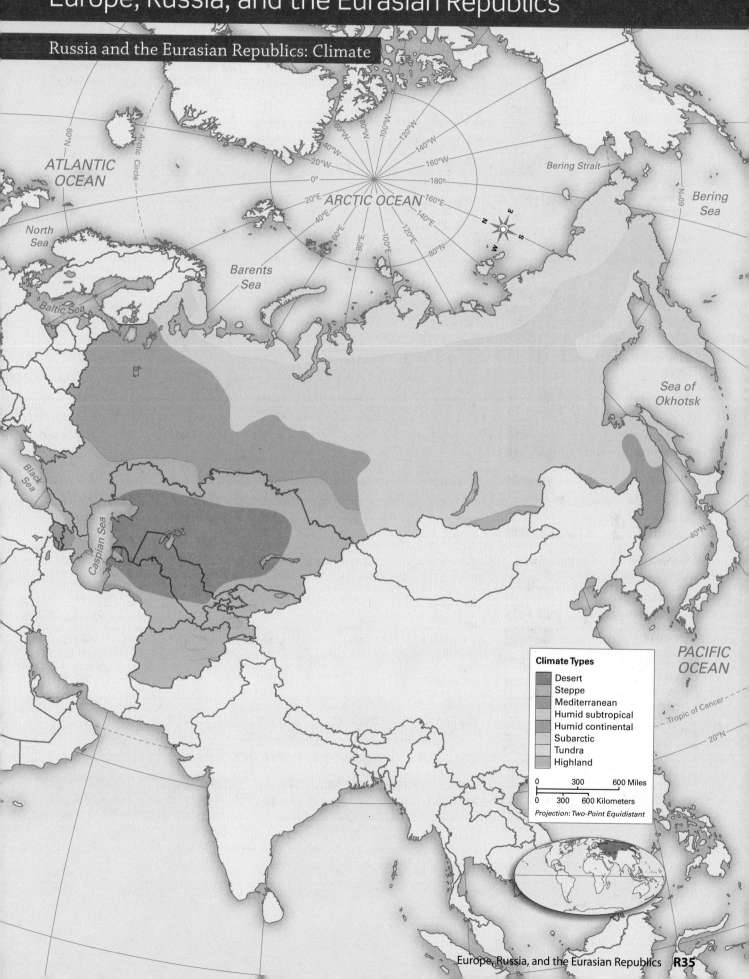

ATLANTIC
OCEAN

60°N

Arctic Circle

ARCTIC OCEAN

Bering Strait

Bering
Sea

60°N

North
Sea

Barents
Sea

Baltic Sea

Black
Sea

Caspian Sea

Sea of
Okhotsk

PACIFIC
OCEAN

40°N

Tropic of Cancer

20°N

Climate Types

	Desert
	Steppe
	Mediterranean
	Humid subtropical
	Humid continental
	Subarctic
	Tundra
	Highland

0   300   600 Miles

0   300   600 Kilometers

Projection: Two-Point Equidistant

Country Capital	Flag	Population	Area (sq mi)	GDP (billions $ U.S.)	Life Expectancy at Birth	Internet Users (per 1,000 pop.)
Afghanistan Kabul		33.3 million	250,001	20.8	51.3	80
Albania Tirana		3 million	11,100	11.4	78.3	630
Andorra Andorra la Vella		85,660	181	4.8	82.8	970
Armenia Yerevan		3 million	11,506	10.5	74.6	580
Austria Vienna		8.7 million	32,382	374.3	81.5	840
Azerbaijan Baku		9.8 million	33,436	54.1	72.5	770
Belarus Minsk		9.6 million	80,155	54.6	72.7	620
Belgium Brussels		11.4 million	11,787	454.3	81	850
Bosnia and Herzegovina; Sarajevo		3.8 million	19,741	16	76.7	650
Bulgaria Sofia		7.1 million	42,823	49	74.5	570
Croatia Zagreb		4.3 million	21,831	48.9	75.9	700
Czech Republic Prague		10.6 million	30,450	185.2	78.6	810
Denmark Copenhagen		5.6 million	16,639	295.1	79.4	960
Estonia Tallinn		1.3 million	17,462	22.7	76.7	880
Finland Helsinki		5.5 million	130,559	232.1	80.9	930
France Paris		66.8 million	248,429	2,420	81.8	850
Georgia T'bilisi		4.9 million	26,911	14	76.2	450
United States Washington, D.C.		324 million	3,794,083	18,040	79.8	750

Country Capital	Flag	Population	Area (sq mi)	GDP (billions $ U.S.)	Life Expectancy at Birth	Internet Users (per 1,000 pop.)
Germany Berlin		80.7 million	137,847	3,365	80.7	880
Greece Athens		10.7 million	50,942	195.3	80.5	670
Hungary Budapest		9.9 million	35,919	120.6	75.9	730
Iceland Reykjavik		335,878	39,769	16.7	83	980
Ireland Dublin		4.9 million	27,135	283.7	80.8	800
Italy Rome		62 million	116,306	1,816	82.2	660
Kazakhstan Astana		18.3 million	1,049,155	184.4	70.8	730
Kosovo Pristina		1.9 million	4,203	6.4	71.3	800
Kyrgyzstan Bishkek		5.7 million	76,641	6.7	70.7	300
Latvia Riga		2 million	24,938	27	69.9	790
Liechtenstein Vaduz		37,937	62	5.1	81.9	970
Lithuania Vilnius		2.9 million	25,174	41.2	74.9	710
Luxembourg Luxembourg		582,291	998	57.8	82.3	970
Malta Valletta		415,196	122	9.8	80.4	760
Moldova Chişinau		3.5 million	13,067	6.5	70.7	500
Monaco Monaco		30,581	1	6.1	89.5	930
United States Washington, D.C.		324 million	3,794,083	18,040	79.8	750

Country Capital	Flag	Population	Area (sq mi)	GDP (billions $ U.S.)	Life Expectancy at Birth	Internet Users (per 1,000 pop.)
Montenegro Cetinje, Podgorica		644,578	5,415	4	75	650
Netherlands Amsterdam		17 million	16,033	750.7	81.3	930
North Macedonia Skopje		2.1 million	9,781	10.1	76.2	700
Norway Oslo		5.2 million	125,021	388.3	81.8	970
Poland Warsaw		38.5 million	120,728	474.8	77.6	680
Portugal Lisbon		10.8 million	35,672	199	79.3	690
Romania Bucharest		21.6 million	91,699	178	75.1	560
Russian Federation Moscow		142.3 million	6,592,772	1,326	70.8	730
San Marino San Marino		33,285	24	1.6	83.3	530
Serbia Belgrade		7.1 million	29,913	36.5	75.5	650
Slovakia Bratislava		5.5 million	18,859	86.6	77.1	850
United States Washington, D.C.		324 million	3,794,083	18,040	79.8	750

Country Capital	Flag	Population	Area (sq mi)	GDP (billions $ U.S.)	Life Expectancy at Birth	Internet Users (per 1,000 pop.)
Slovenia Ljubljana		2 million	7,827	42.8	78.2	730
Spain Madrid		48.5 million	194,897	1,200	81.7	790
Sweden Stockholm		9.8 million	173,732	493	82.1	910
Switzerland Bern		8.1 million	15,942	664	82.6	880
Tajikistan Dushanbe		8.3 million	55,251	7.8	67.7	190
Turkmenistan Ashgabat		5.3 million	188,456	35.9	70.1	150
Ukraine Kiev		44.2 million	233,090	90.5	71.8	490
United Kingdom London		64.4 million	94,526	2,858	80.7	920
Uzbekistan Tashkent		29.5 million	172,742	65.5	73.8	430
Vatican City Vatican City		1,000	0.2	Not available	Not available	Not available
United States Washington, D.C.		324 million	3,794,083	18,040	79.8	750

Gazetteer

A

Albania a country on the Balkan Peninsula in southeastern Europe (p. 545)

Alps a great mountain system in central Europe (p. 470)

Amazon River the major river in South America (p. 325)

Amsterdam (52°N, 5°E) the capital and largest city of the Netherlands (p. 505)

Andes Mountains (AN-deez) a long mountain range along the west coast of South America (p. 323)

Apennines (A-puh-nynz) the major mountain range on the Italian Peninsula (p. 470)

Appalachian Mountains a mountain system in eastern North America (p. 191)

Athens (38°N, 24°E) an ancient city and the modern capital of Greece (pp. 374, 476)

B

Baja California a peninsula in Mexico (p. 277)

Baku (40°N, 48°E) the capital of Azerbaijan (p. 572)

Balkan Peninsula a peninsula in Southern Europe (p. 531)

Barcelona (41°N, 2°E) a large port city in Spain on the Mediterranean Sea (p. 486)

Berlin (53°N, 13°E) the capital of Germany (p. 507)

Bern (47°N, 7°E) the capital of Switzerland (p. 513)

Bogotá (4°N, 72°W) capital of Colombia (p. 343)

Bosnia and Herzegovina a country on the Balkan Peninsula (p. 545)

Boston (42°N, 71°W) the capital of Massachusetts (p. 198)

Brasília (10°S, 55°W) the capital of Brazil (p. 334)

British Columbia a province in Canada (p. 233)

British Isles a group of islands off the northwestern coast of Europe including Britain and Ireland (p. 496)

Brussels (51°N, 4°E) the capital of Belgium (p. 505)

Budapest (48°N, 19°E) the capital of Hungary (p. 542)

Buenos Aires (BWAY-nohs EYE-rayz) (36°S, 60°W) the capital of Argentina (p. 338)

Bulgaria a country in the Balkans (p. 546)

C

Canadian Shield a region of ancient rock that covers more than half of Canada (p. 226)

Caracas (11°N, 67°W) the capital of Venezuela (p. 346)

Caribbean Sea an arm of the Atlantic Ocean between North and South America (p. 297)

Carpathians (kahr-PAY-thee-uhnz) a major mountain chain in central and eastern Europe (p. 531)

Cartagena (kahr-tah-HAY-nuh) (10°N, 74°W) a coastal city in northern Colombia (p. 343)

Carthage an ancient city in North Africa (p. 384)

Caspian Sea an inland sea located between Europe and Asia; it is the largest inland body of water in the world (p. 555)

Caucasus Mountains a mountain system in southeastern Europe between the Black Sea and Caspian Sea (p. 555)

Chechnya (CHECH-nyuh) a republic in Russia that is fighting a violent struggle for independence (p. 569)

Chernobyl (51°N, 30°E) a city in Ukraine; the world's worst nuclear reactor accident occurred there in 1986 (p. 534)

Chicago (42°N, 88°W) a major U.S. city and port in northeastern Illinois on Lake Michigan (p. 213)

Constantinople the former center of the eastern Roman Empire (p. 392)

Croatia a country in the Balkans (p. 545)

Cuzco the capital of the Inca Empire (p. 265)

D

Danube River (DAN-yoob) the second-longest river in Europe; it flows from Germany east to the Black Sea (pp. 495, 532)

Detroit (42°N, 83°W) a large U.S. city in Michigan (p. 213)

Dublin (53°N, 6°W) the capital of Ireland (p. 518)

E

English Channel a strait of the Atlantic Ocean between England and France (p. 494)

Gazetteer

F

Florence (44°N, 11°E) the capital city of the Tuscany region of Italy (p. 405)

G

Grand Banks (47°N, 52°W) a rich fishing ground near Newfoundland, Canada (p. 227)

Greater Antilles an island group in the Caribbean that includes Cuba, Jamaica, Hispaniola, and Puerto Rico (p. 298)

Great Lakes a group of five large freshwater lakes in North America; they are Lake Superior, Lake Michigan, Lake Huron, Lake Erie, and Lake Ontario (p. 192)

Gulf of Mexico a large gulf off the southeastern coast of North America (p. 277)

H

Havana (23°N, 82°W) the capital of Cuba (p. 313)

Helsinki (60°N, 25°E) the capital of Finland (p. 523)

I

Iberia a large peninsula in Southern Europe; Spain and Portugal are located there (p. 483)

K

Kiev (50°N, 31°E) the capital of Ukraine (pp. 540, 561)

Kosovo a country on the Balkan Peninsula in southeastern Europe (p. 546)

L

Lake Maracaibo (mah-rah-KY-boh) (10°N, 72°W) an oil- rich body of water in Venezuela (p. 346)

La Paz (17°S, 65°W) the capital of Bolivia (p. 353)

Lesser Antilles a group of small islands in the Caribbean; they stretch from the Virgin Islands in the north to Trinidad in the south (p. 298)

Lima (10°S, 75°W) the capital of Peru (p. 353)

Lisbon (39°N, 9°W) the capital of Portugal (p. 486)

Llanos a plains region in South America (p. 323)

London (51°N, 1°W) the capital of England and the United Kingdom (p. 518)

M

Madrid (40°N, 4°W) the capital of Spain (p. 486)

Manaus (3°S, 60°W) a major port and industrial city in Brazil's Amazon rain forest (p. 334)

Mediterranean Sea a sea between Europe and Africa (p. 469)

Mexico City (23°N, 104°W) the capital of Mexico (p. 288)

Milan (45°N, 9°E) a major industrial city in Italy (p. 481)

Mississippi River a major river in the United States (p. 192)

Montenegro (43°N, 19°E) a country in the Balkans (p. 546)

Montreal (46°N, 74°W) a major Canadian city in Quebec; founded by the French in 1642 (p. 239)

Moscow (56°N, 38°E) the capital of Russia (p. 555)

N

Naples (40°N, 14°E) a port and the largest city in southern Italy (p. 480)

New York City (41°N, 74°W) a city in the northeastern United States; the largest city in the United States (p. 198)

Niagara Falls a waterfall created by the Niagara River between Ontario and New York (p. 225)

Gazetteer

Northern European Plain a large plain across central and northern Europe (p. 493)

North Macedonia a country on the Balkan Peninsula in southeastern Europe (p. 545)

North Sea a shallow arm of the Atlantic Ocean in Northern Europe (p. 494)

O

Orinoco River (OHR-ee-NOH-koh) a major river in Venezuela (p. 324)

Oslo (60°N, 11°E) the capital of Norway (p. 523)

Ottawa (45°N, 76°W) capital of Canada (p. 240)

P

Palenque a Maya city built by Pacal, located in what is Mexico today (p. 252)

Pampas a fertile plains region in southern South America located mainly in Argentina (p. 326)

Panama Canal (26°N, 80°W) a canal built by the United States in the early 1900s across the Isthmus of Panama (p. 307)

Paris (46°N, 0°) the capital of France (p. 503)

Prague (50°N, 14°E) capital of the Czech Republic (p. 539)

Pyrenees (PIR-uh-neez) a high mountain range between Spain and France (p. 469)

Q

Quebec a province in eastern Canada (p. 232)

Quito (2°S, 78°W) the capital of Ecuador (p. 352)

R

Rhine River a major river in Europe; it begins in Switzerland and flows north to the North Sea (p. 495)

Río Bravo the Mexican name for the river known as the Rio Grande in the United States; it forms the border between Mexico and Texas (p. 277)

Rio de Janeiro (23°N, 43°W) the second-largest city in Brazil; it is a major port city and Brazil's former capital (p. 333)

Río de la Plata (REE-oh day lah PLAH-tah) a body of water in South America (p. 326)

Rocky Mountains a major mountain range in western North America (pp. 192, 225)

Romania a country in Eastern Europe (p. 546)

Rome (42°N, 13°E) the capital of Italy; it was the capital of the ancient Roman Empire (pp. 382, 482)

S

Santiago (33°S, 71°W) the capital of Chile (p. 355)

São Paulo (24°S, 47°W) the largest city in Brazil and South America (p. 332)

Scandinavia a region of Northern Europe that includes the Scandinavian Peninsula, Iceland, Greenland, and Denmark (p. 496)

Seattle (48°N, 122°W) a major U.S. port and city in Washington State (p. 214)

Serbia a country in the Balkans (p. 546)

Siberia a huge region in eastern Russia (p. 556)

Sicily an island at the tip of the Italian peninsula (p. 480)

Sierra Madre (SYER-rah MAH-dray) the chief mountain range in Mexico (p. 277)

Slovenia a country in Eastern Europe (p. 545)

Sparta a city-state in ancient Greece; rival of Athens (p. 378)

St. Lawrence River a river in North America that flows from the Great Lakes to the Atlantic Ocean (p. 225)

Stockholm (59°N, 18°E) the capital of Sweden (p. 521)

St. Petersburg (59°N, 30°E) Russian city, former capital and home to the czars, now a major port (p. 566)

T

Tbilisi (42°N, 45°E) the capital of Georgia (p. 571)

Tenochtitlán the historic capital of the Aztecs, located in what is now Mexico (p. 259)

Toronto (44°N, 79°W) Canada's largest city (p. 235)

U

Ural Mountains (YOORH-uhl) a mountain range in Russia that separates Europe and Asia (p. 555)

V

Vancouver (49°N, 123°W) a city in western Canada just north of the U.S. border (p. 240)

Vatican City (42°N, 12°E) a small country in Rome that is the head of the Roman Catholic Church (p. 479)

Venice (45°N, 12°E) the capital of the Italian region of Veneto in northern Italy (p. 405)

Vienna (45°N, 12°E) the capital of Austria (p. 512)

Volga River (VAHL-guh) the longest river in Europe and Russia's most important commercial river (p. 557)

W

Warsaw (52°N, 21°E) the capital of Poland (p. 538)

Washington, DC (39°N, 77°W) the capital of the United States (p. 210)

Y

Yerevan (40°N, 45°E) the capital of Armenia (p. 572)

Yucatán Peninsula (yoo-kah-TAHN) a large peninsula that separates the Caribbean Sea from the Gulf of Mexico (p. 277)

Explaining a Process

How does soil renewal work? How do cultures change? Often the first question we ask about something is how it works or what process it follows. One way we can answer these questions is by writing an explanation.

1. Prewrite

Choose a Process

ASSIGNMENT
Write an expository essay explaining one of these topics:

- how water recycles on Earth
- how agriculture developed

- Choose one of the topics on the left to write about.
- Turn your topic into a big idea, or thesis. For example, your big idea might be "Water continually circulates from Earth's surface to the atmosphere and back."

Gather and Organize Information

TIP: ORGANIZING INFORMATION
Explanations should be in a logical order. You should arrange the steps in the process in chronological order, the order in which the steps take place.

- Look for information about your topic in your textbook, in the library, or on the Internet.
- Start a plan to organize support for your big idea. For example, look for the individual steps of the water cycle.

2. Write

Here is a framework that will help you write your first draft.

A WRITER'S FRAMEWORK

Introduction

- Start with an interesting fact or question.
- Identify your big idea.

Body

- Create at least one paragraph for each point supporting the big idea. Add facts and details to explain each point.
- Use a variety of sentence structures to add interest to your writing.
- Use chronological order or order of importance.

Conclusion

- Summarize your main points in your final paragraph.

---

3. Evaluate and Revise

Review and Improve Your Paper

- Reread your paper and make sure you have followed the framework.
- Make the changes needed to improve your paper.

Evaluation Questions for Your Paper

1. Do you begin with an interesting fact or question?
2. Does your introduction identify your big idea?
3. Do you have at least one paragraph for each point you are using to support the big idea?
4. Do you use a variety of sentence structures?
5. Do you include facts and details to explain and illustrate each point?
6. Do you use chronological order or order of importance to organize your main points?

4. Proofread and Publish

Give Your Explanation the Finishing Touch

- Make sure to use standard grammar, spelling, punctuation, and sentence structure.
- Check for punctuation at the end of every sentence.
- Think of a way to share your explanation.
- Use social studies terminology correctly.

5. Practice and Apply

Use the steps and strategies outlined in this workshop to write your explanation. Present your paper to others and find out whether the explanation makes sense to them.

Describing a Place

ASSIGNMENT
Write a description of one of these places in the Americas:

- a city
- a country

What are the physical features of a country? What is the weather like? What drives the economy? The answers to questions like these are often cold, hard facts and statistics. But they can bring life to a description of a place.

1. Prewrite

Identify a Topic and Big Idea

- Choose one of the topics on the left to write about.
- Turn your topic into a big idea, or thesis. For example, your big idea might be, "Cuba's government greatly influences life in the country."

TIP: PRECISE LANGUAGE
Describe your place with specific nouns, verbs, adjectives, and adverbs. For example, rather than writing "Buenos Aires is big," write "Buenos Aires is the largest city in Argentina."

Gather and Organize Information

- Look for information about your place in the library or on the Internet. Organize your notes in groupings such as physical features, economy, or culture. Decide which facts about the place you are describing are most important or unique.

2. Write

This framework will help you write your first draft.

A WRITER'S FRAMEWORK

Introduction

- Start with an interesting fact or question.
- Identify your big idea and provide any necessary background information.

Body

- Write at least one paragraph for each category. Include facts that help explain each detail.
- Write about each detail in order of importance.

Conclusion

- Summarize your description in your final paragraph.

3. Evaluate and Revise

Review and Improve Your Paper

- Reread your paper and use the questions below to identify ways to revise your paper.
- Make the changes needed to improve your paper.

Evaluation Questions for a Description of a Place

1. Do you begin with an interesting fact or question?
2. Does your introduction identify your big idea? Do you provide background information to help your readers better understand your idea?
3. Do you have at least one paragraph for each category?
4. Do you use order of importance to organize the details of your description?
5. Are there more details you would like to know about your place? If so, what are they?

4. Proofread and Publish

Give Your Description the Finishing Touch

- Make sure you used commas correctly when listing more than two details in a sentence.
- Check your spelling of the names of places.
- Share your description with classmates or with students in another social studies class.

5. Practice and Apply

Use the steps and strategies outlined in this workshop to write your description of a place. Share your description with classmates. With your classmates, group the descriptions by country and then identify the places you would like to visit.

Writing Workshop 3

An Oral Report

ASSIGNMENT
Write an oral report about the individual achievements of a historical figure such as Queen Isabella, Martin Luther, Napoleon, or Mikhail Gorbachev.

TIP: Think about why you chose this person. Is there something from your own personal experience or knowledge that makes this person interesting?

People have shaped the world. Who are the important people in history? How do individuals contribute to societies, past and present? These are questions we ask as we try to understand our world.

1. Prewrite

Choose a Topic

- Choose a person who affected the history of Europe or Russia.
- Choose a specific achievement in the person's life. For example, you might choose to explain how Mikhail Gorbachev contributed to the end of the Cold War.

Gather and Organize Information

- Look for information about your person in the library or on the Internet. Identify the important main ideas and details about your person's life.
- Organize the main ideas and details in an outline or note cards. Speaking from an outline or note cards will make your speech sound more natural.

2. Write

You can use this framework to help you write your first draft.

A WRITER'S FRAMEWORK

Introduction

- Introduce the person and the event.
- Identify the importance of the event.

Body

- Write at least one paragraph for each major part of the event. Include specific details.
- Use chronological, or time, order to organize the parts of the event.

Conclusion

- Summarize the importance of the person and event in the final paragraph.

---

3. Evaluate and Revise

Review and Improve Your Report

- Read your first draft at least twice, and then use the questions below to evaluate your report.
- Make the changes needed to improve your report.

Evaluation Questions for an Oral Report

1. Do you introduce the person and identify their importance?
2. Do you have one paragraph for each main idea?
3. Do you include specific details about the person?
4. Do you use chronological order, the order in time, to organize the person's achievement?
5. Do you end the paper with a summary of the importance of the person?

4. Proofread and Present

Give Your Oral Report the Finishing Touch

- Make sure your central idea or theme is clear and your oral report supports it.
- Use words or images that reflect your oral report's theme.
- Maintain eye contact with your audience and pace yourself. Do not rush to finish your oral report.
- Vary your tone of voice to help bring out the meaning of your words.

5. Practice and Apply

Use the steps and strategies outlined in this workshop to write your oral report. Share your oral report with a partner. As you listen to your partner's report, organize and interpret the information by creating an outline of the report.

Compare and Contrast

ASSIGNMENT
Write a paper comparing
and contrasting two
countries or regions.
Consider physical
geography, government,
and/or culture.

How are two countries or regions alike? How are they different?
Comparing and contrasting places can teach us more than
studying each one individually.

1. Prewrite

Choose a Topic

- Choose two countries or regions to write about.
- Create a big idea, or thesis, about the two countries.
  For example, your big idea might be "Canada and
  the United States are both large North American
  countries, but they have different natural resources
  and economies."

**TIP: ORGANIZING
INFORMATION**
A Venn diagram (two
overlapping circles) can
help you plan your paper.
Write similarities in the
overlapping area and
differences in the areas
that do not overlap.

Gather and Organize Information

- Conduct research and use data from geographic
  tools, including maps, graphs, charts, databases,
  and models to identify at least three similarities or
  differences between the countries.
- Decide how to organize your main ideas and
  details, for example, by each place or by each
  similarity or difference.

2. Write

This framework will help you use your notes to write a first draft.

A WRITER'S FRAMEWORK

Introduction

- Start with a fact or question
  relating to both countries.
- Identify your big idea.

Body

- Write at least one paragraph for
  each country or each point of
  similarity or difference. Include
  facts and details to help explain
  each point.
- Use block style or point-by-point
  style.

Conclusion

- Summarize the process in your
  final paragraph.

3. Evaluate and Revise

Review and Improve Your Paper

- Reread your draft, then ask yourself the questions below to see if you have followed the framework.
- Make any changes needed to improve your compare-and-contrast paper.

Evaluation Questions for a Compare-and-Contrast Paper

1. Do you begin with an interesting fact or question that relates to both places?
2. Does your first paragraph clearly state your big idea and provide background information?
3. Do you discuss at least three similarities and differences between the places?
4. Do you include main ideas and details from your research?
5. Is your paper clearly organized by country and region or by similarities and differences?

4. Proofread and Publish

Give Your Paper the Finishing Touch

- Make sure you have capitalized the names of countries and cities.
- Reread your paper to check that you have used standard grammar, spelling, sentence structures, and punctuation.
- Share your compare-and-contrast paper by reading it aloud in class or in small groups.

5. Practice and Apply

Use the steps outlined in this workshop to write a compare-and-contrast paper. Compare and contrast your paper to those of your classmates.

English and Spanish Glossary

Phonetic Respelling and Pronunciation Guide

Many of the key terms in this textbook have been respelled to help you pronounce them. The letter combinations used in the respelling throughout the narrative are explained in the following phonetic respelling and pronunciation guide. The guide is adapted from *Merriam-Webster's Collegiate Dictionary, 11th Edition; Merriam-Webster's Geographical Dictionary;* and *Merriam-Webster's Biographical Dictionary.*

MARK	AS IN	RESPELLING	EXAMPLE
a	alphabet	a	*AL-fuh-bet
ā	Asia	ay	AY-zhuh
ä	cart, top	ah	KAHRT, TAHP
e	let, ten	e	LET, TEN
ē	even, leaf	ee	EE-vuhn, LEEF
i	it, tip, British	i	IT, TIP, BRIT-ish
ī	site, buy, Ohio	y	SYT, BY, oh-HY-oh
	iris	eye	EYE-ris
k	card	k	KAHRD
ō	over, rainbow	oh	OH-vuhr, RAYN-boh
ù	book, wood	ooh	BOOHK, WOOHD
ò	all, orchid	aw	AWL, AWR-kid
ä	foil, coin	oy	FOYL, KOYN
aù	out	ow	OWT
	cup, butter	uh	KUHP, BUHT-uhr
ü	rule, food	oo	ROOL, FOOD
yü	few	yoo	FYOO
zh	vision	zh	VIZH-uhn

*A syllable printed in capital letters receives heavier emphasis than the other syllable(s) in a word.

A

absolute location a specific description of where a place is located; absolute location is often expressed using latitude and longitude (p. 16)
ubicación absoluta descripción específica del lugar donde se ubica un punto; con frecuencia se define en términos de latitud y longitud

agricultural industries businesses that focus on growing crops and raising livestock (p. 169)
industrias agrícolas empresas dedicadas al cultivo de la tierra y la ganadería

agriculture the process of growing crops and raising animals to provide food or other products (p. 369)
agricultura proceso de cultivar y la crianza de animales para proporcionar alimentos u otros productos

alliance an agreement to work together (p. 442)
alianza acuerdo de colaboración

Allies Great Britain, France, the Soviet Union, and the United States; they joined together in World War II against Germany, Italy, and Japan (p. 449)
Aliados Gran Bretaña, Francia, la Unión Soviética y Estados Unidos, se unieron durante la Segunda Guerra Mundial contra Alemania, Italia y Japón

alluvial deposition a process in which rivers create floodplains by flooding their banks and depositing sediment along the banks (p. 57)
depósito aluvial proceso en el cual los ríos crean llanuras de inundación inundando sus bancos y depositando sedimentos a lo largo de los bancos

altiplano a broad, high plateau that lies between the ridges of the Andes (p. 327)
altiplano meseta amplia y elevada que se extiende entre las cadenas montañosas de los Andes

aqueducts channels used to carry water over long distances (p. 386)
acueductos canales utilizados para transportar agua a largas distancias

archipelago a large group of islands (p. 298)
archipiélago gran grupo de islas

arms race a competition between countries to build superior weapons (p. 456)
carrera armamentista competencia entre países para construer armas mejores

assets items of economic value that a person or company owns (p. 176)
activos elementos de valor económico que una persona o empresa posee

asylum a place of safety; protection given especially to political refugees (p. 461)
asilo lugar de seguridad; protección que se ofrece especialmente a los refugiados políticos

Axis Powers the name for the alliance formed by German, Italy, and Japan during World War II (p. 449)
Potencias del Eje Nombre de la alianza formada por Alemania, Italia y Japón durante la Segunda Guerra Mundial

B

barter the exchange of one good or service for another (p. 173)
trueque intercambio de un bien o servicio por otro

bilingual a term used to describe people who speak two languages (p. 206)
bilingüe término utilizado para describir a las personas que hablan dos idiomas

biome a large community of living organisms, both plants and animals, that are adapted to a particular environment; a biome may be made up of several ecosystems (p. 78)
bioma comunidad grande de organismos vivos, tanto plantas como animales, que se adaptan a un entorno particular; un bioma puede estar compuesto de varios ecosistemas

birthrate the annual number of births per 1,000 people (p. 109)
índice de natalidad número de nacimientos por cada 1,000 personas en un año

Bolsheviks a radical Russian Communist group that seized power in 1917 (p. 563)
bolcheviques grupo comunista ruso radical que obtuvo el poder en 1917

border a political or geographic boundary that separates one country from another (p. 131)
frontera límite político o geográfico que separa a un país de otro

Byzantine Empire the society that developed in the eastern Roman Empire after the west fell (p. 394)
Imperio bizantino sociedad que se desarrolló en el imperio romano oriental después de que el oeste cayó

C

canton one of 26 districts in the republic of Switzerland (p. 512)
cantón uno de los 26 distritos de la república de Suiza

capitalism an economic system in which individuals and private businesses run most industries (p. 439)
capitalismo sistema económico en el que los individuos y las empresas privadas controlan la mayoría de las industrias

cartography the science of making maps (p. 13)
cartografía ciencia de crear mapas

cash crop a crop that farmers grow mainly to sell for a profit (p. 287)
cultivo comercial cultivo que los agricultores-producen principalmente para vender y obtener ganancias

Catholic Reformation a series of reforms to the Catholic Church; launched by Catholic officials in response to the Reformation (p. 410)
Reforma católica serie de reformas a la Iglesia Católica; lanzada por funcionarios católicos en respuesta a la Reforma

Catholicism the faith of Roman Catholics; the largest branch of Christianity (p. 479)
Catolicismo la fe de los católicos romanos; rama más grande del cristianismo

causeway a raised road across water or wet ground (p. 259)
carretera elevada carretera construida sobre agua o terreno pantanoso

center-pivot irrigation an irrigation technique that uses a sprinkler in the center of a large circular field; the long arms of the sprinkler circle over the field to water crops (p. 120)
riego por pivote central técnica de riego que usa un rociador en el centro de un gran campo circular; los brazos largos circulan sobre el campo para regar los cultivos

chancellor a German prime minister (p. 510)
canciller primer ministro alemán

Christianity a major world religion based on the life and teachings of Jesus of Nazareth (p. 477)
cristianismo una de las pincipales religions del mundo, basada en las enseñanzas de Jesús

circumnavigate to go all the way around (p. 423)
circunnavegar dar una vuelta completa

citizen in ancient Rome, a person who could take part in the government (p. 383)
ciudadano en la antigua Roma, una persona que podía participar en el gobierno

city-state a political unit made up of a city and all the surrounding lands (p. 372)
ciudad estado unidad política compuesta de una ciudad y todas las tierras que la rodean

civil war a conflict between two or more groups within a country (p. 306)
guerra civil conflicto entre dos o más grupos dentro de un país

civilization an organized society within a specific area (p. 249)
civilización sociedad organizada dentro de un área específica

climate a region's average weather conditions over a long period of time (p. 62)
clima condiciones del tiempo promedio de una región durante un período largo de tiempo

cloud forest a moist, high-elevation tropical forest where low clouds are common (p. 300)
bosque nuboso bosque tropical de gran elevación y humedad donde los bancos de nubes son muy comunes

cluster settlement a type of settlement that is grouped around or at the center of a resource (p. 115)
núcleo de población tipo de asentamiento que se agrupa alrededor o en el centro de un recurso

Cold War a period of distrust between the United States and Soviet Union after World War II, when there was a tense rivalry between the two superpowers but no direct fighting (p. 454)
Guerra Fría período de desconfianza entre Estados Unidos y la Unión Soviética que siguió a la Segunda Guerra Mundial; existía una rivalidad tensa entre las dos superpotencias, pero no se llegó a la lucha directa

colony a territory inhabited and controlled by people from a foreign land (p. 198)
colonia territorio habitado y controlado por personas de otro país

Columbian Exchange the movement of people, animals, plants, diseases, and ideas between Europe and the Americas in the 1400s and 1500s (pp. 309, 426)
Intercambio colombino movimiento de personas, animales, plantas, enfermedades e ideas entre Europa y las Américas en los siglos XV y XVI

command economy an economic system in which the central government makes all economic decisions (p. 164)
economía autoritaria sistema económico en el que el gobierno central toma todas las decisiones económicas

commerce the substantial exchange of goods between cities, states, or countries (p. 116)
comercio intercambio sustancial de bienes entre ciudades, estados o países

common good the welfare of a community (p. 139)
bien común bienestar de una comunidad

common market a group of nations that cooperates to make trade among members easier (p. 458)
mercado común grupo de naciones que cooperan para facilitar el comercio entre los miembros

commonwealth a self-governing territory associated with another country (p. 311)
mancomunidad o estado libre asociado territorio autogobernado asociado con otro país

Commonwealth of Independent States (CIS) a union of former Soviet republics that meets about issues such as trade and immigration (p. 541)
Comunidad de Estados Independientes (CEI) unión de ex repúblicas soviéticas que se reúne para tratar temas como el comercio y la inmigración

communism a political system in which the government owns all property and dominates all aspects of life in a country (p. 445)
comunismo sistema político en el que el gobierno es dueño de toda la propiedad y controla todos los aspectos de la vida de un país

conquistador a Spanish conqueror (p. 261)
conquistador conquistador español

constitution a written plan of government (p. 137)
constitución plan escrito del gobierno

constitutional monarchy a type of democracy in which a monarch serves as head of state but a legislature makes the laws (p. 515)
monarquía constitucional tipo de democracia en la cual un monarca sirve como jefe de estado, pero una asamblea legislativa hace las leyes

continent a large landmass that is part of Earth's crust; geographers identify seven continents (pp. 25, 53)
continente gran masa de tierra que forma parte de la corteza terrestre; los geógrafos identifican siete continentes

continental divide an area of high ground that divides the flow of rivers towards opposite ends of a continent (p. 193)
línea divisoria de aguas zona de terreno elevado que divide el flujo de los ríos en dos direcciones, hacia los extremos opuestos de un continente

contraction a reduction in business activity or growth (p. 162)
contracción reducción de la actividad o crecimiento de negocios

cooperative an organization owned by its members and operated for their mutual benefit (p. 314)
cooperativa organización cuyos miembros son los propietarios y que es operada para beneficio de todos

cordillera (kawr-duhl-YER-uh) a mountain system made up of roughly parallel ranges (p. 323)
cordillera sistema de cadenas montañosas aproximadamente paralelas entre sí

cosmopolitan characterized by many foreign influences (p. 505)
cosmopolita caracterizado por muchas influencias extranjeras

coup (KOO) a sudden overthrow of a government by a small group of people (p. 355)

golpe de estado derrocamiento repentino de un gobierno por parte de un grupo reducido de personas

Creole an American-born descendant of Europeans (p. 351)
criollo persona de ascendencia europea y nacida en América

Crusade a religious war in which Christians tried to retake the Holy Land from Muslim Turks (p. 397)
Cruzada guerra religiosa en la que los cristianos trataron de recuperar la Tierra Santa de los turcos musulmanes

cultural diffusion the spread of culture traits from one region to another (p. 99)
difusión cultural difusión de rasgos culturales de una región a otra

cultural universal a cultural feature found in all societies (p. 101)
rasgo cultural universal rasgo de la cultura que es común a todos los grupos sociales

culture the set of beliefs, values, and practices that a group of people have in common (p. 95)
cultura conjunto de creencias, valores y costumbres compartidas por un grupo de personas

culture region an area in which people have many shared culture traits (p. 97)
región cultural región en la que las personas comparten muchos rasgos culturales

culture trait an activity or behavior in which people often take part (p. 96)
rasgo cultural actividad o conducta frecuente de las persona

Cyrillic (suh-RIHL-ihk) a form of the Greek alphabet (p. 561)
cirílico forma del alfabeto griego

czar (ZAHR) a Russian emperor (p. 562)
zar emperador ruso

D

dachas Russian country houses (p. 566)
dachas casas de campo rusas

Declaration of Independence a document written in 1776 that declared the American colonies' independence from British rule (p. 430)
Declaración de Independencia documento escrito en 1776 que declaró la independencia de las colonias de América del Norte del dominio británico

English and Spanish Glossary

Declaration of the Rights of Man and of the Citizen a document written in France in 1789 that guaranteed specific freedoms for French citizens (p. 432)
Declaración de los Derechos del Hombre y del Ciudadano documento escrito en Francia en 1789 que garantizaba libertades específicas para los ciudadanos franceses

deforestation the clearing of trees (pp. 83, 326)
deforestación tala de árboles

degree a unit of measurement indicated by parallels circling the globe (p. 24)
grado unidad de medida indicada por paralelos que circundan el globo

democracy a form of government in which the people elect leaders and rule by majority (p. 137)
democracia sistema de gobierno en el que el pueblo elige a sus líderes y gobierna por mayoría

desertification the spread of desert-like conditions (p. 81)
desertización ampliación de las condiciones desérticas

developed countries countries with strong economies and a high quality of life (p. 171)
países desarrollados países con economías sólidas y una alta calidad de vida

developing countries countries with less productive economies and a lower quality of life (p. 171)
países en vías de desarrollo países con economías menos productivas y una menor calidad de vida

dialect a regional version of a language (p. 310)
dialecto versión regional de una lengua

dictator a ruler who has almost absolute power (p. 447)
dictador gobernante que tiene poder casi absoluto

diplomacy the work nations do to keep friendly relations with one another (p. 133)
diplomacia trabajo que hacen las naciones para mantener relaciones amistosas entre sí

direct democracy a form of government in which citizens meet regularly in a popular assembly to discuss issues, pass laws, and vote for leaders (p. 137)
democracia directa forma de gobierno caracterizada por asambleas populares en las que los ciudadanos se reúnen periódicamente para debatir problemas, aprobar leyes y elegir funcionarios públicos

disarm to give up all weapons (p. 519)
desarmarse renunciar a todas las armas

domestication the process of changing plants or animals to make them more useful to humans (p. 369)
domesticación proceso en el que se modifican las plantas o los animales para que s ean más útiles para los humanos

draft law requiring men of certain ages and qualification to serve in the military (p. 146)
servicio militar obligatorio ley que establece que los varones de edades y calificaciones determinadas deben prestar servicio militar

E

earthquake a sudden, violent movement of Earth's crust (p. 55)
terremoto movimiento repentino y violento de la corteza terrestre

economic interdependence when producers in one nation depend on others to provide goods and services that they do not produce (p. 163)
interdependencia económica cuando los productores de una nación dependen de otros para proporcionar bienes y servicios que no producen

economy a system of producing, selling, and buying goods and services (p. 159)
economía sistema de producción, venta y compra de bienes y servicios

ecosystem a group of plants and animals that depend on each other for survival, and the environment in which they live (p. 78)
ecosistema grupo de plantas y animales que dependen unos de otros para sobrevivir, y el ambiente en el que estos viven

ecotourism the practice of using an area's natural environment to attract tourists (p. 305)
ecoturismo uso de regiones naturales para atraer turistas

El Niño an ocean and weather pattern that affects the Pacific coast of the Americas; about every two to seven years, it warms normally cool ocean water and causes extreme ocean and weather events (p. 329)
El Niño patrón oceánico y del tiempo que afecta a la costa del Pacífico de las Américas;

aproximadamente cada dos a siete años, calienta las aguas normalmente frías del océano, y provoca sucesos oceánicos y climatológicos extremos

empire a land with different territories and peoples under a single ruler (pp. 282, 384)
imperio zona que reúne varios territorios y pueblos bajo un solo gobernante

English Bill of Rights a document approved in 1689 that listed rights for Parliament and the English people and drew on the principles of Magna Carta (p. 430)
Declaración de Derechos Inglesa documento aprobado en 1689 que enumeraba los derechos del Parlamento y del pueblo de Inglaterra, inspirada en los principios de la Carta Magna

Enlightenment a period during the 1600s and 1700s when reason was used to guide people's thoughts about society, politics, and philosophy (p. 427)
Ilustracion período durante los años 1600 y 1700 en el que la razón guiaba las ideas de las personas acerca de la sociedad, la política y la filosofía

environment the land, water, climate, plants, and animals of an area; surroundings (pp. 16, 77)
ambiente la tierra, el agua, el clima, las plantas y los animales de una zona; los alrededores

equator an imaginary line that circles the globe halfway between the North and South Poles (p. 24)
ecuador línea imaginaria que atraviesa el globo terráqueo por la mitad entre el Polo Norte y el Polo Sur

erosion the movement of sediment from one location to another (p. 56)
erosión movimiento de sedimentos de un lugar a otro

estuary a partially enclosed body of water where freshwater mixes with salty seawater (p. 326)
estuario masa de agua parcialmente rodeada de tierra en la que el agua de mar se combina con agua dulce

ethnic cleansing the effort to remove all members of an ethnic group from a country or region (p. 545)
limpieza étnica esfuerzo por eliminar a todos los miembros de un grupo étnico de un país o región

ethnic group a group of people who share a common culture and ancestry (p. 98)
grupo étnico grupo de personas que comparten una cultura y una ascendencia

ethnocentrism the belief that one's own culture or ethnic group is superior (p. 545)
etnocentrismo creencia de que la propia cultura o grupo étnico es superior

European Union (EU) an organization that promotes political and economic cooperation in Europe (p. 458)
Union Europea (UE) organización que promueve la cooperación política y económica en Europa

executive branch the part of government that carries out and enforces laws (p. 203)
rama ejecutiva parte del gobierno que lleva a cabo y hace cumplir las leyes

expansion the action of becoming larger or more extensive (p. 162)
expansión acción de volverse más grande o más extensa

extinct no longer here; a species that has died out has become extinct (p. 79)
extinto que ya no existe; una especie que ha desaparecido está extinta

F

factors of production the basic economic resources needed to produce goods and services. The four main factors of production are land, labor, capital, and entrepreneurship (p. 161)
factores de producción los diferentes recursos que se necesitan para la creación de un bien o servicio. Los cuatro factores de producción principales son: la tierra, la mano de obra, el capital y la capacidad empresarial

favela (fah-VE-lah) a huge slum in Brazil (p. 333)
favela enorme barriada en Brasil

feudal system a system of exchanging land for military service (p. 400)
sistema feudal sistema de intercambio de tierras para el servicio military

fjord (fyawrd) a narrow inlet of the sea set between high, rocky cliffs (p. 497)
fiordo entrada estrecha del mar entre acantilados altos y rocosos

English and Spanish Glossary

foreign policy a nation's plan for how to act toward other countries (p. 133)
  política exterior plan de una nación de cómo actuar hacia otros países

fossil fuels nonrenewable resources that formed from the remains of ancient plants and animals; coal, petroleum, and natural gas are all fossil fuels (p. 84)
  combustibles fósiles recursos no renovables formados a partir de restos de plantas y animales antiguos; el carbón, el petróleo y el gas natural son combustibles fósiles

fracking a process that breaks up rock by injecting large amounts of water and chemicals into cracks; forces cracks in the rock to widen, allowing oil and gas to flow out (p. 123)
  fractura hidráulica proceso que rompe la roca inyectando grandes cantidades de agua y productos químicos en las grietas; forza las grietas con el objetivo de ampliarlas en la roca, permitiendo que el petróleo y el gas fluyan hacia fuera

free enterprise system an economic system in which businesses can compete freely with one another with little government intervention; capitalism (p. 167)
  libre empresa sistema económico basado en la competencia libre entre las empresas con una intervención estatal mínima; también conocida como capitalismo

free trade the removal of trade barriers between nations (p. 184)
  libre comercio eliminación de las barreras comerciales entre las naciones

freshwater water that is not salty; it makes up only about 3 percent of our total water supply (p. 47)
  agua dulce agua que no es salada; representa sólo alrededor del 3 por ciento de nuestro suministro total de agua

front the place where two air masses of different temperatures or moisture content meet (p. 65)
  frente lugar en el que se encuentran dos masas de aire con diferente temperatura o humedad

G

gaucho (GOW-choh) an Argentine cowboy (p. 336)
  gaucho vaquero argentino

Geographic Information System (GIS) a technology system that combines and provides geographic information from many different sources (p. 22)
  Sistema de información geográfica (SIG) sistema tecnológico que combina y proporciona información geográfica de muchas fuentes diferentes

geography the study of the world, its people, and the landscapes they create (p. 5)
  geografía estudio del mundo, de sus habitantes y de los paisajes creados por el ser humano

geothermal energy energy produced from the heat of Earth's interior (p. 498)
  energía geotérmica energía producida a partir del calor del interior de la Tierra

geyser a spring that shoots hot water and steam into the air (p. 524)
  géiser manantial que lanza agua caliente y vapor al aire

glacier a large area of slow moving ice (p. 47)
  glaciar gran bloque de hielo que avanza con lentitud

globalization the process in which countries are increasingly linked to each other through culture and trade (p. 179)
  globalización proceso por el cual los países se encuentran cada vez más interconectados a través de la cultura y el comercio

Global Positioning System (GPS) a technology system that transmits information from satellites to Earth, giving the exact location of a given object on our planet (p. 22)
  Sistema de posicionamiento global sistema tecnológico que transmite información de los satélites a la Tierra, dando la ubicación exacta de un objeto en nuestro planeta

globe a spherical, or ball-shaped, model of the entire planet (p. 20)
  globo terráqueo modelo esférico, o en forma de bola, de todo el planeta

golden age a historical period marked by great achievements (p. 374)
  edad de oro período histórico marcado por grandes logros

Gothic architecture a style known for its high pointed ceilings, tall towers, and stained glass windows (p. 398)

arquitectura gótica estilo conocido por sus techos altos, torres altas y vitrales

Great Depression a global economic crisis that struck countries around the world in the 1930s (p. 447)
Gran Depresión crisis económica global que afectó a países de todo el mundo en la década de 1930

grid a pattern of imaginary lines that circle the globe in east-west and north-south directions (p. 24)
cuadrícula patrón de líneas imaginarias que atraviesan el globo terráqueo en las direcciones este-oeste y norte-sur

grid settlement a type of settlement that is purposefully laid out with a network of transportation routes; the streets form a grid by running at right angles to each other (p. 115)
asentamiento hipodámico tipo de asentamiento que está diseñado de acuerdo a las rutas de transporte; las calles forman una cuadrícula al cruzarse en ángulos rectos entre sí

gross domestic product (GDP) the value of all goods and services produced within a country in a single year (p. 171)
producto interior bruto (PIB) valor de todos los bienes y servicios producidos en un país durante un año

groundwater water found below Earth's surface (p. 48)
agua subterránea agua que se encuentra debajo de la superficie de la Tierra

guerrilla a member of an irregular military force (p. 345)
guerrillero miembro de una fuerza militar irregular

gulag a soviet labor camp (p. 563)
gulag campo soviético de trabajos forzados

H

habitat the place where a plant or animal lives (p. 79)
hábitat lugar en el que vive una planta o animal

hacienda (hah-see-EN-duh) a huge expanse of farm or ranch land in the Americas (p. 283)
hacienda granja o rancho de gran tamaño en las Américas

Hellenistic relating to a period in which Greek culture blended with other cultures; Greek-like (p. 381)

helenístico relativo a un período en que la cultura griega se mezcló con otras culturas; tipo Griego

hemisphere a half of the globe, divided by lines of latitude and longitude; Earth's hemispheres are the Northern Hemisphere, Southern Hemisphere, Eastern Hemisphere, and Western Hemisphere (p. 25)
hemisferio una mitad del globo, dividida por líneas de latitud y longitud; los hemisferios de la Tierra son el Hemisferio Norte, el Hemisferio Sur, el Hemisferio Oriental y el Hemisferio Occidental

heritage the wealth of cultural elements that has been passed down over generations (p. 103)
patrimonio cultural riqueza cultural que se pasa de una generación a otra

Holocaust the Nazis' effort to wipe out the Jewish people in World War II, when about 6 million Jews throughout Europe were killed (p. 450)
Holocausto intento de los nazis de eliminar al pueblo judío durante la Segunda Guerra Mundial, en el que se mató aproximadamente 6 millones de judíos en toda Europa

Holy Land the region where Jesus lived, preached, and died (p. 397)
Tierra Santa región donde Jesús vivió, predicó y murió

human geography the study of the world's human geographic features—people, communities, and landscapes (p. 11)
geografía humana estudio de los habitantes, las comunidades y los paisajes del mundo

humanism the emphasis on the abilities and accomplishments of human beings (p. 406)
humanismo énfasis en las habilidades y logros de los seres humanos

humanitarian aid assistance to people in distress (p. 135)
ayuda humanitaria ayuda a personas en peligro

human rights rights that all people deserve, such as rights to equality and justice (p. 135)
derechos humanos derechos que toda la gente merece como derechos a la igualdad y la justicia

humus (HYOO-muhs) decayed plant or animal matter; it helps soil support abundant plant life (p. 80)

humus materia animal o vegetal descompuesta; contribuye a que crezca una gran cantidad de plantas en el suelo

hunter-gatherers people who hunt animals and gather wild plants, seeds, fruits, and nuts to survive (p. 366)
cazadores y recolectores personas que cazan animales y recolectan plantas silvestres, semillas, frutas y nueces para sobrevivir

hydroelectric power the production of electricity from waterpower, such as from running water (p. 85)
energía hidroeléctrica producción de electricidad generada por la energía del agua, como la del agua corriente

I

ice ages long periods of freezing weather (p. 367)
era glacial periodos largos de clima helado

imperialism the practice of building an empire by claiming lands, setting up colonies, and controlling those areas (p. 441)
imperialismo intento de dominar el gobierno, el comercio y la cultura de un país

income the money or wages earned from a job, or money earned by buying and selling goods and services (p. 177)
ingresos dinero o los salarios ganados de un trabajo, o el dinero ganado comprando y vendiendo bienes y servicios

indigenous (in-DIJ-e-nus) originating or living in, or occurring naturally in, a particular region or environment (p. 287)
autóctono que se origina o vive en, o se produce naturalmente, en una región o medio ambiente en particular

Industrial Revolution the period of rapid growth in machine-made goods that changed the way people across Europe worked and lived; it began in Britain in the 1700s (p. 435)
Revolución Industrial período de rápido aumento de los bienes producidos con máquinas que cambió la forma de vivir y trabajar en toda Europa; comenzó en Gran Bretaña a comienzos del siglo XVIII

inflation the rise in prices that occurs when currency loses its buying power (p. 286)

inflación aumento de los precios que ocurre cuando la moneda de un país pierde poder adquisitivo

informal economy a part of the economy that is based on odd jobs that people perform without government regulation through taxes (p. 339)
economía informal parte de la economía basada en trabajos pequeños que se realizan sin el pago de impuestos regulados por el gobierno

infrastructure the set of resources, like roads and factories, that a country needs to support economic activities (p. 538)
infraestructura conjunto de recursos, como carre-teras o fábricas, que necesita un país para sostener su actividad económica

interest groups organizations that try to influence government policies (p. 149)
grupos de interés organizaciones que tratan de influir en las políticas gubernamentales

interest rate a percentage of the total amount of money in a customer's account (p. 175)
tasa de interés un porcentaje de la cantidad total de dinero en la cuenta de un cliente

investment the use of money today, such as buying stock in a company, in order to earn future benefits (p. 177)
inversión el uso del dinero hoy en día, como la compra de acciones en una empresa, con el fin de obtener beneficios futuros

isthmus a narrow strip of land that connects two larger land areas (p. 297)
istmo franja estrecha de tierra que une dos zonas más grandes

J

judicial branch the part of government that interprets laws (p. 203)
rama judicial parte del gobierno que interpreta las leyes

jury duty obligation to serve as a juror (p. 146)
servicio de jurado obligación que tiene un ciudadano de desempeña la función de jurado

L

land bridge a strip of land connecting two continents (p. 367)
puente de tierra franja de tierra que conecta dos continentes

landform a shape on the planet's surface, such as a mountain, valley, plain, island, or peninsula (p. 52)

accidente geográfico forma de la superficie terrestre, como una montaña, un valle, una llanura, una isla o una península

landlocked completely surrounded by land with no direct access to the ocean (p. 340)

sin salida al mar que está rodeado completamente por tierra, sin acceso directo al océano

landscape all the human and physical features that make a place unique (p. 5)

paisaje todas las características humanas y físicas que hacen que un lugar sea único

latitude the distance north or south of Earth's equator (p. 24)

latitud distancia hacia el norte o el sur desde el ecuador

lava magma that reaches Earth's surface (p. 55)

lava magma que llega a la superficie terrestre

legislative branch the part of government that makes laws (p. 203)

rama legislativa parte del gobierno que hace las leyes

limited government a type of government that has legal limits on its power, usually in the form of a constitution (p. 137)

gobierno limitado forma de gobierno cuyo poder está restringido por la ley, comúnmente la constitución

linear settlement a type of settlement that is grouped along the length of a resource; usually has a long and narrow pattern (p. 115)

asentamiento lineal tipo de asentamiento que se agrupa a lo largo de un recurso; por lo general tiene un patrón largo y estrecho

llanero (yah-NAY-roh) Venezuelan cowboy (p. 346)

llanero vaquero venezolano

longitude the distance east or west of Earth's prime meridian (p. 24)

longitud distancia este u oeste del primer meridiano de la Tierra

M

Magna Carta a document signed in 1215 by King John of England that required the king to honor certain rights (pp. 430, 516)

Carta Magna documento firmado por el rey Juan de Inglaterra en 1215 que exigía que el rey respetara ciertos derechos

maize corn (p. 249)

maíz elote o choclo

manor a large estate owned by a noble or knight (p. 401)

hacienda gran finca perteneciente a un noble o caballero

manufacturing industries businesses where people make finished products from raw materials (p. 169)

industria manufacturera actividad económica en la cual las personas transforman materias primas en artículos de consumo

map a flat drawing that shows all or part of Earth's surface (p. 20)

mapa representación plana que muestra total o parcialmente la superficie de la Tierra

map projection a method of showing our round planet on a flat map (p. 26)

proyección de mapas método para mostrar nuestro planeta redondo en un mapa plano

maquiladora (mah-kee-lah-DORH-ah) a U.S. or other foreign-owned factory in Mexico (p. 288)

maquiladora fábrica estadounidense o de otro país establecida en México

maritime on or near the sea (p. 239)

marítimo en o cerca del mar

market economy an economic system based on free trade and competition (p. 164)

economía de mercado sistema económico basado en el libre comercio y la competencia

masonry stonework (p. 267)

mampostería obra de piedra

Mediterranean climate the type of climate found across Southern Europe; it features warm and sunny summer days, mild evenings, and cooler, rainy winters (p. 472)

clima mediterráneo tipo de clima de todo el sur europeo; se caracteriza por días de verano cálidos y soleados, noches templadas e inviernos lluviosos y más frescos

medium of exchange a means through which goods and services can be exchanged (p. 174)

instrumento de cambio un medio para intercambiar bienes y servicios

megacity a giant urban area that includes surrounding cities and suburbs (p. 333)

megaciudad zona urbana enorme que incluye los suburbios y ciudades de alrededor

English and Spanish Glossary

megaliths huge stones used as monuments or as sites for religious gatherings (p. 371)
megalitos enormes piedras usadas como monumentos o como sitios para reuniones religiosas

megalopolis a string of large cities that have grown together (p. 114)
megalópolis serie de ciudades grandes que han crecido hasta unirse

Mercosur an organization that promotes trade and economic cooperation among the southern and eastern countries of South America (p. 338)
Mercosur organización que promueve el comercio y la cooperación económica entre los países del sur y el este de América del Sur

meridian a line of longitude (p. 24)
meridiano línea de longitud

Mesolithic Era a period, also known as the Middle Stone Age, in which people used smaller and more-complex tools than those used during the Paleolithic Era, or Old Stone Age (p. 369)
Período Mesolítico periodo, también conocido como la Edad Media de Piedra, en el cual la gente usaba herramientas más pequeñas y más complejas que las usadas durante el Período Paleolítico o Edad de Piedra Antigua

mestizo (me-STEE-zoh) a person of mixed European and Indian ancestry (p. 282)
mestizo persona de origen europeo e indígena

meteorology the study of weather and what causes it (p. 14)
meteorología estudio de las condiciones del tiempo y sus causas

metropolitan area a city and its surrounding areas (p. 114)
área metropolitana una ciudad y sus alrededores

Middle Ages the period between ancient and modern times; it lasted from about AD 500 to 1500 (p. 396)
Edad Media período entre los tiempos antiguos y modernos; duró alrededor de 500 a 1500 A. D.

migrant a person who moves regularly in order to find work, or a person who moves to flee poverty or violence (p. 461)
migrante persona que se muda regularmente para encontrar trabajo, o una persona que se mueve para huir de la pobreza o la violencia

migrate move to a new place to live (p. 367)
emigrar mudarse a un nuevo lugar para vivir

migration the process of moving from one place to live in another (p. 110)
migración movimiento de personas de un lugar para ir a vivir a otro lugar

minute the unit of measurement of a globe's surface that is part of a degree (p. 24)
minuto la unidad de medida de la superficie de un globo terráqueo que forma parte de un grado

mission a church outpost (p. 282)
misión asentamiento de la Iglesia

mixed economy an economy that is a combination of command, market, and traditional economies (p. 165)
economía mixta economía de mercado con características de sistemas tradicionales y dirigidas

money any item, usually coins or paper currency, that is used in payment for goods or services (p. 173)
dinero cualquier artículo, generalmente monedas o billetes, que se utiliza en el pago de bienes o servicios

monsoon a seasonal wind that brings either dry or moist air (p. 70)
monzón viento estacional que trae aire seco o húmedo

mosaics pictures made with pieces of colored stone or glass (p. 394)
mosaicos obras pictóricas elaboradas con piezas de piedra o vidrio de varios colores

mulatto (muh-LAH-toh) a term used to refer to a person of mixed European and African ancestry (p. 282)
mulato término utilizado para referirse a una persona de ascendencia mixta europea y africana

multicultural society a society that includes a variety of cultures in the same area (p. 98)
sociedad multicultural área de la sociedad en la que convergen culturas diversas

N

nation-state a country united under a single, strong government (p. 404)
estado-nación país unido bajo un solo gobierno poderoso

national interest a country's economic, cultural, or military goals (p. 134)
interés nacional objetivos económicos, culturales o militares de un país

nationalism a devotion and loyalty to one's country (p. 441)
nacionalismo sentimiento de lealtad a unpaís

natural resource any material in nature that people use and value (p. 82)
recurso natural todo material de la naturaleza que las personas utilizan y valoran

navigable river a river that is deep and wide enough for ships to use (p. 495)
río navegable río que tiene la profundidad y el ancho necesarios para que pasen los barcos

Neolithic Era a period, also called the New Stone Age, in which people learned to make fire, domesticate animals, and grow food (p. 369)
Período Neolítico un período, también llamado la Nueva Edad de Piedra, en el que la gente aprendió a producir fuego, domesticar animales y cultivar alimentos

neutral not taking sides in an international conflict (p. 512)
neutral que no toma partido en un conflicto internacional

newsprint cheap paper used mainly for newspapers (p. 229)
papel de prensa papel económico utilizado principalmente para imprimir periódicos

New World a term used by Europeans to describe the Americas after the voyages of Christopher Columbus; the Americas were a "New World" to Europeans, who did not know they existed until Columbus's voyages (p. 423)
Nuevo Mundo término usado por los europeos para describir las Américas tras los viajes de Cristóbal Colón; las Américas eran un "Nuevo Mundo" para los europeos, que no sabían de su existencia hasta los viajes de Colón

nonrenewable resource a resource that cannot be replaced naturally; coal and petroleum are examples of nonrenewable resources (p. 83)
recurso no renovable recurso que no puede reemplazarse naturalmente; el carbón y el petróleo son ejemplos de recursos no renovables

nonrepresentative government a system of government where power is unlimited and citizens have few, if any, rights (p. 151)
gobierno sin representación sistema de gobierno con poder ilimitado, en el que los ciudadanos tienen pocos o ningún derecho

North Atlantic Drift a warm ocean current that brings warm, moist air across the Atlantic Ocean to Northern Europe (p. 495)
Corriente del Atlántico Norte corriente oceánica cálida que trae aire cálido y húmedo a través del océano Atlántico al norte de Europa

O

observatory a building from which people can study the sky (p. 254)
observatorio edificio desde el cual la gente puede estudiar astronomía

ocean currents large streams of surface seawater; they move heat around Earth (p. 64)
corrientes oceánicas grandes corrientes de agua de mar que fluyen en la superficie del océano; transportan calor por toda la Tierra

opportunity cost the value of something you give up in order to get something else (p. 159)
costo de oportunidad el valor de algo que renuncias para obtener otra cosa

Orthodox Church a branch of Christianity that dates to the Byzantine Empire (p. 475)
Iglesia ortodoxa rama del cristianismo que data del Imperio bizantino

P

Paleolithic Era A period, also known as the Old Stone Age, in which the first humans and their ancestors lived and used stone tools (p. 364)
Período Paleolítico período también conocido como la Edad de Piedra Antigua, en la que los primeros seres humanos y sus antepasados vivieron y utilizaron herramientas de piedra

parallel a line of latitude (p. 24)
paralelo línea de latitud

parliamentary monarchy a type of government in which a king shares power with an elected parliament and a prime minister (p. 486)
monarquía parlamentaria tipo de gobierno en el que un rey rige conjuntamente con un parlamento elegido por votación y un primer ministro

peninsula a piece of land surrounded on three sides by water (p. 277)
península pedazo de tierra rodeado de agua por tres lados

permafrost permanently frozen layers of soil (p. 74)
permafrost capas de tierra congeladas permanentemente

physical geography the study of the world's physical geographic features—its landforms, bodies of water, climates, soils, and plants (p. 10)
geografía física estudio de las características físicas de la Tierra: sus accidentes geográficos, sus masas de agua, sus climas, sus suelos y sus plantas

pioneer an early settler; in the United States, people who settled the interior and western areas of the country were known as pioneers (p. 200)
pionero poblador; en Estados Unidos, las personas que se establecieron en el interior y el oeste del país se llamaron pioneros

plantation a large farm that grows mainly one crop (p. 198)
plantación granja muy grande en la que se produce principalmente un solo tipo de cultivo

plate tectonics a theory suggesting that Earth's surface is divided into a dozen or so slow-moving plates, or pieces of Earth's crust (p. 53)
tectónica de placas teoría que sugiere que la superficie terrestre está dividida en unas doce placas, o fragmentos de corteza terrestre, que se mueven lentamente

political party a group of people who organize to gain political power (p. 148)
partido político grupo de personas que se organizan para ganar poder político

pope the spiritual head of the Roman Catholic Church (pp. 397, 479)
papa jefe espiritual de la Iglesia Católica Romana

popular culture culture traits that are well known and widely accepted (p. 179)
cultura popular rasgos culturales conocidos y de gran aceptación

population the total number of people in a given area (p. 106)
población número total de personas en una zona determinada

population density a measure of the number of people living in an area (p. 106)

densidad de población medida del número de personas que viven en una zona

precipitation water that falls to Earth's surface as rain, snow, sleet, or hail (p. 48)
precipitación agua que cae a la superficie de la Tierra en forma de lluvia, nieve, aguanieve o granizo

prehistory what historians call the time before there was writing (p. 363)
prehistoria el período al que se refieren los historiadores antes de la existencia de la escritura

prevailing winds winds that blow in the same direction over large areas of Earth (p. 63)
vientos preponderantes vientos que soplan en la misma dirección sobre grandes zonas de la Tierra

prime meridian an imaginary line that circles the globe and breaks it into an eastern half and a western half (p. 24)
primer meridiano línea imaginaria que atraviesa el globo terráqueo y lo divide en una mitad oriental y una mitad occidental

profit the money left over after the costs of producing a product are subtracted from the income gained by selling that product (p. 160)
ganancia dinero que queda después de que los costos de producción de un producto se restan de los ingresos obtenidos por la venta de ese producto

Protestant a Christian who protested against the Catholic Church, or whose faith is rooted in the Reformation (pp. 409, 508)
protestante un cristiano que protestó en contra del la Iglesia Católica, o cuya fe tiene sus raíces en la Reforma

province an administrative division of a country (p. 232)
provincia división administrativa de un país

public goods government goods and services that the public consumes; highways are an example (p. 168)
bienes públicos bienes y servicios públicos que el público consume; las autopistas son un ejemplo

public opinion the way large groups of citizens think about issues and people (p. 149)
opinión pública la manera cómo grupos grandes de ciudadanos piensan sobre temas y personas

pulp softened wood fibers; used to make paper (p. 228)
pulpa fibras ablandadas de madera; usadas para hacer papel

Q

Quechua the official language of the Inca Empire (p. 265)
quechua idioma oficial del Imperio inca

R

reforestation planting trees to replace lost forestland (p. 83)
reforestación siembra de árboles para reemplazar los bosques que han desaparecido

Reformation a religious movement to reform the abuses of the Roman Catholic Church (p. 409)
Reforma movimiento religioso para reformar los abusos de la Iglesia Católica Romana

refugee someone who flees to another country, usually for political or economic reasons (pp. 312, 461)
refugiado persona que escapa a otro país, generalmente por razones económicas o políticas

region a part of the world that has one or more common features that distinguish it from surrounding areas (p. 7)
región parte del mundo que tiene una o más características comunes que la distinguen de las áreas que la rodean

regionalism the strong connection that people feel toward the region in which they live (p. 239)
regionalismo gran conexión que las personas sienten con la región en la que viven

Reign of Terror a bloody period of the French Revolution during which the government executed thousands of its opponents and others at the guillotine (p. 432)
Reino de Terror período sangriento de la Revolucíon Francesa durante el cual el gobierno ejecutó a miles de personas, oponentes y otros, en la guillotina

relative location a general description of where a place is located; a place's relative location is often expressed in relation to something else (p. 16)
ubicación relativa descripción general de la posición de un lugar; la ubicación relativa de un lugar suele expresarse en relación con otra cosa

Renaissance the revival of European art and literature at the end of the Middle Ages; *Renaissance* means "rebirth" (p. 405)
Renacimiento renacimiento del arte y la literatura europea a finales de la Edad Media; *Renacimiento* significa "volver a nacer"

renewable resource a resource that Earth replaces naturally, such as water, soil, trees, plants, and animals (p. 82)
recurso renovable recurso que la Tierra reemplaza por procesos naturales, como el agua, el suelo, los árboles, las plantas y los animales

representative democracy an indirect democracy in which people vote for representatives to make and enforce laws (p. 138)
democracia representativa democracia indirecta en la que los ciudadanos votan por los representantes para que creen las leyes y las hagan cumplir

representative government a system of government where people are the ultimate source of government authority (p. 145)
gobierno representativo sistema de gobierno en el que los ciudadanos son la fuente de autoridad absoluta

republic a type of government in which people elect leaders to make laws for them (p. 383)
república tipo de gobierno en el que los ciudadanos eligen a los líderes para que hagan leyes para ellos

retail industries businesses that sell directly to final customers (p. 170)
distribuidores minoristas empresas comerciales que venden directamente a los consumidores finales

revolution the 365¼ day trip Earth takes around the sun each year (p. 42)
revolución viaje de 365¼ días que la Tierra hace alrededor del Sol cada año

rotation one complete spin of Earth on its axis; each rotation takes about 24 hours (p. 41)
rotación giro completo de la Tierra sobre su propio eje; cada rotación toma 24 horas

rural describes areas found outside of cities; less densely populated, with primarily agricultural economies (p. 114)
rural describe las áreas que se encuentran fuera de las ciudades; menos densamente pobladas, con economías principalmente agrícolas

S

savanna an area of tall grasses and scattered trees and shrubs (p. 71)
  sabana zona de pastos altos con arbustos y árboles dispersos

savings the income not spent on immediate needs and wants (p. 177)
  ahorros ingresos no gastados en necesidades y deseos inmediatos

scarcity conflict that exists because wants are unlimited and resources are limited (p. 159)
  escasez conflicto que resulta cuando existe una demanda ilimitada y una oferta limitada de productos

Scientific Revolution a series of events that led to the birth of modern science; it lasted from about 1540 to 1700 (p. 418)
  Revolución Científica serie de sucesos que produjeron el nacimiento de la ciencia moderna; duró desde alrededor de 1540 hasta 1700

Senate the council of rich and powerful Romans who helped run the city of Rome (p. 383)
  Senado consejo de los ricos y poderosos romanos que ayudaron a dirigir la ciudad de Roma

service industries businesses that provide services rather than goods (p. 170)
  empresas de servicios empresas que proveen servicios pero no bienes

settlement any place where a community is established (p. 113)
  asentamiento cualquier lugar donde se establezca una comunidad

slash-and-burn agriculture the practice of burning forest in order to clear land for planting (pp. 119, 287)
  agricultura de tala y quema práctica de quemar los bosques para despejar el terreno y sembrar en él

smelters factories that process metal ores (p. 566)
  fundiciones fábricas que tratan menas de metal

smog a mixture of smoke, chemicals, and fog (p. 288)
  smog mezcla de humo, sustancias químicas y niebla

social institution an organized pattern of belief and behavior that focuses on meeting people's basic needs (p. 101)
  institución social patrón organizado de creencia y comportamiento que se enfoca en satisfacer las necesidades básicas de la gente

social science a field that focuses on people and the relationships among them (p. 6)
  ciencias sociales campo de estudio que se enfoca en las personas y en las relaciones entre

society a community of people who share a common culture (p. 365)
  sociedad comunidad de personas que comparten la misma cultura

soil exhaustion the process of soil becoming infertile because it has lost nutrients needed by plants (p. 326)
  agotamiento del suelo proceso por el cual el suelo se vuelve estéril porque ha perdido los nutrientes que necesitan las plantas

solar energy energy from the sun (p. 41)
  energía solar energía del Sol

sovereign nation a government with complete authority over a geographic region (p. 132)
  nación soberana gobierno con autoridad completa sobre una región geográfica

spatial pattern the placement of people and objects on Earth and the space between them (p. 115)
  patrón espacial colocación de personas y objetos en la Tierra y el espacio entre ellos

steppe a semidry grassland or prairie; steppes often border deserts (p. 71)
  estepa pradera semiárida; las estepas suelen encontrarse en el límite de los desiertos

store of value something that holds its value over time (p. 174)
  depósito de valores algo que mantiene su valor con el tiempo

strike a work stoppage by a group of workers until their demands are met (p. 348)
  huelga interrupción del trabajo por parte de un grupo de trabajadores hasta que se cumplan sus demandas

suburb an area immediately outside of a city, often a smaller residential community (p. 114)
  suburbio área inmediatamente fuera de una ciudad, a menudo una comunidad residencial más pequeña

suffragette a woman who campaigned to gain the right to vote (p. 440)
sufragista una mujer que hicieron campaña para obtener el derecho a votar

superpower a strong and influential country (p. 454)
superpotencia país poderoso e influyente

surface water water that is found in Earth's streams, rivers, and lakes (p. 48)
agua superficial agua que se encuentra en los arroyos, ríos y lagos de la Tierra

T

taiga (TY-guh) a forest of mainly evergreen trees covering much of Russia (p. 559)
taiga bosque de árboles de hoja perenne principalmente que cubre gran parte de Rusia

technology the use of knowledge, tools, and skills to solve problems (p. 104)
tecnología el uso de herramientas, destrezas

terraced farming an ancient technique for growing crops by cutting steps into hillsides or mountain slopes (p. 119)
cultivo en andenes técnica antigua para cultivar la tierra en laderas o pendientes de montañas

terrorism violent attacks against civilians to create fear (p. 215)
terrorismo ataques violentos contra civiles que provocan miedo tradición y en la que la gente suele cultivar su propia comida, hacer sus propios bienes y utilizar el trueque para comerciar

textile a cloth product (p. 437)
textil producto de tela

tool any handheld object that has been modified to help a person accomplish a task (p. 364)
herramienta cualquier objeto de mano que ha sido modificado para ayudar a una persona a realizar una tarea

totalitarian government a type of government that exercises control over all aspects of society (p. 141)
gobierno totalitario forma de gobierno que ejerce control sobre todos los aspectos de una sociedad

trade barrier any law that limits free trade between nations (p. 184)
barrera comercial cualquier ley que limite el libre comercio entre las naciones

trade route a path used by traders for buying and selling goods (p. 113)
ruta comercial itinerario utilizado por los comerciantes para la compra y venta de bienes

traditional economy an economy in which production is based on customs and tradition and in which people often grow their own food, make their own goods, and use barter to trade (p. 164)
economía tradicional economía en la que la producción se basa en las costumbres y y conocimientos necesarios para resolver problemas

Treaty of Versailles the final peace settlement of World War I (p. 445)
Tratado de Versalles acuerdo de paz final de la Primera Guerra Mundial

Trans-Siberian Railway a rail line in Russia that extends about 5,800 miles (9,330 km) from Moscow to Vladivostok; it is the longest single rail line in the world (p. 568)
Ferrocarril Transiberiano línea de ferrocarril rusa de 5,800 millas (9,330 km) de largo, desde Moscú hasta Vladivostok; es la vía de ferrocarril más larga del mundo

trench warfare a style of fighting common in World War I in which each side fights from deep ditches, or trenches, dug into the ground (p. 443)
guerra de trincheras forma de guerra comúnmente usada en la Primera Guerra Mundial, en la cual ambos bandos luchan desde profundas zanjas, o trincheras, cavadas en el suelo

tributary a smaller stream or river that flows into a larger stream or river (p. 192)
tributario río o corriente más pequeña que fluye hacia un río o una corriente más grande

tropics regions close to the equator (p. 45)
trópicos regiones cercanas al ecuador

U

U.S. Constitution a founding document of the United States; it outlines the structure and limits of the U.S. government (p. 202)
Constitución de EE. UU. documento de la fundación de los Estados Unidos; describe la estructura y los límites del gobierno de los Estados Unidos

English and Spanish Glossary

uninhabitable unable to support human settlement (p. 522)
inhabitable que no puede sustentar asentamientos humanos

unit of account a yardstick of economic value in exchanges, such as money (p. 174)
unidad de cuenta unidad monetaria que se utiliza en las transacciones comerciales, como el dinero

United Nations an organization of countries that promotes peace and security around the world (p. 134)
Naciones Unidas organización de países que promueve la paz y la seguridad en todo el mundo

universal theme a message about life or human nature that is meaningful across time and in all places (p. 103)
tema universal mensaje significativo sobre la vida o la naturaleza humana que se conoce en todo tiempo y lugar

unlimited government a type of government in which there are no legal limits set on its power (p. 141)
gobierno ilimitado forma de gobierno en el que no hay límites legales establecidos en su poder

urban areas that are cities and the surrounding areas; heavily populated and developed (p. 114)
urbano áreas que son ciudades y sus alrededores; densamente pobladas y desarrolladas

V

viceroy governor (p. 351)
virrey gobernador

Vikings Scandinavian warriors who raided Europe in the early Middle Ages (p. 520)
vikingos guerreros escandinavos que atacaron Europa al principio de la Edad Media

W

water cycle the movement of water from Earth's surface to the atmosphere and back (p. 48)
ciclo del agua circulación del agua desde la superficie de la Tierra hacia la atmósfera y de regreso a la Tierra

water vapor water occurring in the air as an invisible gas (p. 48)
vapor de agua agua que se encuentra en el aire en estado gaseoso e invisible

weather the short-term changes in the air for a given place and time (p. 62)
tiempo cambios a corto plazo en la atmósfera en un momento y lugar determinados

weathering the process by which rock is broken down into smaller pieces (p. 56)
meteorización proceso de desintegración de las rocas en pedazos pequeños

wholesale industries businesses that sell to businesses (p. 170)
distribuidores mayoristas empresas comerciales que venden productos a otras empresas comerciales

Index

Index

Index

Index

279*m*, 487, 487*m*, 499*m*, 559*m*; computer generation of, 4*f*; features of, 28–29, 28*m*, 29*c*; geographers' use of, 20–21; historical, 411, 411*m*; mental, 243*m*; physical, 31, 31*m*, 89, 89*m*, 192*m*, 226*m*, 278, 278*m*, 298*m*, 324*m*, 325*m*, 327*m*, 470*m*, 494*m*, 497*m*, 532*m*, 556*m*; political, 30, 30*m*, 219, 219*m*, 307*m*, 517*m*, 571*m*; population, 573, 573*m*; projections of, 26–27, 26*m*, 27*m*; sketch, 243, 243*m*; thematic, 31, 31*m*, 317, 317*m*; uses in geography, 21*m*

maquiladoras (factories in Mexico), 288

Mariana Trench, 54

Marie-Antoinette (queen of France), 431

marine west coast climate, 72, 498

Maritime Provinces of Canada, 239

market economy, 164, 165*f*

Marseille, France, 503

Marshall Plan, 452

Martinique, 310, 501

masonry: of ancient Inca, 267

Massif Central, 493

math, link to (feature): number lines, 255*f*; population density, 109*c*, 109*f*; proportion, 474*f*; timelines, 255*f*

Mato Grosso Plateau, 326

May, Theresa, 519

Maya Hiatus, 252

Maya people: civilization height of, 251–253, 251*m*, 252*p*; culture of, 253–255, 253*f*, 253*p*, 254*p*, 255*c*; decline of, 255–256; geography impact on, 250–251; in Guatemala and Belize, 302; in Mexico, 281*f*, 281*p*; overview, 269*c*

media: citizenship and, 149–150, 150*p*

Mediterranean climate, 72, 73*c*, 73*p*, 472

Mediterranean coast. *See* southern Europe.

Mediterranean Sea, 469–470, 470*m*, 494, 494*m*

megacities, 332–333

megaliths, 371, 371*p*

megalopolis, 114

mental maps, 243

Mercator cylindrical map projection, 26

Mercosur trade-promotion organization, 338, 340

merengue music, 312*f*

meridians of longitude, 24, 24*m*, 25

Mesolithic Era (Middle Stone Age), 369

mestizos, 282, 304, 338, 339, 341

metal mining, 559–560, 565, 566–567

meteorology, 14–15

metropolitan areas, 114

Mexican Revolution (1910–1920), 284

Mexico: climate and vegetation of, 279–280, 278*m*, 279*p*; colonial Mexico and independence, 283*f*, 283*p*, 284*f*, 284*p*; cultural regions, 288–290, 289*m*, 289*p*; culture of, 284–285, 285*f*; early, 281–282, 281*p*, 282*p*; economy, 286–288, 287*p*; government of, 140, 140*f*, 286; natural resources of, 280; physical features, 277–278, 278*m*, 278*p*

Mexico City, Mexico, 278, 288

Michelangelo, 407, 407*p*

Mid-Atlantic Ridge mountains, 55

Middle Ages: Black Death, 403, 403*f*, 403*p*; Christian church and society, 396–399, 398*m*, 399*p*; England, political changes in, 402–403, 402*f*; life in, 399–401, 399*f*, 400*f*, 401*p*; power conflicts, 404

Middle Stone Age (Mesolithic Era), 369

Midwest region of United States, 212–213

migrations: to Europe, 461; from Ireland, 110*c*, 110*p*, 111; of prehistoric cultures,

367–368, 367*m*; push-and-pull factors for, 110–111, 110*c*

Milan, Italy, 480*p*, 481

Milosevic, Slobodan, 548

minerals: in Atlantic South America, 326; in Canada, 228, 241; in Mexico, 280; as natural resources, 86–87, 86*p*, 87*p*; in Pacific South America, 329

minutes of latitude from equator, 24

missionaries, 282

Mississippi River, 192, 193*f*

mixed economies, 165

Moche people of Peru, 264

modern democracy: United States as, 198–202

Moldova, 540

monarchies: constitutional, in British Isles, 515–516; Greece as, 474; parliamentary, in Spain, 486

money and banking: economics and, 173–176, 174*f*; management of, 176–178, 176*c*, 177*c*; paper money, 174*f*; purpose of, 173–174

monsoons, 65, 69*c*, 70

Montenegro, 546

Monterrey, Mexico, 288

Montevideo, Uruguay, 336

Montezuma (Aztec emperor), 261

Montreal, Canada, 239

Moors, 483, 483*p*

Morales, Evo, 353

mosaics: in religious art, 394

Moscow, Russia, 555, 566, 567*m*, 567*p*

mountains, 54, 54*f*, 54*p*, 66–67, 66*p*

Mount Elbrus, 557

Mount Kilimanjaro, 74*p*

Mount McKinley (Denali), 193

Mount Pinatubo, 61

Mount Saint Helens, 60–61, 61*p*, 193

Mount Tambora, 120

movement: of Earth, 41–42, 42*f*; as geography theme, 17*f*, 18. *See also* earthquakes; plate tectonics

Index

Table of Contents: *North America* ©ESC/Science Source; *Alberta, Canada* ©Simon Harris/eStock Photo; *Oaxaca woman* ©Dorothy Alexander/Alamy; *soccer* ©Renzo Gostoli/AP Images; *suit of armor* ©Guglielmo De Micheli/Time Life Pictures/Getty Images; *Donan Castle* ©Getty Images RF; *Delphi* ©Digital Vision/Robert Harding; *Bulgarian woman* ©Gregory Wrona/Alamy; *Prague* ©Paul Springett 09/Alamy

Module 1: *Village in Himalayas* ©age fotostock/SuperStock; *Indian girl with goat* ©Anthony Cassidy/The Image Bank/Getty Images; *sandstone formations* ©Digital Vision/Getty Images; *rock climber* ©M. Colonel/Photo Researchers/Science Source; *Sahara Desert, Algeria* ©Frans Lemmens/The Image Bank/Getty Images; *satellite view Europe* ©ESA/K. Horgan/The Image Bank/Getty Images; *Houses of Parliament* ©Sandy Stockwell/Skyscan/Corbis; *Oxford Street, London* ©Kim Sayer/Corbis; *Victoria Falls* ©Torleif Svensson/Corbis; *children dancing* ©Penny Tweedie/The Image Bank/Getty Images; *internet usage map* ©Donna Cox and Robert Patterson/NCSA; *Mojave Desert* ©Kevin Burke/Corbis; *Mount Rainier* ©David R. Frazier/Photo Researchers/Science Source; *Washington, DC* ©Miles Ertman/Masterfile; *(bc) airplane at DFW* ©Paul Buck/AFP/Getty Images; *strawberry picker* ©Morton Beebe/Corbis; *globe* ©D. Hurst/Alamy; *satellite of Italy* ©M-Sat Ltd./Science Source; *satellite of Italy* ©Earth Satellite Corporation/Science Photo Library/Science Source

Module 2: *North America* ©ESC/Science Source; *Monument Valley* ©George H.H. Huey/Corbis; *iceberg* ©Mark Karrass/Corbis; *koala* ©L. Clarke/Corbis; *time lapse sun* ©Paul A. Souders/Corbis; *ocean waves* ©Doug Wilson/Corbis; *hiker in Norway* ©Terje Rakke/The Image Bank/Getty Images; *cruise ship* ©Image Source IS2/Fotolia; *irrigation* ©Alan Sirulnikoff/Photo Researchers/Science Source; *surfer* ©Rick Doyle/Corbis; *hiker* ©Kate Thompson/National Geographic/Getty Images; *Mount Everest Himalayas* ©Marta/Fotolia; *Surtsey Island* ©Yann Arthus-Bertrand/Corbis; *Canyonlands National Park* ©age fotostock/Superstock; *Horseshoe Overlook* ©Owaki - Kulla/Corbis; *cablecar* ©age fotostock/Superstock; *Mount St. Helens* ©David Weintraub/Science Source; *storm cell* ©Minerva Studio/Shutterstock; *tornado on horizon* ©Eric Meola/The Image Bank/Getty Images; *flood rescue* ©William Thomas Cain/Getty Images; *rainforest* ©age fotostock/Superstock; *Tuareg men* ©Ariadne Van Zandbergen/Lonely Planet Images/Getty Images; *Monument Valley* ©Robert Marien/Corbis; *Nice, France* ©Ingram/PictureQuest/Jupiterimages; *zebra by Kilimanjaro* ©Sharna Balfour/Gallo Images/Corbis; *Mount McKinley* ©Robert Glusic/Corbis; *polar bear* ©Paul Souders/Photodisc/Getty Images; *pigeon drawing* Library of Congress; *mushrooms* ©Carl

and Ann Purcell/Corbis; *Wangari Maathai* ©Adrian Arbib/Corbis; *children plant trees* ©Peter Arnold, Inc./Alamy; *oil pumps* ©Bill Ross/Corbis; *Glen Canyon Dam* ©Meinzahn/iStock/Getty Images Plus/Getty Images; *mining* ©James L. Amos/Corbis; *airplane* ©Charles Bowman/Photolibrary; *yard sale* ©Sarah Leen/National Geographic Stock

Module 3: *Olympic closing ceremony* ©Gary M. Prior/Getty Images; *Ganges & Yamuna Rivers* ©Richard I'Anson/Lonely Planet Images; *field workers* ©117 Imagery/Getty Images; *Mongolian musician* ©Jerry Kobalenko/Alamy; *Japanese use chopsticks* ©TWPhoto/Corbis; *Kenyan boys* ©Knut Mueller/Das Fotoarchiv/Photolibrary New York; *boy from Oman* ©Photononstop/Superstock; *Jerusalem* ©Peter Armenia; *Korean baseball* ©Reuters/Corbis; *1909 baseball game* Library of Congress Prints & Photographs Division; *Cuban baseball* ©Timothy A. Clary/AFP/Getty Images; *Pledge of Allegiance* ©David Coates/The Detroit News/AP Images; *students in Peru* ©Mike Theiss/National Geographic/Corbis; *Notre Dame Cathedral* ©Corbis; *Buddhist temple* ©MasterLu/Fotolia; *Hokusai's wave* Library of Congress Prints & Photographs Division; *Tokyo* ©Sean Pavone/Shutterstock; *Noosa river estuary* ©Patrick Oberem/iStockPhoto.com; *Ellis Island* The Granger Collection, NYC — All rights reserved; *wheat field & combine* ©Peter Beck/Corbis; *health clinic* ©Jewel Samad/AFP/Getty Images; *Birmingham, Alabama* ©Darryl Vest/Alamy; *harbor* Photodisc/Getty Images; *Times Square* ©holbox/Shutterstock; *farm* ©David Frazier/Corbis Premium RF/Alamy Images; *highway* © PhotoDisc/ Getty Images RF; *stock trader* ©Spencer Platt/Getty Images; *Sami* ©Franz Aberham/Photographer's Choice/Getty Images; *slash and burn farming* ©Paul Franklin/Oxford Scientific/Getty Images; *terraced farming* ©Glen Allison /Getty Images/PhotoDisc; *irrigation* ©David Frazier/Corbis Yellow/Corbis; *indigo sky tornado* ©Photodisc/Don Farrall/Getty Images; *Hoover Dam aerial* ©Getty Images; *pollution in lake* ©Alamy; *smokestacks* ©tomas/Fotolia

Module 4: *Laura Chinchilla* ©Monica Quesada/AP Images; *Houses of Parliament* ©Jose Fuste Raga/Corbis; *Indian voters* ©Narinder Nanu /AFP/Getty Images; *U.N. Headquarters* ©Arnaldo Jr/Shutterstock; *Great Lakes* ©Stocktrek Images/Getty Images; *soldiers patrolling DMZ, Korea* ©Michel Setboun/Corbis; *Doctors Without Borders* Photo by Kate Geraghty/The Sydney Morning Herald/Fairfax Media via Getty Images; *National Congress* ©VISION/easyFotostock/age fotostock; *Mexico City* ©J. D. Heaton/Picture Finders/age fotostock; *Tanks and protester* ©Jeff Widener/AP Images; *Chinese poster* ©Swim Ink/Corbis; *cadets* U.S. Air Force; *voters* ©Blend Images/Hill Street Studios/Getty Images; *planting tree* ©Kidstock/

Blend Images/Getty Images; *A 1938 Herblock Cartoon* ©The Herb Block Foundation, Library of Congress Prints & Photographs Division, Washington, D.C. [LC-DIG-ppmsca-17190]; *Joe Biden* ©Reuters/Ronen Zvulnun/Alamy

Module 5: *world map in currencies* ©bcracker/iStockPhoto.com; *Moroccan man* ©Shahn Rowe/Stone/Getty Images; *woman sells pickles* ©Godong/Universal Images Group/Getty Images; *NY Stock Exchange* ©Fotosearch/Getty Images; *dump truck* Vince Streano/Getty Images; *factory worker team* ©Andersen Ross/Getty Images; *baker* ©Monkey Business Images/Shutterstock; *tractor* © Getty Images RF; *tractors harvesting* ©Artville/Getty Images; *Rwandan farming* ©Tony Camacho/Science Source; *Times Square* ©Francisco Diez Photography/Getty Images; *Soviet market* ©Peter Turnley/Corbis; *Inuit fishing* ©White Fox/Tips Images/age fotostock; *Madison Robinson* ©Fish Flops; *firefighter* ©TFoxFoto/Shutterstock; *farmer with cattle* ©Owaki-Kulla/Corbis; *cheese cellar* ©Jack Sullivan/Alamy; *cheese counter* ©Kevin Fleming/Corbis; *cheese inspectors* ©Michelle Garrett/Corbis; *Afghan street market* ©Carl & Ann Purcell/Corbis; *train in Sydney* ©Glen Allison/The Image Bank/Getty Images; *Afghan school girls* Patrick ROBERT/Sygma via Getty Images; *Brazilian real bills* DRGill/Shutterstock; *Japanese yen* ©Takeshi Nishio/Shutterstock; *Mexican peso* ©PhotoSpin, Inc/Alamy Images; *Euro note* ©Westend61 GmbH/Alamy; *rupee* ©Steve Estvanik/Shutterstock; *Chinese yuan* ©bendao/Shutterstock; *bank vault* ©Andrew Sacks/The Image Bank/Getty Images; *Hispanic teen girl* ©asiseeit/iStockPhoto.com; *Seattle port* ©Druid007/Shutterstock; *Trump with Xi Jinping* ©Saul Loeb/AFP/Getty Images

Module 6: *Statue of Liberty* ©Tom Grill/Photographer's Choice RF/Getty Images; *teens* ©eStock Photo/PictureQuest/Photolibrary New York; *Grand Canyon* ©Ron Watts/Corbis; *Grandfather Mountain, NC* ©Altrendo Panoramic/Altrendo/Getty Images; *Mississippi Delta* ©NASA/Science Photo Library/Science Source; *ice skating* ©Alan Schein Photography/Corbis; *Hollywood Beach, FL* ©Kord.com/age fotostock; *Hurricane Katrina* ©NASA/Corbis; *Hurricane Katrina* ©Eric Gay/AP Images; *Washington on Delaware* ©The Metropolitan Museum of Art/Bridgeman Art Library; *ox train* Library of Congress Prints & Photographs Division, Washington, D.C. [LC-USZ62-15913]; *Constitution painting* ©Hall of Representatives, Washington, DC/Bridgeman Art Library; *crowd* ©Saul Loeb/AFP/Getty Images; *Brooklyn Bridge* ©Alan Schein Photography/Corbis; *contour strip farming* ©David Frazier/Corbis; *Houston, TX* ©Thinkstock/Stockbyte/Getty Images; *Cake Rock* ©Tony Waltham/Robert Harding World Imagery/Getty Images; *Barack Obama* ©Emmanual Dunand/AFP/Getty

Images; *Clinton and Trump* Mandel Ngan/ AFP/Getty Images; *battle* ©Ted Spiegel/ Corbis; *George Washington* © 2010 A&E Television Networks, LLC. All rights reserved

Module 7: *Newfoundland* ©Darwin Wiggett/All Canada Photos/Superstock; *Canadian Parliament Bldg* ©Steve Vidler/ eStock Photo; *hockey girls* ©Dave Reede/ First Light/Getty Images; *Niagara Falls* ©Photodisc/Getty Images; *Alberta, Canada* ©Simon Harris/eStock Photo; *Ontario* ©CNES, 1988 Distribution Spot Image/Photo Researchers; *totem poles* ©Steve Vidler/eStock Photo; *Halifax* ©Photocanada Digital Inc.; *Samuel de Champlain* Library of Congress Prints & Photographs Division [LC-USZ62-33292]; *mounties* ©Photocanada Digital Inc.; *Canadian railroad* ©Donovan Reese/ Photodisc/Getty Images; *Toronto, Canada* ©Exactostock/Superstock; *Chinese New Year* ©Albert Normandin/ Masterfile; *Nunavut* ©First Light/ Design Pics Inc./Alamy; *logging* ©Pierre Longnus/Photographer's Choice/Getty Images; *canoeing* ©Design Pics Inc./ National Geographic Stock

Module 8: *Tikal* ©Simon Dannhauer/ Shutterstock; *Aztec mask* ©The Trustees of the British Museum/Art Resource, NY; *Mayan art* Justin Kerr, K4806/Kerr Associates; *woman walking by wall* © Kevin Schafer/CORBIS; *arrowhead* ©Justin Kerr/ Kerr Associates; *mask* ©Erich Lessing/ Art Resource, NY; *Mayan stone carving* ©The Trustees of the British Museum/ Art Resource, NY; *Mayan observatory* ©Charles & Josette Lenars/Corbis; *double-headed serpent* ©The Trustees of the British Museum/Art Resource, NY; *Colca Valley* ©Photononstop/ Superstock; *Llama* ©American Museum of Natural History, New York, USA/The Bridgeman Art Library; *Nazca lines* ©Jgz/ Fotolia; *Pachacuti* ©New-York Historical Society, New York/The Bridgeman Art Library; *Incan textile* ©Stuart Franklin/ Magnum Photos; *gold mask* Museo del Banco Central de Ecuador/DDB Stock Photo; *Portrait of Atahualpa* Anonymous, 16th century Portrait of Atahualpa (d.1533), 13th and last King of the Incas. V A 66707. Photo ©bpk, Berlin/ Ethnologisches Museum, Staatliche Museen, Berlin, Germany/Dietrich Graf/ Art Resource, NY; *Francisco Pizarro* Musée du Château de Versailles / Dagli Orti/Art Archive; *Tikal Mayan pyramid* ©Imagebroker/Alamy; *bones* © 2010 A&E Television Networks, LLC. All rights reserved; *Spanish missionary* © 2010 A&E Television Networks, LLC. All rights reserved.; *Palenque ruins* © 2010 A&E Television Networks, LLC. All rights reserved

Module 9: *Mexican dancers* ©Rommel/ Masterfile; *Church of Santo Domingo* ©Danny Lehman/Corbis; *cactus, Mexico* ©age fotostock/Superstock; *Popocatepetl volcano* ©Charles & Josette Lenars/ Corbis; *Mexico beach* ©Sally Brown/

Index Stock Imagery, Inc./Fotosearch Stock Photography & Footage; *Olmec head* ©Kevin Schafer/Corbis; *Aztec turquoise mask* ©Werner Forman/Art Resource, NY; *Mayan pyramid* ©Fred Lengnick/ImageState Media; *mural* Mexican National Museum, Mexico City/DDB Stock Pho; *Father Hildalgo* ©Schalkwijk/Art Resource, NY; *women by graves* ©Liba Taylor/Corbis; *satellite of Mexico* MODIS Rapid Response Team/NASA; *Torre Caballito* ©age fotostock/Superstock; *Oaxaca woman* ©Dorothy Alexander/Alamy; *Mexican cowboy* ©Micheal E. Long/National Geographic/Getty Images; *Guanajuato, Mexico* ©Julie Eggers/Danita Delimont/ Alamy; *Teotihuacan* ©Pictures Colour Library/Travel Pictures/Alamy; *oil rig* ©2010 A&E Television Networks, LLC. All rights reserved; *Hidalgo mural* ©2010 A&E Television Networks, LLC. All rights reserved; *Arrival of the Spanish* ©2010 A&E Television Networks, LLC. All rights reserved

Module 10: *Virgin Islands* ©Don Hebert/ The Image Bank/Getty Images; *Kuna women* ©Mark Eveleigh/Alamy; *El Morro Castle* ©David Sanger/The Image Bank/ Getty Images; *Cuba* ©Bruno Morandi/ Robert Harding World Imagery/Getty Images; *Santa Ana Volcano* ©Robert Escobar/epa/Corbis; *Hurricane Isabel* ©CNP/Corbis; *banana harvest* ©David Alan Harvey/Magnum Photos; *Puerto Barrios, Guatemala* ©Bettmann/Corbis; *scuba diving* ©Look GMBH/eStock Photo; *Panama Canal* ©Danny Lehman/Getty Images; *Guadaloupe university* ©Stuart Cohen/Image Works, Inc.; *Grenadian steel drums* ©Dave Bartruff/Danita Delimont Stock Photography; *Fidel Castro* ©Library of Congress Prints & Photographs Division; *Cuban refugees* ©Hans Deryk/ AP Images; *Cuba* ©AFP/NewsCom; *Lesser Antilles* ©Picture Finders/Pictures Colour Library Ltd.; *homes in Barbados* ©Steve Skjold/Alamy

Module 11: *Venezuelan cowboy* ©Kevin Schafer/Kevin Schafer Photography; *Amazon River* ©Steve Vidler/eStock Photo; *Peruvian funeral mask* ©Peter Horree/Alamy; *Amazon* ©Heeb Christian/Prisma Bildagentur AG/Alamy; *Rio de Janeiro* ©SIME/eStock Photo; *Brazil* ©Moacyr Lopes Jr./UNEP/ Peter Arnold, Inc.; *soccer* ©Renzo Gostoli/ AP Images; *horse race* ©The British Library/HIP/Image Works, Inc.; *Eva Peron* ©Bettmann/Corbis; *Buenos Aires* ©Prisma/Superstock; *Paraguay horsemen* ©Julio Etchart/Photolibrary; *buildings & palm trees* ©Wayne Walton/ Lonely Planet Images; *tunjo* ©Boltin Picture Library/The Bridgeman Art Library; *Cartagena fort* ©Fotoworld/ Photographer's Choice/Getty Images; *bus in Andes* ©Krzysztof Dydynski/Lonely Planet Images; *Ecuadorian market* ©Janice Hazeldine/Alamy; *Lima, Peru* ©Ron Giling/Peter Arnold, Inc.; *Lima, Peru* ©Peter M. Wilson/Alamy; *Lima, Peru* ©Photodisc/Fotosearch Stock

Photography & Footage; *vineyards in Chile* ©Randa Bishop/Danita Delimont Stock Photography

Module 12: *Donan Castle* ©Getty Images RF; *suit of armor* Guglielmo De Micheli/ Time Life Pictures/Getty Images; *Martin Luther* ©AKG Images; *Greek vase* ©Heritage Image Partnership (HIP)/Art Resource, NY; *mural* ©Pierre Vauthey/ Sygma/Corbis; *Svaneti Mestia Georgia* ©Esin Deniz/Shutterstock; *Stonehenge* ©Roger Nichol/Shutterstock; *Pericles* ©Gjon Mill/Time & Life Pictures/Getty Images; *Athena* ©Alinari/Art Resource, NY; *Ulysses* ©National Gallery of Victoria, Melbourne, Australia/The Bridgeman Art Library; *Colosseum* ©Comstock/Jupiter Images; *Westminster Abbey* ©John Lamb/ Getty Images; *statue of David* ©Rabatti-Domingie/AKG Images; *DaVinci helicopter model* The Granger Collection, New York; *Shakespeare* National Portrait Gallery, London/SuperStock; *The Harvesters* ©Giraudon/Art Resource, NY; *Gutenberg Workshop* ©Bettmann/Corbis; *Acropolis* ©Goodshoot/Jupiterimages/Getty Images; *Legacy of Greece* ©2010 A&E Television Networks, LLC. All rights reserved.; *Parthenon* ©2010 A&E Television Networks, LLC. All rights reserved.; *Persian Wars* ©2010 A&E Television Networks, LLC. All rights reserved

Module 13: *Monument to the Discoveries* ©Visual Cortex/Alamy; *Hitler saluting* ©Hugo Jaeger/Timepix/Time Life Pictures/Getty Images; *steam train* ©Ali Meyer/Corbis; *WWI soldiers* Hulton Archive/Getty Images; *astrolabe* ©Heritage Image Partnership (HIP)/ Art Resource, NY; *telescope* Telescope belonging to Sir Isaac Newton (1642–1727) 1671, English School / Royal Society, London, UK / Bridgeman Images; *compass* Réunion des Musées Nationaux/Art Resource, NY; *Salon des Quatre-Glaces* ©RMN-Grand Palais/Art Resource, NY; *Declaration of Independence* ©Houghton Mifflin Harcourt; *signing Magna Carta* ©Bettmann/Corbis; *Magna Carta* ©National Archives, UK/The Bridgeman Art Library; *British Parliament* The Granger Collection, NYC; *English Bill of Rights* Custody of the House of Lords Record Office/Parliamentary Archives; *signing Independence* ©Bettmann/Corbis; *French Declaration* ©Document conservé au Centre historique des Archives nationales à Paris/ Centre historique des Archives nationales (CHAN); *Oath of the Tennis Court* ©RMN-Grand Palais/Art Resource, NY; *Storming the Bastille* ©Gianni Dagli Orti/ CORBIS; *Napoleon's coronation* ©Erich Lessing/Art Resource, NY; *spinning Jenny* ©Hulton Archive/Getty Images; *Bessemer furnace* The Granger Collection, New York; *Suffragettes* ©Hulton Archive/Getty Images; *Lenin Talks to Revolutionaries* The Granger Collection, New York; *Hitler in car* The Granger Collection, New York; *Benito Mussolini* ©Hulton-Deutsch Collection/Corbis; *Anne Frank* ©akg-images, London; *Hitler in Paris* ©Hulton-Deutsch Collection/Corbis; *US soldiers Normandy* ©Bettmann/Corbis; *Yalta conference* ©Bettmann/Corbis; *Holocaust prisoners* ©Margaret Bourke-White/Time & Life Pictures/Getty Images; *Stalingrad in WWII* ©Hulton Archive/Getty Images; *WWII ruins* ©Hulton Archive/Getty Images; *Mikhail Gorbachev* ©Peter Turnley/Corbis; *reunification celebration* ©Robert Maas/Corbis; *Independence rally Prague* ©David Turnley/Corbis; *EURO coins* ©AFP/Getty Images; *Pro-Brexit demonstration* ©Ms Jane Campbell/Shutterstock; *Gorbachev cartoon* ©Estate of Edmund S. Valtman, Library of Congress; *WWII political cartoon* "The Tide Comes In," 1944, by John Collins. M965.1; *solider writing* © Bettmann/Corbis; *celebrating victory* © 2010 A&E Television Networks, LLC. All rights reserved.; *troops in street* © 2010 A&E Television Networks, LLC. All rights reserved.; *soldier and cannon* © 2010 A&E Television Networks, LLC. All rights reserved

Module 14: *Delphi* ©Digital Vision/Robert Harding; *St. Maddalena Church* ©Richard Klune/Corbis; *matador* ©Carlos Cazalis/Corbis; *Tuscany* ©IT Stock Free/eStock Photo; *harvesting grapes* ©Charles O'Rear/Corbis; *Greek church* ©SIME/eStock Photo; *Ibiza beach* ©Jeremy Lightfoot/Robert Harding Picture Library; *Crete* ©Dmitry Kovyazin/Alamy; *Athena on amphora* ©Erich Lessing/Art Resource, NY; *Parthenon* ©Vega/Taxi/Getty Images; *Greek Orthodox procession* ©Roberto Meazza/IML Image Group; *Giuseppe Garibaldi* © Pictorial Press Ltd/Alamy; *tourists in Rome* ©Steve Vidler/Superstock; *Naples, Italy* ©Martin Moos/Lonely Planet Images; *Milan Fashion Week* ©Giuseppe Cacace/Getty Images; *Florence* ©Samot/Shutterstock; *satellite of Venice* ©WorldSat International Inc.; *Belem tower* ©Travel Ink/Digital Vision/Getty Images; *Madrid avenue* ©Nigel Francis/Corbis

Module 15: *Palace of Westminster* ©Steve Vidler/ImageState Media; *Norway snowboarding* ©Fredrik Naumann/Samfoto; *tulips in Holland* ©Brian Lawrence/ImageState Media; *satellite of Alps* ©WorldSat International Inc.; *Norway fjord* ©Stefan Auth/imagebroker RF/Photolibrary New York; *satellite of Norway* ©WorldSat International Inc.; *Charlemagne* ©Superstock; *German WWII tanks* ©Corbis; *Arc de Triomphe* ©Vince Streano/Corbis; *Eiffel Tower* ©William Manning/Corbis; *Holland* ©Goos van der Veen/Hollandse Hoogte/Redux Pictures; *Brandenburg Gate* ©Svetlana Gryankina/Fotolia; *Bavarian castle* ©Exactostock/Superstock; *Bavarian with cow* ©Elfi Kluck/Index Stock Imagery/PictureQuest/Jupiterimages/Photolibrary; *German soccer fans* ©Sean Gallup/Getty Images; *Christmas market* ©Sean Gallup/Getty Images; *Bernese Alps* ©Ray Juno/Corbis; *horse drawn carriage* ©Dallas and John Heaton/Free Agents Limited/Corbis; *Winston Churchill* ©Carl Mydans/Time & Life Pictures/Getty Images; *Scot play bagpipes* ©Andrew Steven Graham/Demotix/Corbis; *London* ©Michael Duerinckx/ImageState Media; *Oslo, Norway* ©Jon Arnold Images/Danita Delimont Stock Photography; *people with reindeer* ©Dave G. Houser/ImageState Media; *blue lagoon, Iceland* ©Hans Strand/Corbis; *Strokkur Geyser* ©Hans Strand/Corbis

Module 16: *Tallinn, Estonia* ©Jon Arnold Images Ltd./Danita Delimont Stock Photography; *Iron Gates Gorge* ©Adam Woolfitt/Corbis; *Prague* ©Paul Springett 09/Alamy; *Bulgarian woman* ©Gregory Wrona/Alamy; *Kazimierz & River Vistula* ©M. ou Me. Desjeux, Bernard/Corbis; *High Tatras* ©Liba Taylor/Corbis; *horse grazing* ©Vadim Kozlovsky/Shutterstock; *radiologists* ©Gleb Garanich/Reuters/Corbis; *Pope John Paul II* ©Bettmann/Corbis; *Polish singers* ©Wally McNamee/Corbis; *St. Sophia Monastery*

©age fotostock/SuperStock; *Kiev* ©John Farrar/VirtualKiev; *Prague* ©sborisov/Fotolia; *Bachkovsky Monastery* ©Ethel Davies/ImageState Media; *Romas* ©Barry Lewis/Corbis; *Old Bridge of Mostar* ©Amel Emric/AP Images; *Bosnian street* ©David Turnley/Corbis

Module 17: *Kremlin, Moscow* ©Steve Vidler/ImageState Media; *Bolshoi dancers* ©Robbie Jack/Corbis; *Yankicha Island* ©Sergey Frolov/Danita Delimont/Alamy; *Baku, Azerbaijan* ©Jeremy Horner/Corbis; *Mutnovskij Volcano* ©Mikhail V. Propp/Peter Arnold Images/Photolibrary New York; *Lenghieri Village* ©Marc Garanger/Corbis; *Red Square, Moscow* ©Maxim Marmur/Hulton Archive/Getty Images; *Russia* ©Oxford Scientific/PictureQuest/Jupiterimages/Photolibrary New York; *Soviet poster* The Granger Collection, NYC — All rights reserved; *Winter Palace* ©Yogi, Inc./Corbis; *Siberian people* ©Maria Stenzel/National Geographic Stock; *Moscow, Russia* ©Harald Sund/The Image Bank/Getty Images; *Batimi, Georgia* ©Vahan Abrahamyan/Shutterstock

Regional Atlas Maps: *Death Valley, CA* ©Gavin Hellier/Robert Harding Picture Library; *Costa Rican coffee* ©Russell Gordon/Das Fotoarchiv/Photolibrary New York; *Flags* ©Image Club/Getty Images

Text Credits

Excerpt from "Charter of the United Nations." Text copyright © the United Nations. Reprinted by permission of the United Nations.

Excerpt from *The Odyssey* by Homer, translated by Robert Fitzgerald. Text copyright © 1961, 1963 by Robert Fitzgerald; text copyright renewed © 1989 by Benedict R. C. Fitzgerald, on behalf of the Robert Fitzgerald's Children. Reprinted by permission of Benedict R.C. Fitzgerald on behalf of the Robert Fitzgerald's Children.